LIFELONG LEARNING FOR ALL

Meeting
of the
Education Committee
at Ministerial Level,
16-17 January 1996

ORGANISATION FOR ECONOMIC CO-OPERATION AND DEVELOPMENT

ORGANISATION FOR ECONOMIC CO-OPERATION AND DEVELOPMENT

Pursuant to Article 1 of the Convention signed in Paris on 14th December 1960, and which came into force on 30th September 1961, the Organisation for Economic Co-operation and Development (OECD) shall promote policies designed:

- to achieve the highest sustainable economic growth and employment and a rising standard of living in Member countries, while maintaining financial stability, and thus to contribute to the development of the world economy;
- to contribute to sound economic expansion in Member as well as non-member countries in the process of economic development; and
- to contribute to the expansion of world trade on a multilateral, non-discriminatory basis in accordance with international obligations.

The original Member countries of the OECD are Austria, Belgium, Canada, Denmark, France, Germany, Greece, Iceland, Ireland, Italy, Luxembourg, the Netherlands, Norway, Portugal, Spain, Sweden, Switzerland, Turkey, the United Kingdom and the United States. The following countries became Members subsequently through accession at the dates indicated hereafter: Japan (28th April 1964), Finland (28th January 1969), Australia (7th June 1971), New Zealand (29th May 1973), Mexico (18th May 1994) and the Czech Republic (21st December 1995). The Commission of the European Communities takes part in the work of the OECD (Article 13 of the OECD Convention).

Publié en français sous le titre :
APPRENDRE A TOUT ÂGE
Réunion du Comité de l'éducation au niveau ministériel, 16-17 janvier 1996

Photo credit: Hubert.

FOREWORD

The fourth meeting of the OECD Education Committee at Ministerial level was held in Paris on 16 and 17 January 1996 around the theme of "Making Lifelong Learning a Reality for All".

This report presents the documentation prepared for the meeting. It explains the nature and background of the issues and challenges, and sets out the implications for strategic policy and reform. Part I describes why Ministers agreed to focus on how to make learning a process extending from early childhood through retirement, and occurring in schools, the workplace and many other settings. This builds on the broad consensus that has emerged since their meeting in November 1990 on the importance of lifelong learning in realising a range of educational, social and economic policy objectives. Part I also describes the main policy issues addressed by Ministers; their *Communiqué* highlights the conclusions, sets out policy targets and reform agendas, and suggests further possible work for the OECD. Part II analyses the main policy issues and the major trends in OECD economies and societies: the widening scope and impact of information and communication technologies; the gathering momentum of globalisation and trade liberalisation; the ageing of the population; the growing cultural and ethnic diversity; and the changing nature of work. It also suggests a number of directions for strategic policies designed to advance the implementation of lifelong learning for all.

While priorities and specific policies will necessarily vary with periodic national differences and reassessments, implementation strategies will require a commitment to new system-wide goals, standards and approaches to certification and qualification. Five broad areas must be addressed: revitalising early childhood education and initial schooling to provide the foundations for lifelong learning; organising flexible and interconnected pathways between formal and non-formal learning and work; re-examining the roles and responsibilities of governments and their partners in implementing lifelong learning; securing the knowledge-base and necessary human and physical resources for improved policy-making and practice; and creating adequate incentives for public and private investment in lifelong learning.

This report results from a collective effort by consultants and members of the Secretariat – the Education and Training Division, the Centre for Educational Research and Innovation (CERI), the Programme on Educational Building (PEB), and the Programme on Institutional Management in Higher Education (IMHE). It was prepared principally by Albert Tuijnman, under the direction of Abrar Hasan of the Education and Training Division. It is published on the responsibility of the Secretary-General of the OECD.

TABLE OF CONTENTS

Part I
POLICY ISSUES AND STRATEGIC DIRECTIONS

Introduction 13
The issues for discussion 15
The Ministers' *Communiqué* 21

Part II
BACKGROUND REPORT

Acknowledgements 26

Introduction 27

Chapter 1
Transitions to learning economies and societies

A. Introduction 29
B. Broad trends in the economy, culture
and society 29
C. Trends and developments in education,
training and learning 40
D. Conclusions 70

Chapter 2
Towards lifelong learning for all: aims, barriers, strategies

A. Introduction 87
B. From recurrent education to lifelong learning 88
C. Barriers to the implementation of lifelong
learning for all 92
D. Towards strategies for lifelong learning 94
E. Conclusions 97

Chapter 3
Establishing the foundations for lifelong learning

A. Introduction 99
B. Culture, values and pluralism in school
learning 99
C. What foundations for lifelong learning? 103
D. Creating "positive" learning environments 107
E. Investing in early childhood education 113
F. Early or late selection and differentiation? . . . 117
G. The foundations for lifelong learning: policy
conclusions 120

Chapter 4
Improving pathways and transitions in lifelong learning and work

A. Introduction 123
B. The policy questions and issues 124
C. Types of pathways and transitions in lifelong
learning and work 125
D. Pathways in formal education and their links
to labour markets 133
E. Education, training and transitions
to employment 140
F. Education, training and work-to-work
transitions 148
G. The value of education and training 155
H. Lifelong learning and work: policy conclusions 157

Chapter 5
Managing autonomy and choice: the role of government

A.   Introduction   163

B.   Developments in governance and
     management of education   163

C.   The governance and management of schools
     and school systems   167

D.   The governance and management of learning
     beyond schooling   178

E.   Government intervention in markets
     for learning   183

F.   Managing autonomy and choice: policy
     conclusions   184

Chapter 6
Using goals and standards in formal and non-formal learning

A.   Introduction   187

B.   Setting education goals, and new approaches
     to steering education systems   187

C.   Standards in the formal and non-formal
     sectors   193

D.   Steering change by the use of standards   200

E.   Using goals and standards: policy conclusions   202

Chapter 7
Strengthening educational resources

A.   Introduction   205

B.   Teachers and other key actors   205

C.   The use of new technologies   210

D.   Physical settings for lifelong learning   213

E.   Information for teaching, learning and policy-
     making   215

F.   Strengthening the resources: policy
     conclusions   219

Chapter 8
How to pay for lifelong learning for all?

A.   Introduction   223

B.   The policy context   223

C.   The benefits of lifelong learning   225

D.   What are the costs of lifelong learning?   231

E.   What is needed to ensure sufficient resources
     for lifelong learning?   239

F.   Financing lifelong learning: policy conclusions   245

Annex: Evidence and key statistics   269

Bibliography   329

List of Charts

1.1.   Components of population growth in
       OECD regions, 1982-86, 1987-91 and 1992   30

1.2.   Shares of high-technology industries in
       total manufacturing exports, 1970 and 1992   33

1.3.   Employment share of agriculture, industry
       and services, 1900-90   34

1.4.   Employment shares for blue- and white-
       collar workers, 1981-91   35

1.5.   Annual hours worked per person per year,
       1870-1993   36

1.6.   Incidence of part-time employment (men),
       1973, 1983 and 1993   38

1.7.   Incidence of part-time employment
       (women), 1973, 1983 and 1993   38

1.8.   The relative size of the population aged 5
       to 14, 1970-2010   41

1.9.   The relative size of the population aged 5
       to 14 and 15 to 24, 1994   42

1.10. Population that has attained less than
       upper secondary education, 1992   43

1.11. Change in educational attainment,
       population aged 25 to 64, 1981-92   44

1.12. Population in four age groups that had
       attained at least upper secondary
       education, 1992   45

1.13. Educational attainment of women
       compared to men for 25- to 34-year-olds
       and 55- to 64-year-olds, 1992   46

1.14. Labour force participation rate of those
       having attained some tertiary education,
       1981 and 1992   47

1.15. Full-time students at all education levels
       except pre-primary, 1985 and 1992   49

1.16. Schooling expectancy for a 5-year-old
       child, 1985 and 1994   49

1.17. Enrolment in early childhood education,
       1970-92   50

1.18. Net enrolment of 3- and 4-year-olds in
       early childhood education, 1994   51

1.19. Net rates of participation in secondary
       education for 16-year-olds, 1985 and 1994   52

1.20. Net rates of participation in secondary
       education for 17-year-olds, 1985 and 1994   52

1.21. Number of students in full-time upper secondary education, 1985 and 1992 53

1.22. Number of full-time students in tertiary education, 1985 and 1992 54

1.23. Employees who received training and its duration, 1994 55

1.24. Sweden: employees who received training by age, 1982-94 56

1.25. United Kingdom: employees of working age receiving job-related training by age groups, 1984-90 57

1.26. Germany (FTFR): enrolments and courses in further education and training, 1965-93 58

1.27. Germany (FTFR): evolution of enrolments and expenditure for further education and training, 1965-92 59

1.28. Germany (FTFR): continuing education expenditure, 1965-92 59

1.29. France: increase in adult education students, hours and expenditure, 1984-93 60

1.30. Public education expenditure as a percentage of GDP, 1970-93 61

1.31. Educational expenditure by initial source of funds, 1992 62

1.32. Expenditure per student from public sources by level of education, 1985-92 63

1.33. Ratio of students to teaching staff by level of education, 1992 64

1.34. Graduation rates in upper secondary education, 1992 65

1.35. Graduation rates in university education, 1985 and 1992 66

1.36. United States: mean scores of college-bound students on verbal and mathematics components of the Scholastic Aptitude Test (SAT), 1976-93 67

1.37. United States: mean science proficiency scores, by sex and age, 1992 68

1.38. Earnings differentials by educational attainment for young and older men in the early 1990s 69

1.39. Unemployment rate by level of education for persons 24 to 64 years, 1992 70

3.1. Percentage of children with special learning needs who are enrolled in schools outside the mainstream education system, late 1980s 107

3.2. Federal expenditure per student for Head Start and enrolments in the programme, United States, 1975-95 116

3.3. Distribution of 9-year-olds in various types of grouping for reading instruction, 1991 . . 118

4.1. Upper secondary students enrolled in public and private general and vocational education, 1992 125

4.2. Net full-time enrolment rates for 17-year-olds, 1992 127

4.3. Youth labour force participation and unemployment, 1994 129

4.4. Enterprise tenure, 1991 132

4.5. Monthly flow into unemployment, 1993 . . . 132

4.6. Type of vocational education and youth unemployment, 1992 144

4.7. Active labour market programmes: training of unemployed adults and those at risk, 1993/94 149

4.8. Participation in job-related continuing education and training by level of education, early 1990s 151

4.9. Participation in job-related continuing education and training by age groups, early 1990s 154

5.1. Percentage of respondents who thought it was "very important" for decisions to be taken by schools themselves, 1993-94 164

5.2. Decisions taken at school level, lower secondary education, 1991 170

6.1. Overall difficulty of examinations: comparative scale 195

6.2. Perceived confidence in important school subjects, 1993-94 196

7.1. Number of teaching hours per year, by level of public education, 1992 206

7.2. Staff employed in education, 1992 207

7.3. Index of computer use for instruction in four subjects, 1989 and 1992 212

7.4. Expenditure on educational R&D as a percentage of total expenditure on education and of total expenditure on R&D, early 1990s 218

8.1. Relative differences in earnings from work by level of education, 1992 226

8.2. Unit costs per student by level of education, 1992 232

8.3. Comparative distribution of adult literacy and numeracy skills, 1994 238

8.4. Percentage of adult education and training courses that are employer-supported, 1994 241

List of Tables

1.1. Foreign or immigrant population and labour force, 1983 and 1993 73

1.2. Aged dependency ratios in OECD countries, 1980-2040 74

1.3.	International specialisation in high-wage and high-technology industries, 1970 and 1992	74
1.4.	Educational attainment in Sweden, 1930, 1970 and 1994	75
1.5.	Incidence of long-term unemployment, 1983, 1989, 1992 and 1993	75
1.6.	Full- and part-time employment situation and individual preferences in European countries, 1989	76
1.7.	Children under 18 years living in poverty in the United States, 1960-92	76
1.8.	Enrolment in public and private early childhood and primary education, 1994	77
1.9.	Enrolment in upper secondary education, 1975-92	78
1.10.	Transition characteristics from secondary to tertiary education, 1994	79
1.11.	Sweden: average number of training days per employee receiving training, 1986-94	80
1.12.	Public education expenditure as a percentage of gross domestic product, 1970-92	81
1.13.	Educational expenditure by initial source of funds, 1985-92	83
1.14.	Direct public education expenditure, 1985-92	84
1.15.	Unemployment rate by level of education for persons 24 to 64 years, various years	85
3.1.	Foreign language education in the European Community, 1990	102
3.2.	Teaching time per subject specified in the intended curriculum in lower secondary education, 1992	104
3.3.	Compulsory school starting and ending ages, 1992	113
3.4.	Transition from home to school, 1992	114
3.5.	Trends in the dependence of educational attainment on social origin	119
4.1.	Trend in the share of vocational and technical education in total upper secondary enrolment	126
4.2.	Percentage of students leaving secondary education without a certificate	127
4.3.	Job turnover and labour turnover, 1985 and 1991	131
4.4.	Summary indicators of pathways in education and transitions to employment	134
4.5.	Differentiation characteristics in initial education and training, 1992	136
4.6.	Differences between structures of education and training systems	139
4.7.	Unemployment rates for those leaving education at different levels, one year after leaving (based on follow-up surveys), and unemployment rates for the total labour force	143
4.8.	Share of technically educated and differences between the net wage rate of technically educated and non-technically educated by education level	157
5.1.	Policy instruments defined	166
5.2.	Decisions taken by level of governance, lower secondary education, 1991	168
5.3.	Decisions taken at the school level by decision mode, lower secondary education, 1991	169
5.4.	Decisions taken at the school level by decision domain, public lower secondary education, 1991	170
5.5.	New strategic roles of governments: characterisation of reform strategies	177
6.1.	Respect for teachers and the quality of teaching in secondary education, 1993-94	197
7.1.	"Older" and "newer" learning resources and tools	211
7.2.	Schools using personal computers for instruction, 1982-92	212
8.1.	Social rates of return to levels of education in selected OECD countries, by gender and ISCED level, 1992	247
8.2.	Private return to schooling in United States and United Kingdom, based on Mincer-type wage equations	248
8.3.	Private rate of return to schooling in the Netherlands, based on Mincer-type wage equations	251
8.4.	Returns to labour market programmes, United States, 1987-89	252
8.5.	Effectiveness of active labour market programmes	253
8.6.	The productivity of training in high-tech and low-tech regimes in selected manufacturing industries in Chinese Taipei, 1986	255
8.7.	Returns to training at work for young workers, 1980s	255
8.8.	Returns to on-the-job training	256
8.9.	Enrolment gaps by level of education and age group, 1992	259
8.10.	Estimated costs of closing the enrolment gaps in early childhood education, 1992	259
8.11.	Estimated costs of closing the enrolment gaps in lower and upper secondary education, 1992	260
8.12.	Estimated costs of closing the enrolment gaps in both university and non-university tertiary education, 1992	261
8.13.	Education expenditure by function, 1992	262

8.14. Examples of higher education cost functions 262

8.15. Examples of higher education cost functions: comparison of teaching costs for different modes of instruction, Australia, 1989-90 263

8.16. Adults likely to be in need of basic education and training: numbers of 25-64 year-olds in the labour force with lower secondary education or less, 1992 . . 263

8.17. Adults likely to be in need of basic education and training, 1994 264

8.18. Unit costs of selected labour market training programmes 264

8.19. Cost scenarios for extending lifelong learning to the least qualified 265

8.20. Cost scenarios for extending lifelong learning to adults with low literacy proficiency 265

8.21. Duration of adult education and training courses, 1994 265

8.22. Evaluation of financing schemes for lifelong learning 266

List of Annex Tables

A.1. Proportion of 0-14, 25-34 and 25-44 year-olds in the population, 1960-2010 271

A.2. Indicators of growth and dispersion of communication technologies, 1982 and 1992 272

A.3. Shares of high-technology industries in total manufacturing, 1970 and 1992 273

A.4. Employment shares for blue- and white-collar workers, 1981 and 1991 274

A.5. Annual hours worked per person per year, 1870-1992 275

A.6. Size and composition of part-time employment, 1973-93 276

A.7. The relative size of the population aged 5 to 14, 1970-94 277

A.8. The relative size of the population aged 5 to 14 and 15 to 24, 1994 278

A.9. The relative size of the population aged 5 to 14, forecast 1994-2010 279

A.10. Population aged 25-64 that has attained a specific highest education level, 1981-92 . . 280

A.11. Average annual change in educational attainment for the population aged 25 to 64, 1981-92 284

A.12. Proportion of the population in four age groups that had attained at least upper secondary education, 1992 285

A.13. Educational attainment of women and men, aged 25-34 and 55-64, 1992 286

A.14. Labour force participation rate by level of education for persons between 25 and 64 years of age, 1981-92 287

A.15. Number of full-time students in all levels (except pre-primary), 1975-92 288

A.16. Schooling expectancy for a 5-year-old child, 1985-94 289

A.17. Net rates of participation in full-time secondary education, 1985 290

A.18. Net rates of participation in full-time secondary education, 14-23 year-olds 1994 291

A.19. Number of full-time students in upper secondary education, 1975-92 292

A.20. Number of full-time students in tertiary education, 1975-92 293

A.21. Employees who received training and its duration, 1994 293

A.22. Sweden: number of employees who received training by age, 1982-94 294

A.23. United Kingdom: participation in job-related training by age, 1984-90 294

A.24. Denmark: students in public adult education and continuing vocational training, 1980-93 295

A.25. Denmark: public expenditure on adult education and training, 1980-93 296

A.26. Germany (FTFR): institutions, courses and enrolments in adult education, 1965-93 . . . 297

A.27. Germany: expenditure on education by the federal government, the *Länder* and local authorities according to expenditure areas, 1965-92 297

A.28. France: development of private sector continuing training financed by public authorities and enterprises, 1984-93 298

A.29. Direct expenditure per student in pre-primary education, from public sources, 1985-92 299

A.30. Direct expenditure per student in primary education from public sources, 1985-92 . . . 300

A.31. Direct expenditure per student in secondary education from public sources, 1985-92 301

A.32. Direct expenditure per student in tertiary education from public sources, 1985-92 . . . 302

A.33. Ratio of students to teaching staff in early childhood education, 1985-92 303

A.34. Ratio of students to teaching staff in primary and secondary education, 1985-92 303

A.35. Ratio of students to teaching staff in tertiary education, 1985-92 304

A.36. Graduation rates in upper secondary education, 1985-92 304

A.37. Graduation rates in general upper secondary education, 1985-92 305

A.38. Graduation rates in vocational and technical upper secondary education, 1985-92 306

A.39. Graduation rates in tertiary university education, 1985-92 307

A.40. United States: mean verbal and mathematics proficiency scores on Scholastic Aptitude Test, 1976-93 308

A.41. United States: mean science proficiency scores, by sex and age, 1970-92 308

A.42. Ratios of mean annual earnings by educational qualifications, early 1970s-90s 309

A.43. Earnings differentials by educational attainment of young and older men, early 1970s-90s 313

A.44. Percentage of children with special learning needs who are enrolled in schools outside the mainstream education system, late 1980s 314

A.45. Federal budget allocations for Head Start and enrolments in the programme, United States, 1975-95 314

A.46. Distribution of 9-year-olds in various types of grouping for reading instruction, 1991 .. 315

A.47. Transitions in initial education and training, 1985 and 1992 316

A.48. Youth labour force participation and unemployment, 1983 and 1994 317

A.49. Monthly flows into and out of unemployment 318

A.50. Distribution of employment by enterprise tenure, 1991 319

A.51. Transition systems and youth unemployment, 1992 320

A.52. Participants in labour market training programmes 321

A.53. Participation in job-related continuing education and training 322

A.54. Participation by age in job-related continuing education and training 322

A.55. Percentage of respondents who thought it was "very important" for decisions to be taken by schools themselves, 1993-94 323

A.56. Perceived confidence in school subjects and cross-curricular qualities, 1993-94 324

A.57. Number of teaching hours per year, by level of public education, 1992 324

A.58. Staff employed in education as a percentage of the labour force, 1992 325

A.59. Index of computer use for instruction in four subjects, 1989 and 1992 325

A.60. Expenditure on educational R&D as a percentage of total expenditure on education and of total expenditure on R&D 326

A.61. Education and earnings, 1992 327

A.62. Unit costs per student by level of education, 1992 328

A.63. Percentage of adult education and training courses that are employer-supported, 1994 328

Part I

POLICY ISSUES AND STRATEGIC DIRECTIONS

INTRODUCTION

The documentation prepared for the January 1996 Meeting of the Education Committee at Ministerial level consisted of two parts, the "Issues for Discussion" and the "Ministers' *Communiqué*", and the Background Report.

Ministers met in order to discuss the possible elements of broad strategies for making lifelong learning a reality for all. The document, "The Issues for Discussion", which was prepared by the Secretariat in advance of the meeting, sets out the main reasons why a strategy for lifelong learning is key to the continued development of OECD countries as they move towards the 21st century.

The large and continuing shift in employment from manufacturing industry to services, the gathering momentum of globalisation, the wide diffusion of information and communications technologies, and the increasing importance of knowledge and skills in production and services are changing the skill profiles needed for jobs. The distribution of employment opportunities is changing, with many unskilled jobs disappearing. With the more rapid turnover of products and services, and with people changing jobs more often than previously, more frequent renewal of knowledge and skills is needed. Along with these developments, confounded by factors such as the ageing of populations, emerging new values and patterns of leisure and work, and changing family relationships, there is the risk of new polarisation emerging between those who participate fully in the acquisition and use of knowledge and skills, and those who are left on the margins. Ministers accepted lifelong learning for all as the guiding principle for policy strategies that will respond directly to the need to improve the capacity of individuals, families, workplaces and communities continuously to adapt and renew.

Success in realising lifelong learning – from early childhood education to active learning in retirement – will be an important factor in promoting employment, economic development, democracy and social cohesion in the years ahead. Ministers focussed their discussion on issues of implementation, and explored three broad concerns:

- improving the foundations for lifelong learning, including the extent and quality of early childhood, primary and secondary education, so that all learners, young and old, obtain and maintain the academic and vocational qualifications they need for work and further learning;

- facilitating pathways and progressions through lifelong learning and work, particularly the transition from school to work and continuing education, and learning opportunities for adults;

- clarifying the roles and responsibilities of all partners – including governments, social partners, educational institutions, families and the learners themselves – in implementing and financing lifelong learning for all.

As a result of their discussion, Ministers agreed to make a commitment to pursue and implement a broad strategy for lifelong learning, suited to the circumstances of each country. The details are included in the official *Communiqué*, which is reproduced in its entirety below.

The *Communiqué* identifies two areas where action is required; foundation learning and the pathways through lifelong learning and work. Ministers agreed that educational disadvantage which is not addressed early in life is likely to persist. They therefore assigned high priority to the goals of improving access and quality in early childhood education and creating "tomorrow's schools" that would effectively combat failure. The latter is to be achieved by ensuring more flexible curricula, introducing individualised learning paths, exploiting better new information technologies and the potential of new teaching and learning methods that foster "cross-curriculum" skills, establishing a closer "parity of esteem" between vocational and academic studies and, above all, by ensuring not only an interest and capacity but continued motivation for learning in all students.

With respect to learning beyond initial schooling, Ministers agreed that large gaps in coverage still exist. In seeking to close these gaps, Ministers underlined the increasing variety of settings, both formal and non-formal, in which learning takes place. Hence the organisation and implementation of pathways through learning and work, in ways that allow broad access, flexibility and mobility, were seen as responsibilities shared between governments, both central and local, employers, educational institutions, teachers and trainers, and individuals. Ministers agreed on the need for a more strategic role of governments, bringing together other ministerial portfolios in addition to education. In their *Communiqué*, Ministers envisage strengthening partnerships among the many actors by establishing clear goals for the system, defining performance standards for both providers and learners, upgrading the knowledge and skills of teachers and trainers, developing career guidance and counselling services, especially for adult learners, and recognising that skills and competences can be gained outside the formal system. But partnerships are called for not only to broaden access and increase participation. They are also needed to create adequate incentives for individuals, employers and those who provide education and training, to invest more in lifelong learning, and to improve quality by delivering "value for money." Ministers are keenly aware that lifelong learning for all will require additional financial resources. But because lifelong learning provides substantial economic and social returns to all partners — individuals, families, employers and the society as a whole — the additional investment must be mobilised by all concerned.

THE ISSUES FOR DISCUSSION

Education and training systems which have made impressive progress over the last three decades are now faced with major challenges. The widening reach and impact of information technologies, the gathering momentum of globalisation and trade liberalisation, the ageing of the population, growing cultural and ethnic diversity and the changing nature of work are combining to create new opportunities in a context in which knowledge and skills will play a more significant role. A new focus for education and training policies is needed now, to develop capacities to realise the potential of the "global information economy" and to contribute to employment, culture, democracy and, above all, social cohesion. Such policies will need to support the transition to "learning societies" in which equal opportunities are available to all, access is open, and all individuals are encouraged and motivated to learn, in formal education as well as throughout life. The public expects and demands high quality and relevant education for all.

These expectations must be seen against a background of unacceptably high levels of unemployment and heightened concerns over future employment prospects, marginalisation and social exclusion. Many young people face a difficult transition from school to work and adult life, in part because they leave school without qualifications or, more generally, with neither an adequate foundation of knowledge and skills nor a positive attitude towards learning itself. It is estimated that one-third of all adults in many OECD countries have acquired only minimum standards of literacy and numeracy. Opportunities and incentives for learning and re-learning continue to be limited and unevenly distributed, and the potential for learning in non-institutional settings has been insufficiently exploited.

THE LIFELONG LEARNING APPROACH

Lifelong learning offers an appropriate framework for addressing these issues. The new idea underpinning "lifelong learning for all" goes beyond providing a second or third chance for adults and proposes that everyone should be able, motivated and actively encouraged to learn throughout life. This view of learning embraces individual and social development of all kinds and in all settings – formally, in schools, vocational, tertiary and adult education institutions, and non-formally, at home, at work and in the community. The approach is system-wide; it focuses on the standards of knowledge and skills needed by all, regardless of age. It emphasizes the need to prepare and motivate all children at an early age for learning over a lifetime, and directs effort to ensure that all adults, employed and unemployed, who need to retrain or upgrade their skills, are provided with opportunities to do so. As such, it is geared to serve several objectives: to foster personal development, including the use of time outside of work (including in retirement); to strengthen democratic values; to cultivate community life; to maintain social cohesion; and to promote innovation, productivity and economic growth.

Investment in education and training in pursuit of lifelong learning strategies serves to address these social and economic objectives simultaneously by providing long-term benefits for the individual, the enterprise, the economy and the society more generally. For the individual, lifelong learning emphasizes creativity, initiative and responsiveness – attributes which contribute to self-fulfilment, higher earnings and employment, and to innovation and productivity. The skills and competence of the workforce is a major factor in economic performance and success at the enterprise level. For the economy, there is a positive relationship between educational attainment and economic growth. Lifelong learning strategies promote equity by reducing barriers, so that opportunities for learning, which are currently accessible in full measure mainly by those who already have relatively high levels of education, are available to and taken up by all. These strategies can play an important role in breaking the cycle of disadvantage and marginalisation and so contribute to social cohesion. Improvements in equity by reducing the costs of longer term remedial action can result in increased efficiency, and so help to "pay" for extending lifelong learning to all. Accordingly, policies aimed at lifelong learning provide an important condition for sustained social and economic development, along with complementary macroeconomic, labour market, social and environmental policies.

There is now a consensus on the need for lifelong learning for all. The question is how the concept can be applied in practice. In implementing lifelong learning, it is important to be clear about the roles and responsibilities of the many actors involved: learners of all ages, parents, employers, unions, teachers and trainers, voluntary and private organisations (profit-making and non-profit) and different government departments at various levels. A rigorous, comprehensive and system-wide approach built on active partnerships of various kinds and at various levels of provision, at local, regional and national levels is needed. Forging the required partnerships is made more difficult by the wide range of education provision which lies outside the formal responsibilities of Education Ministries. This is a challenge that must be met: What, then, must OECD societies do to make lifelong learning a practical reality for all?

LIFELONG LEARNING FOR ALL: THREE BROAD CONCERNS

Three inter-related sets of issues need to be addressed in order to make lifelong learning a reality for all. The first is to improve the foundations for lifelong learning, so that all learners, young and old, obtain the academic and vocational qualifications they need for work and further learning. The second is to facilitate pathways and progressions through lifelong learning and work, especially the transition from school to work. The third is to rethink the roles and responsibilities of all partners – including governments – in implementing and financing the organisation of lifelong learning for all.

Improving the foundations for lifelong learning

The quality of pre-primary and primary education is key to all lifelong learning strategies. Although excellent early childhood education is well established in some countries, most need to improve access and raise quality, including for those with disabilities. Educational disadvantage not addressed early in life is likely to persist. Education at this stage must foster an interest, motivation and capacity for learning in all children. Schools, from early childhood onwards, should provide learning environments

where learners like to be, where they experience a sense of self-worth, of excitement and challenge in learning, and of success and achievement and pleasure of learning. Goals and practices require rethinking, as programmes need to take account of the circumstances of young children and their families and to recognise that solutions to difficulties must be found in partnership with other agencies and actors, especially parents and teachers. Successful schools exist in all countries. It is important to build upon strengths and the progress already made, and to develop ways of disseminating innovations and good practice.

At the secondary level, existing structures and practices often limit effective responses to the diverse aptitudes and backgrounds represented amongst students and weaken their motivation to learn. One consequence is that 15 to 20 per cent of young persons in many OECD countries leave school without a worthwhile qualification. Reducing this proportion is an overriding priority. Ways need to be found in some countries to introduce appropriate flexibility into practices that are at present characterised by detailed and standardised curricula, classrooms organised by age or grade divisions and ability tracking, fixed and narrow timetables, authoritarian teaching styles and assessments and rote learning. Further, steps need to be taken to link subject-based theoretical knowledge better to its practical applications and to provide sufficient opportunities for young people to enjoy learning while developing such critical "cross-curricular" skills as inter-personal and social relations, communication, problem-solving and learning-to-learn. This would help to establish a closer "parity of esteem" between vocational programmes and general academic studies at upper secondary and tertiary levels. There are many highly successful teaching strategies which foster knowledge, skills and a commitment to continued learning in young people and adults returning to basic education. These need to be further developed and more widely applied to encourage new "cultures" of learning and work in individuals, families, institutions and communities.

"Schools of tomorrow" will need to develop and draw on the active participation of learners, to address diverse learning needs and interests of all ages, to emphasize cross-curricular efforts and to adapt methods and contexts of learning in the light of new possibilities opened up by wider use of information technologies and advances in pedagogy. Institutions can be opened up for use by the wider community, including extended learning opportunities for adults seeking training in literacy and numeracy. Strategies to develop and implement successful innovation in foundation learning already include pilot projects, teacher development, incentives for innovation, and various forms of communication among parents, communities and local enterprises. New forms of accountability and governance, broadened autonomy in managing resources and a wider range of funding sources have also been introduced. Where teachers, trainers, institutions, cities and communities are experimenting with innovative approaches, the outcomes need to be examined, assessed and, where successful, extended more widely. Countries differ in the strategies used to extend successful innovation and sustain reform – strong, centrally-co-ordinated efforts as in Spain and the United Kingdom (England and Wales); "steering" as found in some Nordic countries and the Netherlands; a systemic approach which fosters local development and partnership, as envisaged in recent reform legislation in the United States; and close attention to monitoring and evaluation in France.

These developments place new demands on teachers and trainers. Many factors operate to limit the incentive for them to respond to these demands, such as a lack of appropriate pedagogical skills; weak links between schools, the community and local industry; limited scope for, and experience with, professional consultation by teachers; inadequate support services; and overall conditions of work, including remuneration. Policies to increase the capacity and motivation of teachers and trainers to address the challenges range from new recruitment strategies, staffing arrangements and career patterns to new forms of support for in-service training. Any strategy mix will need to be feasible in terms of its overall costs, as well as effective in improving the quality of teaching and learning.

Facilitating transitions through lifelong learning and work

As participation increases in a diverse range of academic and professional education, especially at the tertiary level, and the provision and application of information technology widens, the pathways followed by individuals are becoming more varied and transitions – particularly from school and initial tertiary education to work – more critical. This raises questions about the linkages and balance between academic and professional education, and how relevance can be assured and high quality recognised. Too often the links and articulations between the

pathways within lifelong learning and transitions to and from work and further learning opportunities are rigid and restrict mobility. Training opportunities at these levels are not available to all, and, more significantly, are heavily tilted in favour of the already better-educated and trained. This exacerbates the problem of disadvantage, especially for the unemployed, the low-performing, and those who are "locked-in" by geography or work, home or family circumstances. The need is both to broaden access and to develop more flexible, visible and interconnected pathways. New industry-education partnerships will be needed to support extended and varied forms of training to meet labour market needs. Other possible responses include a strengthening of work-based experience in regular programmes and encouraging both the supply of, and demand for, learning and re-learning opportunities for adults seeking to upgrade their skills, paying special attention to workers in small and medium size enterprises and catering especially to the unemployed.

The wide range of learning environments and diversity among client groups make it difficult to assess and compare quality. But, if information on the contents and relevance of learning opportunities is not available, learners will be unable to exercise the degree of choice implied by a lifelong approach to learning for all. Similarly, employers and education institutions may have insufficient information on which to base their decisions about recruitment, admission or learning needs, if the scope of provision, both formal and non-formal, is not reflected in the range of qualifications and recognised competencies.

Better means are needed to identify the knowledge, skills and competencies required and obtained in all forms of lifelong learning. The challenge is to develop, and put in place, methods of assessment and recognition which serve this purpose. However, as responsibility for providing a diverse range of lifelong learning opportunities becomes more widely shared, one key issue is how to develop partnerships not only within formal education provision but also through co-ordinated action involving Ministries and other actors outside education. Recent initiatives in establishing novel assessment and qualifications frameworks have not yet been successfully extended to all learning. It will be necessary to build on the strengths of such approaches and explore their weaknesses and gaps in order to recognise many more forms of learning. At the same time, in considering how to facilitate transitions to and from work and non-formal learning, attention needs to be given to different ways of improving the capacity of individual-learners – many of whom are adults seeking to re-enter learning – to make choices. This will entail new strategies for education- and work-based career guidance and counselling, and for partnerships amongst education institutions and employers.

Rethinking the roles and responsibilities of governments and partners

Strategies of lifelong learning for all imply new roles and responsibilities for a wider variety of actors and stakeholders – learners of various types, their families, teachers, social partners and governments. There is a task for the partners in revisiting goals, curricula and teaching and learning methods, as well as in redefining governance and management. The roles of government need to be rethought at several levels; a wide range of alternative policy orientations requires close analysis – including direct management, control and regulation; steering and framework setting for accountability; establishing or intervening in education and training markets; and more completely realised forms of privatisation. The mix of policies would go beyond a redistribution of responsibilities among the stakeholders and levels of decision-making and aim to foster a consensus for lifelong learning among the partners and a shared commitment to finance it. The extent to which society-wide agreement can be reached on the role of education and training markets is an open question. Nevertheless, intermediate and local levels of government will have a particular role to play in building partnerships for common action.

Lifelong learning is a challenge principally for Education Ministers, but it also involves other ministerial portfolios. Although there is wide variation among Member countries, none has the equivalent of a single "Ministry of learning". Indeed, given the breadth of lifelong learning, such a combination of ministerial portfolios would probably be impossible. Learning at work and active labour market policies for the unemployed are of particular interest to Ministers of Employment. The search for a systemic, coherent approach to lifelong learning for all requires close connections among the Ministries, as well as at different levels of governance, so that issues do not fall between them.

The implementation of lifelong learning for all requires the cost-effective use of public resources, and raises questions about the allocation of funds by level and type of provision. But it will also require additional resources, which cannot, in view of the current constraints on public budgets, all come from the public purse. Public financing will need to be used more strategically and effectively to support a wider range of learning opportunities, while being directed toward target groups, and to leverage private and public funds available under other ministerial portfolios in favour of gaps in the provision of lifelong learning. Evidence is now emerging that, where benefits are clear and incentives are in place, individuals and the social partners may be willing to shoulder larger investments for learning and skill acquisition. New possibilities of harnessing more effectively this willingness and ability to contribute resources should be explored. While there is some experience in countries with a wide range of policy options, each needs to be considered anew in relation to the new context and against the aim of stimulating and developing a culture of lifelong learning for all. For example, learners at the tertiary level in some countries could assume a greater share in the form of tuition fees, combining their studies with work, income-related loans or increased loan-based components in student financial aid awards. Similarly, in some countries, private employers could be encouraged to finance further education with the leverage of tax incentives and to provide basic learning opportunities to the unemployed within the framework of employment programmes based in part on wage subsidies. Further, financing incentives can be used to "free-up" resources through wider use of low-cost provision options opened up by information technologies and by distance learning in general. Where such initiatives add to the productive capacity of the economy, they might more than pay for themselves in terms of increased earnings and satisfaction for individuals, reduced costs for employers and multiple benefits to the society as a whole.

Making lifelong learning a reality for all requires action by a large number of actors – individuals, parents, teachers, communities, social partners and governments at all levels. They will need a well-developed knowledge base – data, information, research, evaluation and analyses – to support informed decision-making. In an increasingly interdependent world individual choices as well as collective policy decisions must draw on information that goes beyond national frontiers. But expenditures on education R&D are, at present, a minuscule part of OECD countries' total R&D effort and to be effective and relevant they need to be expanded. A revamped knowledge base will be essential in the exercise of a more strategic role for government, both within the formal education sector where new, stronger partnerships will reduce the reliance on detailed rules and regulations, and in non-formal learning where provision is diverse and not under the direct control of Education Ministries. Knowledge and understanding will be particularly needed about the outcomes of education and training, including evaluation of innovations for enhancing lifelong learning for all. The effects of strategies to extend successful and cost-effective innovations more widely need to be systematically assessed. Education Ministers have a particular responsibility for strengthening the local and national as well as the international and comparative knowledge bases. The OECD provides a unique forum for Member countries to exchange ideas and country experiences, research and policy analyses, taking into account specific country circumstances and the increasing importance of internationalisation. OECD's programme of data collection and development, research and analyses has contributed to the understanding of the functioning and development of education systems of Member countries and their links with the economy and society, as has its pioneering work on international educational indicators, and the on-going programme of country-specific and cross-country education policy reviews.

THE MINISTERS' COMMUNIQUÉ

Lifelong learning will be essential for everyone as we move into the 21st century and has to be made accessible to all, OECD Education Ministers agreed today.

"We are all convinced of the crucial importance of learning throughout life for enriching personal lives, fostering economic growth and maintaining social cohesion", said the Hon. Simon Crean, M.P., chairman of the meeting,* "and we have agreed on strategies to implement it. OECD societies have made great strides during the 1990s, but now we need to find more effective ways of offering every one of our citizens such an opportunity. The target may be ambitious, but we cannot afford not to work towards it".

STRATEGIES FOR LIFELONG LEARNING

Strategies for lifelong learning need a whole-hearted commitment to new system-wide goals, standards and approaches, adapted to the culture and circumstances of each country. OECD Education Ministers agreed to:

- strengthen the foundations for learning throughout life, by improving access to early childhood education, particularly for disadvantaged children, revitalising schools and supporting the growth of other formal and non-formal learning arrangements;
- promote coherent links between learning and work, by establishing pathways and bridges that will facilitate more flexible movement between education and training and work, aimed in particular at smoothing the initial transition between the two, and by improving the mechanisms for assessing and recognising

the skills and competences of individuals – whether they are acquired through formal or non-formal learning;

- rethink the roles and responsibilities of all partners – including governments – who provide opportunities for learning;
- create incentives for individuals, employers and those who provide education and training to invest more in lifelong learning and to deliver value for money.

In developing these strategies, Ministers affirm the importance of international co-operation and the value of the exchange of views and information that takes place in the OECD, and request the Organisation to carry out further analyses on how best to implement lifelong learning.

STRENGTHENING THE FOUNDATIONS OF LIFELONG LEARNING

Although excellent early childhood education is well-established in some OECD countries, most still need to improve access, raise quality and identify ways in which pre-school programmes can operate in partnership with the families of young children – since educational disadvantage which is not addressed early is likely to persist throughout life. Since strategies to combat deprivation at this early stage must extend beyond education, Ministers recognise the need to develop stronger, more coherent partnerships with social service, health, housing and employment agencies and voluntary bodies at local, regional and national levels.

Recent years have seen a considerable expansion of participation and completion rates in OECD education systems. The need now is to focus more intently

---

* "Making Lifelong Learning a Reality for All", meeting of the OECD Education Committee at Ministerial level, 16-17 January 1996. The meeting was chaired by the Honourable S. Crean, Minister for Employment, Education and Training, Australia. The vice-chairmen were Mr. J. Ritzen, Minister of Education, Science and Culture, the Netherlands and Mr. F. d'Aubert, Secretary of State for Research, Ministry of National Education, Higher Education and Research, France. Prior to the meeting, consultations took place with the Business and Industry Advisory Committee and the Trade Union Advisory Committee.

on quality, since a sizeable minority of young people still leave school without adequate qualifications, knowledge or skills. This has been a major factor in youth unemployment across OECD countries. A system which elicits high levels of performance from all students, and establishes a sound foundation on which they can build, is essential. Ministers underline the important contribution parental involvement can make in establishing this foundation and supporting motivation to learn. Ministers affirm their commitment to achieving a broadly-based and effective foundation for lifelong learning at the primary and secondary levels – whether academic or vocational – from which no-one is excluded.

Ministers are concerned about education systems' capacity to change quickly, at a time when many factors are combining to influence the shape of tomorrow's schools. In the future, schools should offer individualised and accredited programmes to learners of all ages. This means rethinking the way in which much education is currently organised, with the objective of enhancing motivation for lifelong learning and making it accessible to a much wider range of people – including adults returning to learn, the disadvantaged and those with disabilities. Rigid structures and practices – in curricula, grading students by age, fixed and narrow timetables and emphasis on rote learning – often characterise learning provision in many countries. Lifelong learning provides the opportunity to review curriculum content and methods of delivery. It would benefit from more supple frameworks which encourage self-directed learning, and permit a more flexible response to the diverse aptitudes and backgrounds of students. Institutions in most systems need to provide for a greater diversity of skills including learning to learn and other critical cross-curricular skills, and a better balance needs to be achieved between theoretical knowledge and its practical application. The new information technologies – including mass media and distance learning – offer opportunities for wider access as well as innovative approaches to student-centred teaching methods. Schools are a major social asset and should become "community learning centres" offering a variety of programmes and learning methods to a diverse range of students, and remain open for long hours throughout the year.

Ministers invite the OECD to study promising approaches to the "school of tomorrow" and identify examples of good practice for wider dissemination. The quality of education depends heavily on the skill, experience and motivation of teachers and trainers.

They, too, should be lifelong learners, and their continuing professional development in knowledge and understanding of both their students and their subjects, teaching skills, and the use of new technologies should be a priority. In particular, teachers will be encouraged to participate more fully in curriculum development and school management, and through performance incentives and support structures, to make the best use of their skills. For their part, governments seek to develop strategies that will make it possible to raise the professional status of teaching, to revitalise and renew teachers skills and to reward careers spent in high-performance teaching and training.

PROMOTING BETTER LINKS BETWEEN LEARNING AND WORK

Lifelong learning is not restricted to linear progression through primary, secondary and tertiary education. It increasingly takes place in a variety of formal and non-formal settings, but large gaps in coverage still exist. The 15 to 20 per cent of students who, in many countries, leave school with no useful qualifications face particular difficulties in transition to work – especially as high levels of unemployment persist despite the economic recovery in almost all OECD countries. Many adults have not been able to develop an adequate base for lifelong learning. Up to one in three adults in many OECD countries have attained only minimum standards of literacy and numeracy: they are at particular risk of long-term joblessness. As industry, commerce and services are transformed by technology, many skills – not only of employees, but also of managers and the self-employed – are becoming obsolete. There is a growing diversity of learners' needs, and current opportunities for updating them, especially for less-skilled workers, are limited and unevenly distributed. Pathways through learning and work with interconnecting bridges which facilitate mobility are not available to all. Skills and competences gained outside the formal system are often unrecognised and undervalued.

Ministers agree to give high priority to the availability of a broad range of options after compulsory schooling, especially in upper secondary and the first years of tertiary education, smoothing the transition to working life. A more fluid relationship between learning and work will be needed in the future, where an initial period of full-time education is followed by various combinations of work (full- or part-time), training and education available in enterprises, schools and tertiary institutions. Suitable academic and vocational pathways for learners at all levels and ages should be created, along with more sophisticated and transparent approaches for assessing and recognising competences. It is important to continue to build on the achievements represented by traditional forms of certification and to find ways of improving their relevance to the labour market. The development of career guidance and counselling, especially for adults, should be a priority.

Ministers invite the OECD to identify promising policy options by analysing country experiences in promoting flexible and interconnected pathways for lifelong learning, with particular reference to the transition from school to work. They welcome the recent publication by the OECD and Statistics Canada of the first International Adult Literacy Survey, which documents the nature and levels of literacy and numeracy among adults, and look to the Organisation to continue this work, to review country programmes and to identify policy options which address the problem.

RETHINKING THE ROLES AND RESPONSIBILITIES OF PARTNERS

In a rapidly changing world, a strategy for lifelong learning involves many participants and requires a rethinking of roles and responsibilities. Governments in partnership with learners, their families, public and private providers, teachers, and the social partners are best placed to set the policy framework for developing systems and networks through which individuals learn. Ministries of Education will need to adopt a more strategic role, to set goals and targets and to direct policy toward gaps in provision. On the basis of shared responsibilities, they will aim to foster a common commitment towards action for lifelong learning among the partners. Particular attention should be paid to the changing roles and needs of teachers and trainers, since ultimately it is they who will implement the policy.

Consistent with this new strategic role for government, as schools and other educational institutions are given new responsibilities, their capacity to exercise them must be developed through improved support structures, training and evaluation. The evaluation of learners, institutions and education systems is crucial both in securing greater effectiveness and in ensuring accountability for the resources used. Establishing clear goals, defining acceptable but high standards of performance, and offering teachers and trainers the opportunity to improve their skills will make it easier to focus educational change and to sustain reforms.

Ministers propose that the OECD should study both the roles and the responsibilities of different partners in providing lifelong learning, and ways in which such partnerships – at local, regional and national levels – could be made more effective. Lifelong learning involves ministerial portfolios other than education. Ministers undertake to deepen cooperation with their colleagues in the areas of social, labour market, economic and communications policies, in order to make sure that policies which affect education are coherent and cost-effective.

CREATING INCENTIVES FOR MOBILISING INVESTMENT

There are substantial potential benefits from lifelong learning, and increased investment is likely to be needed if these are to be realised. Incentives must be found which will mobilise new resources, but how the responsibility for such investments is shared will depend on the traditions and circumstances of different Member countries. While some countries are prepared to fund lifelong learning largely from the public purse, others will need to find ways of mobilising new investment if it is to be affordable. Incentives are also required to improve cost-effectiveness and the allocation of resources – which currently does not reflect the needs or priorities of lifelong learning – as well as to promote better co-ordination of the many potential public and private sources of support.

Even at a time of growing pressure on resources, governments will continue to be responsible for the adequate funding of basic education, given the very high social returns which result from investment at this first stage. They also have a responsibility to ensure, in a framework of devolution and sharing of financing at higher education levels, that there is a fair opportunity for all to participate.

Public spending on tertiary education – whether it takes place in universities or other educational institutions, at home through distance learning, or in the workplace – varies markedly from country to country. If this sector is to grow and diversify, new sources of funding will be required. Ministers looked at a range of options, including partnerships with business, charging tuition fees, deferred contribution schemes, and changing the balance between loans and grants to students. Taking account of their different circumstances, countries will need to strike a new balance between the contributions of individuals, employers and workers, and of society collectively. They request the OECD to deepen its analysis of policies which offer incentives for learners, their families, employers and other partners to mobilise larger investments for learning, and which promote cost-effectiveness, equity and quality in tertiary education.

Ministers call upon private- and public-sector employers and the social partners to respond to the demand for increased investment in human capital, to overcome barriers to the expansion of adult education and training and to further develop active labour market programmes, particularly to combat marginalisation and social exclusion. They invite the OECD's Business and Industry Advisory Committee and the Trade Union Advisory Committee to propose new ways of urging businesses to increase their capacity for training and the participation of their employees, and encouraging unions to do likewise for their members. They request the OECD to explore alternative types of incentives to encourage firms to provide more quality training to meet the growing and diverse skill needs of the workplace.

LIFELONG LEARNING IN THE 21st CENTURY

Ministers reaffirm the value of international co-operation and the exchange of information and comparative country experiences in developing national policies – especially in light of the widening reach of information technologies and the gathering momentum of globalisation. They welcome the OECD's role in fostering a fruitful exchange of ideas, its pioneering work in establishing international education indicators, and its ongoing programme of policy reviews. They look to the OECD to continue working on improving understanding of the functioning of education systems through its research, data collection and analysis. In particular, they seek advice on how best to implement lifelong learning for all, especially for the disadvantaged and those excluded from the mainstream. Ministers invite the OECD to:

- assess alternative visions of the "school of tomorrow", in particular in the light of new technologies and advances in pedagogy;

- review and explore new forms of teaching and learning appropriate for adults, whether employed, unemployed or retired;

- monitor progress towards the realisation of lifelong learning for all in OECD Member countries, through thematic reviews of aspects such as early childhood education, vocational

and technical education, including training in enterprises, the transition from school to work, and the roles and responsibilities of tertiary institutions, including universities, and those institutions specialised in adult education;

- identify the benefits of increased investment in lifelong learning, its implications for education and training policies in the effort to move towards a "learning society", and how sharing the costs of such investments can be related more equitably to the benefits;

- deepen its analyses of how more investment for learning by all partners might be mobilised, how education and training providers might be encouraged to achieve greater cost-effectiveness and to improve the quality of what they offer, and how greater coherence might be achieved among policies, especially in relation to active labour market policies;

- continue work on the flexibility of enterprises, with emphasis on the connections between new technologies, innovations and work organisation, and their implications for human resource development.

Future economic prosperity, social and political cohesion, and the achievement of genuinely democratic societies with full participation – all depend on a well-educated population. Governments will seek to establish an environment that encourages individuals to take greater responsibility for their own and their children's learning and, where appropriate, permits a choice as to where they acquire the learning they need. Real commitment involving all partners – including the co-operation of different government Ministries – will be needed to implement coherent, equitable and cost-effective programmes which will cover the needs of all for high-quality learning. Ministers call on their partners in the provision of education, training and those involved in the creation of employment to help them to generate a positive and encouraging climate of opinion in which lifelong learning can flourish, and to establish the mechanisms which will make it a reality. They have jointly committed themselves to taking such action, and are confident that as the 21st century begins, the strategy outlined above will usher in a new era of lifelong learning for all.

Part II

BACKGROUND REPORT

Acknowledgements

We would like to thank the following persons for the significant contributions they made to elements of this report: Edwin Leuven, in consultation with Andreas Schleicher (Chapter 1); David Istance (Chapter 2); Torsten Husén (Chapter 3); Wim Groot (Chapter 4); John Townshend (Chapter 6); John Lowe and Peter Sutton (Chapter 7); and John Addison, Elchanan Cohn, Hessel Oosterbeek, Wim Groot and Edwin Leuven (Chapter 8).

INTRODUCTION

Since the last meeting of OECD Education Ministers in November 1990, there has emerged a consensus on the importance of lifelong learning in meeting a range of educational, social and economic policy objectives. Lifelong learning is a means of shaping the future of OECD societies, by fostering the personal development of the individual, countering the risks to social cohesion, promoting democratic traditions, and responding to the challenges posed by increasingly global and knowledge-based economic and social systems.

The key idea underpinning lifelong learning for all is that while everyone is able to learn, all must become motivated to learn, and should be actively encouraged to do so, throughout life. Lifelong learning is conceived broadly, as learning that occurs variously in formal institutions of education and training or informally – at home, at work or in the wider community. Although this notion of lifelong learning is now widely accepted, and has already become a natural feature of everyday life for certain privileged groups, the next essential step is to make it a reality *for all*.

In agreeing to make lifelong learning for all the focus of the Ministerial discussions, Member countries have laid down an ambitious agenda for reform. The extent of the challenges posed to the education and training systems of OECD countries are described in Chapter 1, while possible policy responses are introduced in Chapter 2. The complexities of implementation in a field that cuts across traditional demarcations and departmental jurisdictions require that the existing evidence be carefully considered as a basis for policy discussions. No single strategy will suffice, given the differences among countries and the fact that lifelong learning is as a moving target. Nevertheless, two priority areas for policy action are identified in Chapters 3 and 4: revitalising schools and other institutions in order to establish a sound foundation for lifelong learning; and improving the pathways and transitions between formal and non-formal learning and work. A strategy needs also to identify the *instruments* to be used in the pursuit of these priorities. Four such instruments are discussed in Chapters 5, 6, 7 and 8.

Building an inclusive learning society is a long-term goal; achieving it will require major and sustained efforts over many years. Although the strategic directions developed in Chapters 3 through 8 are consistent with a long-term approach, their focus is on action that must be initiated in the short and medium term. There is no single, unified and hierarchically structured "system" of lifelong learning that suits all countries. Lifelong learning will need to build upon specific national and cultural heritages, and policies modified to suit particular conditions and needs. Moreover, to be effective, the strategy does not engage the education sector or governments alone. Three elements need to be taken into account. First, a "system" of lifelong learning cannot be imposed; it must depend and thrive on a great variety of initiatives taken by different actors in many spheres of life and work. Secondly, the role of government is not to "invent", manage and pay for a "system" of lifelong learning opportunities, but rather to monitor and steer developments and redistribute resources so that provision is equitable, flexible and efficient. Thirdly, the very nature of lifelong learning – diverse, pluralistic, and undertaken over a lifetime – calls for co-operation and co-ordination among many policy sectors, involving both macroeconomic and structural policies.

TRANSITIONS TO LEARNING ECONOMIES AND SOCIETIES

A. INTRODUCTION

This chapter brings together two spheres: the broad trends and developments in OECD economies, cultures and societies (Section B), and those in the education and training systems of the Member countries (Section C). The two are clearly linked: education and training systems both shape and respond to broad social and economic changes. Aspects of these interactions are examined in the different chapters that follow. The objective here is to identify the long-term contextual changes – challenges and opportunities – faced by education and training systems.

The evidence presented paints a picture of ongoing – indeed sometimes intensifying – trends of globalisation and ageing populations; of widely diffused information and communication technologies; of changes in the organisation of work and patterns of employment; and of changing values with regard to family, community, the environment, leisure and life-styles – all part of the drive towards the post-industrial information society. Most aspects of social activity and economic production are becoming more knowledge-intensive. Meanwhile, because of its deepening links with the economy, the education and training sector is also changing: the types of demand for education, training and skills are diversifying, as are the types of provision. One of the major policy questions that emerges is whether the trends described here contain risks for social cohesion and democratic traditions. If so, how can education and training systems be restructured to combat these risks and strengthen the democratic foundations of OECD countries?

This chapter, then, establishes the context for lifelong learning through the detailed analysis of a wide range of social, economic and educational data. The ideas that underpin this broad principle need to be grounded in an analysis of key facts and developments, and not merely founded on an assertion of anticipated benefits. The facts show that while certain developments are consistent with the broad changes required for lifelong learning to be implemented, they are not emerging everywhere sufficiently clearly to allow education authorities and other relevant policy partners simply to watch matters evolve.

B. BROAD TRENDS IN THE ECONOMY, CULTURE AND SOCIETY

Globalisation

Seen in the narrow perspective of movement of goods and services, globalisation is not a new or even recent process: some speak of a golden age of the 1950s and 1960s; others cite references farther back in history. Today's globalisation process is, however, new in its specificity. The concept has been broadened to encompass movements not only of goods and services, but also of investment, people and ideas across national and regional frontiers. Since the 1970s, three closely-related phenomena have played a central role in facilitating and spurring a new wave of globalisation: market deregulation, the advent and spread of new information technologies based on micro-electronics, and the globalisation of financial markets.

These three aspects are reflected in some simple indicators. Trade within the OECD area grew more rapidly than GDP during the 1970s – sometimes averaging 20 per cent – although the rate declined in the 1980s. In 1993 some $1 trillion of foreign exchange transactions took place every day. Since the mid-1980s, global foreign direct investment (FDI) has been growing at a rate three times that of domestic output. In 1993 there were some 37 000 multinationals with 170 000 affiliates, and a global FDI stock of $2 trillion that produced $5.5 trillion in sales by foreign affiliates – a figure larger than that for the global value of exports. World trade will thus be a major engine of growth over the next ten years. World merchandise trade is projected to grow at more than 6 per cent per year until 2010, faster than at any time since the 1960s (World Bank, 1995). In this global economy, the balance of imports and exports will be closely linked to the skills of the labour force in producing marketable goods and services with high value-added.

Increased movement of people is an important component of globalisation. Travelling abroad comes naturally to a large proportion of the population of OECD countries. Mass tourism has created an entirely new dimension in social and cultural interaction. In the original twelve countries of the European Community, private consumption expenditure on travel and tourism is estimated to grow by 78 per cent from 1995 to 2005 (Tourism Council, 1995). In addition to tourism, there are trends in international migration. Table 1.1 shows that compared to the early 1980s, the share of foreigners and immigrants in the total population has increased in the majority of OECD countries. Exceptions are Belgium and France, due to the importance of naturalisations, and Canada which experienced high levels of migration during the previous decade. Although the foreign or immigrant population is increasing in nearly all countries, the presence of foreigners in the total population continues to vary widely among the European countries (OECD, 1995b). Furthermore, there has been an increase in the number of asylum-seekers in recent

years, especially in the large western European countries and in the Nordic countries. These developments have made foreign encounters in the local environment a common experience. Chart 1.1 shows that migration trends appear to be reversing in Japan in recent years. Migrants must be integrated into the economy and society, and that requires action on the part of governments and the social partners. Language barriers have to be taken into account and an equilibrium must be found in combining new cultures with existing ones. Valuing diversity will be essential as more and more people with different value systems and backgrounds interact in community life and the workplace, which increasingly rely on dynamic team situations, against the backdrop of an increasingly diverse customer base, both in production and in services. The resources of education, training and self-directed learning are essential in addressing the challenge of valuing diversity.

Globalisation brings opportunities for economic and personal development, but it can also create vulnerability. As cultures mix, some of the traditional norms, values and cultural "maps" of communities and families no longer apply. One role of education

◆   Chart 1.1.   ***Components of population growth in OECD regions,
1982-86, 1987-91 and 1992***[1,2,3]
Percentage of total population

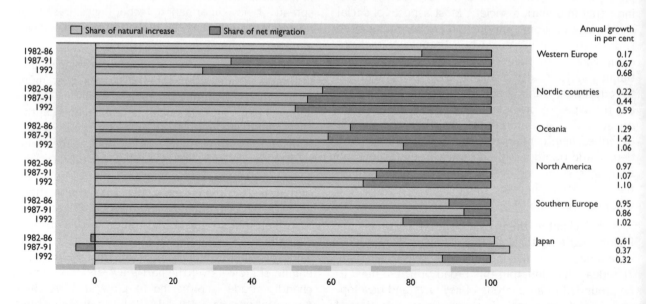

1.   Share of natural increase and net migration in the total increase of population for each period.
2.   Western Europe includes: Austria, Belgium, France, Germany, Ireland, Luxembourg, Netherlands, Switzerland, United Kingdom.
3.   Southern Europe includes: Greece, Italy, Portugal, Spain, Turkey.
Source: OECD (1995b), p. 23.

has been to maintain the stability of society by socialising individuals with knowledge commonly accepted as being necessary for adult life. However, in a complex world characterised by changing values, skills and competencies, this traditional knowledge-base is increasingly being questioned – which presents a major challenge to communities, families and individuals. "Enlightened" communities are responding by creating multimedia houses of culture and learning, where different traditions can meet. Given that national identities and regional and local cultural heritages are, at least in part, transmitted through education, school and adult education are similarly faced with a major challenge.

Demographic developments

The OECD population is ageing. Total dependency ratios will increase; the majority of the dependants will be aged, and often living alone. The consequences for public expenditures will be serious. Lower fertility rates influence not only the quantitative demand for schooling, but also the lower inflow rate into the labour market. Table 1.2 shows the likely result, which is a rapid increase in aged dependency ratios (OECD, 1988a). The share of people aged 65 and over is expected to increase from 18.9 per cent in 1980 to 27.6 per cent in 2020. This shift delivers the equivalent of a "demographic shock" – beginning around 2005 – to a number of OECD countries, including Germany, Japan and, to a lesser extent, the United States.

Annex Table A.1 shows the changing age profiles of populations in OECD countries. The shares of the 25-34 and 25-44 year-olds in the total population have increased in many countries since 1960, and they will continue to grow until at least 2000. To some extent this trend explains the rising demand for adult education and continuing vocational training observed in many OECD countries. Part of this new demand is directed towards tertiary education – in particular the conventional universities, which generally face rising enrolments of non-traditional students. But the trend in the age-dependency ratio suggests that there is also a large and rising demand for adult education among senior citizens. Providing adequate learning opportunities for older adults – who, as a group, are under-represented in adult education in all OECD countries – is a priority for governments, partly because such provision may help reduce or delay dependency. On the other hand, since a large portion of the retired population could well be prosperous and healthy and have a great deal of free time,

the demand for adult education will, to a large extent, be oriented towards personal development rather than economic goals. Flexible and diverse options are required because senior citizens cannot, as learners, be treated as a single group (Schuller, 1992).

Massive diffusion of information technologies

It is widely recognised that the new information technologies represent a structural break from the past (OECD, 1988b and 1992a). They are pervasive – that is, they have an impact throughout economic and social systems and not simply on particular enterprises or a specific sector. Pervasive technological change is not to be equated with certain hardware, or with specific production processes; it is, in its development and application, fundamentally a social process, and cannot be *imposed* on societies. This observation has major implications for education and training systems. Rather than describe the features of the new technologies – from microprocessors to information superhighways – this subsection explores some of the indicators of change, and their implications for education.

The massive diffusion of information technologies is not easy to capture in statistical terms. Nonetheless, there are some indications of the extent of change in OECD societies. For example, the software market grew by 17.5 per cent over the 1991-93 period, and is now in the same league as hardware sales (OECD, 1994a), even though computers are a fast growing commodity in OECD trade. Other high-technology sectors with a growing share in trade include semiconductors, telecommunications, aircraft and pharmaceuticals. The telecommunications sector in particular has become a thriving industry. Annex Table A.2 shows that the number of business mainlines per 100 employees increased from 15 in 1982 to 28 in 1992 across the OECD area. The global dimension is further highlighted by the rapid increase in international telecommunications traffic, which grew by more than 10 per cent per year in the OECD area during the period 1988-92. The data provided in Table 1.3 also indicate a trend in international specialisation, where high technology plays an important part. Japan shifted away from low-wage and low-technology industries towards high-wage and high-technology industries between 1970 and 1992. In the United States the trend was slightly away from low-wage industries and industrial specialisation stayed relatively unchanged. Industry structure appears to be very stable in the European Union with relatively little emphasis on high-technology industries (OECD, 1994b).

The patterns of job creation and job destruction flowing from the introduction of new technologies are normally unevenly distributed from one region, industry or occupation to another – and, if unchecked, can encourage dualism in society. Full exploitation of the new technologies implies a shift from the "taylorist" model of production organisation that dominated the first half of this century, not only in manufacturing but also in services and public administration. New technologies tend to shift the emphasis in work organisation and job content towards qualities like teamwork, initiative, creativity, entrepreneurship, problem-solving and openness to change. The move is away from a pyramid structure, and towards a substantial upgrading and broadening of skills. Table 1.4 illustrates this development for one country, Sweden, where long time-series are available. The data show a massive upward shift in the educational attainment of the population, a movement that will not come to an end in 1996: qualification levels continue to rise with the inflow of young, well-educated people into the labour market; with growth in adult education and training; and with narrow job descriptions being replaced by broader classifications. But the rise in levels of qualification, which parallels the move from the industrial to the post-industrial learning society, does not alter the fact that well into the future, there will be a large group of people who are at the tail-end of the skills distribution. Moreover, whereas highly-trained workers with access to the new learning economy will benefit from the wealth being generated there, they still face careers with frequent job changes, which indicates the need for continuing access to education and training. Many other workers, however, will remain tied to dormant sectors offering only dead-end jobs with low pay, poor benefits and few opportunities for acquiring new skills or qualifications. In this regard it is noteworthy that women's participation in the labour force is estimated to increase in all countries except Japan, commonly to 45 per cent in 2005. Women will contribute much more than men to labour force growth over the period 1995-2005 (OECD, 1994c, Chapter 2).

The education system needs to take these changes into account; it must provide everyone with an adequate foundation for later acquisition of new skills, and facilitate movement of workers between industries, employers and occupations. A high minimum threshold of competencies for all young people

is needed if people are to compete in the fast-changing labour market. Inadequate literacy skills among large numbers of adults need to be addressed (OECD and Statistics Canada, 1995). Workers need to be provided with more opportunities of on-the-job training. New technologies can also have a major impact on education practice by freeing teachers from the constraints of classroom space and time and large classes. They can cut costs and increase teachers' productivity. Teachers, meanwhile, will need frequent retraining, a point elaborated in Chapter 7.

Developments have not been uniform within the industrial sector, since low-technology, low-skill and low-wage industries saw their share in total employment decrease, while that of high-technology, high-skill and high-wage manufacturing expanded (OECD, 1994d). Thus the trends do not signal the demise of manufacturing industries in the OECD area; rather, they indicate that such industries have tended to become more productive with fewer but better-educated and better-trained workers. Chart 1.2, which shows the share of high-technology industries in total manufacturing, confirms the shift from low-skill manufacturing to high-skill, high-technology intensive production.

Changes in industrial, occupational and qualification structures

Technological change affects the industrial, occupational and skill structures of labour markets. The long-run shift in the industrial structure is made clear in Chart 1.3. It is widely recognised that in recent decades the service sector has become the largest single source of jobs, employing more than 60 per cent of the workforce.

The new growth industries are those involved in the creation, processing and distribution of information and knowledge. The share in value-added by high-technology industries has increased from 1970 to 1991, in some countries more than in others. Even though causality cannot be inferred, this finding points to a positive relationship between skills, technology, innovation, productivity and competitiveness. High-technology industries saw real growth in productivity and their performance in trade was exceptional as well. During the 1970s and 1980s the share of high-technology products in trade grew at an average of 20 per cent at current prices. Japan and Germany recorded exceptional annual growth in the percentage of employment in high-tech industries from 1980 to 1991, whereas Australia, Italy and the

◆ Chart 1.2. **Shares of high-technology industries in total manufacturing exports, 1970 and 1992**[1, 2]
Percentage of manufacturing exports

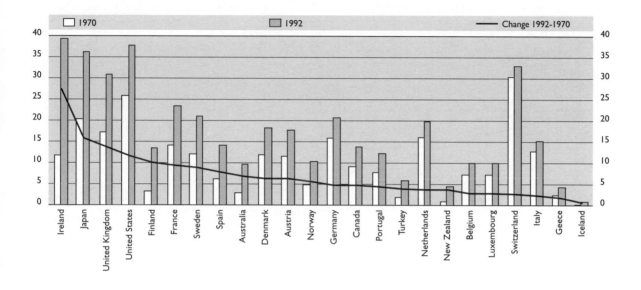

1. Australia and Italy, 1991 data.
2. See Annex Table A.3 for data and notes.
Source: OECD (1994*d*), *The OECD Jobs Study: Evidence and Explanations*, Part I, Table 4.12, p. 149.

United Kingdom experienced a contraction of employment in these industries (OECD, 1994*d*).

Chart 1.4 and Annex Table A.4 show the occupational distribution. The share of white-collar employment has risen in nearly all OECD countries; overall, the increase was from 54 per cent in 1981 to 60 per cent in 1991 (OECD, 1994*c*). Among the white-collar workers, the highly-skilled experienced the largest employment growth, indicating the continuing high demand for qualified workers. Occupational projections for a number of countries suggest a strong demand for highly-skilled professional, technical, administrative and managerial occupations, and a weakening demand for relatively low-skilled agricultural and production occupations. Whereas blue-collar workers in manufacturing and transportation made up about 40 per cent of the United States workforce in the 1950s, they accounted for less than 20 per cent in the early 1990s. This trend will most likely continue, so that by the year 2010 industrial workers may account for no more than between 10-15 per cent of the total labour force in advanced OECD countries.

The lower number of jobs in low-technology manufacturing will be more than offset by the expected rise of non-government services in total employment. However, the service sectors will be a source of employment opportunities mainly for those with intermediate-level skills (OECD, 1994*c*). The new jobs require a good deal of formal education and training, and the ability to acquire and apply analytical knowledge. Further, formal education is expected to exert an even greater influence with regard to allocating and sorting workers, and legitimising social stratification based on qualifications.

Unemployment

The incidence of unemployment was relatively low during the 1950s and 1960s; rates in many OECD countries were in the range of 1.5 to 3 per cent. The impacts of the first and second oil shocks were felt during the 1970s. During the 1980s, Europe especially has experienced relatively high unemployment rates: an average of 9.5 per cent in the European Communities (OECD, 1992*b*). While unemployment has tended to increase in some OECD areas, labour force partici-

◆ Chart I.3. **Employment share of agriculture, industry and services, 1900-90**
Percentage of total employment

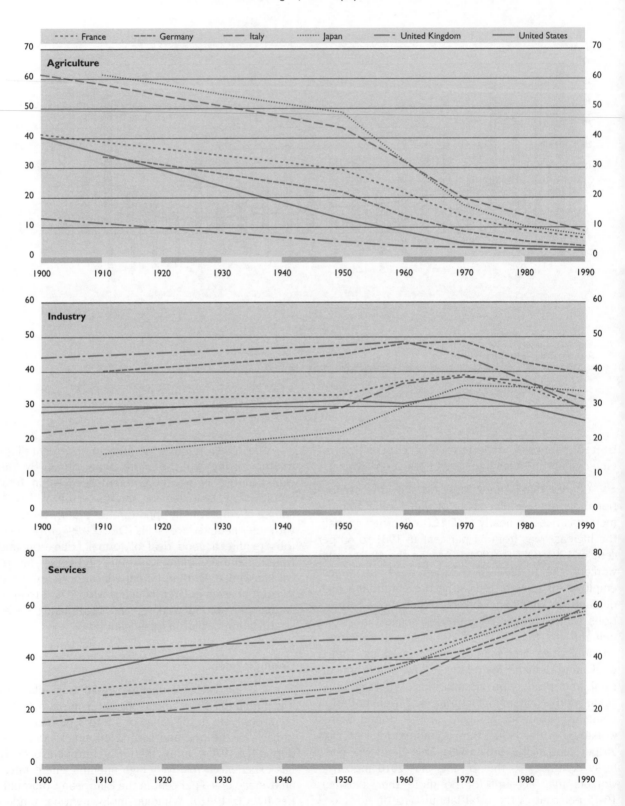

Source: OECD, historical series.

◆   Chart 1.4. ***Employment shares for blue- and white-collar workers, 1981-91*** [1]
Percentage of total employment, average annual change

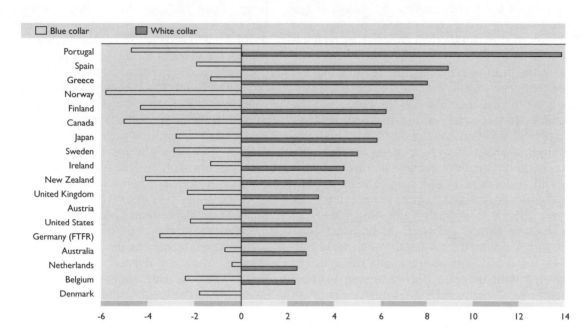

1.   See Table A.4 for data and notes.
Sources: OECD (1994c), *Employment Outlook,* Table 2.3, p. 82.

pation rates have also continued to increase. The capacity of the European economy to generate jobs slowed down during the 1970s and 1980s, whereas the United States experienced continued employment growth (OECD, 1994c, Annex Table A). Many of those unemployed were not able to find work for sustained periods of time. Table 1.5 shows that long-term unemployment of one year and over as a percentage of total unemployment in the European Communities ranged from 27 per cent in Denmark to 58 per cent in Italy in 1992, compared with 11 per cent in the United States and 8 per cent in Sweden. Unemployment in the European Union is generally expected to remain high until the end of the decade, at around 11 per cent; rates of joblessness in the United States are expected to fluctuate around the 6 to 7 per cent mark, and those for Canada around 10 per cent; Japan's rate increased substantially since 1990 (Stevens and Michalski, 1994). This bleak picture of the future job market is bound to have consequences for the education systems of OECD countries; education's role of providing knowledge and skills and bolstering social cohesion will have to be given urgent priority. Youths

are expected to stay on in the education system, and many other people – the unemployed, underemployed, and senior citizens – will be returning.

The changing work environment

As noted above, work arrangements are changing not only with respect to the nature and content of jobs but also in terms of their organisation and location. High-performance workplaces emphasise self-managing teams, study circles, flexible rather than narrow job design, flat organisational structures, employee problem-solving groups, information and office technologies, just-in-time learning and production, the ability to meet customer needs and, particularly, innovation and total quality management. People's knowledge, skills and qualifications are key to all these priorities. The move towards the high-performance and flexible workplace thus calls for a major education and training effort. But the nature of learning in the workplace is also changing: self-directed and team learning is replacing formal classroom instruction.

Before the Industrial Revolution, work was mainly agricultural or craft-oriented, and situated in the vicinity of the home. Jobs in the industrial age required workers to be concentrated in plants and offices, which stimulated urban growth. New technologies now make it possible to place the home, once more, at the heart of economic life. Teleworking and self-employment are two examples of developments that shrink the distance between the home and the workplace. Today, much of the telework involves employees in traditional job patterns who prefer to work from wherever they happen to be. But with greater decentralisation of decision-making responsibility and an increase in task-specific team production, telework is expected to grow in importance. By the year 2000 it is estimated that the number of teleworkers in Europe and North America will have jumped from around 0.6 million (in 1994) to 12 million. As home and work environments become progressively fused, they are also becoming learning environments. Consequently, the distinction between formal education and training and learning in non-formal settings is becoming increasingly blurred. It is critical that educational policy takes these developments into account.

One element of the changing work environment is the long-term decline in the number of working hours. Chart 1.5 and Annex Table A.5 show that a century ago, people worked on average about 2 770 hours per year. Today that figure is approximately 1 700 hours for a majority of countries. This decline has been persistent during the twentieth century; only recently has it begun to level off or, in a few countries, even to reverse. Although average hours worked by men have fallen, female labour supply has increased. Women now work more hours than they did ten years ago. The net effect of the decline in male labour supply and the increase in female labour supply is slightly positive – with families as the unit of analysis, the sum of husbands' and wives' labour time is now higher than it was before. But there are divergencies in this respect. People in the United States appear to have begun to work more hours, on average, than they did ten years ago. In contrast, Japan, where working hours are still relatively high compared to the OECD average, at around 2 000 per person per year, is expecting a decline of 244 hours by the year 2010. Most European countries are also expecting a continued decline. Germany, Norway and Sweden all have well below 1 600 working hours per

◆   Chart 1.5.   ***Annual hours worked per person per year, 1870-1993***[1]

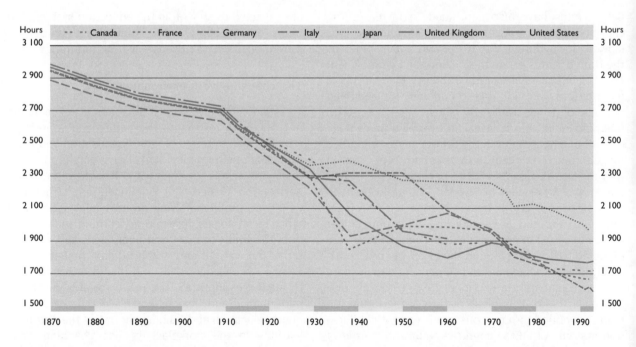

1.   See Annex Table A.5 for data and notes.
Sources: Data for the 1870-1960 period are from Carnoy and Castells (1995). From 1970 onwards the data are from OECD (1994c), *Employment Outlook,* Table B.

person per year, and expect a continued decline. In the case of Norway, annual hours worked may fall to 1 300 by 2010 (OECD, 1994c).

The long-term decline in working hours has meant an increase in the time available for other activities, such as family life, education and training, travel and leisure. In the United Kingdom, which has long recorded time-keeping information, available non-work hours in the average lifetime increased from 118 000 in 1856 to 287 000 in 1981. Over the same period, average working hours fell from 124 000 to 64 000 (Ausubel and Grubler, 1994). This trend is significant, because it indicates that the portion of total lifetime spent at work has fallen from about 50 per cent to less than 20 per cent. However, the increase in time for non-work activities is distributed unevenly between the different life stages. One-fifth of total lifetime is now spent on formal education and training before entering the world of work. This proportion is expected to grow as learning societies mature.

Working arrangements are being altered in many Member countries. Until recently, lifetime employment with a single employer was by no means an exception. But conditions are changing, and so are the expectations and demands of both employers and employees. This results in part-time, temporary, multiple and irregular jobs. Temporary work has become more common in Europe since 1983, especially in France, Ireland and the Netherlands (OECD, 1991a, Table 2.11). Annex Table A.6 shows that the share of part-time employment in total employment has increased for both men and women during the 1980s and early 1990s. The Nordic countries – which in 1983 had a relatively high part-time employment incidence – are an exception, in that the incidence has remained quite stable. In all other OECD regions, both male and female part-time employment has risen in this period. Charts 1.6 and 1.7 vividly illustrate the trends in size and composition of part-time employment for men and women. Some countries have seen a doubling of male part-time employment from 1983 to 1992 as a share of total employment; examples (1992 figures) are Australia (10.3 per cent), the Netherlands (13.4 per cent) and the United Kingdom (6.3 per cent). Female part-time employment increased the most in absolute terms, reflecting (at least in part) the re-entry difficulties women experience.

However, part-time work is not an option for everyone. Inflexible working conditions prevent many from taking up such employment, while for many others the choice is not voluntary. Table 1.6 presents data on full-time and part-time employment and individual preferences for eleven European countries. It can be seen that in France, Greece, Ireland, Italy and Portugal, where part-time employment was under 10 per cent in 1989, a significant group of workers would prefer part-time employment over full-time employment. However, in these countries over 40 per cent of all part-time workers preferred a full-time job. Part-time employment can thus be voluntary or involuntary, reflecting partial under-employment. It may indicate an inability to find a full-time job, or increased consumption of leisure. Available data show that involuntary part-time employment is more common for women than for men (OECD, 1990c, Table 7.1). In parallel, whereas men outnumber women in employer-sponsored training, women are over-represented in many adult education programmes. The demand for such learning opportunities is expected to grow for both women and men.

As work environments change in response to technological innovation and as conditions of work are altered, flexibility becomes a key criterion of success for both employers and employees. This is reflected in the alternative work arrangements mentioned previously, including self-employment. But flexibility depends on – indeed, presupposes – the widespread capacity, willingness and opportunity to continue learning. The development of the information economy and the concomitant transition towards the learning society must nevertheless be accommodated within the context of a broad, non-instrumental view of learning. Developing the creative and adaptive potential of all individuals has intrinsic value: contributing to social and economic adjustment is not the only imperative.

The shapes of the information economy and learning society to come are being influenced by the gradual but ongoing shift from materialist to postmaterialist values, a shift characterised by a reorientation towards enjoyment and self-fulfilment (Lenk, 1994). Although many people will continue to view work as a chore, for many others – especially those who are included in the high-skill, high-wage economy – work can increasingly become a source of personal development and satisfaction. This positive trend is, of course, offset by the growing precariousness of employment. This will change the scope of consumption; there will be increased emphasis on the pursuit of leisure, personal development goals, and aesthetic and intellectual interests. Postmaterialism will involve a redefinition of values, cultural

◆ Chart 1.6. **Incidence of part-time employment, 1973, 1983 and 1993**
Men

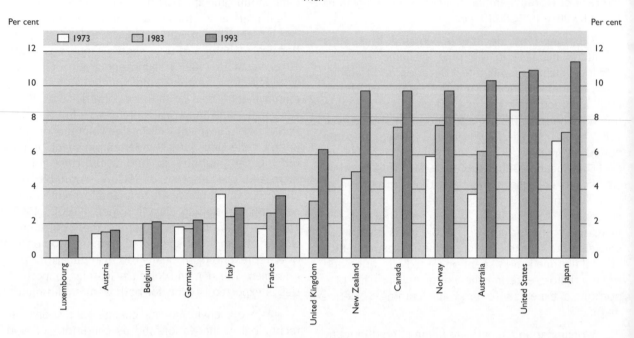

Source: Annex Table A.6; and OECD (1994c), *Employment Outlook,* Table D, pp. 198-199.

◆ Chart 1.7. **Incidence of part-time employment, 1973, 1983 and 1993**
Women

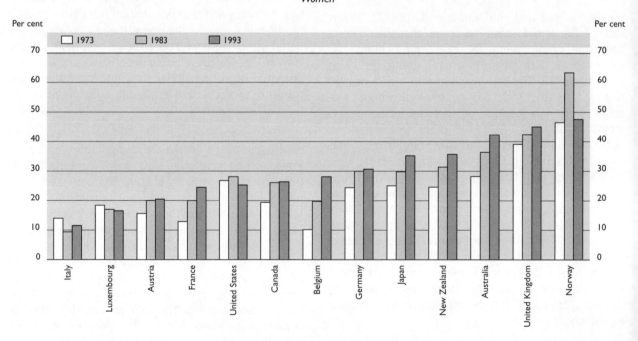

Source: Annex Table A.6; and OECD (1994c), *Employment Outlook,* Table D, pp. 198-199.

norms, institutional structures and communities, and interpersonal and social relationships. The indications are that the OECD countries – and their education systems – are in for a significant cultural revolution in this respect (OECD, 1994c).

Cultures, communities and families

Cultures – a wide concept encompassing languages, traditions, values and belief systems, but also habits and the "art of living" – are being redefined in the information age. As an increasing number of communities and families are linked by mainlines, cable and satellite, entrepreneurs rather than governments are setting the pace, and the choices are multiplying. Networks such as the Internet provide unprecedented supply of often diffuse information. Hence, more than ever people need the knowledge, literacy and analytical skills to search for and select the information they need, and to put it into perspective. While the skills needed to operate personal computers and related equipment come naturally to some people, this is not true for many others. Among the novelties further down the road are the expected growth of digital commerce involving data transfer and banking services, interactive television, home shopping, multimedia kiosks, and cable-based community services. A literate and educated population is the key to unlocking the benefits while safeguarding cherished cultural values. The very notion of literacy has evolved; in addition to reading, writing and numeracy skills, people now also require technological and computer literacy, environmental literacy, and social competence. Educational institutions have a major role to play in preventing the social and economic exclusion, and cultural alienation, that can result from a lack of appropriate literacy skills.

Another task for both schools and adult education has emerged in the wake of changing values and belief systems – not least the rise in individualism. Single-parent families and one-person households have increased rapidly as a proportion of all households. At the same time, new ways of organising family relationships are also emerging (Stevens and Michalski, 1994). These households are vulnerable to economic instability. Single-parent families are especially prevalent in the United States, where one-third of female-headed families are classified as poor. Recent survey data from the United States suggest that an increasing number of families with children face economic hardship, despite a 3.2 per cent annualised increase in real GDP from 1960 to 1990 (OECD, 1992b; NCES, 1994). Table 1.7 shows that for more

than a decade now, one in five children in the United States is considered poor, and African-American children were much more likely than Whites to live in poverty. More than half the children living in poverty lived in a female-headed household (NCES, 1994). But the United States is not alone among the OECD countries. Evidence shows that in European and Pacific countries income gaps are also widening; in Europe this development coincides with a trend of rising unemployment, from a standardised rate of 4.3 per cent in 1975 to 11.4 per cent in 1994 (OECD, 1995d).

Important social and economic issues are at stake, because children living in poverty risk missing out on the social, cultural and economic capital they need if they are to establish the foundations for success in lifelong learning and work. The cost to children living in poverty is especially high in urban areas, where the perpetuation and emergence of new ghettos are a cause of concern. The learning economy represents a rich opportunity for many people, but not for all. With poverty and unemployment continuing at high rates, social assistance remains important for large segments of the population. New ways must be found to secure the welfare of all members of OECD societies. What role can schools and adult education play in combating poverty and its consequences and symptoms? Because knowledge, skills and educational and occupational qualifications are powerful factors in determining access to good jobs with adequate pay, schooling and adult education are necessary components in any strategy for improving the quality of life of disadvantaged populations. Although educational policy cannot offer solutions by itself, there is a growing realisation that education, training and continuing learning more generally have a major role to play in complementing existing social insurance provisions.

For people not in employment, education is expected to hold even greater attraction in the future than it does today. First and foremost, it is the principal means of acquiring the skills and qualifications to enter employment. Education is more than an investment in human capital, however; it is also an avenue for personal development. Moreover, enrolment in education confers a sense of security and respectability, which is to be preferred over the anxieties and low status that are associated with unemployment. For all these reasons, the potential demand for education, training and learning is thus becoming both greater and more heterogeneous than ever before. Flexible learning environments that straddle the divides between the home, the workplace and the community are the key to satisfying this demand. The provision of high-quality education and training early in life is important but not sufficient. This foundation must be complemented by adequate learning opportunities beyond traditional schooling.

Educational policy is a powerful instrument that falls within the competence of OECD Member countries. Providing all citizens with a solid foundation of knowledge and learning skills is of crucial importance in securing equity, sustaining democracy and promoting economic development. In the course of building a learning society, many opportunities will be opened up; the possibility of acquiring new knowledge, skills and competencies will no longer depend on obtaining a formally prescribed education at any given age. Instead, "learning will become the tool of the individual – available to him or her at any age – if only because so much knowledge and skill can be acquired by means of the new learning technologies" (Drucker, 1994).

C. TRENDS AND DEVELOPMENTS IN EDUCATION, TRAINING AND LEARNING*

Changes in skill and qualification requirements bring into focus the need for education, training, and learning more generally as the means of updating skills and acquiring new qualifications. The premise that current education and training systems must adapt to new conditions is based on the analysis of broad transformations in OECD economies and societies presented in the previous section. But that analysis, as well as the review of options and strategies for change given in further chapters, must be informed by an understanding of how education and training systems have evolved over decades.

This section reviews trends in the demand and supply of learning opportunities for children, youth, and young and older adults in OECD countries. The purpose is to show how the demand and supply of learning opportunities have evolved, and who the main beneficiaries of public and private provision have been. Although the focus is on the formal sector of education and training – where internationally comparable data are available – important develop-

ments in non-formal learning are highlighted using examples from individual Member countries.

Trends in the development of education and training systems are organised under four broad themes: *i)* the contexts of education, training and learning; *ii)* access to and participation in formal education and training, as well as participation in adult education and non-formal and self-managed learning; *iii)* the costs and resources associated with the provision of learning opportunities; and *iv)* the internal and external efficiency of education and training systems.

The contexts

Education and training systems and the results they produce are subject to complex influences. In order to appreciate the differences in structures, processes and the outcomes achieved, it is important to note the different conditions and influences under which these systems operate. Thus, contextual information – for example, on the extent to which countries face demand for educational services at the different levels and in sectors of education, or experience resource constraints – should be accounted for in an analysis of the equity and efficiency of education and training opportunities. Many of the factors that shape the contexts of learning are given; they are not susceptible to policy intervention. Population characteristics, for example, play a significant role in the design and achievement of educational policies. The number of children and youths in a population determines the demand for schooling and hence the targets to be achieved for the supply of learning opportunities and the resources that will be required. The number of adults lacking proficiency in basic literacy and numeracy sets the stage for programming a country's adult basic education and literacy efforts.

Youth and population

Of central interest for educational policy is the ratio between the school-age population and the total or working-age population. Countries with larger young populations must allocate a greater proportion of their national income to initial education and

---

* The statistics presented in this section must be interpreted with utmost care because the dynamic nature of the education and training systems challenges the validity of comparisons over time. Many national changes in definitions and methodology have occurred since the data for particular years were collected, especially in the

allocation of national educational programmes to the levels defined in the International Standard Classification of Education (ISCED). Furthermore, the various sources from which the countries derive the data submitted to the OECD are not always entirely compatible.

training in order to devote the same proportion of domestic product to each student compared with countries with smaller youth populations. The proportion of young people aged 5 to 14 has gone through a cycle of modest increase and then decline and stabilisation in all OECD regions for a quarter of a century (see Chart 1.8). Annex Table A.7 provides information on the trend in specific countries over the same period. In some countries, such as Canada, Iceland, New Zealand and Spain, the decline has exceeded 6 per cent. The decline in the number of young people, which reflects a reduced birth rate, has somewhat eased the pressure on expanding school systems at the lower levels of education. As was mentioned in Section B, this long-term decline in birth rates has a knock-on effect on the rate of renewal of labour force qualifications, which will reveal its full impact in the years to come.

During recent years the decline in the proportion of young people has slowed down in many OECD countries – the Czech Republic, Greece, Ireland, Portugal and Spain are the exceptions. The ratio of 5-14 year-olds to the total population in most OECD

countries now lies between 11 and 14 per cent; the proportion of 15-24 year-olds is slightly larger. Although the differences between countries in the relative size of the young population have diminished since 1970, there are still remarkable contrasts, as shown in Annex Table A.8 and Chart 1.9. In 1994, in Mexico and Turkey, more than 20 per cent of the population were aged 5 to 14. At the other end of the spectrum are Austria, Belgium, Denmark, Germany, Italy, Japan, Luxembourg, the Netherlands, Sweden and Switzerland, where the proportion of 5- to 14-year-olds is below 12 per cent.

The population forecasts shown in Annex Table A.9 and Chart 1.8 suggest that over the next decade the proportion of the 5- to 14-year-old population will stabilise in most countries; the exceptions are the Czech Republic, Germany (FTFR), Greece, Ireland, Mexico, Spain, and Turkey, where this proportion is expected to decrease by more than 2 per cent – and, on the other hand, Sweden, Denmark and Norway, where it is expected to increase by around 1 per cent. The forecasts also indicate that overall differences

◆   Chart 1.8.   *The relative size of the population aged 5 to 14, 1970-2010*[1,2,3]
Percentage of total population

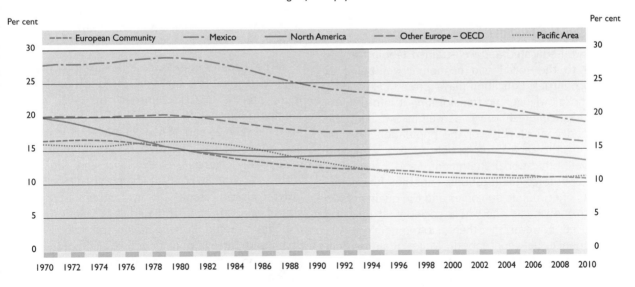

1.   Data for the 1970-94 period are United Nations demographic estimates, those for 1994-2010 are United Nations demographic projections.
2.   The chart shows trends in the relative size of the young population. The young population is the percentage of 5- to 14-year-old people in the total population. The total population includes all persons residing in the country, regardless of citizenship, educational or labour market status.
3.   The category "North America" includes Canada and the United States. The category "European Community" includes the 12 countries that belonged to the European Community in 1992. Other Europe – OECD includes Austria, the Czech Republic, Finland, Iceland, Norway, Sweden, Switzerland and Turkey.

Source: United Nations (1994), *World Population Prospects, 1950-2010.* Data for the Czech Republic were provided by the Czech Statistical Office.

◆   Chart I.9.   **The relative size of the population aged 5 to 14 and 15 to 24, 1994**[1,2]
Percentage of total population

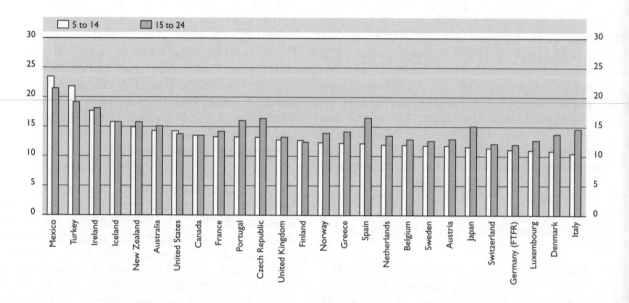

1.   Data are United Nations demographic estimates.
2.   Data for Australia: Australian Bureau of Statistics (1995), *Series A Population Projections* data. Reference month: June.
Source: United Nations (1994), *World Population Prospects 1950-2010,* and national data submissions.

between countries in the relative size of the young population will continue to diminish.

Educational attainment

A well-educated and well-trained labour force is critical to the social and economic well-being of OECD countries. Education plays a role in expanding scientific knowledge and transforming it into productivity-enhancing technology, as well as in raising the skills and competencies of the population, thereby improving the capacity of people to live, work and learn well. Educational attainment – and, by implication, labour force qualifications – are therefore determinants of economic outcomes and the quality of life for both individuals and whole societies. It must be recognised, however, that there is often no close correspondence between labour force qualifications – which can be defined quite precisely – and the skill requirements of jobs, which are difficult to pin down and measure with sufficient accuracy. Furthermore, because educational attainment represents only one aspect of labour force qualification, its use as a proxy for measuring qualifications is limited. Finally, attainment data are usually presented in terms of formal

educational qualifications and often neglect skills and competencies that are acquired through adult education, continuing vocational training, or other non-formal ways of learning at home and in the workplace.

The data in Annex Table A.10 show that there are marked inequalities in levels of educational attainment among OECD countries. In 1992 in most Member countries more than half of the population aged between 25 and 64 had completed at least upper secondary education (level 3). In four countries – Germany, Norway, Switzerland and the United States – around 80 per cent had attained that level. In other countries, especially in southern Europe, the educational structure of the adult population showed a different profile. In Belgium, Ireland, Italy, Portugal, Spain and Turkey, more than half of the working-age population had not completed upper secondary education, with the figures in Portugal and Turkey exceeding 80 per cent (see Chart 1.10). These findings have serious implications for job creation and economic development. Because the annual inflow rates into the labour force are relatively low, countries seeking to bring a large proportion of the population

◆   Chart 1.10.   **Population that has attained less than upper secondary education, 1992**[1]
Percentage of population aged 25-64

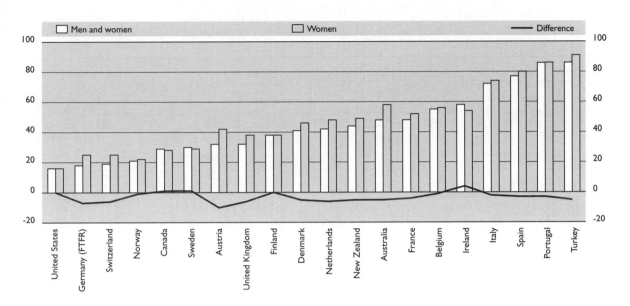

1.   For definitions and notes see Annex Table A.10.
Source: OECD Education Database.

up to the standard of upper secondary education will have to expand enrolments in adult education and continuing vocational training. The demand for such learning opportunities cannot yet be met, especially for people in their mid career.

Overall, the share of persons completing less than upper secondary education (levels 0/1/2) has been shrinking, and the proportion of persons completing upper secondary education (level 3) and going no further has declined significantly. This can be seen in Annex Table A.11 which presents, for a group of OECD countries, estimates of the average annualised changes in educational attainment for the population aged 25 to 64 years from 1981 to 1992. However, this progress has been uneven and substantial differences in educational attainment between countries still remain (see Chart 1.11). There are large differences between countries with respect to how quickly the educational attainment profile of the population has changed. The decline in the proportion of the population without an upper secondary education has been relatively modest in countries such as Canada, Denmark, France, Norway, Spain and the United States. In the case of Norway, this trend may be due

to the fact that the group with a low level of formal education was already comparatively small in 1981. High rates of change are recorded in Finland, New Zealand, Sweden and the United Kingdom. In these countries, the decline over the last decade in the proportion of the population with less than upper secondary education has been substantial.

The proportion of the age group going on to post-secondary education in universities (levels 6/7) or non-university tertiary institutions (level 5) has generally increased. In some countries, such as Canada, Norway, Spain and Sweden, this increase has been substantial. At the tertiary level, the biggest gains in absolute terms (and frequently in proportional terms) are found at the university level in most countries. In some countries – for example, New Zealand and the United States – the share of the population with qualifications below university level has even decreased. It is acknowledged that such interpretations are problematic, however, since university and non-university sectors have not been clearly defined internationally. The trend over the last decade contrasts with that of the 1970s, when the non-university sector experienced the most rapid

43

◆ Chart I.II. ***Change in educational attainment, population aged 25 to 64, 1981-92[1]***
Average annual change of the population-share having attained a specific level of education

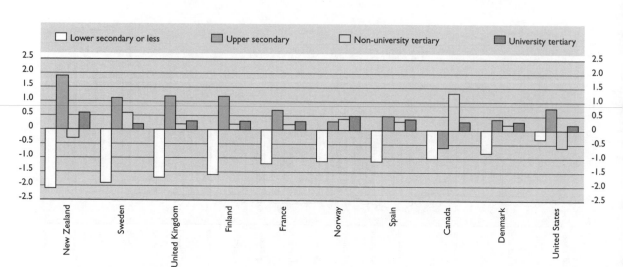

1. This chart shows the estimated average annual changes in population shares for below upper secondary education, for upper secondary education, for non-university tertiary education, and for university tertiary education. Included are all persons in the age group 25-64. Annual changes have been calculated over the period indicated in Annex Table A.11. For countries for which the available data covered less than 5 years, no annual changes were calculated.
Source: OECD Education Database. For details see Annex Table A.11.

expansion. Again, however, comparisons of educational attainment over time must be interpreted with special care.

Another way of looking at trends in educational attainment over time is to examine the attainment levels of different age cohorts. Chart 1.12 indicates for four age groups the percentage of the population that had attained at least upper secondary education in 1992. As can be seen, younger age groups have generally higher levels of attainment. This is a result of the expansion of education over decades. Annex Table A.12 shows that, on average, as much as 72 per cent of persons aged 25 to 34 had attained at least upper secondary education in 1992 in OECD countries. Among those aged 55 to 64, less than 50 per cent had attained this level. The difference between these generations ranges from as much as 51 per cent in Finland to only 11 per cent in New Zealand.

Older persons may increasingly find their comparatively low levels of skills and competencies overtaken by rising qualification requirements, and at the same time encounter difficulties in updating their qualifications through retraining because of limited basic educational competencies (see also Chapter 4). The proportion of the population that has received

tertiary education also varies greatly across countries. In 1992, more than 40 per cent of the population in Canada and around 30 per cent in the United States had attained the tertiary level, whereas in Austria, Italy, Portugal and Turkey, the figure was less than 10 per cent. Here also, however, it must be recognised that educational programmes at the tertiary level differ significantly between countries so that attainment levels must be compared cautiously.

It is important to note that the educational structure is rapidly closing the attainment gap in southern Europe, with younger generations obtaining more education than their elders (see Annex Table A.12). In Italy, Portugal, Spain and Turkey, the proportion of persons attaining upper secondary education in 1992 was three to five times higher among those aged 25 to 34 than among those aged 55 to 64. As regards tertiary education, the proportion for the younger age group was two to four times larger than the older group in these countries.

Even though in all countries except Turkey there has been significant progress towards greater equality in opportunities between the sexes since the 1960s, there is still insufficient opportunity and/or incentive for women to reach the same level of educational

◆ Chart 1.12. **_Population in four age groups that had attained_**
at least upper secondary education, 1992[1, 2]
Percentage of respective age group

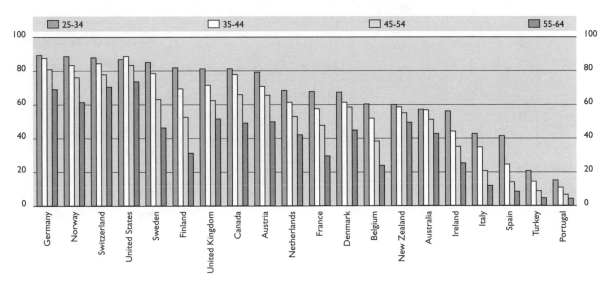

1. Australia, 1993 data. Portugal, 1991 data.
2. Of the 25- to 34-year-olds in Denmark, a relatively large number are still enrolled in education. Data may therefore understate the true values.
Source: OECD Education Database. For details see Annex Table A.12.

attainment as men in many OECD countries. Annex Table A.13 shows that, in 1992, women still formed the majority of those who had attained only primary or lower secondary education. In Germany and the Netherlands, the difference in the expected levels of attainment among those aged 55 to 64 was greater than 20 per cent, while for the age group 25-34 years it was 5 per cent or less (Chart 1.13). The same holds true for the group attaining non-university tertiary education, and in no OECD country did as many women aged 24 to 64 hold university qualifications as men in the same group. Again, these tendencies are much stronger among older age groups; specifically, the high proportion of females having attained only primary or lower secondary education was more pronounced among 45-54 and 55-64 year-olds than among 25-34 or 35-44 year-olds. Similarly, among university graduates, the average proportion of women was only around 35 per cent in the age groups 45-54 and 55-64, whereas this proportion was approximately 10 per cent higher for those aged 25 to 34 and 35 to 44. In addition to these overall differences in attainment, it should be remembered that men and women often choose different fields of study – a tendency that ultimately leads them to different seg-

ments of the labour market, even if they have received the same level of education and training.

Labour force participation and education

The level of educational attainment is a factor influencing participation rates in the labour force and the quality of economic activity: the data in Annex Table A.14 show that labour force participation rises with the level of education. Participation rates, while uniformly high, vary substantially among OECD countries, ranging in 1992 from around 60-65 per cent of the population 25-64 years in Ireland and certain southern European countries to around 80-90 per cent in the Nordic countries, Switzerland and the United States. Differences in participation rates by education levels are much larger among women than among men. This suggests that for women with low levels of educational attainment it is more difficult to obtain access to the labour market.

The influence of educational attainment on labour force participation rates appears to be growing in importance, especially for older males and all females. From 1981 to 1992, participation rates have declined in all countries for the group attaining only

◆ Chart 1.13. **Educational attainment of women compared to men for 25- to 34-year-olds and 55- to 64-year-olds, 1992**[1]
Percentage difference

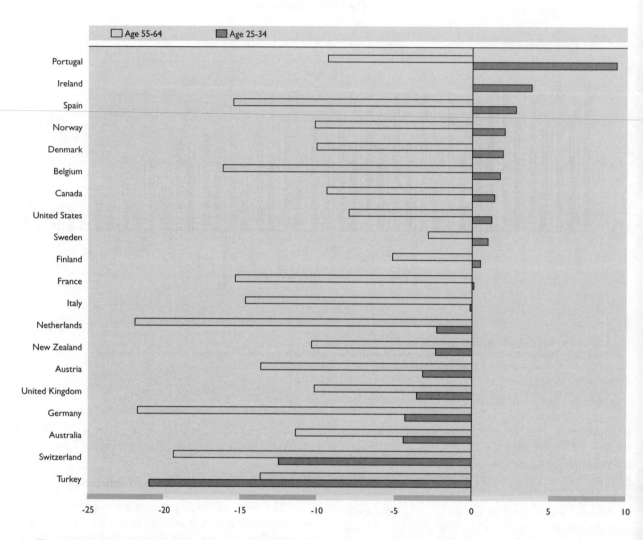

1. This indicator measures the difference in educational attainment between men and women. It is based on the percentage difference between a weighted average of attainment among men and a weighted average of attainment among women. Negative numbers indicate that women have on average a lower educational attainment than men, positive numbers indicate the opposite. The higher the number the higher the degree of inequality. The indicator only shows inequalities between genders. It does not represent inequalities within gender groups.
Source: OECD Education Database. For details see Annex Tables A.10 and A.13.

primary education. The pattern is clearest for older males. It is due to both social and economic changes, especially the structural shift in economic activity from low-skill manufacturing to high-skill services as well as the wider availability of pension schemes and early retirement options. But Chart 1.14 indicates that in the majority of countries that provided data, education is increasingly important in determining labour force participation. The difference in the par-ticipation rate of those having attained lower secon-dary education and those having obtained some terti-ary education is not only substantial in most countries, but also increased from 1981 to 1992 in Canada, Denmark, Finland, Norway, Sweden, the United Kingdom and the United States, whereas the difference was relatively low in New Zealand and remained stable over this period. In France and Spain differences decreased.

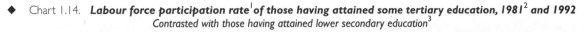

◆ Chart 1.14. ***Labour force participation rate[1] of those having attained some tertiary education, 1981[2] and 1992***
Contrasted with those having attained lower secondary education[3]

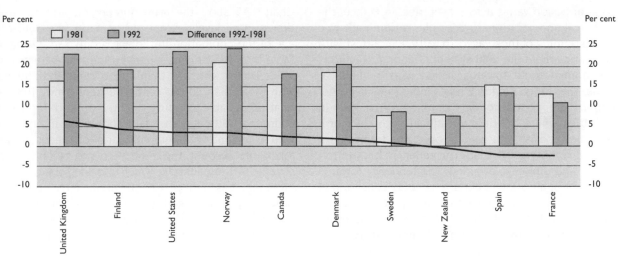

1. The labour force participation rate is calculated as the percentage of the population that belongs to the labour force. The labour force is defined in accordance with *OECD Labour Force Statistics*.
2. Data refer to 1984 for the United Kingdom and to 1982 for Finland.
3. This indicator shows the difference between the labour force participation rate of those having obtained some tertiary education and those having obtained lower secondary education. For example, for the United States, the participation rate of those having obtained tertiary education was 20.1 per cent higher than the participation rate of those having attained only lower secondary education in 1981. In 1992 the difference was 23.9 per cent, the gap therefore widened by 3.8 per cent.
Source: OECD Education Database. For details see Annex Table A.14.

Access and participation

Formal education and training systems vary in their capacity to meet the full spectrum of learning needs of young people. Enrolment statistics reflect the structure of the systems and indicate their relative openness. Indirectly they also provide glimpses of the phenomenon of early school-leaving. The presentation below focuses on systemic factors which reflect the policies and practices of education systems, and which are largely malleable. Part of the problem of early school-leaving is a predictable, if not inevitable, consequence of deeply entrenched practices: secondary education policies in many countries are biased towards young people bound for tertiary education; nearly half of the OECD countries require no more than nine years of compulsory education; and in three-quarters of the Member countries, compulsory schooling ends at age 14, 15 or 16.

New forms of assessment and certification methods and an emphasis on competency-based learning have led to more diverse approaches and, in catering to a broader spectrum of learning needs, have enabled more persons to continue studies longer. The growing variety of forms of pre-primary education also appears to have had positive effects on improving the prospects of many young children. The trend can be attributed to a number of factors, both those internal and external to education systems. Internal changes follow on deliberate reform decisions – the decision in Belgium to extend compulsory schooling to the age of 18 is an example. In countries such as Australia, France and the United Kingdom, the expanded provision of post-secondary opportunities have created powerful incentives for young persons to stay longer in school. The diversification of curricula in those countries as well as in Scandinavia has also had an effect on the character of secondary education – it began better to serve the needs of those not going on to tertiary education.

External factors, such as labour market conditions, have also played a role. High youth unemployment rates since the 1970s – especially in Europe, New Zealand and Australia – and the decline of "youth jobs" requiring few or no skills increased the incentives for young people to stay on in the system and acquire work skills while reducing the opportunity costs of doing so.

The relative importance of "education-led" and "employer-led" vocational training (see Chapter 4) in total provision varies across countries. In France, the technical and vocational *lycées* play a dominant role in the training of those aged 16 to 19, in contrast with Germany, where the dual system of apprenticeship is the normal route towards skilled worker qualifications. The United Kingdom relies more than any other country on post-secondary training provision. In countries where full-time vocational secondary programmes coexist with general ones, the former have tended to outgrow the latter in terms of both enrolments and diplomas awarded. The tendency towards the vocationalisation of upper secondary education in Europe – which is in sharp contrast to the trend observed in Japan and the United States – is especially strong in Belgium, France, Italy, the Netherlands and Sweden. An exception is Germany, where full-time technical upper secondary education complements the dual system of apprenticeship in the system of vocational education.

Apprenticeship is an important component of vocational education provision in many countries although the nature of apprenticeships differs widely between countries. In Germany it has had a central role, catering for about two-thirds of the age group, with government subsidies paid to companies to increase the supply of apprenticeships in line with the demand. In France and Italy, apprenticeship has been overhauled and strengthened; it now caters for the training needs of about 15 per cent of the relevant age group. In the Netherlands, the number of apprentices doubled between 1982 and 1990, reaching 20 per cent of the age group in 1990. In the United Kingdom, apprenticeship declined dramatically from 1975 and has now been virtually replaced by post-school training programmes.

Post-school training programmes have been set up in most European countries, usually under the auspices of the Ministry of Labour. In France, Italy and the Netherlands, about 5 per cent of the 16-18 age group acquire occupational skills through employment/training contracts or some other form of on-the-job training. The United Kingdom has gone furthest in this direction, with over half of all school-leavers receiving training under the Youth Training Scheme.

Participation in formal education

In most countries about half of the 5- to 29-year-olds are enrolled in full-time education, whereas in Australia and the United Kingdom there are also sub-stantial part-time enrolments especially in secondary education (OECD, 1995*y*). Annex Table A.15 and Chart 1.15 show the total number of full-time students (in all levels except pre-primary) as a percentage of the population in the age group 5 to 29 years. More than 20 per cent separated the two extremes in 1992: Turkey with less than 40 per cent, and Finland with more than 60 per cent. The trend since 1985 is relatively stable, sloping slightly upward for most countries. Although the data should be interpreted with care, and demographic variation needs to be taken into account, the trend seems to be fairly consistent: in the countries which provided data, enrolments increased since 1975 by about 1 to 5 per cent of the population aged 5-29. Exceptions are Austria, Finland, Japan and Switzerland, where enrolment increased by 8 to 10 per cent of the age group during the same period.

Another perspective can be obtained by examining the number of years a 5-year-old can expect to be enrolled in school. Chart 1.16 presents estimates of school expectancy in the OECD countries for which time series are available. In 1994, average school expectancy was the lowest – 14 years or less – in the Czech Republic, Greece and Turkey. It was highest, 16.5 years or more, in Belgium, Canada and the Netherlands (Annex Table A.16). School expectancy has generally increased from 1985 to 1994 in all countries that provided data, in some cases by more than two years, as in Norway and Sweden.

Enrolment in early childhood and primary education

Chart 1.17 shows the long-term trend of enrolment in early childhood education, from 1970 to 1992, by OECD regions. The trend in Japan and North America appears rather stable, whereas strong growth occurred in Europe and to an extent also in the Pacific Area. Trends in the coverage of education systems can also be examined using net enrolment rates. These relate the enrolment of a given age group to the total population in that age group. Table 1.8 presents net rates of participation in early childhood and primary education from 3 to 7 years. Early childhood education has become a growth industry, and for good reasons, which are spelled out in Chapter 3. Overall, the rates of participation increase for each succeeding year of age. In 1994, at age 3, six of the 16 countries reported enrolment rates of over 50 per cent (see Table 1.8). However, the variation among countries in access and par ticipation is highly significant, varying, for 3-year-olds, for example, from under

◆   Chart 1.15.   **Full-time students at all education levels except pre-primary, 1985 and 1992**[1, 2]
Per 100 persons in the population aged 5 to 29

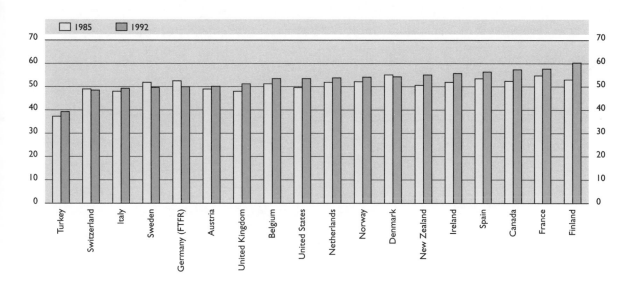

1.   Students enrolled in primary, secondary or tertiary education are counted regardless of their age. Students enrolled at the pre-primary level of education are
     excluded, even if they are 5 years or older.
2.   Enrolment in public and private institutions combined.
Source: OECD Education Database. For details see Annex Table A.15.

◆   Chart 1.16.   **Schooling expectancy for a 5-year-old child, 1985 and 1994**[1, 2]
Head counts

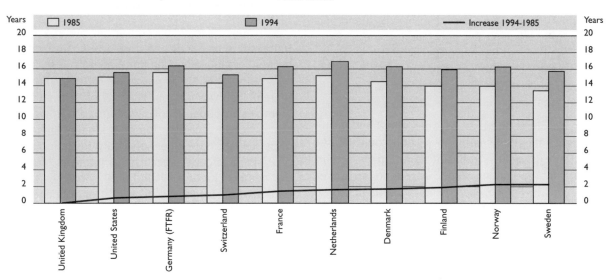

1.   The expectation is obtained by adding the net enrolment rates for each year of age from 5 to 29 and dividing by 100. This indicator therefore presents a hypothetical
     duration assuming a constant length of studies during the ensuing years. Expectancy rates are calculated using head counts. Note that the results would be slightly
     affected if part-time schooling was not taken into account: the loss would be half a year or more for Norway, the United Kingdom and the United States.
2.   1994 covers the whole of Germany.
Source: OECD Education Database. For details see Annex Table A.16.

◆ Chart 1.17. **Enrolment in early childhood education, 1970-92**[1]
Percentage of the population aged 5 to 29

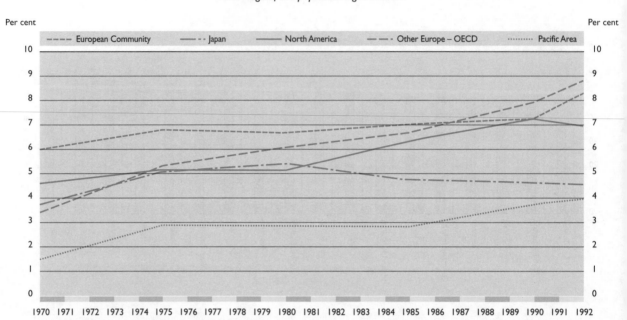

1. North America includes Canada and the United States. Pacific Area includes Australia and New Zealand. European Community excludes Luxembourg. Other Europe – OECD includes Austria, Norway, Sweden and Switzerland.
Source: OECD Education Database.

20 per cent in Greece, Ireland, Mexico and Switzerland to over 80 per cent in New Zealand and France. Rates over 60 per cent are recorded in the Czech Republic and Denmark. Early childhood education has thus become virtually universal in a few countries, while others still have a long way to go in achieving that target.

Chart 1.18 shows that, between age 3 and 4, the enrolment rates rise sharply in several countries. At age 4 there is again significant variation: less than 30 per cent in Finland and Switzerland and over 90 per cent in France, Japan, the Netherlands, New Zealand, Belgium, Spain and the United Kingdom. Table 1.8 suggests, however, that participation is nearly universal at age 6. Over 90 per cent of the age group are enrolled in all but one of the countries reporting data – Finland. At this stage the balance in enrolments shifts to primary schools. However, the majority of 4-year-olds in the United Kingdom are in primary school, whereas in Germany, Ireland, Switzerland and the Nordic countries, a large proportion of 6-year-olds are still enrolled in early childhood education.

Enrolment in secondary education

In lower secondary education, there is virtually universal enrolment. At this level, the variation between countries in the enrolment of 5- to 29-year-olds reflects mainly demographic factors. No data are therefore shown for this level. Choice of study programmes in upper secondary education is an important factor in the retention of students. Higher rates of participation in upper secondary education inevitably imply a broader spectrum of interests and learning needs. Charts 1.19 and 1.20 show net rates of participation in secondary education, depending on the system, for 16- and 17-year-olds, in 1985 and 1994. It will be seen that enrolment increased virtually everywhere, with large increases especially in those countries where participation rates were comparatively modest in 1985. Increases have been most marked in the Nordic countries, societies that have not had a strong apprenticeship tradition (France, Ireland and Spain), and countries which – in addition to lacking the apprenticeship tradition – also had education systems that tended to use upper secondary education exclusively to identify and prepare

◆ Chart 1.18. **Net enrolment of 3- and 4-year-olds in early childhood education, 1994**[1, 2, 3]

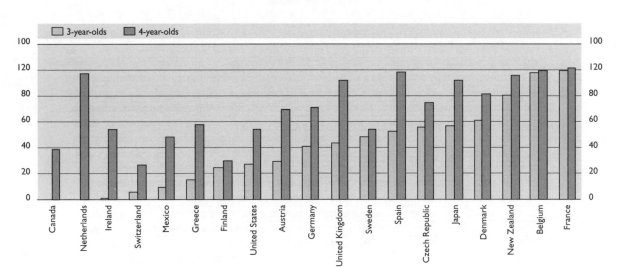

1. Net enrolment rates for each age group are calculated by dividing full-time plus part-time enrolments at that age by the total population of that age. Most countries do not distinguish full-time from part-time enrolment in early childhood education; all children are considered as full-time in this chart.
2. United Kingdom: includes substantial enrolments of 4-year-olds in primary education.
3. Canada: according to national definitions, 3-year-olds are enrolled in child care and *not* in early childhood education.
Source: See OECD Education Database. For details see Table 1.8.

candidates for university (New Zealand and the United Kingdom).

In most OECD countries, full-time secondary schooling continues until age 17 or 18. With a few exceptions, full-time secondary participation rates of 16-year-olds are close to or over 90 per cent. Annex Tables A.17 and A.18 show that the rate exceeded, in 1994, 95 per cent of the 16-year-olds in Belgium, Finland, France, Germany, Japan, the Netherlands, Sweden and the United States. Comparatively low retention rates are observed in Mexico (39 per cent). Australia and the United Kingdom also have substantial numbers of students continuing upper secondary education on a part-time basis. Many countries show comparable enrolment rates at age 17 and 18. It should be noted that while full-time secondary participation ends for most persons before age 19, in 1994 nine countries show participation of 10 per cent or more of the population continuing after that age in secondary programmes. These countries are Canada, Denmark, Finland, France, Germany, the Netherlands, Norway, Spain and Switzerland. It is important to note that for Denmark, Germany and the Netherlands

these rates include students who have completed one secondary programme successfully and are participating in a second programme at that level.

The data in Annex Tables A.17 and A.18 indicate that the highest retention rates at age 17 and 18 occur in European countries with very different models of provision in upper secondary education, including both entirely school-based provision and dual systems. What these countries have in common is a long and continuing tradition of highly organised systems of education and training, with clearly defined and collectively organised and accepted responsibilities. Another feature setting these systems apart is their "inclusiveness". This is particularly evident in the countries with the dual system (Austria, Germany, the Netherlands and Switzerland), whose success so far has resided in their capacity to provide the majority of young people with recognised qualifications and to organise the successful transition of large numbers of young people from education to employment (see Chapter 4).

Table 1.9 shows how the balance between general and vocational education has evolved since 1975.

◆ Chart 1.19. **Net rates of participation in secondary education for 16-year-olds, 1985 and 1994**[1]
Percentage enrolled

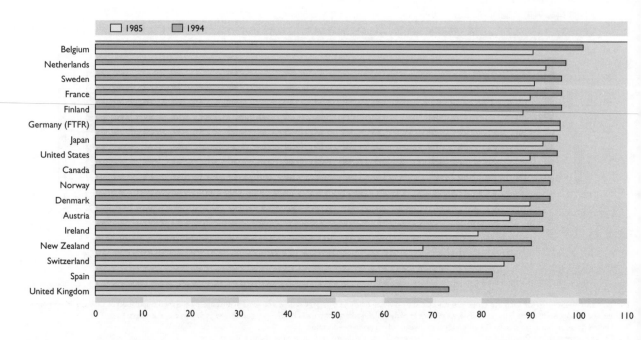

1. 1994 covers the whole of Germany.
Source: OECD Education Database. For details see Annex Tables A.17 and A.18.

◆ Chart 1.20. **Net rates of participation in secondary education for 17-year-olds, 1985 and 1994**[1]
Percentage enrolled

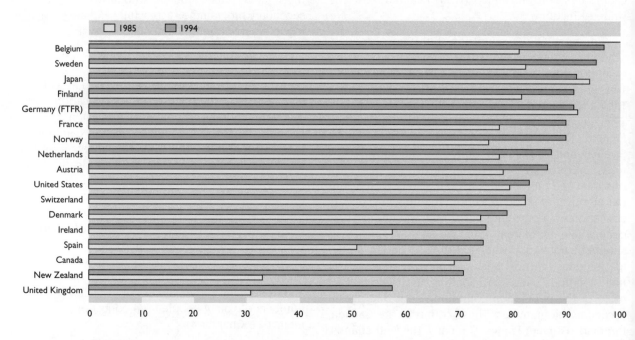

1. 1994 covers the whole of Germany.
Source: OECD Education Database. For details see Annex Tables A.17 and A.18.

In seven out of 14 countries which provided data for 1975, the majority of upper secondary students were in general programmes. In 1992, in Australia, Japan and New Zealand more than 70 per cent of upper secondary enrolments were in general programmes. This is in contrast to Germany, where only 1 in 5 upper secondary students was enrolled in a general programme, as was 1 in 4 in Austria. In more than half of the OECD countries – two-thirds of the 16 countries providing data – the majority of upper secondary students participate in vocational or apprenticeship programmes (see Chapter 4). Among the European countries, Spain and Turkey are the exceptions, with rates below 50 in 1992.

It is of interest to review the trend in enrolment growth at the upper secondary level. Annex Table A.19 shows the percentage of 5-29 year-olds enrolled at that level. Chart 1.21 presents the difference between 1985 and 1992. In Australia, Canada and the United Kingdom enrolments have been fairly stable since 1975, but then they were already relatively high in 1975. In other countries – such as Austria, Italy, the Netherlands, Norway, Spain and Switzerland – enrolments increased by more than 5 per cent since 1975, which indicates a significant expansion in a relatively short time span.

Transition from secondary to tertiary education

Recent years have seen the dissolving of age boundaries in the transition from secondary to tertiary education. The process has widened to include students ranging from 17 to 24 years. Does this represent an opportunity for countries to explore new organisational frameworks for learning that are more gradual and take place outside as well as inside the classroom?

Table 1.10 shows net rates of full-time participation in upper secondary, non-university tertiary, and university education at each year from 17 to 24. There is a gradual shift from secondary to tertiary education as the age increases. As can be seen, the age boundaries are much more pronounced in some countries than others. Overall, rates slope downward for each succeeding year of age. The Czech Republic is the only OECD country that reports full-time participation rates below 65 per cent of the 17-year-olds. As

◆ Chart 1.21. **Number of students in full-time upper secondary education, 1985 and 1992**[1,2]
Per 100 persons in the population aged 5-29

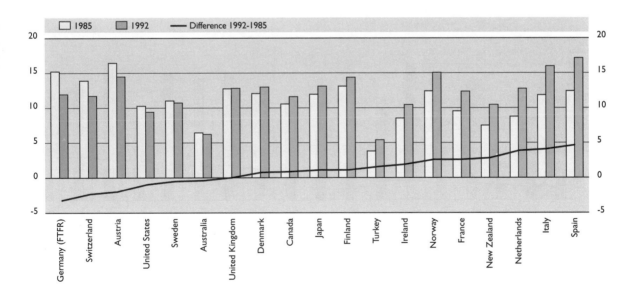

1. Students enrolled are counted regardless of their age.
2. Enrolment in public and private institutions combined.
Source: OECD Education Database. For details see Annex Table A.19.

full-time upper secondary education ends, the number of countries with participation rates below 50 per cent increases. By age 19, ten of 18 countries reporting complete data have full-time enrolment rates (upper secondary and tertiary combined) below 50 per cent.

After age 19, the decrease in full-time education is gradual but steady. For 20-year-olds, 15 out of 18 countries with complete data report overall full-time participation rates of 30 per cent or greater, with the majority of those participants in tertiary education in all but four countries – Denmark, Germany, the Netherlands and Switzerland. Those four allow students who have completed upper secondary education to pursue additional upper secondary qualifications. For those aged 22, eight out of 18 countries report full-time participation rates above 30 per cent of the age group, and all countries except Germany report a majority of their full-time participants in tertiary education. For the 24-year-olds, only Denmark, Finland and Norway report full-time educational participation at more than 25 per cent.

Enrolment in tertiary education and training

Annex Table A.20 shows the number of full-time students in tertiary education expressed as a percentage of the 5-29 year-old population. There is considerable variation – from fewer than 3 in Turkey to 10 in Canada and Finland in 1992. Whatever the causes of these differences, countries are similar in one respect: Chart 1.22 indicates that enrolments in tertiary education increased everywhere during the period 1985-92. Since 1975, in seven of 21 countries enrolments more than doubled. The expansion of tertiary education is a major achievement of the past 25 years, and the process is far from complete. The impact of tertiary education provision on public education budgets is considerable. Public pressure to reduce the unit cost is rising. In this context, the discussion about the allocation of resources in the perspective of lifelong learning can have major consequences. The issue of financing tertiary education is discussed in Chapter 8.

◆ Chart 1.22. ***Number of full-time students in tertiary education, 1985 and 1992***[1, 2, 3]
Per 100 persons in the population aged 5-29

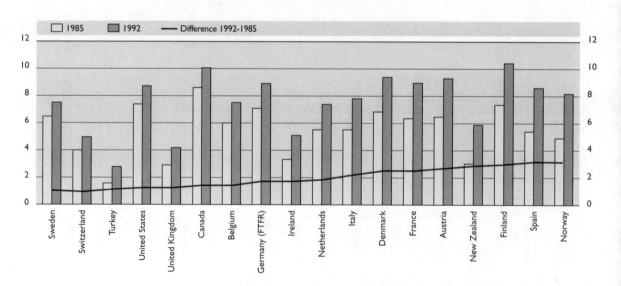

1. Students enrolled are counted regardless of their age.
2. Enrolment in public and private institutions combined.
3. The number of students in Austria is slightly overestimated due to multiple counts.
Source: OECD Education Database. For details see Annex Table A.20.

Participation in adult education and continuing vocational training

Lifelong learning becomes reality in the further education and training market. This section will review the evidence that the demand for and supply of further education and training opportunities are rising. Research and data collection in this area are still in a developmental phase; reliable data are scarce and inferences have to be made with caution.

One recent source of comparable data is the International Adult Literacy Survey, with data collection in 1994. This survey was conducted in six OECD countries and Poland (see OECD and Statistics Canada, 1995). Chart 1.23 shows the percentage of employees who received training during the six months preceding the interview. Training rates are highest in Switzerland, the United States and Sweden, around 42 per cent, closely followed by Canada and the Netherlands with rates of 38 per cent. In Poland 15 per cent of the employees received training.

Chart 1.23 also shows the length of the training – an indication of intensity that has implications for costs. Eighteen to 49 per cent of workers received training lasting one week or less. Of the people trained in the Netherlands, 18 per cent received this brief training, in Sweden this was 49 per cent. The Netherlands is the only country in which training tends to be for a prolonged period. Put in another way, in all countries except Sweden and the Netherlands, about half of the people who receive training are trained one to four weeks, the other half is trained for a month or longer (Annex Table A.21).

Time-series data that allow international comparisons of adult education and on-the-job training are not readily available. In order to investigate the evolution some country examples are examined below.

• Sweden

In Sweden a relative high percentage of the employed receives training that is fully or partially financed by their employer. The data in Chart 1.24 show the percentage of the employed in different age

◆ Chart 1.23. **Employees who received training[1] and its duration, 1994**
Percentage of employed population

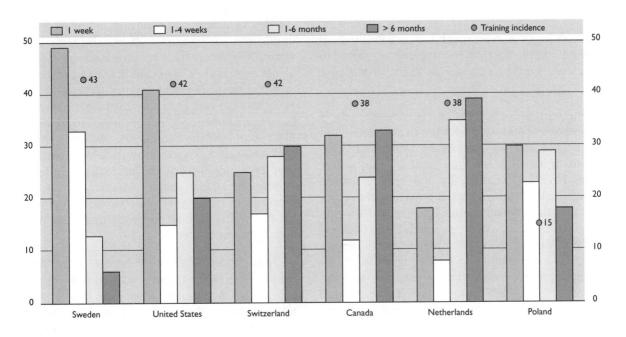

1. Since the previous six months.
Source : OECD and Statistics Canada (1995). See Annex Table A.21 for source data.

◆ Chart 1.24. **Sweden: employees who received training by age, 1982-94**[1]
Percentage of employed population

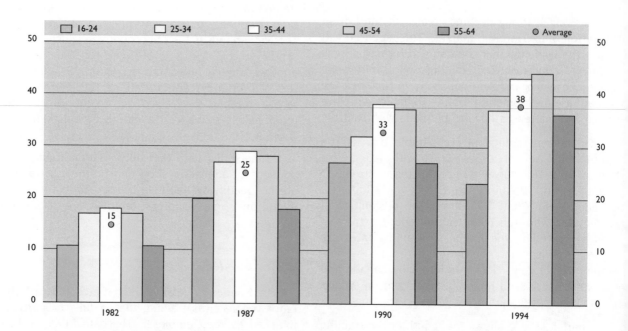

1. Refers to the first six months of the year.
Source: Statistics Sweden, *Personalutbildningsregistret.*

groups that received training during the first six months of the relevant year. In all age groups the trend is upwards, being more pronounced for middle-aged and older workers than for young employees. Compared to 1982, the probability of being trained increased overall. The total training rate amounted to 15 per cent in 1982 and increased to 38 per cent in 1994.

One remarkable feature of the Swedish data is the parabolic relationship between the probability of being trained and age (see Annex Table A.22). One possible explanation for this could be that young workers have up-to-date skills and require limited training. Workers above 55 are approaching the retirement age, thus making large training investments unattractive. In contrast, those aged 25 to 54 need training to update their skills; they will also remain productive long enough to render investments in training profitable. Table 1.11 shows the average number of days the training lasted, which was 6.7 days in 1994. There is no clear trend over time – average duration ranges from 5.7 to 7.3 days since 1986. In general, training duration tends to decrease with age, although not uniformly.

• **United Kingdom**

Annex Table A.23 and Chart 1.25 show the percentage of employees receiving job-related training during the previous four weeks. The total share of workers receiving training increased by more than 50 per cent, from 9.1 per cent in 1984 to 15.4 per cent in 1990. The incidence of training decreases by age. In 1990, 25.2 per cent of the 16- to 19-year-olds received training as opposed to 8.3 of the 50- to 59-year-olds. Relative to 1984 the training rates increased by 25 per cent for the employees aged 16 to 19, about 50 per cent for 20- to 29-year-olds, and 70 per cent for 30- to 39-year-olds. Older workers experienced the highest increases in training rates. Rates more than doubled for 40- to 49-year-olds and were nearly six times as high for workers aged 50 to 59.

Annex Table A.23 and Chart 1.25 allow the training practices in the United Kingdom to be contrasted with those in Sweden. Whereas in the lataer the relation is parabolic, it is linear in the United Kingdom. Like Sweden, however, the United Kingdom shows an increase in training participation. This evidence does not account for different types of training,

◆   Chart 1.25. **United Kingdom: employees[1] of working age receiving job-related training[2] by age groups, 1984-90**
Percentage receiving training during the previous 4 weeks

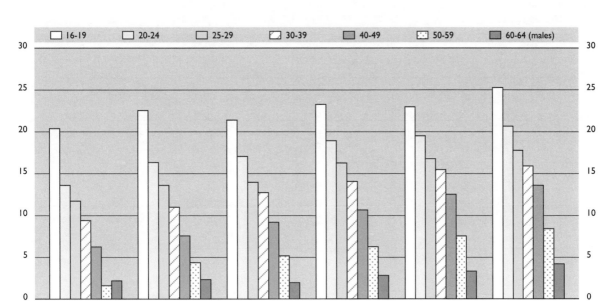

1.   Excluding the self-employed and people on government employment and training programmes.
2.   "Training" includes both on-the-job and off-the-job training; four-week reference period.
Source: Labour Force Survey, 1984; 1986-90 (preliminary estimates for 1990).

however, or their duration or intensity. A second point is the lack of international standards for the classification of training.

• Denmark

Annex Table A.24 shows the number of students enrolled in public adult education and continuing vocational training. Stability is the most striking feature. Enrolments are fairly constant except for Open University students, adults in regular formal education and day high-school students. The fact that the increases in enrolment are found in general education points to adults updating their formal qualifications. Whether this is driven by labour market or private considerations is not clear. Enrolment in publicly-supported vocational training remained relatively constant or showed slight increases. The evidence reviewed for Sweden and the United Kingdom suggests that the increases in vocational training are found mainly in employer-sponsored training.

The expenditures on public adult education and continuing vocational training are listed in Annex Table A.25. Nominal expenditures slope mildly upwards, areas that demanded more expenditures are those with increased enrolments. A striking example

of the benefits of distance education is the Open University. Although enrolments increased, expenditures remained relatively constant, because of the high fixed-cost component in distance education.

• Germany (former territory of the Federal Republic)

The concept of adult education in the German tradition of humanistic education was replaced by the notion of further education and training in the early 1970s. This more encompassing term pointed to both general and vocational education and training. Policy efforts in this area were directed to make it a fully endowed independent sector under public responsibility. Chart 1.26 and Annex Table A.26 show the development since 1965.

The trend is markedly upwards. In 1965, 1.7 million people were enrolled in further education and training. In the first half of the 1970s enrolments increased rapidly, reaching 3.7 million people. Growth slowed down in the second half of the 1970s, but by 1980 4.6 million adults took part. In the first half of the 1980s enrolments dropped slightly to 4.5 million in 1982. After 1985 growth picked up; in 1993 about

◆ Chart 1.26. **Germany (FTFR): enrolments and courses¹ in further education and training, 1965-93**

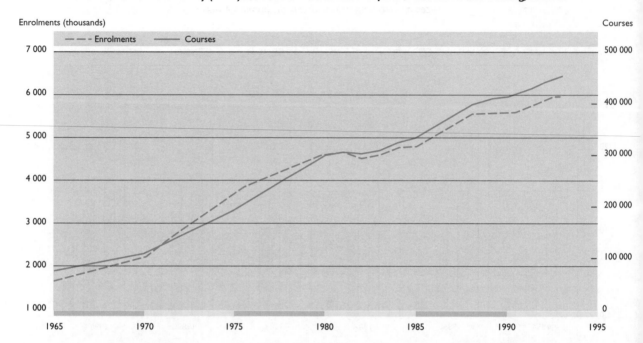

Enrolments (thousands)

Courses

- - - Enrolments   ——— Courses

1. Courses in 1991-93 include lecture series.
Source: Federal Ministry of Education, Science, Research and Technology (1994-95), *Basic and Structural Data; Education Statistics for the Federal Republic of Germany.*

6 million people participated in further education and training.

Chart 1.27 shows the development of public expenditures compared with enrolments. In the 1960s and 1970s expenditure growth was equal to enrolment growth. Throughout the 1980s there was an increased commitment to further education and training, and outlays increased more than enrolments.

Chart 1.28 presents the budget share of further education and training in total public education expenditures. There is a clear cyclical movement with a low share in the first half of the 1970s and an increase after 1974. From 1979 the budget share decreased slightly until 1983, when the trend reversed, reaching a peak in 1986, with 3.5 per cent of total public education expenditures allocated to further education. After 1986 the budget fluctuated. The general trend is upwards, although not impressively so: it increased from 2 per cent in 1965 to about 3.3 per cent in 1992. But again, it should be recalled that the bulk of the investment in further education and training is supplied from private, not public, sources.

● **France**

Further education and training in France expanded steadily since 1984. Annex Table A.28 shows that 5.7 million people were engaged in 1993. In 1984 this number was 3.5 million; the average growth rate was 5.6 per cent. In France, enterprises have to spend 1.5 per cent of their wage bill on training. Firms spent about FF 44.8 billion on continuing education in 1993, more than twice the amount in 1984. Expenditures thus increased by an average growth rate of over 10 per cent. Public expenditures equalled FF 28.4 billion in 1993, more than double the outlay on further education and training in 1984. Annex Table A.28 also shows that the training lasted on average 297 hours in publicly provided courses. Training duration in enterprises was significantly shorter (81 hours). During the second half of the 1980s and the first half of the 1990s expenditures on adult education increased substantially in France, as can be seen in Chart 1.29. Expenditures by enterprises increased more rapidly than government outlays. This increase in expenditures was not so much the result of more people being engaged in continuing training, but to the longer duration of this train-

◆ Chart 1.27. **Germany (FTFR): evolution of enrolments and expenditure[1]**
for further education and training, 1965-92
Enrolment in public institutions and public expenditure

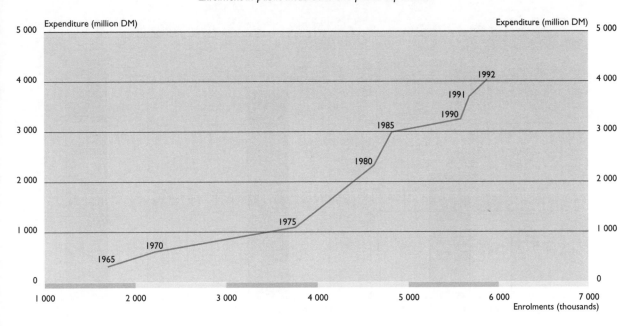

1. Net expenditure.
Source: Federal Ministry of Education, Science, Research and Technology (1994-95), *Basic and Structural Data; Education Statistics for the Federal Republic of Germany.*

◆ Chart 1.28. **Germany (FTFR): continuing education expenditure,[1] 1965-92**
As a percentage of total public education expenditure

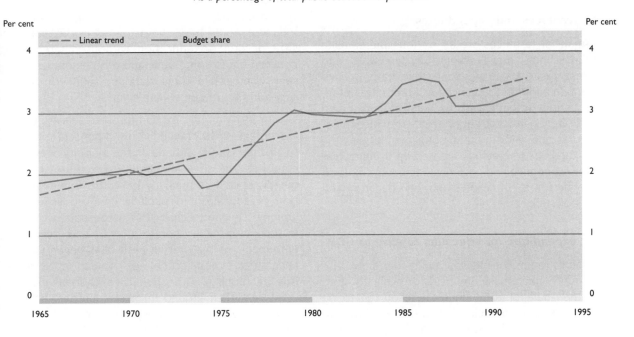

1. Net expenditure.
Source: Federal Ministry of Education, Science, Research and Technology (1994-95), *Basic and Structural Data; Education Statistics for the Federal Republic of Germany.*

◆   Chart 1.29.   *France: increase in adult education, students, hours and expenditure, 1984-93*
Percentage points increase by source of funding

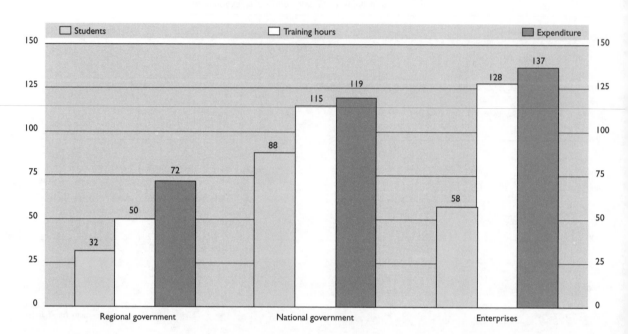

Source: Ministry of Education, Higher Education, Research and Vocational Integration (1995), *Repères et références statistiques sur les enseignements et la formation.*

ing; in enterprises the average training duration more than doubled.

Costs, resources and expenditures

Financial resources are an obvious prerequisite to build schools, hire teachers, buy textbooks, and otherwise create a safe and supportive learning environment. In addition to financial resources, the intangible qualities of dedicated teachers, principals and parents are of utmost importance. The incentives, both costs and rewards, that bring people with the "right" qualities to teaching are tied up in many features of economies and societies, including the local and public control of schools and the education and salaries of staff.

Public expenditure for education relative to GDP

One of the major financial policy decisions that each country must make, implicitly or explicitly, concerns the share of total financial resources to be devoted to education. A closely related task is then to divide the allocated resources among the various levels and sectors of education and training. Table 1.12 shows the trend in public expenditure on

education as a percentage of gross domestic product from 1970 to 1992. Chart 1.30 shows a plot of data for four countries; the trend lines are suggestive of convergence in public education expenditure. Ideally this indicator would have shown trends in the shares of GDP devoted to education without differentiating between funds from public and private sources. However, comparable trend data for total educational expenditure are not available yet.

In 1970, public expenditure on education as a percentage of GDP ranged from 2.4 per cent in Mexico to 10.2 per cent in Canada. In the majority of Member countries, the share of public expenditure was well over 5 per cent. In the early 1970s the dominant position of education in publicly financed social programmes began to change as a consequence of two factors: slowing economic growth, and decreasing enrolments as the drop in birth rates began to influence the size of the school-age population. Nevertheless, in terms of GDP, public educational expenditures held their ground in most countries. By 1980, expenditure was at or above 5 per cent in all countries except Germany (4.8 per cent), Greece (3.2 per cent), Italy (4.5 per cent), Mexico (4.6 per cent), Portugal (3.7 per cent), and the United States (4.9 per

◆ Chart 1.30. **Public education expenditure as a percentage of GDP, 1970-92**[1,2]
Selected countries

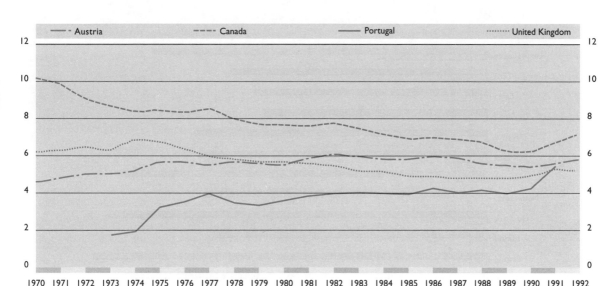

1. Data for gross domestic product (GDP) and expenditure are shown for selected countries, indicating the typical convergence of education expenditure among OECD countries since 1970.
2. For 1992 and 1993 data, possible inconsistencies may arise with earlier years, because of changed definitions in the data collections.
Source: OECD Education Database. For details see Table 1.12.

cent). By 1988, public educational expenditures as a percentage of GDP had declined in most countries, including Australia, Belgium, Canada, Germany, Ireland, Japan, the Netherlands, Sweden, Switzerland and the United Kingdom. Between 1980 and 1988 public expenditure remained at the same level, or even increased, in Italy, New Zealand, Portugal and the United States – countries that had a comparatively low position during the 1970s. By 1993 public expenditure was below the relative level in 1970 in the countries which provided data, except Australia, Austria, Germany, Mexico and Switzerland. The increase was most remarkable in Portugal, where expenditures rose from 1.8 per cent of GDP in 1973 to 5.3 per cent in 1993. This increase reflects a massive reform and expansion effort carried out as part of that country's democracy-building and modernisation drive in the years following the 1974 Revolution.

Private and total education expenditures

Education and training expenditures can generate economic growth, reduce social inequality and secure democratic values. They are therefore a productive investment. Moreover, education and training are a source of personal growth and satisfaction, and require continued commitment. However, public education budgets are under pressure in many OECD countries. This has led to a debate over the privatisation of educational activities, institutional diversity and the extent of public subsidies for privately controlled schools. As Table 1.13 indicates, some OECD countries have reassessed the balance between public and private education finance since 1985.

The share of private education expenditure has been constant in many countries, but there are notable exceptions, such as Finland, the Netherlands and the United States (see Table 1.13). The most important increases in the demand for learning opportunities are thus beyond the sector of initial schooling.

Chart 1.31 shows that private expenditures for educational institutions were in 1992 less than 1 per cent of GDP for all countries except Germany (FTFR), Japan, Spain and the United States. In the Nordic countries – Denmark, Finland and Sweden – the role of the government is predominant. The data for Germany (FTFR) suggest that the institutional arrangements and the existence of partnerships that go beyond financing are important factors in increasing private funding.

◆ Chart 1.31. **Educational expenditure by initial source of funds, 1992[1,2]**
As a percentage of gross domestic product

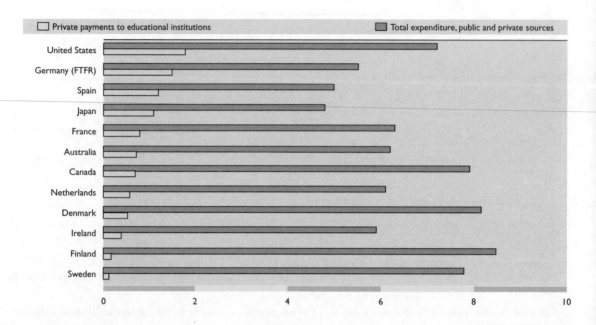

1. See notes to Table 1.13.
2. Data for Germany (FTFR) and Ireland refer to 1991.
Source: OECD Education Database.

Share of education expenditures in total public expenditures

Table 1.14 shows that most OECD countries spent between 10 to 15 per cent of the total public budget on education in 1993. The pattern is relatively stable and points to a continued effort to maintain current levels of investment. Variation among countries in the share of education spending in the public budget can be partially explained by the division of responsibilities between the public and private sector in the financing of education. This applies especially to tertiary education, where the importance of private funding differs considerably among countries.

In the aggregate, measures of education expenditure can estimate the total cost of education at the various levels of education. They do, however, not account for differences between countries in participation rates. An indicator on expenditure per student (also called the unit cost) provides an estimate of the financial resources that are invested each year for the education of a student at given levels of formal education. Summing such estimates over the duration of studies would yield an estimate of the total cost of education per student.

Two points should be considered in interpreting such unit cost data. Firstly, variations across countries or years may not reflect true differences in the resources provided to students, because there may be differences in relative prices. Secondly, unit costs need to be interpreted carefully, because of differences in reporting practices. At the tertiary level, for example, some countries include research expenditures whereas other countries report them separately. The data presented in Annex Tables A.29-A.32 should therefore be taken as a first approximation.

There is large variation among the countries in per student expenditure at all levels of education. Annex Table A.29 presents estimates of the unit cost of pre-primary education from 1985 to 1992. In 1985, spending per student ranged from 912 US dollars in Spain to 4 410 dollars in Norway. By 1992, the range had shifted from 1 240 dollars for the Czech Republic to 6 300 dollars for Denmark. Expenditures per student were higher in 1992 than in 1985 for all countries that provided data for this period. Some of the variation is explained by differences between countries in what constitutes early childhood education. True costs may be overstated, because of the inclusion of costs for extended day and evening programmes, as in the Nordic countries, or understated because of a failure to distinguish between full- and part-time programmes.

In 1985, per student expenditures in primary education ranged from 1 320 US dollars in Ireland to 4 356 dollars in the United States (Annex Table A.30). Spending per student increased from 1985 to 1992 in nearly all countries. In 1992, per student expenditures were lowest in Ireland (1 770 dollars) and highest in the United States (5 600 dollars). Annex Table A.31 presents unit costs in secondary education. Expenditures seem to have increased since 1985, at least for the countries that could provide the date. Portugal spent the least per student in 1985, and the United States the most. In 1992, the unit costs ranged from 2 620 dollars in New Zealand to 6 470 in the United States.

In tertiary education, expenditures per student were relatively stable or showed only slight increases from 1985 to 1992. As can be seen from Annex Table A.32, of the countries reporting data in 1985, spending per student was lowest in Spain and highest

in the United States. In 1992, the Czech Republic spent 3 590 dollars per student, compared with 12 350 dollars for Canada and 12 900 for Switzerland.

Chart 1.32 shows country averages of expenditure per student by level of education for the years 1985 to 1992. Typically, per student expenditures increase with increasing levels of education, with the highest costs incurred for tertiary education. The variation in per student expenditures by levels is expected to decrease, however, as expenditures per student in pre-primary seem to be growing more rapidly than those at subsequent levels. The growth in per student spending appears to be the lowest in tertiary education.

Ratios of students to teaching staff

An important indication of the educational resources that are available in a country is the ratio of students to teaching staff. But the allocation of teaching resources to the different levels of education is also an important policy issue. In almost all countries, older students have more access to teaching

◆   Chart 1.32.   *Expenditure per student from public sources by level of education, 1985-92*[1,2,3]
Country average,[4] constant 1992 US dollars

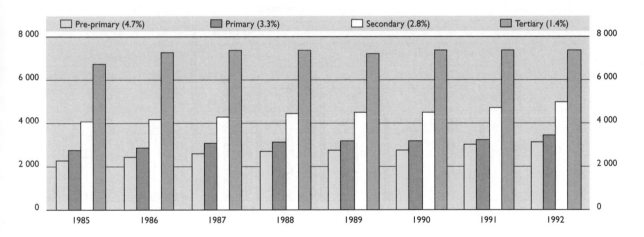

1. The number of students used to calculate expenditure per student from public sources is the number enrolled in public schools or in private schools that are predominantly publicly funded.
2. Direct expenditure per student from public sources is calculated by dividing direct gouverment expenditure for educational institutions at the corresponding level of education by the corresponding full-time equivalent enrolment. The result is converted into US dollars using the purchasing power parity (PPP) exchange rate for GDP.
3. Number in brackets in the legend is the average annual growth rate.
4. Calculated using data from countries that report full series. Norway, Spain and the United States, report data for all levels. Belgium reports data for all levels except tertiary education. Austria and Denmark report data for all levels except pre-primary education. Ireland reports data for all levels except secondary education and the United Kingdom reports data for pre-primary and primary education.

Source: OECD Education Database. See Annex Tables A.29 to A.32.

resources than younger students. This pattern of a progressively declining ratio of students to teachers can be thought of as producing a "bonus for age".

Annex Tables A.33-A.35 show the trend in student:teacher ratios at the levels of pre-primary, primary and secondary combined, and tertiary education from 1985 to 1992. Chart 1.33 shows the situation in 1992. In that year, of the 13 countries reporting information for both public and private early childhood education, six had ratios between 12 and 19; one had a ratio under 11; and six had ratios above 23. Of the 15 countries reporting data in 1992 for primary and secondary education, eight had ratios between 15 and 20, and another five had ratios below 12. For most countries reporting lower and upper secondary education separately, the ratios between the two levels are relatively similar. In tertiary education, in 1992, the ratios ranged from 10.7 in Germany (FTFR) to 23.1 in Turkey.

Examining the trends over time, at the pre-primary level there is a picture of sharply declining ratios in a few countries, notably Austria, Denmark, Spain and Turkey, and a sharp increase in ratios in the Netherlands. At the primary and secondary levels

of education, student:teacher ratios have decreased constantly since 1985 in most OECD countries for which such data are available, most markedly in Denmark, Germany (FTFR), Japan and Spain.

At the tertiary level of education, the reverse trend can be observed: the increases in participation have outpaced the increase in teaching staff in most OECD countries over the period 1985-92, most markedly in Ireland and the Netherlands. However, due to substantial problems in measuring educational staff at the tertiary level of education, the comparisons are not fully reliable.

Internal and external efficiency of education and training

The overall picture of important trends in education and training is not complete without information on student, system, and labour market and social outcomes, so that the results achieved can be assessed and possible shortcomings identified. There are many kinds of results, reflecting the multiple goals or purposes of education – including access to and completion of schooling; academic learning; job

◆   Chart 1.33.   **Ratio of students to teaching staff by level of education, 1992[1]**

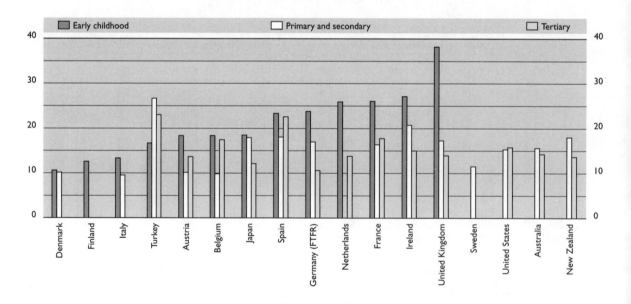

1.   The student:teacher ratio is obtained by dividing the number of full-time equivalent students at a given level of education by the number of full-time equivalent teachers at the same level. Note that the student:teacher ratio is not an indicator of class size. Note further that all children in early childhood education are counted as full-time even though they may attend school only half-day.

Source: OECD Education Database. For details see Annex Tables A.33 to A.35.

placement, continuation into tertiary education, or other dispositions after schooling, such as values, attitudes and social skills; and satisfaction of the public with school performance. In addition to outcome measures in the form of basic national aggregates, indicators of disparity between major regional and socio-economic groups are also of interest.

Graduation rates in upper secondary education

It will be seen that achieving upper secondary education is of utmost importance not only to secure employment and labour market participation, but also to serve as a basis for subsequent learning later in life. One measure of how systems perform in providing the population with upper secondary education is the graduation rate. Annex Tables A.36-A.38 provide the graduation rates in upper secondary education for different types of programmes.

Graduation rates measure "first-time" graduates as a percentage of the persons in the population at the typical age at which individuals complete the relevant programme. As can be seen from Chart 1.34, the proportion of students completing their first

upper secondary programme varies substantially among countries. However, 12 in 19 countries providing data show rates above 80 per cent. Austria, Denmark, Germany, Ireland, Japan, the Netherlands and Norway have first-programme graduation rates exceeding 90 per cent. The extent to which students graduate from general or vocational programmes also differs among countries. Of the 17 OECD countries providing data in 1992, eight reported that the majority of first-programme graduates came from institutions with general programmes and the others reported that they came from vocational or apprenticeship programmes.

Upper secondary graduation has expanded significantly since 1985. Denmark, France, and Turkey experienced increases of 10 per cent, and Italy, the Netherlands, Portugal, Spain and Norway of 20 to 40 per cent. Graduation rates in other countries were relatively stable. The distribution of graduates between general and vocational education has also been fairly constant for most countries. In France, however, the overall increase in graduation rates is mainly due to an expansion of general education,

◆   Chart 1.34.   ***Graduation rates in upper secondary education, 1992***[1]

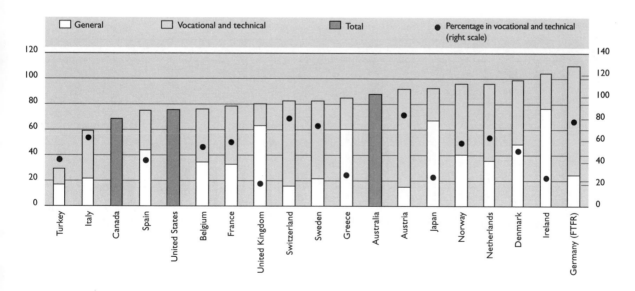

1.   Graduation rates are calculated as the ratio of first-time upper secondary graduates to the number of persons in the population who are at the typical age at which persons in that country complete the corresponding educational programme. Upper secondary graduates are persons who successfully complete the final year of upper secondary education (success may or may not be established through a final examination). As a consequence, graduation rates may exceed 100 per cent because graduation can occur before or after the theoretical age of graduation.

Source: OECD Education Database. For details, see Annex Tables A.37 and A.38.

whereas in the Netherlands and Norway the increase was mainly due to a substantial rise in vocational and technical graduates.

Graduation rates in tertiary education

Annex Table A.39 presents the graduation rates for tertiary university education. These rates are of interest because they show the proportion of young people who are highly qualified. The graduation rates presented in Chart 1.35 include advanced degrees; however, they exclude non-university tertiary education, which is a large segment in some countries. As can be seen, the tertiary graduation rates vary from 7 to 11 per cent in Austria, Switzerland and Turkey, to 36 per cent or more in Australia, Canada, Norway and the United States, with the remaining countries spread over the percentage range. The rise in graduation rates in some countries points to an increased demand for learning. Although birth rates tend to slow down or decline, in the future, the pressure on tertiary education is expected to continue because of continuing high demand.

Student learning outcomes

OECD education systems have expanded, and increased enrolment rates made attainment levels rise. But what about the quality of education that is actually delivered? Assessment must be an integrated part of educational policy. Bishop (1995) observes that "high-stakes" examinations at the end of secondary schooling are probably necessary if high achievement levels are to be attained. Based on Canadian data he finds that examination systems have pervasive effects on students, school administrators, teachers and parents. In provinces with external examinations, schools were not only likely to employ better qualified teachers, but the school infrastructure was of higher quality, and more attention was being paid to science and mathematics instruction.

Chart 1.36 shows the mean proficiency scores on the Scholastic Aptitude Test (SAT) in the United States since 1976. The SAT is the test most frequently taken by college-bound students. It is designed to predict success in the first year of college and to provide information about student performance over time. Since 1976 the mean SAT scores decreased until

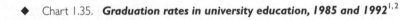

◆ Chart 1.35. *Graduation rates in university education, 1985 and 1992*[1,2]

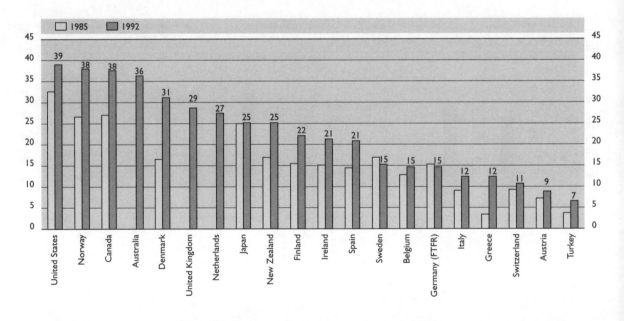

1. Ratio of public and private university education graduates to population at theoretical age of graduation, men and women.
2. For the Netherlands, 1992 data include non-university education graduates. For Norway, data refer to 1991.
Source: OECD Education Database. For details see Annex Table A.39.

◆   Chart 1.36. ***United States: mean scores of college-bound students on verbal and mathematics components***
of the Scholastic Aptitude Test (SAT),[1] 1976-93

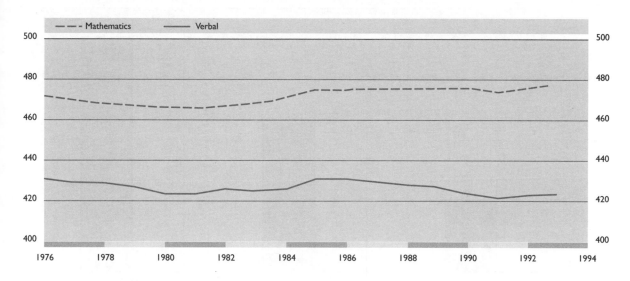

1.   The Scholastic Aptitude Test is the test taken most frequently by college-bound students. The proportion of high-school graduates who take the examination varies over
     the years, a development that can influence the mean scores. The highest score possible on each scale is 800; 200 is the lowest. The raw mean score on the tests in 1941
     was 500 with a standard deviation of 100. Since then the tests have been psychometrically anchored to this scale. For source data, see Table A.40.

Source: National Center for Education Statistics (1994), *The Condition of Education*, p. 64 and p. 228.

1980 when performance increased. Test scores worsened after 1985 only to rise again in 1991. This pattern is more or less consistent for both verbal and mathematics test scores. Mean scores in mathematics were higher than the scores on the verbal tests. More detailed data show that performance is highly correlated with family background and ethnicity.

As the complexity of working life increases and technology enters daily life, competence in science becomes a crucial determinant of success in education and life career. Chart 1.37 indicates the science proficiency of 9-, 13- and 17-year-olds in the United States, for 1992. Time series data are presented in Annex Table A.41. Mean science performance is higher for all groups than it was ten years ago. Another indication of success in the improvement of science education in the United States is that the gender gap in performance has decreased.

Education, unemployment and earnings

There are numerous conceptual problems in evaluating the external efficiency of education and training systems, and few reliable and internationally comparable indicators are available. A major aspect of efficiency is captured by trends in labour force qualifications as measured by the educational attainment of the working-age population. Another aspect is the relationship between educational attainment and earnings. Further indicators examine the relationships between education, labour force participation and unemployment.

• *Education and earnings*

Chart 8.1 (see Chapter 8) indicates that earnings differentials are closely related to education, for both men and women. Earnings from work is an indirect measure of the extent to which education enables the recipient to find and hold gainful employment. Earnings also represent a useful indicator of the value of education, since they are closely related to other important outcomes, for example health and dependency on social assistance (see Chapter 8). While the specific gaps in earnings between different attainment levels vary in size and in the degree to which they have changed over time, there is a clear tendency for mean earnings differences to widen persistently from the more to the lesser educationally quali-

◆ Chart 1.37. **United States: mean science proficiency scores,[1] by sex and age, 1992**

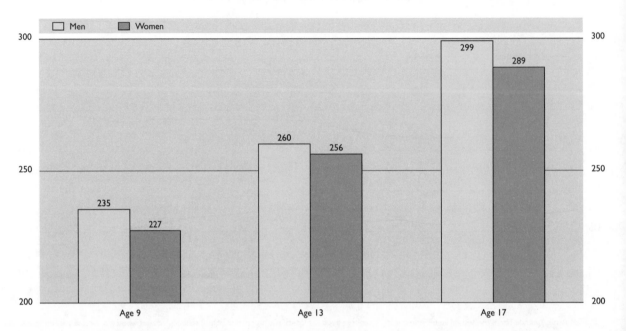

1. The science proficiency scale has a range from 0 to 500. The science tests are administered as part of the National Assessment of Educational Progress since 1970. See Table A.41 for details.
Source: National Center for Education Statistics (1994), *The Condition of Education*, p. 56.

fied workers. Tertiary education normally offers a substantial earnings advantage in comparison with upper secondary education. In 1992, among men aged 25 to 64, the average earnings of tertiary graduates were between 45 to 75 per cent higher than those of upper secondary graduates. In the Netherlands, however, this earnings advantage was much smaller than this percentage range. The earnings advantage for university-educated women also lies in the range of 45 to 75 per cent in most countries. In 1992, however, it was much smaller in Austria, Denmark, Italy and considerably larger in the United Kingdom.

Persons lacking an upper secondary qualification have considerably lower earnings than those educated at upper secondary or higher levels. In 1992, men aged 25 to 64 without an upper secondary qualification typically earned 10 to 25 per cent less than those who had attained that level. In the United States, this difference was as large as 35 per cent. Among women as well, the typical earnings disadvantage of those lacking an upper secondary qualification is 10 to 25 per cent. As is the case with men, women in the United States who had not completed an upper secondary education earned around 35 per cent less than those who had.

The multiple disadvantages suffered by people with low educational attainments have, in some countries, increased with time. In cases where relative wages have declined in response to declining demand for less-skilled labour, employment losses may have been less, but at the cost of increased poverty and hardship. Annex Table A.42 presents ratios of mean annual earnings by educational qualifications from the early 1970s to the early 1990s. During the 1980s, a fairly sharp increase in earnings differentials occurred in the United States, the United Kingdom (men only), Canada, and Sweden (men only), especially for workers without qualifications at the upper secondary level. In these countries, the largest increase in differentials occurred between those with university qualifications and those with the lowest levels of attainment. This represented a reversal of the trend observed for the 1970s, when there was some compression in average earnings differences. In contrast, little change was observed in Australia, Denmark and Japan, and some decline seen in the Netherlands and Norway during the 1980s.

Chart 1.38 shows that important differences emerge when trends are examined separately for younger and older age groups. Younger workers

◆ Chart 1.38. ***Earnings differentials by educational attainment[1] for young and older men in the early 1990s[2]***
Ratio of mean annual earnings by qualifications, ages 25 to 34 and 45 to 54

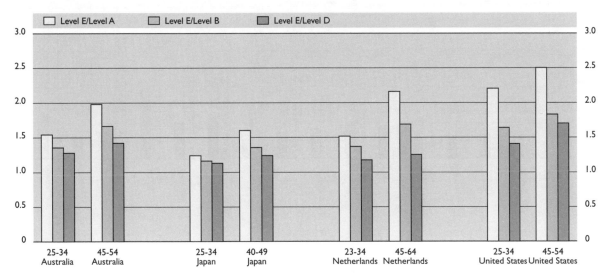

1. For the definitions of the education levels see notes to Annex Tables A.42 and A.43. The following classification can serve as a rough approximation: level A = ISCED 0/1/2, level B = ISCED 3, level D = ISCED 5 and level E = ISCED 6.
2. For the Netherlands, educational level B includes upper secondary vocational (defined as level C in Table A.42) and general upper secondary education.
Source: OECD (1994d), *The OECD Jobs Study: Evidence and Explanations,* Table 7.A.1, pp. 160-161. See also Table A.43.

entering the labour market in the 1990s without an upper secondary qualification are especially disadvantaged; their mean earnings have fallen relative to the others. Especially in Australia and the United States, the career chances of the least qualified deteriorated sharply during the 1980s. In Japan and the Netherlands, on the other hand, there was little or no change. Among older workers, the well-known tendency for earnings to rise with age for the more educationally qualified workers is evident in all four countries. Beyond that, there are no common patterns. The United States is the only country where the pattern observed in the 1970s differs clearly from that of the 1980s. Whereas earnings differentials declined or rose very little during the 1970s, the 1980s witnessed a substantial increase in the earnings of older college-educated workers relative to others. In conclusion, those who enter the labour market without an upper secondary qualification are at risk of low earnings – both at the beginning of their career and throughout it. While low levels of attainment are consistently associated with low relative earnings, the gap is more variable in its size, and changes over time, at higher levels of educational attainment.

• *Education and employment*

As occupational qualifications are rendered obsolete more quickly, the notion of a once-and-for-all career preparation is disappearing. There is evidence of market failures in education and training, a point elaborated in Chapters 4 and 8. For example, even during spells of high unemployment there is evidence of skill shortages, which can be interpreted as a sign of qualitative mismatches between labour supply and demand. Education enhances an individual's position on the labour market. Those with less schooling are more likely to be caught in jobs characterised by frequent turnover, low wages, and high unemployment (OECD, 1994d). Chart 1.39 shows that unemployment rates are generally much higher for those with a primary, lower secondary or upper secondary education than for those with a university or non-university tertiary education. Educational attainment thus has a consistent influence on the employment experience.

However, the relationship between educational attainment and unemployment is not linear, because the largest difference in experience is usually found between the least educated and all other groups. The

◆   Chart 1.39.   **Unemployment rate[1,2] by level of education for persons 24 to 64 years, 1992**
Compared with unemployment rate for tertiary graduates

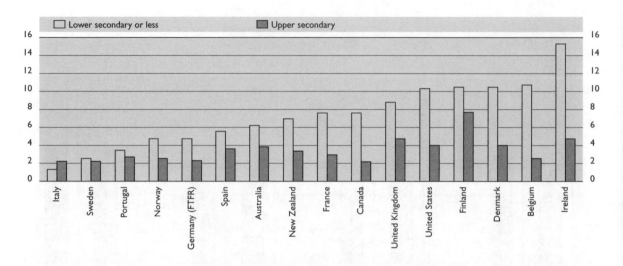

1.   In some cases the data are unreliable due to small sample sizes.
2.   The unemployment rate is the percentage of people in the labour force (the currently active population) without work (*i.e.* not in paid employment or self-employment). Labour force participation is defined as the proportion of the population that: *a)* is working for pay, *b)* is self-employed, or *c)* meets the following two conditions: seeking work (*i.e.* taking specific steps in a specified recent period to seek paid employment or self-employment) and currently available for work.
Source: OECD Education Database. For details on sources, see Annex Table A.10.

risk of unemployment is especially high for young school-leavers: educational attainment conditions that risk. In all countries, and over time, individuals without an upper secondary qualification have the highest rates of unemployment. That risk has grown since the late 1970s, concomitant with the rise of the "minimum threshold" of skills and competencies required in the labour market.

The relationship between educational attainment and unemployment tends to be irregular at the highest levels of education. The fact that this pattern is widespread may be a sign of rigidities in wage adjustments for occupations requiring advanced education, or a sign of extended job search by more educated persons. In some countries the differences in unemployment rates by level of educational attainment have widened considerably (Table 1.15). This is true even when adjusting for changes in the shares of the labour force for each educational attainment group. Within countries, however, the differences in unemployment experience for different attainment levels (at least those above the level of the least qualified) diminish as workers get older and experience progressively substitutes for formal qualifications. Since the late 1970s, educational attainment also seems to have more to do with differences in

unemployment for older workers. This could be linked to structural change and the difficulty encountered by those with low qualification levels when they try to leave jobs in declining industries.

D.   CONCLUSIONS

Section B reviewed a number of broad trends affecting life in the OECD area, including demographic change and ageing, globalisation, the diffusion of new information and communication technologies, trends in employment and shifts in the distribution of occupations, qualifications and skills, and developments in the worlds of work, community and family life. Together, these trends and developments point to an array of gradual but profound changes. Analysis of some of the symptoms of the ongoing transformation of OECD economies, cultures and societies revealed both risks and opportunities. Despite continuing productivity gains and a gradual increase in overall standards of living, unemployment, poverty and social exclusion remain widespread, and the aspirations and needs of many are unfulfilled. The emerging high-skill, high-wage learning economy accommodates a growing share of the workforce in OECD countries, but the divisions between those who are included and those who are excluded are sharp, and could deepen. Long-established patterns of job entry and career progression are "in doubt" or called "into question" as the knowledge content of jobs is altered and low-skill mass production systems are replaced. Turnover in the labour market is rising, and skills tend to become obsolete more rapidly. But if the future is uncertain, it is also rich with opportunity. Ongoing transformations hold promise for major advances in the quality of life. Realising these improvements in living conditions – and securing a fair distribution of the efforts and benefits – will depend heavily on a sense of solidarity and on the knowledge, skills and qualifications of the population. The central importance of the human factor underscores the imperative of reorienting policies to build and strengthen the learning society.

As a necessary condition for – and complement and balance to – the post-industrial economy, the very concept of the learning society raises a fundamental question, addressed in Section C: Are the trends in education and training consistent with the development of the post-industrial society, or do education systems continue to develop in accordance with the model of an outmoded industrial society? The analysis of trends in education and training offers mixed answers.

Impressive progress has been achieved in many areas of education and training policy since the 1970s. The evidence presented in this chapter points to rising overall levels of educational attainment. In most Member countries more than half of the population aged between 25 and 64 has completed at least upper secondary education. But progress has been uneven. There were large differences in educational attainment between countries in the early 1980s; some of these differences still exist today. Levels of educational attainment are, moreover, rising faster in certain countries than in others – a development that will have an impact on the comparative advantage of nations. To complicate matters further, within countries, there is an uneven distribution of attainment levels by age groups. In certain European countries more than half of the working-age population has received little education beyond primary schooling. Evidence shows that those people are at risk in changing labour markets. In these countries there is a large, but unmet, demand for adult education and training, especially among people in mid-career.

Early childhood education has become a growth industry, and for good reasons, which are spelled out in Chapter 3. At age 4, enrolment rates rise sharply in most countries. But the variation among countries in access and participation is highly significant. Early childhood education has become virtually universal in a few countries, but others have a long way to go in opening up learning opportunities for young children. Policy dilemmas are posed, because resources are limited and because an expansion of pre-primary education affects the relationships between families and schools. Moreover, as early childhood education expands, the boundary with primary schooling tends to blur, which creates both new opportunities and difficulties.

The evidence indicates that all OECD countries pursue a policy of expansion in secondary education. A few countries now retain nearly all youth in secondary school until age 17. But many education systems fall short of this target. A quarter or more of 17-year-olds is no longer enrolled in full-time education in Australia, New Zealand, Greece, Ireland, Portugal, Spain, Turkey and the United Kingdom. Young people without an upper secondary qualification face a difficult transition to work, with high unemployment, high turnover, and low-paying jobs that offer few opportunities for personal development and further education and training. Whereas this situation is not necessarily indicative of school failure or inadequate student performance, increasing the retention rates in secondary education and discouraging early school leaving must feature highly on the policy agendas of governments. But, however ambitious, achieving a full cycle of broad-based secondary education for all students until age 17 is not enough. Upper secondary education must be relevant and of high quality. Merely keeping increasing numbers of youths in schools for more and more years does not present an attractive option. Graduation rates in upper secondary education are well below the participation rates in many countries, suggesting that a significant number of youths attend school but do not obtain qualifications. Although there is evidence that a certain number of these youths will obtain this qualification at a later age, it is desirable that qualifications are acquired earlier on, because failures tend to cumulate, and because it is difficult for schools and communities to reach out to at-risk youths beyond a certain age. Thus, in conclusion, it appears that – despite the progress towards the shared goal of providing universal upper secondary education – achievements to date fall short in all Member countries.

Countries have, moreover, dramatically expanded enrolments in tertiary-level institutions, in a few cases reaching 40 per cent of the age group leaving secondary schools. Despite the growth in enrolments, tertiary education reaches less than 25 per cent of an age group, in some cases less than 10 per cent. Some countries are thus likely to face increasing pressures for expansion. The prospect of further growth in mass tertiary systems highlights a range of policy dilemmas and problems. Employment considerations, finance and staffing are large-looming issues for all countries. How to define the proper balance between traditional university education and newly emerging forms of post-secondary vocational education is another contentious issue. Maintaining quality and controlling costs while accommodating a larger student body are the overriding challenges.

The data on educational attainment suggest that there is a large and unmet demand for adult education and forms of continuing vocational training. OECD data sources indicate that around a third of the labour force in certain countries participates in job-related education or training in a year. Although impressive, this figure suggests that two-thirds of the labour force do *not* participate in organised learning activities each year. The data further suggest that many of the least-qualified receive training lasting only one or two days – an amount that is unlikely to count much towards the goal of acquiring new skills and qualifications. Moreover, there are many people who are not counted in labour force statistics; their learning needs must also be accommodated. The inevitable conclusion is that, despite the increasing volume and diversity of supply, the learning needs and demands of many adults go unmet. Reaching out to such adults is a high priority for all countries. In pursuing a necessary policy of development and expansion in adult education and continuing vocational training, countries will have to come to grips with a number of thorny issues, ranging from financial and legal problems and questions about the proper division of responsibilities, to the institutional frameworks and the supporting arrangements that will need to be put into place.

The above review of developments in education and training suggests that the moves, as yet uncompleted, towards mass education systems have reached a new plateau. But the analysis also underscores the problems and weaknesses, which pose large challenges: the underdevelopment of early childhood education, less than full retention in upper secondary education, graduation gaps in secondary education, insufficient participation and in other cases unchecked growth at the tertiary level, and uneven development of adult education and training. The financing of expansion and reform is an additional factor. But the problems clearly go beyond the management of quantities. At a time when education and training systems are confronted with a wide range of new and intensified challenges, the question must be asked whether merely continuing to expand education and training systems – more of the same – will suffice as a policy strategy for gearing up to the demands of the twenty-first century.

The challenges clearly go beyond the mere noting of a growing demand for education and training among learners of all ages, and an increase in the diversity of providers. There is a need for a different quality and content of education, which signals a generic and paradigmatic shift from education to learning. New information and communication technologies can change the way education is organised. Instead of a supply-led and heavily institutionalised system, the new conditions allow for a demand-led, client-driven approach, where the learners can shop for education from diverse sources and in ways they themselves plan. These developments will have repercussions on governments' near-monopolies of supplying education and training, prescribing the curriculum and textbooks, and assessing and certifying the outcomes. In so far as current education systems are not proactive in meeting the new and diverse demands under flexible conditions, educational arrangements in OECD countries fall short of what is needed.

On balance, the data analysis presented in this chapter supports the conclusion that more of the same will not be enough, and that continuing to expand currently front-loaded systems without rethinking their purpose and design is a mistake. The challenges posed cannot be dealt with in isolation. For example, the policy decisions taken with regard to the development of adult education and training will have an impact on policies for tertiary education, and they in turn will influence policies designed to ease the transition from school to work. Addressing the challenges thus requires not only major redirections of education and training policies. What is needed, above all, is that the reforms are planned as part of a coherent blueprint for change – a new organising framework for the long-term development of learning societies.

Table 1.1. **Foreign or immigrant population and labour force, 1983 and 1993**

(percentage and numbers in thousands)

	Foreign population and labour force [1]		
	Foreign population		Foreign labour force
	% of total population		% of total labour force
	1983	1993 [2]	1993
Austria	3.9	8.6	9.6
Belgium	9.0	9.1	8.3
Denmark	2.0	3.6	1.9
Finland	0.3	1.1	. .
France	6.8	6.3	6.2
Germany [3]	7.4	8.5	8.8
Ireland	2.4	2.7	3.0
Italy	0.7	1.7	. .
Japan	0.7	1.1	. .
Luxembourg	26.3	31.1	38.6
Netherlands	3.8	5.1	3.9
Norway	2.3	3.8	4.5 [4]
Spain	0.5	1.1	0.5
Sweden	4.8	5.8	5.1
Switzerland	14.4	18.1	21.7 [5]
United Kingdom	2.8	3.5	3.6

	Foreign-born population and labour force [6]					
	Foreign-born population				Foreign-born labour force	
	Thousands		% of total population		Thousands	% of total labour force
	1981	1991	1981	1991	1981	1991
Australia	3 004	4 125	20.6	22.7	2 184	25.7
Canada	3 843	4 343	16.1	15.6	2 681	18.5
United States	14 080	19 767	4.7	7.9	11 636	9.3

Note: . . Data not available.
1. Data for the foreign population are from population registers except for France (census), the United Kingdom (labour force survey), Japan and Switzerland (register of foreigners). Data for foreign labour in EU countries are taken from the Community labour force survey. For the other European countries data are based on work permits.
2. 1990 for France, 1992 for Ireland.
3. Data for 1993 cover Germany, and for 1983 the former Federal Republic of Germany.
4. Excluding the unemployed.
5. Number of foreigners with an annual residence permit or a settlement permit who engage in gainful activity. Seasonal and frontier workers are excluded.
6. Census data (1980 and 1990 for the United States), except for Australia (labour force survey).
Source: OECD (1995b), *Trends in International Migration, Annual Report,* Table 1.2, p. 27.

Table 1.2. **Aged dependency ratios in OECD countries, 1980-2040** [1]

	1980	2000	2020	2040	% Change 1980-2040	% Change 2010-2040
Canada	14.1	19.0	28.9	37.8	168	77
France	21.9	23.3	30.6	38.2	74	56
Germany	23.4	25.4	33.5	48.2	106	58
Italy	20.8	22.6	29.3	41.0	97	60
Japan	13.5	22.6	33.6	37.8	180	28
United Kingdom	23.2	22.3	25.5	33.1	43	48
United States	17.1	18.2	25.0	32.3	89	72
Average of the above	*19.1*	*21.9*	*29.5*	*38.3*	*108*	*57*
Australia [2]	14.8	18.3	26.1	36.2	144	80
Austria	24.2	22.6	30.4	40.8	69	53
Belgium	21.9	22.0	26.9	36.0	64	53
Czech Republic [3]	18.1	19.6	31.2	43.0	137	97
Denmark	22.3	21.5	30.5	42.1	89	73
Finland	17.7	21.2	34.8	38.8	119	56
Greece	20.5	22.6	27.4	34.0	66	32
Iceland	15.8	16.1	20.9	33.2	110	106
Ireland	18.2	16.9	18.7	27.1	49	66
Luxembourg	20.0	25.5	31.9	36.4	82	32
Netherlands	17.4	19.7	28.9	42.0	141	90
New Zealand	15.4	16.3	23.0	35.8	132	105
Norway	23.4	22.8	27.9	38.2	63	71
Portugal	16.1	20.8	23.7	33.1	106	55
Spain	17.2	21.8	25.3	38.2	122	66
Sweden	25.4	25.1	33.1	37.4	47	41
Switzerland	20.8	25.0	39.9	49.9	140	57
Turkey	8.5	8.0	10.3	15.9	87	94
OECD average	*18.9*	*20.8*	*27.6*	*36.6*	*98*	*63*

1. (Population 65 +/population 15-64) × 100; 1980 actual ratios; 2000 to 2040 projected ratios.
2. Australian Bureau of Statistics, 1995, *Series A Population Projections* data. Reference month: June.
3. The data for 2000 and 2020 are from a projection made by the Czech Statistical Office (Projection of the population of the Czech Republic until the year 2020, Czech Statistical Office, Praha, 1995); the data for 2040 are raw estimates based on this projection. The data for 1980 are from the demographic yearbook published by the Czech Statistical Office.
Sources: OECD (1988a), *Ageing populations: The social policy implications*, Table 14; and national data submissions.

Table 1.3. **International specialisation in high-wage and high-technology industries, 1970 and 1992** [1]

	Japan 1970	Japan 1992 [2]	United States 1970	United States 1992 [2]	European Community 1970	European Community 1992 [2]
High wage	64	107	136	118	101	98
Medium wage	122	121	95	95	94	92
Low wage	102	56	64	82	110	116
High technology	124	144	159	151	86	82
Medium technology	78	114	110	90	103	100
Low technology	114	46	64	74	103	113

1. The specialisation (or revealed comparative advantage) index for a particular type of industry has been calculated by dividing the share of a country's exports in a particular industry relative to its total manufacturing exports by the total OECD exports in that industry type relative to the total OECD manufacturing exports.
2. Total OECD and EC exports for 1992 were calculated using 1991 data for Italy and Australia.
Source: OECD (1994b), Table 26, p. 134.

Table 1.4. **Educational attainment in Sweden, 1930, 1970 and 1994** [1]

(distribution of population 16-59 years by education level, in per cent)

Education level	1930 [2]		1970		1994	
	Men	Women	Men	Women	Men	Women
Early childhood and primary education	84.3	86.9	46.7	48.8	11.7	9.6
Lower secondary education	5.9	5.4	13.0	17.0	17.5	16.6
Upper secondary education	8.1	7.4	33.0	27.6	46.8	48.0
Tertiary education	1.6	0.3	7.3	6.6	21.0	23.1

1. The data from 1970 and 1994 are fully consistent. Some minor problems were encountered in the conversion of 1930 data to the ISCED classification system.
2. Age group 15-60 years.
Sources: Statistics Sweden, Census 1930, 1970 and *Utbildningsregistret*, Statistics Sweden (SCB), situation on 1st January 1994.

Table 1.5. **Incidence of long-term unemployment, 1983, 1989, 1992 and 1993** [1,2]

(per cent of all unemployed)

	1983		1989		1992		1993	
	6 months and over	12 months and over	6 months and over	12 months and over	6 months and over	12 months and over	6 months and over	12 months and over
North America								
Canada	28.8	9.9	20.8	6.8	33.4	13.1	31.4	14.1
United States	23.9	13.3	9.9	5.7	20.6	11.2	20.4	11.7
Pacific Area								
Australia	52.7	27.5	40.6	23.1	58.7	34.5	57.1	36.5
Japan	31.5	12.9	37.3	18.7	36.2	15.9	34.4	17.2
New Zealand	..	..	34.5	14.7	53.2	31.9	52.5	33.2
European Community								
Denmark	60.6	33.0	50.8	25.9	49.9	27.0	..	25.2
France	67.0	42.2	63.7	43.9	58.1	36.1	58.2	34.2
Germany	64.8	39.3	66.7	49.0	55.4	33.5	..	40.3
Greece	60.7	35.0	73.5	52.4	70.3	49.7	..	50.8
Italy	83.0	57.7	58.7	70.4	69.7	58.2	..	57.7
Netherlands	75.1	50.5	66.1	49.9	76.9	44.0	..	55.2
Spain	72.8	52.4	72.7	58.5	66.1	47.4	69.6	50.1
United Kingdom	68.0	47.0	57.2	40.8	57.3	35.4	..	45.5
Other Europe – OECD								
Norway	20.3	6.3	29.5	11.6	41.1	23.6	45.6	27.2
Sweden	24.9	10.3	18.2	6.3	25.7	8.0	32.0	10.9

Notes: .. Data not available.
1. Data derived from surveys in OECD countries. While data from labour force surveys make international comparisons easier compared to a mixture of survey and registration data, they are not perfect. Questionnaire wording and design, survey timing, differences across countries in the age groups covered, and other reasons still mean that care is required in interpreting cross-country differences in levels.
2. Data refer to persons aged 14 and over in Italy and Greece; aged 15 and over in Australia, Canada, Denmark, France, Germany, Japan, the Netherlands and New Zealand; and aged 16 and over in Spain and the United States. Data for Norway refer to persons aged 16-74 and data for Sweden refer to persons aged 16-64. Data for the United Kingdom refer to men aged 16-69 and women 16-64.
Source: OECD (1994c), *Employment Outlook*, Table P, p. 206.

Table 1.6. **Full- and part-time employment situation and individual preferences in European countries, 1989**[1]

(percentage)

	Full-time jobs	Part-time jobs	Would you prefer a part-time job (full-time workers)?		Would you prefer a full-time job (part-time workers)?		Would you prefer a full-time or part-time job (unemployed)?	
			Yes	No	Yes	No	Full-time	Part-time
Belgium	71	22	13	77	19	47	51	30
Denmark	83	17	13	84	6	89	52	27
France	92	8	17	79	57	32	28	70
Germany	82	18	17	83	8	92	22	19
Greece	97	2	14	86	78	22	87	10
Ireland	87	7	7	90	. .	. .	87	11
Italy	94	6	32	68	49	51	. .	. .
Netherlands	69	27	12	86	18	78	39	54
Portugal	94	5	24	70	40	29	76	23
Spain	85	15	24	73	63	35	72	24
United Kingdom	78	21	25	75	6	94	71	20
Total	*85*	*15*	*21*	*77*	*30*	*66*	*52*	*34*

Note: . . Data not available.
1. When the figures do not add up to 100 per cent, the difference is the percentage of respondents who provided "no reply".
Sources: Commission of European Communities, *European Economy*, No. 47, March 1991, Annex 2, Table 23; and OECD (1994d), *The OECD Jobs Study: Evidence and Explanations*, Part II, Table 6.14, p. 93.

Table 1.7. **Children under 18 years living in poverty in the United States, 1960-92**

(by ethnicity, selected years)

	Percentage of all children living in poverty			Percentage of children living in poverty who live with a female householder[1]		
	Total	White	Black	Total	White	Black
1960[2]	26.5	20.0	65.5	23.8	21.0	29.4
1965[3]	20.7	14.4	47.4	31.7	27.0	49.7
1970	14.9	10.5	41.5	45.8	36.6	60.8
1975	16.8	12.5	41.4	51.4	41.7	70.1
1980	17.9	13.4	42.1	52.8	41.3	75.4
1985	20.1	15.6	43.1	53.8	43.0	78.4
1990	19.9	15.1	44.2	57.9	46.9	80.3
1991	21.1	16.1	45.6	59.0	47.4	83.1
1992	21.1	16.0	46.3	57.9	45.4	81.8

1. No husband present. The householder is the person in whose name the housing unit is owned or rented.
2. Data presented are for 1959 for Blacks and 1960 for Whites and total.
3. Data presented are for 1967 for Blacks and 1965 for Whites and total.
Sources: US Department of Commerce, Bureau of the Census, *Current Population Reports, series P-60*, "Poverty in the United Sates", various years (based on March Current Population survey), and National Center for Education Statistics (1994), *The Condition of Education*, p. 132.

Table 1.8. **Enrolment in public and private early childhood and primary education, 1994**

(net enrolment rates[1] by single year of age, 3 to 7, head counts)

	3-year-olds			4-year-olds			5-year-olds			6-year-olds			7-year-olds		
	Pre-primary	Primary	Total	Pre-primary	Primary	Total	Pre-primary	Primary	Total	Pre-primary	Primary	Total	Pre-primary	Primary	Total
North America															
Canada	n.a.	n.a.	n.a.	39.2	–	39.2	87.0	11.7	98.8	0.6	98.7	99.3	–	99.2	99.2
United States	27.6	–	27.6	54.1	–	54.1	74.8	6.1	81.0	13.3	84.6	98.0	0.5	101.5	102.1
Mexico	9.7	n.a.	9.7	48.4	n.a.	48.4	71.8	5.5	77.3	1.7	98.8	100.6	3.4	100.7	104.1
Pacific Area															
Australia	..	–	–	91.8	n.a.	91.8	96.2	74.6	96.2	..	99.2	..	–	99.4	99.4
Japan	57.0	n.a.	57.0	91.8	n.a.	91.8	96.2	n.a.	96.2	n.a.	101.9	101.9	n.a.	102.8	102.8
New Zealand	80.4	–	80.4	95.7	0.2	95.9	2.4	102.3	104.6	–	101.8	101.8	–	100.0	100.0
European Community															
Belgium	98.2	–	98.2	99.7	–	99.7	98.0	1.4	99.4	4.2	95.6	99.8	0.1	99.1	99.2
Denmark	61.0	–	61.0	81.7	–	81.7	84.7	–	84.7	92.7	3.8	96.5	5.7	93.4	99.1
France	99.3	–	99.3	101.4	–	101.4	99.9	2.1	102.0	1.1	100.1	101.2	0.1	100.8	100.8
Germany	40.9	–	40.9	71.4	–	71.4	81.5	–	81.5	70.7	43.8	114.6	1.3	96.8	98.0
Greece	15.3	–	15.3	57.6	–	57.6	48.3	20.0	68.3	1.1	91.6	92.6	–	93.3	93.3
Ireland	1.0	–	1.0	54.2	–	54.2	100.1	0.3	100.4	55.5	45.3	100.8	2.3	98.5	100.8
Netherlands	n.a.	n.a.	n.a.	97.1	0.4	97.5	98.0	0.6	98.7	0.9	98.2	99.1	0.1	99.5	99.6
Spain	52.7	–	52.7	98.5	–	98.5	102.0	–	102.0	0.2	103.3	103.5	0.1	104.1	104.3
United Kingdom	39.4	4.1	43.5	10.9	81.3	92.0	102.0	100.2	100.2	0.1	99.3	99.4	0.0	98.5	98.5
Other Europe – OECD															
Austria	29.5	–	29.5	69.3	–	69.3	87.0	–	87.0	37.9	61.2	99.1	0.1	98.2	98.3
Czech Republic	55.6	–	55.6	74.8	–	74.8	81.4	–	81.4	34.1	65.9	100.0	4.2	95.8	100.0
Finland	24.4	–	24.4	29.9	–	29.9	34.8	–	34.8	56.8	0.8	57.6	0.6	99.0	99.6
Sweden	48.6	–	48.6	54.5	–	54.5	61.2	–	61.2	92.8	5.3	98.1	–	97.4	97.4
Switzerland	5.4	–	5.4	26.5	–	26.5	77.7	0.2	77.9	70.0	28.7	98.7	2.6	97.2	99.8

Notes: .. Data not available. n.a. Not applicable. – Magnitude is either negligible or zero.
1. Net enrolment rates for each age group are calculated by dividing full-time plus part-time enrolments at that age by the total population of that age. Most countries do not distinguish full-time from part-time enrolments in early childhood education; all children are considered as full-time in this table.
Source: OECD Education Database.

77

Table 1.9. **Enrolment in upper secondary education, 1975-92**[1]

(percentage of upper secondary students enrolled in public and private general and vocational education;[2] head counts)

	1975		1980		1984		1988		1992	
	General education	Vocational education and apprenticeship	General education	Vocational education and apprenticeship	General education	Vocational education and apprenticeship	General education	Vocational education and apprenticeship	General education	Vocational education and apprenticeship
Pacific Area										
Australia	62.1	37.9	68.0	32.0	71.1	28.9	71.6	28.4	75.5	24.5
Japan[3]	..	..	..	..	..	..	68.5	28.1	72.5	27.5
New Zealand	..	..	..	..	97.2	2.8	97.0	3.0	81.2	18.8
European Community										
Belgium	40.0	60.0	37.0	63.0	54.5	45.5	..	..	40.8	59.2
Denmark[4]	40.7	59.3	41.6	58.4	35.0	65.0	31.3	69.3	43.8	56.2
France[5]	19.2	80.8	21.0	79.0	42.2	57.8	43.7	56.3	45.9	54.1
Germany[4]	..	..	21.0	79.0	21.0	79.0	20.3	79.7	20.4	79.6
Ireland	27.0	73.0	..	..	82.8	17.2	76.4	17.6	..	..
Italy[6]	58.7	41.3	25.0	75.0	24.0	76.0	31.7	68.4	32.6	67.4
Netherlands	..	..	57.9	42.1	47.6	52.4	33.7	66.3	29.9	70.1
Portugal	..	..	..	..	..	..	73.9	26.0	..	..
Spain[5]	58.0	42.0	59.0	41.0	55.0	45.0	56.7	43.5	58.6	41.4
United Kingdom[7]	64.0	36.0	..	..	84.6	15.4	81.9	17.6	42.4	57.6
Other Europe – OECD										
Austria	45.6	54.4	41.4	58.6	39.3	60.7	24.3	75.7	24.0	76.0
Finland	49.0	51.0	49.0	51.0	49.0	51.0	45.6	54.5	45.6	54.4
Norway	56.4	43.6	50.0	50.0	44.8	55.2	44.1	55.9	40.2	59.8
Sweden	29.0	71.0	29.0	71.0	23.0	77.0	23.2	76.7	..	..
Switzerland	66.7	33.3	63.6	36.4	65.6	34.4	23.1	76.9	26.8	73.2
Turkey	56.0	44.0	60.0	40.0	58.0	42.0	58.2	41.8	56.5	43.5

Note: .. Data not available.
1. Due to the revision of the OECD Education Statistics questionnaire in 1985 there may be some differences in coverage prior to that date.
2. Vocational education includes vocational, technical and apprenticeship programmes.
3. Students enrolled in special training colleges (about 100 000 in the relevant age group) not included.
4. Including part-time education.
5. Students enrolled in special education excluded.
6. Figures for programmes lasting less than three years not reported.
7. Vocational course figures are inflated by large numbers of adults taking courses at the upper secondary level.
Source: OECD Education Database.

Table 1.10. **Transition characteristics from secondary to tertiary education, 1994**

(net enrolment rates[1] by single year of age, 17-24-year-olds, head counts[2])

	ISCED[3]	Age							
		17	18	19	20	21	22	23	24
North America									
Canada	3	70.6	40.1	16.2	14.6	. .	. .	. .	. .
	5	4.9	14.1	19.7	20.7	23.6	24.7	10.8	12.1
	6/7	11.9	22.7	29.0	27.4	25.9	22.0	16.3	11.7
United States	3	81.3	26.0	7.0	1.3	0.6	0.3	0.1	0.4
	5	1.2	14.4	17.5	12.1	10.4	7.7	6.5	6.8
	6/7	1.7	20.5	20.8	21.4	22.5	19.9	15.6	11.8
Pacific Area									
Australia	3	72.3	29.1	17.3	13.9	8.0	6.3	5.6	5.1
	5	2.9	9.6	9.9	8.6	7.0	5.9	5.4	4.9
	6/7	12.6	23.0	23.3	20.3	16.1	11.4	8.6	7.2
New Zealand	3	75.6	30.7	13.8	8.6	5.1	4.0	3.3	2.9
	5	1.6	6.2	8.2	7.7	6.3	4.9	4.0	3.3
	6/7	1.5	19.9	26.4	26.5	22.3	15.6	10.5	7.6
European Community									
Belgium	3	97.8	53.5	29.2	16.8	6.8	5.5	4.7	4.7
	5	0.2	12.2	20.6	23.5	18.7	12.2	7.1	4.4
	6/7	0.6	18.9	20.3	18.4	16.8	13.8	9.4	5.9
Denmark	3	70.8	61.5	43.4	27.2	16.8	10.5	6.8	4.4
	5	0.0	0.0	0.7	2.0	3.0	3.6	3.3	2.9
	6/7	0.0	0.2	3.4	10.2	16.3	19.4	20.4	19.4
France	3	85.8	59.1	34.0	14.7	4.8	1.7	0.4	0.2
	5	0.2	4.5	10.5	13.1	10.9	6.3	2.9	1.3
	6/7	2.0	18.6	24.0	25.7	24.4	21.2	16.2	10.8
Germany	3	79.9	80.4	57.2	31.4	15.9	21.2	2.1	0.8
	5	0.8	1.8	2.6	2.9	2.4	1.8	1.7	1.7
	6/7	0.0	1.0	5.5	11.7	15.3	15.5	16.7	15.8
Ireland	3	74.3	60.3	10.9	3.9	. .	. .	. .	. .
	5	×	×	×	×	×	×	×	×
	6/7	7.4	32.7	36.7	31.9	21.5	13.2	7.9	5.4
Netherlands	3	70.9	62.5	43.9	29.7	17.6	10.7	7.0	5.3
	5	×	×	×	×	×	×	×	×
	6/7	2.0	12.2	21.5	26.3	27.1	24.7	21.1	16.1
Spain	3	74.0	43.1	25.8	20.0	13.0	8.6	4.4	3.2
	5	0.0	0.4	0.5	1.0	0.2	0.1	0.1	0.1
	6/7	0.0	19.2	25.5	29.9	26.8	24.7	18.9	14.9
United Kingdom	3	71.7	31.3	15.3	9.7	7.9	7.3	6.5	6.1
	5	0.3	3.8	5.7	4.9	3.5	2.7	2.1	1.9
	6/7	1.3	16.9	22.1	21.3	16.0	9.4	6.0	4.6
Other Europe – OECD									
Austria	3	85.7	55.2	21.3	7.8	4.1	1.2	1.0	. .
	5	. .	. .	. .	. .	. .	. .	. .	
	6/7	0.0	5.3	12.0	14.7	15.1	14.5	13.9	12.5
Czech Republic	3	62.5	24.9	3.6	0.9	0.4	0.0	0.0	0.0
	5	0.0	3.6	5.8	5.0	6.4	5.2	1.4	0.0
	6/7	0.0	7.6	13.8	12.5	11.9	12.0	8.7	3.9
Finland	3	89.6	80.0	23.7	17.4	16.1	13.5	9.0	6.1
	5	0.5	1.7	4.0	7.0	9.3	9.4	8.4	6.2
	6/7	0.0	0.5	9.3	15.7	20.6	22.9	21.8	20.3
Norway	3	90.4	82.1	35.1	20.2	14.1	10.5	7.3	5.3
	5	0.0	0.3	8.7	11.5	10.2	8.6	6.8	5.3
	6/7	0.0	0.2	6.4	12.2	17.2	19.8	19.5	17.0
Sweden	3	95.6	82.4	22.8	10.6	8.7	8.3	7.8	6.7
	5	×	×	×	×	×	×	×	×
	6/7	0.0	0.8	11.7	17.8	18.2	18.5	16.4	14.3
Switzerland	3	76.6	73.8	51.5	22.6	8.9	4.8	3.1	2.2
	5	0.2	0.5	1.3	3.0	4.6	5.8	6.4	5.8
	6/7	0.0	0.5	2.9	7.1	9.7	10.1	9.3	8.1

Notes: . . Data not available. × Data included in another category.
1. Net enrolments rates for each year of age are calculated by dividing full-time plus part-time enrolments at that age by the total population at that age.
2. Public and private institutions.
3. For the definitions of the education levels (ISCED), see Annex Table A.10.
Source: OECD Education Database.

Table 1.11.   **Sweden: average number of training days per employee receiving training, 1986-94** [1]

Age group	1986	1987	1989	1990	1992	1993	1994
16-24	6.8	6.8	8.8	8.3	5.3	6.9	6.1
25-34	7.3	6.4	8.1	8.8	6.6	6.7	7.3
35-44	6.1	5.7	6.2	7.3	7.3	6.9	6.8
45-54	5.2	4.8	6.9	6.9	5.3	5.8	6.7
55-64	4.5	4.2	4.5	4.1	4.4	4.7	5.5
Total	*6.2*	*5.7*	*6.9*	*7.3*	*6.2*	*6.3*	*6.7*

1.   Refers to a six-month reference period.
Source: Statistics Sweden, *Personalutbildningsregistret.*

Table 1.12. **Public education expenditure as a percentage of gross domestic product, 1970-92**

	1970	1971	1972	1973	1974	1975	1976	1977	1978	1979	1980	1981
North America												
Canada	10.2	9.9	9.1	8.7	8.4	8.5	8.3	8.6	8.0	7.7	7.7	7.6
Mexico	2.4	2.6	2.9	3.0	3.3	3.9	4.3	4.7	4.8	5.0	4.6	5.0
United States	6.0	6.0	5.7	5.5	5.5	5.7	5.6	5.3	5.0	4.9	4.9	4.8
Pacific Area												
Australia	4.6	4.7	5.0	5.4	6.4	6.2	6.1	6.2	5.9	5.8	5.6	5.7
Japan	5.0	5.1	5.0	4.9	5.4	5.3	5.3	5.4	5.7	5.6	5.9	5.5
New Zealand	..	..	5.7	5.8	5.9	6.5	6.0	6.4	6.4	6.2	6.7	6.1
European Community												
Belgium	..	..	..	5.7	6.2	5.9	5.8	6.1	6.0	6.0	5.7	5.7
France	..	..	..	..	5.5	5.6	5.5	5.4	5.3	5.2	5.1	5.5
Germany (FTFR)[1]	3.7	4.2	4.4	4.5	4.9	5.1	4.9	4.7	4.6	4.6	4.8	4.8
Greece	2.8	2.7	2.9	2.8	3.4	3.4	3.4	3.7	3.8	3.5	3.2	3.4
Ireland	6.2	6.3	6.4	6.5	7.3	6.5	6.6	6.5	6.6	6.6	6.4	6.6
Italy	..	5.0	5.1	5.1	4.8	4.8	5.0	4.9	4.5	4.7	4.5	4.6
Netherlands	7.5	7.5	7.4	7.3	7.1	7.4	7.2	7.1	7.1	7.0	7.1	7.2
Portugal	..	..	..	1.8	2.0	3.3	3.6	4.0	3.5	3.4	3.7	3.9
Spain	..	..	..	..	..	..	..	..	..	..	..	..
United Kingdom	6.2	6.3	6.5	6.3	6.9	6.8	6.4	6.0	5.8	5.7	5.7	5.6
Other Europe – OECD												
Austria[2]	4.6	4.8	5.0	5.0	5.2	5.7	5.7	5.5	5.7	5.6	5.5	5.9
Czech Republic	..	..	..	..	..	..	..	..	..	..	..	..
Finland	..	..	..	..	..	..	..	..	6.5	5.9	5.8	5.9
Norway	..	..	6.2	6.4	6.0	6.4	6.2	6.4	6.3	6.0	5.8	5.8
Sweden	7.9	8.0	7.9	7.6	7.3	7.1	7.2	7.7	8.0	8.6	8.5	8.0
Switzerland	3.9	4.2	4.4	4.7	5.0	5.3	5.5	5.4	5.3	5.2	5.2	5.1

Table 1.12. **Public education expenditure as a percentage of gross domestic product, 1970-92** (cont.)

	1982	1983	1984	1985	1986	1987	1988	1989	1990	1991	1992[3]
North America											
Canada	7.8	7.5	7.2	6.9	7.0	6.9	6.8	6.2	6.2	6.7	7.2
Mexico	5.0	3.6	3.9	3.8	3.5	3.3	3.3	3.6	4.0	4.5	4.9
United States	4.9	4.8	4.6	4.6	4.8	4.8	4.9	5.0	5.2	5.5	5.4
Pacific Area											
Australia	5.7	5.6	5.4	5.4	5.3	5.1	5.5	4.6	4.6	5.0	5.3
Japan	5.3	5.1	4.9	4.7	4.7	4.5	4.4	3.7	3.6	3.7	3.6
New Zealand	5.6	4.9	4.7	5.1	5.8	5.9	6.1	..	..	..	6.5
European Community											
Belgium	5.7	5.6	5.5	5.6	5.5	5.3	5.0	5.7	5.3	5.4	6.0
France	5.6	5.7	5.7	5.7	5.7	5.6	5.5	5.1	5.1	5.4	5.5
Germany (FTFR)[1]	4.7	4.8	4.6	4.6	4.5	4.4	4.3	4.2	4.1	4.1	4.1
Greece	3.6	3.6	3.8	4.0	3.8	3.8	3.4	..	..	..	..
Ireland	6.1	6.3	6.0	6.0	6.3	6.2	5.4	5.1	5.0	5.2	5.5
Italy	4.7	4.8	5.1	5.0	5.0	4.8	4.9	5.0	5.2	..	5.1
Netherlands	7.2	7.0	6.6	6.6	6.7	6.9	6.1	5.7	5.7	5.6	5.6
Portugal	4.0	4.1	4.0	4.0	4.3	4.1	4.2	4.0	4.3	5.5	..
Spain	3.1	3.4	3.4	3.6	3.6	3.7	3.9	4.2	4.4	4.5	4.6
United Kingdom	5.5	5.2	5.2	4.9	4.9	4.8	4.8	4.8	4.9	5.3	5.2
Other Europe – OECD											
Austria[2]	6.1	6.0	5.8	5.8	6.0	5.9	5.6	5.5	5.4	5.6	5.8
Czech Republic	..	..	..	..	..	..	..	4.1	4.2	4.4	4.8
Finland	5.8	5.8	5.5	5.7	5.7	5.8	5.7	5.7	6.0	6.1	8.3
Norway	6.0	6.0	5.8	5.6	5.5	5.6	5.7	7.0	6.0	6.8	..
Sweden	7.8	7.4	7.2	7.0	7.0	6.9	6.5	5.4	5.6	6.5	7.7
Switzerland	5.2	5.3	5.2	5.1	5.1	5.0	5.1	5.0	5.2	5.5	5.7

Notes: .. Data not available. Vertical lines denote break in series.
1. From 1974 onwards, an increased coverage of financial statistics. Since 1983, including university research. Since 1991, including East-Berlin. The figure for 1992 is an estimate.
2. From 1970-75 including "private education"; data have not been allocated separately over this period.
3. Possible inconsistencies may arise with earlier years, because of changed definitions in the data collection.
Sources: OECD (1992c), Table 2.3, p. 84, and OECD Education Database.

Table 1.13. **Educational expenditure by initial source of funds,** [1] **1985-92** [2]

(as a percentage of gross domestic product)

		1985	1986	1987	1988	1989	1990	1991	1992
North America									
Canada	Private	0.6	0.6	0.7	0.6	0.7	0.7	0.7	0.7
	Total	7.0	6.9	7.2	7.0	6.9	6.9	7.4	7.9
United States	Private	..	..	..	..	..	1.4	1.5	1.8
	Total	..	..	..	..	..	6.6	7.0	7.2
Pacific Area									
Australia	Private	..	..	..	..	..	..	0.8	0.7
	Total	..	..	..	..	..	..	5.5	6.2
Japan	Private	..	..	..	..	1.2	1.1	1.3	1.1
	Total	..	..	..	..	4.9	4.7	5.0	4.8
European Community									
Denmark	Private	–	–	–	–	–	–	–	0.5
	Total	6.9	6.5	6.2	6.4	6.4	6.3	6.1	8.2
France	Private	..	..	..	..	0.6	0.6	0.6	0.8
	Total	..	..	..	..	5.7	5.8	6.0	6.3
Germany (FTFR)	Private	..	..	..	..	..	..	1.5	..
	Total	..	..	..	..	..	..	5.5	..
Ireland	..	..	..	..	..	..	..	0.4	..
	..	..	..	..	..	..	..	5.9	..
Netherlands	Private	0.2	0.3	0.3	0.3	0.3	0.3	0.4	0.6
	Total	6.4	6.5	6.8	6.5	6.1	6.0	5.8	6.1
Spain	Private	1.3	1.3	1.2	1.1	1.1	1.1	1.1	1.2
	Total	4.9	4.9	4.9	5.0	5.3	5.5	5.6	5.0
Other Europe – OECD									
Finland	Private	0.4	0.5	0.5	0.4	0.5	0.5	0.6	0.2
	Total	6.2	6.3	6.3	6.2	6.2	6.5	6.6	8.5
Sweden	Private	..	–	–	–	–	–	–	–
	Total	..	6.0	5.9	5.7	5.4	5.6	6.5	7.8

Notes: .. Data not available. – Magnitude is either negligible or zero.
1. The distinction between education funds originating in the public and private sectors is based on the initial source of funds and does not reflect subsequent transfers between the public and private sectors. The expenditure shown under "private" payments consist mainly of tuition and other fees paid to educational institutions by students or households but exclude public subsidies to households and other private entities. The expenditure shown under "total" expenditure from public and private sources combined reflect direct government expenditure for public and private institutions and payments of households and other private entities to educational institutions. Public subsidies have been netted out where necessary to avoid double counting.
2. Possible inconsistencies may arise with earlier years, because reporting practices changed in 1992.
Source: OECD Education Database.

Table 1.14. **Direct public education expenditure,** [1] **1985-92**

(as a percentage of total public expenditure)

	1985	1986	1987	1988	1989	1990	1991	1992 [2]
North America								
Canada	13.7	13.4	14.1	14.1	14.1	13.6	13.8	14.0
Mexico	12.8	12.2	13.0	13.9	15.2	15.7	18.2	20.3
United States	13.1	13.2	13.4	13.6	14.0	14.3	14.7	14.2
Pacific Area								
Australia	15.5	14.9	14.3	14.9	12.7	12.2	12.5	13.1
Japan	. .	12.5	12.0	11.7	11.6	11.3	11.4	11.3
European Community								
Belgium	10.3	10.1	9.8	9.7	10.3	9.5	9.5	10.5
Denmark	11.6	11.7	10.8	10.7	10.6	10.6	10.4	12.5
France	. .	. .	. .	. .	10.3	10.3	10.6	10.6
Germany (FTFR)	9.6	9.5	9.4	9.1	. .	. .	8.0	8.5
Ireland	. .	11.2	11.8	11.5	12.6	12.2	12.4	13.7
Italy	9.1	9.4	9.6	9.6	9.8	9.6	. .	9.5
Netherlands	10.2	10.4	10.4	10.2	10.0	9.9	9.8	9.5
Portugal	. .	8.7	9.3	10.3	10.5	. .	. .	. .
Spain	8.6	8.7	9.1	9.7	10.0	10.1	10.0	10.4
United Kingdom	11.1	10.8	11.1	11.4	11.6	11.9	11.6	11.9
Other Europe – OECD								
Austria	7.7	7.8	7.7	7.5	7.4	7.5	7.5	7.4
Czech Republic	8.1	8.3	8.2	8.1	8.1	8.1	8.7	10.3
Finland	12.9	12.6	12.6	12.7	13.2	12.9	14.7	13.9
Norway	13.2	13.0	13.1	12.4	12.8	. .	12.1	14.0
Sweden	. .	9.4	9.6	9.7	9.0	9.3	10.4	11.7
Switzerland	15.0	15.2	15.1	15.1	15.2	15.4	15.5	15.2

Note: . . Data not available.

1. Direct public expenditure for educational services include both the amounts spent directly by governments to acquire educational resources and the amounts provided by governments to public and private institutions. The latter include expenditure such as scholarships and other financial aid to students plus certain subsidies to other private entities.

2. Possible inconsistencies may arise with earlier years, because reporting practices changed in 1992.

Sources: OECD Education Database; OECD National Accounts Database.

Table 1.15. **Unemployment rate by level of education for persons 24 to 64 years, various years** [1]

		Level of education			
		Lower secondary or less	Upper secondary	Tertiary	All levels
North America					
Canada	1981	7.8	5.2	3.5	5.7
	1989	10.0	6.8	4.3	6.7
	1992	15.2	9.7	7.6	10.0
United States	1981	10.1	6.5	3.2	5.8
	1989	8.9	4.6	2.6	4.4
	1992	13.5	7.2	3.2	6.6
Pacific Area					
Australia	1989	7.3	4.2	4.3	5.4
	1991	9.1	6.0	5.7	7.1
	1993	11.2	8.9	5.0	8.8
New Zealand	1981	2.8	1.9	1.5	2.3
	1990	8.1	4.9	4.4	6.0
	1992	11.2	7.5	4.2	8.1
European Community					
Belgium	1989	11.1	4.7	2.4	7.5
	1992	13.0	4.7	2.2	7.8
Denmark	1981	8.3	5.7	2.7	6.3
	1988	12.1	7.1	3.6	8.3
	1992	15.6	9.1	5.1	10.6
France	1981	6.7	4.7	3.2	5.6
	1989	11.0	6.6	3.2	8.1
	1992	12.1	7.4	4.5	8.8
Germany	1989	13.7	6.8	4.2	7.3
	1992	8.9	6.4	4.1	6.2
Ireland	1989	20.9	6.6	3.2	13.8
	1992	19.8	9.3	4.5	13.6
Italy	1989	6.4	7.7	4.8	6.6
	1992	7.3	8.2	6.0	7.4
Netherlands	1990	9.7	4.8	4.7	6.6
	1992	8.0	4.4	. .	5.0
Portugal	1989	4.0	4.7	4.7	4.1
	1991	5.3	4.5	1.8	4.9
Spain	1981	8.6	7.8	4.5	8.2
	1989	13.3	13.1	10.7	12.9
	1992	16.0	14.1	10.5	14.7
United Kingdom	1984	11.4	7.6	3.8	8.5
	1989	9.8	5.8	2.6	6.5
	1992	12.3	8.3	3.5	8.4
Other Europe – OECD					
Finland	1982	4.9	3.5	0.0	3.7
	1989	4.0	3.0	1.4	3.0
	1992	14.9	12.1	4.4	11.4
Norway	1981	2.1	1.1	0.7	1.3
	1989	6.3	3.7	1.6	3.7
	1992	7.1	4.9	2.3	4.5
Sweden	1981	2.7	1.7	0.6	2.0
	1989	1.4	1.1	0.9	1.1
	1992	4.6	4.3	2.1	3.8

Note: . . Data not available.
1.   Consult explanations given in Chart 1.39.
Source: See Annex Table A.10.

TOWARDS LIFELONG LEARNING FOR ALL: AIMS, BARRIERS, STRATEGIES

A. INTRODUCTION

Chapter I described broad demographic, technological, economic, social and cultural trends, as well as major developments in education and training. There is a reciprocal relationship between societal change and developments in education and training. Change opens up new opportunities for education and training, but it also poses new challenges; they are summarised in the increased importance of the human factor in underwriting social and economic progress, and wider participation in an increasingly globalised world.

Another way to review the opportunities and challenges for education and training is to underline the importance of increasing diversity of settings in which learning takes place as well as in the diversity of demand for learning opportunities tailored to individual interests, aspirations and needs. Current education and training systems have neither exploited the opportunities, for example those offered by new technologies, nor fully met the challenges. As agreed by Education Ministers in 1990, piecemeal changes to the systems are not sufficient; broader, system-wide reforms are called for (OECD, 1992d). "Lifelong learning" constitutes a framework for coherent reform planning. This is the message given in the *OECD Jobs Study* (OECD, 1994d). The same message was repeated at the informal Forum of Ministers in September 1994, and reinforced by the Ministerial Council in May 1995.

"Lifelong learning" defines a broad set of aims and strategies around the central tenet that learning opportunities available over the whole life-span and accessible on a widespread basis should be key attributes of modern societies. To add the demanding qualification that this must be "for all" is to stress that for lifelong learning to be limited to a privileged group is to create unacceptable divisions in society that could well threaten social cohesion.

At the dawn of the 21st century, the need for lifelong learning is pressing. OECD countries now must establish the framework conditions for making it a reality for all. Strategies for achieving these conditions will be a major preoccupation of countries for the foreseeable future. No single strategy will suffice, given the differences among countries and regions and the complexity of the work to be undertaken. Strategies are needed to gain general acceptance of the basic principle, that a lifelong learning framework is useful in addressing three fundamental objectives shared by all Member countries:

i) *personal development*: by focusing on and exploiting the active learning potential of the individual, lifelong learning strategies place the individual at centre stage; the quality and relevance of provisions are tailored to interests and needs, by giving individuals greater choice and opportunity for initiative;

ii) *social cohesion*: by emphasising that lifelong learning has until now remained the privilege of the few, and that halting and reversing social polarisation requires that systematic opportunities be extended to all, the framework offers a rallying point for strengthening the democratic foundations of OECD societies;

iii) *economic growth*: by improving the conditions, equity and efficiency of investment in skills formation, the framework is fundamental to improving flexibility, raising productivity and promoting economic growth and jobs creation. Against the above, the question is not whether OECD countries can pay the price for lifelong learning, but whether they can afford not to.

These issues determine the coverage of this chapter. Firstly, in Section B, it elaborates why "lifelong learning for all" is now such a central ambition for OECD countries, showing that it contributes to an array of goals rather than a single aim. This section also traces how the concept has evolved. Different proposals for recurrent and lifelong education have been advanced since the 1960s (Faure *et al.*, 1972; OECD, 1973). Although successes were booked on certain fronts, the proposals did not go all the way to successful implementation. As a prelude to the discussion of the present-day policy context, Section C reviews the main barriers that have stood in the way of successful implementation in the past. Section D describes the elements and broad outlines of strategies through which lifelong learning is to be realised. These broad guidelines for policy are the subject of the more detailed analyses advanced in Chapters 3 to 8.

B.   FROM RECURRENT EDUCATION TO LIFELONG LEARNING

There has long been an awareness of the importance of lifelong learning for a whole set of objectives – personal, economic, social and cultural – at the core of the dynamism and prosperity of Member countries. Earlier discussions, including those around the OECD concept of "recurrent education", have stated that case in powerful terms. Nevertheless, long-standing barriers and new problems meant that those earlier concepts were rarely realised in full, and in some quarters there remained scepticism that the radical reforms being called for were either necessary or feasible. Developments since have shown that the earlier case was indeed justified, and many of the original arguments and propositions remain as pertinent as ever. That Ministers of Education now discuss "Realising Lifelong Learning for All" demonstrates as much.

The concept of recurrent education, which emerged in the late 1960s, was defined by the OECD (1973) as follows: "Recurrent education [is] a comprehensive educational strategy for all post-compulsory or post-basic education, the essential characteristic of which is the distribution of education over the total life-span of the individual in a recurring way, *i.e.* in alternation with other activities, principally with work, but also with leisure and retirement" (p. 16). The goal was the modification of the entire education system so that access would be made available throughout the lifetime of individuals. It was seen as desirable that access to post-compulsory education should be guaranteed to all individuals at appropriate times over the life-cycle; that it should be possible to alternate formal education and work in an intermittent way; and that each adult should have a legislated right to study leave (Bengtsson, 1985). The following

were among the original principles of recurrent education:

- Promoting complementarity between school and adult education. Qualifications should not be seen as the "end result" but as steps in a process of personal development and growth throughout life.

- Modifying the upper secondary curriculum so that the final grades of secondary schooling offer the students a real choice between further study and work.

- Introducing compensatory education at the primary and secondary levels.

- Increasing the participation of adults in tertiary education, by recognising the value of work experience and "opening up" the universities.

- Extending the provision of formal adult education to a wider audience.

- Abolishing "terminal stages" in the formal education system so that all programmes lead on to other programmes.

- Alternating formal education and work at the upper secondary and tertiary levels.

- Alternating work and education careers in an intermittent way, which necessitates paid study leave, maternity leave and general income maintenance during periods of "significant non-work".

Many of the above principles of recurrent education still apply today. This is not surprising, given that recurrent education was advocated as a strategy for achieving lifelong learning, which was seen as the longer-term goal. But as the description below of what we now mean with lifelong learning will show, there are some important differences between the strategies advocated in the early 1970s and those that appear appropriate today. These differences are less conceptual than contextual; they derive not from a new understanding of education or learning, but from major changes in wider economic and social contexts in which education policies are shaped and implemented.

Changing contexts and conditions for policy-making

Recurrent education emphasised the correspondence between formal education and work, and implied some instances of interruption in the lifelong process of education. It also considered that educational opportunities should be spread out over the entire life-cycle, as an alternative to the lengthening of formal schooling early in life. In contrast, today's notions of lifelong learning pay less regard to the role of formal institutions and more to non-formal and informal learning in a variety of settings – at home, at work and in the community. Another major difference concerns the role of government. Partly because it emphasised formal education, the recurrent education strategy assigned a large role for government in organising, managing and financing the system. The past years have seen a partial retreat from this principle, and partnership and shared responsibility have become the norm. This shift is reflected in recent policies to strengthen the development of continuing vocational training, especially on-the-job training, rather than expanding formal adult education in institutions fully or partly financed from the public budget. The notion that work ought to be alternated on a sporadic basis with formal education has been replaced by strategies to promote learning while working and working while learning. Another difference is that full retention in broad-based secondary education until at least 17 or 18, and even the expansion of tertiary education, are no longer considered problematic in certain countries; achieving a full cycle of secondary education for all has, as argued below, become one of the cornerstones of strategies for realising lifelong learning for all. Increased reliance on the responsibilities of employers and individual learners is also reflected in the reluctance of many countries to legislate and implement arrangements for paid study leave. Concomitantly with the rising emphasis on accountability, choice and even, in certain OECD countries, "markets for learning" (OECD, 1996a; see also Chapter 5), the concept of "social demand", which was central in the recurrent education philosophy, appears to have been replaced with "individual demand" as key to the provision of adult education, training and learning more generally. As will be seen, this move has implications for equity, efficiency and flexibility.

In reviewing the changing educational policy contexts in OECD countries since the 1960s, Papadopoulos (1994) refers to the "double challenge" posed by recurrent education: vertically, to the established patterns of progress through education, and horizontally, to education's place in broader social policy. He concludes: "Few governments, even if they were willing to accept this double challenge, had the machinery to confront it effectively. Yet it must not be assumed that the effort had been wasted. Many of the elements of the recurrent education strategy in fact gradually found their way into national education pol-

icies and practices. Above all, the long debate around recurrent education helped to bring about greater awareness among educationists as well as other stakeholders of the inter-relatedness of their concerns and the need for concerted action" (p. 115).

The meaning of lifelong learning today

The meaning of lifelong learning is still open to selective interpretation; it depends, to a degree, on the political and philosophical allegiances of the beholder. Yet there exists a core of common elements in most interpretations (Sutton, 1994; Titmus, 1994; Tuijnman, 1994). These include, firstly, a strong belief in the intrinsic as opposed to instrumental value of education and learning. Secondly, there is a common desire for universal access to learning opportunities, regardless of age, sex or employment status. A third common denominator is the recognition of the importance of non-formal learning in diverse settings not confined to those of educational institutions. Fourthly, most observers agree that what distinguishes lifelong learning from more conventional approaches is the diversity in means and methods of teaching and learning. Another common element is the promotion in learners of the personal characteristics required for subsequent learning, including the motivation and capacity to engage in self-managed, independent learning. Finally, the lifelong learning concept is advanced as a critique of, and an alternative to, conventional, "front-end" educational philosophies.

Lifelong learning is now understood to mean the continuation of conscious learning throughout the life-span, as opposed to the idea that education stops at 16, 18 or 21. This understanding involves two aspects (OECD, 1991b). Firstly, it encapsulates the blueprint of recurrent education but in an adapted form: the opportunity to return repeatedly to formal educational institutions *and* non-formal learning that is in some way conscious, planned and systematic. Secondly, it implies recognition by individuals, employers and governments of points where there is a social and/or economic need to update knowledge and skills. This second aspect is distinguished from the first because it does not just see lifelong learning as a right to be exercised, but as a necessary requirement of participation.

"Learning" is not associated only with formal education and training. People learn not only in classrooms, but informally at work, by talking to others, by watching television and playing games, and through virtually every other form of human activity.

Although few would deny that valid learning does take place in such ways, it is difficult to analyse non-formal learning with any rigour. That is why the discussion on lifelong learning still tends to concentrate on activities where "learning" is organised, structured, conscious, and in some way "measurable".

"Learning as consumption" is an imperfect term to describe learning activities that contribute directly to the quality of life rather than aiming mainly to enhance economic potential. The essential difference between learning as consumption and learning as investment is the time perspective. If the education activity is being undertaken with a view to immediate satisfaction, then learning is a consumptive activity. If the learning activity is undertaken with the aim of increasing utility or satisfaction in the future, then the investment motive determines the choice for education. There are two main problems with making crude distinctions between learning for investment and for consumption. The first is that many learners have mixed motives. Even learning that takes place at work can have strong socially related motives, while learning associate with "leisure" activities can accomplish confidence-building that will serve well in the workplace. The second is that learning can be used for a multiplicity of purposes, regardless of the main motives behind it.

The development of learning over the whole life-cycle – with initial education as an introduction and pre-school learning as a prelude – has important implications for the school curriculum in terms of developing long-term self-sustaining study skills and habits. It also presents personal and policy choices about when learning should take place, raising the possibility of re-allocation of resources and potentially a deferral of some of the learning traditionally associated with full-time initial education.

A further essential element of an understanding of the concept involves lifelong learning as an attitude, both of individuals and societies. Although such things as the willingness to learn from experience may seem like a psychological matter with little direct policy relevance, it can be extended to cover the way communities, employers and whole societies operate, and in this sense is relevant for the macroeconomic and structural policy changes being planned and experienced by OECD societies.

Current approaches to lifelong learning differ from those put forward previously in that they now stress the importance of various kinds of partnership in learning, rather than concentrating chiefly on the role of governments as monopoly providers of formal education and training. The new approaches clearly carry considerable implications for the changed role of governments and the expanded type and number of roles that can be played by other stakeholders. Because of its fluid, dynamic, and cover-all character, "lifelong learning" does not lend itself readily, particularly as regards orientation and programming, to the imposition of precisely specified government norms, controls and regulations, nor to the specification of a set of organisational, administrative, methodological and procedural criteria by which its progress and success may be measured.

Five arguments for lifelong learning

As described above, the concept of lifelong learning is broad and inclusive. Five sets of arguments in favour of the lifelong learning approach can be distilled from the foregoing. In distinguishing these, it is important to note that not all these expectations regarding lifelong learning will be met in equal measure, precise results will depend on the concrete shape that is given to it in the different countries and communities for, as observed at the outset, there is no single path to its realisation. Tensions may exist between the different aims and ambitions: for instance, to what degree are broad learning strategies geared to raising and maintaining employment-relevant skills consistent or in competition with those for social cohesion or cultural renewal? The possible tensions that arise need to be addressed and resolved if lifelong learning is to be realised for all.

There is the "learning economy" argument, which recognises the extent to which OECD economies and societies have moved towards a dependence on the creation and manipulation of knowledge, information and ideas. This case is central to the recent OECD-wide formulations of the necessity for lifelong learning referred to above, including the OECD Jobs Study (OECD, 1995e). Since these defining features of the knowledge and information-intensive society affect everyone, the learning involved is for those of all ages, not just the young; mature adults are just as much part of it as are children and youth. There is a warning inherent in this argument – those countries and regions that do not follow its logic to create learning societies, and those individuals who do not participate in them, are increasingly disadvantaged and left behind. There are thus international, equity, and inter-generational outcomes at issue.

The "speed of change" argument is closely related, but focuses especially on the ubiquity of rapid technological change and of growth in knowledge and information. In the future, such change and growth is unlikely to reverse and slow down, so that the ramifications of rapid change will in all likelihood become still more pertinent as time goes by. These ramifications are economic, social and cultural, although economic arguments tend to dominate many policy agendas. They all point to the need not only for there to be excellent and widespread learning opportunities (consistent with the "learning economy" case), but also for knowledge and skills to be *constantly renewed*. Partly, this is a matter of "keeping up" with change. But is also about securing human capacity for flexibility and coping with change, and maintaining cultural coherence and quality in the face of knowledge and information "overload". As the report on *OECD Societies in Transition: The Future of Work and Leisure* (OECD, 1994e) underlines, however, a full perspective is needed that incorporates the whole range of social and cultural concerns, not only the skills dimension. This case for lifelong learning contains an implicit warning about the risks – for countries, enterprises and individuals – of being "left-behind".

The "life-cycle redistribution" argument is more speculative and open-ended, but may be just as telling in the long term as those mentioned above. As economic and labour market activity is increasingly being compressed into the middle period of life, between a prolonged education at the beginning and an extended retirement period at the other end, serious questions arise about the rationality and sustainability of the pattern, if for no other reason than the growing expenditure burden on the "shrinking middle". Might not education and training be strategic elements in general policy approaches that seek to reverse this compression and spread activities more evenly over the life cycle? Instead of promoting the increasingly delayed start to working life, there is a case for re-thinking the life cycle distribution of organised learning resources. Temporal factors are also at the centre of social issues posed by the combination of ageing societies and limited employment openings. Life cycle considerations already play some part in educational arrangements, such as grant and loan systems; implementing lifelong learning will require that such considerations are further extended. The equity dimension is important to this discussion. Strategies for lifelong learning should thus address the distribution of opportunities, across generations and across social strata; they invite new thinking to devise more integrated, equitable and efficient life

cycle arrangements in which education and training constitute an important part.

There is the "active policies" argument for lifelong learning, which picks up and extends the theme current in much economic and social policy that an underlying broad aim should be to move away from essentially passive approaches based on transfer payments – especially in response to unemployment – towards active policies that contribute directly to the formation of human capital and to the psychological and social well-being of individuals. As regards education and training specifically, policies permitting access to high-quality and relevant learning opportunities represent prime examples of active approaches. However, those education and training programmes representing little more than the passive operation of holding or "parking" mechanisms – offering participants a place but few prospects of active learning – cannot themselves rightly be counted as "active". In other words, education and training programmes – especially for those who are unemployed, seeking to enter the labour market or otherwise disadvantaged – should not automatically be assumed to be preferable to transfer policies aimed at income maintenance, unless there is a genuine learning component that confers knowledge, skills and qualifications, and improves life and career chances. Meeting the more exact conditions implied by the promotion of "activity" would, however, contribute substantially to the well-being of OECD countries.

This leads, finally, to the "social cohesion" argument. In part, this stems from all the foregoing: given the importance of the learning foundations and of continued learning in knowledge-intensive societies characterised by rapid change, those who miss out – either initially or later on – suffer effective exclusion. Further, given the close and cumulative links between successful learning in childhood and youth, and the motivation and capacity to continue to learn throughout life, social cohesion is undermined by the failure to put firmly in place these virtuous circles of successful learning. The social cohesion argument extends also to other broader social, cultural and economic fields. There are, for instance, the pronounced socio-economic inequalities of income and personal resources which recent OECD analyses have shown to have increased in many countries during recent years, markedly so in some cases. The prospects here, without innovative policy strategies, could be bleak indeed as underscored by the report, *OECD Societies in Transition: The Future of Work and Leisure* (OECD, 1994e). Learning is the most necessary insurance against exclusion and marginality; educational activity represents a particularly important source of involvement and participation in light of the many pressures now putting social cohesion at risk.

Strategies for lifelong learning must be "for all"

It follows from all these arguments that strategies for realising lifelong learning for all are broad, open-ended and future-oriented. They address learning in all its forms; they accept neither narrow demarcations between education and training, academic and vocational programmes, nor restrictions to learning opportunities in formal structures. Yet, it is this very breadth and diversity that call for a close examination of the balance and direction that should be taken if lifelong learning is to be more than a chaotic, unarticulated collection of structures and functions.

The value of spelling out these different rationales is also that they serve to reinforce the starting point that the broad ambition of lifelong learning loses its policy impact if it is regarded as an idea that is relevant for some individuals but not generalised across society as a whole. The relevance of lifelong learning to contemporary societies derives from its being a concept for national and international application, guiding large-scale strategies. The meaning of the different cases for lifelong learning – the "learning economy", "speed of change", "life-cycle redistribution", "active policies", and "social cohesion" arguments – stems from their general relevance across OECD countries, not to individual persons. For this reason, it is valuable to examine the barriers inhibiting the generalisation of learning to all parts of the community, seeing non-participation not as an individual failing but as a result of structured conditions affecting individuals in manifold, complex ways.

C. BARRIERS TO THE IMPLEMENTATION OF LIFELONG LEARNING FOR ALL

A number of major barriers to adult learning have been identified in the research literature and in OECD's work on adult learning and recurrent education (OECD, 1975; OECD, 1977-81; Levin and Schütze, 1983; Schütze and Istance, 1987; Kawanobe et al., 1993). Based especially on the framework devised by Cross (1981), the distinction can be drawn between barriers that operate at the structural/contextual level, those at the institutional level, and individual/dispositional barriers to learning. The value of elaborating these different dimensions is to show that all of these are in play: lack of participation cannot be

attributed exclusively to the presence of hostile learning environments or lack of suitable learning opportunities or lack of individuals' interest and motivation – they arise from combinations of *all* of them. It serves the purpose of clarifying that a range of policy approaches is relevant to overall strategies for lifelong learning.

Structural/contextual barriers refer to many of the factors outlined above as among the most pertinent aspects of the changed context for lifelong learning. Thus the socio-economic, labour market, financial and political conditions include some of the most powerful influences on participation in learning. The nature of people's lives, living conditions, communities, and sense of security shape not only whether they will enrol in education or become involved in other forms of learning; they help to form what people regard as relevant to their lives and what they might expect from active learning. These structural/contextual factors influence both the "supply" side of provision, programmes and opportunities and the "demand" side of individual expectations and motivations. One problem is that while these are not outside the reach of policy, they will often not be the direct province of the education authorities, nor will their impact on learning be a direct or exact one. They may indeed operate at the most general level of the values, belief systems, habits and traditions that constitute the very fabric of OECD societies. The lack of precision and diffusion of their operation does not lessen their importance.

Institutional barriers refer in essence to the "supply" side of the education, training and learning opportunities in place, rather than the "demand" of individuals and groups. What individuals and groups perceive as the learning possible and relevant to their lives is closely shaped by such factors as the programmes available; their timing and accessibility; the quality and ethos of teachers, trainers and support staff; the location of institutions; the environment for non-formal learning to flourish, and so forth. Indeed, these "institutional" factors are those most accessible to reform through educational policy-making, though in decentralised, pluralistic systems even this range of factors will often only be open to influence rather than prescription. Examples of institutional barriers include the factors that prevent students from progressing along their routes or that limit access. Inadequate use of new technologies and insufficient and ineffective guidance and counselling services that assist people in creating individually relevant pathways for lifelong learning are other limiting factors. Or, most simply, suitable programmes and pathways may just not be in place.

Individual/dispositional barriers comprise the dispositions, values and attitudes of individuals to education and learning more generally. They are, of course, closely shaped by the structural and institutional factors outlined above – factors which are both more directly shaped by and further removed from the influence of education systems and their authorities. These individual factors, in their turn, shape the play of those structural and institutional forces. While this dimension becomes manifest in the dispositions and attitudes of individuals, it does not follow that it reflects the purely personal and hence lies outside the realm of legitimate policy intervention. Personal attitudes are very closely shaped by broad cultural contexts. Attitudes to learning are especially sensitive to the general culture, the respect that this gives to the improvement of knowledge and skills, and the extent to which this improvement is regarded as rightfully "for all", or only for certain sections of society.

Valuable though it is to identify these inhibiting factors and pressures, they are still only a framework, not a precise model for action, as in reality these different dimensions are all interactive and some are more powerful in certain circumstances than others. They show, however, that policy strategies should be operating on a number of fronts simultaneously, rather than on a narrow range of variables. They also show the scope for strategies that do attempt to be comprehensive to set in train positive developments that are mutually reinforcing.

Addressing the bottlenecks to a systemic culture of lifelong learning

The theme of this section is that realising lifelong learning is not exclusively a matter of creating and sustaining widespread, high-quality learning opportunities, challenging as this is. It is also about overcoming the obstacles that inhibit its development. In the foregoing, some of the principal conditions and dimensions outlined that act to inhibit both the widespread implementation of lifelong learning and the take-up of opportunities by adults. Below, the barriers are described in terms of some of the main "publics" who need to be targeted to make lifelong learning a reality.

- Among *individuals*, there is often a lack of insight into what is possible, as well as an innate conservatism about venturing into new fields of learning in order to create a valuable and relevant foundation of knowledge and skills. This points to the need for guidance and counselling services.

- Among *teachers*, protection of professional self-interest can stand in the way of the structural, organisational and pedagogical changes – at the system, institutional and individual levels – that the realisation of lifelong learning entails.

- Within many of the discrete sectors of *education and training systems*, as well as the separate government departments, are the territorialism and viewpoints that prevent the emergence of the larger, holistic visions implied by lifelong learning.

- Among *employers* in many countries, there is often a marked inconsistency between the demands made for the creation of a high-level knowledge and skills base on the one hand, and willingness to match such demands with corresponding support for the educational enterprise in general and the preparation of their workforce in particular.

- Among *politicians* and *decision-makers* there is too often only a superficial espousal of the grand principles and no real willingness to confront the consequences for action stemming from that espousal. "Lifelong learning" is one such principle that may well receive rhetorical support but not the corresponding radical agendas for governance and finance.

- Among *parents*, there are – depending on the system in question – examples of efforts to maximise the comparative advantage of their own children's education, and – in so doing – ensure that much-needed reforms for the general good cannot take place, or that the learning opportunities available to those who need them most are either inadequate or not available at all.

- In some *communities*, including those most in need of educational and cultural investment, the attitude may prevail that learning is something for the specialist education and training bodies with little connection with those in the community.

These are only examples, not meant to typify all individuals, teachers, employers and politicians. The "types", however, are sufficiently widespread to illustrate the value of addressing target "players" who sometimes act as obstacles to lifelong learning. There needs to be a common acceptance of the demanding nature of "learning societies"; a capacity for change, some of which will be radical; the high level of involvement of all groups and communities, and not just specialist educational bodies; and the victory of large visions over narrow viewpoints. It is unrealistic to imagine that this environment will simply emerge unaided, except in those countries and settings where lifelong learning has taken strongest root.

The importance of a strategic vision that addresses and meets these obstacles is critical. Providing that vision may well be a role for education authorities and their counterparts in labour and social affairs departments to undertake, not through prescriptive plans but through an understanding of the bigger picture and consequent information needs. Clearly, there are profound implications for investment and consumption. The goals associated with lifelong learning are ambitious – expanding early childhood education, making upper secondary education a common experience for all youth, opening up post-secondary education and training, developing employer-led pathways from education into the world of work, pursuing active training policies for the unemployed and disadvantaged, further developing distance education and general adult education, and improving the equity and efficiency of provisions in the markets for learning and training. Realising these goals may well call for increased public and/or private investments, even if some of the resources could be freed by efficiency gains or the redistribution of costs by levels and types of education and training provision. The case for new investment will hardly be convincing in the absence of a full elaboration of the strategy for lifelong learning, including estimates of the costs of alternative futures, and a full calculus of expected benefits.

D. TOWARDS STRATEGIES FOR LIFELONG LEARNING

The above review of barriers to the implementation of lifelong learning strategies has indicated a number of weaknesses and problems, which pose major challenges to policy-makers. These problems cannot be appropriately addressed in a piecemeal fashion; meeting the challenges requires system-wide reform. Lifelong learning provides an appropriate framework for pursuing this system-wide reorientation of education and training policies. This section examines the overall feasibility of implementing the

all-embracing concept of lifelong learning and proposes the broad outlines of possible strategies. It aims to identify the policy directions that might be considered – guidelines that are analysed indepth in the subsequent chapters.

The policy directions and guidelines are aimed at improving equity, coherence, flexibility and efficiency of the pathways in lifelong learning and work; by improving the relevance and quality of the foundations and extending it to all; by enhancing articulation between the various pathways and system components; by renewing the resources and "assets" of the system; and by improving flexibility and increasing efficiency through better policy co-ordination, new approaches to governance, including new partnerships, and a reassessment of the priorities and means of financing the system.

Building an inclusive learning society will take major and sustained efforts over the long term. Yet, the need for action is urgent, for unless countries are already moving towards lifelong learning now, the likelihood that they will meet these long-term objectives become still more remote. Although the policy guidelines developed below are consistent with this long-term vision for the development of education systems in OECD countries, the focus is also on action that must be initiated in the short and medium term, until the turn of the century. "Long-term" does not mean "dispensable in the immediate term"; it refers instead to the large scale of the undertaking and hence the investment of time and resources in order to see the project fully through into practice. There is a particular value, given the theme of partnerships, of identifying the strategic contribution where each of the main partners has particular responsibilities. It is obvious that the education authorities, by no means the only partner in the lifelong learning enterprise, have a central role; it cannot be realised without the lead and integral involvement of education and training systems.

In considering the scope and content of strategies for lifelong learning, three questions are pertinent. Firstly, what are the goals and objectives a lifelong learning strategy is supposed to serve? Secondly, what are the constituencies for lifelong learning, and what are their respective roles and responsibilities? And thirdly, what are the requirements in terms of monitoring, assessing and evaluating progress towards achieving the goals? These questions imply directions for strategic analyses which are elaborated in the subsequent chapters.

Strategic goals and objectives

A commitment to lifelong learning will necessitate a review of the goals and objectives of education, training and learning more generally. Although the priorities and specific emphases will differ among countries, six interrelated sets of goals deserve attention:

i) *Enlarging access to high-quality early childhood education.* Because the first years of life are crucial for continued learning, and since disadvantage which is not corrected in the early years can persist, enlarging access to high-quality early intervention programmes and early childhood education is a central goal in any strategy for lifelong learning.

ii) *Revitalising foundation learning in primary and secondary schools.* Providing a solid and secure basis of learning in primary and secondary schools will require attentiveness to both the capacity and motivation to learn. In order to sustain motivation and develop abilities, "positive" learning environments are needed. Such environments should facilitate the use of individualised teaching and learning strategies, and employ assessment and examination procedures that value and take account of individual progress in learning. A rethinking of the curriculum and the very organisation of schools, continued attentiveness to students with special needs, the underserved and slow learners, and more generally a focus on those who are "at risk" of failure, are further requirements.

iii) *Overcoming problems of transition.* In all Member countries, young adults, communities and employers are faced with the individual, social and economic consequences of difficulties in managing the transition from school to work. Building an inclusive learning society requires that the barriers that hinder this transition be removed. Appropriate guidance and counselling services are a major element in any strategy for achieving this.

iv) *Encouraging adult learning.* Beyond schooling and initial tertiary education, the most common times for adults to undertake major learning projects have been at points of crisis or substantial change in their lives or careers. There is a need for learning to become a part of the on-going process of everyday life, as a function of continuing self-development and adaptation to new conditions and environments. This highlights the importance of creating a better framework to motivate, facilitate and reward continued learning, and in so doing increase the demand for learning opportunities among adults. Because evidence suggests a strong bias in participation in favour of those who already have a good education, there is a role for governments in securing fairness; this must be reflected in strategic policy decisions. Because over 20 per cent of adults in some of the most advanced OECD countries have literacy skills at only the most basic level (OECD and Statistics Canada, 1995), adult basic education must feature centrally in any strategy for realising lifelong learning for all.

v) *Addressing the lack of coherence in the system.* A comprehensive system of lifelong learning opportunities implies a fluid relationship between learning and work, where an initial period of full-time schooling is followed throughout working life by sequences and combinations of organised learning at school and/or at work, which accompany or alternate with full- or part-time work. Under current arrangements, most of the elements of the system are in place, but the articulation between them is far from perfect. University education exerts a disproportionate influence on the structure of some education systems, and the pathways that should connect general and vocational education are often non-existent or inflexible. Priority must be given to the creation of a framework for linking the formal and non-formal elements of lifelong learning in flexible sets of pathways and progressions in education and working life, taking account of the differing needs and potential of individuals, and including arrangements for the assessment of knowledge and skills which recognise the value of all forms of learning. Important elements of a coherent system are more developed arrangements for the assessment and recognition of acquired skills and competencies, including well-developed mechanisms for assessing prior learning and validating skills acquired outside the formal sector. Frameworks of standards for assessment, recognition and certification of training are needed to encourage investment in skills and to facilitate mobility.

vi) *Renewing the resources and "assets" of the system.* The goal of creating "positive" learning environments calls for new capital investment in buildings and other physical infrastructures. But the "assets" of education systems lie only partly in their buildings. The greater share is in the knowledge and experience of teachers and non-teaching staff. In many OECD countries these human resources are underdeveloped. Teachers and administrators need access to information and research about the structures they are working in, at local, national and international levels. The continuing professional development of staff, especially but not exclusively teachers, must be taken far more seriously. However, informed decision-making cannot take place in the absence of an adequate information base. Hence there is a need to strengthen the research and information base at the national and international levels.

In order to give substance and focus to the formulation of these goals and objectives, the main purposes of lifelong learning, the "cases" outlined above, come to the fore to ask how each – the "learning economy", "speed of change", "life-cycle redistribution", "active policies", and "social cohesion" arguments – can be implemented on a widespread basis. The focus of each emphasises the need to seek ways in which these broad ambitions are actively developed across OECD countries as: continuous training and retraining on the basis of an advanced foundation of learning; openness to new learning and the ability to manage knowledge "overload"; the promotion of active lives and policies; social inclusion not exclusion; "life-cycle sensitive" perspectives and practices that break away from rigid (and inappropriate) age compartmentalisation patterns.

It is also necessary to recognise that practices and policies that promote one of these may not promote the others in equal measure. Hence the inclusion in the goals and objectives listed above of the need for "visions" that set out the nature and priorities of lifelong learning, bringing in all the relevant partners and players. Obviously, too, objectives by themselves are much easier to identify than to put into practice, for they depend on a range of means and instruments through which they are made possible. Certain of these are elaborated in the following section, focusing on those aspects that are closer to those fields where the education authorities are likely to play a lead or major role.

Means and instruments

The key instruments for implementing a strategy for lifelong learning include: *i)* the redefinition of the roles and responsibilities of Education Ministries and their partners; *ii)* the appropriate human resources, physical infrastructure and knowledge base to provide high-quality lifelong learning; *iii)* adequate financing arrangements to implement an inclusive programme of lifelong learning and to provide sufficient opportunities and incentives to the partners in the system.

The insight that lifelong learning is not restricted to formal education provides a useful starting point for a strategic discussion about roles and responsibilities. A strategic question is how far the responsibility of governments for education should be extended to the areas of lifelong learning that lie beyond formal education and training, for example continuing vocational education and learning on the job. Instead of extending the role of governments in organising and funding an integral system of lifelong education, extending from pre-school years to old age, policy-makers now tend to opt for a more limited approach, one in which the responsibilities of other interest groups – especially the individual and the social partners – are emphasised. This approach has been accompanied by a tendency to increase the scope for private constituencies to assume more responsibility for provision.

There is wide agreement that governments need to assume a significant role in co-ordinating the provision of lifelong learning: for example, it is clear that governments have a role in disseminating information and guidance on the options that are available. It is the responsibility of governments to establish the appropriate framework conditions for lifelong learning; but governments cannot become monopoly providers. Partnerships are central in any strategy for achieving an inclusive approach to lifelong learning. Notions of partnership differ, however, depending on the levels and sectors of educational provision; partnerships for better schools will be very different from partnerships for adult education and training.

Strategies for lifelong learning must be financed; the success of any strategy stands or falls with its success in mobilising and reallocating resources. Because of the high costs involved, the financing of mass tertiary education is a real issue for governments. If it is widely acknowledged that education and training have the characteristics of investment, little has been done in OECD societies to account properly for human capital. As a result, countries are unable to make appropriate investment decisions. In OECD (1996a), it is put this way: "In the context of a growing body of evidence that investment in human capital is playing an even greater role in determining the outcome of competition amongst firms (...) the question [arises] of the extent to which the systems for information and decision-making regarding the stocks and flows of human capital impede or facilitate structural adjustment and optimal choices. In the light of today's competitive pressures and pervasive changes in the realm of production (...) the need [is] to rethink the rules and traditions that govern human capital formation and decision-making systems."

E.   CONCLUSIONS

The strategic directions suggested in this chapter do not apply only to the education sector or to governments alone. Coherent strategies for lifelong learning must take three framework conditions into account. Firstly, a "system" of lifelong learning cannot be imposed; it must depend and thrive on a great variety of initiatives taken by different actors in many spheres of life and work. Secondly, the role of government is not to invent, manage and pay for a unified, comprehensive "system" of lifelong learning, but rather to monitor and steer developments and redistribute resources so that the available opportunities will be equitable, systematic, flexible and efficient. Thirdly, the very nature of lifelong learning – diverse, pluralistic, and undertaken over the lifetime – calls for

co-ordination among many policy sectors, involving both macroeconomic and structural policies.

These strategic issues, aims and instruments, especially as they are pertinent to the particular contribution that the education authorities in OECD countries will make to realising lifelong learning, lead directly into the chapters that follow. The next two chapters examine the main issues confronting education and training systems for which those authorities have substantial responsibility. This is done, firstly, in Chapter 3, which examines the foundations laid for lifelong learning through schools and initial education systems; secondly, in Chapter 4, which addresses the pathways and transitions that take place between the worlds of education, learning and work. On this basis, Chapter 5 then looks at the nature of governance and constituencies that have become so crucial to educational debate and policy formulation today. From this, the more detailed focus is developed on the means and instruments through which lifelong learning is to be realised, and the major issues that are raised in relation to these: the role and use of educational goals and standards (Chapter 6); maintaining and renewing key educational resources – the professionals, buildings and research and development (Chapter 7); and the ubiquitous questions raised above, costing and financing lifelong learning strategies (Chapter 8). Their contribution as background to the contemporary discussion about taking the lifelong learning project forward to become reality lies thus both in the cumulative form of analysis – from the main sectoral and transversal issues to detailed means and instruments – and in the compilation of a very detailed body of evidence and experience from across the OECD range of countries.

ESTABLISHING THE FOUNDATIONS FOR LIFELONG LEARNING

A. INTRODUCTION

This chapter considers the far-reaching implications for schools of a successful reorientation of policy towards lifelong learning. Change must be considered and it must be persuasive, reinforcing public commitment to early childhood education and intervention programmes, and primary and secondary education. Lifelong learning is not synonymous with adult education; it begins from the earliest years. Because the first four to five years of life are the period of most rapid growth – critical in the child's cognitive, emotional and social development – enriching the learning environment early on, developing a sound foundation for subsequent growth of knowledge, skills and values, and a positive attitude towards learning are the key features of any coherent strategy for continuing growth and development throughout the life cycle, the ultimate goal of lifelong learning. If the early foundations are not properly mastered, it will serve little purpose to develop a learning society that targets adults. This chapter aims to identify points of intervention up to, and including, the completion of a full cycle of secondary education by all students.

The importance of formal schooling for the overall success of lifelong learning calls for a new and searching scrutiny of its nature – schools as institutions, the processes that govern them, and the "fit" between these characteristics and processes and the aims they seek to realise. In this, it is necessary to include the examination of the earliest pre-school years and how integrated with or distinctive from the rest of the schooling cycles this phase should be. And it is important that the focus is systemic and not just institutional; it should extend beyond the questions of what are good schools and how they can be realised in individual cases, to ask how good schools can be put in place in *all* cases. Such is the speed of change in so many social, economic and cultural domains, as amply illustrated in Chapter 1, that such an examination of the nature of schools should address how far they should also be subject to rapid

change; this report concludes that they should embrace change while offering essential stability for pupils, parents and the wider public. While all this calls for specific policies, it also depends on creating a general environment that is strongly supportive of the enterprise of schooling. Through the creation of such a "positive" climate, many of the more detailed reforms will be substantially facilitated.

Section B considers the common values and principles that underline school curricula in OECD countries. Issues encountered in defining and selecting the content of the core curriculum are reviewed in Section C. Section D addresses the question of how this common content might best be offered, and in what settings. Section E takes up the issue of individual differences in ability, needs and interests, including the tensions between policy measures to promote equality and those intended to increase quality and efficiency in school learning. Section F analyses evidence on the effectiveness of early childhood education and intervention programmes, and concludes that public attention, resources and effort should focus on the children who most need community support to help them acquire the foundations for lifelong learning and work. Section G presents a summary of the main findings and the strategic considerations for policy.

B. CULTURE, VALUES AND PLURALISM IN SCHOOL LEARNING

Today's multicultural, pluralistic and increasingly technocratic societies are faced with fundamental questions that are at the heart of the debate about values and purposes in school education. Given that schools are embedded in their local communities, which differ a great deal in terms of affluence, cohesion, and social and cultural outlook, what core of common humanistic values and civic principles, if any, shall constitute the guidelines for the curriculum to be taught in the compulsory school? How can we ensure that these common values and principles complement or are compatible with those taught at home and in the community?

The elementary or primary school, with its essential features of universality and full-time attendance, developed as an institution for children concomitantly with the industrial society and was a powerful instrument in the establishment of the modern nation-states in the OECD area. It was the main instrument in establishing a common identity, backed by a policy of making the populations within the various national borders literate in one or two standardised languages. Children were taught the history of their country, often with a strong nationalistic bias. Basic skills constituting literacy and numeracy were a staple for all, as were a moral code and a general or "factual" curriculum. Notions of "good" conduct or behaviour and a set of facts to be mastered defined the competence required in the progression towards either secondary school or entry into the workforce.

Traditional primary school systems have had clear purposes, goals and expectations, which naturally related to the main characteristics of the societies they served. Schools have responded to the expectations not only of governments but also of religious bodies and other powerful groups (Husén, 1979).

In tomorrow's world, schools will continue to play a role in establishing a basis for national identity. But the goals and objectives the schools are expected to pursue have widened, partly in response to internationalisation and resultant changes in culture, economy and polity (Husén, 1987). Governments are challenged to find overall policy frameworks that are unifying, coherent and orderly on the one hand, and receptive to diversity on the other. As in the past, literacy, numeracy, a common sense of history and cultural identity, concepts of nature, and an understanding and appreciation of the larger society and civic order have to be acquired by all children, so as to establish a framework of reference for the citizens of countries and to provide the human resources for continuing growth. However, the school must also foster critical self-awareness and the capacity to reflect constructively on experience, and thereby contribute to educating independent, critical and responsible citizens ready to live comfortably with one another and to exercise their duties in democratic and pluralistic societies that extend across the various borders of the traditional nation-states. More than ever, schools will be called upon to emphasise co-operation in learning and in living. Today, schools

are organised in an individualistically competitive mode, where a high grade for one student often means a low grade for a classmate; success for some means failure for others. There are many alternative ways of motivating students and assessing performance, an issue taken up below and explored further in Chapter 6.

In a lifelong learning framework designed to meet the conditions of modern life and serve a more global, post-industrial society, curricula need to be considered differently from the way they were at the time when school for most students was not only the beginning but also the end of formal education, and commonly equated with "filling up" for the rest of life. Since there is no way of predicting precisely the changing conditions in work, culture and everyday life, it is difficult to foresee what specific elements should be part of the foundations for lifelong learning. However, one of the few things that can be predicted with certainty is that the individual in tomorrow's world will be called upon to learn and relearn throughout life. There is widespread agreement that everyone should be motivated – and have the capacity – to be actively involved in continuing learning processes. The implication is that the schools should capture and hold the interest of all children from an early age and concentrate on teaching those competencies which constitute the ability to learn systematically, consistently and enthusiastically.

Determining the content of the curriculum is a major challenge. It must be changed from near-encyclopaedic information on disconnected subjects and items to a source of intellectual instruments and strategies for learning. Paradoxically, in several countries, recent years have seen the emphasis in curriculum work move away from the "cross-curriculum" competencies that this challenge implies. In the United Kingdom and the United States, for example, the trend is towards a tightening of the curriculum and a return to well-defined subjects complemented by an appropriate system of formal assessment (see also Chapter 6). The "back to basics" movement may be seen as an attempt to find an anchor of stability in an unstable social and economic context. Lifelong learning strategies invite reflection on how to restructure a curriculum to prepare young people for a life with more uncertainties, risk-taking, entrepreneurial opportunities, and perhaps periods of unemployment or "significant non-work". Two seemingly opposed forces are influencing the development of school curricula, one that steers "back to basics" and one that concentrates on "cross-curriculum" or "survival" skills, which involve problem-solving and theoretical-analytical competencies not related to any specific discipline or subject; information search, decoding and synthesis skills; critical reflexiveness; learning-how-to-learn; and social competence (Trier and Peschar, 1995). Ultimately, though, the issue is not one of "basics" or "no basics", but what is meant by basics for contemporary life and in a lifelong learning context.

In re-examining the school curriculum, countries are faced with the question of how the breadth and depth of knowledge should be balanced (OECD, 1993d). Breadth is necessary – it is essential to be familiar with different subjects and well-articulated fields of human enquiry in order to identify key competencies and learning strategies. Moreover, breadth in the curriculum is important for capturing students' interest, for motivating them to enlarge their view of the world. But breadth does not and should not preclude depth. The aim of curriculum design and teaching is to find ways in which the deeper challenges of enquiry can be encompassed within a broad framework of forms of knowledge and experience.

Schools are expected to impart not only substantive knowledge and "applicable" skills, but also the core values that are central in a society. Such core values can develop and change over time, however, as is the case of environmental awareness (OECD, 1994o and 1995x). Chapter 1 showed how national cultures have been deeply affected by the pluralism and multiculturalism accompanying the processes of industrialisation. The question is, to what extent is a core of shared values – which constitute a common frame of reference with regard to socially, culturally, and in some instances religiously anchored norms – a necessary prerequisite for consistent foundation learning for all? If there is a need, how is such a core best defined? This question is taken up in the next section.

The problem of shared values and consistencies between the various actors in education has become acute in OECD countries, because of mass media, urbanisation, migration, tourism and international communication – all of which bring together people of various backgrounds and expose them to different values (Husén et al., 1992). The issue will become even more pronounced in a framework for lifelong learning, because it encourages increased diversity in the supply and demand for learning opportunities, and because it calls attention to the need for complementarity of different agents and their roles in formal and non-formal learning.

School curricula in OECD countries need to rise to these challenges and indeed to be part of social, cultural and economic vitalisation, rather than a pale reflection or, as it sometimes appears to be, a reactionary force. School itself needs to be proactive and creative. There are also the specific issues of pluralism and diversity. Pluralism, in terms of the right to hold another opinion and tolerance and respect for other people's values, is already a shared norm among OECD countries. But the implications of this for the organisation and operation of schools and the content of learning are not always well understood, or are resisted. Attitudes towards ethnic or religious minorities, and towards immigrants, are a case in point. Language policies are another important aspect of multi-culturalism and tolerance for diversity in school practice. In many countries, schools enrol large numbers of students for whom the language of instruction is not their first or even second language. School systems must resist pressure to turn what amounts to an advantage into a disadvantage and a barrier to learning and achievement.

In practical terms, the problem is whether and to what extent nationally-based syllabuses should be tailored to a "common standard". Given the link between trade and labour markets, there are practical reasons for harmonising – though not standardising – the syllabuses in certain respects, if for no other reason than to render the skills, competencies and qualifications attained in different countries transportable. But what about national history and geography, cultural values, and language imperatives? Table 3.1 suggests that the European countries generally teach not one but two foreign languages in lower and upper secondary education. The Netherlands has the highest mean number of foreign languages per student, but allocates relatively few hours to language instruction. In England and Wales, secondary students are taught on average one language for between two and four hours per week.

OECD countries – together or in various regional groupings – are faced with adjusting to ongoing integration, mainly economic but in some instances with substantial cultural and political implications. There are increased migration, cross-border trade and global communication on the one hand, and on the other a new wave of ethnic and cultural claims by peoples and minorities residing within national borders, for whom political and cultural self-determination is a cherished goal. Will foreign language learning have to be extended to cover international language differences? How the OECD countries pro-

Table 3.1. **Foreign language education in the European Community, 1990**

	Number of hours of instruction per week				Mean number of foreign languages per student in secondary general education
	First language		Second language		
	Age 14/15	Age 17/18	Age 14/15	Age 17/18	
Belgium (French community)[1]	6	6	4	4	1.4
Belgium (Flemish community)[1]	6	6	5	6	1.9
Denmark[2]	2	3	3	3	1.4
France[1]	3	3	3	3	1.5
Germany[1, 3]	4	6	4	6	1.3
Greece[2]	3	..	3	..	..
Ireland[2, 4]	3	..	3	..	1.0
Italy[2]	4	..	3	..	1.0
Luxembourg[1]	3	4	5.5	5	..
Netherlands[2]	2.5	2.5	2	2.5	2.2
Portugal[2]	3	4	3	4	0.8
Spain[2, 5]	4	3	3	3	1.0
United Kingdom[6]	2	4	2	4	0.9

Notes: .. Data not available.
1.   Maximum possible number of hours per week.
2.   Mean number of hours per week.
3.   Instruction in the *Gymnasium*.
4.   Full-time instruction only.
5.   Refers to the situation before the school reform.
6.   England and Wales only.
Sources: Survey conducted by *Eurobarometer* in December 1990; EUROSTAT (1995), *Les chiffres clés de l'éducation dans l'Union européenne*, Luxembourg.

pose to cope with this phenomenon will profoundly affect the shape and orientation not only of the school curriculum but the very fabric of future learning societies that depend on formal institutions and community-based movements. What is to be taught? On whose authority? To whom and by whom? Pluralism and acknowledgement of the values of diversity do not mean abandoning the idea of a common set of shared values.

This leads us back to the question raised in the opening paragraph of this section. What core of common values and civic principles, if any, shall constitute the guidelines for the curriculum to be taught in the compulsory schools of individual countries, and perhaps more widely across the OECD area? Governments have a role in establishing frameworks in which these common values and principles complement or are compatible with those of particular subsets of society and with those of home and community.

The idea of a common core of values and principles underpinning curricula thus emerges both as a necessity in the modern democratic state and as an acute challenge to governments attempting to achieve a balance of potentially conflicting and divisive interests. For schooling, however, there are several clear implications. First, most systems have in

place or under review frameworks of national goals, objectives and guidelines for a core curriculum (Skilbeck, 1990). Nations have increasingly demonstrated a capacity to define common goals and purposes for schooling (Knutsen, 1995). They have created and continue to review curricular frameworks and the outlines of core curricula in schools (Papadopoulos, 1994). These frameworks and outlines need to be reappraised and perhaps modified to meet both the increasing diversity and mobility of populations and the principle of basic formal schooling as a foundation for continuing learning instead of an endpoint. A further challenge is to modify and strengthen these frameworks and curricula to acknowledge the ongoing internationalisation process, whereby countries become intimately linked economically and new political structures emerge.

Although the conditions and contexts in countries are very different, there are certain shared objectives for school education that transcend national boundaries (see Chapter 6). Democracy and respect for diversity are two such objectives. But the goals and principles underpinning the curriculum may be at odds with one another, and countries can face difficulties in ensuring that the national values espoused in the curriculum are compatible with those of their neighbours, or even those of the cultural and linguistic minorities residing within their borders. As the

OECD Member countries press forward in creating an interconnected, post-industrial world, the differences – if not the tensions – over what constitutes accepted values may increase. New opportunities are, of course, in the offing as well. The legacy of universal basic schooling is there to build on, but the structures need to be more comprehensive in acknowledgement of an increasingly globalised environment.

C. WHAT FOUNDATIONS FOR LIFELONG LEARNING?

There is a consensus that all children must master a core of essential knowledge and skills, and acquire the values and attitudes that prepare them effectively for adult life and the worlds of work and continued learning. Some people think that schools give too much weight to "academic" subjects, whereas others feel that the "basics" are being neglected. Others claim that schools do too little to prepare young people for jobs, and that the vocational orientation of programmes as well as the relations with employers must be strengthened. In the perspective of lifelong learning, what sort of foundation should all young people acquire? What should be the basic elements? How do these differ from the elements schools have traditionally sought to impart? Are these differences sufficiently important to demand a complete overhaul of current curricula and the methods of teaching and learning? Finally, what are the implications for children with special learning needs?

Few empirical studies have been conducted with the aim of identifying the skills that constitute a common core of competence in a learning society. This is not surprising, since there is still a great deal of debate about what constitutes such a society. A recent study – on the broad theme of what European business expects of schooling – was conducted under the auspices of the European Round Table of Industrialists (1995) in co-operation with the Conference of European University Rectors. When questioned about the shape of the school curriculum of the future, leading business executives outlined a broad humanistic educational philosophy. Far from seeking vocationally trained specialists, or wishing to see schools concentrate on a limited set of basic skills, they advocated a modern liberal education, structured around three key learning areas: mathematics, science and technology; the humanities; economics and social sciences, as forming the basic chain extending from pre-school to adult education.

The position of these leading executives is in striking contrast to that often taken by other representatives from the world of work, who do not focus on a perceived lack of orientation in history, languages and the natural and social sciences, but criticise school-leavers' competence in arithmetic, writing, communication and analytical skills – competencies which are seen by many to be at the heart of the school curriculum.

What kind of competencies and skills are called for in a society that tries to enhance the capacity for learning and relearning throughout life? Clearly, these competencies must reflect the multidimensional nature of the goals for education mentioned previously. The essential elements constituting a common foundation might include the following areas of knowledge and experience (OECD, 1994f): moral reasoning and action; mathematical-analytical skills and their applications; scientific ways of mastering and applying technological knowledge; information and communication science; cultural, civic and economic studies; arts; health; and the environment. Core learning processes might include learning and thinking techniques; ways of organising knowledge; forms of expression; and interpersonal and social relations. Some of these areas refer to the "cross-curriculum competencies" (Trier and Peschar, 1995) seen by many to hold increasing significance: problem-solving; critical thinking; communication; democratic values; understanding of political processes; self-perception; and self-confidence.

"Cross-curriculum" skills are not normally identified in the syllabus, which still tends to be organised around discrete subject areas. Table 3.2 shows teaching time per subject specified in the curriculum as a percentage of all teaching time in public lower secondary education. Many countries devote a substantial portion of teaching time to reading, writing and foreign languages. The amount of time devoted to mathematics and science is consistent across the countries. The data suggest that the teaching of foreign languages in the Netherlands may reduce time for mathematics and science teaching. For all countries, the data give an impression of a full and possibly "overloaded" curriculum. How, in such a context, can room be created for new subjects and new curricular emphases? Cross-curriculum skills will need to be accommodated within the time devoted to existing subjects – arrangements that will represent a major challenge to teachers.

Table 3.2. **Teaching time per subject specified in the intended curriculum in lower secondary education, 1992[1]**

(percentage of total teaching time)

	Reading and writing[2]	Mathematics	Sciences[3]	Social studies[4]	Foreign languages	Technology	Arts	Physical education	Religion	Vocational skills	Other
Pacific Area											
New Zealand	20	16	9	9	7	11	7	12	..	6	3
European Community											
Belgium	15	13	6	11	13	2	5	8	6	..	23
France	18	14	10	13	17	8	7	11	..	..	1
Germany (FTFR)	13	12	11	11	18	..	9	9	6	3	9
Ireland	19	10	8	16	12	6	12	4	5	..	10
Italy	22	10	10	14	10	10	13	7	3	..	..
Netherlands	16	8	9	14	26	..	10	11	2	2	1
Portugal	11	13	14	16	17	14	6	6	3	..	..
Spain	20	13	10	10	13	6	12	10	6	..	..
Other Europe – OECD											
Austria	14	12	13	11	11	6	11	11	6	2	3
Finland	12	12	12	12	9	..	6	9	4	..	24
Norway	16	12	9	10	10	..	9	9	7	..	19
Sweden	10	12	13	17	9	2	7	9	..	..	21
Turkey	20	13	13	11	10	..	9	7	7	7	3
Country mean	**16**	**12**	**11**	**13**	**13**	**6**	**9**	**9**	**5**	**2**	**10**

Notes: ... Data not available.
1. Refers to the percentage of the total available teaching time per subject category in public lower secondary education. "Teaching time" is expressed as a number of lessons of standard duration.
2. Refers to mother tongue instruction.
3. Includes physics, chemistry, biology and earth science.
4. Geography, philosophy and history.
Source: OECD (1995d). *Education at a Glance – OECD Indicators*. p. 165.

A crucial element concerns the skills referred to in the expression "learning to think, thinking to learn", used in a CERI (Centre for Educational Research and Innovation) conference report (Maclure and Davies, 1991). These skills are not a priority in schools where the overriding objective is to impart encyclopaedic knowledge. In contrast, the position receiving much support today is that detailed and factual knowledge in specific areas can be taught – and mastery in them achieved – as they are needed later on. Learning-to-learn skills (Smith, 1994) refer to the ability to find information and to extract the relevant from the less relevant, to relate it to previously acquired knowledge, to contextualise it, and put it to use – again, as needed. On the whole, what is required of students is familiarity with the sources of information that can be used, as well as the techniques of using them.

Active and experiential learning have been a priority in enlightened approaches to vocational education in OECD countries. The role of general education in contributing to vocational preparation is now more widely recognised. Vocational education is no longer viewed as a matter of training students for a set of specific competencies for which there is a high demand on the labour market at any given moment. Today, in compulsory schooling the emphasis is on broad knowledge and generic competencies, and vocational education is regarded as a part of work-related lifelong learning. Separate structures may be maintained, but there is strong consensus about the need for a more unified framework, with a clear alignment of subject content.

How can lower secondary schools provide high-quality academic preparation for those who are going on to universities and other tertiary institutions, and at the same time satisfy the more pragmatic needs of others who are not? How can the school develop the broad and generic abilities that will allow students to acquire the specific skills and competencies that make them "productive" on a job?

It is now generally agreed that part of the answer to the above question is that the best vocational preparation for tomorrow's uncertain labour market is a solid and broad general education, on the strength of its generic character. Another part is that the best general education will incorporate understanding of, and wherever possible also experience of, the world of work. Such an approach will, however, only work if the pathways in initial education and training are kept open to all students. At present they are not, and a major challenge for most systems is to remove bar-

riers and provide adequate career guidance and counselling, particularly at the key transition points (Killeen *et al.*, 1992).

It is therefore imperative not to stream the students too early with regard to what are deemed, often prematurely, to be different cognitive abilities. Postponing the rigid separation of "academic" and "practical" students until after the completion of a common foundation programme in lower secondary education is the best means of securing options open to all students. At the same time, in the interest of reducing the discontinuity between school and the world beyond, "employer-led" and work-based learning activities need to be introduced or extended in upper secondary education. For some students, this might provide a break in the routine during their involuntarily lengthy school careers. Students taking pre-university academic programmes can also benefit from out-of-school learning. The issue of education-led vocational training versus employer-led work-based learning is explored further in the next chapter.

There are many indications of a convergence between general and vocational education. Within general schooling, there has been a steady introduction into the vocabulary of such terms as work experience, school-business partnerships, and practical "hands-on" learning experiences. Within the vocational sector, in countries where it continues to exist as a separate sub-system, there is a growing recognition of the need for students to acquire not only more specialised skills that provide links to professions, but also a broad and theoretically-based knowledge of principles in the natural and social sciences – as well as social competence, and information search, processing and synthesising skills. All of this paves the way for a unified curriculum, combining the liberal and life-preparation traditions of "academic" schooling with work-oriented technical and vocational education. For its part, vocational education will have a much stronger general education component, as workplaces increasingly demand broad and flexible skills.

In reaction to the narrowness of "traditional" vocational qualifications acquired through apprenticeship or secondary schooling, a movement to broaden vocational education and training – supporting "foundation skills", "core skills" and "key qualifications" – gained momentum throughout the 1970s and 1980s, and gave rise to concrete innovations in the curricula of general and vocational programmes at the secondary level of education. It has also fostered the view that occupational expertise is not a major concern of schools and that vocational specialisation should start at the post-secondary level, if at all. There is widespread agreement today that "taylorist" forms of specialisation in secondary education do not work. However, many analysts also suggest that labour markets are no longer organised according to the traditional occupations and professional qualifications for which programmes are intended. Consequently, there are voices pointing to a need to redefine "professionalism" as a principle and "professionalisation" as a lifelong process; the new definitions would in turn need to be "translated" in terms of learning objectives and conditions at various education, working career and life stages.

In many countries there is a tendency for specific vocational education to be postponed until a second phase of upper secondary or even post-secondary stages of education. Even though vocational preparation in these cases is scheduled after the completion of general programmes, there is a new realisation that embedding certain work-related learning encounters in general secondary education is an attractive means of diversifying and contextualising the learning environments to which students are exposed (OECD, 1995f). As noted in Chapter 4, a further link is being pursued in some countries through the idea of *generic* vocational competencies as achievements for students by the end of their schooling period.

It is thus clear that the imperative of developing lifelong learning alters and broadens several of the traditional emphases of school curricula. The former emphasis on the three "Rs" – reading, 'riting, and 'rithmetic – has now been broadened to include, for example, scientific literacy, environmental literacy and computer literacy. That multiple literacy now needs to cover a wide range of human activities: mathematics and natural science, the humanities, technology, economics, politics and the environment. Literacy in this sense is a continuing quest, one cannot become fully "literate" at school (OECD and Statistics Canada, 1995).

Initial schooling should be conceived not as a unique, self-contained period of schooling leading on to vocations, professions or tertiary education, but a phase in a process, albeit a crucial one. The notion of value-added learning, which presupposes individualised instruction and personal growth targets in learning achievement, is worth exploring in this connection (OECD, 1995g).

Children and youth at risk

What might be the implications of the new perspectives on curriculum and school organisation for *special education*? Current notions of democratic entitlement and accompanying concerns for equality and social justice bring into force the educational needs of disadvantaged children or those with severe learning difficulties. These concerns pose a major challenge to OECD governments committed to the goal of making lifelong learning a reality for all (OECD, 1995f). Chart 3.1 shows that while there are some differences between countries, the vast majority of children with special learning needs are enrolled in mainstream schools. This reflects the point that policies across countries now favour the full integration of children with special learning needs into mainstream schools (OECD, 1995h). There are certain prerequisites. First, all children must have access to the curriculum, which implies a need to modify buildings and equipment and to reconsider certain modes of instruction. In addition, the organisation of the school is a significant factor: streaming and grade repeating are obstacles to genuine integration. Attention thus needs to be given to teacher training and to ways of involving parents as fully as possible in the education of their children. Integrating students with learning difficulties and special needs into mainstream schools is part of the commitment to lifelong learning for all – a policy that serves not only the equity goal but also the efficiency perspective, because students with special needs can develop more effectively in an integrated learning environment.

At their last meeting in 1990 the Ministers of Education addressed "the urgent need" to open access further, to allow all to achieve their full potential, and to overcome failure. They were concerned about the reality that despite the considerable national efforts made since the early 1960s to offer equal educational opportunities to all and to overcome the problem of failure, a significant percentage of young people in many countries were leaving school without an employable qualification and with no interest in further studies. Under-achievement was occurring from the beginning of the primary school stage; pupils who started behind frequently remained behind throughout the whole period of compulsory schooling.

What can be done to prevent people from failing at school that has not been tried and tested already? The recommendation offered in a recent study (OECD, 1995f) is that the top priority should be to

◆ Chart 3.1. **Percentage of children with special learning needs who are enrolled in schools outside the mainstream education system, late 1980s[1]**

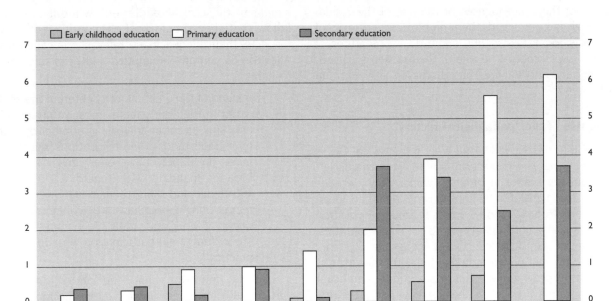

1. Data refer to selected years from 1987 to 1991.
Source: OECD (1995*h*), *Integrating Students with Special Needs into Mainstream Schools*, p. 41. See also Table A.44.

adopt proactive measures during early childhood and primary education while continuing to maintain and refine those programmes for the whole of schooling and the transition to working life that are clearly having some impact. It is essential to detect and help pupils with learning difficulties at the earliest possible moment. A second conclusion is that the problem of failure is closely associated with social and economic disadvantages and cannot be solved by schools on their own. The road to overcoming failure lies through co-ordinated national, local and community policies over a broad range of actions, including income transfers, welfare housing, health and, above all, active employment measures concerted with the social partners.

D. CREATING "POSITIVE" LEARNING ENVIRONMENTS

Current experience and insights derived from research findings offer some guidance on the question of how and in what environments the foundations for lifelong learning and work might best be developed. To begin with, adults must be capable of, and willing to, engage continuously in personal development tasks and learning projects. Their capac-

ity and motivation to learn naturally depend on whether they draw positive experience from their compulsory stay in schools and other institutions. A first prerequisite, therefore, is that schools must be places where children and young adults *like* to be, where they experience a sense of self-worth, challenge and lasting achievement. The second prerequisite is that all children before leaving the formal education system must have "learned how to learn" under self-motivated and self-managed conditions. How should schools and classrooms be organised to create such "positive" learning environments? What are the best methods to enable and encourage children to acquire and develop the foundations, and to what extent is this consistent with current provision and teaching-learning strategies? What should governments do to improve the learning environments that schools now offer?

Since the mid-19th century, when compulsory schooling became universal by law in the leading industrial nations, the competencies needed for adult life have been imparted more or less according to a standard model of instruction. Usually the school in that model is age-graded and the students are divided into separate classrooms, all of which are about the same size, have identical tools, and have the teacher at the front. This section first examines some of the consequences of the rise of the "pedagogical factory", and then employs a critique of schools today to describe some desired features of tomorrow's school. The role of the teacher is considered only briefly here, but discussed at length in Chapter 7.

The rise of the "pedagogical factory"

Up to the Second World War, in the typical OECD country, the vast majority of 13- to 14-year-olds left compulsory school in order to work. A few decades later, the legislated school-leaving age had been raised to 15 or 16. Today, upper secondary education is mandatory until age 17 or 18 in a few countries. Instead of only 5 per cent of an age group fifty years ago, today half or more qualify for entry into tertiary education programmes. This represents a significant shift towards a belief in the need for formal, structured learning to be extended progressively into early and middle and now late adolescence and early adulthood.

The basic physical unit, the school building, has grown in size following urbanisation and the consolidation of school districts and catchment areas; however, with notable exceptions, it has not been modified to match the wider changes occurring in society. The time of the "little red schoolhouse" has passed. In the early 20th century, many children went to schools that enrolled up to a hundred pupils; today such schools are exceptions. With the consolidation of school districts, increases in enrolment and retention, and differentiation among programmes, compulsory schools have become large public institutions, or "pedagogical factories" (Goodlad, 1984). The size and number of school units falling under the jurisdiction of school administrations, as well as the number of children enrolled, has grown markedly over the decades. On the whole, the school system has become much more complex, and the need for increased co-ordination has meant employing more non-teaching and administrative staff. These factors in part explain the trend of rising unit costs in education, reviewed in Chapter 8. A superficial analysis may conclude that productivity in school learning has declined. It is argued in Chapter 6 that this is not the case, because goals have been widened and new standards evolved.

Within a relatively short period, a revolution has occurred as regards the status and role of schools as institutions and the needs and attitudes of young people in OECD countries. Yet the basic structures and procedures of schooling are often recognisably similar to those of an earlier era. While it does not follow that they should be radically different in all respects, their adequacy and relevance is called into question as certain ambiguities and problems come to light:

- Instead of the great majority entering the adult world in their early teens, most young people now stay on for an increasing number of years in schools and other institutions which, at least on paper, have been given a much broader mandate with regard to imparting knowledge and skills; the fact is, however, that many young people have little contact with the world of work and adult life outside school. Their "functional participation" in adult life is practically nil.

- The limitations imposed on children and youth have been reinforced by the rapid pace of urbanisation spurred by economic growth: increasing numbers of children are growing up in cities and densely-populated suburban areas, places which can impose constraints on the freedom to move about, explore nature, and interact with the community beyond the immediate home neighbourhood.

- The reduced sense of security in the urban environments in which the majority of children grow up reinforces their separation from "normal" community life, as many can no longer go to school by themselves but must rely on adult supervision and organised transportation.

- Although working hard to open up schools to the surrounding environment, communities have been compelled to isolate their buildings and grounds by putting up walls, fences and other physical barriers.

- With both parents tending to work outside the home, schools have had increasingly to assume caretaking functions beyond the regular school hours, further isolating children from the community.

- Because they are expected to provide education as well as to care for a large number of children and adolescents, schools have a strong incentive, for financial, organisational and managerial reasons, to become standardised – almost industrial – in their approach to allocating all children of a given age to a closed classroom where fixed sylla-buses for defined grades are taught, most often still in a "frontal" mode.

– Over the years supervision by authorities – whether locally, regionally or nationally organised – has also been tightened, as OECD countries' school systems have matured and it has become increasingly important to enforce compliance with defined norms and regula-tions. As mentioned in Chapter 5, this trend towards technocratic supervision and control, which again reinforced separateness from communities and families, has begun to reverse in certain countries.

– The model of "frontal" classroom instruction has become dominant as the school classes have gradually become more homogeneous in both age and ability. Previously it had been common, in certain types of school, for more advanced pupils to help teach their less advanced classmates.

– Despite the significant changes that have occurred, on the surface very little has hap-pened with regard to the modes of operation and strategies for teaching and learning employed in schools. The overriding problem is that schools have become increasingly "information-rich" but "action-poor".

– Given the lack of self-initiated activity in school, many young people are not well pre-pared to shoulder adult responsibilities after a long sequence of uninterrupted schooling. They have become used to having their work planned in minute detail by the teachers, hour after hour, day after day. The subject-matter is carefully prepared and dispensed in measured doses by teachers who are concerned that they may lack the time needed to cover the syllabus.

– While schools try to impart an ever-swelling subject-matter to increasing numbers of stu-dents for more and more school years, society beyond the school is undergoing sea changes. In the information economy, other institutions and agencies are poised to take over some of the school's traditional tasks.

– Standardisation within countries of syllabuses, textbooks and pedagogical regimes has been further reinforced by the introduction of national assessments of student performance and, in certain countries, standardised exami-nations leading to recognised qualifications – all children are expected to progress at a certain pace through the same trajectories, with tests that fail a significant portion of them as a "reward" at the end of the path.

– Standardised achievement tests, because of the way they are constructed, often involve the recall of memorised, factual knowledge in narrow areas of competence; the outcomes they measure are at odds with the "cross-curriculum" skills most sought in a framework for lifelong learning: motivation and self-confidence; social and communication skills; self-managed learning; and capacity for inde-pendent information search, retrieval and analysis.

– As it stands, the standardisation of school learning, and testing, can be at cross-purposes with the cherished ideals of diversity, individu-alisation and, in the long run, the incentives to learn.

This picture of the "standard school" in today's post-industrial world is a bleak one. The picture is of course not universally valid; many schools look quite different. But the tendencies of alienation and dis-continuity between the school, the home, the wider community and the world of work are common, and they point to serious problems for today's and tomorrow's schools.

The symptoms are clear. Lack of trust leads some parents to pay themselves for the schooling of their children, even though it can be obtained virtually free of charge in government-dependent schools. Aliena-tion and distrust are also behind the deliberate choice of certain adolescents and young adults to become truants. In the former industrial society, young people had a choice of leaving school early, because there were still "entry jobs" to be found. In today's world, however, the number of unqualified jobs that can be taken up by young people who are tired of school is decreasing. Many young people who would like to enter the world of work have little choice but to carry on in the system in the hope – which for many may be in vain – of improving their prospects. These developments may lead to further strains in the relations between schools and the outside world.

For many different reasons, the "pedagogical fac-tory" described above cannot survive the transition to the information economy and learning society. But what is to take its place? How might tomorrow's "ideal" school look? Before turning to this question, however, some insights derived from recent research into new possibilities for teaching and learning are presented; special attention is given to the options opened up by new information and instructional technologies.

Possibilities of a "new" pedagogy

Raizen (1994) has tried to summarise recent research on what makes learning effective. A first perspective is that instruction should take account of the learner's own ideas and experiences, and use these to stimulate a range of responses. Secondly, learning should occur as far as possible in context. Research studies suggest that learning in many cases is most effective when it takes place through "situated" activity: groups of learners engage on a common task, using "real-life" tools. The hallmarks of successful environments for the worlds of learning and work are identified by Raizen (p. 97):

– Any learning experience must be meaningful and motivating for learners: they must be able to make sense of it and understand its purpose.

– Any learning experience must take into account what the learner brings to it; individuals come to any learning experience with prior knowledge and experience, which may either facilitate or impede the intended learning.

– Learning experiences should interweave domain-knowledge, problem-solving strategies appropriate to the domain, and real-world applications of both: most people learn best when declarative knowledge ("the what"), procedural knowledge ("the how"), and strategic knowledge ("the when"), are integrated.

– Learners must be actively involved in their own learning, even as they are provided with models of expert performance to emulate. They need coaching and error-correction, in diminishing amounts – a "fade" – that will allow them to become autonomous and independent.

– Learning sequences should introduce increasing complexity, yet students should learn at any level of complexity to attend to the general nature of a task before attending to its details.

– Learning experiences should help each person to build strategies for controlling his or her own performance – setting goals, planning, checking work and monitoring progress, and revising their courses of learning. Most importantly, learners need to develop strategies for acquiring additional knowledge and expertise.

– Learning experiences should introduce the learner into the community of participants in a given domain or occupation, so that the individual will come to understand the physical, conceptual, symbolic and social tools of the community and their use.

This analysis suggests that the learning process is not "roughly the same" for all learners in a particular age group, and that learning does not routinely proceed in a linear fashion. The implication is that the traditional classroom approach – in which the learning process was largely teacher-centred and instructive in mode, linear in progression, and didactic in character – may be less effective than is often assumed, at least for certain categories of students and for many areas of the curriculum. The realisation that learning is most solid when students are involved in directing and monitoring their own progress – and that a co-operative rather than a competitive approach to learning is of immense help to students – has major implications for the design of "positive" learning environments. For the learners, this means that the process has less to do with passive acquisition of knowledge for recall later on, and more with becoming active in structuring and organising the encounter. Thus, the importance is placed on learners' own interaction with the phenomena that confront them, rather than on the assumption that learning processes must be dominated by teacher-centred authority and that knowledge must be externally transmitted, received and reproduced. According to this view, "knowledge cannot be conveyed, it can only be constructed" (Maclure and Davies, 1991). Osborne and Freyberg (1985) put this succinctly:

"[This] view of learning with understanding focuses on the proposition that learners themselves must actively *construct* or *generate* meaning from sensory input (...). No-one can do it for them (...). Piaget, too, considered that knowledge is *constructed* by the individual as he or she acts on objects and people and tries to make sense of it all (...). Knowledge is acquired not by the internalisation of some given outside but is constructed from within (...)."

The implication is that the skills of research, enquiry, and expansion of the concepts and categories one already has are essential to *meaningful* learning. A further step involves applying, monitoring, correcting and extending the knowledge and skills acquired in the actual situations in which those skills are to be used. The concept of "learning to learn" captures this constructivist view of "active learning". Smith (1994) puts this as follows:

"Learning to learn is a matter of both aptitude and personal experience, and people can typically be said to learn to learn in a relatively haphazard manner. From in-school and out-of-school experience people constantly acquire new information and behaviours. While so engaged, they gradually develop personal learning strategies and personal knowledge about the optimum conditions for learning. Each person develops a concept of self-as-learner. The learning to learn process is understood as haphazard, because it results not so much from deliberate interventions on the part of teachers or trainers to improve learning capacity and performance, as from personal interpretations over time of learning-related experience. These interpretations often prove dysfunctional as far as becoming an active, flexible, confident learner in a variety of contexts is concerned. Hence the growing interest in the deliberate enhancement of learning capacities, dispositions, and strategies, through such means as curriculum planning, instruction and training."

In developing the foundations for lifelong learning, then, it will be important to consider the ways in which people learn effectively. For policy-makers and curriculum-developers, the challenge is to ensure that learning-to-learn ceases to be a haphazard enterprise and instead becomes an integrated part of the style and organisation of all learning endeavours carried on in school. The aim is twofold: to achieve effective learning for all students and to foster and stabilise a readiness to go on learning once the school has been left behind.

The above discussion demonstrates that there is strong pressure on schools for students to acquire cognitive, metacognitive, social, cultural and practical competencies. But it is obvious that schools alone cannot perform all these tasks, and that a reconceptualisation of the core curriculum should discuss not only the type of subjects to be learned, but more fundamentally their contents, in order to reduce them, leaving more time for other, non-cognitive activities. The question is not, therefore, whether and how much mathematics or science, environmental or health education should be taught, but what the content of these subjects should be and how they

should, for some learning activities, relate together in an interdisciplinary approach. At the elementary level, this can more easily be arranged, because one teacher tends to be in control of all subjects. This presupposes, however, that the teachers have at their disposal an "open" curriculum, for which they will need to be prepared. Moreover, learning takes place in other settings as well; the responsibility of families, communities and societies in fostering and supporting learning must be more generally recognised. The idea of the "educative society" is not new; the time has now come to translate it into practical reality on the basis of partnerships for educational advancement.

New technologies, especially the personal computer, offer a means of reconstructing both the contents and processes of learning, particularly at the primary and lower secondary levels of education. Such technologies can execute algorithmic functions rapidly, and memorise facts that constitute a major part of today's school curriculum. Furthermore, such technologies can be used by students in self-directed learning activities that do not require teacher attendance. This may mean that some resources can be freed and reallocated (see Chapters 7 and 8). For example, less time needs to be spent on acquiring the factual knowledge base indicated in Table 3.2, and so more time is available for the questions of "what", "why", "how" and "when" – in other words, on the metacognitive skills now deemed so important in the perspective of lifelong learning (OECD, 1995f and 1995i). Computers are also powerful tools for helping students learn some of these metacognitive skills. Finally, multimedia learning packages hold promise for developing, de facto, technological literacy.

It is expected that education systems are at the beginning of a major transformation, a few glimpses of which are given below. At the same time, it should be realised that major changes in education require a long time to take effect. Despite the urgency with which educational reforms are sometimes launched, the formal school systems tend to change only slowly.

Glimpses of tomorrow's schools

Although the new information and communication technologies represent the potential for major change to occur, until now they have frequently been used in ways that merely reproduce "traditional" pedagogical practices. In the next stage, the newly available technology should lead to real innovation in teaching, learning and the administration of education. This is the realm of interactive technologies, such as networks and multimedia. Finally, technology will be used to transform education – its purpose and content.

It should not be understood that "traditional" procedures are all obsolete: some, such as group teaching, remain in use because of their effectiveness and resource efficiency. The point is not to abandon practices because they are rooted in the past, but to assess and modify them as necessary in the light of new challenges and possibilities. Again, the orientation should be towards effective, stimulating and enjoyable learning, by means of efficient teaching, and to instil in students a commitment to continuing that learning beyond the end of schooling.

The programme for change must be generated and driven forward not by technology *per se* but by considerations of how society, and the teaching profession in particular, can exploit technology in order to provide the most effective education for a democratic, socially inclusive and economically advanced community. Hebenstreit (1994, p. 117) identifies the elements of a programme to integrate information technology into tomorrow's schools:

– All students will need to become computer-literate as well as literate and numerate in the familiar sense: they should be able to handle current information technology at a level appropriate to their discipline or field of study, and be equipped to employ it appropriately to further their cognitive development in the future.

– New technology can contribute to the redesign and implementation of the curriculum and to assist in applying new methods of assessment and certification.

– Students and teaching staff will need to have ready access to workstations and networks in order to benefit from the growing availability of services.

– Collections of software for use in teaching can become accessible anywhere on the network and in the educational establishment.

New information technologies should open up and increase access to educational establishments and agencies for the development of open learning organisations or dual mode institutions. It will be important to capitalise on the fact that educational pathways may not be rooted in time or place; they could be accessible electronically from anywhere and at any time. Institutions could consist of, or be rendered open through, a mix of physical and electronic access points, thus meeting the needs of new categories of learners.

Another element is that, in the school of the future, students of various ages can mix with the participants using a personal computer, and with multiple interactions among individuals. Thus, learning will be less a matter of jumping – or failing to jump – fixed hurdles at set intervals, and more a self-paced or small-group activity in which students of mixed ages and backgrounds address objectives by multiple means.

The concept of a school as a "community learning centre" is of interest in this regard. A typical centre would welcome people of different ages and the range of services would extend well beyond those provided by conventional primary or secondary schools. The home and the workplace would be extensions of the centre, linked by computer and telecommunications and operating during hours that are determined by the learners rather than the availability of teachers. Classrooms will be needed but at times and for groups very different from those at present. Conventional media such as the blackboard and textbook will be complemented and in some cases replaced by multimedia, learner-driven equipment. Indices such as teacher:student ratios need to be replaced by indices reflecting that teacher workloads will be determined less by the number of students and more by the nature of the "subject" and the availability of software. The resource implications of this concept are considered in Chapter 7.

Despite the promise of the new technologies and their value in transforming several key elements of the learning process, it is not sufficient, in visualising "the school of the future", to focus on more efficient and flexible ways of learning specific elements of subject-matter. One of the great achievements of the school as an institution is that it provides a well-structured social setting in which young people can address a wide array of developmental tasks. Their emotional needs, interpersonal relations, physical development and artistic expression – not to mention a wide array of activities requiring the manipulation of physical materials – cannot be provided for satisfactorily in a one-to-one relationship with a computer screen. The school is also a community functioning on many levels. Identification with that community and its values is part of the process of maturation and, for many students, will be the point of departure for a continuing involvement with education. In other words, a sense of place and people is just as important as a sense of handling specified learning tasks. Good schools will continue to be needed for social learning.

E. INVESTING IN EARLY CHILDHOOD EDUCATION

Early childhood education and early intervention programmes in primary schooling are important aspects of a strategy aimed at equal opportunities in foundation learning and assisting children and young people at risk. At what age should early childhood education begin? What factors and conditions can make early intervention programmes successful? What are the beneficial effects of intervention programmes, and do these effects justify an increase in public and private expenditures?

It is widely recognised that the early years of education play a decisive role in a child's future, for they shape attitudes to learning and provide basic social skills that come into place in later school years. Many families have no financial choice but to arrange

for institutional day care and early childhood education. Even those with a choice often opt for some form of pre-school at age 3 or 4, as it is felt that children benefit from the interaction with adults and children other than family. A 1981 study on this subject indicated that many parents would make use of day care if they could (OECD, 1981). Things have not changed since then. For a variety of reasons, child care, pre-school and early intervention programmes have become dominant policy concerns across OECD countries.

The conditions under which a child spends the first years of life tend to set the stage for the career to come. For instance, the academic promise that teachers express in rating cognitive ability when the child reaches the end of primary school is related to attainments during the later years of formal schooling (Husén, 1969; Rist, 1970); moreover, follow-up studies show that there are enduring effects on attitudes to education and the willingness to continue learning in adulthood (Tuijnman, 1989). Table 3.3 shows starting ages for early childhood education and compulsory

Table 3.3. **Compulsory school starting and ending ages, 1992**

	Early childhood education	Compulsory schooling	
	Starting age[1]	Starting age[1] (full-time)	Ending age[2] (full-time)
North America			
Canada	4	6	16
United States	3	6	17
Pacific Area			
Australia	..	..	15
Japan	3	6	15
New Zealand	2	5	16
European Community			
Belgium[3]	2.5	6	16
Denmark	3	7	16
France	2	6	16
Germany[3]	3	6	15
Greece	3.5	5.5	14
Ireland	4 to 5	6 to 7	15
Italy	3	6	14
Luxembourg	..	..	15
Netherlands[3]	4	6	16
Portugal	3	6	15
Spain	2	6	16
United Kingdom	2	5	16
Other Europe – OECD			
Austria	3	6	15
Finland	3 to 6	7	16
Norway	3	7	16
Sweden	3	6 to 7	16
Switzerland	4 to 5	6 to 7	15
Turkey	3	6	15

Notes: .. Data not available.
1. Typical starting age.
2. Legal compulsory school-leaving age in 1993.
3. Compulsory part-time attendance until age 18.
Sources: OECD (1995d), *Education at a Glance – OECD Indicators*; EUROSTAT (1995), *Les chiffres clés de l'éducation dans l'Union européenne.*

schooling. In the majority of OECD countries compulsory schooling starts at age 6; by age 4, however, nearly all children are in organised programmes in such countries as Belgium, France, the Netherlands, New Zealand, Spain and the United Kingdom. In these countries there are proposals to reorganise the link between pre-school and primary school. Data on the transition from home to school are given in Table 3.4.

In OECD countries, early childhood education has increasingly become a public provision and thus an integral part of the service society. Table 3.4 suggests that, in some countries (Belgium and France are examples), formal instruction begins much earlier; many children are in preparatory classes from age 2. It is argued that better educational use could be made of the receptivity in very young children, and

that certain elementary skills such as reading, singing and playing musical instruments can be fostered much earlier. The question here is not whether provision should be organised for 2- to 6-year-olds, but rather, what kind of provision would ensure school readiness.

It is generally acknowledged that preschooling brings real benefits to disadvantaged children, although how and to what extent these benefits last is a matter of debate. Furthermore, preschooling can provide children with compensation for the lack of an extended family. The role given to pre-school education and its implementation varies across countries. Most countries share the aim of familiarising children with life in society. Some countries, such as Denmark, Germany, Ireland and the Netherlands, view preschooling as complementary to children's family

Table 3.4. **Transition from home to school, 1992**

Net enrolment in public and private early childhood and primary education, ages 4 to 7

(percentage)

	Age				
	3	4	5	6[1]	7[2]
North America					
Canada	..	45.9	99.2	103.7	..
United States	28.5	53.0	88.6	102.3	1.1
Pacific Area					
Japan	23.1	57.6	65.7	101.9	..
New Zealand	73.7	92.6	99.7[3]	100.8	..
European Community					
Belgium	97.7	99.3	99.7	99.8	0.1
Denmark	37.9	53.6	61.1	96.4	8.4
France	98.8	101.4	99.8[3]	100.6	..
Germany (FTFR)	30.8	68.5	78.5	115.1	1.4
Greece	11.2	48.9	85.2	102.5	..
Ireland	1.2	55.7	99.9	99.1	2.5
Netherlands	..	98.0[4]	98.8	97.7	0.8
Spain	37.2	95.8	100.4	103.2	..
United Kingdom	37.0	90.1[4]	98.8	98.5	..
Other Europe – OECD					
Austria	29.0	66.3	86.2	98.4	0.3
Finland	24.3	28.1	32.0	57.6	0.6
Norway	44.0	56.5	65.1	79.3	1.2
Sweden	45.2	50.8	60.6	99.9	..
Switzerland	7.4	26.2	77.3	99.0	2.7
Turkey	..	0.3	1.5	14.2	..
Country mean	**33.0**	**62.6**	**79.2**	**93.2**	**1.0**

Notes: .. Data not available.
1. Enrolment in early childhood and primary education; figures over 100 per cent arise because the demographic year and the school year do not always correspond.
2. Enrolment in early childhood education only.
3. Primary education only.
4. Enrolment in early childhood and primary education.
Source: OECD (1995d), *Education at a Glance – OECD Indicators*, p. 132.

life, and see its main role as that of socialising children. Other countries, including Belgium, France, Greece, Italy, Luxembourg and Spain, further aim to introduce learning skills and familiarise children with school life (Euridyce, 1994).

Country differences in the age at which children enter preschooling aside, there are many approaches to early childhood education. These are most evident in the private sector. Some approaches focus on experiential education (involving, for example, frequent field trips); others emphasise skills development (sports, games), academic development (regular reading and story times), the visual arts (drawing and painting), or a particular religious faith. Montessori schools see constructive play as an educational tool. Waldorf schools emphasise musical education. In addition, there is great variation in the cost and quality of private day care and pre-school education. For these and many other reasons, universal, publicly-funded and regulated pre-school education is increasingly a sought-after goal in OECD countries.

Even though – as noted above – pre-school systems in OECD countries operate differently depending on the historical context in which they evolved, they currently face similar challenges, and high-quality research is needed to illuminate the options for policy and practice. Given limited financial resources, should more public funds be allocated to reach more children, or should funding focus on maintaining and improving existing services? At what age is it most appropriate to begin pre-school activity? How much preschooling is effective? How shall quality in child care be defined? Any attempt to respond to these questions entails a consideration of aspects such as the ratio of staff to children; group size; space in square metres as well as the equipment and materials required for an effective play-learning environment; the type and level of training of the care-providers, and their salaries and benefits; and the interaction and involvement of parents in the pre-school setting.

Despite the progress in research, most questions cannot be answered yet. Synthesising the available knowledge base for early childhood education, and undertaking reviews of recent policy initiatives and of "good practice" appear to be urgent tasks. The brief survey of the experience of three countries, given below, suggest that a thematic review of policies for early childhood education can reveal interesting country differences, and offer insights useful for decision-making.

A survey of three countries

France

France has long begun schooling children at age 3 and preschooling has also been available to children under 3 for almost a decade. While many view French pre-school as a model worthy of emulation, others would argue that it has gone too far. Currently, approximately 30 per cent of children between ages 2 and 3 go to school, and lively debate continues over the question of the most appropriate age for children to enter. Pre-school for 2-year-olds initially aimed at accommodating disadvantaged children living in "priority education zones" (ZEPs). If such children begin earlier, the argument goes, they would have better chances of educational success later on.

The Marne Valley suburbs to the east of Paris provide an example. This area, faced with an ageing population and a declining birth rate, decided to convert surplus space into kindergartens. Rather than risk cutting classes, and to meet the growing demand of parents, children were increasingly accepted at the age of 2. More generally, the increased number of women workers, the shortage of day care places, and parents' perception that earlier education can improve their childrens' chances all have led to the gradual extension of preschooling to those under 3. Finally, the financial savings over day care centres or other forms of child care are considerable, as kindergarten is free of charge.

In June 1992, measures were announced to facilitate the entry of children into kindergarten (école maternelle) from age 2. The rationale was in part based on a study that showed a positive influence of preschooling on subsequent performance (Jarousse et al., 1992). In the meantime, policy remains flexible; schools decide on entry on a case-by-case basis, and according to local needs. Lowering the age limit for entering school raises important issues, as most écoles maternelles are not sufficiently equipped, in terms of either teaching staff or facilities, to provide for the physical and emotional needs of 2-year-olds. There are also concerns that, with more 2-year-olds in the classroom, the école maternelle will be confined to playing a supervisory rather than educational role.

United States

Head Start, launched in 1965, is a comprehensive pre-school development programme whose main goal is to improve the social competence of 3- to 5-year-old children from low-income families. It delivers a wide range of services: health, education, parental involvement and social services. In 1990, 20 per cent of the total population of 3- to 5-year-olds whose family income fell below the poverty line were in Head Start. That year, the programme served over half a million children at a cost of approximately $1.45 billion. Current policy is geared to providing one year of coverage for 4-year-olds (Chafel, 1992). Chart 3.2 shows the expansion of Head Start since 1975.

To date, the results of much of the research on the effects of compensatory pre-school education are ambiguous (Currie and Thomas, 1993; Maynard, 1995). The pessimism surrounding some studies of Head Start is based on the failure to find lasting effects on the IQ of children involved in the programmes. However, other studies – such as for example the Perry Pre-school Project in Ypsilanti, Michigan – concluded that long-term cognitive gains were not adequately measured by IQ tests (Barnett, 1992; Zigler and Muenchow, 1994). In addition to educational benefits, such studies have noted that children who went through the programme are more likely to improve their lives, both socially and eco-

nomically, and less likely to be unemployed and poor and, in the case of girls, less likely to become teenage single mothers.

A study of sixteen American day care centres (Endsley, 1993) suggested that directors who promote formal parent involvement are likely to run high-quality programmes and facilitate parent-staff communication. Another study (Replogle, 1994) describes the activities of two Head Start programmes, one in Kentucky and one in Iowa, that integrate families into the wider community and bring community resources into their programmes to better serve parents and children. They illustrate how Head Start can become a community hub for families.

United Kingdom

The National Union of Teachers and Leeds University researchers carried out a study entitled "Testing and Assessing Six- and Seven-year-olds" on 1 395 children who had had pre-school and 933 who had not. The results showed that the first group, which had a lower socio-economic profile than the children who had no nursery education, scored higher in all subjects (Blackburne, 1992). On a related theme, a

◆ Chart 3.2. *Federal expenditure per student[1] for Head Start and enrolments in the programme, United States, 1975-95*

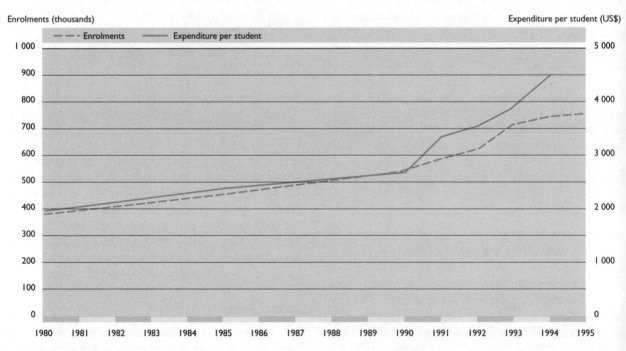

1. Expenditure per student is obtained by dividing total federal expenditure for Head Start by total enrolments.
Source: United States Department of Education (1994*a*), *Digest of Education Statistics,* Tables 349 and 360. See also Table A.45.

study done in 1994 by the University of London tracing the school careers of 900 pupils over nine years, showed that the quality of teaching at a primary school affects childrens' performance right through to GCSE (General Certificate of Secondary Education) (Hopkins, 1994). The "primary school effect" appears to influence children's long-term retention, attitudes towards school, study skills, motivation and self-esteem (cited in *Times Educational Supplement*, 9 September 1994). One could hypothesise about a similar "pre-school effect".

F. EARLY OR LATE SELECTION AND DIFFERENTIATION?

This section describes and analyses the structural and institutional changes OECD countries might need to consider in establishing tomorrow's schools. Dilemmas faced by the school as an educational as well as social institution are described, and tensions between approaches involving early versus late student differentiation noted.

Life chances are determined by many personal factors and conditions in the social and economic environment, including the educational level of parents and their expectations for their children. In post-industrial society, schools play an increasingly central role in mediating the effects of the home and the social environment of children's educational and eventual occupational careers. Learning is a cumulative process, and successful acquisition of knowledge, values and attitudes early on sets the stage for negotiating further learning encounters successfully. Given the tensions between policies to promote equal access and a fair distribution of educational outcomes and policies to raise the quality of provision and improve efficiency, what should policy-makers do in terms of early versus late selection and differentiation? To what extent, and up to what age level, should the core curriculum be common to all children, despite their differences in interests and aptitudes? What, in particular, can be done to provide equal opportunities for all, combat school failure and assist children and youth at risk?

A major issue has been how to make secondary schooling universal but at the same time comprehensive, so that it caters to the needs and interests of all young people between 10-11 and 17-18 years-old. At two major conferences in 1961, important questions were asked about the capacity of highly selective and structurally differentiated school systems to offer the best learning opportunities to all students, and to

exploit fully what was then called the "reserve of talent" (OECD, 1962; Halsey, 1961).

Despite the "rolling reforms" pursued by many OECD countries since then, the practice of "streaming" or "tracking" children after four to six years of primary schooling still prevails in the few European countries where structural reform has been most vehemently resisted. The data in Annex Table A.46 give an indication of the extent of early grouping or streaming. Chart 3.3 reports the distribution, in percentages, of 9-year-olds in various types of grouping for reading instruction, a "common core" subject. Organisational differentiation during or immediately following primary school is common in New Zealand (83 per cent) and the Netherlands (87 per cent); it also occurs in the United States (45 per cent), Ireland (49 per cent) and Iceland (48 per cent).

The large majority of OECD countries have moved beyond the early tracking model, and now employ a "mixed" approach, characterised by uniform syllabuses and modes of provision in lower secondary education until about age 15 or 16 and differentiated services thereafter. Fully comprehensive schools that lack differentiation until the age of 17 or 18 exist in very few countries outside North America, Australia and, albeit to a lesser extent, Japan.

Formal equality of opportunity is endorsed by all. Yet policy-making aimed at promoting equality in education is beset with dilemmas that are not always made explicit. In the Netherlands, for example, after a protracted and disruptive debate, all lower secondary schools were made comprehensive in the sense that a standardised curriculum was introduced, but the mechanism of structural differentiation at age 12 remained firmly in place. In the United States, to take another example, there is a strong commitment to meritocracy – a notion used to describe a social system where status depends entirely on documented ability and merit, and not on ascription (Young, 1958); thus, fully comprehensive schools have developed in the United States but not, generally, in mainland Europe. Although the principle of meritocracy is widely endorsed across the OECD area, so are the practices that contradict and negate equal opportunities: vast differences in funding between schools and school districts, large quality differences between public and private schools, and selective entry requirements in certain public and private schools.

A first problem derives from the fact that the education system is there to impart knowledge and skills, which by necessity amplify individual differences. The school is expected, simultaneously, to

◆ Chart 3.3. **Distribution of 9-year-olds in various types of grouping for reading instruction, 1991**[1]
Percentage distribution

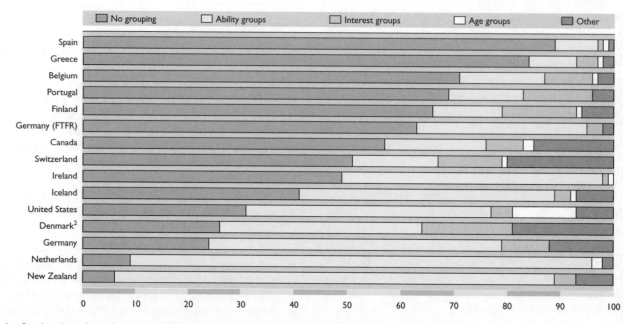

1. Based on data collected for the International Association for the Evaluation of Educational Achievement reading literacy study.
2. "No grouping" is probably underestimated due to an inaccurate translation in the Danish survey.
Source: Elley (1992) and OECD (1995d), *Education at a Glance – OECD Indicators,* p. 172.

serve as an "equaliser" of opportunities and outcomes, and as an instrument that establishes, reinforces and legitimises distinctions. These two functions are incompatible as long as there is only one approved pathway to mainstream educational success, which is assessed using yardsticks very similar to those applied when elite systems of education were still the rule. If the criteria of success and the approach to assessment are standardised and applied in a linear fashion – a measurement of one cognitive dimension rather than multiple intelligences (Gardner, 1987) – then a significant group of students will *a priori* be destined to fail. Comprehensive systems that employ comparative examinations therefore do not necessarily improve formal equality of opportunity, although the evidence shows that the between-school differences are smaller in such systems compared with differentiated ones (OECD, 1993*a* and 1995*z*). However, by making a broader spectrum of options available to young people, the forces that work in the direction of inequality are given more scope. Equality of opportunity can be achieved only if multiple options based on different values are provided – options that are *not* ranked along only one dimension. It is this realisation that

uniform provisions within the education system are not necessarily the solution to realising a more egalitarian society that undergirds the policy pursued in the Netherlands. A policy of lifelong learning – which calls for multiple pathways and the abolition of "dead end" tracks, as well as parity of esteem among programmes – thus offers a key to reconciling the educative and sorting functions of the education system.

The second problem is that between equality and meritocracy mentioned above – an issue that cuts across various types of social and economic organisation. The movement towards the "new centrality of theoretical knowledge, the primacy of theory over empiricism, and the codification of knowledge into abstract systems of symbols that can be translated to many different and varied circumstances" (Bell, 1973) puts rationality and systematised knowledge before property and political status as a basis for influence and power in the post-industrial society. The dilemma lies in the fact that the handing down of achieved status from one generation to the next is, in the meritocratic society, a substitute for inherited privileges in the ascriptive society. As educational qualifications become the key determinant of life chances and social status, the meritocratic tendencies associated with educational selection also become a mechanism of social reproduction – and everywhere, children with poorly educated parents seem unable to take full advantage of opportunities (Hansen, 1994). Research evidence overwhelmingly supports the finding that inequalities in educational careers among children from different social backgrounds have not diminished but remained remarkably stable, despite increases in the standard of living, rises in enrolment and reforms implemented to promote equal opportunities (Shavit and Blossfeld, 1993). Table 3.5 offers a summary of the research evidence for a number of OECD countries. Ishida et al. (1995) conclude that the effect of educational qualifications on social reproduction and mobility is remarkably uniform over time across ten OECD countries. Thus, meritocracy in the fabric of post-industrial OECD countries works against equality.

Diverging pathways can either encourage or hinder the completion of a qualifying initial education and participation in further learning. Diversity can lead to segmentation and exclusion. In order to encourage the largest possible number of individuals to pursue effective, successful and continuing learning routes, pathways should not only be open towards the higher levels of education and training in different learning environments, but also offer multiple exit and re-entry points, clearly defined and truly enabling qualifications that have value in the labour market, and allow pursuit of further and higher-level studies or lateral switching to other pathways, without the need to repeat what is already known and mastered.

Initial education should lead to broad qualification profiles. The responsibility for the "fit" between skill requirements on the labour market and skill profiles produced through initial education and training should not be left primarily to young people and their parents. As will be discussed more fully in Chapter 6, modular courses seem a far more efficient alternative in the context of lifelong learning.

However, "foundation learning" at the primary and secondary stage cannot be fundamentally redefined or reorganised so as to become more integrated, broad, open and motivating with regard to further learning as long as tertiary education, in particular the university, in its present form, continues to govern the entire education system. Openness and integration must logically start at the level of tertiary and continuing adult education. This is currently not the case. For example, the Fachhochschulen that parallel the universities and the Grandes écoles point to a reproduction of "academic" and "occupational" streams at the post-secondary level. Similarly, adult education in most countries has not become integrated with tertiary education. As long as "destinations" of exclusive types are offered as alternatives at the upper end, the preceding stages of learning will inevitably tend to be selective.

Table 3.5. **Trends in the dependence of educational attainment on social origin**[1,2,3]

	Changes in independent variables			Trend
	Father's education	Father's occupation	Additional variables	Age cohorts
Germany	0	0	None	1916-1965
Italy	–	+	None	1920-1967
Japan	–	0	None	1905-1955
Netherlands	–	–	None	1891-1960
Sweden	–	–	Community size (–)	1902-1967
Switzerland	0	0	None	1950-1960
United Kingdom[4]	0	0	None	1913-1952
United States	0	–	Mother's education (–)	1910-1964

1. Legend: "+" means increasing dependence; "0" means no change in the dependence; "–" means decreasing dependence.
2. Estimates derived from studies employing nationally representative data for successive cohorts born between the second decade of the twentieth century and the 1960s. Data for even older cohorts are employed in the case studies of Japan, the Netherlands, Sweden and the United States. Data do not extend to the most recent cohorts in England and Wales. The study on Switzerland analyses data for only two age cohorts. The data sets range in size from about 1 000 to 25 000 cases. Most include data for men and women, but for Japan and England and Wales, data were only available for men.
3. All studies analyse cohort differences in the effects of socio-economic origins on the length of schooling. The effects on length of schooling are estimated in Ordinary Least Squares regressions of highest school grade completed (or attended). The exception is the study for England and Wales in which the dependent variable is defined as the highest qualification attained. In all studies, socio-economic origin is represented by father's education and by father's occupation. In most studies, father's occupation is measured by occupational status or prestige-like scales, but in a few, it is measured by a set of categories approximating occupational classes. Father's education is usually measured by the highest school grade completed by the father.
4. The studies refer to England and Wales only.
Source: Shavit and Blossfeld (1993), pp. 11, 13 and 16.

The conclusion is, therefore, that the reorientation of policy in a framework of lifelong learning offers fresh possibilities of overcoming dilemmas caused by the structural differentiation still present in the school systems of certain, mainly European, countries. But for this to work, OECD countries will need to take a critical look at the organisation and functions of universities as forming the cornerstones of mass tertiary education. This point is explored further in Chapters 5 and 8.

G. THE FOUNDATIONS FOR LIFELONG LEARNING: POLICY CONCLUSIONS

Schools are no longer the only experience of education for the majority of the population. Nor are they adequate. Instead, schools are becoming the principal agencies for developing, in children and young adults, the foundations for further learning throughout life. Schools are also invited to play a wider role as focal points for educational and cultural activities that engage the adult population.

The embedding of schools in a lifelong learning approach to education raises questions about their status as social and cultural institutions, and about their curricula, methods of teaching and learning, instructional technologies, and assessment and certification. There are implications for the goals and values underlying what is taught, for career guidance and counselling services, and for the physical environment in schools. If schooling is to provide a foundation for lifelong learning, an expansion of pre-school education is in many cases also called for.

There is at least some convincing evidence to support the assertion that early childhood education and intervention programmes in primary schooling can produce important value-added results for individual children, their families and the community at large. Meeting the expanding demand is a serious challenge for some Member countries. Targets might be to offer a minimum of half-day education four or five days per week to all 4-year-olds, and to 3-year-olds deemed to be at risk of school failure on account of their social environment or other reasons. The principle of individual treatment should be extended to pre-school children, so that some may enter formal education at an earlier age than the norm, when they are "school ready". Social maturity should be a factor in such decisions.

However, given the costs involved, and considering the anticipated individual and social benefits (see Chapter 8), it is clear that a thorough review of current research, policies and practical approaches to early childhood education in the OECD area is in order.

Initial schooling should be a phase in a process that provides a broad, solid foundation of knowledge and skills as a basis for further learning, and continued motivation for it. In many instances, this will require that attention be paid to the way in which the various disciplines in university education are structured, as well as to the close correspondence between disciplines, competitive selection and admission procedures, and the secondary school curriculum. The "wash-back" effects on the curriculum of competitive entrance examinations for post-secondary education that are administered by universities or, in certain countries, by national authorities, are a cause for concern in this respect. Such examinations, to the extent they are subject-matter oriented, can hinder curriculum reform and reduce the scope for experimentation with new pedagogical approaches.

In order for the school to be a place where all learners like to be, and feel motivated not only to perform optimally given their conditions and interests but also to continue to learn actively throughout life, a means needs to be found to link assessment for selection and assessment as a tool for developing the individuals' capacity and motivation to learn. The notion of value-added learning, which presupposes individualised instruction and personal growth targets in learning achievement, is worth exploring in this connection.

In order to allow schools to develop into community education centres which prepare students for continuing learning, and which provide a focus for adult learners, governments will need to take a number of policy initiatives.

First, there is a need to re-examine the values and beliefs traditionally assumed or actively taught in schools, to compare these with those exposed by other significant groups, and to reconcile the two wherever possible. Communities, schools and teachers ought to be given some scope for developing their own imprints and signatures. At the same time, however, the process of schooling must be consistent and coherent across the nation. Hence, a broad consensus should be reached on a common core of values, with sufficient scope left for schools and their curricula to confront differences in a spirit of tolerance and respect. A suitable framework for this exercise will involve consultations with students, communities, parents, teachers, and organisations in civil society.

A parallel review of the broad goals and objectives of foundation learning, within a coherent framework for lifelong learning, should be undertaken, involving the social partners and other interested parties and sectors of education. Any recent surveys may be taken as a starting point, and this will form part of the wider exercise in setting goals discussed in Chapter 6.

In the light of the above, the curricula of primary and secondary schools should be reviewed, and revised where necessary. The following guidelines may be anticipated:

- The curriculum of primary education should be revised, where necessary, to concentrate on core skills for further learning. This will include familiarity with new information technologies for all primary pupils.

- The factual content at primary and lower secondary levels should be reduced further in favour of "cross-curriculum" skills, including learning-to-learn skills, social competence, and information retrieval and processing skills. Such skills will provide the basis for later learning, and help to avoid an overloaded curriculum.

- A reduction in factual knowledge should not mean the abandonment of the principles of the natural and social sciences, of moral reasoning, or knowledge and practice of the performing and visual arts. Awareness of the history and geography of the country of residence should be set against a widening background which matches the age-related spatial and temporal perceptions of the learners, and contemporary concerns for the environment.

- In secondary education, there should be continuing emphasis on metacognition and the teaching of core subjects in upper secondary education, mainly mathematics and sciences, social studies, and foreign languages, next to cross-curriculum competencies.

- At all levels, particular attention will need to be given to foreign language learning, in response to the growing linguistic diversity in Member countries. Second or third languages, and those of the linguistic minorities residing within borders, should attain a higher status, next to the principal language, and should in consequence be taught in school.

- Specific vocational preparation should be postponed, at least until the stage of upper secondary schooling. There should also be a convergence between general and vocational curricula, so that pupils who do not expect to transfer to tertiary-level institutions receive a broad and general education on which subsequent vocational training can repeatedly build at later stages in life, while keeping open the possibility of their entering tertiary education at a later date.

- In tune with the greater individualisation made possible by new learning technologies and the principle of a general primary and secondary education for all, pupils should not be sorted too early into pre-tertiary academic and pre-employment practical groups. Those likely to proceed directly to tertiary education ought also to take part in practical activities. The links with the world of work are discussed in the next chapter.

- Given the above requirements, the articulation of upper secondary and tertiary education programmes needs to be seriously reconsidered.

Particular attention should be given to students with special needs, and those at risk of school failure and social alienation. Increased flexibility in the grouping of students will provide some response to this challenge, and the greater involvement of parents and the local community, as discussed in Chapter 5, will strengthen the environment for such pupils.

Young people and adults should be permitted to return to regular secondary schools and other institutions of secondary education at later ages, to join particular classes. This will make efficient use of resources, and help to break down the alienation between young people in school and the world outside.

Clear norms should be devised for the acquisition and use of new information technologies by schools and teachers. Connectivity with the outside world should be an important criterion. The development of appropriate software and multimedia packages needs further encouragement. To this end, governments should team up and pool resources, in order to expand their markets and offer better incentives for firms focusing on the development and marketing of learning technologies.

Teachers will need to adopt new pedagogical methods in order to exploit the opportunities offered by new learning technologies, and to teach the learning-to-learn and information retrieval skills that are deemed so important in a framework for lifelong learning. Active or constructive rather than passive learning techniques are required. This presupposes that students, parents and teachers work out a personal learning plan for each student and young adult, incorporating challenging subjects and special interests, relevant information-based learning, a tutorial relationship with teachers, and an aligned assessment system that encourages value-added learning based on progress in attaining personal growth targets. For purposes of transparency and portability, such learning will still require accreditation by existing or modified certification procedures, at least at the end of school cycles. Further, heterogeneity will increase as many young adults stay longer in school, and as adults return to study in increasing numbers. Accommodating their learning needs will require flexibility, suggesting the adoption of a modular approach to teaching and learning.

Accordingly, serving teachers are faced with a number of challenges deriving from likely changes in their work environments. As discussed in Chapter 7, a major retraining programme should be an element in national strategies for creating tomorrow's schools. There are implications also for pre-service teacher training. Given the demands placed on tomorrow's teachers, recruitment into teacher training institu-

tions and the study programmes they offer should guarantee a high-level preparation. Governments should make provision for this in advance, through their inspectorates and in consultation with teachers and other sectors of educational provision.

Lifelong learning presupposes continuity between initial education and training, and the organised learning experiences that take place thereafter, during working life. What is sometimes overlooked is that continuity is absolutely essential *throughout* initial education and training. Articulation must be assured from one school year to the next and, above all, from one stage to another, notably, from early childhood to primary education, from primary to secondary education, and from secondary education to further studies and working life. This chapter has indicated how secondary education should be organised and delivered so as to equip young people with a solid foundation of useful knowledge and skills. The next chapter is concerned with the challenge of how to guarantee continuity and articulation, when most young people are no longer in compulsory schooling but are free, at least in principle, to make their own choices in respect of learning and work.

IMPROVING PATHWAYS AND TRANSITIONS IN LIFELONG LEARNING AND WORK

A. INTRODUCTION

Chapter 3 took up the basic principles of lifelong learning. This one places those principles into a context at once wider and more concrete: that of pathways and transitions through lifelong learning and work. A learner is like a traveller faced with a choice of routes to a destination. More than one route is possible; each entails costs and benefits. Policy-makers and their partners can have a hand in shaping the infrastructure of these learning "routes", by encouraging an itinerary through incentives here, and by strongly suggesting an alternate route there. In the end, however, the route is the learner's own: he or she chooses among the types and sequences of available courses and programmes, and decides on the time to be invested. This necessary emphasis on the individual means that career guidance, whether based in educational institutions, employment centres or enterprises, has an important role to play in lubricating the relationship between the learner's own development and the demands of the labour market. Factors influencing these choices will naturally include the specific opportunities and constraints facing the learner – for example, gender, resources, ethnic origin, age, the geographical availability of learning opportunities, and the quality of information and guidance which is available.

To the extent that learning pathways are open-ended and interconnected, they invite learners to progress from one type and level of education and training to another, and to move back and forth between, or to combine, learning and work activities. The notion of pathways stems from the conviction that human beings at all life stages are able to learn and develop.

Indeed, the meaning of the very word "career" is currently being extended to take in not only progress within an occupation, but the overall lifelong development of an individual in terms of both learning and work.

Some aspects of individual pathways can be usefully measured and certified in terms of established levels of achievement and recognised qualifications. They imply that continuing learning not only enhances the freedom and adaptability of learners, but also leads to a potentially useful accumulation of knowledge and skills, thus increasing the learners' personal "capital" of competence and qualification.

Inherited structures and the organisation of pathways vary strongly across countries. Some have highly differentiated education and training systems; others more homogeneous ones. In some systems, pathways diverge with few interconnecting routes; in others there are frequent cross-roads and junctions, allowing learners to take short cuts or detours. The underlying difference is that some systems rely on education and training courses that are modular and can be relatively freely assembled into individual routes, whereas others continue to use inflexible ones. A flexible and interconnected system of pathways, in comparison with the discontinuities of some structurally differentiated systems, enhances learning opportunities and facilitates continuity.

Lifelong learning necessitates movements and linkages enabling learning to be undertaken in combination with other activities and phases of life. These depend critically on the arrangements for education and training, in particular the extent to which they enable these movements and linkages to take place. They also depend on the organisation of labour markets, firms, social and private arrangements and the ways that these permit individuals, supported by career guidance, to move through the different pathways in realisation of lifelong learning trajectories. These are examined in this chapter, which seeks to summarise the lessons from research and offers concrete illustrations of national experiences. Many of the findings of research and country examples are taken from the early post-compulsory and post-secondary phases, reflecting the volume of research and work on the initial years of adulthood. Ultimately, lifelong learning policies will call for a comprehensive description and analysis of pathways and transitions throughout the entire life cycle.

This chapter considers the characteristics of a coherent framework from several perspectives. Section B formulates the policy questions and issues. Section C describes four types of pathways and transitions, and examines evidence about their frequency. Section D examines a range of issues related to the articulation between education, training and the labour market. The focus is on the weaknesses and structural barriers that block transitions, particularly to and from employment. Questions are raised about trade-offs between equity and efficiency, and the role of governments *vis-à-vis* that of other stakeholders. Section E addresses the transition from education or training to the labour market, and considers particularly the advantages and disadvantages of employer-led and education-led systems of vocational education. Section F reviews the role of adult education and continuing vocational training in flexible labour markets, for example, in facilitating the transition from one job to another, and considers the wider social returns to all adult education. For each of the pathways and transitions considered, the chapter reviews the impact of recent policy initiatives and their contribution to the coherence of the overall system and smooth transition to employment. Section G examines arguments for the value of education to employers, to individuals and to society. Finally, Section H offers conclusions and directions for policy.

B. THE POLICY QUESTIONS AND ISSUES

Transitions between the world of learning and the world of work take several forms – from home to school, from school to work, and from work back to education. To this must be added "learning while working" and "working while learning". This chapter considers the progressions between different programmes and levels of education and different labour market conditions. Some of the policy issues, for example the structures of differentiation and the nature and role of secondary curricula in facilitating the transitions, were discussed in Chapter 3. This chapter concentrates on the transitions from education to work and *vice versa*. To date, the policy analyses and research studies conducted in the area of life-cycle transitions have examined the narrow set of issues described below. The intention here is to present the "state of the art" of an underdeveloped yet important field. Further analyses would include the

study of barriers to realising coherence and smooth transitions; the study of transitions in values and beliefs, in life experience, and in inter-personal relations; the role of guidance in support of lifelong career development; the study of life-cycle transitions in relation to concepts such as "new professionalism", "value-added in lifelong learning", and "work-learning-culture-democracy interfaces". These are only touched on here.

Lifelong learning can perform at least three functions with regard to transitions to and from work. It provides the foundations of values, knowledge, skills and qualifications that facilitate initial access to the labour market. It offers an avenue to obtaining new skills and qualifications that improve re-entry possibilities for those who have become unemployed or underemployed, or who have voluntarily left the labour market for a while. Thirdly, lifelong learning provides the conditions and means for the continuing formation and updating of the skills of the employed labour force, at least in some cases, facilitating within-firm and job-to-job mobility. This chapter addresses these three functions and seeks answers to the following questions: Are the current levels and the current direction of investment adequate to meet the requirements of a coherent approach to lifelong learning for all? What should be the proper balance between general and vocational education, both in initial and in further education and training? Given the objectives of lifelong learning specified in Chapter 2, what changes in education and training systems might improve the transitions from school to work, from unemployment to employment, and from one job to another?

These three broad questions are analysed by examining evidence regarding the scope and magnitude of problems in lifelong learning and work transitions, and how these differ among OECD countries. The conditions and arrangements that put young people at risk in these transitions are identified. The chapter also studies the policies, strategies and innovations that countries have undertaken, and the forms of government intervention that are likely to increase the efficiency and equity of pathways, transitions and outcomes. The issues addressed here are large, complex and – to an extent – country-specific, so that complete and universally valid answers cannot be obtained. But analysis of the issues provides many insights – not least by revealing the gaps in the comparative knowledge base about transitions in lifelong learning and work.

C. TYPES OF PATHWAYS AND TRANSITIONS IN LIFELONG LEARNING AND WORK

This section describes four major types of transition: from one education or learning institution or programme to another; from education to work; from unemployment or inactivity to work; and from one job to another. The limited descriptive statistics, which are offered here without much analysis, are intended to provide the background. The data are used for analytical purposes in subsequent sections.

Pathways within initial education and training systems

Table 1.9 in Chapter 1 shows the distribution of upper secondary students in general and vocational education and apprenticeship programmes from 1975 to 1992. It provides one indication of the pathways leading through general and vocational education. Chart 4.1 indicates that there is considerable variation among countries. For five of the 16 countries for which data are available, the share of students in

◆ Chart 4.1. ***Upper secondary students enrolled in public and private general and vocational education, 1992***[1,2,3,4,5]
Percentage

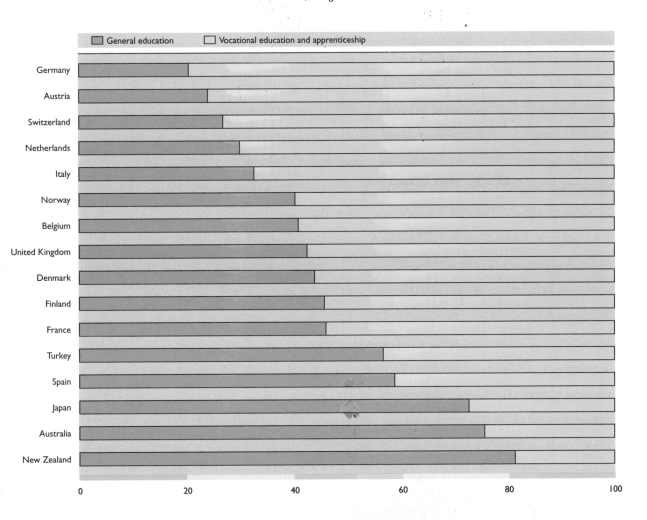

1. Students enrolled in special training colleges (about 100 000 in the relevant age group) not included in Japanese data.
2. Data for Denmark and Germany include part-time education.
3. Students enrolled in special education not included in the data for France and Spain.
4. Figures for programmes lasting less than three years not reported in Italian data.
5. Vocational course figures are inflated by large numbers of adults taking courses at the upper secondary level in the United Kingdom.
Source: OECD Education Database.

vocational education was high in 1992. In Austria, Germany, Italy, the Netherlands and Switzerland, more than two-thirds of all students in upper secondary education were enrolled in programmes classified as vocational or technical. In three countries – Australia, Japan and New Zealand – about a quarter or less of the students were in such programmes. In the other countries, between 40 and 60 per cent of the students were enrolled in vocational upper secondary education.

Table 4.1 shows the trend in the share of vocational and technical education in total enrolment in upper secondary education. Two periods are distinguished: 1975-84 and 1984-92. Japan was the only country where the relative importance of vocational education diminished over both periods, a development consistent with the redirection of policy in a framework for lifelong learning (see Chapter 3). The share of vocational education increased in Austria, Denmark, the Netherlands and Norway. No discernible change, or very minor fluctuations, were observed for Finland, France, Germany, Spain, Switzerland and Turkey. As argued in Chapter 1, these developments must be examined in the context of the requirements for lifelong learning.

Transitions from education to employment and other activities

The transition from education to work and other activities takes place at different ages. This can be inferred from the net full-time enrolment rates in secondary and tertiary education and training given in Annex Table A.47, and can be illustrated by using the concept of median school-leaving age – the age by which 50 per cent of the relevant age groups have left full-time secondary education. There is considerable dispersion across the countries. The unweighted median for all countries is at age 19, but in some countries (Australia, Greece, New Zealand and the United Kingdom), it is at 18, whereas in some others (Belgium, Denmark, France, Netherlands and Switzerland) it is attained at age 20.

At age 17 – the age by which compulsory education has ended in most countries – on average three-quarters of all young people are in school on a full-time basis. Countries in which enrolment at age 17 is well above average are Belgium (where compulsory education ends at age 18), Denmark, Finland, France, Germany, Netherlands, Norway, Sweden and Switzerland. In the Nordic countries, on average, 15 per cent of the 17-year-olds have left full-time schooling behind. Chart 4.2 shows that, in 1992, the enrolment rates are above 90 per cent in three countries: Belgium, Germany and the Netherlands. Nearly one in three 17-year-olds in New Zealand and Spain are no longer enrolled in the regular school system.

A particular problem of transition is associated with early school-leaving. This term can be defined as leaving the formal system before completing a full cycle of upper secondary education or acquiring a recognised vocational qualification. Although completion rates from initial schooling have increased since the mid-1980s (see Chapter 1), it can be inferred from the net enrolment rates shown in Annex Table A.18 that, in 1994, a significant number of young persons still leave school without a qualification. This is a major failing of education and training systems, since lifelong learning opportunities for this group are severely constrained.

Over 5 per cent of 14-year-olds were no longer enrolled in full-time secondary education, in 1994, in Denmark, Greece and Mexico (Annex Table A.18). In some countries where the legal school-leaving age was 16 years in 1992, the enrolment rate of 16- and

Table 4.1. **Trend in the share of vocational and technical education in total upper secondary enrolment**[1]

	Time period	
	1975-84	1984-92
Pacific Area		
Japan	–	–
European Community		
Denmark	+	..
France	0	0
Germany	0	0
Italy	0	–
Netherlands	+	+
Spain	0	0
Other Europe – OECD		
Austria	+	+
Finland	0	0
Norway	+	+
Sweden	+	..
Switzerland	0	0
Turkey	0	0

Note: .. Data not available.
1. Based on percentage of upper secondary students enrolled in public and private general and vocational education, 1975-92.
Legend:
"+" means increasing enrolment in vocational education;
"0" means no discernible or non-significant change in vocational enrolment;
"–" means decreasing enrolment in vocational education.
Sources: OECD Education Database, and Table 1.9 in Chapter 1.

◆   Chart 4.2. ***Net full-time enrolment rates for 17-year-olds, 1992***[1,2]

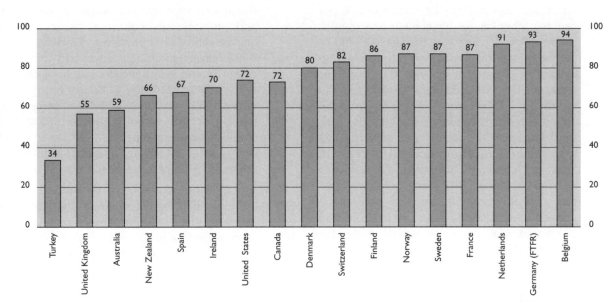

1.   Total enrolments in secondary and tertiary education.
2.   If part-time students are considered, the enrolment rates are substantially higher in the United Kingdom. In 1992, 20 per cent of 17-year-olds were enrolled on a part-time basis.
Source: OECD Education Database.

17-year-olds was still above 90 per cent; in other countries the retention rate in secondary schooling began to decline steeply once schooling was no longer compulsory for all students. According to the *OECD Jobs Study* (OECD, 1994*d*), Norway is one of the few countries in which less than 10 per cent of 20-year-olds have received less than an upper secondary education. Table 4.2, which shows the percentage of students leaving secondary education without

Table 4.2. **Percentage of students leaving secondary education without a certificate**

		Leavers without certificate
Finland[1]	1992	12
France	1986	19
Germany	1988	12
Greece	1987	36
Ireland	1989	9
Italy	1988	11
Netherlands	1986	26
Spain	1988	23
United Kingdom	1989	8

1.   Drop-outs per 100 students in upper secondary schools and vocational and professional upper secondary institutions.
Sources: OECD (1993*a*) and EURYDICE (1994*b*).

a certificate for several countries, provides further evidence of the scale of school failure that must be addressed if programmes of lifelong learning are to be implemented.

In the absence of internationally comparable statistics, it is useful to refer to data for individual countries, to gain a broader perspective on the nature as well as extent of "drop-out", a term used in different ways and contexts:

– Some countries refer to retention in upper secondary, post-compulsory schooling. In Japan, "of those who graduated from lower secondary schools in March 1993, 96.2 per cent advanced to upper secondary schools or colleges of technology in April 1993" (Japanese Ministry of Education, Science and Culture, 1994). In the United Kingdom (England), the staying-on rate beyond compulsory schooling "is now 73 per cent, rising to 80 per cent when part-time study is taken into account. In Scotland, the current figure for full-time post-compulsory education is 82 per cent" (OFSTED, 1994).

– Other countries use "drop-out" to denote those students who leave before completion of compulsory or all of secondary education. In

France, "of the generation born in 1968 (the latest one to complete its education), 8 per cent left school at 16" (French Ministry of Education, 1994). In Australia, the year 12 (end of secondary school) completion rate reached an estimated 72 per cent in 1992. The "apparent retention rate" of secondary school students to year 12 (*i.e.* the estimated proportion of the cohort entering secondary schooling who continued to year 12) was 77 per cent in 1992 (Australian Education Council, 1992). In Sweden, "a survey carried out by Statistics Sweden in Spring 1987 among 20-year-olds, four years after they left compulsory schooling, showed the following results: 77 per cent had completed upper secondary school; 4 per cent had never entered a programme in the upper secondary school but were studying in special courses; 9 per cent had entered, but never completed, upper secondary school; 10 per cent had never applied or been admitted to upper secondary school" (Swedish Ministry of Education and Science, 1992). In the United States, by 1992, 11.6 per cent of the 8th-grade class of 1988 were neither enrolled nor had received a high school diploma or equivalent credential. 1992 would have been the "theoretical year" of secondary school completion for these young adults (US Department of Education, 1994b). However, it is noted that this may overstate the eventual rate of attainment in the United States: "Of those in the 10th-grade class of 1980 (who should, 'theoretically', have graduated in 1982), 83.6 completed on time (in 1982); 8.3 per cent completed between 1982 and 1986; and 1.7 per cent completed by 1992. An estimated 7 per cent dropped out and did not eventually complete secondary schooling" (US Department of Education, 1994b).

– For a third group of countries, available data refer specially to leaving school before the acquisition of vocational qualifications. In Denmark, "7 per cent of a year group do not continue in the education system after basic school (...). Of the 93 per cent of a year group who commence a course of education after basic school, only 77 per cent complete it". Not all of these post-compulsory courses lead directly to vocational qualifications, so "in total, it is 25 per cent of a year group who do not get any vocationally-qualifying education" (Danish Ministry of Education, 1993). In the Netherlands, "in 1985/86, 29.7 per cent of those leaving full-time junior secondary vocational education, general secondary education and pre-university education do so without any qualifications. However, 52 per cent of these leavers go straight on to part-time education (some eventually to acquire qualifications)" (Dutch Ministry of Education and Science, 1989). In Germany, "the percentage leaving school without any certificate has stabilised at about 6 per cent. However, about one-quarter of these persons obtain the apprenticeship certificate" (OECD 1994d).

While it is not possible to be precise, a few generalisations might be drawn. An estimate of drop-out referring to the "theoretical" age of secondary school completion fails to take into account that some young people complete secondary schooling later than the "theoretical" age and qualifications may be acquired in ways other than through completion of upper secondary schooling. A reasonable question is whether delayed alternatives to schooling at the "upper secondary" level are, in fact, "equivalent". The motives for drop-out vary, but include perceptions of a lack of relevance and limited success in schooling (as reported from surveys carried out in the United Kingdom) as well as possibilities for employment (one of the explanations in the Dutch case). It is not possible to judge the extent to which the drop-out situation has changed, and importantly, why improvement or deterioration may have occurred. Attention is inevitably drawn to responses on the part of education authorities [*e.g.* Education Priority Programme in the Netherlands; education priority areas (ZEP) in France] or to broader economic and social developments (including sustained, high levels of youth unemployment).

High drop-out rates may signal a range of problems, such as unattractive schooling environments, lack of motivation in students, values and beliefs that cast doubt on the relevance of schooling, or limited success in initial learning. Some students may drop out because they expect to be better off without finishing the education programme. At least part of the problem of early school-leaving stems from inappropriate education policies and practices. For example, policies in many countries favour young people who seek to continue in tertiary education; they are not focused on those at risk of dropping out. Nearly half of the OECD countries require no more than nine years of compulsory schooling; in three-quarters of the countries, compulsory schooling ends at age 14, 15 or 16 (see Table 3.3). Policies to combat dropping out should target such conditions.

The problem of early school-leaving extends further than policies governing the age of compulsory school attendance. As mentioned in Chapters 1 and 3, social factors also contribute: poverty, ethnic minority status, and factors in the home environment such as level of family education, and quality of housing. Other factors include poor knowledge of the majority language, the type of school attended, the location of the school and wider community influences. The schools themselves also play a role. Early school-leaving may be caused by the school "ethos" as reflected in the programmes of study, school organisation, and the incentives or disincentives facing the individual. Rumberger (1995), using data from the US National Educational Longitudinal Survey of 1988, found that a number of family and school experience factors influence the decision of adolescents to leave school, with class repeating being the single most powerful predictor. At the institutional level, the study revealed that mean drop-out rates vary widely between schools, and that much of the variation can be explained by differences in the background characteristics of students.

The enrolment rates in full-time education shown in Chart 4.2 suggest that the highest retention rates occur in the "continental" European countries, where provision of upper secondary education is very different from that in the English-speaking countries. There are separate institutions for vocational training and education as well as dual systems; in addition, governments and educational institutions in these countries have a long tradition of highly organised support systems that take responsibility for young people who are at risk of early school-leaving.

Strategies for combating early school-leaving have focused on diversifying upper secondary education to meet a wider spectrum of learning needs and student preferences. Recent actions in this vein include: targeting pupils with learning disabilities (Belgium); curriculum reforms aimed at overcoming inequities across different socio-economic groups with different risks of dropping out at an early age (Ireland); changes in governance providing for greater school autonomy; involvement of parents and industry in new partnerships (Portugal); and the pursuit of a "standards-driven" approach to educational reform.

Additional indicators of the transition from school to work are the youth labour force participation and unemployment data given in Chart 4.3. In five countries, the youth participation rate – mea-

◆　Chart 4.3.　***Youth labour force participation and unemployment,***[1,2] ***1994***
Percentage

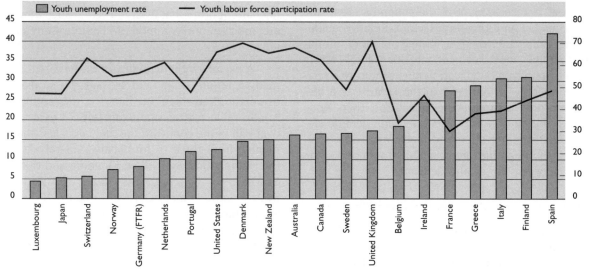

1.　Youth refers to ages 15-24. Unemployment and labour force participation rates are defined in accordance with *OECD Labour Force Statistics*.
2.　1993 data for Belgium, Denmark, Germany, Greece, Ireland, Italy, Portugal and the United Kingdom.
Source:　OECD (1995j), *Employment Outlook*, Table B, p. 205. See also Annex Table A.48.

sured as a percentage of 15-24 year-olds who are active in the labour force – is less than 45 per cent: Belgium, Finland, France, Greece and Italy. It is between 45 and 60 per cent in Germany, Ireland, Japan, Luxembourg, Norway, Portugal, Spain and Sweden. Participation rates over 60 per cent are found in Australia, Canada, Denmark, the Netherlands, New Zealand, Switzerland, the United Kingdom, and the United States. Of these countries, Denmark, the Netherlands and Switzerland have a developed apprenticeship system.

Youth unemployment rates were above 25 per cent in six countries in 1994 (OECD, 1995e): France, Greece, Ireland, Italy, Spain, and Finland. In all of these countries except Italy, where youth unemployment was high to begin with, the unemployment rates have increased significantly since 1983. Youth unemployment rates at, or below, 10 per cent occur in Germany, Japan, Luxembourg, the Netherlands, Norway and Switzerland. Particular circumstances explain the low youth unemployment rates in Japan and Norway. In the cases of Germany, Luxembourg, the Netherlands and Switzerland, the apprenticeship system may have been a factor in keeping unemployment down.

The unemployment of school-leavers is not necessarily a sign of educational failure. For example, a strong increase in the supply of young people, resulting from high birth rates, may also be a contributing factor. A proper indicator would measure the unemployment of young people relative to overall unemployment to take account of the general state of the labour market and long-term factors. Relative unemployment rates by type of schooling are more informative. A high unemployment rate for school-leavers with a certain type of education might indicate a relative oversupply in that type. In the context of a lifelong learning strategy, the questions then arise whether the education provided enough generic elements and whether alternative pathways and opportunities of retraining are available to improve the match between supply and demand.

Labour turnover and occupational mobility

Labour turnover measures movements of workers among jobs and may have implications for the process of skill acquisition and, especially, for the extent and nature of enterprise-based training. Table 4.3 contains data on labour turnover: both accessions (hirings) and separations, whether or not they involved an unemployment spell. In the latter, in the 1980s, 20 to 30 per cent of existing staff left enterprises or establishments each year, while another 20 to 30 per cent were hired. Though cross-country comparisons are difficult, there are indications that the difference between a number of European countries and North America (best represented by Canadian estimates) is not nearly as marked as might be expected (OECD, 1995w). Labour turnover is highest in the United States and Canada and lowest in Japan, with the European countries falling in between, though closest to North America as represented by Canada.

Tenure in a job is closely related to turnover rates. As can be seen from Chart 4.4, the distribution of workers by their tenure varies widely from one country to another. Nearly 29 per cent of workers in the United States in 1991 had tenures of one year or less, while the corresponding proportion in Japan in 1990 was less than 10 per cent. Four countries (Australia, Canada, the Netherlands and Spain) have a figure close to that of the United States; among them, the proportion of workers with tenure under one year ranges from 21 to 24 per cent (Annex Table A.50). In four others (Finland, France, Germany and Norway), the percentage is closer to Japan's. Finally, the situation in Switzerland and the United Kingdom – with roughly 18 per cent of the workers having less than one year of tenure – reflects the average across the OECD countries. These differences at the short end are mirrored at the long end as well. Only about one in four workers in Australia, the Netherlands and the United States has been at his or her current firm for at least ten years. Such long spells are much more common in France, Germany and Japan.

A useful synthetic indicator of the distribution is median tenure: that held by half the workers. The unweighted average median for the countries in Annex Table A.50 is approximately 5.4 years. In just over half of the countries the median is less than this, ranging from three to four years (Australia, Canada, the Netherlands, the United Kingdom and the United States) to roughly five years (Finland and Switzerland). France, Germany, Japan, Norway and Spain have much higher medians, ranging from 6.3 years in Spain to 8.2 years in Japan. A second synthetic indicator of this distribution is average tenure, a measure which is more affected by long-lasting jobs. The unweighted OECD average is 8.7 years. Five countries are below that average (Australia, Canada, the Netherlands, the United Kingdom and the United States), and seven are above (Finland, France, Germany, Japan, Norway, Spain and Switzerland).

Table 4.3. **Job turnover and labour turnover,[1] 1985 and 1991**

(annual rates as a percentage of total employment)

	Unit of observation	Job turnover[2]		Labour turnover	Share of job turnover in labour turnover (per cent)
		1985	1991		
Australia	Establishments (manufacturing)	29.3[3]	..	..	..
Canada	Firms	23.3[4]	30.4[4]	75.2 (89.0)[4]	34.8[4]
Denmark	Establishments	30.0[5]	28.5[5]	57.9[5]	45.0[5]
Finland	Establishments	19.5[6]	25.3	77[6]	25.7[6]
France	Firms	23.8[7]	25.6[7]	58[7]	12.4[7]
Germany	Establishments	16.6[8]	16.3[8]	56.1[8]	28.7[8]
Italy	Firms	22.8	20.1[9]	68.1[9]	31.2[9]
Japan	Establishments (continuing)	7.8[10]	..	36.6	21.3
Netherlands	Based on labour flows	19.3[11]	24.7[11]	..	31.8[11]
Sweden	Establishments	30.8	28.4	37	37[12]
United Kingdom	Establishments	17.5[13]	14.4[13]	40.0[13]	59.3
United States	Establishments	19.7[14]	23.3[14]	43.6 (quart.)[14]	30.8[14]

Note: .. Data not available.
1. Job turnover is the sum of changes in employment levels across all firms or establishments. Labour turnover measures change in individuals among jobs. Greater total job turnover should be associated with higher labour turnover but high labour turnover needs not to be the result of high job turnover.
2. Sampling months/periods vary across countries. Periods are as follows: *Australia*, June; *Canada*, annual averages; *Denmark*, November; *Finland*, annual averages; *France*, November; *Germany*, June; *Italy*, December; *Japan*, January-June; *Netherlands*, September; *Sweden*, November; *United Kingdom*, March-June; *United States*, June (biannual).
3. For manufacturing only. Job turnover for 1984-85.
4. Job turnover is an average of 1984-85 and 1985-86 and 1989-90. Labour turnover figures in brackets include temporary hirings and separations.
5. Job turnover is an average of 1985-86 and 1986-87 and 1989-90. Labour turnover and share for manufacturing only for 1984-85 to 1990-91.
6. Job turnover for 1986-88. Labour turnover for 1984. Share based on job turnover 1986-88 and labour turnover 1984.
7. Job turnover is an average of 1984-85 and 1985-86 and 1989-90. Labour turnover based on continuing establishments only.
8. Job turnover is a weighted average of |0.5(1982-83) + 1983-84 + 0.5(1984-85)| and |0.5(1988-89) + (1989-90)|. Labour turnover refers to 1985 and the share of labour turnover accounted for by job turnover for 1980-85.
9. Job turnover is an average of 1990-91 and 1991-92. Labour turnover for 1985-91.
10. Job turnover for 1984.
11. Job turnover for 1990 constructed from labour market flows. Data on share of labour turnover for 1990.
12. Share of job turnover in labour turnover for manufacturing only using job turnover.
13. Job turnover for 1985-87 and 1989-91. Labour turnover for manufacturing only; and the share of labour turnover for manufacturing uses job turnover for 1987-89.
14. Data on job turnover are an average of 1980-82 and 1982-84 and 1989-91. Share of job turnover in labour turnover for 1979-83.
Source: OECD (1995w), "Employment dynamics in firms", mimeo, Employment, Labour and Social Affairs Committee, Paris.

In Japan, as a consequence of the long-term tenure system, the stability of employment and the fostering and application of higher skills and competencies of employees in firms have been promoted, and these have been the driving forces of high economic growth. Therefore, the low rate of turnover does not indicate a weakness in lifelong learning or the acquisition of skills. The importance of long-term tenure has not changed until very recently, and the promotion of the fluidity of the labour market does not necessarily contribute to the protection of workers and the facilitation of lifelong learning.

Transitions between employment and unemployment

One component of labour turnover are flows into and out of unemployment. These differ widely among OECD countries, particularly between Europe and North America. As shown in Chart 4.5, flows in the latter are larger than those in the former. Data on inflows and outflows reveal that in many countries, the increased duration of unemployment resulted from a relative decline in outflows. Relatively low and falling outflows may be an indication of employers' reluctance to hire, owing to, *inter alia*, the high cost of dismissals (OECD, 1994c and 1994d). As shown in Chapter 1, unemployment rates in Europe are now close to 10 per cent, while in the United States they are substantially lower.

Annex Table A.49 shows that the flow rate into unemployment, in 1994, was particularly high in Canada, Denmark, Finland and the United States. In all four countries, more than 1.5 per cent of the employed workforce became unemployed each month. The Nordic countries excepted, the flow into unemployment in Europe and Japan is lower, comprising less than 0.5 per cent of the workforce. Australia and New Zealand are somewhere in between. The inflow rates into unemployment for

◆   Chart 4.4. ***Enterprise tenure,*[1] *1991*[2]

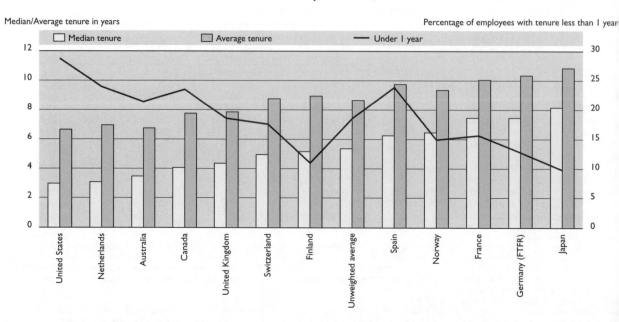

1.   The data are not perfectly comparable across countries, because of differences in data sources, population and sector coverage, reference years, and definitions. For more details, consult the source.
2.   1989 data for Norway, 1990 data for Germany, Japan and the Netherlands and 1992 data for Spain.
Source: OECD (1993*b*), *Employment Outlook,* Table 4.1, p. 121.

◆   Chart 4.5. ***Monthly flow into unemployment, 1993*[1,2,3]

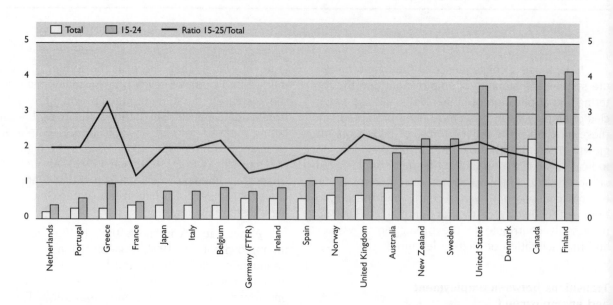

1.   Inflows refer to those unemployed for less than one month (two months in the case of Finland).
2.   As a percentage of the working-age population (15-64 years) less the unemployed.
3.   For some countries, data may refer to 1992 or 1994. For details see Annex Table A.49.
Source: OECD (1995*j*), *Employment Outlook,* Table 1.9, pp. 27-28.

youth aged 15-24 years are generally double the rates observed for the entire labour force. This is another indication of the difficulties experienced by many youths in finding stable employment. The incidence of unemployment in the United States and Canada is thus almost three times that of Europe and Japan. In the United States the burden of unemployment is much more evenly distributed over the workforce than in Europe, where a large share of the labour force has low risk of unemployment, and a small share are long-term unemployed.

European countries are in general characterised not so much by low labour turnover rates but by low inflows and outflows from unemployment. The character of labour turnover may also differ, with labour turnover tending to be concentrated in relatively fewer positions in Europe than in North America (OECD, 1995w). Though flows into and out of unemployment are apparently significantly lower in a number of European countries than in North America, there are indications that job-to-job flows play an important role in some European countries (OECD, 1995w). With respect to the transition between employment and unemployment, there is a cleavage between European countries and Japan on the one hand and the United States, Canada and the Nordic countries on the other.

The implications of these data have not fully been analysed. High labour turnover (including job-to-job flows) in general provides some advantages, such as flexible reallocation of resources across firms. However, it may also reduce the investment in employer-based knowledge and skills because employers less certain of reaping the benefits. Limits on the incentives for investment in employer-based training stemming from high labour turnover represent a weakness in the provision of lifelong learning opportunities. High flows and short spells of unemployment may be more efficient from the point of view of the operation of the labour market than, for example, a combination of low incidence and duration. This is because unemployment erodes the value of human capital.

In summary, this section has provided empirical baseline information on pathways in education and transitions between education and employment. Some indication of a relationship between types of education and training systems, early school-leaving rates, and youth unemployment rates are also provided. It is clear that there are major deficiencies in the provision of lifelong learning for a small but significant percentage of the youth cohort.

Table 4.4 summarises the main findings on indicators of pathway use in education and the transition from school to work with the notions "low", "medium" and "high". A comparison of the entries in the different columns reveals that all of the four countries which have both "low" youth unemployment and a "high" rate of participation in secondary vocational education – Austria, Germany, Luxembourg and Switzerland – all have employer-led systems of vocational training (see also Annex Table A.51). The only other country classified as having a "high" rate of secondary vocational preparation is Italy, where the system is led by educational institutions, and here the rate of youth unemployment is high. Japan and Norway, the only other two countries where youth unemployment is classified as "low", also have education-led systems of vocational education, with low and medium rates of participation. The latter two countries have, however, experienced favourable economic conditions during much of the 1980s and early 1990s. The pattern in the data implies that a high rate of participation in vocational education is associated with low youth unemployment if the vocational training system is employer-led. Otherwise, a high rate of participation in secondary vocational education is not related to the level of youth unemployment.

In three of the eleven countries where youth unemployment is high, the median school-leaving age is early; in the six others the median age is about average. These findings suggest that there is no clear relationship between school-leaving age and youth unemployment. There is also apparently a weak relationship between the school-leaving age and the youth labour force participation rate: in three countries the participation rate is high whereas the median school-leaving age is early; for five others the former is high and the latter medium to high.

D. PATHWAYS IN FORMAL EDUCATION AND THEIR LINKS TO LABOUR MARKETS

This section considers whether the evidence available shows that the organisation of pathways in education and training systems – and countries' approaches to differentiating types and levels of institution, and to sorting and selecting students – have consequences for achieving the objectives of lifelong learning. The section also considers the place of vocational education; the extent and nature of differentiation; how and at what age it occurs, the ease of entry and what role, if any, social background plays in the selection process. The flexibility or rigidity of student differentiation in Member countries is also examined,

Table 4.4. **Summary indicators of pathways in education and transitions to employment**

	Pathways use		Transition from school to work[1]	
	Share of students in upper secondary vocational education	Median school-leaving age	Youth unemployment	Youth labour force participation
North America				
Canada	..	Medium	High	High
United States	..	Medium	Medium	High
Pacific Area				
Australia	Low	Low	High	High
Japan	Low	..	Low	Medium
New Zealand	Low	Low	Medium	High
European Community				
Belgium	Medium	Medium	High	Low
Denmark	Medium	High	Medium	High
France	Medium	High	High	Low
Germany (FTFR)	High	..	Low	High
Greece	..	Low	High	Low
Ireland	..	Medium	High	Medium
Italy	High	..	High	Low
Luxembourg[2]	High	..	Low	Medium
Netherlands	High	High	Medium	High
Portugal	..	..	Medium	Medium
Spain	Medium	Medium	High	Medium
United Kingdom	Medium	Low	High	High
Other Europe – OECD				
Austria	High	..	Low	High
Finland	Medium	Medium	High	Low
Norway	Medium	Medium	Low	High
Sweden	..	Medium	High	Medium
Switzerland	High	High	Low	Medium
Turkey	Medium	Low	Medium	Medium

Note: .. Data not available.
1. The countries are classified on the basis of the 1993 data provided in Annex Table A.49. Youth unemployment is considered "Low" if it is under 10 per cent. "Medium" rates are those between 10 and 15 per cent; and "High" rates are those over 15 per cent. Youth labour force participation rates are considered "Low" beLow 45 per cent; "Medium" between 45 and 55 per cent; "High" above 55 per cent.
2. The rating from Luxembourg is based on 1988 data (OECD, 1992f).
Source: OECD Education Database.

for example in terms of accommodating student choice. Given the objectives of lifelong learning – inclusion, equity and efficiency – and noting the evidence on the effects of good quality education and training, what is or should be the role of governments in improving pathways and facilitating progressions?

Approaches to differentiation in education systems

Chapter 3 described how education systems vary in the way they differentiate between type and level of education and training, and in the way they sort and select students. All school systems teach the basic cognitive skills (reading, writing, elementary mathematics) in the first grades. Labour market participation requires generic and more vocational skills,

which build on the basic and meta-cognitive skills, imparted by schooling. The trajectory from general to vocational skills differs widely among OECD countries. Chapter 3 concluded that not all the more specific vocational skills need to be developed prior to employment; in fact, there is a widespread consensus about the value of general knowledge and competencies as laying the foundation for the acquisition of specific vocational skills at the workplace. This consensus notwithstanding, OECD countries differ in the following six respects:

– *Extent and nature of differentiation.* School systems differ in the age at which students choose or are directed into separate schools or separate curricula; criteria may include, for example, differences in cognitive abilities or the vocational interests of students. A major issue here is the degree of choice available to students and families.

- *Flexibility or rigidity of differentiation.* In some systems, choices have to be made at an early age and are virtually irreversible. In others, choices are made later or permit flexibility in changing earlier choices.

- *Ease of entry.* Some systems are more or less open, with students enjoying easy access to the schools of their choice. Others are more or less closed, with strong selectivity at entry levels for advanced learning.

- *Positioning of vocational education.* In some education systems vocational education is positioned at the secondary level; in other systems it occurs increasingly at the post-secondary level of education. Some apprenticeship programmes combine schooling with on-the-job training and work experience. Certain countries – notably Germany and the Netherlands – have seen an increase of enrolment in post-secondary institutions with a strong "applied" character, in a shift away from the specific vocational tracks and programmes formerly considered as "terminal" education (OECD, 1994*g* and 1994*k*).

- *Quality of educational services.* In some systems there are large quality differences between schools and between classes within schools, whereas in others the differences are less marked (see OECD, 1994*h*). The wider dispersion of quality in certain systems implies that greater effort in enforcing a uniformly high-quality level of provision is required. The sharing of the benefits of successful innovative approaches on a larger scale by all institutions is an important avenue for improving quality.

- *Nature of the transition to the labour market.* In some systems there is a gradual transition from education and training to the labour market, whereas in others the transition is more discrete. This juxtaposition mirrors the involvement of employers in vocational training. In the former, employers frequently take the lead in developing partnerships that can be characterised as employer-led. When the transition from school to work is of a more discrete nature, educational institutions are in a dominant position *vis-à-vis* employers, that is, education-led.

Differentiation varies not only in type and timing, but also in extent; regulation, subsidisation and/or direct government activity may be involved. Little is known about the effects of such differences on equitable outcomes or the efficiency of producing the desired individual and labour market results.

Table 4.5 summarises certain characteristics of differentiation in the initial education systems of Member countries. Compulsory education starts at age 6 in most countries. The first structural differentiation of pupils takes place in either lower or upper secondary education. On average, it occurs at the age of 14 years. Countries with early differentiation include Austria, Belgium, Germany, Ireland, the Netherlands, Turkey, the United Kingdom and the United States. In contrast, in Australia, Canada, Denmark, Finland, New Zealand, Norway and Sweden, the first structural differentiation occurs at a relatively older age and has more to do with individual interest than assumed or estimated ability levels. On average, students can choose between three and four different types of educational institutions at the first stage of differentiation. It will be noted that Japan has six options to choose from and Italy seven.

The factors determining differentiation cannot be inferred with certainty, but are likely to include talent and ability, interest and motivation, and social and home background. Kellaghan *et al.* (1993) and Maynard (1995) conclude that family background exerts a strong set of influences on the educational success of children, some of which are direct and enduring – for example, those resulting directly from the socio-economic status of the family and the physical environment of the home. Factors such as the amount and quality of time parents spend with their children, the number and spacing of children, changes in the composition of family and residential mobility have more episodic influence.

The structure of pathways

The different pathways between organised learning and work in OECD countries, both during and after initial education and training, are described by three illustrative or stylised types of situations or "models", which do not necessarily correspond fully to the experience of any specific country. Actual country experiences are staged, in reality, across a continuum rather than three discrete "models". The purpose of this stylised description is to highlight certain patterns of interconnection between institutional arrangements, qualification structures, and labour market outcomes.

Table 4.5. **Differentiation characteristics in initial education and training, 1992**

| | Compulsory schooling age | | First differentiation | | | | Initial Vocational education | | | |
	From	To	At age	By ability level	By type	Levels or types	From age	To age	During compulsory schooling	Form
North America										
Canada	6	16	18	Yes	Yes	4	18	27	No	Vocational colleges
United States	6	17	12	Yes	No	5	18	20	No	Community colleges
Pacific Area										
Australia[1]	6	15	16	No	Yes	3	16	18	No	Traineeships
Japan	6	15	15	Yes	Yes	6	15	18	No	Vocational education
New Zealand	6	16	18	Yes	Yes	5	15	18	Yes	Vocational education
European Community										
Belgium (Flemish)	6	18	12	Yes	Yes	2	12	18	Yes	Vocational education
Belgium (French)	6	18	12	Yes	Yes	2	12	18	Yes	Vocational education
Denmark	7	16	16	No	Yes	3	16	18	No	Vocational education
France	6	16	15	Yes	Yes	3	15	18	No	Vocational education and apprenticeship
Germany	6	18	10	Yes	–	5	16	19	Yes	Vocational education and apprenticeship
Greece	5.5	15	14.5	Yes	Yes	4	14.5	17.5	No	Vocational education
Ireland	6/7	15	12	Yes	Yes	3	15	18	No	Vocational education and apprenticeship
Italy	6	14	14	Yes	Yes	7	14	19	No	Vocational education
Netherlands	5	16	13	Yes	Yes	4	16	19	No	Vocational education and apprenticeship
Portugal	6	14	15	Yes	Yes	2	15	17	No	Vocational education
Spain	6	16	14	Yes	Yes	2	14	17	No	Vocational education
United Kingdom[2]	5	16	11	Yes	No	2	–	–	–	–
Other Europe – OECD										
Austria	6	15	10	Yes	No	2	14	19	No	Apprenticeship
Finland	7	16	16	Yes	Yes	2	16	19	No	Vocational education
Norway	7	16	16	Yes	No	2	16	18	No	Vocational education and apprenticeship
Sweden	7	16	16	Yes	Yes	3	16	19	No	Vocational education and apprenticeship
Switzerland	6/7	15	15	Yes	Yes	4	15	18	No	Vocational education and apprenticeship
Turkey	6	15	12	Yes	Yes	5	12	15	Yes	Vocational education and apprenticeship

Note. – Not applicable.
1. Form includes traineeship, apprenticeship and technical and further education colleges.
2. Since 1992 new vocational qualifications have been introduced.
Sources: OECD (1995d). *Education at a Glance – OECD Indicators*, and national submissions to OECD.

Model 1 represents a situation where vocational education is underdeveloped and where general education and vocational education (to the extent that the latter exists) are distinct and mutually isolated. Transition from school to work is regulated either through the labour market (low youth wages, absence of occupationally segmented markets) or through *ad hoc* programmes. Learning on the job and internal labour markets allow workers to advance to higher levels of responsibility and remuneration. Credentials are obtained mainly in initial schooling and tertiary education.

Model 2 shows a configuration in which general education and vocational education are, again, organised in mutually isolated tracks. Vocational education, however, is highly developed at the post-compulsory stage and is closely linked to the labour market. Effective linkages between education and employment are created through organised combinations of school- and work-based learning, through industry involvement in the design of curricula and certificates, and through close correspondence between educational qualifications and job classifications. Progression in this model takes place through prolonged routes of formal education and training, both general and vocational. Both types of tracks lead to recognised qualifications, but they are associated with different destinations and there are no links between them.

Model 3 represents a situation appropriate to a lifelong learning strategy in which the different branches of education and training are connected by a series of "bridges" and "ladders" at all stages and levels of post-compulsory, tertiary and adult education and training. This situation also suggests a fluid relationship between learning and work, where an initial period of full-time schooling is followed throughout working life by sequences and combinations of organised learning on or off the job, which accompany or alternate with part- or full-time work.

National configurations of education and training pathways

As noted above, current systems in OECD countries do not exactly fit any of these three stylised and descriptive models; they can, however, be examined in terms of their relative closeness or dissimilarity. Historically, some English-speaking and southern European countries come close to Model 1, whereas the education and training systems in the German-speaking countries traditionally have been close to Model 2. In reality, all systems incorporate elements of both, and most seek to progress towards the third model.

The French system, for instance, is close to Model 2 in that vocational-technical progression routes have been organised in the form of secondary and tertiary technical education, and that transition to employment at this intermediary level (and from traditional vocational education and apprenticeship in some areas of activity) takes place on the basis of strong traditional links between educational certificates and industrial classifications (OECD, 1994c). Nevertheless, the French system also has features of Model 1, in that increasing numbers of young people unsuccessfully try to enter the labour market without any occupationally relevant certificate either directly after general or vocational secondary education or after an incomplete tertiary education.

Although no national education system is altogether close to Model 3, it can be used as a goal for lifelong learning. Most countries currently appear to be seeking ways to approach it. The diversification of the vocational-technical routes in many European countries illustrates this tendency. The Netherlands is illuminating in that it continues to have a highly structured and non-unified system of general and vocational education, but has gone far to provide bridges back and forth between the two streams in secondary education. The Netherlands is also of interest because it is among the few countries that have recently been able to attract more young people into vocational than general education at the secondary level (OECD, 1994k). This seems to be partly due to the widespread perception that young people who leave secondary education with vocational qualifications have better chances of finding satisfactory employment in the long term. Another explanation may be that these vocational programmes at the secondary level are no longer "terminal", in that successful graduates can pursue further studies at either the secondary or post-secondary levels. The possibility of switching among different vocational programmes and between general and vocational tracks thus does more than enable young people in vocational education to progress to higher levels of vocational-technical education or eventually continue into tertiary education. It allows young people at any stage of post-compulsory education who decide not to proceed to the next level to turn to a relevant vocational programme providing recognised labour market qualifications.

Other steps towards Model 3 can be observed in countries where the borderline between secondary and post-secondary education has become increasingly blurred through the development of multipurpose further education since the 1960s. Community Colleges in North America, Technical and Further Education (TAFE) in Australia, and further education colleges in the United Kingdom offer alternative, non-academic routes to tertiary education as well as vocational and technical programmes to both young people and adults. It remains to be seen, however, whether these efforts will be successful in developing bridges to high-quality tertiary education.

A radical innovation in developing tracks has been undertaken in the United Kingdom, where since the mid-1980s the expansion of further education has been accompanied by another fundamental move towards system flexibility: the introduction of National Vocational Qualifications (NVQs) and, more recently, General National Vocational Qualifications (GNVQs), which are seen as a bridge towards academic educational qualification for upper secondary students. Together with academic qualifications equivalence arrangements, NVQs and GNVQs are expected to enable young people and adults to progress via routes that combine academic and vocational courses or modules according to the learner's choice. Only longer-term experience will show whether these strategies actually lead to a situation in which vocational and academic education become equally valuable elements in a unified system of integrated routes of lifelong learning.

Pathways through tertiary education

In existing provision which broadly follows Models 1 and 2, the division between vocational and general secondary education is as starkly present in most tertiary education. The term "high-quality tertiary education" is frequently applied exclusively to "academic" education, which is only considered to be job-related if it leads to one of the traditional professions, notably medicine and law.

An exception to the lower status accorded to vocational or technical tertiary education are the French *Grandes écoles*. However, relatively few young people continue from secondary vocational education to technical education at the tertiary level (about 15 per cent). Only 1 per cent enter the *Grandes écoles*, via the technological *baccalauréat* and *classes préparatoires*. The competition among candidates from the most selective streams of upper secondary education increases with the level and prestige of the technical education. In this case, bridges and ladders across the two sub-systems exist, but they are one-way. They lead most often, and most successfully, from general education to higher levels of technical education.

The general absence of bridges between vocational secondary and non-technical tertiary education reinforces the argument advanced in Chapter 3 for a convergence between general and vocational education at secondary level. This is not to say that there should be automatic parity of esteem between vocational-technical and general academic education at the tertiary level. However, countries have attempted to strengthen upper secondary and post-secondary vocational studies (France), created or reinforced apprenticeship-style training (Australia, Canada, Italy, Portugal, the United Kingdom and the United States), and increased the capacity for advanced technical studies by developing tertiary-level polytechnic institutions (Austria, Finland and Switzerland). A major thrust of new policy initiatives is to make the university system more flexible and responsive to the emerging needs of the economy. Countries have upgraded their more technically oriented tertiary-level education institutions into universities (Australia and the United Kingdom), fostered institutional autonomy and competition between polytechnics (New Zealand), and made it easier for students to move between the apprenticeship system and tertiary studies (Germany).

Entry into tertiary education immediately after secondary education provides a solid basis for learning later in life, and reinforces the habit of education. But initial tertiary education can no longer meet potential needs for the whole of working life, and it can be assumed that much subject-knowledge is never directly applied. An argument can therefore be advanced for the postponement of part of tertiary education until a time when entrants are sure of the uses to which they intend to put it. Alternative learning models such as enterprise training, distance education, adult education in the humanities, physical sciences and technologies, and non-formal learning for either job-related or personal development purposes, can fulfil some of the functions of existing tertiary education structures. This has implications for employers' recruitment policies; greater testing of applicants will be required, rather than reliance on certificated tertiary education, which may or may not be relevant.

Access to tertiary education also needs to be kept open to as wide a section of the population as possible. Access courses, refresher courses and a modular approach, with full recognition of prior learning, both vocational and non-vocational, are already contributing to such developments. Tertiary establishments will respond to increased demand for high-level courses, both from those able to meet the entry requirements which establishments lay down for such courses and from those in need of preparatory bridging courses.

Differences between structures of education and training systems

Education systems are still very different. Table 4.6 indicates some of the major differences between the education and training systems of Germany, the Netherlands and the Nordic countries, on the one hand, and those of English-speaking countries – Australia, Canada, New Zealand, the United Kingdom and the United States – on the other. Abstracting from country-specific details, these can be characterised as the difference between "systemic" and more "fragmented" structures. The dual systems of Germany, Austria and Switzerland are generally regarded as examples of the former, which have been quite successful in helping young people make the transition from school to work. Decision-makers and researchers have seen employers effectively mobilised in these countries to provide apprenticeship places. They have also learned about collective efforts to standardise the content and methods of training within industry. Through such efforts, former apprentices have access to the careers of "Meister",

technicians and engineers. The systems of the German-speaking countries are now often taken as role models for the vocational training of youth.

The dual system has long been perceived as immutable, and fixed. Today, though, critical questions are being raised in Austria, Germany and Switzerland. Young people no longer wish to enter certain types of industrial and craftsmanship apprenticeship, but prefer more attractive programmes in services or high-tech activities, after which they tend to move on to post-secondary education. Consequently, the universities are becoming overcrowded and the duration of initial education continues to increase. Displacement of the vocationally and technically trained by the graduates from post-secondary education casts a cloud over the successful continuation of the dual approach.

Largely stimulated by the successes booked by dual systems, other European countries such as Denmark, France and the Netherlands have experimented with periods of enterprise-based learning interspersed in school-based vocational education. Such efforts raise questions as to the complementarity of theoretical and practical learning in the work environment as part of formal education (see Chapter 3).

In the English-speaking countries, initial vocational training has developed mainly in the form of school-based alternatives to academic education.

Table 4.6.   **Differences between structures of education and training systems**

Characteristics	Fragmented structures	Systemic structures
Balance of general and vocational education and training	Emphasis on general education; vocational training weak; parity of esteem problem	Strong vocational training systems
Certification	"Market" plays large role in individual course certification; government may take lead in setting up certification system	Based on industry consensus; employer associations and unions play major role within state framework
Customising possibilities	Emphasis on modularity; individuals can package and choose timing of courses; certification more concerned with achieved competencies than course definition	Well-defined long-term courses; less possibility of individual modification; well-defined requirements for courses
Entry requirements	Entry requirements less important	Clear minimum entry requirements
Subsequent employment opportunities	Relatively wide range of employment opportunities	Well-defined "good" employment opportunities at end, but in narrow area
Company involvement and location of training	Largely in public and private sector colleges; weak company commitments	Strong company involvement; much company-based training, and close links between companies and school-based training

Source: OECD.

Thus, the United States established community colleges; the United Kingdom expanded further education colleges at post-compulsory level and developed a new qualification system; and Australia developed TAFE and embarked on the process of award restructuring, which included revision of qualifications as well as collective agreements. In addition, these countries rely heavily on transition programmes and active labour market policies targeted towards young people. At the same time, they have experimented with "partnerships" between schools and firms. Due to the marked decentralisation of education, and the weakness or absence of collective organisation (except in Australia), these efforts have remained less systematic than those in continental Europe, despite the success of some of these experiments.

In addition to the differences between national education systems – which are significant in many respects – there are important similarities, which have not been mentioned. Various types of imbalance testify to flaws in the articulation of the education systems of OECD countries: high youth unemployment, paradoxically associated with the recruitment difficulties reported by some employers for certain categories of jobs; problems of transition, affecting even highly-qualified young people; and the doubts cast over the role of diplomas and certificates in recruitment and access to employment. The direction of change in OECD countries has also been described. All are seeking to remove the traditional barriers between vocational and general education in order to improve the parity of esteem between programmes and to provide better preparation for lifelong learning. Model 3 identified some of the features of a flexible system of pathways, which may serve as a direction for programmes of lifelong learning.

E. EDUCATION, TRAINING AND TRANSITIONS TO EMPLOYMENT

This section reviews the advantages and disadvantages of different approaches to facilitating the transition from education or training to the labour market. The causes and consequences of transition problems are examined in the light of evidence on changing skill requirements. Concern is directed to various transitions from employment due, for example, to early school-leaving, career interruptions and returns to learning from retirement. Policy issues arise because some approaches are more successful than others.

Models of transition from education to employment

Two modes of transition from school to the labour market can be distinguished: a discrete or sequential one, and a gradual one. The two types of gradual transition are working while learning and learning while working. The latter involves a specific form of partnership between educational institutions and the world of work. The dual model approach was reviewed previously, but other less systemic, extensive and institutionalised forms of co-operation have emerged as well. Most of these projects involve simple forms of co-operation between an enterprise and a school (OECD, 1992e).

Work-experience placements are the most common activity in the United Kingdom, as in many other European countries, if only because they are often required by governments. In France, for example, the *séquences éducatives en entreprise* have been a standard feature of vocational upper secondary schools since the late 1970s. Reinforcing this link with the workplace, visits to enterprises by students and teachers, work-shadowing (observation of a worker's daily routines) and teacher secondment have become increasingly popular. But much activity also goes on within schools, notably curriculum development projects and the establishment of mini-enterprises. In the United States, significant emphasis has been placed on employers giving direct help to schools and students – career academies, company employees acting as mentors to individual students, "adopt a school" initiatives, and donation of equipment are all examples (Stern *et al.*, 1995).

Coalitions between schools and enterprises have been established in a variety of forms. In one version, employers in an area agree to give jobs to students who meet certain educational objectives; even this form has a number of variations. Big companies in the United States are becoming more action-oriented, and inclined to launch their own programmes rewarding innovation across an entire school system. Other coalitions are based around programmes originated by public, semi-public or other non-profit-making bodies. Such programmes may aim, for example, to promote enterprise in schools, improve career guidance and counselling services or retrain teachers with co-operation from employers. Such co-operation as well as that between schools and firms in general, tend to concentrate on upper secondary schooling, and are designed in particular for students engaged in pre-vocational and vocational studies. There is thus a tendency for public authorities as well as employers to direct partnership efforts towards students close to making the transition from school to work.

The involvement of employers in vocational education frequently stems from their perception of the failings of an education system managed and financed almost entirely by the public authorities. Three shortcomings in particular lead employers to believe they are not getting what they require (OECD, 1992e):

– *Relevance*: schools are criticised for running vocational programmes that are out of touch with the changing skills needed by industry. This perception stimulates schemes to give learners greater experience of the wider world, and brings greater knowledge of that world into the curriculum.

– *Standards*: there is an impression in some countries that educational standards have been declining precisely when they should be rising. Even those who dispute this allegation would generally not deny that education systems still fall short of providing a high-quality and relevant education for all. Employers thus seek general improvement in education, for example by adding their voices to calls for schemes designed to help improve the teaching of specific subjects – most commonly science and mathematics – which too few workers are thought to have mastered.

– *Skills*: employers fear that without being pushed, schools, colleges and universities will go on teaching as if their students were destined for jobs in enterprises organised in old-fashioned or outdated ways. This relevance imperative is another powerful focus for partnerships.

There are conflicts between the three concerns. Possibly the starkest conflict is between reinforcing traditional standards and teaching "new" skills – an issue taken up in Chapter 6. From these concerns, two questions can be raised that underlie the debate on vocational education and training. The first is, how much should be provided, and to whom? The second is, how should it be delivered, and what should be the respective roles of schools and employers? At the heart of both issues is the problem of how to prepare workers for the increasing number of occupations requiring combinations of technical and general competence. Countries that aim at improving the efficiency of vocational routes would do well to ensure that employers perceive those routes as appropriate.

Three elements are important in this regard: the *relevance* of specific skills being taught in a vocational field to current practices in the workplace; the *method of combining* these specific vocational studies with broader, and more general learning; and the *efficiency* with which young people acquire these skills.

Co-operation between vocational schools and employers can be one way of making studies more relevant to employers' needs. But employers have an incentive to emphasise the skills they think are applicable in the workplace, which may be taught at the expense of general skills. How should firms be involved in vocational education and training? This question can be studied by comparing education-led and employer-led systems.

Education-led and employer-led systems

In most countries and for most young people, the "transition" from full-time education to full-time employment is no longer a matter of crossing a short bridge between two stable structures. Rather, it is part of a continuous journey of discovery that starts well before students leave school, and ends well after they start employment. This realisation of the fluidity of the boundaries between education and employment provides a powerful rationale for the advocacy of lifelong learning. More and more students have a part-time job, as the figures on youth labour force participation rates presented in Chart 4.3 demonstrate. In the United States, three-quarters of high-school seniors are already working in their spare time, mainly in relatively low-skilled and temporary jobs. Work experience of this type does not necessarily improve the chances of entering higher-quality jobs; it is, however, beneficial to the extent that it shapes desirable attitudes such as perseverance and team spirit. The description of Model 3 in Section D outlines features of a system of flexible pathways which can help realise some of the goals of lifelong learning.

In an education-led system of vocational education, the emphasis is on classroom teaching of vocational skills. Employer-led systems place more emphasis on learning on-the-job with additional instruction through formal teaching. The main example of an employer-led system of vocational preparation is the dual system, dominant in Germany, Austria and Switzerland (OECD, 1994i). Apprentices recruited and paid by employers spend one or two days a week in vocational schools and the remainder with the firm, learning a trade. Such employer-led systems appear to have at least five advantages:

- The drop-out rates appear to be lower than those from formal vocational education in schools. Because school failure is a major deterrent to achieving lifelong learning for all, lower drop-out rates may signal a comparative advantage in several respects.

- The learning efficiency of an employer-led system appears to be higher than that of formal classroom education, because new and "applicable" skills are learned more rapidly and thoroughly, and students have an earlier introduction to up-to-date technologies. Because constructivist learning is facilitated by the variety and challenge inspired by "real-world" learning environments, employer-led systems are in a better position than education-led ones to take full advantage of the new opportunities opened up by a shift to a lifelong learning approach.

- In an employer-led system, enterprises learn about the productive qualities of students as prospective workers. This information is more valuable than the diplomas awarded in formal schooling. Although the certificates conferred by the firm at the end of the training period may have value as a device for signalling achievements, the firm at which the student receives the training benefits more from this information transfer. Aptitude, interest and motivation to continue learning are among the qualities sought by employers, but they are usually only very indirectly signalled by educational credentials.

- The cost-efficiency of an employer-led system may well be greater, for both governments and employers, because the total costs are lower than those of providing relevant and high-quality vocational preparation within the formal school system.

- Using the enterprise as a site for education and training gives students practice in learning at the workplace, which helps to prepare them for a lifetime of learning at work.

Employer-led systems introduce a wider diversity of learning environments for students. Although variety in settings for learning is desirable from a pedagogical viewpoint, it can increase inequality, as students in a good learning environment will fare better than others. Employer-led approaches also lead to "creaming off" of the most capable students by firms offering the highest wages and the best career prospects, which will compound existing inequities. Because firms may be short-sighted, the number of open training places will vary over the business cycle, resulting in too few places during a recession. A further point is that a dual approach may be at odds with the goal of creating a more flexible workforce, because it puts more emphasis on the transfer of skills specific to one employer. Employer-sponsored training increases internal flexibility through promotion or replacement within the firm, but decreases external flexibility and job-to-job mobility. Apprenticeships have proved an excellent means of passing on specific craft skills, but are employers able to cater for the broader body of knowledge and competencies required in many occupations today? Uncertainty about the duration of the employment and fear of running risks by employers may cause under-investment in the more general competencies acquired on the job. Another concern is the early break with general education made by many students following a dual track programme. With more initial education, there is on average a greater likelihood of a young person's returning to education and training as an adult. On the other hand, the relatively early age at which young people change from full-time to part-time education in a dual system may prevent some of them from dropping out altogether.

Systemic approaches to managing the transition from education to the labour market influence the nature and extent of early school-leaving. The data suggest that countries with a well-developed system of gradual transition from education to the labour market are more successful in preventing early school-leaving than countries with a discrete school-based system of transition. A strategy for lifelong learning would need to take these considerations into account, within the specific national context of each country. Further evidence on the ability of employer-led systems to reduce the problems of school-to-work transition can be inferred from Table 4.7, which gives the unemployment rates for leavers from different school levels one year after dropping out. In almost all countries, the unemployment rate declines as the level of education rises. Among school-leavers with lower secondary education in Australia, France, Ireland, Spain and the United States more than a third are unemployed one year after leaving school. Among university graduates, the unemployment rate is 12 per cent or less, except in Italy and Spain. In almost all the countries surveyed in Table 4.7, the unemployment rate among the 15- to 24-year-olds is

Table 4.7. **Unemployment rates for those leaving education at different levels, one year after leaving (based on follow-up surveys), and unemployment rates for the total labour force**

		Unemployment for leavers from:				Unemployment in the labour force	
		Lower secondary education	Upper secondary education	Non-university tertiary education	University education	Age 15-24	Age 25-64
North America							
Canada	1988	..	..	8	9	18	10
United States[1]	1991	37	12	6	8	14	7
Pacific Area							
Australia[2]	1992	33	..	..	..	18	9
European Community							
Denmark	1991	9	15	11	12	11	11
France[3]	1992	57	24	8	12	21	9
Ireland[4]	1992	35	24	21	10	23	14
Italy	1992	..	..	..	39	33	7
Spain	1991	34	36	13	26	34	15
United Kingdom[5]	1993	15	13	..	..	15	8
Other Europe – OECD							
Finland	1990	17	6	2	−1	23	11
Sweden[6]	1992	16	5	..	..	11	4
Switzerland	1993	..	..	3	6	7	3

Note: .. Data not available.
1. The population of recent leavers was deduced from data collected by means of a retrospective household survey.
2. Data for all school-leavers have been used since the statistics on transition from education to work do not distinguish between those who obtained their Secondary School Certificate (ISCED 3) and those who did not (ISCED 2).
3. Seven months after leaving education instead of one year. Data for tertiary education are from 1989.
4. Leavers from ISCED 2 include both persons who left full-time education after having successfully completed ISCED 2, and persons who left school while attending ISCED 3, but who did not complete it. The data in all cases relate to short-term perspectives, i.e. one year following departure from full-time education. Persons who left school while attending ISCED 3 but who did not complete ISCED 3 are included in the total of ISCED 2 leavers.
5. Data refer to England and Wales only.
6. Data for lower secondary education are from 1990.
Source: OECD (1995d), *Education at a Glance – OECD Indicators.*

on average double that for workers aged 25-64. The exceptions are Denmark, Italy and Ireland. The higher relative unemployment rate among school-leavers compared to the total unemployment rate signals efficiency and equity problems in the transition from school to work.

What can be said about the relative outcomes of different systems? No country has a perfect system for providing a problem-free transition from school to work (OECD, 1994j). Yet, some systems appear to work better than others. Consider, for example, Annex Table A.51, which presents data on youth and adult unemployment rates, classified by the nature of vocational preparation in Member countries. Whether the observed differences are due to education systems, labour market institutions or country-specific conditions is an open question. Caution must be exercised in inferring a direct relationship between institutional arrangements for vocational preparation and youth unemployment rates, even though Chart 4.6 seems to

indicate that the countries with work-based apprenticeship systems linking skill development with employment are associated with low rates of youth unemployment. Regression analysis shows that even after controlling for certain differences between education systems, the countries with an apprenticeship system have a youth unemployment rate 4 percentage points lower than that of countries which do not have employer-led systems. This difference is highly suggestive, as it equals almost half the average youth unemployment rate among all countries.

Of the countries with mainly school- or college-based vocational education systems, only Japan has so far escaped high youth unemployment. Although Japan does not have a dual system, in practice training takes place very largely in enterprises. Vocational high schools and colleges prepare young Japanese people for certain occupations, but in practice the recruitment system judges candidates according to their performance in general education. Employers

◆ Chart 4.6. **Type of vocational education and youth unemployment, 1992**[1]
Difference between youth and adult employment rates

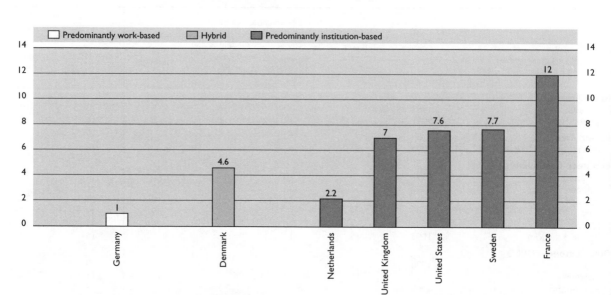

1.   Youth unemployment is measured as a percentage of the labour force aged 15-24 years. Adult unemployment is measured as a percentage of the labour force aged
     25-64 years.
Sources: OECD (1995d), *Education at a Glance – OECD Indicators*, Table C12(b), p. 42; and OECD (1995j), *Employment Outlook*, Table P, p. 218.

then rely on on-the-job career development to foster work-related skills and desired attitudes. In short, the countries that have witnessed the lowest youth unemployment rates are the ones in which employers are mainly responsible for training. These systems also share certain characteristics of stability, predictability and legitimacy: they are readily accepted by all those involved and provide clear routes. Young Japanese and German people know far more precisely than young American and French people what they have to do to get a particular kind of job. Thus, there is strong evidence that employer-led systems are more successful in facilitating the transition into employment than education-led ones.

That conclusion is forceful. However, successful employer-led systems depend on conditions and characteristics that are lacking in many OECD countries. Simply concluding that all countries should develop the apprenticeship model will not be helpful therefore to some policy-makers. How, then, can the efficiency of education-led systems be improved? The section below, based on findings in Stern (1994), explores this question by reviewing recent policy changes introduced in a range of OECD countries.

Policy changes in education-led systems

Chapter 3 noted that, in order to prepare individuals for work that demands intellectual curiosity and continuing learning, many employers now call for education and training that promote higher-order thinking for all students, not just for the élite, as in the past. Vocational education, which has traditionally concentrated on practical abilities, is now being reformed and, in some places, radically reorganised. Changes include strengthening the general content of vocational classes and making it easier to attract more intellectually talented students into vocational programmes, by offering them sufficient theoretical grounding to deal with new technology and problems as they appear. As noted in the previous chapter, the line between vocational and general education is becoming blurred. The blending of vocational and general education mirrors the convergence of working and learning in the workplace to a greater or lesser degree in all OECD countries.

In the United States there is now a proliferation of new programmes designed to integrate general and vocational education (Grubb *et al.*, 1991; Rosenstock,

1991). This followed revision in 1990 of the federal law on subsidising vocational education programmes run by states and localities. Prominent spokesmen for employers complained in the 1980s about the poor preparation of vocational graduates from secondary schools (National Academy of Sciences, 1984; Committee for Economic Development, 1985; Kearns and Doyle, 1988). Since employers had traditionally provided decisive political support for vocational education as a separate track, their complaints had a major impact. The 1990 law requires that all federal money for vocational education must be spent on programmes that integrate academic and vocational instruction. Examples include career academies, which organise the core curriculum of the secondary school around an occupational theme. Graduates from these academies may enter the workforce full-time, or they may pursue further studies at a college or university either continuing in the same field or transferring to an entirely different one. Evaluations have found that students in career academies achieve higher grades and are more likely to complete high school (Stern *et al.*, 1992). Another recent innovation in the United States is "tech prep", which combines the academic and vocational curricula and also links the last two years of secondary school with the first two years of post-secondary education (Hull and Parnell, 1991). These and related innovations have received additional impetus from the passage of the 1994 School-to-Work Opportunities Act.

Japan has just created a new, "integrated" vocational-academic upper secondary curriculum. Until 1994, such schools offered either a prescribed general curriculum as preparation for university or a specialised vocational curriculum. However, the proportion of students attending vocational secondary schools fell from 40 per cent in 1955 and 1965 to 26 per cent in 1992. Therefore, beginning in 1994, upper secondary schools were permitted to offer an integrated curriculum focusing on career development. Students in the integrated programme have fewer required subjects and are given career guidance to help them design their own course sequence. In 1994 very few schools introduced the integrated curriculum, but it was expected that the idea would catch on and promote "convergence of vocational and general education" (Yoshimoto, 1994, p. 5). This convergence has already occurred to some extent at the tertiary level, through the growth of special training colleges offering higher diplomas in industrial, commercial and other vocational fields. Enrolment in these institutions stood at 862 000 in 1992 – double the 1978

number, and more than one-third the 1992 enrolment level in universities.

France has created three sets of upper secondary diplomas: general, technical, and vocational *(baccalauréat professionnel)*. At age 15, after four years of lower secondary school most students either continue in a three-year upper secondary programme towards a general or technical diploma, or enter a two-year vocational programme. In 1985, the vocational diploma was introduced, giving graduates of two-year vocational programmes the option of receiving an upper secondary diploma after an additional two years. As of 1991/92, the number of students enrolled in the vocational diploma programme had grown to 114 000, compared to 707 000 preparing for general and 290 000 for technical diplomas (Kirsch, 1994). At the post-secondary level, students holding a general or technical diploma may continue studying for tertiary diplomas in technology. The majority of graduates from the university institutes of technology continue into further studies. The system thus allows students to enter a vocational programme at various ages, and to pursue occupational studies at a high level.

The dichotomy between vocational and academic routes will not disappear quickly or without struggle, since the traditional disciplines have been sanctified by time and it is still not sufficiently clear what will take their place. But there is pressure to create something new, in part because it is difficult to attract talented or ambitious students to vocational education.

High youth unemployment rates also indicate continuing problems with the school-to-work transition in most countries. Countries are following three principal approaches to improve the transition: *i)* augmenting the supply of high-quality vocational and training opportunities and redressing the balance between technical and academic education; *ii)* creating frameworks for the assessment, recognition and certification of training; and *iii)* introducing co-financing arrangements to even the sharing of costs and benefits.

Work-based learning for students

Apart from teaching knowledge and skills required on the job, the approach of education through work gives students practical experience for the purpose of learning. School-based enterprises that combine learning and productive work are another recent development. Examples of new initiatives can be found in many OECD countries:

- Sweden now requires students in the new three-year upper secondary programmes to spend 15 per cent of their time in a workplace. Most of these placements are unpaid. Students use the experience to conduct projects related to their courses (Vickers, 1994).

- Australia is creating "student traineeships" to allow those in grades 11 and 12 "to combine their school-based studies with work experience and off-the-job training". The government will fund the purchase of off-the-job training "for up to 5 000 students by 1995-96" (Keating, 1994, p. 93).

- France is making greater use of *alternance* (work-based learning). Traditional apprenticeship still exists in France on a minor scale (mainly in the craft industries), and work-based training contracts are used for unemployed young people. However, the placement of students in enterprises as part of their schooling did not begin on an extensive scale until the introduction of the vocational, secondary diploma (*baccalauréat professionnel*) in 1985. Students are required to spend at least 16 weeks in enterprises during the two-year programme. The traditional separation between formal education and employment in France has meant that these work experiences are often not closely connected with what is being studied in school. For instance, performance in the workplace has no effect on whether a student receives the diploma. Nonetheless, the fact that hundreds of thousands of students have been placed in enterprises has encouraged the education authorities to extend the practice of *alternance* to the two-year vocational programmes that begin at age 15 and precede the vocational diploma programme. The technical universities are also currently in the process of adding a third year that will consist mainly of traineeships in the workplace.

- The United Kingdom, where an initiative to create "modern apprenticeships" for 16- to 17-year-old school-leavers is being launched, offers government-funded training credits which students can cash in with employers who are able to provide the training required. Unlike traditional apprenticeships, these new schemes will not require trainees to spend a fixed length of time in an enterprise. Prototype programmes were developed in 1994 in 12 sectors, including agriculture and commercial horticulture, business administration, chemicals, child care, construction engineering, information technology, and retailing. There are expected to be 150 000 apprentices in training when the new system is fully up and running (Employment Department, 1994).

- Korea has restructured its vocational secondary curriculum to include one full year in enterprises during the three-year programme. It is hoped that this will help attract more students into vocational secondary schools, thus reducing the perceived oversupply of students going to university. At the same time, however, opportunities for vocational secondary school graduates to enter university will be expanded, again to increase the attractiveness of the vocational programme. The year of work experience for vocational upper secondary students is intended to enhance their adaptability in actual work situations (Cho, 1994).

While enterprises are developing methods of "just-in-time" learning and schools are giving more students the opportunity to learn in workplaces, the emergence of the knowledge- and learning-intensive economy is creating demands for hybrid organisations that combine education with production. One such hybrid is the school-based enterprise, which for the most part has been connected to vocational programmes in order to give students an opportunity to practice what they learn. Placements in firms may not be available or may not offer as much opportunity to learn as a school-based enterprise (Stern *et al.*, 1994). In addition, school enterprises are now taking on other tasks, including technology transfer and the development of better methods to build learning into the work process. Examples from three countries follow:

- In the United States, the school-based enterprise is a common feature of vocational and professional education. A 1992 survey for the National Assessment of Vocational Education (US Department of Education, 1994*b*) found that 19 per cent of secondary schools were operating some kind of enterprise that involved students in producing goods or services for other people as part of their school activities; most of these were associated with vocational programmes. For example, students in construction trades may build a house; those preparing for food service occupations may run a restaurant; classes in automotive trades often repair cars; a child care class may provide day care for clients outside the school. Similar programmes are offered in Community Colleges. These school-based enterprises are analogous to teaching hospitals run by medical schools, or law journals produced by law students. The school enterprise provides practical experience that helps prepare students for subsequent work in a particular occupation or industry.

– In Denmark, school-based enterprises, which are part of the apprenticeship system, provide experience for students who are waiting for training contracts with enterprises (Danish Ministry of Education, 1994, p. 101). Printing, retailing and construction are examples of activities carried out by school enterprises. Students normally expect to stay in the occupation for which they receive training. There are some indications that employers prefer to have trainees work in school-based enterprises during the early part of their training, when they are less profitable for firms.

– A particularly good example of school enterprise for the learning-based economy is the German-Singapore Institute (GSI) in Singapore. Founded in 1981 as a joint venture between the Economic Development Board of Singapore and the German Agency for Technical Co-operation, GSI calls itself a "teaching factory". It carries out development projects for local manufacturers while preparing technicians and middle managers in the fields of technology, factory automation and robotics, plastics manufacturing technology, and (since 1992) manufacturing software. Having enrolled about 1 100 students in 1994, GSI plans to admit 2 000 students a year in the next six years. Students spend most of their two or three years in laboratories equipped with state-of-the-art production equipment. The GSI model has been adopted in other countries, including Brazil and Malaysia.

In economies in which much or most work is becoming less routine, workers will need above all to respond flexibly to changing demands, to solve problems, to take responsibility and to work in teams with relatively flat hierarchies. General education may provide a better preparation for young people to learn skills at later stages of the occupational career than vocational training. On the other hand, vocational skills are better preparation for a smooth transition into employment than general education. There is a need to supply young people with both general and broad vocational skills. Thus a tension is created between the need for greater contact with the workplace – to ensure that learning is relevant – and the need for continued learning in formal institutions. This tension can only be addressed through greater convergence between general and work-oriented learning. The challenge posed – to both education systems and labour markets – is formidable. The response to that challenge might be a convergence of systems that, under a variety of institutional arrangements, seek to create balanced packages of learning in both workplaces and educational institutions – packages that will require co-operation between employers and educators at the final stages of pathways through initial education and training.

The role of guidance and counselling

Guidance and counselling are neglected in many national systems. They must play a more central role if lifelong learning is to become a reality – since a framework characterised by choice and individual pathways through learning and work must entail information and guidance if appropriate decisions are to be made. At present, too many students are obliged to rely on reputation and rumour for information. Effective guidance makes it easier for workers to continue learning and developing, by helping them to make good choices, by smoothing transitions of all kinds, by giving individuals access to information, and by encouraging them to take continuous responsibility for their own careers – whether inside or outside the workplace. At the same time, good guidance can reduce unemployment by improving the fit between the knowledge and skills of individuals and the opportunities offered to them on the labour market. A further potential benefit is the upgrading of the skills and qualifications of the workforce – as the result of alerting them to education and training opportunities – and a consequent increase in job satisfaction and, possibly, a reduction of inequality of opportunity.

Guidance services can be based in educational institutions, employment centres, or they can be independent. The education-based services are usually offered by school counsellors or guidance teachers, who have the important advantage of knowing and understanding the young people they are advising – but who sometimes lack information concerning job opportunities and the demands of the labour market. Moreover, their services are not generally available to young people who have left education or to adults. Employment centres often supply information to a wider age range, but their counselling services are sometimes confined to the unemployed, and those who work in them are not always qualified to offer a more broadly-based guidance service. This typical division of responsibility between education and labour authorities means that there may be some duplication, and sometimes conflicting agendas. Employers may feel that school-based guidance services do not pay enough attention to their interests, while educators tend to believe that the developmental needs of the young people sometimes risk being overlooked by the labour authorities.

So far as young people are concerned, careers education normally takes place in schools – but not always on a very consistent basis. In Mexico, for example, the needs of young drop-outs may be relatively neglected; in Austria, many university students lack appropriate guidance. Ideally, careers education should be part of the secondary school curriculum, integrated into an individual programme of learning. Constructive links with local enterprises can help individuals to develop the skills to create a personal learning project, which can be extended through further education, training and work.

Although various forms of educational guidance are well established in many OECD countries, most offer a rather patchy and incoherent service. The extent and quality of guidance for adults in transition varies widely but is generally inadequate. Some enterprises have career planning facilities for their employees – either in-house or using external consultants. Independent counselling services are perhaps the best solution for adults, but they have to depend on public funding, rely on voluntary help, or charge for their services.

Most OECD countries need to improve the operation of their systems if lifelong learning is to become a reality. In particular, training and updating for guidance counsellors needs to be markedly improved in terms of both quality and quantity. Many governments could have a positive effect on their national systems for relatively little financial outlay by sponsoring high-quality training packages, guidance materials and computer programmes – along the lines of the highly successful materials produced by Human Resources Development Canada and by the Canadian province of Alberta. Employers, also,

should be encouraged to take educational and career guidance more seriously. While the issue of wasteful duplication should be addressed, a pluralistic model, based in both education and labour, is likely to be the most effective in meeting the needs of a very diverse range of clients, especially adults, who require several different access routes. But unnecessary duplication should be minimised by rigorous auditing of the activities of different parts of the service, and effective liaison between different elements and interests is essential.

F. EDUCATION, TRAINING AND WORK-TO-WORK TRANSITIONS

This section addresses the relationship between coherent approaches to lifelong learning and labour market flexibility. It reviews the evidence of trade-offs in the effects of lifelong learning on both internal (within firm) and external flexibility, and considers the wider social benefits of adult education. Other issues include the relationship between on-the-job training and internal work organisation within firms; the effects of an ageing labour force on the need for lifelong learning; and the effects of training certification and standardisation on the demand for and supply of learning opportunities for adults.

Training programmes for the unemployed

Rising unemployment has focused attention on the issue of the transition between the worlds of work and education. Governments have attempted to devise a range of training measures designed to help those who have already left school to obtain qualifications in order to secure a worthwhile job. This is clearly a narrow focus and interpretation of the interface between lifelong learning and work. As argued above, what is required, in the perspective of lifelong learning, is to equip individuals to move between various alternatives, and back and forth within the realms of working while learning and learning while working. Active labour market programmes, particularly but not exclusively youth training schemes, need to be related to both general and vocational adult education. Adult basic and secondary education organised by Education Ministries exist all too often side by side with active labour market programmes governed by the employment services; in a lifelong learning framework, these separate provisions need to be better co-ordinated and linked more directly with the world of work, as in employer-led vocational training systems that emphasise *alternance*.

As shown in Chart 4.7 between 0 and 5.3 per cent of the labour force in OECD countries participate in training programmes for the unemployed. These programmes are distinguished by:

- Their timing: programmes in some countries commence after six months of unemployment; in others a person must be unemployed for at least two years to be eligible for training.

- Their targeting: some programmes are aimed at special target groups, whereas others select on the basis of motivation or trainability.

- Their type and duration.

- Their relation to work after training: some programmes guarantee participants work; others expect trainees to find a job themselves.

Training programmes for the unemployed are often complicated by multiple objectives that are not complementary. The two most common objectives are to help those finding the transition to employment difficult, by allowing them to have contact with the labour market and practice in work habits, and to offer an avenue for upskilling by providing high-quality training. Programmes created as a response to youth unemployment sometimes claim to have the latter objective but become dominated by the former. Ways of coping with this problem are to make a clear distinction between the different audiences involved, to improve guidance and counselling, to strengthen co-ordination between policy fields, and to create bridges between different programmes of active labour market and education policy.

Box 1 surveys some of the empirical research on the effectiveness of training programmes for unemployed workers. OECD (1993b) presents a summary of seventeen evaluation studies and concludes that the available evidence offers meagre support for the hypothesis that such programmes are effective. However, most studies show that the effects of training programmes are greater for women than for men. Haveman and Hollister (1991) claim that "in general, employment and training programmes have had their greatest impacts and largest social returns for those who have had the least previous labour market experience and are most disadvantaged. Most evaluations found that programmes work better for women than for men, for those less educated and poorer than for those better educated and with higher income". They also conclude that intensive, firm-based skill-training

◆ Chart 4.7. ***Active labour market programmes: training of unemployed adults and those at risk, 1993/94***[1]
Percentage of the labour force

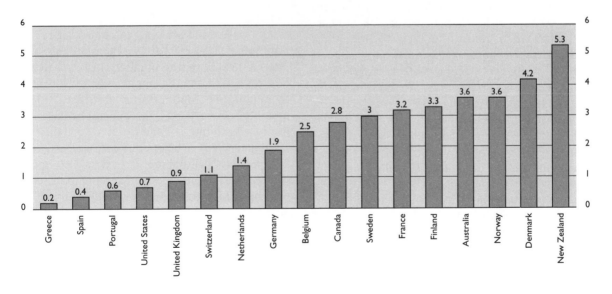

1. 1992/93 data for the United States.
Source: OECD (1995j), *Employment Outlook*, Table T, pp. 222-230. See also Table A.52.

Box 1.   **Effectiveness of training programmes for the unemployed**

Moffit (1992) surveys the effects of training programmes on welfare recipients in the United States. The main conclusions of this survey are: *i)* training programmes clearly have positive earnings effects; *ii)* calculation of the net monetary social benefits – which acknowledge the costs of implementing the programme, the transfer payment costs, and the value of output produced by the welfare recipients – generally shows positive effects; *iii)* these programmes however, are no panacea for the problems of low incomes among female-headed households – a large change in the poverty rate of female-headed households.

Barnow (1987) and Riddell (1991) survey the effects of the Comprehensive Employment and Training Act (CETA) in the United States. They conclude that women are generally found to benefit more from training than men. In terms of the different services offered by the programme, public service employment and on-the-job training generally had the highest estimated impact, and classroom training and work experience the lowest. However, the range of estimates of the various studies is quite large, which mars the conclusions.

Björklund (1991) surveys evaluation studies of Swedish training programmes. The results of this review are ambiguous: half the studies cited find that training programmes have negative earning effects, while the other half find (weakly) positive effects. Björklund and Moffitt (1987) analysing the wage effects of training programmes for the unemployed in Sweden, find that the average is 6.5 per cent. They further find that the marginal wage effects are negative. The implication of this finding is that the average wage would decrease if everyone were to receive training. Unlimited access to training is therefore not efficient.

Ridder (1986) evaluates employment programmes, wage cost subsidies and training programmes in the Netherlands. The results suggest that training programmes have no effect on the stability of re-employment for unemployed workers who are older than 35. They are most effective for women, ethnic minorities and younger workers, in that order.

---

programmes for youth may be very effective, and that job search and placement efforts generate at least short-term benefits at low cost. With regard to seriously disadvantaged men, it is difficult to draw conclusions because of the lack of evaluation studies, which points to a general problem: Europe lags behind the United States in the availability of good evaluation studies of labour market programmes (Buechtemann and Ryan, 1996). In conclusion, it appears that even within the narrow perspective of training for pursuing employment, there are difficulties with such programmes, particularly those that are disconnected from both the education system and the job market, in that the evidence appears unfavourable to labour market policy interventions for youth and young adults. The results are, however, not entirely negative: the broad attributes of employer-led systems, which link more general education, specific vocational skills training, and work-based learning, are expected to yield greater benefits than partial, short-lived and institutionally detached youth training schemes. This, again, points to the necessity for efficient policy co-ordination in the perspective of lifelong learning.

Training and work-to-work transitions

This section examines evidence on the incidence, distribution, effectiveness and value of on-the-job training for workers. According to *The OECD Jobs Study*, on-the-job training increases labour market flexibility (OECD, 1994*d*). Two types are relevant here: internal flexibility (the number of tasks a worker can be assigned to and the employment of workers within the enterprise) and external flexibility (job-to-job mobility). Investments in "general" human capital increase both internal and external flexibility (Becker, 1962 and 1975). Higher-educated workers are more "employable" within the firm; they also voluntarily change jobs more frequently than poorly-educated workers. Investments in "specific" human capital also increase internal flexibility, in particular if the training takes the form of "multi-skilling" (Cappelli, 1993). However, on-the-job training may decrease external flexibility; and the value of the shared investment in specific human capital may be reduced when workers move to another enterprise.

Labour market flexibility also has an effect on training provision. Workers with a high propensity to quit are less interested than others in investing in on-the-job training. Workers may be more inclined to quit if the opportunities for promotion are small. Less internal flexibility may therefore increase external flexibility, and higher external flexibility may decrease the opportunities for profitable investments in on-the-job training. Workers who frequently change jobs are also less likely to be selected for training by the employer (Booth, 1992). As a result, higher external flexibility leads to less investment in specific human capital. As was shown previously in Chart 4.4, turnover rates are lowest in Japan and highest in the United States; European countries are somewhere in the middle. Accordingly, it is to be expected that the Japanese and European economies are more characterised by low turnover and high training intensity, and the United States' economy relatively more by high turnover and low training intensity.

Non-formal learning at work and the economic returns

Access to both formal and non-formal learning in the workplace is not equal for all workers. The conclusions that can be drawn from a vast body of research on this subject are as follows:

– The likelihood of participation in on-the-job training increases with the level of education: higher-educated workers receive more on-the-job training than poorly educated ones.

– Men receive more on-the-job training than women.

– Full-time workers receive more training than part-timers.

– The participation rate decreases with age, work experience and tenure.

– The probability of receiving training is to a large extent determined by occupational and industrial characteristics. Workers in higher-level positions participate in training more frequently. Public sector workers participate in training more frequently than private sector workers.

Chart 4.8 presents figures on participation in job-related continuing education and training by education level for some Member countries (OECD, 1995k).

◆ Chart 4.8. **Participation in job-related continuing education and training by level of education**[1]
Percentage of the employed population aged 25-64, early 1990s

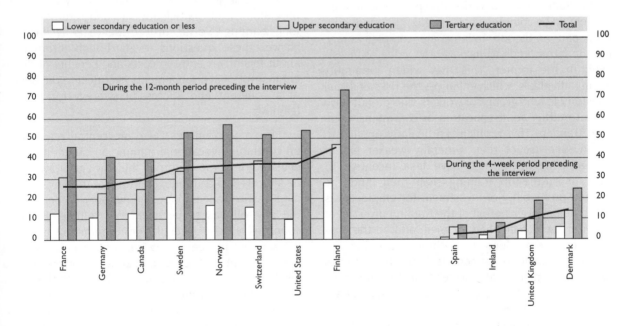

1. A definition of job-related continuing education and training for adults is given in OECD (1995d), p. 366.
Source: OECD (1995d), *Education at a Glance – OECD Indicators*. See also Table A.53.

Between 30 and 40 per cent of workers in the countries surveyed had participated in training in the 12-month period preceding the survey. The participation rate among highly-educated workers was three to five times higher than among poorly-educated workers. Between 10 and 20 per cent of the latter had participated in training, while in all countries surveyed participation was over 40 per cent among highly-educated workers (see also Chapter 8).

What factors can explain this uneven distribution of learning opportunities? Employers use observable characteristics of individuals – such as education – as a selection device for hiring new workers. Education is seen as a proxy for the amount of formal on-the-job training and non-formal learning at work that the employer will need to invest in the worker, since higher-educated workers are expected to need less training, at least initially. Thus employers hire the highest-educated worker, irrespective of the requirements of the job. This theory, therefore, predicts a positive return to educational attainment over and above that which seems to be required by the job, and a negative effect of perceived "overschooling" on the participation rate in firm-based training.

However, results from the empirical research on the costs and benefits of continuing vocational training – summarised in Box 2 – suggest that initial formal education and on-the-job training are complementary rather than alternatives. In OECD (1991a) it was concluded that "education and post-school training seem to be complements" (p. 152). If formal education and on-the-job training are complementary, then the latter tends to increase the value of investments in the former. This may widen inequality among individuals, which enhances the risks of social exclusion of some groups of workers who do not have access to either adult education or continuing vocational training. This problem particularly applies to women. Because of their generally weaker labour force attachment, women have less incentive to invest in on-the-job training than men, and the expected profitability of investment for employers is lower. The pay-back period of the training investment is shorter for women than for men, and so the economic returns to female on-the-job training are reduced. As their investment is less, the earnings growth for women is also lower than that for men, thus increasing the male-female wage gap (see Chapter 1). This completes a vicious circle of lower labour force attachment: less on-the-job training → lower wage growth → lower wages → weaker labour force attachment.

Occupational stratification may be another part of the explanation of why workers with higher levels of initial education also receive more education and training on the job. University graduates and holders of advanced degrees are usually given preference in hiring for positions at managerial and professional levels. These are also the levels at which greater amounts of in-service education and training are provided.

Differences in the "pay-back" period of the investment in work-related lifelong learning for adults explain why full-time workers tend to receive more training than part-time workers. This profitability rationale extends to older workers as well. What are the effects of the "greying" of the labour force – reviewed in Chapter 1, Section B – on the need for lifelong learning? Productivity may decrease with age, but this can be compensated by training. Nevertheless, Chart 4.9 shows that, with the exception of Sweden, participation in continuing vocational training among older workers is lower than among younger workers. The participation rate among workers aged 45-64 is only one-quarter to two-thirds that among workers aged 25-34. This situation has adverse effects on the labour force flexibility of older workers, who change jobs less frequently than younger workers and are also less mobile within the establishment. A relevant question is how labour market flexibility can be increased, and what are the possible effects of institutional arrangements, such as early retirement programmes, on participation in and returns to lifelong learning? So far, little evidence is available to answer these questions, even though information about incentives and the costs and benefits of different institutional arrangements is critical to the design of a coherent and successful strategy for lifelong learning.

In some countries there are central regulations on continuing vocational training; in others it is deregulated. In some countries the amount of money to be allocated to continuing vocational training is specified – as in France, where a mandatory 1.5 per cent of the pay-roll has to be spent on training. In other countries with such regulation, the amount is lower: 0.7 per cent in Spain, 0.25 per cent in Belgium, and 0.20 per cent in Greece. In Sweden, workers have a legal entitlement to educational leave. At the other end of the spectrum there are countries where the government refrains completely from imposing regulation. In Germany, continuing vocational training is regarded as a market good which should remain as free as possible from government intervention. A self-

Box 2. **The effects of training**

Almost all available evidence suggests that continuing vocational training has substantial productivity effects. Barron *et al.* (1989) use an employer rating of the productivity of new hirings on a scale of 0-100, where 100 equals the maximum productivity rating an employee can obtain at this position, and 0 is absolutely no productivity by the employee. The productivity rating of the new employee is compared with the productivity of a typical employee after two years on the job. The results show that on-the-job training has a significantly positive effect on productivity and wages: a 10 per cent increase in training time raises productivity growth by 3 per cent and raises wages by 1.5 per cent. Similar findings are reported by Bishop (1987 and 1989*b*). Apart from training, few variables appear to affect wage and productivity growth. They also find that the effect of relevant previous experience on wage and productivity growth is U-shaped.

Bishop (1991), using the same data set as Barron *et al.*, finds that the elasticity of productivity growth with respect to training time is 0.09 at establishments with 18.5 employees and about 0.12 for companies with 200 employees. The impact of training on wage growth is small, and less than one-fifth of the impact on productivity growth.

Groot (1993) uses data on individual productivity ratings of employees in the Netherlands to generalise both the individual wage and productivity growth of workers who received training, and the wage and productivity differences between trained and non-trained workers. The duration of training has a positive effect on productivity growth, wage growth, productivity differences and wage differences. The average productivity growth of training is 16 per cent, and the average productivity difference 8 per cent. The average wage growth is less than a quarter of the average productivity growth.

Research on the wage effects of continuing vocational training in the United States includes Mincer (1988), Barron *et al.* (1989), Brown (1989), Holzer (1988), Lynch (1991), and Lillard and Tan (1986). A survey of this research leads to the conclusion that the wage effect of continuing vocational education is between 4 and 16 per cent (OECD, 1991*a*).

Evidence for positive wage effects of continuing vocational training in the United Kingdom can be found in Greenhalgh and Stewart (1987), Booth (1992), and Groot and Oosterbeek (1995). Greenhalgh and Stewart find that vocational training yields significant returns, but the marginal benefit of further weeks of training falls to zero once the individual has accumulated four weeks. They also find evidence to suggest that the acquired skills depreciate within a decade or so.

For the Netherlands, Groot *et al.* (1994) find higher values for the wage and welfare effects of participation in continuing vocational training. They find that on average, participants in continuing vocational training earn 11 per cent more than non-participants. They further find that participants are better off with firm-sponsored training than self-financed or self-directed learning. For a representative worker in the sample, the wage effect is 21.2 per cent.

Blanchflower and Lynch (1992) compare the structure of post-school education and training for young non-university graduates in the United Kingdom and the United States. Their principal finding is that non-college graduates in the United Kingdom receive much more post-school training than similar youths in the United States. They further find that the rates of return to post-school training in both countries is high, especially in the United States.

regulating system also operates in the Netherlands. In Italy, government intervention is limited; further training being seen as the responsibility of the enterprise or public sector employers.

The following conclusions can be drawn from the findings in Box 2:

– Continuing vocational education of a formal type and non-formal learning in the workplace both increase worker productivity.

– Training has a substantial effect on wages; workers typically receive between one-third and half of the substantial benefits accruing to the investments in learning made by employers.

Despite the fact that employees receive a substantial benefit from enterprise-based training, other research indicates that they do not pay much of it (Stern and Ritzen, 1991). This means that employees receive a very high rate of return to their small invest-

◆   Chart 4.9.   *Participation in job-related continuing education and training by age groups*[1]
Percentage of the employed population aged 25-64, early 1990s

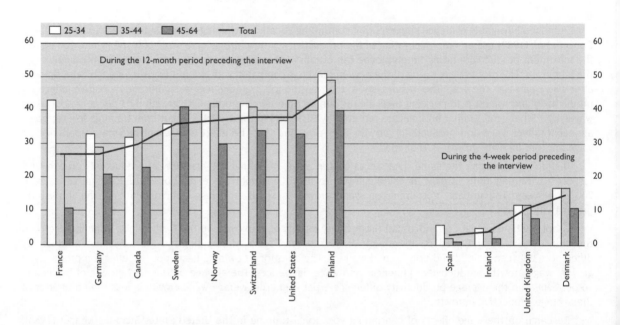

1.   See notes to Table A.53 and A.54.
Source: OECD (1995d), *Education at a Glance – OECD Indicators.*

ment in enterprise-based training – in some cases higher than the rate of return received by the sponsoring employers. Yet employers exercise more control over the amount of training provided. Presumably, employers' decisions will tend to reflect the rate of return they themselves receive, not the higher rate of return received by their employees (see also Chapter 8). This implies that the amount of training provided will be less than what would be warranted by the social rate of return, where the social rate of return is an average of the rates of return received by employers and workers. Additional explanations supporting the case for under-investment in training are put forward by Stern and Ritzen (1991): *i)* uncertainty about the returns; *ii)* liquidity constraints: *iii)* wage legislation; *iv)* displacement by subsidised training for the unemployed; *v)* complementarity between general and specific training; *vi)* restrictions imposed by labour contracts; *vii)* unemployement insurance and transfers which facilitate the substitution of older by younger workers.

Social returns to adult education

There has frequently been under-investment in training because the full returns are not easily quanti-

fied. Appreciating the returns to adult education which is not immediately tied to vocational needs is even more difficult, given the near total absence of a statistical knowledge base. A common-sense belief is that there are two principal benefits of such provision: social cohesion and personal development.

As discussed in Chapter 3, there is a divergence between the culture of youth and that of the surrounding society. In association with rising unemployment and individualisation at the workplace, this poses a threat to social cohesion. The continued ability and opportunity to relate to other members of the community are therefore of crucial importance to the functioning of democratic societies. Such ability and opportunity can be gained by some work-based relationships, but will for many others depend upon the accessibility of educational activities.

Personal development, which can only be ensured through some form of lifelong learning, contributes both to performance and productivity, and to general physical and mental health. A number of employers have already recognised the importance of the personal development of staff, and support general education in the arts and other non-vocational fields.

In the interests of equity and social cohesion, adult education should be available to all members of the community and not restricted to those working for certain employers. The question of funding is dealt with particularly in Chapter 8, but the principle should be acknowledged that provision should not cease at the normal age of retirement, since active life extends well beyond that age, and the social integration of those above it can also be ensured through education. It will become commonplace to learn while working, but lifelong learning by definition also embraces the unemployed, the poorly-educated, women with weak attachment to the labour market, the retired and every other member of the community, and it includes learning which may be regarded as general and at first sight unconnected with paid work.

G. THE VALUE OF EDUCATION AND TRAINING

In determining the need for and value of lifelong learning in a human capital perspective, two questions must be answered. Is there under-utilisation of the skills of inefficiently-allocated workers and, if so, is this a temporary phenomenon? Secondly, is there evidence that poorly-educated workers are displaced by more highly educated workers?

Under-utilisation of knowledge and skills leads to an allocation of people to jobs that is less than economically efficient, and frustrating for the individual. Under-utilisation is associated with the displacement of poorly-skilled by higher-skilled workers, resulting in higher unemployment rates for the poorly-skilled and a decrease in the private rate of return to education and training. The problems of under-utilisation and displacement are highly relevant in a policy strategy designed to increase learning opportunities and attainments for all people regardless of age, sex or employment status. Will lifelong learning merely aggravate the "diploma disease", and restrict even further the opportunities to work, learn and prosper of those who missed out, for whatever reasons, in their initial education trajectory? Fortunately, the evidence offered in Box 3 suggests that the incidence of skill under-utilisation decreases with age and work experience (Groot, 1995). This finding suggests that the problem is to an extent only a temporary one, and that displacement is concentrated among entrants into the labour market.

The signals from the labour market to young people are often mixed. On the one hand, employers say they want workers with immediately relevant skills. On the other, it is clearer than ever that high levels of general education lead to better job prospects. In most OECD countries, an adult with a university degree can expect to earn 1.5 times to twice as much as one with only an upper secondary qualification; university graduates are only half as likely, on average, as all adults to be unemployed (OECD, 1995d). Education is not a homogeneous good, and the returns also differ by the type of education received. The annual wage growth rates for university graduates in the United Kingdom in the 1980s varied from 2 per cent for theology to 24 per cent for law (Dolton, 1992). Table 4.8 shows for four countries the share of technically-educated workers in the labour force and the difference between the average net wage rates of technical and non-technical workers. Both in the United States and in the United Kingdom, technical workers (on average) earn substantially more than non-technical workers. In the Netherlands and Germany, the net average wage differentials between technical and non-technical educated workers are much smaller, but the share of technically-educated workers in the workforce in these countries is higher than in the United States and the United Kingdom. The four-country comparison seems to suggest that the lower relative earnings prospects for technically-educated workers in Germany and the Netherlands have not, so far, caused their share to drop below the level observed in other countries. The results in Table 4.8 rather seem to suggest that a relatively large share of technically-educated workers causes a lower wage differential between the two groups.

Model 3, reviewed in Section D, offers one way of dealing with allocation and distribution problems which can, potentially, lower the benefits expected from a lifelong learning strategy: to make academic and vocational routes in secondary and tertiary education less separate, and to establish "parity of esteem". This is the option chosen by Germany. Attempts are under way in the United Kingdom and France to develop vocational equivalents to academic qualifications, although in neither country has genuine equal esteem yet been achieved. Denmark, however, has come a long way. Of the 42 per cent of each age cohort entering tertiary education, slightly over half come from the academic *gymnasium*; the rest come directly from various vocational and technical upper secondary programmes that automatically qualify students for further education. Thus, the 94 per cent of young Danes who enrol in upper secondary education following compulsory schooling do not seal their futures by taking up a particular option. There seems to be a delicate balance, therefore,

Box 3. **The screening theory of education**

Screening theory actually refers to a range of theories that challenge the human capital assumption of the productivity-augmenting role of education. The general term "screening" is often used to indicate that education serves as a signal for pre-existing abilities, or as a means for the already better off to get the best jobs. In the first view – education as a signal – wages still equal marginal productivity. In the latter view – the credentialist view of education – which can be ascribed to Berg (1970) and Thurow (1970) – education only serves as an admission ticket for certain professions. The existence of a relation between productivity and wages is questioned. Since productivity is not altered by schooling, total output is not raised.

According to the signalling view, education yields useful information to identify individuals with a higher expected productivity. This set of theories includes the filtering theory (Arrow, 1973,) the screening theory (Stiglitz, 1975) and the signalling theory in the strict sense (Spence, 1974; Riley, 1976). In these theories the (empirical) relation between education and wages is a result of the productivity-identifying role of education; the exact extent to which education has a productivity-augmenting effect as well remains an open question. In either case, educational achievement serves as signals for employers and results in an efficient allocation of employees over jobs.

If education serves as an admission ticket or credential for a better job with higher earnings, there is a premium for completion of a course with a certificate. Early school-leavers or drop-outs would thus have, averaged over their years of schooling, a lower return to education than those who completed their course with a certificate. Layard and Psacharopoulos (1974) compare the returns and conclude that there are no significant differences between these two groups. Hungerford and Solon (1987) also compare year-to-year returns and find that the rate in the first and last year is higher than in the years in between. The first finding confirms the prediction by Arrow (1973) that admittance to higher education (college) itself yields an income benefit.

Groot and Oosterbeek (1994) divide actual years of education into effective years (the shortest, most efficient path to attain a certain level of education), inefficient routing years (skipping and repeating classes, and years spent inefficiently), and drop-out years (spent in education without receiving a diploma). This division is such that the actual number of years of education is equal to the sum of effective years, repeated years (minus) skipped years, inefficient years, and drop-out years. This decomposition allows the screening theory to be tested against the human capital theory. This test relies on two predictions of the screening theory: first, that years spent in education without obtaining a degree should not increase earnings, and second, that a more rapid completion of a degree signals greater ability and should therefore lead to higher earnings. For males, the results strongly support the human capital theory and refute the predictions of the screening hypothesis. Skipped years have a significantly negative influence on future earnings. According to the screening hypothesis this effect should be positive, since skipping a class gives a positive signal to potential employers whereas within a human capital framework the finding can be explained as the manifestation of a less-than-thorough understanding of the curriculum. Repeated years have no effect on future earnings. This is in accordance with the human capital theory, whereas the screening hypothesis predicts a negative effect because of the negative signal repeated years give to employers. The absence of influence on earnings from inefficient years of education agrees with both the human capital and screening predictions. Finally, a positive return on drop-out years is found. This is in line with the human capital theory and refutes the screening theory. For women too, all results are in line with the human capital predictions and reject the screening theory.

between maintaining the option of further study so as to avoid stigma, and maintaining a sufficient flow of graduates going directly into employment so as to justify employers' investment. As long as pathways in lifelong learning and work are connected by a series of bridges and ladders, at all stages and levels of education, and during all phases of the work career, skills under-utilisation and displacement in the labour market are less of a problem than that of under-investment in lifelong learning.

Several countries have launched initiatives to improve the relevance and marketability of educational programmes. New Zealand has established a single national framework for the recognition of school, vocational and higher academic qualifications. The United Kingdom has introduced a system that awards upper secondary education certificates for a combination of academic and vocational studies, and that meets agreed workplace standards – a controversial approach whose results are yet to be

Table 4.8. **Share of technically educated and differences between the net wage rate of technically educated and non-technically educated by education level**[1, 2]

	Upper secondary education		Tertiary education	
	Share of technically educated	Difference in average net wage rate	Share of technically educated	Difference in average net wage rate
Germany	51.3	Technically educated earn 1% more than non-technically educated	45.4	Non-technically educated earn 9% more than technically educated
Netherlands	46.0	Non-technically educated earn 5 to 8% more than technically educated	23.0	Non-technically educated earn 1.5% more than technically educated
United Kingdom	37.1	Technically educated earn 17% more than non-technically educated	39.9	Technically educated earn 5.8% more than non-technically educated
United States	23.0	Technically educated earn 17% more than non-technically educated	20.8	Technically educated earn 14% more than non-technically educated

1. Upper secondary education refers to completed ISCED 3 or less; tertiary education refers to the attainment of a degree, diploma or certificate at ISCED 5, 6 or 7.
2. Share of technically educated in the labour force.
Source: Groot (1995).

assessed (see Chapter 6). Germany has attempted to put qualifications for part-time vocational studies on an equal footing with those for intermediate general education, and university entrance certificates are being awarded by vocational institutions. Japan has taken steps to ensure that qualifications acquired in special training schools are fully recognised by the universities. Canada has established a system for the recognition of prior learning on the basis of testing. But these steps, while promising, are still rather modest in relation to the perceived need to enhance the recognition of skills and competencies and to ensure their value in the domains of lifelong learning and work.

H. LIFELONG LEARNING AND WORK: POLICY CONCLUSIONS

This chapter has addressed a range of policy questions and issues surrounding the relationship between progressions in education and lifelong learning and transitions to and within the labour market. The focus has been on employment rather than the links between transitions in lifelong learning, culture and democracy. This narrow focus is to an extent determined by the type, quantity and reliability of the evidence available. Further studies will need to inquire into the wider aspects of transitions within the lifelong learning framework. This section seeks to

answer the three questions posed in Section B of this chapter before offering directions for policy.

Are the current levels and the current direction of investment adequate to meet the requirements of a coherent approach to lifelong learning for all? Participation in initial schooling, tertiary education and further training can be less than efficient. When it is, is under-investment in human capital the result? Inefficiency arises mainly because of the uncertainty about individual and social returns. The costs are immediate, but the returns accrue in the future and are imprecise and uncertain. If individuals are averse to risk, they will be reluctant to embark on major learning tasks. Another reason for insufficient investment in lifelong learning is that many people do not have the funds to pay fees, and need to take out loans in order to do so. Banks and financial institutions are generally unwilling to finance investments in education and training since human capital cannot, at present, be treated as a collateral security. To counter this deficiency, governments can step in with student loans and subsidies.

Two problems affect the education system. Firstly, young people do not stay in the system long enough. Early school-leaving and dropping-out are particularly worrying phenomena. Because employers use certificates as a mechanism for screening prospective workers and the process of job entry often determines career prospects, including opportunities for further learning and training at work, governments need to ensure that all young people acquire the necessary foundations before leaving the formal education system – the contribution of the social partners in employer-led systems must be noted here. Secondly, some students stay too long in the initial education system, that is to say, they could have been better off had they acquired the skills needed in the workplace. Inefficient routings through the system and stacking of different types of education within the same level are examples of problems that can lead to a massive, but often counterproductive, enrolment in the initial formal system, especially at the tertiary level. Thus, the skills some employees eventually bring to the job may, at least in the beginning of their work careers, be under-utilised. But the analysis presented in this chapter suggests that "over-education" is not a serious problem in the long term because the additional knowledge and skills workers bring to their jobs make them more flexible and enhance their capacity to continue learning throughout life.

In general, more public money is spent on formal initial education than on adult education and training. For certain groups, under-investment at the post-school stage presents a serious obstacle. The first of these groups is composed of unemployed workers, who have less access to opportunities for lifelong learning – especially employer-sponsored training – than employed workers. A second group consists of adults with poor initial education, who are often considered less trainable by employers and incur more cost and effort in acquiring the knowledge and skills they need. A third group comprises older workers and senior citizens for whom the monetary benefits of lifelong learning are lower than for younger workers, because fewer years remain to reap the returns on their investment. Older workers have less incentive to invest in job- or career-related training, although motivation to take part in consumption-oriented general adult education may be high. The final group is composed of women who, in many countries, participate less in job-related training than men. Because women tend to have weaker ties to the labour market than men, their returns to vocational training tend to be lower. Conversely, women in certain countries are over-represented in more general adult education programmes.

The conditions under which employers are willing to finance or sponsor programmes for initial or continuing vocational training do not always coincide with those sought by governments or educators.

Costs are important because high-quality programmes are expensive (see Chapter 8). Moreover, there is the possibility that an apprentice will opt for further study rather than immediate employment after completing a programme or that an employee who undergoes training may terminate his or her employment once a better qualification has been achieved. A straightforward policy solution to this problem, as in France, is to offer public subsidies to employers who provide work experience or training to young people or to their workers in general on the grounds that in a mobile labour market – above all a mobile learning market – the benefits accrue not just to the host employer but also to individual trainees, to other employers and to the economy as a whole. A similar rationale creates a case for taxing companies that fail to provide a sufficient quantity of training. As labour market flexibility increases, it seems inevitable that at least some public intervention of this type will be needed to sustain a satisfactory overall level of investment in lifelong learning and skill formation.

The high rates of return to individuals from job-related adult education and training may point to under-investment. Insufficient provision can be remedied if the risk premium to firms and individuals is reduced by public subsidies. Improving skill certification procedures, or creating them where they do not already exist, should also help to remedy the under-provision of enterprise-based training, by enabling individuals to demonstrate what they have learned, and thereby encouraging them to invest more in training. Another option is collective action by the social partners, especially joint initiatives launched by employers and unions within sectors and branches of the labour market. Distortions can also be adjusted by allowing a multiplier on the direct training cost as tax-deductible. The multiplier can be made to vary with the business cycle, to prevent firms from cutting back on training expenditures during periods of recessions. Subsidising counter-cyclical training has been effective in countries including Japan and Sweden. Other possibilities might include arrangements by which firms can borrow money from governments on financial markets to finance training for their workers and in which the pay-off period is linked to the time the worker remains with the firm. If the worker leaves the enterprise, and the investment has to be written off, the outstanding part of the loan is paid through capital insurance funds.

Chapters 5 and 8 further explore the question of what governments can do to redress the problem of under-investment in lifelong learning for adults, and offer concrete suggestions for determining policy. Meanwhile, the next question for policy-makers has to do with the inaccessibility of lifelong learning opportunities for some groups, resulting in disadvantages and even social exclusion, and what governments can do to improve the social distribution of learning opportunities. This question raises again the issue of foundation learning, reviewed in Chapter 3. *In the perspective of lifelong learning, what should be the proper balance between general and vocational education, both in initial and in further education and training?*

Initial formal education is the foundation for learning later in life. It is sometimes argued that general qualifications lower the cost of training in the future, and that the greater participation of higher-educated workers in on-the-job training can be seen as proof. This suggests that general knowledge and skills improve the efficiency of lifelong learning, while specific vocational skills do not, or do so to a lesser degree. From a lifelong learning perspective it may be preferable to endow young people with general knowledge and skills rather than with narrow vocational qualifications. However, young people with vocational qualifications have smoother transitions from school to work, if those qualifications are acquired in an employer-led system. Further, within the same education level, starting wages in most Member countries are higher for school-leavers with vocational qualifications than for young workers with general education.

This may indicate that there is a trade-off between efficiency in the short and long run, that is, between a rapid, smooth transition to employment with vocational qualifications and a delayed transition offering better and more durable lifetime career perspectives with a general education. However, it may be that a smooth transition from school to work does have a positive effect on lifelong learning opportunities and long-run efficiency. If there is a state of dependency in unemployment, if youth unemployment has long-lasting effects on career prospects, if unemployment at the start of working life implies a higher risk of being locked into a sequence of unstable jobs with few opportunities for training and advancement, then there are evidently also long-term benefits accruing from broad vocational qualifications. The same holds true if unemployment leads to a depreciation of human capital, because skills become out-of-date and obsolete, and few new skills are acquired during spells of unemployment.

In all OECD countries the main dividing line between pathways in education runs between general and academic education on the one hand, and employment-oriented vocational education and training on the other. Clear-cut differentiation occurs in North America mostly at the tertiary stage, while in most European countries it originates in the structures of upper secondary education. Further, in all countries there are questions about the parity of esteem and comparative value of general-academic and vocational-technical education at the tertiary level. These concerns are being addressed by attempts to integrate general and vocational content in the same programmes, and to build bridges and ladders between separate general and vocational tracks.

Given the objectives of lifelong learning, what changes in education and training systems might improve the transitions from school to work, from unemployment to employment, and from one job to another? Inefficient transitions from school to work result in spells of unemployment by school-leavers. Some vocational qualifications facilitate the immediate school-to-work transition. There are, essentially, two models for the provision of vocational education: one has employers taking the lead, the other assigns the larger role to educational institutions. In either case, there are both equity and efficiency implications. However, the evidence suggests that the former is more effective in smoothing the transition from school to work. The best-known example of an employer-led system is the dual system.

Inefficient transitions from unemployment to employment are those that do not result in relatively stable employment. Training programmes for unemployed workers are meant to provide the answer. However, programmes do not always achieve the desired results and may even have a counterproductive effect. The programmes need to be linked therefore, both structurally and through effective career guidance, with the mainstream pathways in the education and training system.

Job-to-job transitions point to the need for flexibility of workers and enterprises. Firm-specific on-the-job training strengthens employment because trained workers are less likely to quit or to be made redundant. Lower turnover rates, however, may be at odds with a policy of increasing the flexibility of the labour market. The apparent paradox is that training may do both: improve the flexibility of workers and enterprises while reducing that of the labour market as a whole. Therefore, it is also necessary to encourage enterprise-based training that has some general, transferable content. Some of this training can be provided more cost-effectively in enterprises than in schools. Attention needs to be given to measures which will actively encourage labour flexibility, including certification of on-the-job learning, portability of such certification, and access to career guidance.

Bridging these three factors is a key objective: What is, or should be the role of governments and their partners in implementing strategies to avoid early school-leaving and dropping out, improving school-to-work transitions, and enhancing the supply of well-educated and trained workers ready to learn and face tomorrow's challenges?

Possible directions for policy

The main conclusions and suggestions for policy can be summarised as follows:

– The conditions and types of pathways in lifelong learning and transitions to the labour market are related to many country-specific features of education and training systems and their relationship with labour markets. Any action aimed at improving coherence or linkages must take these particularities into account. It must be based on careful analysis of the specific relationship in each country between employment and unemployment, wages, the provision of organised learning opportunities, and whether such learning leads to recognised qualifications.

– The amount and quality of the knowledge and skills acquired initially determine not only occupational and life careers, but also future investments in learning. This implies that unless counter-measures are adopted, the expansion of lifelong learning opportunities in a "free marketplace" will increase inequality among individuals and social groups.

– Enabling young people to acquire broad general and vocational skills by means of modern apprenticeship or *alternance* systems improves the efficiency of the transition from school to work. In countries where there are close links between educational institutions and firms, the transition is more efficient than in systems where there are weak links. The conditions for fruitful and enduring co-operation between schools and enterprises are specific and not easy to achieve.

– In countries where an employer-led or apprenticeship system is not already in place, a range of policies is required, given the variety of individual learning needs and interests as well as differences in objective and functioning of enterprises and public administrations:

• Institutions and programmes must be flexible and responsive to changing labour market conditions as well as to the changing behaviour and priorities of employers and young people.

• Programmes must maximise collaboration among employers, educators and public agencies, in both decision-making and the creation of appropriate incentives for people to participate.

• To give young people practice in using the workplace as a site for learning, enterprises should be encouraged to provide opportunities for work-based learning, and schools can organise productive activities under their own auspices.

• An alternative approach to bringing work experience into schools is to provide educational institutions at all levels with a legal framework enabling them to offer paid services to the public. Examples of such school- and college-based enterprises are construction, catering, vehicle repair and software development.

• Programmes must create a favourable balance between the initiation of young people into the workforce and measures aimed at their longer-term development. The idea of lifelong learning indeed challenges the very notion of a single "transition" period between education and employment.

• The needs and hopes of each young person must be the focus of any strategy. Individuals must have more control over their own learning and career development instead of being expected to follow predetermined pathways.

• Early school-leaving, drop-out should be discouraged and school failure prevented not only by the relevance of the curriculum and school-work links discussed in this chapter and in Chapter 3, but also by reconsideration of the statutory age limit for compulsory education. Pupils not attaining an adequate basic level of secondary education could be obliged to continue in education beyond the compulsory age. This might be part-time if they enter employment.

• Social assistance transfers and unemployment benefits should not pose undue obstacle to people wishing to pursue studies to acquire new skills and qualifications.

• Firms should be encouraged by appropriate tax regimes or other incentives to provide training for their own employees and, where practicable, for other learners. Conversely, higher taxation may be applied to employers which do not provide or support training.

• Employers, banks and financial institutions must be encouraged to devise accounting procedures so that investment in human capital can be treated on the same grounds as investment in real property, plant and securities; human capital should be useable as collateral.

• Governments should recognise the importance for social cohesion of non-vocational adult education which tends generally to raise the self-confidence, social participation skills and hence employability of participants, as well as their capacity to contribute to the further development of democratic institutions and whole societies.

• Particular emphasis should be placed on ensuring that the formal and non-formal learning needs of the following groups are met: the unemployed, both short- and long-term; those with low levels of educational attainment; older workers and senior citizens; women entering or returning to employment.

– The evidence shows that skills depreciate with unemployment. Yet many formal training programmes for unemployed workers do not appear to be very efficient in upgrading or restoring these skills, or in helping them to obtain jobs. Such programmes must not be one-off but be set in a lifelong learning perspective.

– A significant proportion of employees are in jobs in which their skills are under-utilised. Workers with more formal education than required for the job may require less on-the-job training than others. However, the empirical evidence on this point is ambiguous. The fact that part of the workforce has more formal qualifications than required raises the question of the timing of skills investment, as well as that of appropriate government financing. Might it be more efficient for individuals to postpone a certain part of their formal education, to take up a job, and to return to organised learning as the need arises?

– Lifelong learning systems based on enabling more individuals to construct their own pathways of learning and work will require education and career guidance to be available on a continuing basis throughout life. Much current provision is concentrated upon young people and the unemployed. A key policy issue for the future is how access to educational and career guidance can be ensured for all adults, where such guidance services should be located, and the respective roles of government, employers and individuals in paying for such services.

MANAGING AUTONOMY AND CHOICE:
THE ROLE OF GOVERNMENT

A. INTRODUCTION

There have been many discussions over the years of the objectives to be met by lifelong learning; these are much easier to identify than the means through which it will be realised. Yet, policy discussion will remain at the level of ideas unless attention is directed to such practical considerations, which will mean to address the institutional arrangements for governance and management concerning lifelong learning. This is already a complex undertaking if it can be assumed that those arrangements are the exclusive province of a central government agency. That assumption obviously does not hold. Educational and social policies are increasingly devolved from the centre, and are founded on partnerships between public bodies and a wide range of other interests. In an area as transversal as lifelong learning – cutting across educational, labour market, social, and cultural policy responsibilities – the need for attention to be paid to institutional arrangements and issues of governance becomes still more pressing. What does it mean to devise policies for lifelong learning in this context? Who is responsible for what, given the various levels and interests in play? These are the questions addressed below. Specifically, this chapter provides an analysis of the role of government in the implementation of approaches to lifelong learning.

This chapter has six elements. In Section B the challenges to traditional approaches to management and governance are presented, and key policy issues identified. Sections C and D analyse developments in governance and management, and indicate new directions for government in bringing about lifelong learning; the former reviews key developments at the level of compulsory schooling, the latter developments in education and training beyond schooling. Section E evaluates the arguments for a government role in markets for learning. Conclusions and recommendations for policy in a lifelong learning framework are presented in Section F.

B. DEVELOPMENTS IN GOVERNANCE AND MANAGEMENT OF EDUCATION

New approaches to governance and management in education and training are emerging in response to economic, social, political and educational developments. Until the 1970s, there was wide acceptance of what Wildavsky (1979) termed the "rational paradigm" in planning. This method favoured the organisation of highly centralised education systems and emphasised central government responsibility. During the 1970s, it became increasingly apparent that centrally administered reforms had not been implemented as planned in many areas of social policy – education and training included. In line with broader trends to loosen central direction and control in other spheres of social and political life, arguments were put forward in a number of countries for increased decentralisation and devolution in education and training – that is, a reduced role for central government.

In the 1980s, the emphasis shifted once again. In the United States and the United Kingdom (England and Wales), for example, changes in educational policy seemed to be more in the direction of greater central control than autonomy at the level of the establishment, or greater choice for individual learners. In certain countries a reinforcement of responsibilities of both central and regional authorities and schools took place at the same time. This was the case in Sweden, for example, where a bill passed by the Parliament in 1988 called for decentralisation at the same time that the central school board proposed a set of examinations that would exert a heavy influence on the content of what was to be taught.

These examples reveal a more general tendency. Demands from economies undergoing restructuring appeared to call for strong, centre-directed initiatives and renewed interest in skill requirements. These new demands, however, were seen to be more effectively met through a boosting of management and governance at the level of the institution. Thus, the pattern was for central governments to specify goals and directions and assess outcomes, whereas the means to achieve them were left in the hands of the individual institution, students and their parents, and the local community.

The response was more complex, however. Governments introduced expanded forms of partnership, a wider diversity of provision within the formal education sector, and various forms of privatisation. Such changes push toward a wider diffusion of responsibilities, not only from the centre to the region, institution, teacher and learner, but also to "stakeholders" outside the institution – parents, employers and municipal authorities among them. The evolution of markets for learning partly reflect this shift, but some countries have gone further by placing publicly-provided education and training on the same basis as privately-organised learning opportunities. Importantly, however, many governments have at the same time strengthened their strategic roles through approaches intended to guide or steer other partners and providers.

Recent developments have added to the pressures for this redefinition of the role of governments.

There is a growing loss of confidence in political processes and, by extension, in the public administration put in place to give effect to policies. This reflects, in part, a scepticism in the public at large about the ability of public authorities to respond effectively to the new challenges confronted by societies in the 1990s. The decline in public confidence in government has occurred at a time of growing interest on the part of multiple groups to take part more fully in decisions concerning the management and governance of education.

Some indication of the importance of these developments may be discerned in voting patterns and public opinion surveys. OECD's survey of public attitudes to education (1995*l*) is an example. The survey results indicate that, for management areas in which decisions traditionally have been taken at levels above the school (often at central level), there appears to be a substantial segment of the public that favours locating the responsibility for such decisions at the school. As shown in Chart 5.1, about two-fifths (41 per cent) of respondents across the twelve countries surveyed believed it was "very important" for decisions to be made by the schools themselves

◆   Chart 5.1.   ***Percentage of respondents who thought it was "very important" for decisions to be taken by schools themselves, 1993-94***[1,2]
Country averages, percentage

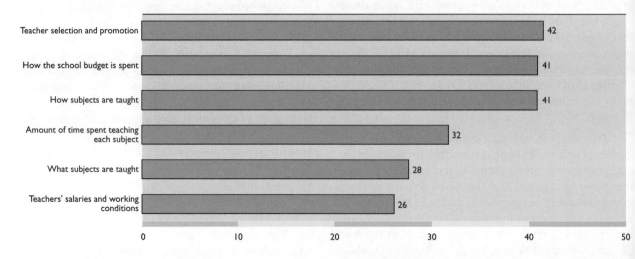

1.   The data are derived from a questionnaire distributed to a sample of the general public in each of the participating OECD countries. The questionnaire referred specifically to the final years of compulsory secondary education and a common set of questions were asked in all countries. The organisation of the survey was undertaken within each country and the surveys were administered by reputable national survey organisations. The recommended sample size was 1 000 individuals.
2.   The average was taken with respect to: Austria, Belgium (Flemish Community), Denmark, Finland, France, the Netherlands, Portugal, Spain, Sweden, Switzerland, the United Kingdom and the United States.

Sources: OECD (1995*l*) and OECD (1995*n*).

about how the school budget is to be spent. A similar percentage (42 per cent) believed it was "very important" for the schools to make decisions on teacher selection and promotion. Although public opinion differs among countries on the extent to which schools should assume decision-making responsibilities generally (ranging from an average 17 per cent of those surveyed in Spain, to 60 per cent in the United States who believed that it was "very important" for schools to take decisions in all of the areas identified), survey respondents in all countries were more likely to believe that schools themselves should take decisions in the areas of budget and teacher selection or promotion (Annex Table A.55). A preference on the part of the public to locate decision-making at the level of the provider weakens the power of the government to direct or control provision, and it also sets the context in which government roles in management, governance and pedagogy are being redefined.

A second recent development is the pressure for reform in the management of public administration. This, too, is partly related to the loss of confidence in central government action, but it is also due to growing competition for resources within the public budget. Weight is given to improving efficiency – and increasingly, the key to improved efficiency is perceived to be a relaxation of regulation by the centre. By the late 1980s, public sector reform strategies were incorporating what seemed to be the "positive" results of new management approaches. These suggested that the delegation of decision-making was popular with those so empowered. One particularly attractive feature of delegation was that it ensured that the "producers" of goods or services would be more closely and directly influenced by "consumers". That kind of experience was widely believed to be relevant in the delivery of a range of public services (Osborne and Gaebler, 1993). Not all countries have followed this path, and for those that have done so in the field of education and training, evidence on efficiency effects is mixed and limited (as discussed in Sections C and D below).

Another development, closely related to the second, is the broader policy debate about whether education and training should be considered as a "public good" or as a "commodity" to be purchased on the market. This debate derives in part from questions of efficiency, but also concerns the balance to be realised between individual choice and community interests in democratic societies. If education is supplied as a market commodity, competitive forces are assumed to induce providers to use resources efficiently and to offer education services in response to the preferences, needs and interests of learners as consumers. It is a view of education that gives full weight to the freedom of individuals to choose, and by implication minimises the direct role of government.

One set of concerns raised about this "education as commodity" view relates to imperfections in the market for education and training, such as lack of timely and accurate information, or certain externalities that could occur when the longer-term effects of education and training are not captured solely by the learner (see Chapters 4 and 8). In either situation, choices may not lead to the most efficient provision. Such imperfections can be addressed with appropriate intervention from government. A second set of concerns relates to the broader, community-wide purposes education is intended to serve. For example, free operation of the market could lead to a wide differentiation in the opportunities available to young people, on the basis of wealth and other socioeconomic characteristics. Again, some of the potential adverse consequences of such a differentiation can be addressed indirectly through the market, with public subsidies for education and training (targeted vouchers, tax expenditures), including criteria attached to subsidies to encourage providers to respond to the preferences, needs and interests of those in target groups. Intervention of this type represents a departure from the "free" market philosophy.

Other outcomes of education considered as "public good" may not be easily generated through the market, even if the government intervenes with subsidies and information. When weight is given to the full range of education outcomes, a case can be made for *public* rather than *market* provision. Following Musgrave (1959), the argument is based "on the qualitative nature of the educational services desired". Thus, "public schools may be desired because they make for political and cultural tolerance, serve as a melting pot, and pass on a common cultural heritage" (p. 44). As Blaug noted, "all modern societies have struck some sort of uneasy compromise between freedom of choice in education and the community interest in shared values" (1970, p. 119). To date, the compromise has permitted some private provision, but under considerable State control.

Thus, the present debate about the markets for learning extends beyond the question whether markets can improve efficiency. The debate is partly ideo-

Table 5.1. **Policy instruments defined**

	Primary elements	Expected effects	Costs	Benefits	Examples
Mandates	Rules	Compliance	*For initiators:* Enforcement *For targets:* Compliance Avoidance	*For individuals:* Specific benefits *For society:* Long-term, diffuse benefits	Non-discrimination requirements
Inducements	Money (procurement)	Production of value; short-term returns	*For initiators:* Production Oversight Displacement *For producers:* Overhead Matching Avoidance	*For initiators/producers:* Increased budget authority *For clients:* Value received	Grants-in-aid to governments, providers and individuals In-kind grants to individuals
Capacity-building	Money (investment)	Enhancement of skill, competence; long-term returns	*For initiators:* Short-term costs	*For providers/agencies:* Short-term, specific benefits *For society:* Long-term, diffuse benefits	Basic research
System-changing	Authority	Composition of public delivery system; incentives	*For "old" providers:* Loss of authority	*For new providers:* Gain in authority	Vouchers Desinstitutionalisation New providers

Source: Adapted from McDonnell and Elmore (1987).

logical, concerned with the appropriate balance between individual choice and broader interests. Whatever the balance to be struck, there is a government role in ensuring that conditions exist to support the appropriate functioning of such markets for learning.

A fourth development is the growth of learning opportunities outside the formal education sector. Private and voluntary efforts by individuals, communities and enterprises – as well as the impact of the media, telecommunications, and the diffusion of new information technologies – have widened the field of learning. Such non-formal learning is projected to assume greater importance in overall lifelong learning provision. The sheer breadth of that provision not only draws government interest into learning activities for which there has been little regulation or public financial involvement, but also increases the complexity of governance and management tasks. Direct government control across this wide field seems neither feasible nor desirable.

From these perspectives, new approaches to management and governance are best interpreted as responses by governments to wider pressures for a new balance to be struck between choice and autonomy and, at the same time, the complementary need for overall "steering" to ensure that the outcomes of education and training meet the needs of the economy and society. Thus, while authorities are counting on pressure from both empowered "producers" and influential "consumers" to raise standards, increase efficiency and mobilise fresh efforts at the level of providers and learners, they are acquiring greater experience with new strategies which seek to "steer" such effort in formal and non-formal settings for the benefit of all.

Further, on the basis of the analysis provided in Chapters 3 and 4, government will have a new role to play in fostering, within the framework of a lifelong approach to learning, new linkages among levels and types of education and training. Such links include new relationships between schools and tertiary institutions, among tertiary institutions and programmes, and between formal and non-formal education and training. The linkages can be fostered through government policies that enable individuals to make their own choices, provide public funding at least partly on the basis of those choices, and widen the scope for government purchase of education and training services from public or private entities.

The above developments describe a number of changes in the strategic government role in bringing about reform. In the perspective of lifelong learning, such a role needs to balance publicly supported learning, learning at the workplace and individual choice. The issues include the selection of the most appropriate mix of government policies and the most effective approaches to management. Details and options such as standard-setting, assessment and evaluation, teacher development and financing (among others) are analysed in-depth in Chapters 6, 7 and 8. The specific policy options manifest different roles of government. As characterised in Table 5.1 these options comprise:

- *mandates*, which may create uniformity as well as adversarial relations between the government "regulator" and the education or training provider;
- *incentives*, such as formula funding, demonstration grants or performance awards;
- *capacity-building*, to include investment in staff development for teachers, to use a wide variety of methods and environments, and to accommodate learners with more varied interests and backgrounds;
- *system-changing*, to include privatisation and contracting out.

There is an apparent trend away from mandates and towards other types of policy instruments. Changes of this nature in the roles of government can give rise to unpredictable and unanticipated results. For example, the expected benefits of combining the Ministries of Education and Labour, in a few countries, or of creating national employment and training boards, have not yet fully emerged.

The key questions for policy include: What are the new strategic roles for government in a framework of lifelong learning? What balance is to be realised between central regulation, institutional autonomy, participation in decision-making by local authorities and other parties, and individual choice? Does this balance differ among sectors and types of education and training? Given the new perspectives raised by these questions, the analyses needed to provide answers are limited. More complete answers await further, detailed work.

C. THE GOVERNANCE AND MANAGEMENT OF SCHOOLS AND SCHOOL SYSTEMS

Since the mid-1980s, two trends in educational administration can be observed across OECD countries. Firstly, authorities have increased autonomy at the level of the school. Importantly, it is now widely asserted – if not agreed – that many attempts to improve education outcomes by centrally directing actions in schools have led to insufficient results – because they were too slow, patchy or impermanent. On the basis of work carried out into the 1990s, the OECD has called for greater attention to provider-level development including in-service education and the training of teachers (OECD, 1974; 1982; 1989; 1990*a*; 1992*h*; 1994*l*; van Velzen *et al.*, 1985). Secondly, there has been increased emphasis placed on the authority of government to formulate goals, provide steering guidelines and monitor quality.

Country patterns in the distribution of management and governance responsibilities

If these two trends apply across most OECD countries, the individual country patterns nonetheless vary in significant ways. Although international comparisons may conceal unique and meaningful features of management and governance, a description of the distribution of responsibilities is provided by a set of indicators on decision-making in education, shown in Tables 5.2, 5.3 and 5.4 (OECD, 1993*a* and 1995*o*). The data refer to the distribution of

Table 5.2. **Decisions taken by level of governance, lower secondary education, 1991**[1,2]

(as percentage of all decisions)

	School level	Intermediate level 1	Intermediate level 2	Country level
	Public			
North America				
United States	26	71	3	–
Pacific Area				
New Zealand	71	–	–	29
European Community				
Belgium	25	50	25	–
Denmark	41	44	–	15
France	31	–	36	33
Germany	33	42	18	7
Ireland	73	8	–	19
Portugal	40	–	3	57
Spain	28	26	13	33
Other Europe – OECD				
Austria	38	8	26	28
Finland	40	47	–	13
Norway	32	45	–	23
Sweden	48	48	–	4
Switzerland	10	40	46	–
	Private			
North America				
United States	95	5	–	–
European Community				
Belgium	73	–	27	–
France	63	–	21	16
Portugal	88	–	–	12
Spain	65	11	2	22
Other Europe – OECD				
Austria	66	–	6	27

Note: – This specific decision-making level does not exist.

1. The indicator is based on decisions in four areas: education planning and structures (7 decisions), personnel management (12 decisions), organisation of instruction (8 decisions), and resources (7 decisions). The measure refers to the level at which the primary decision-maker is located and not to participation from another level, but in a different, subsidiary role (*e.g.* consulted by the primary decision-maker). For this table, the raw data have been weighted to give equal overall weight to each of the four areas. The results depend on the list of decisions that were selected for inclusion in each category and must be interpreted within this context.

2. Four levels of decision-making are distinguished: "School level", referring to decisions taken by its own governing board, the school principal or head teachers, teachers, parents and students; "Intermediate level 1", referring to the level that is institutionally closest to the school, usually the local authority; "Intermediate level 2", referring to the level that is closest to the central government (state, province, canton; this may also be regional agency of the central government); and "Country level", referring to the central government, national or federal.

Sources: OECD (1993*a*) and OECD (1995*o*).

Table 5.3. **Decisions taken at the school level by decision mode, lower secondary education, 1991**[1,2]

(as percentage of all decisions)

	Total[3]	Decisions taken		
		Autonomously	Jointly with other level	Freely within a framework
		Public		
North America				
United States	26	5	1	19
Pacific Area				
New Zealand	71	38	–	33
European Community				
Belgium	25	22	–	3
Denmark	41	19	9	12
France	31	12	–	19
Germany	33	3	4	26
Ireland	73	21	20	32
Portugal	40	9	2	29
Spain	28	10	3	15
Other Europe – OECD				
Austria	38	14	–	23
Finland	40	20	–	20
Norway	32	14	–	18
Sweden	48	15	–	34
Switzerland	10	–	–	9
		Private		
North America				
United States	95	66	4	25
European Community				
Belgium	73	32	17	24
France	63	44	4	16
Portugal	88	59	–	28
Spain	65	40	–	25
Other Europe – OECD				
Austria	66	41	3	22

Note: – This specific decision-making level does not exist.
1. See Table 5.2.
2. Three decision-making modes are identified: "Autonomously", subject only to the constraint of legislation external to the education system (or very general); "Jointly", in consultation with another level (excludes joint decision-making at the same level); and "Freely", within a framework decided at a more central level (binding legislation, regulations, or a fixed budget).
3. From Table 5.2, column one.
Sources: OECD (1993a) and OECD (1995o).

responsibilities as confirmed by public authorities, and so cannot convey the more complex range of formal and informal relationships, either among levels or with partners outside the education system. What is most striking is the variety of patterns. As shown in Chart 5.2, of the 34 decisions identified for assignment – covering areas of educational planning and structures, personnel management, organisation of instruction and resources – Irish public lower secondary schools were found to have principal responsibility for 73 per cent of decisions while, in Switzerland, such schools exercise responsibility over 10 per cent of decisions. Among those countries

reporting on decision-making in private lower secondary education, a similar range in the distribution of formal responsibilities applies: private lower secondary schools in the United States have principal responsibility for 95 per cent of the decisions examined; in France, Spain and Austria, such schools are afforded responsibility for about two-thirds of those decisions.

The scope for decisions to be taken by the individual school is limited in most countries studied (OECD, 1995d). In 12 of the 14 countries in Table 5.3, public lower secondary schools have formal responsibility for less than half of the decisions. Meanwhile

Table 5.4. **Decisions taken at the school level by decision domain, public lower secondary education, 1991[1]**

(as percentage of all decisions taken by schools)

	Decision domains			
	Organisation of instruction	Structures	Personnel management	Resources
North America				
United States	73	19	8	–
Pacific Area				
New Zealand	35	15	35	15
European Community				
Belgium	72	20	–	29
Denmark	54	26	11	9
France	64	–	13	23
Germany	67	22	–	11
Ireland	30	23	23	24
Portugal	48	9	26	17
Spain	80	–	8	12
Other Europe – OECD				
Austria	58	13	–	29
Finland	39	36	16	9
Norway	56	22	–	22
Sweden	46	22	17	15
Switzerland	100	–	–	–

Note: – This specific decision-making level does not exist.
1.   See Table 5.2.
Sources: OECD (1993*a*) and OECD (1995*o*).

◆   Chart 5.2. ***Decisions taken at school level, lower secondary education, 1991[1]***
Percentage

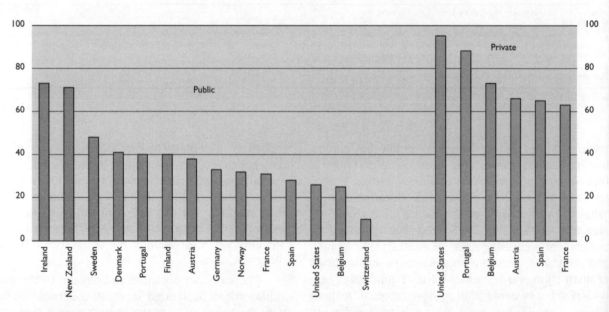

1.   Decisions made autonomously by public or private lower secondary schools as a percentage of all decision domains considered in the respective sectors. See notes to Table 5.3.

Sources: OECD (1993*a*), *Education at a Glance – OECD Indicators*; OECD (1995*o*), *Decision-Making in 14 OECD Education Systems*.

– as displayed in the second column of Table 5.3 – in one-third of the countries, public lower secondary schools have formal autonomous responsibility for one-fifth or fewer of the decisions. Even in private lower secondary education, the scope for autonomous decision-making by the school is limited. In four of the six countries on which comparable information was obtained, less than half of the decisions examined were subject to autonomous decision-making by the school itself. This conclusion applies more to some decision domains than to others. As can be seen in Table 5.4, in nine of the 14 countries, more than half of decisions taken primarily at the level of the school concerned the organisation of instruction. In contrast, in most countries less than one-quarter of decisions taken primarily at the level of the school concerned personnel and financial resources.

These patterns convey a complex picture of the distribution of responsibilities in school systems. Rather than defined solely along a centre-periphery continuum, responsibilities are divided between schools and other levels of the system, but also shared across levels with other "stakeholders" within and outside the school – including students, parents, employers, professional associations and community groups. Thus, country authorities have introduced:

- *governance* of public schools by a plurality of entities, with local authorities and national or jurisdictional authorities assigning important new roles to "user" bodies, while churches, charter-holders and client groups are also being encouraged to assume new roles – for example, in participation, quality review and inspection;

- new forms of *accountability* undertaken within new governance arrangements and – in some countries – financial accountability according to normative protocols;

- broadened *autonomy in resource management* – particularly as regards student and teacher time, but also in relation to organisational matters generally, such as the grouping of students, professional development or links with business and industry, sometimes with explicit reference to the modes of decision-making within the school;

- greater possibility for a *diversity of funding sources*, including tuition fees and contributions from enterprises as well as a structure for sharing the costs of provision through the organised use of volunteers and community and private sector resources;

- *circumscribed autonomy in the curriculum* offered through regulation of obligatory and optional curriculum elements, and through permitting sanctioned differentiation in the curriculum;

- the idea of *school choice* as a means of increasing the attention paid by schools to parents' satisfaction, sometimes associated with changes in school governance.

The new focus suggests that former "bureaucratic" concepts, based on hierarchical arrangements within a school system, are becoming outmoded. Such arrangements fail to respond to the long-standing interest of the teaching force to obtain greater autonomy in order to exercise professional judgement on matters of teaching and learning. Other alternatives, such as the "de-schooled" society functioning simply to provide a set of "community resources" (Illich, 1968), similarly have not emerged, in part because they do not respond to the need for continuity in the early years of formal education or the need to take account of the activities of other partners in the society.

Thus a set of relationships emerges that represents a partial drawing back from a completely autonomous or self-governing school. To be sure, a certain amount of school autonomy may be readily extended in certain areas of decision-making. However, autonomy develops within the framework of a relationship with the system and the community based on a mutuality of benefits and interests. In such a relationship, government authorities assume the role of ensuring the basic protection of rights for all students and establishing frameworks for the provision of resources while the community also participates, in the sense that parents and other significant groups have a role in setting fundamental values and goals, in supporting the teaching and learning process, and in providing resources within the frameworks established by the government. There is also a relationship within the school among school-based personnel, as decision-making is shared and mutually supported. In return, the school (with its local partners) is provided with a greater degree of autonomy in the selection of community-related goals and improved self-management in the fitting of resources to the realisation of those goals. The expected result is to develop improved self-management within schools, and to promote better relations with the community. Such a new partnership role would permit governments to encourage diversity of provision; tap into private resources; give greater attention to articulation and transition; and provide more scope for innovation and creativity – all of which are likely to favour the implementation of a lifelong approach to learning.

Country experiences

Results with regard to the implementation of the partnership models identified have not been fully assessed. Yet enough is known to describe the tensions and conditions that will need to be taken into account if government is to develop a partnership role in support of lifelong learning. A key challenge is for governments to establish a balance between encouraging the realisation of national and/or system-level priorities on the one hand and fostering initiative and innovation and enabling devolved decision-making on the other.

A reorientation at the centre

A crucial policy issue is the choice of decision-maker: central authority, local authority, school or staff governing body, markets (with or without public intervention), and individual learners. Each has its own strengths and weaknesses. The choice will depend partly on the capacities of various decision-makers to achieve the goals set down nationally and locally. If the goal is standardisation, then the central government role is likely to be more appropriate than that of local institutions or private alternatives. If the need is to link isolated institutions involved in lifelong learning, then a new decision-making body such as a stakeholder or co-ordinating board may be desirable.

The difficulties in establishing the necessary conditions for a more "strategic" government role have been frankly recognised in the *Review of National Policies for Education in France* (OECD, 1996b). It is noted that in such a previously centralised system there is a need for *new guidelines* on a wide range of matters. Those mentioned are: promoting equal opportunity, and avoiding the exclusion of minorities; improving quality and effectiveness in the context of mass education provision and unavoidable public spending restrictions; achieving a better match between the types of education and training available and the employment prospects of graduates; and monitoring a changing education system while promoting innovation. There is concern, however, about a "technocratic delusion [under which] decision-makers at the top (...) consider themselves able (...) to solve all the key problems (...) and there is a great danger in partners [such as parents, pupils, local and regional officials] (...) often without realising it (...) incorporating [the consequences of these delusions] into their own outlook when they ought to be defending *vis-à-vis* the Ministry of National Education. [It] will take some time before regional and local authorities (...) learn exactly just what powers and challenges they have to contend with".

In the *Review of National Policies for Education in Denmark* (OECD, 1995m), the examiners note that "the government does not have the means to implement national goals (...); essentially the government lacks the overall co-ordination necessary for allocating funds and other resources in accordance with national policy. [Increasing] institutional autonomy is severely restricted in practice by the Ministry of Education's continued control of course procedures and practices, and the Ministry of Finance's control of teachers' pay and conditions".

The above implies a reorientation in the nature of work performed by central authorities. Policy-makers must begin to see themselves as partners and adjust policy to focus on goals and on the support necessary to secure those goals; to shift from seeking administrative compliance to a role in which there is scope for others to work with regional authorities in new ways; and to trust, enhance and endorse teacher professionalism in conjunction with parents and others in the community. Such a reorientation is an important condition for the implementation of lifelong learning, with greater attention being paid to continuity and linkages, across sectors and levels of formal and non-formal education (OECD, 1995i). A related issue is how these strategic arrangements can be designed, so as to ensure centrally determined or agreed direction and equality in educational opportunity, and at the same time encourage local initiative. Arrangements must also reflect the wider sharing of decision-making with institutions.

Equity and high standards are often seen to be assured by a central role of government in the allocation of targeted funding, specification of curriculum content and assessment, and regulation of teacher preparation and staffing. But to what extent – and in what way – should diversity and initiative be encouraged? In the United States, where there is a tradition in schooling of locally controlled actions, the Goals 2000 legislation proposed a National Education Standards Improvement Council to oversee the preparation and operation of new national content and performance standards. As Howe (1995) points out, these standards go beyond curriculum guidelines to include elements of the learning process in schools. In this regard, a question posed by Howe (1994) can be put more broadly: To what extent can professionals at the school level be expected to adhere to more detailed central guidelines in their areas of competence, and yet "remain willing and able to put forth the kind of energy and commitment that are necessary to make the shift from passive to active (roles)?"

The management of schools – A supporting role

As more responsibilities for decision-making are devolved or shared, governments have sought to strengthen school management. The lack of school-level decision-making capacity can weaken the ability of government to realise overall goals. The roles and leadership styles assumed by principals and head teachers in schools successfully exercising greater responsibilities furnish good examples. In the United Kingdom (England), a study of successful schools under the new structure of local management found that head teachers acted as initiators of proposals; in schools where staff participates in resource management, heads also supported proposals made by others. These two styles of leadership were also observed in schools in Germany (Bavaria). In most schools, the principal delegated responsibility for implementation to the faculty. In a much smaller number, the principals clearly understood their role to be that of a leader, or "pedagogical manager". In the latter schools, the key feature is seen to be "an openness (...) to the fact that [new initiatives] need time for (...) development"; for "those whose profession is structuring schools, this indicates less a requirement for a technical [means of] innovation; more a philosophical, pedagogical consciousness" (OECD, 1996c).

These styles of leadership are "ideal" types; in England and Germany there are concerns that principals or head teachers lack, and are perhaps unable to adopt, those styles likely to be effective in schools having greater autonomy over academic and administrative matters. In Australia, "some schools believe devolution is making principals into managers instead of educational leaders, and are concerned that parents now see teachers working harder at management tasks than on educational tasks" (OECD, 1996c).

Experience with teacher participation in shared decision-making is also mixed. In many countries, teacher participation in decision-making on matters

of curriculum and assessment is an accepted feature of a teacher's job. It has not proved easy in every case to build on those arrangements in order to deepen teacher co-operation and participation in decision-making. In Germany (Bavaria), for example, "teachers all reported difficulties and hindrances (...) for objective reasons such as lack of up-to-date teaching material or the brief period for co-ordinating classroom instruction with colleagues, but also for subjective reasons such as a desire to retain something proven and to avoid the challenge of something new. Teachers emphasised that teamwork cannot be prescribed; it must develop slowly through the initiative of individual teachers" (OECD, 1996c).

In countries where a more strategic role for government has been established, teacher participation in decision-making has been strengthened and focused in part through requirements for school plans and new governance arrangements (favourable experience is reported in the United Kingdom, the Netherlands and the United States). In two countries, Belgium (Flemish community) and Spain, new reforms established formal structures for teacher participation in decision-making within the school. A recent study of the experience in Belgium (Flemish community) with participation councils in private schools and local councils in community schools reported that, while these new bodies were criticised from several standpoints, staff agreed that participation in decision-making was important. In Spain, the school-level co-ordination bodies established as a result of legislation seem to have improved team teaching (OECD, 1996c).

Authorities differ in the extent to which they provide advisory and staff development services to schools. In Australia, the policy framework for devolution in one state led to the "abolition of the curriculum branch of the Ministry and of the position of subject superintendents, leaving responsibility for the management of curriculum issues to heads of departments and to the development of networks between schools" (OECD, 1996c). This fully devolved approach contrasts with the strategies adopted in Spain and Belgium (Flemish community). In Spain, the inspection service remains a system-level responsibility, even if it has been decentralised and given a teaching advisory role. Belgium (Flemish community) has established a new inspectorate and pedagogical counselling service. While it is not possible to compare the effects of these different approaches, there appears to be more uncertainty or criticism of the approaches taken in Australia and Spain, and initial indications of satisfaction with the centralised approach adopted in Belgium (Flemish community). Staff development also figures prominently in policy and reform frameworks, and in this connection the trend in the OECD area is to emphasise school-based or -initiated efforts (OECD, 1994*l*).

A new role for parents and communities

The changing relationship between parents, communities and schools has introduced new challenges (OECD, 1994*p*). Among these are the ways in which parents and communities can strengthen and enhance the effectiveness of their contributions to education. Experiences with education priority areas in the Netherlands and France, and a policy framework affording scope for creative and flexible action at the municipality level in Sweden, are concrete examples of approaches that have elicited effective parent and community involvement (see Boxes 1 and 2). Specific approaches naturally reflect the particular ways in which education is organised in each of the countries concerned. Nonetheless, a number of principles seem to apply to each case.

One necessary condition would appear to be clarity in aims. The Dutch experience illustrates the problem that arises when objectives, particularly of supporting authorities, are not clearly established. At the same time, it appears that local community involvement in the development of participation not only provides a certain responsiveness to local circumstances and interest, but also offers some assurance that developments are sustained. Both the Swedish and French examples demonstrate reliance on local involvement in the development of initiatives. A third feature, found in the Swedish and French approaches, is coherence and a community-wide reach. However, the forms of parent and community participation examined here were not without cost. In the Swedish case, new initiatives were financed through the "creative" reallocation of public resources already available to the local authorities. A second approach, seen in a number of settings, involves the use of time and material resources provided by the community itself. The arrangement for education priority areas in France, for example, set out explicit expectations for wide community support.

Regionalisation

If central authorities are to develop a strategic role, the functions of intermediate levels of government merit attention. There is much to be learned from experiences in countries with federal structures, where the national authorities have some expressly reserved responsibilities but must work in different ways with individual states or autonomous regional communities. Bodies comprised of representatives of individual state authorities address common issues, which, by definition, have national reach. Bodies such as the Australia Education Council, Council of Ministers of Education Canada (CMEC), the Conference of Ministers of Cultural Affairs (KMK) in Germany, the Conference of Cantonal Directors of Public Instruction (CDIP) in Switzerland, and the Council of Chief State School Officers (CCSSO) in the United States, have a largely consultative and advisory role for the executive at state level.

It is significant, however, that even in federal systems, national authorities retain responsibilities in a number of specified domains. In Mexico, although the "National Agreement for the Modernisa-

---

Box 1. **Sigtuna municipality, Sweden**

Sigtuna welcomed relatively large numbers of workers from Southern Europe and Finland in the 1970s, when development centred around Stockholm's international airport, Arlanda. Financing of all education activities was provided through government appropriations (about evenly split between the central government and the municipalities), with special funding for specified purposes such as home language instruction.

The municipality adopted a flexible and creative approach to meet parent and community needs and interests. Categorical funding made available for the children of target minorities, for the training and job placement of parents in these families, and for other social support services were combined to employ counsellors from these minorities. The approach both enabled and encouraged participation by the minority communities and, importantly, addressed in a coherent way their needs and interests. The approach succeeded because officials in the municipality had the flexibility to apply funds as needed, in support of the particular goals established.

Box 2. **Education priority areas**

Policies for education priority areas have been established in one form or another in several countries since the 1960s. These areas are established on the basis of disadvantage and risk of school failure. Once a priority area is designated, additional resources are made available. The education priority area policy provides for local initiative within a well-defined framework that is given relatively stable support.

In France, the *Zone d'éducation prioritaire* (ZEP) policy has as some of its key features: *i)* promotion of the use of facilities in ways that will reach groups that do not ordinarily use them (including museums, community centres and so on); *ii)* provision of regular interpretation services free of charge, for schools and other public agencies; and *iii)* reduction of service and activity charges. None of these features are particularly new, but the ZEP policy envisages a much broader utilisation of the community's resources. The utilisation is reciprocal: various community facilities are made available for school children, while school facilities and expertise (in the technical *lycées*) are made available for community use. There are several other important administrative features: *i)* the ZEP are geographically small; *ii)* they establish formal links among school authorities, social service officials, parents and local politicians; and *iii)* they provide for a three-year cycle of funding.

Evidence on the effects of the ZEP initiative is mixed. In OECD's *Review of National Policies for Education in France* (OECD, 1996b), some positive results are noted, but it is also mentioned that the potential for the approach to generate more substantial, long-lasting gains is inhibited by: *i)* the continuing use of traditional methods for supporting students who are experiencing difficulties; *ii)* an insufficient targeting of resources on schools most in need, including experienced teachers and specialists, owing both to ambiguous criteria for selection into ZEP and rigid personnel policies; and *iii)* insufficiently developed and creative co-ordination with new urban or social policies.

In the Netherlands, the Education Priority Policy provides extra funding for teaching facilities in schools with disadvantaged children. A second component of the policy is the education priority area. The latter are local or regional co-operative networks of schools and welfare institutions; schools can take part in the network if they have a relatively high proportion of disadvantaged students. Co-operation among schools, public libraries and institutions is voluntary; funding is provided, however, only on the basis of an area plan developed and agreed by those schools and welfare institutions taking part.

Evaluation studies of the Dutch Education Priority Policy reveal mixed results (Kloprogge, 1991). One positive indicator is that a number of initiatives have been continued in the face of tight budgets. However, five weaknesses have been identified: *i)* it has been difficult to encourage schools of different denominations to work with each other; *ii)* there was an overly bureaucratic structure for the development and implementation of the plans; *iii)* welfare institutions held an uncertain position in the priority areas, for two reasons: lack of clear interest and support on their part and concern from schools about their competence in educational matters; *iv)* the area plans of work seemed overly ambitious; and *v)* there was a lack of clear direction or purpose so that resources tended to be applied in conventional rather than creative, possibly more effective ways.

---

ion of Education" signed in May 1992 by the national government, the 32 state governments and the teachers union put in place 32 state-level systems of education, "the federal government retained (...) a strong normative and evaluative role: it has exclusive powers over the content of the national curriculum and the evaluation of student performance across the country. It also retains an important compensatory role" (Rizo, 1995). In Spain, the Ministry of Education and Sciences "is responsible over the country as a whole for the functions and services which are essential to ensure basic uniformity in the educational system" (Spanish Ministry of Education and Sciences, 1994). By contrast, in Germany, "the responsibilities of the Federation [national government] (...) are strictly limited by the constitution. They include, in particular,

in-company vocational education, [financial] aid for students and some school pupils, promotion of scientific research, and framework legislation for the general principles relative to the higher education system" (Jobst, 1995). Through such responsibilities as regulating occupational law for specific professions and the civil service, including teachers, federal authorities have an important, indirect impact on education.

Further, the role in governance of the intermediate or lower level – district offices, local education authorities, municipal departments of education – appears to be evolving. In the United Kingdom (England and Wales), the United States and Canada (Alberta), the importance of this level of governance has weakened with the vesting of greater responsibilities at school level. The reforms underway in Mexico and Spain envisage limited roles for municipal authorities. In the reorientation of policy in Sweden in 1992, the new government gave emphasis to the freedom for the individual school to "create their own profiles". This implies that "individual municipalities [must] organise their school activities in such a way that decentralisation does not stop at the central municipal level" (Swedish Ministry of Education and Science, 1992).

These developments have potentially important implications for the strategic role of national governments in the implementation of a lifelong approach to learning. On the one hand, a structure for schooling with responsibilities divided across intermediate levels may "lack flexibility and transparency", a point the examiners raised in relation to the federal system in Switzerland (OECD, 1993c). On the other hand, a strategic role for national governments might be more effective if partners can be engaged at each level. There is the further advantage that, at the regional and local levels, governance and administration arrangements permit and can be used to encourage the participation of partners outside the formal education system (e.g. employers, social services) and so bring about links seen as crucial for the implementation of lifelong learning.

Privatisation – Contracting out

New forms of privatisation are emerging in some countries. One of these is contracting out, in which the government's role is to establish the learning outcomes desired for school populations, and then specify certain conditions a contractor must meet. The contractor is free (within the terms) to use any method to reach the specified outcomes. This strategy differs from the decentralising trend described earlier, in that the delivery function is bid competitively among private vendors for a specific contract term. Contract renewal depends on satisfactory performance, and bonuses may be paid for successful results beyond the minimum requirements of the contract.

The strategy has not yet been widely adopted, and experience is too limited and recent to permit evaluation. Views on the approach tend to be as much ideological as educational. For example, it can be argued that "contracting out": i) is more efficient because it harnesses competitive forces, particularly for inefficient schools; ii) enables governments to take advantage of specialised skills not readily pre-

sent in the school systems; iii) permits a rapid response to new needs and facilitates experimentation in new programmes; and iv) can reduce dependence on a single provider and so lessen vulnerability. To some extent, each of these considerations could be handled through reforms in publicly provided schooling. In this regard, the underlying question is how far market forces should be harnessed.

Implementation and reform strategies

A key policy question is how to implement and sustain the change needed at all levels to provide a framework of lifelong learning for all. At national level, the challenge is to change what Education Ministries do: How to change from a "maintenance" structure to a "development" structure? In school systems, while much is known already about the change process, it has been difficult to extend changes "system-wide". The problem is made more difficult in systems where responsibilities are shared among partners. Why, for example, in systems with devolved responsibilities, should regional and local authorities, local communities and schools accept the powerful overall national control which the State wishes to exercise through its central agencies? As devolution may limit the call of education on the central budget, it also strengthens the argument for local autonomy in decision-making and freedom even from national frameworks that, on other grounds, are legitimate and persuasive. Thus, local bodies and stakeholders have additional leverage and, where they are in disagreement with the central authorities or lack sufficient knowledge or support to take decisions, opportunities for paralysis are greatly enhanced. Evidence of this type of difficulty may be seen, for example, in the case of efforts to establish a national curriculum in the United States.

Government reform strategies differ among countries. Skilbeck (1994) broadly characterises such strategies along a continuum ranging from "comprehensive legislation to much more diffuse, less dramatic, more participative, slower processes whereby local initiative is fostered" (see Table 5.5). Somewhere between these extremes is a Northern European approach, evident in the Netherlands and Sweden, for example, usually referred to as "steering by goals". This refers to the functions of a central government in establishing a framework of goals, broad curriculum outlines, monitoring, assessment and evaluation. With this framework, there is enlarged scope for regional and local authority, school and teacher initiative and for community participation

Table 5.5.   **New strategic roles of governments: characterisation of reform strategies**

Reform strategies		Countries/systems
Government-imposed, comprehensive, legislative-backed reform		New Zealand Spain England and Wales
"Steering by goals"		Netherlands Sweden
Local autonomy, variety of action, plurality of decision-making	– nation-wide strategy in partnership with regional and local authorities; professional associations; unions; parents	
	– loose national structures; teacher professionalism; "grass roots" participation	Independent private schools Tertiary education institutions

Source: Adapted from Skilbeck (1994).

Skilbeck (1994) places the United Kingdom (England) further towards the model of "government-imposed, comprehensive, legislative-backed reform". It is more difficult to identify countries or systems following a model of "local autonomy, variety of action and plurality of decision-making". A stronger version of this model – close to "steering by goals" – is a nation-wide strategy in which government is a partner working together with regional and local authorities, professional associations, unions, and parents. A weaker form of this model, characterised by looser national structures, teacher professionalism and "grass roots" participation, might be found in independent private schools and tertiary education institutions.

Effects on learning

The effects of moves towards new strategic roles for government on student learning have not been easy to gauge. It has been difficult to demonstrate direct links between school organisation and student outcomes. Nonetheless, to the extent that schools operating under the new policy frameworks are found to be more likely to adopt measures known to improve student performance, there is *a priori* justification for such frameworks. A strategic role for government in which schools assume responsibility for deciding on means (OECD, 1996c):

- "[Leads] to greater effectiveness through greater flexibility and better use of resources; to professional development at the school level; to more knowledgeable teachers and parents, and so to better financial decisions; to whole-school planning and implementation with priorities set on the basis of data about student (outcomes and) needs" (Australia).

- "[Through] devolution, produces a valid framework for initiatives taken by communities while taking advantage of possibilities offered by the legal framework. It is important that schools should be able to set their own objectives, to organise their management and curricular development processes in their own agreed manner, and create their own ethos. This all appears to have important consequences for the educational climate and, through this, for the anticipated end product of the school" (Spain).

- "[For] innovations in the curriculum directed at profile development (*i.e.* schoollevel adaptations of programmes), may lead to an increase in the effectiveness of schools" (Germany, North Rhine-Westphalia).

There is also broad agreement that an important dimension of such a strategic role is partnership – as noted in Australia, where "it makes a difference to financial resource management when the notion of partnership is introduced. Consensus breeds greater understanding and satisfaction [and] effectiveness of schooling is enhanced when a partnership is developed between parents, principal, staff and students in a school community (...). Using the partnership to establish the membership of decision-making groups, and to apply the benefits of that decision-making across all functional areas of the school's operations, leads to a strong sense of mutual support, a strengthening of purpose, a commitment to decisions made and an empowerment of participants" (OECD, 1996c).

That the necessary conditions are not always present is confirmed by a range of research findings. Meuret *et al.* (1995) compared the OECD's indicators of decision-making with upper secondary graduation rates and performance in reading at age 14. In comparing the fourteen countries for which information was available, no apparent relationship could be discerned between the proportion of decisions taken at the school, intermediate or system level and schooling outcomes. An extensive body of research in the United States has not persuasively demonstrated that site-based management – a strategy which calls for an indirect but guiding role for government – affects educational outcomes one way or another. Indeed, some United States research suggests that there may be additional costs for site-based management, in terms of both effort and possible unintended effects on children.

While the evidence remains limited, a role for government which favours improved effectiveness can be advanced, by way of hypothesis: improvements in effectiveness result both from augmenting decision-making responsibilities at the level of the school and from conditions which support the informed and effective exercise of those responsibilities. Key conditions appear to be clarity in decision-making responsibilities at the school level and sufficient knowledge and expertise on the part of school staff, parents and partners from the wider community. In adopting a more strategic role as part of a framework of lifelong learning, government should seek to ensure that the needed conditions are established and maintained and to draw on and engage partners in such an effort.

D. THE GOVERNANCE AND MANAGEMENT OF LEARNING BEYOND SCHOOLING

While governments have long and substantial experience in directing the provision of school systems, their roles in supporting non-formal learning have been more diffuse and indirect. Non-formal learning lies generally outside the direct control of governments, not only because they lack the resources to finance provision but also because learning patterns are determined by a complex array of influences and stakeholders. In short, education and training beyond secondary schooling are influenced by a complex interplay of supply and demand factors (OECD, 1995i).

The challenge to government is to rethink its roles in relation to tertiary, adult and continuing education and training, with the aim of developing policies to influence demand and supply. New approaches involve the more strategic use of public financing; an opening up of regulations in the tertiary education sector to accommodate diversity; new efforts of assessment and evaluation; and targeted support for provision which may reduce certain barriers to lifelong learning (see Chapter 2). New roles for government need first of all to be considered in relation to post-school and tertiary education.

Post-school and tertiary education

Although post-school and tertiary opportunities are expanding and becoming more diverse, there is evidence that they are not adequately matching demand. In Germany, Chancellor Kohl has expressed the concern that, overall, education at the tertiary level was "too academic". There is some indication that young people in Germany agree: a survey of university students found that 12 per cent would have enrolled in *Fachhochschulen* if spaces were available. There is evidence drawn from Australia and New Zealand that tertiary education students are seeking to align their skills and competencies with the needs of employers by obtaining "double degrees", undertaking post-graduate study or, in some instances returning to obtain higher vocational qualifications in TAFE in Australia or polytechnics in New Zealand (Committee for Quality Assurance in Higher Education, 1995; New Zealander Ministry of Education, 1995). The latter development has also been noted with regard to community colleges in the United States, and in programmes offered by special training schools (*Senshu Gakko*) in Japan (Box 3).

Current arrangements for the management and governance of tertiary education have been found by both governments and institutions to be inadequate. Government strategies involve the use of two policy "levers", namely regulation and financing.

Regulation

Most countries continue to regard a supportive legal framework as a necessary condition for the effective "steering" of tertiary education. Such a legal framework sets down the respective responsibilities. Yet, in some OECD countries, steps are being taken to address rigidities in regulatory frameworks or uncoordinated approaches linked to them. In the United States, state-level initiatives are addressing a

---

Box 3.   **Special training schools in Japan: a private sector response to demand**

One indication of the lack of responsiveness of tertiary institutions is how many learners seek education outside publicly organised or regulated programmes. The evolution of enrolments in special training schools (*Senshu Gakko*) in Japan is an example. These schools are mostly private and offer education and training for work requiring "mid-level" skills. Qualifications from higher-level courses in these schools (the large majority of courses) are recognised by employers (in some cases, the curriculum is established by "employers", *e.g.* the Health Ministry sets down requirements for dieticians), but as the curricula do not fall under the regulatory control of *Monbusho*, the schools do not confer qualifications that are recognised in tertiary education.

Special training schools have developed at a very rapid rate, with enrolments more than doubling since the early 1980s – in spite of the lack of academic recognition or standing. Given unfavourable employment prospects for many young adults and stagnating enrolments in tertiary education, some institutions have begun to develop articulation arrangements which permit students in special training schools to gain advanced standing and, eventually, to receive tertiary-level degrees in addition to their training school qualifications.

There are other examples of fully private, "external" provision in the OECD area, even if the numbers involved remain relatively modest. In France and Germany, for example, such programmes are found in institutions offering advanced studies in business and management.

---

perceived need to streamline functions and open up structures which now are seen as overly inflexible. New Jersey has abolished its State Board of Higher Education, while the much-applauded California Master Plan has been criticised for its rigidity. In Sweden, while policy development until 1993 aimed to reduce government oversight of tertiary education substantially (widening the scope for the establishment and programmes of institutions), the present direction is to restore some regulatory control through new framework conditions monitored by the National Agency for Higher Education. As part of its reform of tertiary education, the United Kingdom (England) established the Higher Education Funding Council which, while independent of direct government control, nonetheless works to a much narrower set of specifications than the former University Grants Committee.

The implementation of a framework of lifelong learning may call for a new balance in regulations covering tertiary education, in which authorities will assume increased responsibilities for establishing means for assessment and quality assurance while relinquishing even more of their responsibilities for oversight of the structure, organisation and management of provision. In this regard, there is a need to look closely at present legislation and proposed reforms.

Governments have taken steps to widen the scope for input and influence from students, employ-

ers and regional governments or municipalities in decision-making. In France, the contracting policy has sought to emphasise institutional accountability, to ensure the effective use of public funding allocated for international co-operation, and to stimulate joint effort among tertiary institutions, local and regional authorities and enterprises (French Ministry of Higher Education and Research, 1993; OECD, 1995n). The experience with the development of partnership within contracts warrants close attention as a model to be pursued by national authorities seeking both to harness support by local partners and to "steer" provision.

Countries have also adopted different approaches to stimulate the supply of learning opportunities for students who do not continue on to "conventional" tertiary education. In Australia, the National Training Council has – with the agreement of the federal, state, employer and labour interests represented – provided advice on training to the National Board for Employment, Education and Training and the government. It also has helped establish a new way to provide for training outside the wage-setting process. Denmark makes use of a range of governance bodies, including the Ministry, the Council on Vocational Education which advises the Ministry, trade committees which oversee specific training courses, and local education committees which advise technical and commercial schools. The range of bodies corresponds to the diversity of training opportunities in that country. Germany's dual system of vocational and technical education is governed by legislation. The Federal Institute for Vocational Training, operating under the Federal Ministry of Education and Science, oversees training at the federal level and writes guidelines which are approved by the state authorities, relevant industry chambers and trade unions.

Several countries now rely on high-level bodies to advise the Ministry about future development at the tertiary level. In Australia, the Higher Education Council responds to government requests for advice on policy matters. A similar structure has been used in Japan, where the University Council, comprised of members drawn from within and outside tertiary education, has developed for *Monbusho* (Ministry of Education) recommendations for reform. OECD examiners of tertiary education in the Czech and Slovak Republics recommended the establishment of such an advisory body; in Poland, a council established close to the Minister serves this purpose. In New Zealand, a Tertiary Consultative Committee (TCC) has been organised by the Chief Executive of the Ministry of Education in order to foster an exchange of views on policy development and impact. The TCC has no formal or legal status. In all these countries, such bodies are advisory. Government authorities retain full responsibility for decisions regarding the adoption of any of the recommendations. In this respect, authorities in these countries – and in individual States in the United States – have reserved full scope to respond flexibly and directly to newly-identified policy aims.

At the tertiary level, the reduced influence of "buffer bodies" and increased use of advisory bodies may be seen as an expansion of the government role beyond the state-institution relationship, to include a specific role in balancing the roles and responsibilities of other actors, most particularly those from industry. In the United Kingdom (England), for example, co-operative financing and training and research initiatives are promoted through government policies. Thus, governments may be seeking to foster "joint responsibility" insofar as "the sum of institutional interests is not in the public interest" (McGuinness, 1995). This wider perspective includes students, as development will be influenced by the choices they make.

Authorities in several countries are seeking to bolster strategic decision-making in tertiary institutions. In Japan, recent attention is aimed at building up participation in decision-making at the institution-wide level, in the hope that faculties and departments will be encouraged to see their work in relation to the efforts of the university as a whole. The approach adopted in recent reform in Belgium (Flemish community) is to lodge decision-making responsibility at the institution, with only indirect "steering" through financing mechanisms and a broad and light regulatory framework.

Financing

In most OECD countries, public financing is increasingly being used to direct tertiary education provision. Box 4 illustrates the main feature of the approaches, which is to shift the basis of funding from inputs to outputs and outcomes, and thereby to call upon providers to justify the funds received in terms of these outputs or outcomes. One example is Australia's Quality Assessment initiative, undertaken by the Committee for Quality Assurance in Higher Education, which provides for financial awards to institutions based on an assessment of actions and achievements rather than proposed activities (Committee for Quality Assurance in Higher Education, 1995). Outcome criteria are also used to allocate core funding. Williams (1994) points out a key paradox in this new strategic approach to institutional finance: "[With the] advent of output budgeting, governments and external funding agencies become involved in at least as much detailed regulation as they were in line item budgeting". In this respect, the government role is changed, not diminished.

In spite of these innovations, in no OECD country is funding made available to tertiary institutions solely on the basis of a "free market" of choice. The introduction of market forces – including incentives introduced through new funding formulas – mask the extent to which authorities retain responsibility for the allocation of direct institutional appropriations. Governments have retained scope for addressing unintended consequences of the application of formula funding and market incentives, including the rigidity such mechanisms may introduce over time. This flexibility does have drawbacks, however, because the incentives introduced through particular funding criteria and market forces are weakened if governments step in to protect programmes or institutions that are not responsive. On the other hand, the initiatives illustrate concerns about the ability of governments to "steer" the development of tertiary education. Issues in the finance of tertiary education and non-formal learning more broadly are taken up in more detail in Chapter 8.

Box 4.   **Incentives linked to financing mechanisms**

Among the methods used to allocate public subsidies to tertiary education, the following incentives may be found in the countries indicated (Wagner, 1996).

For providers:

- "rationalisation" in the Netherlands and "consolidation" in Australia and Belgium (Flemish community), in which the number of institutions have been (or are being) reduced to permit larger enrolments per institution;
- institutional "profiling" in Australia and "contracts" in France and Finland, in which differentiation and specialisation among institutions permit larger average enrolments across institutions for study programmes in specific fields;
- funding mechanisms which favour development in less-expensive provision; including alternatives to universities (as in Germany), part-time and distance study options, and so on;
- funding mechanisms which provide for a ceiling on funding, as in the new funding formula applied in the United Kingdom and proposed in the Czech Republic, and the allowance for a "self-financing" expectation for institutions in Australia and New Zealand (the latter takes the form of a policy permitting institutions to impose tuition fees to cover a planned reduction in student public funding);
- funding mechanisms which tie public funds to performance indicators or service standards, including "contracts" in France and Finland; "credit points" or units corresponding to the volume of course work completed in Sweden and Norway; "active students", defined as the volume of examinations passed in Denmark; the volume of doctoral degrees in Norway; or accreditation in the United States.

For learners:

- funding mechanisms which directly affect participant eligibility for support, as in limits in Germany on the number of terms for which public support is made available (8-10 terms in universities; 6-8 terms in *Fachhochschulen*), requirements for progress in the Netherlands (students must pass half of their course work each year), and additions to the annual fees paid by students for those who do not complete their studies within a fixed time period (proposed in Australia);
- funding criteria which indirectly encourage learners to be "efficient", in particular tuition fees (a direct application of the market model in a number of countries);
- guidance on the content and methods of participation in programmes of study, as discussed in Germany and France.

Within institutions:

- extending autonomy within institutions in which there are consequences for programmes, departments or faculties stemming from the choices they make in organising instruction and research. A number of large private universities in the United States have adopted the approach, which includes "gain-sharing" through which a unit, faculty, department or centre keeps a portion of the surplus it generates;
- "benchmarking" of costs, in order to evaluate the variation among institutions for identified services.

The emerging infrastructure for learning beyond schooling

While much of the time and resources for learning beyond schooling is devoted to traditional tertiary institutions, possibilities for open and distance learning are developing rapidly. Mainstream education and training continue to adapt, if not fully, to make better use of the possibilities. New learning opportunities are more closely linked to work and work environments; are scheduled during the day and week to accommodate the varying needs of learners; and introduce a shift in the relationship between teacher and learner, towards a more "open" structure for learning. Such opportunities represent a large growth potential for lifelong learning. Governments can encourage changes in institutional cultures in recruiting and training personnel, in funding regimes and in applying information technologies appropriately for educational purposes. A specific approach is to add a "mode" of distance education to conventional tertiary provisions. "Dual mode" institutions introduce considerable flexibility in provision: to shift emphasis from one mode to the other, depending on changes in the pattern of demand for particular courses; to open up continuing professional education at a time when innovations in telecommunications are making interactive learning at a distance a realistic possibility; to accommodate increased enrolments in a context of limited or uncertain levels of resources; to permit an entrepreneurial response to market possibilities for off-campus learning; and to enable improvements in quality for on-campus provision (OECD, 1995*i*).

In establishing flexible arrangements for learning the main role of government is to promote the development of new links between formal and non-formal education providers and enterprises, and more varied use of new information technologies. This implies new methods and arrangements for institutions and other providers, but also new patterns of participation in non-formal learning. Because authorities are unlikely to support all such activities, a related government role is to encourage financing arrangements that promote widespread participation in open learning.

There are now few technical barriers to prevent education and training provision from moving beyond national boundaries. The dimensions of the growth are well documented. In the OECD area, foreign students in tertiary education increased at an average annual rate of over 10 per cent from 1960 to 1980, and by an average annual rate of 2 per cent from 1980 to 1990 (Ebuchi, 1989). Nonetheless, with some exceptions, such student flows account for a small percentage of total tertiary enrolment, in the order of 5 per cent, after the flows have been adjusted to exclude students who are "resident foreigners" (Gordon and Jallade, 1995; Wagner and Schnitzer, 1991). There has been rapid development of new structures and means of provision, including joint programmes (as in the European Union's ERASMUS programme, or University Mobility in the Asia-Pacific region); "split site" arrangements which divide the period of study between the host institution and an institution in the sending country; "branch" campuses, sometimes organised as a co-operative or joint venture with a foreign institutional, government or corporate sponsor; local infrastructure development, as in the Commonwealth Higher Education Support Scheme (CHESS) established by the Commonwealth Secretariat; distance learning opportunities extended across borders by individual institutions or national agencies (*e.g.* the German *Fernuniversität* linked to study centres in Austria; free-standing, multilateral entities such as the Commonwealth of Learning); and the

proposal for "regional" universities, such as an Asia-Pacific Industrial University (Wagner and Schnitzer, 1991; Perraton, 1993). These international initiatives represent major opportunities for accommodating the demand for lifelong learning.

However, the practicalities of international exchange and co-operation in approaches to lifelong learning require further development. Policies now would need to take into account more concrete forms of co-operation, moving beyond a general openness for a sharing of experiences to cross-border funding of university-based research; fees (levels of subsidies) for tertiary students from other countries; recognition of qualifications and contents of degree studies in other countries; and delivery of instructional services across borders. Negotiations in the recently-concluded GATT round gave attention to the trade in international services, including education. Information is accumulating on the outcomes of various types of international arrangements in teaching and learning (Bremer and van der Wende, 1995; van der Wende, 1995; Opper *et al.*, 1990), and on alternative approaches for the recognition of learning beyond borders.

In sum, several emerging themes in the governance and management of post-school education and training can be identified:

– New post-school learning opportunities are emerging in some countries, as the full range of education and training providers are being given more responsibility for determining their objectives and taking initiatives within broad policy guidelines.

– Public funding arrangements are now becoming more strategic, shifting from the specification of fixed inputs to the realisation of agreed outcomes or outputs; at the same time, tertiary providers are expected to move towards mixed public/private funding: students, particularly in graduate and continuing professional education, are now being expected to contribute tuition fees, and institutions are being encouraged to become more entrepreneurial.

– Governments are removing barriers to private sector initiatives: as a matter of policy, some authorities are encouraging private entities to compete for contracts; long-standing distinctions between public and private providers are becoming blurred as access and funding are made more widely available.

– There is growing interest in identifying and assessing skills and competencies. Establishing a national framework of qualifications and standards might reduce the fragmentation of certification and diversify provision by rendering neutral the source of learning. However, no country has implemented a fully developed qualifications framework to date. Thus, the assumptions concerning direct and indirect costs as well as the potential benefits emerging from such frameworks remain untested.

More generally, the role of governments in guiding and funding learning beyond schooling remains an open area for policy development. Even more than in the school sector, the trend is for governments to adopt a strategic role in those tertiary and non-formal sectors where they choose not to be, or cannot be, the main provider of services, but where there is nonetheless great value in "guiding" change. The strategic role involves partnerships with providers and includes regulation, finance, monitoring results and fostering strategic development.

E. GOVERNMENT INTERVENTION IN MARKETS FOR LEARNING

In recent years there is increased interest in "markets for learning". Markets are advocated because they "create the right incentives", that is, they are seen as an effective mechanism to direct resources to their most appropriate uses. The means include enrolment-based funding mechanisms; school choice; contracting arrangements; tax incentives for providers, third-party payers, and learners and their families; vouchers; and a mix of private and public funds. Experience with these approaches varies among countries and across levels of education and training. There is relatively little experience with a market approach to compulsory schooling, and the most substantial experience in adult education and training. In the latter case, the "market" has developed to an extent independently of government.

Yet even with increased interest in market approaches and the long-standing possibility for private provision of schooling, government intervention is observed in every OECD country. Intervention takes the form of either regulation or financing (usually a combination of both), and with formal education there is direct provision through public schools and tertiary institutions. So far, the motives for such intervention usually have been related to efficiency and equity concerns; sometimes, particularly at the post-compulsory level, criteria such as "broadening the financial base" or "feasibility" are used (Eicher and Chevallier, 1993).

According to the efficiency argument, a market for learning relies on government intervention if the learning activity produces benefits for persons other than the provider or learner, under the condition that the net additional benefits outweigh the added costs of the intervention (de Vijlder, 1993; Windham, 1979). The common view is that, on balance, significant positive externalities exist in markets for learning, which are manifested in better health, improved social cohesion, enhanced technological development, higher economic growth, a more balanced income distribution, enhanced democracy, and more active political participation (Haveman and Wolfe, 1984; McMahon, 1995). There is also agreement that such externalities diminish with the level of education – that is, externalities for primary schooling are higher than those for secondary schooling; and the latter are higher than those for post-secondary education. A further reason for government intervention is that risk and incomplete information can lead to inefficient investment (when individual learners make choices that are inappropriate in terms of the subsequent social effects) and under-investment for a country as a whole (when the market fails to permit risks to be averaged). Under such circumstances, government intervention in a market for learning can be used to compensate for the risk assumed by funders and learners. Government subsidies (explicit or implicit) in various tertiary education loan schemes have the effect of overcoming such uncertainty and risk.

Importantly, the foregoing arguments favouring government intervention in markets for learning apply also to adult education and training (Middleton et al., 1993). In this case, however, employers figure more prominently than in the case of formal schooling. To the extent that adult education and training are "general" (Becker, 1962), the motivation for government intervention in the market corresponds to those discussed above for formal education. But, even where adult education and training programmes are "specific", intervention may still be warranted. This is the case when there is uncertainty about turnover and worker leisure, which may lead to under-investment on the part of employers. The training levy, in which all enterprises are obliged (as in France) to set aside a certain percentage of their wage bill for training, is an example of government intervention which seeks to respond to these concerns (see Chapter 8).

Probably the most accepted reason for government intervention in any market for learning is the view that access to educational opportunities should not depend decisively on factors such as social background, gender or ethnic origin. Until the recent expansion of participation at upper secondary and tertiary levels of education and the growth in the need for retaining and upgrading of skills, this view had the greatest cogency at the primary and secondary levels of education. In the framework of lifelong learning for all, full access to learning opportunities in all forms and of all ages for the disadvantaged, un- or under-employed, or otherwise marginalised individuals constitutes an important cornerstone.

The foregoing discussion sets out the main arguments for government intervention in a market for learning. However, the market-based approach as a means of "steering" education and training has been challenged since, even with government intervention, there is no certainty that the externalities and equity aims have been sufficiently taken into account. There is a need for further analysis of existing policies. Importantly, the problems that have been identified in relation to certain "higher order" values for society as a whole are based on perspectives of social relationships that extend beyond those defined through the market. Such values may warrant direct government involvement (through regulation or public provision) as opposed to indirect influence via intervention in the market (Wringe, 1994; McLaughlin, 1994; Henig, 1994; Chubb and Moe, 1993).

F. MANAGING AUTONOMY AND CHOICE: POLICY CONCLUSIONS

In a lifelong learning approach, it is the role of government to promote the development of appropriate "bridges" and "ladders" and to provide frameworks in which the various elements of education and training provision can be articulated. Although such frameworks are not yet in place, recent policy developments in the OECD area reveal new directions in governance and management which may offer bases for redefining the roles of government in support of lifelong learning. Across the range of existing provision of education and training, a number of countries have moved to establish a more strategic role for government. At school level this has meant a reinforced role in specifying desired learning outcomes and at the same time a more supportive, less-directed role in decisions about how the outcomes are to be achieved (through, for example, policies calling for increased school autonomy and

privatisation). At the tertiary level, the strategic role has called for new evaluation mechanisms and information policies, now linked more closely with financing mechanisms. These developments signal a potential convergence in broad policy directions across the different levels of education and training, and a basis for developing a more coherent lifelong approach in the roles of government.

In education at all levels, some countries appear to place the emphasis on establishing intermediary bodies or consulting intermediary levels of government for advice rather than decision-making. That emphasis would result in a direct link between government and its policies on the one hand, and individual education and training providers, public and private, and learners, on the other. However, through intermediary bodies and levels of government, system authorities have scope to work with and influence partners in support of management and financing strategies. The pattern is by no means uniform across countries or levels of education. The roles of regional and local authorities in education and training are unsettled – but apparently changing – in a number of countries. In training, different governance arrangements can be seen in relation to country circumstances and structures. Nonetheless, the emphasis in some countries on new roles for intermediary bodies and local and regional governments might be considered as a point of departure in the development of one element of a strategic policy framework for the implementation of lifelong learning for all.

In a number of countries, a parallel approach to funding is being applied across education levels and segments. In these countries, governments directly fund education providers, establish explicit links between outcome criteria or evaluation and public funding (in whole or in part), and introduce more private participation (with in-kind contributions from communities and enterprises, contracting out, and learner/family participation in funding). In a few countries, a single funding mechanism is being applied across all education provision at tertiary level and is being extended, in part, to upper secondary education. Again, a convergence of financing approaches opens up possibilities for a more coherent approach to the use of financing as a means to steer provision more closely in line with a lifelong approach to learning.

School education

- Education Ministries should adopt and strengthen their strategic role, to advance development of a lifelong approach to learning for all; such a role involves primary responsibility for the setting and assessment of goals and standards and the provision of a supportive framework within which schools are expected to meet these as well as other locally-developed goals.

- In the implementation of policies which balance assurance of quality and opportunity with guidance and support for the increased scope for initiative at the level of the school, intermediate bodies and levels of government should be encouraged to serve as the means to connect schools with partners outside the education system. Curriculum guidelines as well as monitoring and evaluation should emphasise and build on linkages in learning among levels, with non-formal learning and with work.

- Support systems should encourage schools to build on strengths and complementarities, in partnership with parents, communities and enterprises. Policies which establish support systems and structures should aim to encourage improvement and effectiveness, not simply replication.

- Schools should be able to seek funding and in-kind support from a range of sources, subject to the requirement of equal access. Government retains the responsibility to ensure a fair distribution of resources, so that gaps and special needs are covered after all available resources (public and private) are taken into account.

Learning beyond schooling

- Education Ministries should revise and further refine legislative frameworks and financing mechanisms to permit flexibility, but also to guide provision towards greater coherence across the range of tertiary education and to ensure improved responsiveness. Central authorities should retain a limited, but nonetheless direct, power to intervene (*e.g.* through the allocation of a reserve pool of uncommitted funds).

- Education Ministries should move beyond traditional State-institutional relationships to encourage and further build on local partner-

ship among providers and with authorities and enterprises. The roles of buffer bodies and intermediate agencies in monitoring performance, providing support and developing partnership should be strengthened.

- Education Ministries should assume as a principal responsibility the encouragement and promotion of innovation in learning beyond schooling. Support should be provided indirectly, through a more flexible regulatory framework which permits a range of providers and programmes to be established, and directly, through support for innovation outside as well as within formal education institutions and across national frontiers.

- In facilitating participation in and pathways through the range of post-initial learning opportunities, government should develop further a role in providing for an assessment of skills and competencies wherever acquired (as a "transaction facilitator"). Such a role needs to be developed in partnership with providers, clients and a range of government departments.

At all levels

- A general principle is that provision should be influenced by learners as well as other "clients", including government representing society-wide interests and enterprises reflecting their own interests.

- In this connection, government should establish and continue to monitor the conditions under which markets for learning can lead to responsive and efficient provision. Government retains the primary responsibility for access to and equity in lifelong learning in all forms and at all ages, whether the opportunities are afforded through the market or provided directly by the government.

- Governments should explore possibilities for strengthening the linkages between employment and education functions to ensure that general education, training and employment offer mutually reinforcing opportunities for personal growth and development throughout life. Linkages with health and social service functions should also be established and strengthened.

USING GOALS AND STANDARDS IN FORMAL AND NON-FORMAL LEARNING

A. INTRODUCTION

This chapter argues that re-examining educational goals and standards is an indispensable part of the reform process; there is currently a lack of articulation between the objectives pursued at different levels, programmes, and other components of the education and training systems of many OECD countries. Duplication, contradictions and other forms of incoherence arise in part because of a lack of clarity with regard to the goals of education and training systems. They also arise from the conflicting aims of different interest groups inside and outside the education and training sector.

All countries are concerned about the quality and relevance of their formal education and training systems, but the expression of this concern can take different forms. For instance, in the English-speaking countries especially, there is debate over the "standards" that signal high performance. In Japan and most European countries, there has been less anxiety about quality; concern has tended to focus instead on issues related to curriculum and vocational and technical training, *i.e.* on input and process. In some countries there is concern about school standards but relative confidence in the performance of tertiary education institutions. In other countries, the reverse is true.

The starting point for the examination of these issues is the analysis of what countries are currently implementing or seeking to implement in their education systems, both to clarify goals and to articulate standards. This shows the range of experience and varying degrees of success with which the many tensions that arise have been resolved. This discussion also warns that some of the most readily available measures will rarely add up to a comprehensive set of benchmarks, and may often not be the most appropriate, whether from an educational or a public accountability viewpoint. This chapter relies mainly on evidence from school systems but references are also made to tertiary education. While this, of course,

refers only to a part of the range of opportunities that together constitute the full lifelong learning picture, it is the part that comes most within the province of the education authorities and hence warrants such scrutiny here. By clarifying the goals and standards within education systems, the articulation between these and non-formal learning arrangements, as well as with tertiary education and the different partners and organisations involved, is also likely to be facilitated.

Section B sets the stage by examining the issues that constantly re-emerge in the debate over which goals are most appropriate for formal education and training systems; the tensions that can arise as institutional structures are reformed to meet lifelong learning goals are also considered. Section C introduces various approaches to defining education and training standards in both formal systems and non-formal networks. The factors that have led to increased focus on the need for performance standard-setting and assessment are analysed. Section D explores the experiences and strategies of Member countries in setting, assessing and monitoring standards as a means of steering change towards objectives deemed compatible with the goal of lifelong learning for all. Strategies for monitoring school effectiveness and promoting parental choice of schools are also examined. Finally, Section E offers conclusions and directions for policy.

B. SETTING EDUCATION GOALS, AND NEW APPROACHES TO STEERING EDUCATION SYSTEMS

A major challenge faces national policy-makers as they set about reorienting their education systems to meet the challenge of lifelong learning in the 21st century. There is currently widespread dissatisfaction with the functioning of education systems in many countries – as the conclusion of a recent publication from the top-level European Round Table of Industrialists (1995, p. 6) makes clear:

"In nearly all European countries there is an ever-widening gap between the education that people need for today's complex world and the education they receive. Too many disillusioned young students drop out of educational systems through failure or rebellion, or come through with only minimal skills. This is a major economic and social concern particularly at a time when fewer new people than before are available to enter the labour markets. It is time to raise a cry of alarm to alert society to this educational gap."

The unavoidable conclusion is that education systems are not doing enough of what is genuinely needed, and when they are doing the right thing they are not doing it well enough. An indispensable first step in the urgent process of refocusing education systems is clarifying, explicitly, and if necessary establishing new educational goals. In many countries, goals and agendas of different parts of the system are implicit or have not recently been reassessed and, consequently, may pull in different directions. For example, Chapters 3 and 4 reviewed the reasons why conflicts arise between the goals of general and vocational education, and between those of secondary and tertiary education. Moreover, the goals of the formal education and training systems do not always relate clearly to those of non-formal activities (Colletta, 1994).

In spite of – or perhaps because of – such conflicts, reaching a consensus on explicit and reachable goals is essential, if systems are to be steered in a new and more productive direction. The OECD countries have in fact already agreed on a set of general goals for their education systems which broadly meet the concerns of the industrialists quoted above (OECD, 1995*p*, p. 186):

– *To achieve equal access to educational opportunity.* The education system intends to make educational opportunities equally accessible to all members of society regardless of age, ethnic background, race, gender, region, language, religion, or disability.

– *To achieve basic levels of literacy throughout the population.* A "basic" level primarily involves reading, writing, numeracy, and other communication and language skills, but may also involve familiarity with scientific and technological principles.

– *To achieve excellence throughout the education system.* The education system intends to strive for excellence and high levels of achievement for all students, in traditional academic areas as well as in those areas that cut across the familiar boundaries.

– *To achieve lifelong learning.* The education system intends to achieve high levels of participation in programmes tailored to the needs of learners of all ages, including early childhood education, adult education, and continuing vocational training.

Transparency as a goal

To attain these goals requires a refocusing of effort in national education systems; the goal of achieving lifelong learning, in particular, entails a much improved understanding of how the formal and non-formal systems in each country relate to each other. When goals are clear and systems transparent, barriers to goal attainment are easier to negotiate. Indeed, transparency itself needs to become a goal in order to make the others easier to attain.

The OECD Jobs Study (OECD, 1994*d*) recommended that transparency be improved, an opinion seconded by many countries. But transparency means different things to different people. One generally accepted sense is the movement towards making the management and administration of the system and its institutions more open and accountable to the public. The more specific sense used here focuses on the transparency of certification. For Australia, Canada, Mexico and the United States, for example, improving transparency means working towards the creation of a national framework for standards accepted and understood by all. The New Zealand National Qualifications framework is intended to unite all education and training qualifications within one national framework (Qualifications Authority, 1995). In countries such as France and Germany, which already have such frameworks, improving transparency means that new pathways between different levels and sectors of the education and training system will have to be created as the range of choices available to learners becomes wider and more complex, and modular programmes become the norm.

But transparency itself is also a complex goal which includes a variety of elements, and is best assessed using three separate though related criteria (Colardyn, 1994; Colardyn and Durand-Drouhin, 1995):

– *Transferability of skills and competencies.* This focuses on the use of certification within the education system to qualify individuals to move from one programme or level to another; routes taken may link general and vocational education, or secondary and tertiary education.

– *Visibility.* This clarifies the value of certification outside the education system, especially when social partners have been involved in the design and assessment of skills, knowledge and competencies; what someone knows, understands and can do should be fairly and clearly represented by his or her qualification.

– *Portability on the labour market.* This represents the economic value of certification in finding a job, achieving promotion, or generally enhancing career development.

Innovations and changes in assessment and recognition, leading to an improvement of transparency, can usefully be assessed against these criteria – although the form they may take varies depending on the country. Lack of transparency in education systems signals a major problem in relation to lifelong learning: the lack of fit between formal and non-formal provisions when it comes to certification; both transferability and portability need to be improved. Currently, there are several key issues: certification is rarely adequately transferable within formal education systems; it is not portable enough on the labour market; it is not sufficiently visible for firms and other employers, who often do not know what it means; and it often does not correspond to the needs of individuals.

Moving from goals to standards

The general goals outlined above need to be translated into more specific national goals. Can such goals be encapsulated in standards for education and training? Is it helpful to relate goals to specified standards for resource provision, curriculum content, and performance? Identifying goals – and improving the structures through which they might be achieved – must be followed by some form of standard-setting which would indicate the level of performance necessary in order to achieve the new goals. Again, some countries are revising established standards, whereas for others the process is relatively new.

In revising their frameworks, OECD countries have shown increasing interest in linking their national goals and policies to new assessment and certification mechanisms. New standards cannot simply be imposed from above; it is important to develop a consensual approach that unites students, teachers,

parents, employers, and the local community. Moreover, for practitioners, it is not only a matter of putting the new standards into operation; they often have a role to play in making sure that the standards are realistic. If a system is to be refocused successfully, there must be input from all the interested parties.

Common trends

Efforts to improve transparency, increase participation and devolve responsibility from the centre are now under way in many countries. The common trends identified below illustrate how goals, standards, assessment and certification are linked (OECD, 1994*m*; 1995*g*; 1995*l*; 1995*v*). Obviously, goals cannot be achieved everywhere through identical reforms, because countries may already have traditional national standards, a decentralised education system, or a strong tradition of involving the social partners. All the same, many countries are:

– Making student performance standards more explicit, and aggregating and reporting test results at various levels, especially the national level.

– Involving representatives from the world of work and local communities in the educational process. This is especially true for vocational and technical education, but it is also happening in general education.

– Giving parents more influence and choice.

– Devolving more responsibility for defining and managing the educational process to school principals and teachers, and holding them more accountable for outcomes.

– Defining a new balance between general and vocational education – first by aligning and, where possible, integrating separate tracks; secondly, by creating and implementing pathways between the two systems, with the aim of improving parity of esteem; and thirdly, by establishing new pathways from vocational education to tertiary education.

– Diversifying the approaches to assessment and certification of skills and competencies. This trend takes two inter-related forms: improving the flexibility of institutional arrangements (pathways, modules, credit transfers), and focusing on individuals (assessing and certifying prior learning, creating transportable student portfolios, and establishing assessment centres).

Less common, however, is an understanding of the need for professional development for teachers if new goals and standards are to become a reality. Once new performance standards for students have been devised, teachers need to internalise them – but then they need to raise their own level of performance so that they can elicit the required higher achievement levels from their students. As Selden (1994) observed with regard to the United States: "Most of us feel that massive amounts of 'unprecedentedly' effective professional development of teachers is needed to bring about significant changes in student learning". The recently published White Paper on the reform of the Irish education system describes a reform plan that puts the professional development of teachers at the centre of the change process (Irish Department of Education, 1995).

One difficulty with large-scale initiatives of this kind is that they are expensive at a time when all countries are trying to contain costs, and such refocusing – and the restructuring it may entail – must be carried out as economically as possible. (The financial implications of such moves are addressed in Chapter 8.) Nevertheless, some countries (Mexico, New Zealand, Norway, Spain, Sweden, the United Kingdom) have made radical changes to the structures of educational administration and governance. These countries and others (France, the Netherlands) have also developed national systems of monitoring student, school and system outcomes as a means of measuring and evaluating progress. Moreover, the content of curricula and the approach to assessment and certification have been reviewed and adapted in many OECD countries since the mid-1980s.

Flexibility and coherence in the curriculum

The above developments call attention to tensions between flexibility and coherence. Decentralisation tends to promote flexibility, while centralised systems emphasise coherence. This is especially true with regard to the curriculum. The attempt to offer choice and diversity while at the same time raising overall standards and avoiding fragmentation has produced several types of policy reaction in Member countries:

– Some hitherto decentralised education systems (Australia, New Zealand, the United Kingdom and the United States) have attempted to define and implement a common core curriculum for all schools. In the past these decentralised systems commonly promoted flexibility, but sometimes at the cost of fragmentation. These attempts reflect a search for explicit coherence: an agreed framework in which decentralised elements can be connected to each other, and eventually compared. Improving coherence will in turn contribute to transparency in goals and standards as well as in assessment and certification.

– Traditionally centralised systems are increasingly concerned with reducing central curricular prescriptions, in order to give more autonomy to regions/municipalities, institutions, or both. This applies in Mexico, for example, where the national authorities agreed, in 1992, to reform the structure of basic education. Improving the transparency of pathways should increase the flexibility of the system and contribute to a better fit between its various components. Examining ways of accrediting skills and competencies is important in assessing progress towards the attainment of coherence and flexibility.

– Many countries with high-stakes, curriculum-related leaving examinations are seeking to modify them in order to widen access and diversify provision in upper secondary education. Meanwhile, countries such as the United States, which lack such examinations, are discussing whether they should be introduced, and countries such as Denmark, Norway and Sweden, which had highly diversified upper secondary vocational courses, are seeking to streamline them into fewer, broader routes with larger general education components.

– Several countries (for example, England, France, Mexico, New Zealand, Sweden and Spain) have introduced or are intending to introduce national testing for students at key stages – either as part of system evaluation following major reforms, or to influence pedagogical practices (or both).

Most of these developments are occurring within the formal education system. How do they relate to lifelong learning? In general they result from an awareness that the rapidity of change in economies and social conditions requires more flexibility and transparency in educational provision, but also higher standards of foundation learning, so that all students can be trained and retrained. However, reforms which start from this premise of higher standards should not lose sight of the broader goal of promoting life-long learning for all by becoming overly concerned with elite selection. Excessive competition between students and schools at the upper secondary level can result in a narrowing of the implemented curriculum at earlier stages (Japanese Ministry of Education, Sciences and Culture, 1995).

In non-formal education for adults, there has been less coherence in the setting of goals, which reflects the diversity of the field. However, one trend is noticeable. In the 1970s, industrialised countries became aware of the fact that a proportion of their adults demonstrated low levels of literacy. In due course, literacy evolved into the concept of proficiency in applying reading, writing and mathematical skills in daily activities, including work. "Computers literacy" was added to the functional skills thought necessary for adult life, and subsequently "social skills" also, further extending the need for what came to be called "basic skills". Results from the International Adult Literacy Survey show that between 10 and 25 per cent of the adult population aged 16-64 years have literacy skills that might be deemed insufficient, given the demands of modern life.

Goals and standards in tertiary education

Many OECD countries are moving towards systems of mass tertiary education. Traditional tertiary goals and standards are challenged by the need to cater for a more heterogeneous student body and a proliferation of courses designed to meet new demands. These developments are occurring in a context of budgetary constraints on public expenditure. Not surprisingly in these circumstances, there is growing public concern in some countries about the quality of tertiary education. To clarify the goals and set standards for the tertiary education sector may be a useful strategy in those countries where concern with the quality of tertiary education is most acute.

Countries with "open" entry requirements for tertiary education, such as France, Germany and Italy, where institutions have little control over the selection process, are most severely affected. At the other end of the spectrum, the United States – with its mixture of private and state universities and its diverse range of institutions – has been able to offer a wide range of courses to a very heterogeneous student body. The Canadian and Japanese tertiary systems closely resemble the American one, with competitive entrance examinations. In the United Kingdom, although there are very few private tertiary institutions, universities can select their students. In

Sweden, there is a national competition for entry into tertiary education. Setting goals and standards calls for different strategies corresponding to these national contexts. The question for countries with open entry requirements is whether a decentralised approach, allowing institutions to define their own missions within a national goals strategy, is compatible with open entry. In these systems the maintenance of standards apparently involves high student attrition rates. In those countries with a more diverse range of entry standards the wastage rate appears to be much lower but the corollary is that the standards of both degrees and other tertiary qualifications vary widely across the institutional spectrum.

Tertiary education institutions play an important role in the various forms of lifelong learning – and the potential is there for even greater involvement. They can offer specialised courses designed both for those who want to raise their skill level from a low base and for the more highly qualified, as well as courses for adults who seek access to tertiary education.

Long- and short-term continuing education courses are found, under different names, in tertiary education institutions in many Member countries (including Australia, Canada, France, Germany, Mexico, the Netherlands, the United Kingdom and the United States). Long-term courses normally follow on from initial education; adult students tend to be either self-funded or government-supported. Private sector employers are in certain cases enlarging their support as well. Admission typically depends on conventional standards and initial formal qualifications (although some institutions do offer access courses, or base some of their admission criteria on portfolios, interviews or other evidence of prior learning). Pursuit of this type of education can also be facilitated by flexible institutional arrangements such as single-subject courses or modules, part-time studies, and distance learning. Short-term education includes courses, seminars, workshops and conferences lasting from a few days to a month or so; admission requirements may be flexible or highly specific, and such courses are usually subsidised by employers.

Post-graduate programmes are growing in popularity as a way of consolidating previous academic studies, increasing the depth of a student's specialist knowledge, and enhancing his or her chances on the labour market. In these cases, tertiary education is aimed mainly at young adults, and clearly fits into the framework of initial education.

Co-ordination between initial and continuing tertiary education needs to be of two types, since there are two characteristic forms of traditional tertiary education. Courses tend to be either long and thorough, producing graduates who are fully trained in their particular discipline and aware of the latest developments; or short and specialised, producing a less technically accomplished but more adaptable graduate who appreciates diversity and can cope with unforeseeable changes in the organisation of work.

The choice of one or the other type of course affects not only the length and content of initial education, but the balance between general and specialised education. It also has implications for the recognition of initial degrees and continuing professional education, and the balance between the professional, social and cultural experience of the individual. No single model, however, can meet all employers' needs.

There is still a great deal of work to be done in co-ordinating traditional and continuing tertiary education – which is where lifelong learning often takes place. Goals at this level are rarely properly articulated, and common standards need to be evolved across the two sectors; but universities in particular are often fiercely independent, and there are powerful vested interests involved.

Tensions

Several main categories of conflicts or tensions have already been identified. These arise both from efforts to reform traditional systems and from attempts to bring non-formal provision into a more structured relationship with the formal education system. Such tensions should be reviewed in the process of designing and implementing links between formal and non-formal provision; they can form the basis for policy action (OECD, 1996e).

- *Systems*: formal and non-formal provision both offer learning opportunities, but they work within very different perspectives and pursue distinct goals. Globalisation and technological changes have contributed to the development of non-formal provision, whose new values often contrast with those of the more traditional formal systems. Until now, there have been few attempts to develop links between formal systems and non-formal provision.

- *Schools*: schools and teachers are perhaps becoming less important as the sole source of foundation learning, but more important in the socialisation of many young students due to changes in family structure. Education systems are casting around for indicators of civic and social learning to reflect this role (OECD, 1995*l*), which is crucially important for lifelong learning.

- *Governance*: devolved responsibilities are often an acknowledgement of the need for increased professional autonomy for schools and teachers in complex educational processes – but the stress on accountability for outcomes and on new supervisory processes may inhibit creative and flexible professional responses to new needs.

- *Curriculum*: on the one hand, there is stress on raising general standards, encouraging parental aspirations, and elite selection; on the other, social and civic values, core competencies for lifelong learning, opportunities for all to succeed and cross-curricular initiatives are increasingly recognised as important for society as a whole. Curriculum frameworks often reflect these tensions, which question the continued relevance for all students of traditional subject disciplines. Tertiary education, with its traditional disciplines and competitive entrance examinations in certain countries that stress traditional cognitive knowledge, can exert powerful effects on the secondary education curriculum. General secondary schools in countries with high-stakes curriculum-related examinations for advancement to tertiary education, such as Japan, tend, in response to public demand, to concentrate on teaching those academic subjects that are tested. As school performance is judged in relation to students' performance on such tests, schools are prevented from experimenting with approaches that might prove more meaningful in a lifelong learning perspective.

- *Assessment*: national testing of student populations is increasingly employed as a means and gauge for system accountability – students' attainments as a measure of school and system performance. Assessment is undertaken in order to track and guide students, for diagnostic/pedagogic purposes, or to certify student competencies and performance in learning; sometimes these aims are combined.

There is a danger of over-assessment in some systems and confusion of purpose in others.

- *Standards*: there is some tension between medium- and long-term goals and immediate priorities. In formal education systems, standards are formulated to apply over a relatively long period. Non-formal approaches, in contrast, tend to pursue more immediate goals – as exemplified by the competency-based approach, which is evolving at a rapid pace.

- *Accreditation systems*: recognition of skills and competencies can result either from a long structured learning process, or from a competency-based approach focusing only on outcomes. Recognising and certifying prerequisite and acquired knowledge and competencies is one of the major problems for tertiary education institutions confronting lifelong learning. These institutions award socially and professionally recognised degrees and diplomas and therefore have a major impact on certain sectors of working life. In some faculties – medicine, engineering, education, law – universities have made substantial contributions to linking academic research and learning to real-life situations. In other faculties, teaching and research take little account of students' skills and competencies acquired outside formal education. There is a real economic and professional need for new types of certification that link them to work experience. That need, together with the rise of education and training in the non-formal sectors, will create pressure for change. Certificates ought to become "transferable" or "portable" from one work situation to another, from an academic to a professional position and *vice versa*, and new elements can be added to existing evaluation schemes to reflect advancement over time, learning performed in different places, and the individualisation of learning geared to employment and career development.

C. STANDARDS IN THE FORMAL AND NON-FORMAL SECTORS

For the purposes of this section, a policy-relevant definition of the "formal" and "non-formal" sectors of education and training provision is needed. The distinction between formal and non-formal learning is a function of the degree of institutionalisation, the structuring of the curriculum, and the relationships among the various people involved in the learning encounter. A more operational definition is that the formal system refers to all those aspects of education within the sphere of responsibilities and influence of the Minister of Education, together with private schools, universities and other institutions which prepare students for Ministry-recognised qualifications. The non-formal sector comprises learning activities taking place outside this formal system, such as those carried out within companies, by professional associations, or independently by self-motivated adult learners.

Today, a great deal of learning is already taking place in the non-formal sector. In many countries it is the formal sector that needs to adapt in order to find its proper role within a lifelong approach to learning for all. However, the formal sector in many ways represents the "education system", and is currently by far the most important agency for educating and training populations. As Chapter I makes clear, there is also far less systematic information concerning the non-formal sector. Inevitably, then, this section will be somewhat uneven in its treatment of the two sectors – although the non-formal sector clearly has very important implications for lifelong learning, and many of the most fruitful developments with regard to establishing relevant standards are taking place there.

Both the nature of educational standards and the definition of the term vary across OECD countries. Indeed, in some languages there is no exact equivalent of the English word "standards" or the concepts it conveys. One definition is related to the use of standards in industry as norms to which manufacturers must conform. Standards can also be benchmarks against which performances can be measured, as in sports, for example. There is also a politicised connotation, as in the "standards movement" which has become such a feature of educational debate in certain English-speaking countries. Standards in education can refer to curriculum, performance, teaching, or accommodation and resources; generally there are four types:

- Input (or process) standards, which specify the nature and level of resources allocated to the educational process, including those that impact on the quality of teaching. In the United States such standards are often referred to as "opportunity to learn" standards; in the United Kingdom they are known as "process" standards, in order to distinguish those measures which govern the teaching and learning process from those which are related to levels of performance and outcomes.

- Content standards, which define those areas of the curriculum all students should master.

- Performance standards, which describe how well students are expected to perform in those content areas.

- Outcome standards, which refer to the results achieved by institutions and the system as a whole. Often, these results are evaluated on the basis of aggregate measures of student performance.

In educational policy terms, the focus in many countries has shifted from standards of input or process to those of student performance and system outcome – a clear signal of doubt that higher standards of provision, whether material or human, can in themselves guarantee higher achievement.

As to setting standards, there are in the main two approaches. The *inputs approach* can be characterised as the provision of a structured learning setting in which, as a rule, content and organisation of curriculum are predefined; in other words, the duration and place of study are specified, and organised assessments of various kinds lead to an accredited certification. The specifics of this approach vary, since school and post-school curricula, organisation and examinations differ greatly among countries. In most Member countries, there has been substantial curriculum development in primary and secondary education, and regulation of initial vocational training. Much attention has also been directed to the professional development of teachers.

The *outcomes approach* recognises the results of a learning process which can take place at school or in any other setting (at home, at work, or through community activities). The focus is on proof of learning. No single predefined structured setting is needed; the outcome will be considered without regard to the duration of education or training, or even where the learning took place. "Conventional" examinations or forms of continuous assessment may be replaced by a competency-based approach which draws on learning modules and leads to the recognition of units of competencies; these can sometimes be joined to form the basis for new learning systems. It is thus easier for individual students to move between the formal and non-formal sectors: for example, a student with accredited competencies gained at work may negotiate entry into university.

The formal system

OECD Member countries differ sharply in the use they make of standards in educational policy. What are the experiences of Member countries in externally setting and monitoring input, context and performance standards in pursuit of high-quality formal education and training provision? Why have some Member countries with recognised high-quality education systems eschewed this approach? This section reviews policy and practice in Member countries, drawing particularly on recent OECD studies (OECD, 1995*k*; 1995*q*; 1995*v*; 1996*d*).

The degree and direction of public concern for educational standards vary sharply (OECD, 1995*l*). In Denmark, Norway and the German-speaking countries, and to some extent in Japan, public confidence in educational professionals is relatively high, and concern for standards is directed mainly at ensuring selection and training of high-quality teachers and the provision of adequate resources. By contrast, confidence is relatively low in Australia, Canada, Mexico, New Zealand, the United Kingdom and the United States, where there is political pressure for setting explicit standards against which students will be assessed and, in some cases, institutions and staff held accountable.

The debate has also been fuelled in many Member countries by reference to the allegedly better performance of students in other countries – though until now the only sources of evidence for such statements are the International Association for the Evaluation of Educational Achievement (IEA) and the International Assessment of Educational Progress (IAEP). Despite consistent progress in the development of measurement technology, problems of reliability and validity still beset such studies, especially when the context is an international comparative setting where accounting for external factors is particularly difficult. IEA and IAEP data have sometimes been invoked in a partisan or ideological way (OECD, 1995*p*).

In the European tradition, and in Japan, an indication of expectations of student performance is usually incorporated into the national syllabuses. Student performance standards can be defined, *a priori*, as those expected at a particular stage of education, or *a posteriori*, when cut-off points are established on student achievement scales in order to differentiate between levels of performance (pass/fail, gradations in between) (Tuijnman and Postlethwaite, 1994). In practice, the establishment of standards has been an *a posteriori* or normative process, especially for the secondary leaving examinations often associated with university selection. There is a tension here between the beneficial effects of upper secondary academic examinations – such as high standards, links with university scholarship, trickle-down effects on the rest of the school – and the less desirable effects, which include early tracking of students, downgrading of non-academic vocational routes, and rigid subject demarcation. Addressing the inequities that arise from these selection processes has been a major concern of post-war governments in many OECD countries. From a lifelong learning perspective they are still a serious problem, especially in those countries where no structured vocational pathways exist (see Chapter 4).

The traditional curriculum-related approach to setting standards still applies in most European countries. Well-defined subject boundaries are monitored by inspectorates and university specialists. Hierarchies of subject knowledge are embedded in national curriculum and assessment criteria indicating expected student performance levels. Standards in upper secondary examinations are set *a posteriori* in a combination of overall pass/fail and cut-off ranges for certification and selection purposes.

Examination systems are most demanding when students bear a heavy load of required subjects and undergo lengthy tests, and when – as in Germany and France – the test questions call for high-level cognitive skills as well as broad and detailed knowledge. In their survey of examination systems, Eckstein and Noah (1993) found that examinations in France and Germany stand out among the seven countries studied as placing the heaviest burdens on candidates. Chart 6.1 shows that, by contrast, examinees in Sweden and the United States face far lighter tasks.

In countries with a national curriculum, examinations are organised and monitored by State officials. Marking is usually done by secondary teachers; sometimes the latter work more or less autonomously, and sometimes the process is organised by inspectors or officials, or by free-standing examination boards. However, these traditional approaches to standard-setting have been increasingly strained by the growth in student numbers, especially in upper secondary courses, and the increasing heterogeneity of the student population. While there is little evidence that outcome standards are falling, there is concern that rising expectations from parents and employers are not being met. The acute problem of young people who are excluded from participation in employment by the collapse of traditional occupations requiring low levels of literacy and numeracy, and who cannot meet the requirements of new technologies, has sharpened the focus on this issue. The problem is not simply how to raise traditional standards – although that is an important aim – but how to assess key competencies and attitudes such as willingness and capacity to learn, and the ability to work in teams and to communicate. The data in Annex Table A.56 show that the general public in all OECD countries surveyed feels that such "cross-curriculum" competencies and qualities are developed less well than traditional subject-matter knowledge.

Chart 6.2 reports on a recent survey of public expectations and attitudes to lower secondary education (OECD, 1995*l*). It was found that the general public in countries with highly demanding exit examinations, such as Austria, France and Switzerland, were on average much more confident that central subjects featuring in those examinations were well taught, compared to the lower public expectations in countries such as Sweden and the United States, which – according to Eckstein and Noah (1993) – do not have such a demanding examination system, perhaps partly because in the latter countries entrance into tertiary education is governed not by performance on *exit* examinations but by nationally or institutionally determined *entry* tests, such as the Scho-

◆ Chart 6.1. **Overall difficulty of examinations: comparative scale**

◆ Chart 6.2. **Perceived confidence in important school subjects,**[1] **1993-94**
Percentage

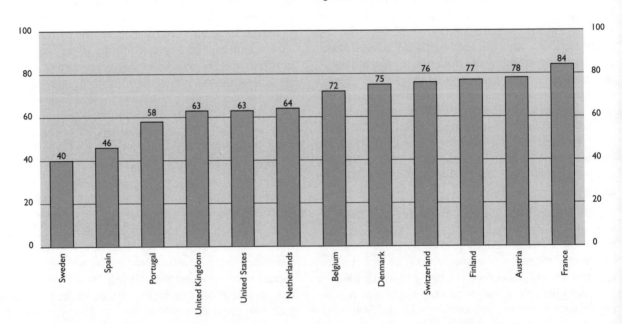

1. Percentage of respondents who viewed subjects as important and who thought they were taught well in schools. See Annex Table A.56.
Source: OECD (1995*l*), *Public Expectations of the Final Stage of Compulsory Education*, Table C23, p. 132.

lastic Aptitude Test (SAT) or the American College Board's Test (ACT) in the United States.

One of the features dividing those countries where there is public debate and anxiety about outcome standards from others is the status of teachers. Table 6.1 presents subjective indicators of teacher respect and perceptions regarding the quality of teaching in mathematics and foreign languages. It might be suggested that where teacher status is high, concern tends to be lower and performance standards are left in the hands of professionals but the data are as yet insufficient to shed full light on this assumption. However, it seems likely that high standards of learning and teaching cannot be imposed. Content and performance standards have to be interpreted by teachers in various contexts. An approach which defines standards too inflexibly and measures performance in too narrow a way will interfere with the professional process and may even lower standards, particularly in those areas which relate most closely to lifelong learning – many of which are not easily assessable.

In Germany and Japan, standards are curriculum-related and set by educational professionals, mainly teachers and inspectors. There is a State core curriculum in Japan. In Germany, although the individual *Länder* control education, there is a substantial degree of national consensus about curriculum and assessment. Teacher selection and training and national or State approval of textbooks are instruments for the standardisation of student performance and teaching in both countries. Marking of examination papers and determination of the level of student performance are left to individual teachers in Germany, with some moderation from colleagues and State officials. This power of certification adds greatly to teacher status, but it also raises questions of inter-rating reliability and hence of equity. In Japan also, assessment and certification are largely in the hands of teachers, but it could be said that a degree of meritocracy is ensured by the fact that students have to take national university entrance examinations before they enrol for specific admission examinations set by the individual universities.

In the United States, which has neither a national curriculum nor curriculum-based national examinations, the approach to standard-setting has necessarily been different. Curriculum and assessment policies and frameworks vary from state to

Table 6.1. **Respect for teachers and the quality of teaching in secondary education, 1993-94**

	Teacher salary index[1]	Respect for teachers[2]	Mathematics well taught[3]	Foreign languages well taught[3]
Austria	2.3	74	87 (0.8)	79 (1.0)
Finland	1.8	58	84 (1.1)	81 (1.2)
France	. .	55	92 (0.7)	87 (0.9)
Netherlands	2.0	61	71 (1.5)	73 (1.5)
Portugal	3.7	59	58 (1.4)	61 (1.4)
Sweden	1.2	48	49 (1.6)	43 (1.6)
United Kingdom	2.4	56	65 (1.4)	51 (1.4)
United States	1.6	68	70 (1.3)	53 (1.4)

Notes: . . Data not available. Standard errors in parentheses.
1. Ratio of maximum lower secondary teachers' salaries to per capita GDP converted using purchasing power parities, 1992.
2. Percentage of respondents who answered "very respected" or "fairly respected" to the survey question: "How respected are lower secondary teachers as a profession?" (1993-1994).
3. Percentage of respondents who were "very confident" or "fairly confident" that the subject was well taught in secondary schools, 1993-94.
Sources: OECD (1995*l*) and OECD (1995*d*).

state, although some common ground is established by the use of nationally distributed textbooks. Despite the passing of the Goals 2000 legislation in 1994 (United States Department of Education, 1994*b*), there is still no specific federal role in implementing a national curriculum framework, although a degree of national consensus over content standards in mathematics and science is beginning to emerge. Standards have commonly been set *a posteriori* on the basis of multiple-choice testing. However, such testing cannot influence classroom practice or serve as an indicator of teaching/learning outcomes in the way that curriculum-related examinations do. Realisation that outcomes-based approaches to standards have little impact on teaching and learning has led to the growth in the United States of portfolio or performance assessment. This puts assessment in the hands of teachers and makes it "formative", that is, a useful tool in promoting learning. But there may be some loss of reliability in measuring and reporting standards. The great diversity of standards of student performances between schools, districts and states has also led to greater emphasis on opportunity-to-learn standards. This is less an issue in those countries where content standards are not so diverse and are set out in national curricular frameworks.

Similar concerns have led both Australia and Canada to revise content and student performance standards at state/province level, and at interstate level in Australia, where *de facto* national curriculum frameworks are being established for most states. Public concern over outcome standards led the United Kingdom government to introduce a national curriculum and assessment system in the late 1980s.

In France, the Netherlands, Japan, Spain, Sweden and England and Wales, testing based on a national curriculum co-exists with traditional secondary leaving/university entrance examinations. The former is usually directed at whole cohorts of students and may prove a better instrument of monitoring, evaluation and guidance in the hands of teachers. Its purpose varies across countries from pedagogical – especially in France, where the tests are taken at the beginning of the school year to make clear their diagnostic function – to the monitoring of student and school performance – for example in England and Wales, where their primary function seems to be monitoring student and school performance. The degree to which the tests are set and marked by teachers or by external bodies also varies. The latter (A-levels, *baccalauréat*) are being forced to adapt to increasing numbers of students and heterogeneity of pathways, but retain their selective function. In general, at this level, testing is primarily external, though sometimes associated with teacher assessment.

Although the empirical data to support this claim are disparate and insufficient, it may be postulated that the teachers' responsibility for assessment and certification – the implementation of standards – is thus a central issue in the public's perception of their status and confidence in their judgements. Where the latter is high, there will be less pressure for the external monitoring of students' performance, except possibly at the level of selection for university. Where it has traditionally been low, assessment is taken out of the hands of teachers, lowering their status and making it more difficult for testing to be used to improve teaching and learning. Trusting the teachers involves a degree of risk by policy-makers, particularly in systems where there is no strong teacher "assessment culture". Given the stability of the teaching force in most Member countries (see Chapter 1), however, investment in professional development programmes which focus on assessment for improved learning are likely to be effective.

The focus on standards within the formal system reflects both increased public concern with educational standards and the increasing importance of formal education qualifications in the workplace. Education matters more, both for individuals and the economy. There is also increasing concern about social exclusion, a process which often begins within the formal system. For these reasons, the debate about standards is of central importance to lifelong learning. While the latter may to some extent have the function of compensating for failure within the formal system, it is greatly facilitated where the formal system has succeeded in developing adequate foundation skills and the ability to learn in its students.

Non-formal provision

Standards set within the formal system inevitably have repercussions on non-formal provision. How should learning progress outside the formal education and training systems be judged against the standards, and how can recognition of achievement best be credited and signalled to the labour market? Outside the formal systems, several kinds of outcomes approach can be distinguished: some are focused on individuals, such as accreditation of prior learning (APL) for access to tertiary education or to employment (mobility, job classification); some are linked to "complete learning" systems as advocated by the National Council on Vocational Qualifications in the United Kingdom.

Outcome assessment takes several forms in non-formal education and training, all of which are crucial in a strategy of lifelong learning:

– *The individual-based approach for educational purposes.* Several countries have developed accreditation of prior learning systems (Canada, France). In these examples, an outcomes approach is linked with the more common input approach; credit is given for skills, knowledge or competencies that have been acquired through work and non-work experience. This frees individuals from the obligation of "relearning" what has been learned. The

final certification will be identical to one achieved through the full educational programme. In France, a recent law on certification (1993) has two objectives: to provide incentives for adults to engage in lifelong learning, and to offer a route to traditional certification (OECD, 1990*b*; 1996*d*).

– *The individual-based approach for employment purposes.* Several countries use the source tools (prior learning assessment, recognition of prior learning) to help the unemployed develop career projects. This approach is widespread in France, through the *Agence nationale pour l'emploi* and the Assessment Centre, through which many long-term unemployed (or other young people or adults) can have their skills and competencies assessed in order to help them redefine their employment strategy, which might or might not include additional education and training.

– *The institution-based approach and new learning systems.* An institution-based approach has emerged in countries with labour force shortages. A decade ago, for various educational reasons, Australia, New Zealand and the United Kingdom were confronted with qualification shortages which were seen as a major obstacle to economic development. These countries put great emphasis on raising schools' attainment and on recognising skills and competencies of adult workers.

In the above, the focus is on school qualifications as well as on new assessment and accreditation policies, including the introduction of the competency-based approach, which allows for recognition of learning irrespective of where it takes place. Developments are aimed mainly at adult populations; for example, under the National Vocational Qualifications (NVQs) system in the United Kingdom, skills and competencies can be assessed and accredited anywhere. This approach is pushed strongly by public authorities, who have called on employers to participate further in defining the skills and competencies needed, as well as assessing them. Doubts are raised, however, with respect to employers' prospective views of those skills and competencies: Were they defining past jobs, or future jobs? How could the future jobs be defined in terms of prerequisite competencies?

Currently, a second development can be seen: these "new" concepts, held in equal esteem, are being integrated into the traditional education system. For the institution, this means the co-existence of both "input" course design, and recognition of learning outcomes. Also, these concepts are intended to serve the age group 16-19 – which raises questions about the foundations of learning and equal accessibility to tertiary education and employment, as well as to further education and training in working life.

Australia and New Zealand are undergoing similar developments, with a stronger emphasis on the training market approach – which permits a more rapid increase of education and training supply. In New Zealand this approach is expected to be implemented fully by 1997. It is based on two principles: first, national qualifications have been developed by a recognised national standards-setting body, and the New Zealand Qualifications Authority (NZQA) is responsible for managing them. Secondly, education and training provision can take place anywhere – in the workplace through self-managed learning projects, or in educational institutions – and can be assessed in the workplace or by the institutions. Assessment leads to the awarding of credits culminating in final certification. This national structure does not differentiate between vocational and academic qualifications: it is a national credit transfer system. Accredited providers and workplace assessors record student results on a national database. Leavers receive an annual printout as they accumulate credits towards a desired qualification or skills profile.

The approach, if it proves successful, will address both the problem of temporary shortages in the labour force and the limits imposed on public authorities in providing ever-increasing amounts of formal education and training. It will also help individuals to have their skills and competencies recognised – an incentive for lifelong learning.

Assessment

Assessment is a key component in the maintenance of standards. In most systems at primary and lower secondary levels assessment is in the hands of professionals, and its purpose is mainly pedagogical: to diagnose weaknesses in students' understanding and facilitate lesson planning by teachers (Smith and Levin, 1995). However, national testing for system accountability is becoming more widespread at these levels. At upper secondary level, assessment for selection and certification, often conducted externally, is the norm in OECD countries. These examinations are a means of maintaining, and perhaps raising, standards in conventional disciplines but they

sometimes make adaptation to new approaches to curriculum and learning difficult. They may also be used to exclude groups of students from access to further education or training.

Competency-based practices are among the innovations that can lead to widening access and help avoid duplication in learning, for they recognise that learning takes place outside the formal education system as well as within it. Competency-based assessment emphasises outcomes, meaning that neither the place of learning nor the learning process is regulated. The conventional course is broken down into discrete, easily assessed skills and competencies, and candidates simply have to demonstrate that they can do what is required. Outside the formal system, firms and public enterprises can develop assessment and certification procedures so as to link them more easily to job classification and remuneration mechanisms.

This competency-based approach represents an important challenge to more traditional forms of assessment, recognition and certification. However, while modularisation has facilitated the assessment of easily assessed skills, it is still a matter of debate how far it can be extended into the domain of existing secondary and tertiary provision. The conventional certification approach remains the main benchmark for tertiary education as well as for labour markets.

Nevertheless, a shift in emphasis to competency-based assessment practices may help change the current limited focus of accreditation. Sources of learning other than conventional institutions will be finally recognised; Open College and Open University in the United Kingdom, *TV Cinq* in France, in-house training programmes in firms, professional associations and non-profit associations, are among the examples.

That recognition should prove particularly advantageous when it comes to promoting lifelong learning, because these other learning modes are often concentrated in the non-formal sector. As was indicated in Chapter 3, the goals associated with lifelong learning are increasingly acknowledged in formal education, and are reflected in the emerging focus on core competencies – first-language literacy, mathematics, study skills, communication skills – as providing the foundations for later learning, and on the importance of coherence between initial and further education. The goals must also address the problem of individuals having to prove not once but several times in their life and career that they have acquired a basic knowledge and set of useful skills.

D. STEERING CHANGE BY THE USE OF STANDARDS

Monitoring and evaluation

This section addresses the problems likely to be encountered in integrating standard-setting, monitoring, and the evaluation of schools and education systems, into a strategy for steering reform and improving the equity, quality and efficiency of the development of human resources. Member country experiences support the theoretical analysis.

A distinction can be made between monitoring education systems and evaluating them, although frequently the two concepts – and practices as well – merge. Essentially, monitoring involves ensuring that regulations and legislation are being complied with, and keeping track of, both inputs and outcomes over time. Monitoring for the purpose of tracking development over time does not necessarily require explicit standards or criteria.

Evaluation may include monitoring activities, but the crucial difference is that it involves qualitative judgement by professionals and others – who are asking whether a given level of resourcing or performance is good enough. Evaluation may utilise explicit or implicit standards or criteria, or may form part of the development of such standards or criteria.

A second distinction should be made, between procedures that monitor or evaluate the standards of a whole education system and those approaches which focus on individual schools or other educational establishments. In some countries, recent anxiety over students' levels of performance has led to increasing emphasis on evaluating the schools themselves – frequently in the context of more general educational reform. Several countries, notably Sweden, Mexico, the Netherlands and the United Kingdom have set up arrangements for evaluating tertiary courses and institutions based on peer review and self-evaluation. In some cases these evaluations have financial consequences.

Monitoring and evaluating education systems

In a framework of lifelong learning, as new standards or targets are set – often through changes in the curriculum or in the content and form of tests and examinations – it becomes increasingly necessary to monitor progress towards achieving them. At the same time, systems of quality assurance, adapted from the private sector, have become more widespread in the public sector in some countries. These

often focus not on outcomes, but on the essential inputs – particularly monitoring procedures – without which the outcomes presumably would not be achievable.

The governments of all OECD countries keep track of financial inputs into their education and training systems through their normal accounting procedures, although different degrees of decentralisation mean that the systems vary greatly in the degree of control they have over how the money is spent – or indeed in how much knowledge they have of local spending decisions.

As far as performance outcomes are concerned, the authorities in France, Scotland, Spain, New Zealand, and England and Wales have set up mass testing systems of various kinds that aim to determine the level at which students across the country are performing, and to compare results over time. These countries are exploring the possibility of linking their testing systems in ways that would allow them to produce comparable information for use in the construction of international indicators of student performance (OECD, 1995*p* and 1995*r*).

International indicators are another way in which governments can both monitor and evaluate different aspects of their education systems: inputs and outcomes can be looked at over time, or be compared with those of other nations (OECD, 1994*m*). International comparisons can highlight differences in relation to other countries; however, such comparisons need careful interpretation, and performance outcomes – what policy-makers are often most interested in – are especially difficult to compare in a meaningful way (OECD, 1994*m*).

National inspectorates may also have a monitoring role to perform, especially in relation to reform; in Spain, for example, school inspectors are asked to report on how the implementation of the new education law is progressing in schools across the country. They are also sometimes asked by governments to judge whether the entire education system is performing sufficiently well. Although most inspectorates focus on the performance of individual schools or teachers, it is widespread practice for government to ask them to evaluate specific aspects of the system, or its workings as a whole – identifying strengths and weaknesses, and perhaps prescribing solutions to problems.

Following the evaluation of a specific aspect of the system – for example, pathways in vocational and technical education – governments may devise standards in the form of targets that must be met in order to raise the general level of performance. A good example is the national assessment of vocational education in the United States (US Department of Education, 1994*b*).

Monitoring and evaluating the performance of schools

The main reasons for focusing on the performance of individual schools can broadly be divided into two categories. The first is accountability – the idea that since society pays for them, public sector schools should fulfil the purposes society defines for them and reach the standards that society requires; the second is school improvement, for a school's performance must be assessed if it is to be analysed and improved, and if expert advice and services such as staff development are to be offered where they are most needed.

In the past, inspectorates in most countries were largely concerned with monitoring compliance within schools. In line with the current general trend, there is a tendency to have them focus more explicitly on school performance in terms of outcomes, although they still perform an important monitoring function, notably in the United Kingdom, the Netherlands, New Zealand and Germany.

Accountability is a complex concept; schools in different countries are accountable in many ways, sometimes to more than one stakeholder. The term itself has a number of different senses, all closely related to the goals of the education system and the standards it is charged with achieving (Kogan, 1988). Simply making schools "accountable" (whether to the State, parents, the community, or to others) is unlikely on its own to lead to improvements in standards of performance. It is, however, a desirable policy in the interests of transparency and democracy in education.

School improvement, too, is intimately related to the setting and monitoring of standards, since schools which are trying to improve their performance need first to raise their expectations. This entails evaluating their strengths and weaknesses, identifying areas which need improvement, and agreeing on an action plan which incorporates higher levels of performance.

The two main methods used for externally evaluating schools are performance indicators and inspection of various kinds. Currently, a number of countries are engaged in a search for reliable performance indicators – mostly based on the results of tests or examination – which accurately reflect achievements. Countries such as Belgium, France and the United Kingdom, which have well-established public examination systems, are using information derived from these results as an index of school quality. The "value added" performance indicators developed by the French, which are based on the *Baccalauréat* results and attempt to identify those *lycées* that offer a wide range of pupils the best chances of success rather than simply producing the highest raw pass rate by ruthlessly selecting their pupils, seem to be the most well-developed indicators currently in use (DEP, 1994).

Many OECD countries have some form of national inspectorate, and consider that there is no substitute for actually visiting schools to see if the standards are being met. In national efforts to raise the performance of individual schools, both objective evaluation from external inspectors and "friendly" advice from professionals or peers who know the school well are important. An evaluation system needs to have credibility in the outside world, while at the same time enabling schools to improve their performance by taking their particular situation into account.

As hinted at above, performance evaluation of individual schools may be undertaken for different purposes:

- to identify the strengths and weaknesses of individual schools as part of a national improvement strategy aimed at raising standards of performance;
- to identify those schools with serious problems and attempt to address those problems;
- to assess the professional competence of teachers;
- to impose or encourage new or more effective ways of operating;
- to encourage the creation of "learning organisations" – institutions that embody a culture of self-managed improvement and evaluation;
- to raise levels of student performance whether at the national, local or individual level.

Hence, "monitoring" standards is not enough if a strategy has not been devised for identifying strengths and weaknesses against a clear set of criteria, enabling those schools which are not reaching a satisfactory level to improve their performance. Procedures – which differ from country to country – need to be followed up to make sure that recommendations are taken, and that any weaknesses are effectively addressed. In this way, the new standards can become progressively more embedded in the system.

Member country experiences

To some extent, the experiences of Member countries in using goals and standards for the explicit steering of their education systems are determined by the nature of their political system. In certain political systems, there has been a move towards setting national goals and standards for achievement by schools, even though the latter operate with increased autonomy over processes (Sweden, France, England); and monitoring by national testing and a focus on outcomes in terms of student and school performance standards. The powers of local or intermediary authorities have been redefined – reduced in the United Kingdom and increased in France, Mexico, Spain and Sweden. Generally this has narrowed the differences between these countries in the distribution of control and in defining national responsibilities more clearly.

Most federal systems have been working to define an agreed national core curriculum of content and performance standards. A spectrum of interstate co-operation and federal initiative ranges from Canada – where there is least central control – through Australia and the United States; in the latter country the federal initiatives have been thwarted by states' rights movements. At the other end of the spectrum is Germany, where aspects of a central tradition continue to operate by consensus among autonomous *Länder*.

This division into federal or nationally centralised systems does not fit all Member countries comfortably; some might best be described as "quasi-federal". Belgium has evolved into an effectively federal system based on language, as far as education is concerned, whereas Spain shows some of the characteristics of both unitary and federal systems. Within the hybrid United Kingdom political system, Scotland and Northern Ireland enjoy a degree of autonomy in educational matters comparable to regions within the Spanish quasi-federal system.

In each of the three broad categories, central or state governments operate with varying degrees of power and with a range of means. Some have national or local inspectorates (or both); some have agencies for national testing and monitoring. In the matter of using standards to raise performance and steer the development of education systems, the experience of those countries where central power is strong (England and Wales, France and New Zealand) has been on balance positive. However, the appropriate balance between central direction, local authority and institutional autonomy is still a matter of some controversy. Limits have been placed on federal initiative in Australia, Canada and the United States. Interstate consensus on limited objectives has been effective to varying degrees in Canada and Germany.

To some extent, public opinion about educational standards is an important factor in governments' ability to change the system. Indeed, in some countries concern about standards has been used to make reform of the system publicly or politically acceptable, as have international comparisons more generally. The problem here is that public perceptions may not relate to future-oriented or lifelong learning goals. The role of pressure groups in diverting the course of change is also a matter of concern.

In some countries, especially the United States, sharper focus on academic standards and student performance through curriculum-related testing – especially if linked to high stakes (for graduation, university entrance) – may jeopardise the older aim of promoting the educational and social inclusion of minority groups. The question of how to reconcile academic standards with wider access and greater emphasis on practical competencies remains largely unanswered.

E. USING GOALS AND STANDARDS: POLICY CONCLUSIONS

The question that arises from the foregoing discussion of Member countries' experience in this area is whether the goals, standards and methods of quality control now used to govern education and training systems are consistent with a lifelong approach to learning.

- *Redefining goals for education systems is an urgent policy requirement in the light of social and economic developments and in the perspective of lifelong learning.* Setting out coherent purposes and redefining links with non-formal educational processes can enhance system performance and improve access for individuals.

- *There is currently a danger that what can be most reliably assessed will become the criterion of quality.* Other skills and areas of knowledge that are vital in establishing a foundation for lifelong learning may consequently be neglected. Performance in key competencies that will enable students to respond to the exigencies of economic and social change needs to be assessed validly and reliably. Until such an assessment is possible, these skills and competencies will not be given the place in educational provision that their importance in the broader economic and social environment warrants.

— *New approaches to assessment and certification are therefore a high priority*. To ensure that these are related to the world of work, continuing consultation with the social partners and the various professions and trade associations is called for. In many cases, current standards of educational resource provision are not adequate to meet these challenges.

— *But the identification and assessment of quality is too complex to be reflected adequately by a set of quantitative indicators, however wide-ranging*. Indeed, some approaches may hinder the quest of improving quality, which should be at the heart of the education process.

— *The goal of improving quality must engage those most centrally involved: teachers and students*. Measures to help teachers and students evaluate their own performances effectively are those most likely to improve quality. This suggests that the continuing professional development of teachers is likely to be an effective approach to steering education systems. Professional development should have two important goals: to acquaint teachers with the nature of changes in the social and economic environment in which their students will live and work, and with the desired educational outcomes which this environment requires of students in a lifelong learning perspective; and to develop in teachers a formative approach to assessment that can serve to promote all students' capacity to learn and to evaluate their own progress across the entire range of curricular and extra-curricular activities. These considerations, which are developed more fully in Chapter 7, also apply to training that occurs outside the formal systems.

— *Curriculum standards, regularly revised to reflect advances in knowledge and the emergence of new social and economic needs and skills, can serve as useful frameworks for teachers, and for teacher development programmes.*

— *Student performance standards, whether a priori statements of expected levels of performance or a posteriori analyses of national test results, can serve as useful indicators for schools and teachers in their own self-assessments.* Such data can also serve governments in their steering of the system: revision of curriculum statements, allocation of resources and planning of teacher development programmes can all be usefully informed by analysis of the strengths and weaknesses of student performance.

— *Standards related to inputs (teachers' qualifications, pay and conditions of work, textbooks, physical resources) and processes (curriculum and assessment frameworks) are also useful in steering the system.* In countries where centrally-directed education systems have existed for many years, this approach has sometimes ossified and requires more flexible and decentralised administration without losing the normative standards of provision which it has usually ensured. Other countries could benefit from more equitable implementation of opportunity-to-learn standards which can only be achieved within national frameworks. In federal systems a coherent national approach is difficult to achieve, but not necessarily incompatible with state or local control of education.

— *Clearly expressed standards, and related monitoring, can also serve the purpose of democratic regulation and accountability at the macro level of nationally aggregated performance.* In this context, the publication of performance outcomes is of crucial importance. Schools and teachers identified as not meeting "standards" (expressed as a cut-off point in aggregated student performance data) need professional help.

— *Such applications of "standards" raise a further question about comparability and the "value added" to student learning by schools and individual teachers.* Put simply, standards alone cannot adequately reflect quality, either of teaching or learning, given the huge variety of student backgrounds and social contexts in which teaching occurs in contemporary society. As part of a broader strategy, in some Member countries inspectorates are finding a new role as mediators between schools and governments, interpreting student performance data in the light of their own professional evaluation of the quality of teaching and learning, and the context in which it occurs. The crucial question facing inspectors in these circumstances is whether they can go beyond diagnosis to promote improvement. Identification of failure, whether by individual students, teachers or schools, is not in itself an adequate strategy for improvement.

– *Opportunities to learn outside the formal system of education and training will continue to develop. They need to be recognised and articulated with the formal systems.* Specifically, governments need to introduce a national credit transfer system. In the best of outcomes, these non-formal approaches can help overcome the major problem of exclusion of students and adults from the benefits of lifelong learning. In the worst, they may intensify and prolong the inequities which to varying degrees are a feature of current national education and training systems.

– *The need is not for new bureaucratic structures or procedures,* but rather for a new focus within formal structures on the needs of all students in a lifelong learning perspective; for recognition of the value of knowledge and skills acquired elsewhere; and, perhaps, for a new emphasis on underpinning civic values to offset the negative effects of the current emphasis on individual performance.

STRENGTHENING EDUCATIONAL RESOURCES

A. INTRODUCTION

This chapter discusses the implications of the trends, issues and policy shifts mentioned in the previous chapters for the human and physical as well as intangible "assets" and resources of education systems (teachers, principals and other staff, governors and managers; buildings and equipment and the supply of useful information of various kinds). Section B examines the implications – not only for the teachers themselves, but for education authorities, administrators, teacher training institutes, and professional organisations – of the shift towards lifelong learning. Section C focuses on the proper uses of new information media and instructional technologies in facilitating learning. Section D deals with the implications for school buildings and the physical "assets" of the system. Section E reviews the information needs of governments and their partners in education. The necessity for policy-making itself to be grounded in a solid knowledge base is also examined. Section F advances suggestions for possible policy directions.

B. TEACHERS AND OTHER KEY ACTORS

Good teachers and school leaders remain the key to efficient education systems. It is false to imply that the new technologies to be studied in a subsequent section will remove the need for teachers, although they doubtless call for some changes in teaching styles, methods and techniques. The policy questions raised are fundamental. What are the new teaching and learning roles predicted by high-quality education systems that are well prepared to meet the challenges implied by a lifelong learning framework? How can teachers, trainers, administrators and all those concerned be helped to perform these roles effectively? The experience of recent years shows that many new educational goals have not been attained because comprehensive initial and in-service training programmes for teachers have not been an integral component of reform. In what ways should training be tailored to the changing roles of teachers? What kind of training is required for school leaders and managers? Specifically, what are the implications for professional training of the new information and instructional technologies?

The transformation of education and training in response to social and economic processes has wide-ranging implications for the duties and tasks of teachers and all those concerned with education. The institution of a lifelong learning framework will only be possible if all educators are committed to maximising their own professional development. New policies are needed for upgrading or retraining personnel and reforming initial education and training in order to ensure that everyone is ready to accept and promote innovation.

A career for teachers

Thoroughly professional teaching remains at the heart of nearly every endeavour to improve the quality of education. As already stated many schools still inculcate knowledge and skills in old-fashioned ways in spite of all the "progressive" efforts to improve the quality and efficiency of teaching and learning. Studies show that "frontal instruction" is still preponderant in many schools (Goodlad, 1984; Slavin, 1995). Lectures and the question-and-answer method often take up most of the time while independent work, whether by individuals or small groups, is limited.

The new policies recommended in previous chapters heighten public expectations of teaching competence and call for a wider interpretation of the tasks and duties of teachers and their relations with education authorities, parents and local communities. They should become accustomed to taking on new tasks and seeing others disappear. Thus, they must respond to the need for whole-school approaches to organisation, school-based innovation, and curricular design, and for new learning strategies, including developing personal development plans with students, mastering learning, cross-age learning, and group learning.

Initial teacher education and training have not always aroused concern. Today, however, the pace and breadth of change within and outside schools have led to demands for their comprehensive reform. OECD studies have recommended that teacher training institutions should get rid of traditionalist courses and outdated theories that inhibit change and prepare teachers who are adaptable and keen on innovation (OECD, 1990*a* and 1994*l*). Aspiring teachers must be given not only a solid grounding in the relevant subject-matter, pedagogical techniques and classroom management, but also an awareness of the overall developmental needs of pupils.

Greater attention is being paid in some countries to the induction of newly-trained teachers on taking up their first posts. In Australia, for example, the Schools Council has recommended a comprehensive review of current practices with a view to ascertaining what induction methods work best. In some countries, experienced teachers are being asked to extend their traditional supervision of student teachers and to be responsible for guiding and counselling newly-appointed teachers over a period of one or more years.

Historically, teacher training has consisted of three main elements: mastering a discipline or set of disciplines, learning and pedagogical theory, and classroom practice. A major issue over many years has been how to achieve a proper balance between subject mastery and teaching skills. In many countries, primary school teachers have been deemed competent to teach all the subjects in the curriculum, with the possible exception of music or gymnastics. For secondary school teachers priority has been given to subject-matter preparation in specific disciplines. Today, the balance between the two fields of competence is affected by the increasing specialisation of some disciplines, and the overwhelming flow of new information.

In some instances, due to the difficulty of recruiting a sufficient number of teachers, there has been a tendency to reduce the extent of subject-matter preparation of teachers in primary and especially secondary education. One proposed solution is to remould the teaching profession to allow outstanding teachers to do nothing but teach. Today, highly-qualified teachers must carry out many routine duties both inside and outside the classroom which do not require pedagogical competence. If teaching assistants were to be employed on a part- or full-time basis, there would be more scope for individualisation, and experienced teachers would be able to

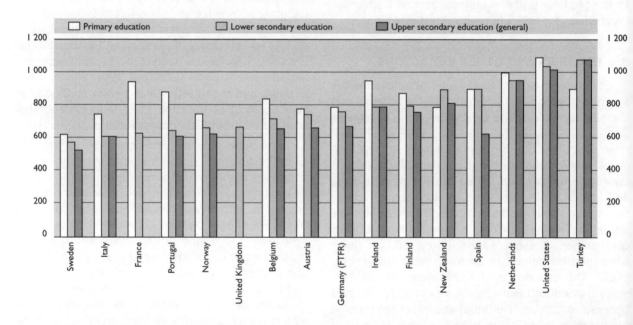

◆ Chart 7.1. ***Number of teaching hours per year, by level of public education, 1992***

Note: See Annex Table A.57.
Source: OECD (1995*d*), *Education at a Glance – OECD Indicators.*

devote more time to their primary tasks. Experiments in which more advanced students have been in charge of teaching their less advanced peers have yielded encouraging results, not least in terms of saving teachers' time and reducing costs.

Chart 7.1 shows substantial cross-national variation in the number of teaching hours per year by level of public education. In primary education, the workload is above average for teachers in France, Ireland, the Netherlands, Spain, Turkey and the United States. In upper secondary education, the spread is from 1 080 hours in Turkey and 1 019 hours in the United States to 612 in Italy and Portugal, and 528 hours in Sweden. There may be scope, therefore, in certain countries for teachers to have more contact hours. Quality and efficiency could be improved in this way, and costs kept down. Moreover, it could be envisaged that teachers in certain countries would be asked to teach more hours, in exchange for periods of educational leave to be used for pursuing their professional development. The most valuable return from increased investment in the education and training of teachers will come from the careful planning and construction of a system-wide induction and in-service

framework using the concept of a teaching career as the foundation.

If essential reforms are to be implemented the main challenge is how to retrain or orientate the teachers already in service, especially given that the rate of entry of new recruits into the teaching profession remains modest in many countries. Chart 7.2 shows the size of teaching staff relative to other education staff, as a percentage of the labour force, in 1992. It can be inferred from the data that many established teachers were educated and professionally trained before the electronic revolution, and some are very firmly set in their ways. In order to keep all teachers motivated and responsive it is essential to promote teaching as an attractive as well as secure career and to offer stimulating incentives for professional development. It is especially important to enable many of the best teachers to stay in the classroom rather than seek others posts.

In-service training

For years education authorities have declared in-service training to be a high priority. In practice, it is still weakly organised and under-funded in a majority

◆ Chart 7.2. **Staff employed in education, 1992**[1,2]
Percentage of the labour force

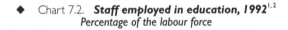
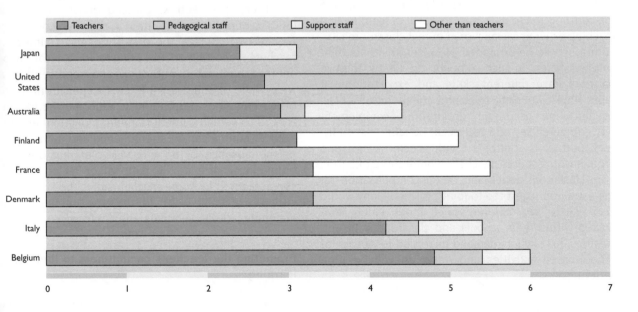

Notes: See Annex Table A.58.
1. Data refer to full-time equivalent staff.
2. Public and private education; primary, secondary and tertiary levels of education.
Source: OECD (1995d), *Education at a Glance – OECD Indicators.*

of countries. Yet all teachers can benefit from further training and it is imperative for those who are not up to standard. Instead of regarding the continuing professional development of teachers as an optional and voluntary experience, education authorities, teachers themselves and communities should regard it as necessary and normal.

The delivery of in-service training can be made by an array of providers and interest groups. Tertiary institutions already offer some courses but make much greater provision if financially enabled to do so. The availability of advanced diploma or certificate courses in special educational fields and of courses leading to post-graduate degrees could be increased. Teachers' centres for professional development could offer *ad hoc* courses on topical matters and facilities for meetings and the conduct of practical projects.

It is essential to link in-service training with research and development programmes (see Section D). Universities and other tertiary institutions should be the major partners of schools in contributing to the in-service training of teachers through collaborative research. Universities have acquired considerable knowledge of learning and teaching processes and techniques including computer-assisted learning. Their service function requires them to share that knowledge with schools.

Co-operative projects between universities and schools, which have revealed the great potential of "action research" for in-service teacher training and the contribution to university research of learning and teaching experiences anchored in real classroom situations, should be expanded. However, there are difficulties inherent in such co-operation. Firstly, the two partners have different skills and expectations. It takes time to nurture trust and collaboration on an equal footing based upon recognition of complementary competencies and reciprocal benefits. Secondly, each partner is confronted with specific issues and problems. In schools, teachers require more free time from classroom duties and better compensation for the extra hours devoted to joint projects. Many would also like to see action-research more widely conducted within their schools and classrooms. In universities, researchers demand increased resources for school-based activities undertaken in collaboration with teachers.

Teachers and new technologies

A recent report by the Center for Educational Research and Innovation concludes that whereas initial training should include a component on the use of information technologies based on the present practices identified in schools, only a few countries have taken appropriate action. This is a grave deficiency since nearly all teachers will be faced sooner or later by the challenge of how to apply technologies. Existing in-service training usually consists of short courses organised away from the school or through formal arrangements within schools (the "cascade model" where experienced teachers are expected to train their colleagues). But this type of familiarisation is not sufficient. The real need is to train teachers in the use of interactive technologies for practical application in the classroom, such as simulation and model-building, problem-solving, complex microworlds or exploration and discovery and even judicious use of basic software packages such as word-processing, spreadsheets or databases.

The required training is demanding because knowledge about what a given student could learn and how he or she learns when using software is only slowly being revealed. It is being introduced at the classroom level mainly by teachers acting as researchers who analyse the effects of different software packages and experiment with alternative ways of using them. Hence the need for collaboration between schools and all the institutions, apart from universities, where research on learning with the aid of information technologies is being conducted.

There has been widespread debate in several OECD countries on whether a national council is required to oversee the education and training of teachers, reporting to the Minister of Education or another nominated authority, and representing a wide range of educational interests apart from those of teachers. Most educationists welcome the idea. It is hard to see how initial training, induction, and in-service training can be strengthened and harmonised in the absence of an effective planning and coordinating centre at the national or regional level supplemented by some mechanism at the local level such as a teaching centre for the provision of courses materials, advice, seminars and conferences.

Promoting the teacher's commitment to lifelong learning

Many barriers inhibit teachers from welcoming the lifelong learning model:

– The segmented organisation of many schools discourages interdisciplinary learning, team teaching and greater use of the learning resources, externally available.

- Teacher training provides little experience of "real life" activities and problems.
- The links between schools and communities are often few and fragile.
- Methods of assessment are often at odds with the development of meta-cognitive and learning-to-learn skills.

If teachers are not actively interested in adopting new methods, students are apt to react to them negatively. OECD (1994*l*) found that whereas some teachers are independently inquiring and innovative, others felt comfortable only when working with colleagues. Encouraging a school climate that fosters collaboration without stifling the creativity of teachers who prefer to work alone is one of the challenges for school improvement strategies. Suitable measures include: forming semi-autonomous teams to overcome the cellular structure of teaching; allocating time for planning, development, reflection and negotiation; using training modules to make teachers familiar with relevant research findings and experiences available outside the school.

A large-scale staff development policy presupposes, however, improvements in incentives and in the general status and esteem accorded to schools and teachers. Many of the conditions and factors associated with modern and "positive" learning environments – reviewed in detail in Chapter 3 – have a much stronger likelihood of coming into being if teachers are appreciated and supported by parents and the larger community. International comparisons support this systemic approach: the countries that are commonly regarded as setting the pace – including Germany, Finland, France, Japan and Switzerland– are distinct more in the regard and esteem accorded to teachers and the enterprise of schooling than in the specific organisational practices that are difficult to translate into other national and cultural settings. This suggests that a major – perhaps principal – role of the education authorities is to help increase and enhance public support for the school system. Criticising the standards achieved by students, teachers and schools may prove counter-productive in the long run. To the extent that high esteem and expectations are extended to schools and teachers, this can be passed on to the many students, parents and communities who themselves have only modest expectations. An outstanding policy challenge is thus to raise expectations as well as the general attractiveness of the system, and especially to ensure that this is felt in those hard-pressed schools that do not match the criteria and conditions of high-performing schools. That challenge may appear excessively ambitious but it only follows from the radical agenda represented by lifelong learning. Meeting it calls for hard scrutiny of the arrangements now in place.

The costs of retraining such a large labour force as that of teachers may be assumed to be substantial, although there is a lack of comparative data on the amount of time already devoted to in-service training in Member countries, some of which at least could be devoted to preparation for the lifelong learning approach. The financial implications of training are taken up in Chapter 8.

School leadership and effective schools

Especially in certain English-speaking countries in recent years, guidelines and policies for schools have made extensive reference to the models offered by business and the market place. Detractors have sought to reject the comparisons, claiming that teaching children is a very different undertaking from manufacturing, buying and selling. As a result, many valuable aspects of the comparison have not been widely developed. One obvious parallel is with the current widespread promotion of enterprises and offices as flexible "learning organisations".

Like the "effective school", the exact list of desirable characteristics of a "learning organisation" may vary. A standard characterisation might, however, include such defining features as: high levels of professional commitment and teamwork; flexible and multi-skilled personnel; flat organisational structures grouped around problems rather than hierarchical structures; very strong emphasis on learning, training and staff development. The "learning organisation" recognises the importance of the "human factor", both in its emphasis on staff development and in incorporating an understanding of human relations into its corporate culture. This is not at the expense of organisational efficiency; it is simply a means to a more comprehensive realisation of efficiency. Bureaucratic constraints are minimised, and the time and attention devoted to the main business of the organisation are maximised ("time on task").

While such parallels between schools and enterprises may not hold in every detail, there is much to be learned from the comparison. That can be done both in terms of analysing where the model is an appropriate one for education and of identifying where current policies and practices appear to be working in a counter direction. The professional communities of educationists and management analysts, far from belonging to entirely different traditions of learning and business with no common reference points, may actually engage in a very useful dialogue.

Schools organised in this way would not be plagued with the constant doubts about standards now experienced in some countries. The inflation of "credentialism" would be halted or even reversed if employers were confident that all who come from the school system have received a solid foundation of the highest quality. Sufficiently high levels of investment and professionalism would obviate the need for burdensome quality checks. Assessment could then focus on the important educational matters of providing formative information for diagnostic purposes and recording student achievement towards qualifications. Concerns about teacher quality and relicensing requirements would diminish if the profession were such an attractive one to enter and schools were able to devote substantial time and resources to staff development.

In many education systems the key responsibilities are being increasingly concentrated at the school level. Schools are taking on managerial tasks from above (national, regional and local authorities) and below (the individual teacher). When responsibility for determining whole-school goals and priorities for designing the curriculum in detail, for relocating and placing personnel, for allocating the budget, and for evaluating pupil and teacher performance is shifted to the school level, all principals and responsible teachers must possess administrative and management skills.

In some systems the new managerial tasks cover only specific areas and their application is confined to experimental schools. In others, however, these tasks have begun to cover wide areas of governance, finance and administration and to apply to all schools or, at least, to all schools within certain defined categories. All this depends on the capacity of school managers (board members, principals, teachers with special responsibilities and committed parents) to provide leadership and organisational skills.

Many OECD countries are paying particular attention to the capacity of school principals or head teachers to offer "positive" school leadership. In a few countries the latter are still regarded as *primus inter pares* but in a number they are considered as the main guarantees of high standards, the manager of innovations and the person to be held accountable if

things go wrong. Where this is so, it has become clear that principals require intensive training in leadership and management skills before taking up their posts and occasional opportunities for continuing training when fully established, especially whenever they are required to assume new responsibilities. Some countries have also realised that school board members or governors can also profit from courses devoted to their powers and duties.

For the benefit of school leaders, teachers with special responsibilities and managers, education authorities can issue guidelines and set up national advisory centres offering practical advice on how to cope with the problems arising from major reforms or specific innovations. Some countries have a "telephone help line". Education authorities can also provide opportunities for experiencing management in other sectors of society such as industry and services and in other schools that have conspicuously succeeded in handling complex managerial problems. Education authorities can also develop among interested teachers an interest in middle management by offering appropriate in-service courses.

C. THE USE OF NEW TECHNOLOGIES

When Richard W. Riley, the US Secretary of Education, testified before the Senate in May 1994 on educational technology and, more specifically, on the role of the "National Information Infrastructure" (NII), he made a strong statement about the potential of new technologies:

"[Information and communication] technologies are a way to individualise instruction; a powerful resource for supporting teachers and their professional development; a vehicle to connect student learning to the real world; a way to connect schools to the home and community; and a means to extend learning beyond the traditional 9 to 3 school day. The National Education Commission on Time and Learning recently published a report showing that we must increase both the amount and the quality of instructional time for our students, and the NII will help to make this possible by allowing students to learn in homes, libraries and other sites, both during and after school. Small schools, schools in remote rural areas, and schools wracked by poverty would all have access to the same rich learning resources. It will be absolutely impossible to give a world class education to every American child without the proper use of these new information tools."

If such optimism surrounds the introduction of new technologies in education, there is a certain scepticism as well. In the past, there were high expectations each time technological innovation such as television, video or language laboratories was brought into the schools. Advocates predicted that the organisation of schooling and teaching methods would be transformed. Results have often not measured up to the expectations. Will this not always be so?

The answer is in the negative. The new technologies are increasingly cheap, fast, flexible and interactive and there is widening access to global networks. Technology-based assessment of prior learning (APL) is becoming slowly a reality in OECD countries. Table 7.1 compares the older devices with newer learning tools and resources.

Personal computers have invaded the school. Table 7.2 shows the percentage of secondary schools that use computers for instruction in five OECD countries. In Austria, Germany, Netherlands and the United States, all secondary schools use computers for instruction. Chart 7.3 shows an index of computer use for instruction in secondary education calculated for five OECD countries. The index is based on the proportion of schools that have computers and actually use them for instructional purposes in four subjects – mathematics, science, mother tongue, and technology or computer education – in grades 7, 8

and 9 (Tuijnman and Brummelhuis, 1993; Brummelhuis, 1995). Germany, Japan and the Netherlands show similar increases in use. In 1989, the United States was far ahead of the other countries, and only a minor increase took place until 1992. The situation was the opposite in Austria, where as a result of massive government intervention computer use in the four subjects increased dramatically in only three years, from about 28 per cent in 1989 to 74 per cent in 1992.

However, barriers remain (OECD, 1995*i*). There are three kinds of obstacles to the full use of new information and communication technologies in the provision of education. First, there are those specific to the technologies in question. Difficulties stem less from the cost, quality and reliability of hardware than from the lack of appropriate software, although that is also a major constraint. To contain costs and ensure that new learning resources become more rapidly and more widely available, OECD countries should explore ways of intensifying co-operation in the development of educational software. They also should make the private sector better aware of the new opportunities for product development. Secondly, obstacles arise at the interface of technology, education and society, which involve attitudes, values and beliefs. Thirdly, the major obstacles to be overcome are those inherent in the education system, including the resistance of management and staff,

Table 7.1. **"Older" and "newer" learning resources and tools**

Function	Learning resources	
	Older technologies	Newer technologies
Live conversation	Classroom with round table and blackboard	Audio conferencing Audiographic conferencing 1-way live video with audio talkback; 2-way video Other real time writing
Time-delayed conversation	Mail, regular and express	Fax E-mail and computer conferencing Videotape

Learning by doing	Typewriter
	Library (research material)
	Laboratory
	Studio
	Internship programme
		Computer for designing, composing, simulating,
		    and analysing results
		Use of authentic video from a foreign country
		    to study that country's language and culture
		On-line use of distant libraries, computer-based
		    research tools, and data

Directed instruction	Lecture hall Slide projector Textbook	Live and taped video Computer tutorial, drill

Source: OECD (1995*i*).

Table 7.2. **Schools using personal computers for instruction, 1982-92**

		Percentage of lower (L) and upper (U) secondary schools					
		1982	1984	1986	1988	1990	1992
Austria	L	5	13	29	50	92	100
	U	7	21	40	62	99	..
Germany	L	10	40	70	86	96	99
	U	20	59	79	92	99	..
Japan	L	0	..	9	18	45	71
	U	..	7	12	31	58	..
Netherlands	L	8	45	76	89	98	100
	U	15	64	83	94	100	..
United States	L	40	70	86	95	100	100
	U	55	80	91	98	100	..

Note: .. Data not available.
Source: Brummelhuis (1995), p. 40.

inappropriate infrastructures, inflexible timetables, financial constraints, and an array of practical difficulties. For example, the allocation of staff to educational institutions at all levels is still largely based on outdated concepts of classrooms, class groups, 9-to-4 timetables and teacher:student ratios that assume all students are in direct contact with a teacher at all times.

The impact of new technologies on educational settings

Every formal educational institution will increasingly need to relate to external sources of knowledge and information. Libraries will continue their transformation into learning resource centres. Many families and individuals will have access to information

◆   Chart 7.3. *Index of computer use for instruction in four subjects, 1989 and 1992*[1,2]

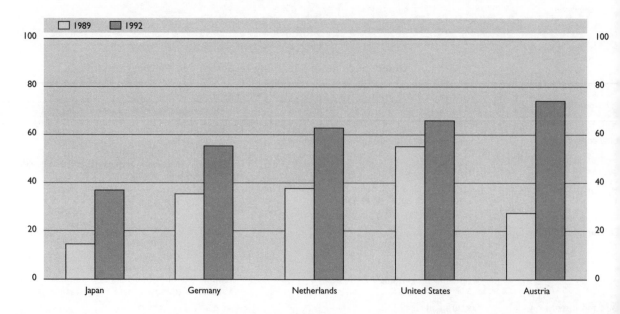

Notes: See Table A.59.
1.   The subjects are mathematics, science, mother tongue and technology or computer education.
2.   The index is based on a yield score that shows the degree of computer use in four subjects in grades 7, 8 and 9 of lower secondary schools using computers.
Source: Brummelhuis (1995), p. 53.

through their own networked computers. Education authorities will have the responsibility of extending that access to everyone, just as in the past public libraries made books available to those who could not afford to buy them. So far, the most frequent response has been to set up the equivalent of a "reading room" where simple but functional machines and software are available for use by learners on a scheduled basis. The equivalent of "computer rooms" serves a similar purpose.

The introduction of new technologies inevitably leads to modifications in the educational setting. Thus, when buildings are linked by interactive networks, including video, it makes little sense to continue to regard them as separate institutions. The question of what modifications may be needed is considered in Section D below.

Increasingly, students in secondary schools will have access to personal portable computers. There will be a concomitant increase in the demand for individual and small-group work-spaces. A larger socialising space for approximately 100 students and a self-contained unit or "neighbourhood" for approximately 400 students are also required. This larger site offers a range of spaces designed to accommodate student activities rather than teacher or content-oriented activities. The concept of the "dispersed school" – with specialised learning spaces separate from the main school buildings and attached to centres provided by local employers, office complexes or the community library – is neither new nor likely to be widely adopted, but it does gain from the power of information and communication technologies to make distances much less important (OECD, 1992h).

Individuals can now work together in learning and production through information technology. As the OECD Programme on Educational Building (PEB) stated in its 1992 seminar: "Learning will become a more diverse networked activity for all ages of students and only part of it will take place in permanent community facilities, designed to provide a social and resource focus in the form of a welcoming and technologically democratic architecture" (OECD, 1992i). The use of buildings for educational purposes thus needs to be more flexible, in light of the new demands and new possibilities of supplying learning opportunities. The main point is that the new communication technologies allow organised learning to occur in increasingly varied settings that are often separate from schools and teachers, and in ways that were open to very few in the past. A greater choice of

options and methods is thus available to individuals, enabling them to become "autonomous" learners.

The fact that learning opportunities can be enriched and extended at low marginal costs with the aid of these new instruction technologies should mean that everyone has the possibility of achieving excellence, defined in terms of individual benchmarks of progress in learning rather than measured against a group norm. The new information and communication technologies thus provide both the rationale and the means of building tomorrow's learning society – one that is networked, with ample and equal access to knowledge and information, and made up of communities and individuals who are in charge of their own learning environments (Stuebing, 1995). The learning society is seen by many as a worthwhile goal; however, it is equally important to proceed in stages rather than attempt wholesale changes for which the teachers are not prepared nor the resources available. Its realisation will require a close examination of the content, style and organisation of modern methods and technologies of learning, particularly in respect of the new possibilities offered by student-centred and self-directed modes of progression, together with an examination of the purpose and function of educational institutions and their use of electronic technologies to meet new educational needs.

D. PHYSICAL SETTINGS FOR LIFELONG LEARNING

Just as there is sometimes a misconception that new forms of learning reduce the importance of teachers, so the observation that new forms of delivery coexist with traditional, fixed-site schools can be misunderstood to imply that schools themselves no longer matter. This again is quite false reasoning. Just as learning often is directed and mediated through teachers, so does it mostly occur in particular places designed for the purpose. It is thus now most important to ask, following the issues of teaching and learning raised above, what sorts of institutions are available, whether they are equipped for the tasks and new forms of educational organisation being demanded, and whether more can be achieved within the existing physical resources that are available. How far, for instance, have countries developed "community learning centres", open to the community as a whole, serving a wide range of learning needs with resources of the highest quality? And, what are the implications of "the information age" for the institutions that specialise in learning?

Learning takes place in a great variety of settings other than schools: in art galleries and museums, at home, and during excursions – but for most young people the school is the principal centre of learning. The physical setting of schools influences the quality and effectiveness of education in a number of ways. Buildings must not only be safe, weatherproof, and conducive to work, but also appropriate for the activities occurring within them. The traditional classroom, with desks in rows, emphasised the teacher's dominant didactic role and discourage interaction between pupils. Windows were often positioned high on the wall, to allow daylight in but make it difficult for pupils to see out.

The 1960s saw the introduction of open plan layouts in some schools with a view to encouraging use of a wider range of teaching methods. Not surprisingly, some teachers were unmoved. Today's school buildings are the product of a different emphasis, as flexibility of use and adaptability of design have become watchwords for architects in recent years. Thus, a secondary school typically consists of a number of classrooms of a standard size, some spaces for special purposes, and some multi-purpose spaces designed to offer flexibility.

The school of the future will continue to be designed to match real learning requirements (OECD, 1995s). Schools must be places where children like to be and where they feel secure and safe. At the current rate of replacement it will be at least 50 years before the educational facilities already in use are decommissioned. The renovation, reorganisation and re-equipping of existing buildings will therefore be an important element in implementing lifelong learning. The scope for making better use of what already exists is considerable.

Using facilities efficiently

Many educational buildings are left unused at weekends and during holiday periods. The barriers to their wider use are more frequently administrative and bureaucratic than structural. Tax-payers are proving less and less willing to accept the under-utilisation of public assets. In countries where educational facilities are controlled by local rather than national authorities, schools are more likely to be regarded as community facilities available to all (OECD, 1995t).

As learning becomes more individualised and less teacher-centred, the idea of flexible hours will become increasingly attractive. The idea of schools for "all ages" is part of the vision of lifelong learning. Institutions, or parts of them, will be encouraged to stay "open at all hours". Equipment and facilities made available for one purpose can be used for others. It has never made sense to keep machines and rooms idle when they could be used by others but administrative complications have stood in the way of better utilisation. Where schools and other institutions have devolved responsibility for their budgets, they are far more likely to take steps to ensure that funds are used to best effect. Thus, universities today commonly use their lecture rooms for summer schools, and their residences for holiday accommodation. Some schools are used as activity centres in the summer, or as centres for evening classes. However, this intensive use of space remains rare for a variety of reasons including the typical difficulties of shared use: cost-sharing, managerial problems and the allocation of responsibilities for cleaning, access and security.

The relative importance of the several levels of education varies from country to country and according to the age of the learner. Even in the context of lifelong learning, there are good reasons for separating learners of different ages, at least for some of the time. Under other circumstances, however, there are good educational and organisational reasons for bringing them together. There already exist centres where school classes, adult education courses, child care, small business advice centres and other services are together under one roof. These may be the forerunners of the "community learning centres" of the future. The potential advantages of bringing together different services at one community centre are several: many common services and facilities (heating plant, kitchens, car parking, computer centres) can be shared, thus reducing the overall cost; the facilities themselves may be more intensively and effectively used; parents, especially mothers of young children, can pursue their own studies while their children are being educated close by; children, as part of their general development, can contribute to the case of elderly and disabled people (OECD, 1995t).

The process that is seeing teachers become "facilitators", "managers of learning" or "guides in a forest of information" will continue. The advantage of schools is that they facilitate learning in groups over a long period. Increasing numbers of jobs demand people who can work in teams and co-operate with others. Learning spaces will become still more varied. Schools will contain a mix of small work stations, group rooms, and large classrooms, and will have access to spaces where hundreds of people can meet for larger events.

Similar arguments apply to tertiary education institutions, which also have a wider function as centres of lifelong learning open to adult learners. Already, more flexible provision has expanded the pattern of learning beyond full-time courses for young adults. The increase in the diversity and quantity of learning is reflected in the spread of a modular approach with recognition of prior learning. Adults are thereby enabled to return to take up new studies as to pursue refresher courses in the disciplines previously studied.

Wastage of tertiary education resources may be assisted by a modular approach but financial arrangements should nonetheless provide incentives for the completion of courses by learners. Greater attention to the intensive exploitation of the physical resources of tertiary education institutions, through co-operation with secondary schools and employers, might also be fostered.

There is the likelihood that employers will increase investment in general adult education, as they come to understand that provision which promotes personal development and satisfaction can also enhance job performance and productivity. Governments can also be expected to continue to support that part of lifelong learning which relates to non-economic objectives, such as personal development and leisure interests. Such provision will thus be centred, as at present, on the physical facilities of many schools and tertiary education institutions. However, governments cannot meet total demand through the institutions over which they have control, and other providers should be welcomed subject to the safeguards over quality discussed in Chapter 6.

To sum up: it is a question of redeveloping and transforming existing educational buildings in order to be able to take advantage of the new learning technologies, and to respond flexibly to such likely trends on the following:

- Declining requirement for "computer rooms" as each learner has access to a laptop computer.

- Locating specialised facilities such as science laboratories in the "real world", linked electronically rather than on site.

- Emphasising the provision of personal workstations, small group interaction areas and large social spaces.

- Implementing an "open all hours" approach as learner-centred programmes complement teacher-centred ones.

- Encouraging institutions to develop distinctive specialisations, which may necessitate purpose-designed buildings.

In recent times, architects and managers of educational buildings have had to learn to live with the increasing pace of change. They cannot predict how the buildings for which they are responsible will be used in the future. The forces that have led them to co-operate more closely with other agencies will continue. The educational institution of the future must provide a sophisticated, functional, efficient, convenient and attractive working environment if it is to survive in the face of competition from other providers of knowledge and learning programmes.

The implication for policy is that the maintenance of the building stock can no longer be regarded as an optional extra. In many countries the condition of schools has been allowed to deteriorate to unacceptable levels. If dangerous buildings are rare, those in which teaching and learning are hindered or limited by poor maintenance are common. Apart from educational considerations, it is uneconomic to allow facilities to deteriorate to the point where expensive repairs become necessary. A second point is that, as the management of school buildings is gradually devolved to the immediate users, and as educational institutions in certain countries find themselves in competition for pupils, there may well be efforts to improve the appearance of buildings. It is, however, the substantial backlog of deferred major maintenance, particularly on the many buildings constructed during the 1960s and 1970s, that will need to be remedied.

E. INFORMATION FOR TEACHING, LEARNING AND POLICY-MAKING

Information is not "external" to the education system and mediated through it; information about and for education itself is a key part of such a dynamic, high-quality system. The information and the knowledge base for teaching, learning and policy-making, and the R&D that generates them, are thus essential elements for the dynamism and quality to be sustained. It would be unthinkable in other "knowledge industries", which are as subject to constant change and decentralised as schools and classes, for there not to be substantial investment in the generation of knowledge, information and innovation.

Given the extent of the decentralisation in education, there are thus strategic questions about realising economies of scale so that a substantial up-to-date knowledge base is generated that is widely accessible. There are questions about the roles of the different partners, and especially the education authorities, in a situation of policy partnerships where either no party may feel responsible for generating and sustaining the information base or else there may be a proliferation of competing sources of professional information. How can countries, in times of budgetary stringency, generate the R&D on the scale appropriate for lifelong learning societies? And what information, for whom, is relevant to lifelong learning when information needs potentially cover such a vast field? Is focus needed, and how can priorities be decided?

The information base for teaching, learning and policy-making varies according to national traditions and priorities and the level of expenditure on data collection and R&D (OECD, 1995u, Appendix A). In most countries the level is certainly small in relation to the volume of educational activity. In countries for which figures are available, R&D accounts for only around a quarter of 1 per cent of educational expenditure, a percentage far lower than in any respectable branch of private industry. Yet, in all countries today new policies and strategies call for reliable and comprehensive information. The shift towards lifelong learning certainly requires a mass of intelligence on the reform of structures, curriculum, pedagogy, financing and control and management, particularly in view of the general trend towards decentralisa tion and autonomous schools.

Although there is no clear-cut relationship between educational reforms and the demand for knowledge and information, policy shifts do affect the demand for research-based knowledge. During the 1950s and 1960s, policy-making was primarily concerned with inputs. During the 1970s, the concern shifted towards structures and processes. From the mid-1980s, student and system outcomes in preferably measurable form became the focus of attention (OECD, 1992j). In the 1950s and 1960s, the central value endorsed was that of equality; until the 1980s, the assumption was that education would be largely led by professionals. In the 1990s, there is an insistence on efficiency, quality and accountability with the devolution of powers to institutions and client groups.

If R&D traditions are affected by modes of government, cultural traditions and existing institutional structures, it is also true, as in Sweden, that the

agenda can be changed by government action. New policies lead to new R&D agendas. The shift in policy towards lifelong learning will lead to new information needs in several fields, and R&D should shift its priorities accordingly. Knowledge about the state of the art in relevant fields is a prerequisite for ensuring that changes in the orientation of policy towards lifelong learning objectives are grounded on reliable evidence and systematically evaluated. Research on research, or "meta-analysis", is particularly important in this context, because it involves policy change at all levels of systems, institutions, practitioners and clients (Walberg et al., 1993).

Elements of a national knowledge base for education

Countries exercise a wide range of choices in the ways they resource, staff and administer their educational knowledge bases, which are strongly anchored in national, political and social contexts, and intellectual traditions. Yet some policy needs are common to almost all countries, even if their detailed resolution ultimately assumes different forms. Governments need information in order to develop and implement current and new policies and to steer and manage educational change in a context of accountability, choice and responsibilities shared with groups in the larger society. They must generate both information to inform their own strategies and to help meet the requirements of other stakeholders – a process that involves sensitive negotiations between government and practitioners in different competing positions. Education authorities will have a dominant role in determining the R&D agenda, while seeking the views of skilled practitioners and respecting the right of researchers to incorporate scholarly and theoretical considerations into their inquiries. They should regard the process of negotiation on agendas as part of the data conditioning both their agendas and their methods.

A national knowledge base for educational policy-making comprises elements such as:

- Knowledge derived from the collation of statistics and indicators that enable national, regional and local systems to monitor inputs and outputs, depending on the degree of desegregation required. The data can be used for a multiplicity of purposes including determining the rates and composition of participation in initial and post-initial education and training; the allocation of funds by levels and functions; the composition of the teaching force; student performance standards; and education and labour market outcomes.

- Knowledge derived from research and development. Research should raise questions and identify problems. The practical usefulness of R&D in education is strongly affected by the degree to which its conditions are negotiated with those being researched and those who sponsor it (OECD, 1995u).

- Assessment and evaluation, which provide the basis for action either for system-wide policy-making or for individual development and which can result from rigorous investigative methods so that findings can be subjected to objective professional appraisal or interactive and intuitive ly inspired judgements.

At the national level these three forms of knowledge creation are complementary, although researchers, in practice, may well resort to all three forms of enquiry. But the findings are seldom brought together for improving or evaluating policy or pedagogical action. In particular, the results of inspections and other forms of monitoring are not always collated to influence assessment needs and, often, allocation of resources. Data generated by evaluation are insufficiently synthesised to be of use in policy planning. All too often, the evaluation of the capacity of existing educational provision to meet the requirements of a lifelong learning model is unsophisticated and of limited usefulness. Policy-makers at the different levels of control and management should be able to draw upon all three kinds of knowledge for a variety of purposes.

The knowledge base in most OECD countries is not only insufficiently synthesised, but also heavily biased in its coverage towards mainstream schooling. There is lack of R&D in the early childhood and adult education and training sectors. Whereas empirical comparative studies of school systems have been undertaken since the early 1960s, the first such study directed at adults became available only in 1995 (OECD and Statistics Canada, 1995). A further weakness is the lack of systematic information about performance standards both in schools and in education and training, partly because of the technical difficulties of securing comprehensive and reliable data and partly because of opposition from many of the actors (OECD, 1995v).

The agenda for R&D is potentially very long, and the various stakeholders always order the priorities differently (Gruber, 1995). Governments will therefore need to decide which are the greatest areas of need within the following broad categories (OECD, 1995u, pp. 173-175):

- *Studies of learning and teaching:* particular concerns here may be the institutional arrangements, for curriculum and outputs of early childhood education, and measures to combat school failure and drop-out.

- *Teacher training and staff development:* an example could be the time and resources already devoted to in-service training.

- *Government and policy:* the effects on budget expenditure of administrative decentralisation according to categories might be examined under this heading.

- *Structural issues:* such concerns as the relationship between the streaming of pupils and school failure might be investigated.

- *Tertiary education and employment:* the equity, efficiency and effectiveness of tertiary education in meeting labour market requirements are examples of topics that might usefully be studied.

- *International issues:* comparative data on adult education supply and demand are largely lacking.

- *Methodologies:* longitudinal studies could be exploited more fully in policy-making, which is subject to many short- and medium-term exigencies.

In the area of lifelong learning, much of the R&D might take place away from the formal sector. Information on needs and "what works" derives less from theory than from sustained enquiry among, and interaction with, users, employers and trade unions. This will call for the application of a wide range of research and enquiry methods and for active feedback and effective dissemination of the findings. Its use for professional development is not well exploited. A proper balance between the several forms of enquiry at the national level will ensure that adequate attention is paid to outcomes as well as to the creation of optimum conditions for good educational practice.

Co-operation at the international level

There are many areas where comparative studies could be conducted fruitfully by researchers from a number of countries. The findings of one country can sometimes be applied in another. Many international associations of researchers already promote exchanges of knowledge, and share information on effective research methods.

The implications of implementing a lifelong learning strategy are so vast and complex that international co-operation in R&D is a precondition for success. Establishing and helping to enlarge the comparative knowledge base for educational policy-making continues to be a major task of the OECD. Steps to strengthen international R&D in education and training might include:

– Creating an international market.

– Intensifying dialogue in international settings and forums so that common problems and possible projects can be identified.

– Looking for forms of international collaboration to address common problems, for instance in terms of pooling resources and creating joint centres of excellence, particularly when the subject of the research would be advanced by adopting comparative perspectives.

– Establishing international bidding procedures so that the best equipped and qualified

researchers, from whatever country, would be appointed and the international dissemination of knowledge, insights and ideas promoted.

– Facilitating the development of an international and comparative knowledge base through networking and the use of information highways, staff and student exchanges, shared training events for junior researchers, shared research programmes and projects, and joint dissemination activities.

Financing and the inadequate volume of R&D

The level of expenditure is the most explicit indication of a country's commitment to educational R&D. Judging by the data supplied to OECD (OECD 1995u), educational R&D is a marginal activity. In the six countries for which relevant data are available, on average only 0.27 per cent of total educational expenditure is thus allocated. Chart 7.4 shows that the range is from 0.37 per cent in Australia to 0.18 per cent in Ireland. Educational R&D also accounts for only a small proportion of total R&D expenditure: the average for the nine countries considered is 0.92 per cent, with a range from 1.5 per cent in Australia to

◆   Chart 7.4. **Expenditure on educational R&D as a percentage of total expenditure on education and of total expenditure on R&D, early 1990s[1, 2]**

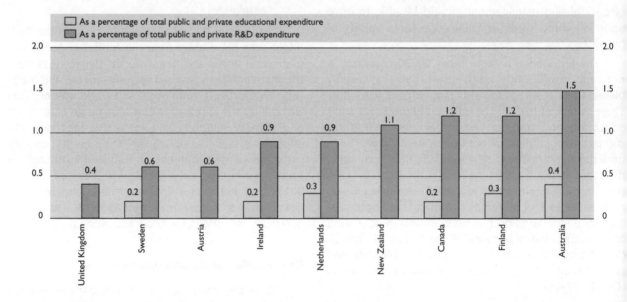

1.   See notes to Annex Table A.60.
2.   In millions of local currency and at current prices.

Source: OECD (1995u), *Educational Research and Development: Trends, Issues and Challenges*, p. 45.

0.4 per cent in the United Kingdom. Government is the principal source of funds for educational R&D in all countries, either directly through its own research units or through grants to tertiary institutions. There is little funding for educational R&D from non-government sources, although these can be important sponsors of independent critical or developmental R&D.

Educational R&D is a highly labour-intensive process. For this reason, it is important to ensure cost-effective work through the high-quality training of researchers and productive use of their time. The scale of the resources allocated for personnel is a second indicator of a country's commitment to R&D. Relevant data, available for eight OECD countries (OECD, 1995*u*), show that the full-time equivalent personnel involved in R&D on education constitute only a small part of the total allocated to R&D: on average, 1.1 per cent.

In short, the scale of financing for educational R&D, which varies among countries, is generally a small proportion of the amount spent on education or on research as a whole. Since many countries are facing the same problems relating to policy and practice, this large disparity implies an ignorance of or indifference to knowledge requirements. Countries should thus review their priorities with a view to increasing their expenditure on R&D and directing it to areas of rising importance such as lifelong learning. Having teachers and other practitioners join in the pursuit of knowledge will help strengthen the resource base of an otherwise weakly nourished activity. It will also increase the capacity of practitioners to identify obstacles to school improvement and ways of securing beneficial change. Teacher training should introduce this possibility to prospective teachers, and broaden professional interests to include lifelong learning. Many countries should review the career paths of educational R&D personnel in order to ensure that the returns to public and individual investment in training are maximised.

F. STRENGTHENING THE RESOURCES: POLICY CONCLUSIONS

It has been implicit in the arguments proposed in earlier chapters that educational resources need to be both expanded and more effectively exploited. Input of advice, materials, work experience, technology and cultural activities is needed from many and varied sources in order to turn schools into community learning centres. Outside schools, a wide range of providers of education has to be encouraged by

government action and by establishing an appropriate framework. The potential of the information age can be tapped both centrally and by individual educational and training institutions. Changes in the consequent role of teachers will demand an extensive national programme of teacher training, both to raise the quality of teaching and to prepare teachers to cope with the consequences of a lifelong approach to learning and greater stress on individual learning paths. Greater knowledge of educational provision and performance is needed by learners, teachers, providers and government so that the enterprise of lifelong learning is purposefully and effectively managed.

The resources for lifelong learning are very largely already in place. However, changes in the way they are used, in attitudes among teachers and administrators, and extensive continuing consultation are required. There are particular implications for access to, and exploitation of, school buildings, for teacher training, and for the expansion of the national knowledge base.

Educational institutions as community learning centres

– Educational institutions, particularly schools and junior colleges should be encouraged by government action to forge closer links with their surrounding communities, not only through learning with production schemes, partnerships with employers and sponsors, and the presence of returning adult learners, as proposed in previous chapters, but also by opening the doors to the voluntary assistance of adults with teaching and other functions, to workers who can demonstrate the realities of different occupations, to recruitment agencies, to cultural groups and organisations in the civil society.

– Educational libraries should become multimedia learning resource centres. Access for local communities, in association with public library services, would ensure full exploitation. Such a development would require government stimulation to ensure the necessary co-operation, and reasonable equity of provision throughout the system.

– Educational institutions at all levels should also be encouraged to develop interactive electronic network links with other providers of education and research centres, including enterprises. Appropriate incentives should be offered to firms to provide input into institutions, particularly in the fields of science and technology.

- School buildings should be adequately maintained in the interests of security and continuing efficiency. Any redesign of an existing building or new construction should take into account the need for flexible teaching spaces as young people stay longer in education and increasing numbers of adults wish to complete their secondary education.

Teacher training

- Initial teacher preparation should be the first stage of a continuing staff development programme that gives teachers professional support in the classroom.
- As foreshadowed particularly in Chapters 3, 5 and 6, a major retraining effort is required to equip teachers and administrators, particularly in primary and secondary education, to face the challenges of the lifelong education approach. Governments should make provision for this in advance, while carrying out the consultations necessary for its effective delivery.
- Given the present and impending changes in national curricula, a rolling programme of training in knowledge about, and teaching of, learning-to-learn and information retrieval skills will be needed. Teachers themselves will require such skills in increasing measure in order to keep abreast of developments in technologies and cognitive knowledge in all subjects. Such training should take place both outside and within schools, through the allocation of time for team reflection and internal development and planning.
- Subject-specific training will need to be updated at regular intervals, possibly by a programme of refresher training attached to the initial training package.
- An integral part of teacher training will be concerned with ways and means of establishing links with local communities and importing outside knowledge into schools. The effects of the presence of larger numbers of adults in schools will also need to be anticipated. This does not imply a threat to the professionalism of teaching, but a redefinition of teaching as

the art of managing learning resources of all kinds.

- Teachers should be encouraged to work in teams, not obligatorily within classrooms or for teaching specific subjects, but for the purpose of ensuring mutual professional support in the face of challenging tasks.
- Governments may wish to consider how non teaching staff might take over some of the administrative and supervisory duties presently performed by teachers, so that they can concentrate on meeting the new demands on their knowledge and skills. In certain countries, teachers' regular contact hours could be increased through a process of consultation.
- Within schools and other learning institutions more advanced learners can play a part in the teaching of other learners, thereby deepening their understanding, increasing social solidarity and relieving teachers of part of their burden.

Knowledge base

- The long-term role of government in fostering and managing lifelong learning will need to be underpinned by the collation and synthesis of information from a variety of sources: teachers, principals and other administrators, non formal education providers, school and post school inspectorates, client groups, social partners, and the wider civil society. A review of information-processing systems will be required, possibly by outside analysts.
- It will be particularly important to gather information on early childhood education, adult education, and continuing vocational training
- At the same time, the reporting requirements placed on education providers in receipt of public funding or being officially accredited will need to be kept within bounds. New frameworks need to be drawn up, therefore, so that providers can analyse their own needs and performance, making use of local knowledge, can take appropriate local action and report in summary form to government. The principle should be followed that information should only be demanded where its exact purpose is known. Information retained locally can be requested subsequently if the need arises.

– Information should not only flow upwards, but also downwards, so that education providers know whether they are, in the view of government, meeting standards and fulfilling goals. Statistical comparisons between institutions should, however, make allowances for the "value added" factor as discussed in Chapter 6. School and post-school inspectorates will have a significant role to play in providing more qualitative feedback. One of the criteria of inspection should be to seek and process external as well as internal information, and to advance understanding. Similarly, information about provision and performance must reach the general public, all being potential learners. The educational guidance and counselling services referred to in Chapter 4 will be a major provider of such information. Governments may also consider promoting education and training through the media, as has been done for national literacy campaigns.

– Knowledge production and knowledge application have been so far poorly articulated. In many countries, there is a lack of mechanisms to ensure that relevant knowledge is presented to policy-makers when critical decisions have to be taken. Close co-ordination is called for between the production of research and its potential users, so as to ensure that relevant and up-to-date knowledge is available at the appropriate time. Policy-makers should influence the orientation of research, and researchers should heed the requirements of policy-makers. This will increase the demand for short-cycle investigations and reinforce the case for developing new modes of knowledge production. Governments should also ensure that the social partners and other interested groups in civil society are aware of the channels for making their views known at local as well as national level.

HOW TO PAY FOR LIFELONG LEARNING FOR ALL?

A. INTRODUCTION

Previous chapters argued that because of rapid technological change, knowledge and skills tend to depreciate at a faster rate than ever before. This increased turnover of skills makes that workers need to be flexible in order to stay productive. Adapting to technological and societal change calls for opportunities for learning new skills. Present-day provision of educational services is not in line with this concern. The best option presently available to achieve flexibility is an arrangement of lifelong learning. Actions that stimulate lifelong learning are therefore likely to increase both personal well-being and economic growth. Although this point is being recognised by OECD countries, most current institutional arrangements clearly discriminate against lifelong learning and favours "it's now or never" initial schooling.

Lifelong learning defines a broad principle that, while all can agree to its desirability, it can appear quite unrealistic in its demands on resources and its need for institutional reform. This chapter does not avoid the conclusion that the sums involved may well be high, just as it proposes that the potential benefits are also enormous. In order that these questions can be addressed, and the policy debate move beyond the level of assertion and counter-assertion, it is necessary to clarify as far as possible the following questions: What are the costs and benefits of lifelong learning, who is enjoying the benefits and who is paying the bills? What are the implications for both financial arrangements and public education budgets? Radical solutions will have to be considered. These are the issues contained in this chapter.

Section B summarises the policy context in which the issue of resources needs to be addressed. Section C offers a sample of evidence, collected from a variety of data sources available in a few Member countries, on the benefits accruing to investments in education, training and learning. To the possible extent, evidence on the non-monetary and social benefits of education and training is also presented. These insights into the distribution of the returns are

of instrumental interest, not least because they influence the thinking about the possible ways of sharing the costs of the initial investments. Section D then examines the principal cost implications of reorienting current provision into a lifelong learning perspective. Section E explores the alternative options for the financing of adequate learning opportunities for all. The lead question undergirding this analysis is what priorities and distribution of sources of funds, costs and benefits might best promote coherence, fairness and efficiency in implementing approaches to lifelong learning for all.

B. THE POLICY CONTEXT

So far, formal education and training systems in the OECD countries have proven to be investments that to a large extent pay for themselves. They yield substantial and measurable returns in the form of rising standards of living, economic competitiveness, and security for society and individuals. Initial and continuing education are seen to contribute to promoting social cohesion and progress, and developing a strong base of shared values that are vital to democratic pluralism.

However, these formal systems of mostly initial education and training are limited in their capacity to meet the variety of learning needs that people face at the close of the twentieth century. Although nearly universal in their coverage at the foundation levels, there remain sizeable minorities whose basic learning needs are not met. Equally crucial, although lifelong learning is already a reality for a select group of individuals, the systems have not sufficiently extended access beyond the "front-end" model of schooling and initial mass tertiary education, to make lifelong learning a reality for all. Thus, current systems are still characterised largely as providing education and training to all "school age" children, youth, and an increasing proportion of young adults. Societal, technological and labour market developments notwithstanding, this approach remains biased towards a "once-and-for-all" educational career.

In this context, the actual and potential returns from lifelong learning need to be contrasted with the rising economic and social costs of the lack of access to lifelong learning opportunities. The data analysis presented in Chapter 1 has shown that where the updating of knowledge, skills and competencies is not possible, individuals face increased risks of low earnings, high unemployment and even social marginalisation.

Renewed and widespread agreement about the importance of lifelong learning notwithstanding, it is not yet a reality for all people regardless of labour market status and age. There are important barriers to its implementation. Aside from those impeding the effort to make lifelong learning more accessible, there is the vital question of human and financial resources: Can OECD countries afford lifelong learning, and how can they pay for it? The other side of this question is whether OECD countries can afford not to pay for lifelong learning?

Even with the firmest political commitment to making lifelong learning a reality for all, Education Ministers face particularly thorny problems in trying to resolve the resource questions.

- The first problem is *accountability*. In order to make informed policy decisions, based on cost-benefit and cost-effectiveness considerations, it is of utmost importance to have access to information on the distribution of both cost and benefits. Although there is strong evidence that expenditures on further education and training, both formal and non-formal, are "productive investments", the returns are spread over time, and often they take the form of private returns (profits to employers and wage premiums to individuals), as opposed to the substantial social returns that accrue to much initial schooling. Furthermore, returns are generally insecure, and past returns may not be an accurate guide to future returns, for example, in expanding systems of mass tertiary education.

- The second problem is *budgetary pressure*. As it was expressed in the most recent OECD Council Ministerial meeting, there is a need for "fiscal consolidation and sustainable fiscal positions in order to free national savings for more productive investment" (Ministers' *Communiqué*, May 1995). Even when lifelong learning can be shown to be a "more productive investment", the sheer weight of fiscal pressures may limit the amount that government can contribute.

- The third problem is the need for *partnerships*. This arises from the fact that lifelong learning embraces much more than the initial education and training systems that lie within the usual area of authority of Ministers. Thus, even if Ministers had the resources to pay for an extended approach to lifelong learning for all, they would not have the full leverage or accountability to affect what happens in labour market programmes, enterprises, trade unions, or the home where much lifelong learning takes place.

- A fourth problem concerns the necessary *institutional reform*. Institutional arrangements are not well adapted for lifelong learning; current provision is delivered through an outdated set of institutions. In order to address the social and economic challenges facing the OECD countries, institutions must be re-thought and re-designed. This applies to curriculum, educational infrastructure, teaching methods and, as importantly, financial arrangements.

Ultimately, ensuring that lifelong learning is affordable and can be implemented depends on three conditions: increasing the level and predictability of its benefits, holding its costs down, and creating finance mechanisms and regulations that provide the right incentives for public authorities, individuals and social partners to invest in it. The purpose of the discussion in this chapter is to shed light on possible ways of overcoming these tensions. In the main, the chapter aims at answering three broad questions:

- *What is the evidence that lifelong learning yields substantial benefits?* Making lifelong learning a reality for all will extend the benefits of initial and subsequent learning to those who are underserved. But what is the nature and magnitude of these benefits, and who enjoys them? To what extent are they dependent on institutional arrangements and other factors? How will the extension of learning opportunities in a lifelong perspective affect the social and individual rates of return? Might "over-education" be likely?

- *What are the short-term costs of extending lifelong learning?* Time-series information on the costs of education and training provision at different levels offers one basis for estimating the costs – particularly for public budgets – of making lifelong learning a reality for all. But how reliable a guide are they? To what extent should the objective of achieving lifelong learning for all be accomplished through the expansion of existing arrangements? To what extent might they be achieved through a departure from the "front-end" model of education? How might the cost-effectiveness of different components of education and training systems otherwise be improved?

– *Who is going to pay for lifelong learning?* Even if lifelong learning can be shown to be a "worthwhile investment", there may be less-than-optimal resources devoted to it, because of the difficulty of public budgets to internalise long-term benefits as an offset to current expenditure. More generally, market failures may also lead to under-investment. There also may be over-spending on certain parts of the system due to subsidies or factors that distort the incentives for various actors to pay for it.

C. THE BENEFITS OF LIFELONG LEARNING

The affordability of lifelong learning depends, in part, on what the benefits from it are. In principle, governments, individuals, and employers will pay for lifelong learning insofar as it is "worthwhile" – insofar as the anticipated marginal benefits are greater than the expected marginal costs. But what is worthwhile depends on how and from whose perspective "worth" is defined and measured. This section considers evidence on the nature and magnitude of the benefits accruing to lifelong learning investments. In presenting and analysing the data, lifelong learning is considered in its component parts.

A macroeconomic view of the benefits

One crude approach to evaluating the benefits of lifelong learning is growth accounting, by which the contribution of education to productivity, output and growth is compared across countries. Because of its aggregate perspective, its value in the context of this discussion is to signal the importance of worker qualifications to overall economic performance and standards of living. For example, one study of 29 countries found education accounting for up to a quarter of economic growth (Psacharopoulos, 1984, pp. 340-346). A more recent study of 24 countries, seven of which are OECD countries, reached similar conclusions (OECD, 1994d, Part II, pp. 115-116). This suggests that investment in education and training produces a substantial economic return. But analysis

at this level says nothing about the distribution of the returns to individual actors, or about the presence of benefits or costs of education and training that occur to someone other than the person who paid for it ("externalities"), or more generally, about the incentives and disincentives facing individual participants.

Another study of interest that examines economic growth is Mankiw *et al.* (1992). In this study an augmented Solow growth model is estimated. Both physical and human capital are specified; the latter is measured by the percentage of the working-age population attending secondary school. The effect of this variable on productivity levels is significant for the whole sample of countries and for a sub-sample of 22 OECD countries. This implies that investment in human capital generates economic growth. Pencavel (1990) decomposes the effect of education on economic growth into the contributions of tertiary and non-tertiary education. For several countries it can be concluded that the contribution of tertiary education falls short to the contribution of non-tertiary education, pointing to diminishing social returns to education.

Monetary returns to formal education and training

An approach more useful for capturing the possible returns from lifelong learning is to focus on the "micro level", and to consider the returns falling to individuals from different levels of education and training. The most readily observed returns are obtained using cross-sectional data to compare the earnings of individuals by level of educational attainment. Chart 8.1 provides a first approximation of the monetary returns to various levels of education. It suggests that the negative consequences of failing to complete upper secondary education is substantial in some countries (in the United States, average earnings of those with a lower secondary education or less are more than a third lower than for those who have completed high school). Earnings for those who have acquired tertiary-level qualifications – university qualifications especially – are typically half again higher than for those with just a secondary education. This approach is weakened by the fact that it fails to take account of individual characteristics other than educational attainment and employment experience in trying to explain differences in earnings, and would therefore over-estimate the returns to schooling.

Another way of assessing the returns to education is by comparing the "private" with the "social" returns to lifelong learning. The first is based on

◆ Chart 8.1. **Relative differences in earnings from work by level of education, 1992**[1,2,3,4]
Mean earnings ratios relative to the earnings of upper secondary graduates; percentage difference

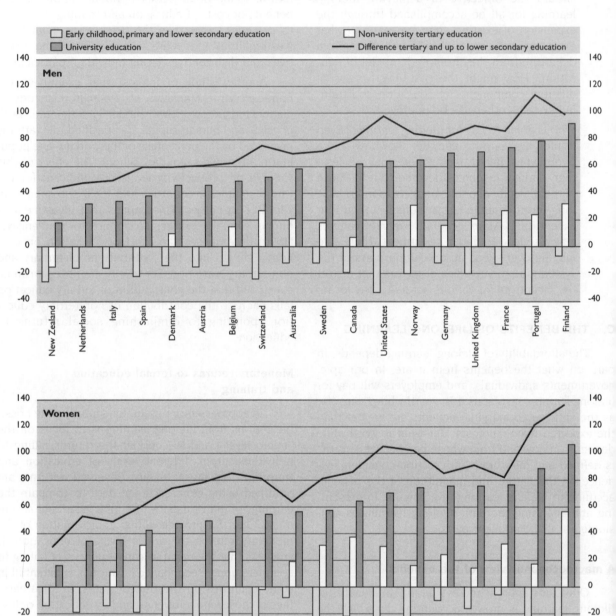

1. Ratio of mean annual earnings by level of educational attainment to mean annual earnings at upper secondary level (x 100) in the population 25 to 64 years of age by gender.
2. Data for non-university tertiary education is included in the data for university education for Austria, Italy, the Netherlands and Spain.
3. 1991 data for Australia, Canada, Denmark, Finland, Italy and Spain.
4. 1993 data for Portugal.
Source: OECD (1995d), *Education at a Glance – OECD Indicators*, p. 233.

comparing the net income gains accruing to an individual that are attributable to education with the costs of acquiring it. Ideally, the social rate of return is based on comparing the net increase in gross earnings from more education to the public and private costs of acquiring it. Private and social rates of return should indicate the period of time over which earnings are counted. This can be done by incorporating a "discount rate" by which the stream over time of benefits and costs can be discounted to a "present value" which can then be compared (Alsalam and Conley, 1995, pp. 86-88).

Much of the literature on rates of return to education and training is constrained by a lack of data and the resulting need to make unrealistic assumptions. Costs are often limited to estimates of foregone earnings; while this may be a reasonable approximation for adults in training, the value of direct costs of formal education – relative to the opportunity costs – is much higher at the primary and secondary levels, and tends to be important even at the tertiary level. This lack of data on direct costs explains, at least partly, why the "rate of return" literature has tended to emphasise private instead of social rates of return. The result has been that the social rates of return have often been overstated. Private rate of return studies tend to be based on before-tax earnings; such studies overestimate the returns in countries with high average and marginal tax rates on income.

Table 8.1 reports social rates of return that have been calculated for selected countries. Included into the data analysis are the direct costs, based on average unit costs, and estimates of foregone earnings, though earnings gains and foregone earnings are assumed to equal the average earnings of persons of the same age who did not go on to that level of education. The average earnings of persons aged 16 to 24 were imputed (Alsalam and Conley, 1995, pp. 99-100).

Another approach is to estimate individuals' earnings using cross-sectional data for different age groups, or data from longitudinal panels, in wage equations that take account of educational attainment as well as labour market experience and a variety of factors. Table 8.2 summarises the findings from more recent research based on this approach conducted in two countries. In the United States, such analyses show rates of return in the order of 5 to 10 per cent for additional years of schooling, increasing with higher levels of education. Though the returns for males compared with females are mixed, returns for Blacks tend to be lower than for Whites. In the United Kingdom, the evidence is more mixed with regard to the experience of men relative to women, though broadly consistent in showing rising returns for men over time, and rising returns with higher levels of education. Factors influencing the size of rates of return include the industry and occupation in which individuals are employed, as well as detailed measures of performance in education, such as grade point averages (Cohn and Addison, 1995).

Table 8.3 reviews some studies on the private return to schooling in the Netherlands, again based on Mincer-type wage equations (Mincer, 1974). Returns in the Netherlands appear to vary between 3 and 9 per cent. There are three key findings. Firstly, Hartog and Oosterbeek (1988) find that there is a significant return to "over-schooling". Secondly, Oosterbeek and Van Ophem (1995) find additional evidence for decreasing returns to schooling. Thirdly, returns on human capital declined during the 1980s. This is at odds with expectations and with the rising return to human capital in the United States, but it is a well-documented phenomenon (see Hartog *et al.*, 1994).

Usually, skill-intensive technological change and, therefore, increased demand for skills are seen as explanations for the increased returns to human capital observed in the United States (Bound and Johnson, 1992; Juhn *et al.*, 1993). The decreasing returns to human capital during the 1980s in the Netherlands contradict these expectations. Teulings (1995) offers an alternative explanation for the Dutch experience: increased skill levels and stable job complexities have led to decreasing returns to education during the 1980s. Accordingly, the rising returns to education in the United States might not be due to technological change. Teulings (1995) suggests another, "more stringent explanation: the rising return to skill should be associated with a declining level of skill for a given industry or occupation". This supply-side argument covers both the Dutch and the American experience. Whichever is the correct explanation, the supply or demand-side argument, the inevitable conclusion is the same: there is a constant need for up-skilling in economies pursuing growth and equity goals.

There is a widespread agreement that the social rates of return to primary and secondary education are higher than the social rate of return to tertiary education (Psacharopoulos, 1993). Moreover, it is also found that private rates of return are generally higher than social rates of return, especially for higher levels of education. OECD countries spend a major part of their education budgets on tertiary education, with expenditure per tertiary student being on average 2.5 times as high as in primary education and nearly twice as high compared to secondary education (OECD, 1995d). This, and the continuing growth of mass tertiary systems, calls into doubt the desirability and sustainability of current arrangements of education finance.

Certain important observations can be made on the basis of the analyses of rates of return to formal education:

- First, the returns to various levels of formal education and training are substantial in virtually all countries, comparing favourably with rates of return observed in alternative forms of investment.

- Rates of return vary according to the occupation and industry in which individuals work.

- Rates of return for women frequently are below those for men, suggesting that their lower rates of labour force participation, and higher likelihood of withdrawing from the labour force to raise children, have a negative impact on lifetime earnings patterns.

- There are sufficient exceptions to the above generalisations to suggest that the patterns are not uniform. The estimates obtained for Belgium, Finland, France, Spain and the United States give rise to the possibility that alternative patterns of labour force participation and lifelong learning may be consistent with earnings gains for individuals and others.

- Rates of return decrease with higher levels of education.

- All of the above is confirmation that formal education is justified as an investment in the OECD countries.

However, it does not necessarily follow that the rates of return calculated for current programmes will also be observed in the future. Returns may decline, for example, if education participation rates are increased. Because of factors that are inadequately captured in rate of return analyses – individual ability or discrimination by employers – the correct rate of returns may be less than studies tend to show. However, the opposite may be true as well, since the costs of not educating and training those who are at risk are very substantial. As shown in Chapter 1, these costs take the form of higher rates of unemployment and higher incidence of economic dependency.

Non-monetary returns to formal education and training

Despite the caveats noted previously, the "true" returns to initial education and training are most likely underestimated. Although the monetary returns from initial education are more readily observed, there are important non-monetary or "non-market" returns, including "externalities" (costs or benefits that are passed on to someone other than whoever finances education). Jorgenson and Fraumeni (1989) estimate that these benefits, which include household work, travel, and leisure, are double the observed monetary returns for men, and five times those for women.

More generally, the consumption value of education, though it is not necessarily reflected in either the monetary or social returns to education, should count among the benefits. This takes the form of education as a leisure pastime in and of itself, and education that is used in leisure or related activities (reading a book or a newspaper) that are not linked to wages or earnings. Citing a survey of studies on returns to education, Schultz (1967) noted that "[all these studies omit the consumption value of education. It is a serious omission (...)". The available estimates of the benefits of education in this respect all underestimate the value of education (McMahon, 1995, p. 9). While estimating the consumption value of education is difficult to do empirically, its presence or absence should be accounted for. Thus, while monetary returns from a basic literacy programme and a trade training programme may be similar, the higher "consumption value" of the former (enabling persons to read after work, and during retirement) might imply higher overall returns.

Other recent studies suggest that education and training do yield returns in terms of positive impacts on environmental quality, crime and health, although the magnitude of such impacts is difficult to estimate. Grossman and Kaestner (1995) review the literature on the impact of schooling on health. In their conclusions they state: "Our interpretation of the extensive literature dealing with the first issue [does schooling have a positive causal impact on good health?] is that the weight of evidence suggests that more schooling does in fact cause better health". The impact of education on crime is less clear cut. Witte (1995) states "Neither years of schooling completed nor receipt of a high-school degree has a significant effect on an individual's level of criminal activity. However, greater amounts of time in school are associated with lower levels of criminal activity". The literature on the effects of education on environmental quality is very limited. Smith (1995) reviews some evidence and considers how education might influence the environmental quality people experience. He states: "The lessons from my selective review of links between education and people's behaviour in learning about sources of environmental externalities and what people can do to protect themselves from these hazards, confirms education's role as enhancing learning."

The implication is that rates of return based just on monetary costs and benefits probably lead to results that understate "true" rates of return, insofar as the non-monetary benefits are greater than the non-monetary costs.

The returns from non-formal education and training

Evaluating the returns from non-formal education and training, or more broadly, from all the learning activities that are undertaken in adult life both within formal institutions of adult education and continuing vocational training, and informally at home and at the workplace, is a very complex endeavour for at least four reasons. Firstly, the content of what is learned is more difficult to define and measure. In contrast to the rates of return analyses reviewed above, there exist no recognisable benchmarks, such as ISCED level or years of education that can be defined as the input (see OECD, 1995d; Lynch, 1995). Secondly, the costs of such learning are difficult to evaluate. Even if costs are restricted to the value of foregone income or lost production, they are difficult to estimate insofar as the learning process itself is difficult to observe. Thirdly, the returns to several forms of lifelong learning, such as courses undertaken for personal enrichment and development, yield non-monetary returns or are more purely classified as learning for its own sake. The difficulty of separating consumptive and productive learning is, however, acknowledged. Finally, the returns to lifelong learning for older persons, including those retired, may appear to be more limited because they are less likely to reflect a change in wages or earnings.

For all these reasons, the literature on returns to both formal and non-formal learning beyond schooling and initial tertiary education is sparse, tending to focus on particular cases or otherwise being constrained in the extent to which they might be generalised. To the extent that adult learning takes place in formally organised and structured programmes, often with public subsidies attached to them, calculating the rates of return may be feasible, provided that

appropriate data are available. One approximation of such returns can be obtained by examining the experience of adults participating in education and training programmes not leading to a degree or other measurable outcome that corresponds to the qualifications recognised in the ISCED system. An analysis of longitudinal data in the United States suggests that studies in vocational subjects yield higher returns than those in academic subjects (see Chapter 4). Further, there seem to be important differences according to the kind of institution in which such studies were pursued. Those taken in four-year colleges or universities appear to produce substantially higher returns than those undertaken elsewhere (Grubb, 1992 and 1995).

Another approach is to examine the post-training experience of unemployed adults. Table 8.4 shows the results of one such evaluation study of labour market programmes in the United States. The evidence shows that among adults, classroom training produced higher wage-returns for females than for males; but on-the-job training and/or job search assistance produced still higher returns for both males and females.

Table 8.5 gives an overview of the outcomes of active labour market programmes in a number of countries. A number of studies investigate the effect of the Comprehensive Employment and Training Act programme (CETA) in the United States. There seems to be a clear indication that enrolment in this programme has a significant positive effect on both earnings and the probability of being employed. In general the results for the United States suggest that active labour market programmes are effective. The outcomes for the European countries listed in Table 8.5 are mixed. There seems to be an indication that training programmes are more beneficial for those who had relatively good initial employment conditions. There are, however, positive effects, especially for employment programmes in the Netherlands.

Because of the interest in evaluating the returns to employers from enterprise-based training – one major aspect of lifelong learning – a rather separate line of analysis has emerged recently, focusing on productivity. This work has been hindered by the difficulty of linking data on training occurrence to productivity measures. One analysis (Bartel, 1991) estimated that an increase in training expenditure yielded a 16 per cent return after a certain period of time.

More recent studies, undertaken as part of an ongoing effort to evaluate the relationship between training, technological change and productivity, found that for manufacturing firms in the United States, a 10 per cent increase in the proportion of workers trained led to a 1.4 per cent increase in total sales within 3 years. Importantly, though, the beneficial effects of training are found to depend on collateral investment in technology (Lynch, 1995). Table 8.6 shows the results of a more detailed analysis of similar kinds of data for the case of a non-OECD country, Chinese Taipei, where the productivity impact of training varies greatly by industry in which a firm operates, and by how advanced a firm's technology is (Aw and Tan, 1995). Similar conclusions were found to apply for Mexico (Lima, 1995). All of this is constant with and amplifies on earlier evidence from the United States that the more technologically advanced an industry is, the more likely employees are to be trained, and the more likely workers are to enjoy higher rates of return on initial formal education (Lillard and Tan, 1992).

However, high as the productivity (and eventual wage) returns from firm-based training might be, participation is not universal. The likelihood of individuals receiving such training depends heavily on their level of initial educational attainment: the more qualified they are, the more likely they are to receive more training (OECD, 1994d). It also depends on the industry and occupation in which an individual is employed. This suggests that, as in the case of formal education and training, the returns from expanded participation in at least the firm-based component of lifelong learning may differ from those observed in the past.

One complication in the consideration of returns to firm-based training is the fact that the wage and productivity returns to training are not always congruent. For example, Table 8.7 shows that comparing returns to training according to where it occurred shows that gains from training in connection with previous employment are less than those from training provided by a current employer, or through apprenticeship. Another analysis finds that although the wage returns from training in a previous job had no effect on initial wages for individuals, their initial productivity was 9.5 per cent higher, and their training requirements were reduced by 17.3 per cent (Bishop, 1994).

Table 8.8 offers an extensive overview of studies that examine the effects of on-the-job training on wages and productivity. Results overwhelmingly point to substantial positive effects on wages, typically ranging from 5 to 15 per cent, but sometimes as high as 20 per cent. The effects of on-the-job training on productivity are positive, and there is also a clear indication that the effects of training on productivity exceed those on wages. This is not surprising because it is unlikely that employers would invest in non-profitable training. As a direct consequence, only those are trained who are likely to be "good" learners. This is observed in practice, since training incidence increases with educational attainment. Selectivity plays therefore a major part in training decisions.

Concluding remarks on returns to lifelong learning

Evidence on the returns to lifelong learning is confined largely to the monetary returns to formal education and training, and to a variety of forms of firm-based training. The evidence, as far is it goes, supports the assumption of lifelong learning as an investment that more than pays for itself. However, the evidence provides only limited guidance as to the likely future returns from expanded participation in lifelong learning. There are a number of reasons for this. Firstly, the returns from increasing participation in formal education and training, as well as firm-based training may not be as high as past observed returns, insofar as expanded enrolments occur among persons who have greater difficulty learning. There is evidence (Björklund and Moffitt, 1987; Groot et al., 1994) that selection is very important in this respect, implying that those who did not receive any training would not benefit from it, or the benefits would be less than the costs. If training would prove to be beneficial (from an economic or social point of view) for those who are presently not trained, government action might be needed to create incentives for employers. Secondly, there is no evidence on the monetary or non-monetary returns to lifelong learning that is not firm-based or otherwise aimed at improving productivity and earnings. This absence of evidence is particularly troubling since it concerns precisely the kind of learning that could prove so crucial in ensuring that citizens are well-informed and active participants in social and cultural life, even after retirement.

The implication is that these latter forms of lifelong learning may be difficult to justify as investments, either because the returns are empirically difficult to measure, or because such forms of learning have a high value in their own right (essentially, they can be seen as "consumption"). Either case could be used to justify individuals assuming a greater share of the costs.

D. WHAT ARE THE COSTS OF LIFELONG LEARNING?

Even if lifelong learning attracts broad political support and yields substantial rates of return, the costs are important because resources are limited. Thus, within a given resource constraint, the extent to which governments – or employers, or individuals – can expand opportunities for lifelong learning depends on how much it costs to provide an additional "unit", whether it is one more place in a preschool programme for young children, an additional place in university, or an opening in adult basic education classes.

Marginal costs (rather than rates of return) are even more important as a determinant of the opportunity to participate in lifelong learning insofar as such learning yields non-monetary returns. Yet costs are not easy to measure reliably. Unit costs for classroom instruction are "lumpy" in the sense that the extra cost of adding one more student to a half-empty class is far less than the extra cost of adding an additional teacher and classroom. Comparisons of unit costs across countries are complicated by the fact that national data include varying levels of administrative (non-teaching) costs. More fundamentally, measured current unit costs may not be reliable indicators of future unit costs, insofar as costs might be reduced, on the one hand, through the elimination of inefficiencies. On the other hand, some components of unit costs for reaching at-risk children and youth might be pushed higher because of the addition of guidance and support services, for example, whereas other components of unit costs may be reduced through the reconfiguration of various teaching and learning inputs (e.g. the mix of fully qualified instructional staff and assistants, or the use of teaching and learning technology).

The use of unit costs as the building block for estimating the overall costs of lifelong learning, therefore, provides only a first approximation of such costs. However, they do provide an estimate that is historically based. Insofar as the extension of lifelong learning requires expanding elements of existing institutional arrangements, estimates derived from unit costs are a reasonable guide to orders of magnitude for future cost scenarios. They also provide a baseline for the consideration of policy measures that could fundamentally alter unit costs.

The additional costs of pursuing policies to make lifelong learning a reality for all consists of two main components. The first is the cost of changing existing education and training practice to ensure that it provides the necessary foundation for subsequent learning. The second is the cost of extending and deepening those subsequent opportunities.

In the analysis that follows, cost scenarios are presented for changes within the systems of education and training that currently are within or closely related to the areas of competence of Education Ministers: early childhood education; secondary education; tertiary education. The next sub-section examines the main components of these costs, and considers evidence on where cost reductions might be achieved, through improved efficiency or by reconfiguring various inputs. A third sub-section surveys in a more cursory manner cost scenarios related to extending opportunities for lifelong learning beyond the system of initial formal education and training. This last sub-section is the least detailed owing to the lack of appropriate data.

The cost of the foundations for lifelong learning

The discussion below reviews estimates of the cost of providing an adequate foundation for lifelong learning, within the framework of formal education and training systems. These costs are presented in terms of their impact on overall education and training expenditure. The analysis then examines the main components of costs, and considers how cost scenarios might vary in response to different policies and programmes and other actions by public authorities.

What constitutes an "adequate foundation" for lifelong learning is dependent on country-specific traditions, such as the patterns of educational attainment reviewed in Chapter 1, and the extent of arrangements for adult education and continuing vocational training, mentioned in Chapter 4. But, as *The OECD Jobs Study* (OECD, 1994d) and the preceding chapters suggest, at the individual level, educational attainment corresponding to the completion of upper secondary education (or its vocational equivalent) seems a bare prerequisite. From the point of view of national education and training systems, this translates into educational attainment patterns characterised by relatively few early school-leavers, and substantial numbers of persons participating in academic and vocational programmes at the tertiary level.

With this in mind, an approximation of the first element of the cost of lifelong learning is the cost of bringing participation rates in national education systems roughly in line with this overall pattern. Thus, the cost of raising participation rates can be approximated by a function of the "unit cost" of educating persons at different levels of education, and the "enrolment gap" – the number of persons who remain to be brought up to given participation targets. Chart 8.2 provides estimates of the unit cost at the pre-primary, secondary and full-time tertiary levels of education.

Table 8.9 estimates the number of student-years by which enrolment levels must be increased in order to reach the participation targets. These target rates must be met by the age cohorts that correspond to the assumed enrolment ages for the different levels of education. For early childhood education the assumed enrolment ages are 3 to 6 years. The target is set in this way, because in some countries primary education starts at 7. In certain countries the enrolment gap will be zero at age 6 because primary education is mandatory from that age. Enrolment ages for secondary education are assumed to be 14 to 17 years. The target for tertiary enrolments is split up in two age groups: 18- to 21-year-olds and 22- to 25-year-olds. This is the case because tertiary education enrolments occur at a later age in the Nordic countries. The participation targets, intended to

reflect "good" practice, are roughly equal to the average enrolment rates by single years of age achieved by the two best performing countries. For pre-primary and secondary education, the target rate is set at 90 per cent, whereas for tertiary education, the target has been set at 25 per cent for 18- to 21-year-olds and 16 per cent for 22- to 25-year-olds.

The enrolment gap is defined as the number of additional persons that ought to be enrolled in order to raise the net enrolment rate to the target rate. It should be noted that the outcomes are sensitive to the assumptions about enrolment ages. National definitions differ. The gaps presented in Table 8.9 are therefore rough estimates. They indicate which countries face large enrolment gaps if the targets are to be attained. They also show which countries are close to achieving the targets.

Table 8.9 suggests that Belgium and France have reached the target rate in early childhood education. The other OECD countries all face considerable enrolment gaps ranging from about 4.1 per cent of the target group (the number of persons aged 3 to 6) for New Zealand to about 86 per cent for Turkey. Countries that face above average enrolment gaps are

♦ Chart 8.2. ***Unit costs per student by level of education, 1992***[1,2,3]

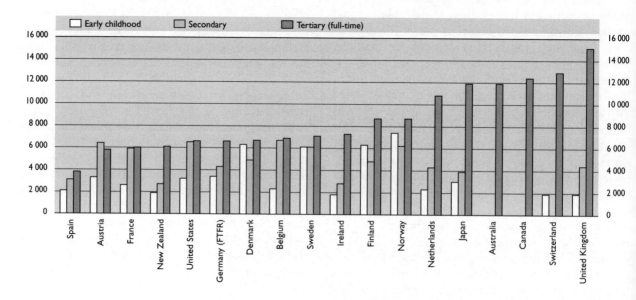

1. Expressed in US dollars, adjusted using purchasing power parities (PPP). Rounded to nearest 100 dollars.
2. Public institutions only.
3. Data refer to public and government dependent private institutions for the Netherlands.
Source: OECD (1995d), *Education at a Glance – OECD Indicators*, Table F.03, pp. 88-92.

Australia, Finland, Switzerland and Turkey. Seven countries have an enrolment gap of one-third of the age group: Canada, Denmark, Greece, Ireland, Norway, Sweden and the United States.

In secondary education enrolments are high for all countries except Turkey. Enrolment gaps range from about 1 to 10 per cent of the target group to be enrolled. The enrolment gaps for Australia and the United Kingdom are relatively high because the calculations are based only on full-time equivalents, whereas part-time enrolments are high in these countries. However, no distinction is made between lower and upper secondary education.

As regards tertiary education for 18- to 21-year-olds, the United States and Belgium reach the target enrolment rate of 25 per cent. As with secondary education, there is little variation between countries. Except for Denmark, Sweden, Austria, Switzerland, Norway and to a lesser extent the United Kingdom, the countries face enrolment gaps up to 18 per cent of the target population. However, in the Nordic countries and Switzerland enrolments in tertiary education tend to be high in the age range above 21. Some countries have a significant share of part-time enrolment which, if counted, would reduce the enrolment gaps considerably. The main examples are Australia, the United States (already a zero gap at full-time enrolments, but there is considerable part-time enrolment in the system as well) and New Zealand. In calculating the gap, upper secondary enrolment is not taken into account in order to get comparable results. Among the 22- to 25-year-olds the enrolment target of 16 per cent is reached by Denmark and Finland. For the remaining countries enrolment gaps range from less than 1 per cent in Austria and Norway to 10 per cent or more in Australia, Greece, Ireland, the United Kingdom and Turkey.

When calculating the cost of raising enrolments, the assumption is made that cost only have a variable component. When assessing the cost it is clear that economies of scale could keep costs relatively low, whereas the fact that providing additional infrastructure could require large starting investments which could weigh heavily on government budgets. These dimensions are not accounted for, as information on the cost of education is sparse and mixed, and accounting practices differ. The cost of filling the enrolment gaps is therefore assumed to be equal to the gap multiplied by the unit cost. The costs are expressed in US dollars, adjusted for purchasing

power parity, and as a percentage of public education expenditure, total public expenditure and GDP.

In interpreting the cost estimates given in Tables 8.10, 8.11 and 8.12, the same caution besetting the data on enrolment gaps should be applied. An additional reservation has to be made because of the assumption about the cost structure. What is clear, however, is that the costliest element of improving the foundation of lifelong learning is likely to be expanding the provision of early childhood education. Cost increases are in general more than twice as high than the cost of raising secondary education enrolments. The costs of increased enrolments in tertiary education are less clear-cut, largely due to the problems in calculating the enrolment gaps, but would be in the region of 1 per cent of the public education budget. The countries with zero enrolment gaps and therefore zero costs are on the lower end of the cost spectrum. For most countries the cost of living up to the three targets – raising enrolments to 90 per cent in pre-primary and secondary and to 25 per cent in full-time tertiary education for 18- to 21-year-olds and 16 per cent for 22- to 25-year-olds – will, according to the crude methodology used here, range from 0.1 to 1.5 per cent of GDP.

More generally, without trying to produce exact numbers, providing OECD societies with a firm base for lifelong learning will require increases in education resources. Although some countries are closer to the goal than others, the costs involved could still be considerable, and more importantly, be politically infeasible. It is therefore necessary to carefully design policies so as not only to provide participants with adequate incentives to invest in their own learning but also allocate the costs to those who benefit most. There is a growing need for lowering foundation costs, pursuing accountability and putting financial arrangements into place that are cost-effective, equitable and do not preclude lifelong learning.

Lowering foundation costs

The decision of whether the foundation costs for lifelong learning are "affordable" is essentially a political one. It depends on the overall fiscal stance of public authorities, the room for manoeuvre in reallocating expenditure between different levels of education, as well as the priority attached to lifelong learning relative to other areas of public expenditure. Whatever the political position may be on what constitutes an "appropriate" level of expenditure, however, there are recurring technical questions. These concern what comprises such costs and how they might be lowered in order for public authorities to achieve greater impacts, given fixed resources, or to improve efficiency to offset the loss of resources?

What are the main components of education costs today? Although the relative importance of different cost components varies considerably across countries (see Table 8.13), it is fair to say that education expenditures are dominated by the "labour-intensive" nature of the typical schooling model. Recurrent expenditures typically comprise nine-tenths of total expenditures; nearly two-thirds of recurrent expenditures are taken by compensation of education staff. Capital expenditures take up less than 10 per cent in most countries (OECD, 1995*d*).

However, detailed comparisons of expenditure composition across countries are hindered by variations in definitions and the allocation of costs. For example, high salary costs for personnel other than teachers in the United States reflect not only the use of teacher assistants and other support personnel, including health, social services, and counselling, but also the high costs associated with student transportation provided by schools in rural and suburban areas. In other countries, such costs may not be incurred or they may appear in other parts of the public budget. Capital expenditure tend to be even more difficult to compare. Some countries fund it as current expenditure (leading to high levels during construction, and negligible levels at other times); other countries take account of repayment schedules for borrowed funds. Accordingly international cost data are only crude indicators of cost. With this caveat in mind, the discussion below considers factors that might have an effect on costs by examining differences in the structure of costs at different levels of education and across countries.

The first point to consider concerns the factors that might explain the differences in unit costs that are observed at different levels of formal education and training. Unit costs in tertiary education exceed those in early childhood and secondary education – often by margins of 100 per cent or more – in all countries for which data are available, except Austria. Annex Table A.62 and Chart 8.2 have shown that unit costs in secondary education exceed those in early childhood education in three-quarters of the countries. The larger unit costs found in tertiary education appear to derive from at least three factors. One is the relatively high salary cost of education personnel in tertiary-level institutions. A second is the relatively high ratio of non-teaching/teaching personnel that is supported by such institutions. In two-thirds of the countries for which data are available, the non-teaching share of recurrent expenditure in tertiary education exceeds that share at the primary and secondary levels. At least part of the difference in overhead may be a statistical artefact, related to differences in the administration of community-based schools (in which certain maintenance costs might be shared), as compared to more self-contained and self-managed university institutions. But some of the cost differences must reflect genuine variation in the provision of educational services and the management of institutions; these differences may, for example, relate to the shares of research and administrative personnel.

A third factor in explaining the larger unit costs found in tertiary education is the relatively large share of expenditures devoted to capital costs. This is in part a function of high-cost special-use tertiary education teaching and research facilities combined with high capital outlays for student residential housing. But the two are pushed along by the increases in capital expenditure that have been undertaken to increase physical capacity in response to the dramatic growth in enrolments at the tertiary level (see Chapter 4).

Differences in unit costs can be explained by examining how they vary across countries. This will show whether there are country-specific institutional arrangements or circumstances that contribute to particularly high or low unit costs. Besides certain exceptions discussed below, there tends to be relatively little variation across countries in the unit costs at the pre-school and tertiary education levels. In most countries, the unit costs for the former are around US$ 3 000, and double that for the latter. The exceptions tend to reinforce the point. For example, while Denmark stands out with one of the highest unit costs for early childhood education, it is also characterised by having the smallest ratio of pupils to teaching staff at that level (OECD, 1995*d*). The opposite pattern exists in the United Kingdom, with the lowest unit costs and the highest pupil:teacher ratio. At the level of tertiary education, among the five countries that stand out with exceptionally high unit costs, those in Japan and the United States are less constrained because they are financed to a much greater extent than anywhere else by private sources. Those in Switzerland and the United Kingdom are systems that include heavily resourced cores that have been made affordable by comparatively low enrolments. Canada stands alone as a country with one of the highest unit costs in tertiary education, the highest participation rate at that level, and a system that is nearly completely state-supported. As a consequence, Canada has, by a wide margin, the highest share of GDP taken up by direct public expenditure for education institutions (OECD, 1995*d*, p. 75).

The patterns of cross-country consistency in unit costs break down at the level of secondary education, suggesting that there are important variations in the organisation and provision of education at this level. There are a number of factors that may explain these variations. Class sizes and teacher qualifications tend to be more variable across countries at that school level than at either the pre-school or tertiary education level. There are also important differences among countries in the mix of vocational and general studies, the year at which vocational studies begin, as well as differences in post-compulsory schooling patterns.

How might unit costs be reduced, or cost-effectiveness increased? The cost scenarios presented above are intended to provide a first estimate of the cost implications of increasing enrolments in the initial education system as a step towards strengthening the foundations for lifelong learning. They are based on the assumption, which may be questioned, of unit costs staying the same over time. In fact, one objective in setting the overall policy framework for lifelong learning might be how to control the generally rising trend in unit costs. But for that, there is a need for more detailed information than is currently available on the costs of different strategies.

In reflecting on ways to control or reduce costs, a certain number of observations are worth keeping in mind. One is the labour-intensive character of initial formal education and training. The largest single component of education expenditure is for teachers. Because there are limits to how much that component can be reduced through the substitution of lower-cost teacher assistants or technology (see Chapter 7), formal education is susceptible to a "cost disease", in which unit costs depend largely on trends in teachers' salaries. However, to the extent that the expansion of enrolments in foundation learning requires a proportional expansion in the teaching workforce, the cost scenarios presented above may overstate costs, at least over the first few years, because of the considerable differences between starting salaries of newly hired teachers, and the salaries of experienced teachers. The average ratio of maximum to starting salaries in OECD countries is 2.1 (OECD, 1995*d*, p. 189), meaning that a newly hired teacher is half as expensive as an experienced one. Since three-fifths of the teaching force in OECD coun-

tries is earning the maximum salary, historical unit costs may be significantly higher than the actual cost of accommodating expanded enrolments.

Another factor that may reduce teachers' costs in some countries is the expected decline in school age populations (see Chart 1.4 in Chapter 1). In more than half of the OECD countries, including those with some of the lowest secondary education completion rates, declines in the number of 10-14 year-olds will at least partially offset the cost of increasing secondary education completion rates.

Finally, it is important not to overlook the possibility that some substitution of "technology for teachers" might occur (see Chapters 3 and 7). The bulk of experience in this respect has been with the delivery of distance learning at the tertiary level. Distance education and distance learning techniques, well established in a number of countries, based on technologies ranging from print modules and correspondence courses, to video cassettes and television broadcasts, interactive video and video conferencing, tend to be cost-effective, especially for governments.

Experience with distance learning has demonstrated the feasibility not only of sharply lower unit costs, but, for some methods, of powerful economies of scale. Using such technologies, the input of teachers is focused on curriculum development, on the front end, and, to varying degrees, on student assessment and feedback throughout the course. Once material is developed, however, the number of students that can be handled is, depending on the approach used, limited only by the costs of delivering courseware. For more traditional methods, involving print material as well as approaches delivered through video and audio cassettes, the unit cost of adding students (the "marginal cost") depends on the recurrent cost of production and distribution of material. Table 8.14 shows the results of one analysis of the Open University in the United Kingdom, which found that unit costs declined by more than 85 per cent, with a ten-fold increase in students (Bates, 1995). For more flexible approaches based on radio and television broadcast and video conferencing, the unit costs of additional students, though higher, also decline steeply with large increases in students. Thus, unlike classroom-based methods in which unit costs are fairly constant, whether one is adding 300 or 3 000 students, unit costs for distance learning decline sharply with larger numbers of students.

Another analysis of a distance education centre in Australia compared costs for the off-campus (distance learning) mode of instruction, the on-campus (face-to-face) mode, and a mixed mode. Table 8.15 shows that the difference in total costs between the off-campus and face-to-face mode is negligible. However, the difference in marginal costs, the costs of adding students (reflected in the delivery costs) are substantial, with the face-to-face mode being over a third more costly (Taylor and White, 1991).

Even at the level of primary and secondary education, different configurations of computer-based teaching and learning technologies show promise of lowering unit costs or limiting the increase in unit costs that might otherwise occur. One approach to reducing unit costs, or at least improving cost-effectiveness, is by using computer-based instructional technology to shift away from the traditional one-teacher to one-classroom configuration. In Canada it is estimated that introducing such technology in primary and secondary schools would require a 3- to 4-fold increase in expenditure on instructional supplies (Stager, 1995). The offsetting benefits were not estimated, though it was expected that this technology would reduce learning time and allow more flexible use of facilities. Moreover, although the initial costs would be substantial, unit costs could be "much less than for traditional methods", because of the possibility of reaching large numbers of students.

How realistic are participation rate targets? Another factor to take into account in evaluating the costs of improving the foundations for lifelong learning is to reconsider the target participation rates for various levels of educational attainment, used for the calculations in Tables 8.9 through 8.12. Those targets are based on "best practice" among OECD countries. But it should be remembered that insofar as Member countries are heterogeneous in their structure and circumstances, the notion of a best practice benchmark may be of only limited usefulness. Thus, not only would it be expensive for the United Kingdom or Switzerland to increase the number of university graduates to the level found in the United States, but it might also pose a shock to their labour markets to have such an increased supply of highly-qualified job-seekers.

Rather, the participation rate targets are better seen as a first option for a change in policy. Such options need to be considered not only in the light of their costs, but in the light of alternative approaches for achieving similar ends. Thus, it might be possible to set lower targets for the completion of upper secondary education, if a smoothly functioning apprenticeship system is put in place, or if there are ample opportunities for individuals to continue formal education and training during adulthood.

The costs of expanded lifelong learning outside formal systems

Estimating the costs of ensuring access for all to lifelong learning outside the formal education and training systems is a formidable task. It is made difficult partly by the scarcity of time-series information on cost development. This owes to the diverse nature of institutions and settings – public and private providers, the workplace, the home – as well as to the conceptual difficulty of defining such costs, when they may entail costs of foregone production, income or leisure time.

In a more profound sense, however, estimating the costs is impossible because of the open-ended nature of the objectives of lifelong learning. In contrast to the case of initial education and training systems, where the criteria for adequate foundations can be specified, the objectives elsewhere are indeterminate. There are two sources of this indeterminate nature. One is the uncertainty around the additional number of persons needing access to "learning beyond initial education". The second is uncertainty about the "volume" of lifelong learning that is needed to achieve certain outcomes, because desired outcomes themselves are so elastic. In the "real world", the "optimum" level of lifelong learning will be variable, depending both on costs and on the usefulness of it for purposes of investment (generating economic returns) and consumption (generating personal satisfaction and other returns in line with individuals' preferences).

However, it is a fact that a certain amount of lifelong learning occurs, that there are certain costs that are incurred and observed, and that there are identifiable population sub-groups who are likely targets of subsidised opportunities for lifelong learning. It is useful, therefore, to martial the available evidence and to establish, within the constraints of explicit assumptions, a baseline of cost estimates and then to consider the implications of changes in the breadth and depth of opportunities for lifelong learning.

As a first step in approximating the costs of extending lifelong learning opportunities beyond the initial phases outlined above, Table 8.16 provides an estimate of the number of persons who might be priority targets for new lifelong learning opportunities, measured in terms . The table provides a breakdown of the number of working-age persons who have at most obtained a lower secondary education or equivalent.

If lifelong learning should be accessible for all persons, the estimates in Table 8.16 understate the number of persons that might be covered in one way or another by lifelong learning arrangements. However, lifelong learning is already a reality to some degree, for many persons. Surveys in a number of countries in the early 1990s found that between a quarter and a half of adults had participated in job-related training in the preceding year (OECD, 1995k). The total number having access to just job-related training on a regular basis (perhaps less than every year), is therefore somewhat above those figures. However, whereas a significant number of persons participate already, their likelihood of doing so is conditioned to some extent on their level of initial qualifications. In this respect, persons with a lower secondary education or less are systematically less likely to participate. Thus, the figures presented in Table 8.16 provide what is probably a credible lower boundary for the focus of eventual policy action in this area.

A recent survey of adult literacy and numeracy levels in the populations of seven OECD countries (OECD and Statistics Canada, 1995) demonstrated that over 20 per cent of adults in some of the world's richest countries have literacy and numeracy skills at only the most basic levels. Chart 8.3 shows the percentage of adults who perform at each literacy and numeracy level on the 5-point scale in the countries surveyed (countries are ranked by the percentage of adults scoring at Level 1, in ascending order). The pattern of distribution is not consistent in various countries or in the different domains. The countries with the highest percentage of people scoring at the basic level (Level 1) do not necessarily have the lowest percentage performing at the top end (Level 4/5). Some countries perform considerably differently on both scales.

Table 8.17 estimates the universe of need for a limited number of countries on the basis of demonstrated performance on the literacy test, which was administered in 1994 (OECD and Statistics Canada, 1995), rather than nominal educational attainment levels. This method yields estimates that range from being only slightly greater in Sweden, to more than 5 times larger in the United States.

Estimating costs from these crude estimates of the "universe of need" adds one more level of uncer-

tainty, since transparent unit cost data are even more difficult to come by here than in the area of formal education. One crude estimate for selected countries is presented in Table 8.18. These estimates are based on "per-participant" costs, rather than "training-years", for example. The result is that they over- or under-estimate costs if the actual duration of training were to be shorter or longer than the average in the year reported. These estimates are also distorted for the reasons discussed previously, in connection with the costs of formal initial education and training.

Two stylised cost scenarios are presented, on the basis of different assumptions, in Tables 8.19 and 8.20. Crude as these estimates are, they suggest that the scale of the problems posed by large numbers of adults in need of lifelong learning, is likely to dwarf that found at the levels of pre-primary, secondary and tertiary education.

In making even stylised estimates of costs at the different levels at which lifelong learning occurs, "indirect costs" loom large in importance with respect to learning that occurs above the foundation level. These costs are over and above the costs to government, for example, in providing classrooms, teachers and administrative support. They include the "opportunity costs" of earnings that are foregone when an individual stops work to participate in training. For employers, such opportunity costs include the value of the goods and services that are foregone when workers are trained. Regardless of the direct costs to government of such lifelong learning, the opportunity costs to individuals and employers impose an additional cost on government in the form of tax revenues that are lost because of the foregone earnings and output. Estimating these costs is difficult at any level above that of the individual in the workplace. Aggregation depends very much on particular working conditions such as the availability of training leave and work organisation – to what extent do colleagues and supervisors participate in the training and learning process?

Given the bias in the accessibility of lifelong learning away from the least qualified, it can be assumed that the indirect costs of extending lifelong learning would be less than the costs that are already incurred for those who presently receive it. Two principal reasons are the higher likelihood of unemployment and lower average earnings among the least qualified – the ones most in need of expanded opportunities for lifelong learning.

◆   Chart 8.3. **Comparative distribution of adult literacy[1] and numeracy[2] skills, 1994**

Proportion of population aged 16-65 scoring at the lowest two literacy levels,[3] prose scale

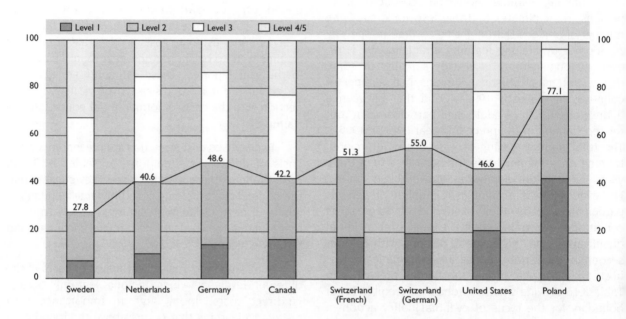

Proportion of population aged 16-65 scoring at the lowest two numeracy levels,[3] quantitative scale

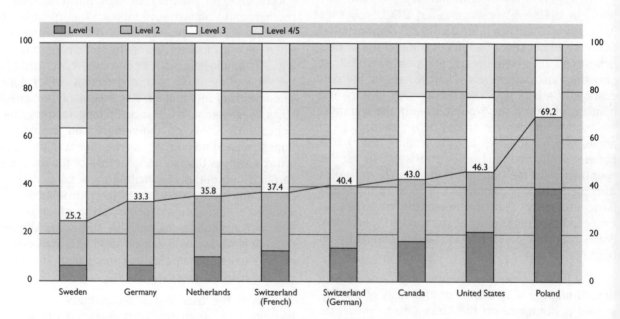

1.   Literacy (prose scale) is defined as the knowledge and skills needed to understand and use information derived from texts, such as editorials, news stories, poems and fiction.
2.   Numeracy (quantitative scale) is defined as the knowledge and skills required to apply arithmetic operations, either alone or sequentially, to numbers embedded in printed materials, such as balancing a chequebook, figuring ou a tip, completing an order form or determining the amount of interest on a loan from an advertisement.
3.   Within the literacy domains a scale from 0 to 500 was constructed, upon which tasks of varying difficulty were placed. A person's literacy ability in each domain can be expressed by a score, defined as the point at which he or she has an 80 per cent chance of successfully performing a given task. People are grouped into five levels of literacy, corresponding to the following ranges for scores achieved: level 1, 0 to 225; level 2, 226 to 275; level 3, 276 to 325, level 4/5, 326 to 500. This measurement system is described in more detail in OECD and Statistics Canada (1995).
Source: OECD and Statistics Canada (1995).

Concluding comments on costs

This section has provided a first approximation of the costs of making lifelong learning a reality for all. This analysis complements the preceding section on rates of return by providing separate detail on costs, and a basis for exploring alternative strategies by which they might be reduced. The main focus has been on the costs of changes in the foundations of lifelong learning. This focus is due partly to the fact that public cost data, for all their shortcomings, are more comparable across countries than data from other sectors in which lifelong learning opportunities exist. But the focus also reflects the fact that regardless of the role which non-public providers might eventually play in providing lifelong learning, the public role will be central in providing the foundations for lifelong learning, and as a main actor in creating the opportunities for the post-foundation forms of lifelong learning.

E. WHAT IS NEEDED TO ENSURE SUFFICIENT RESOURCES FOR LIFELONG LEARNING?

Even if lifelong learning is judged to be "worthwhile" insofar as it leads to monetary and non-monetary returns that more than offset its costs, its affordability hinges on limiting the size of the investment required by keeping costs under control, and on financing it in such a way as to ensure that there is reasonable symmetry between the benefits enjoyed by each actor, and the respective share that each pays.

In this regard, there are a number of points that can be noted about past and current patterns of provision and participation in lifelong learning.

- Historic costs are of limited use as indicators of future costs. The costs of making lifelong learning a reality for all are a function of extending the education foundation to a larger number of persons than are served in most countries, and expanding opportunities beyond the foundation, throughout the individuals' lives. Past cost patterns provide the basis for first approximations of the cost of expanded provision. But they are limited, firstly, by the fact that they measure average rather than marginal costs. Thus they may understate "true" future costs if it proves more expensive to satisfy the learning needs of those who are presently underserved; conversely, they may understate future costs to the extent that significant economies of scale

are possible. Secondly, historic cost patterns fail to reflect the cost structures of innovations in teaching and learning.

- Externalities are widespread. There is broad acceptance of public support for elementary and secondary education because of the social gains from foundation learning. This has been the principle underlying public finance of universal compulsory education in the OECD countries: as society benefits from having an educated population, society should pay. However, this consensus breaks down at the tertiary level. In the case of tertiary education, high levels of public subsidy often lead to large private earnings gains for individuals. The fact that the productivity gains from employer-sponsored training are not necessarily captured in the wages of individuals suggests that there are "externalities" that arise from such training (see Chapter 4). Another point to note is that some employers benefit from the training provided to workers by their previous employers.

- There is lag between when costs are paid and when benefits are realised. Although some lifelong learning is undertaken for its own sake, as a form of leisure or to serve other than work-related purposes, much of it is a form of investment. It is undertaken at a particular time (when most or all of the costs are paid), and the benefits are reaped later. This creates difficulties where capital markets or other institutional arrangements, such as public budgeting practices, do not allow the comparison of costs and benefits across time periods. It has the effect of squeezing out lifelong learning activities that do not produce benefits quickly and, by implication, rationing lifelong learning opportunities to those individuals who are likely to demonstrate the desired benefits most quickly, or who are capable of financing the costs on their own.

In this context, the key to progress in making lifelong learning affordable, is to ensure that there exist the framework conditions that: *i*) encourage innovation in the provision of learning opportunities so as to keep costs under control; *ii*) overcome the problems arising from the presence of externalities, and the delay between when the costs of lifelong learning are incurred, and when the benefits are realised.

A prerequisite to controlling costs of expanded opportunities for lifelong learning is to put cost analysis on the research agenda. Generally, little attention has been given to detailed questions about the average and marginal costs of education and training interventions. And, though there exist crude estimates of public and private expenditure for various levels of education (OECD, 1995*d*), there is insufficient basis for accurate estimates of average or marginal costs for different programmes of study, different methods based on variations in staff/space/technology configurations, for groups of individuals with different learning needs. Evaluations of innovations in teaching and learning methods need to place greater emphasis on considering, *ex post*, all elements of costs. But it is also needed to consider, prospectively, where and how the various elements of cost can be managed and controlled more efficiently. In addition to improving the accounting for financial costs of training, there is need to evaluate economic costs more comprehensively and transparently. This is particularly important if individuals and employers bear considerable "opportunity" costs, for example, in the form of the value of earnings and production that are foregone during participation in lifelong learning.

A complementary, more dynamic approach to better control of costs of lifelong learning is to ensure that "markets" for lifelong learning are open and competitive. This is to ensure that there are sufficient incentives for, and no unreasonable barrier to entry of, potential providers who have demonstrated ability to achieve measurable outcomes at less financial cost, and/or in less time. While this is analogous to enhancing product market competition more generally, it is likely to be a more complicated proposition than in other sectors, because of the large role of public providers in formal education and training. Such "liberalisation" of markets for lifelong learning is likely to require political action and decisions in a number of areas:

- The extent to which public authorities choose to preserve a large role in the provision of various forms of lifelong learning. This may vary according to the level of provision in question, as well as the population being served.

- For those areas of lifelong learning in which public authorities wish to encourage "open provision", there will be need to evaluate whether certain advantages of existing public providers (for example, low overhead costs because of pre-existing facilities), constitute barriers to entry of other providers.

- Lifelong learning, in contrast to more formal forms of education and training, is defined in terms of the individual. This would suggest that there is a need to evaluate the sufficiency of existing educational guidance and counselling services. Such arrangements would include mechanisms for the assessment and recognition of qualifications and competencies that individuals acquire in lifelong learning, as well as arrangements for guiding and counselling individuals on participation in lifelong learning.

Addressing the problem of externalities requires identifying those phases in the spectrum of lifelong learning in which there is significant asymmetry between who benefits and who pays, and shifting the burden of finance appropriately, possibly by putting in place mechanisms that enhance benefits or the willingness to pay. The analysis from Section C, on the benefits of lifelong learning, suggests that the high rates of social returns justify a dominant public role in the financing of learning through the level of upper secondary education. Even at this level, though, the public role is not necessarily automatic. Arrangements such as the dual system of apprentice training existing in Austria, Germany and Switzerland are based on important levels of employer support to provide training, in return for output with a value that exceeds the training wage paid, and trainee support through the acceptance of low training wages, that is similarly offset by allowing access to high-quality training and a proven mechanism for making the transition to employment. The level of public support for private primary and secondary schooling is dependent on a more complicated web of factors that range from constitutional separation of Church and State (that forbids public support of religious schools in the United States), to more technical regulatory issues (that allow full public support of private school teachers' salaries, if the educators are properly certified, and teach according to a State-approved curriculum, in France).

It is less clear as to what constitutes an appropriate public and private share of financing burdens at the level of tertiary education. The issue is clouded at this level by the fact that it produces substantial private returns to individuals, in the form of higher earnings and increased employability. This can be mitigated in countries in which high marginal tax rates on income reduce the effective (after-tax) returns to teriary education. But a countervailing argument is that, regardless of marginal tax rates on earnings gains, high levels of public support for tertiary education are hard to justify on the grounds that, in contrast to elementary or secondary education, participation is far from universal. Thus, public support leads to a net transfer from the less educated and less well-off, to the better-educated and higher-paid individuals.

The finance of lifelong learning opportunities beyond formal, initial education is more ambiguous. "Active labour market policies" as they are practised in OECD countries, are based on high levels of State support for training aimed at compensating for deficiencies in the basic skills of the unemployed (OECD, 1992g). Training undertaken by enterprises, or in connection with employment, is generally financed by employers and, sometimes, employees. Only in exceptional circumstances, such as risk of redundancy, is public support available for enterprise-based training. Chart 8.4 shows the share of employer-supported adult education, by length of the activity. Between 30 and 51 per cent of the learning activities were employer-supported, the highest frequency being in the United States and the lowest in

Quebec Province of Canada. Of the courses with brief duration, between 45 and 66 per cent were employer-supported. Of the high-duration, learning activities, 0 (Quebec) to 23 (Poland) per cent were employer-supported.

Table 8.21 shows the course duration by type of support. Consistent with the data in Annex Table A.63, employers sponsor mainly brief courses; 66 to 86 per cent of the courses are in this category. Non-employer-supported learning activities are distributed more evenly in terms of duration, even though, the bulk of them are short-term. Of the non-employer supported training courses, 23 to 45 per cent are long-term, compared to 0 to 15 per cent of employer-supported learning activities.

It is more difficult to evaluate financing burdens for lifelong learning that are not linked to work or do not have clear consequences for employment performance. This can include learning undertaken by individuals for the purposes of cultural enrichment or self-development. The Nordic traditions of the Folk High School or Study Circles, though relatively cheap, involve some degree of State support. But that financing burden is offset to an extent by direct contribu-

◆ Chart 8.4. ***Percentage of adult education and training courses that are employer-supported, 1994[1,2]***
By duration of training

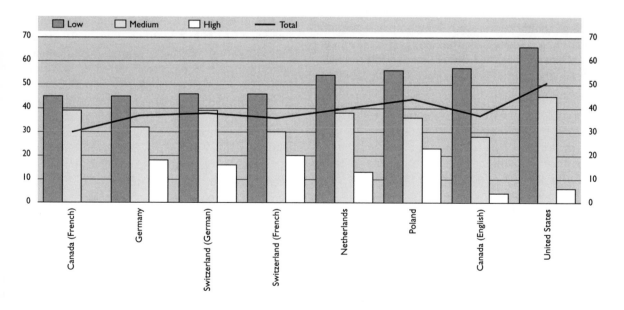

1. Based on the first reported course being taken in the six months preceding the interview.
2. Low: 0-59 hours. Medium: 60-300 hours. High: > 300 hours.
Source: OECD and Statistics Canada (1995).

tions of individuals, who also assume the opportunity costs of foregone work or leisure time. In other countries, a non-trivial share of enrolments in post-secondary institutions, such as Technical and Further Education colleges in Australia, the Open University in the United Kingdom, and junior and community colleges in Canada and the United States, also fall into the category of "leisure education" undertaken for non-vocational purposes. Here too, the financing burden is shared. In none of these cases is it possible to lay down precise criteria for who pays how much. Where individuals benefit, society benefits; how much society can afford is a political choice.

Regardless of how financing burdens may be resolved, externalities are inevitable because of the inevitable asymmetry that arises as a result of the unpredictability of at least some elements of costs and benefits. Although they may exist in connection with "leisure education", there is special need to address them with regard to lifelong learning that occurs in connection with employment. In that regard, a strong argument can be made that employers underinvest in lifelong learning (spend less than is justified by the rate of return) because of uncertainty over being able to capture all the benefits (Stern and Ritzen, 1991). They face risks of other employers "poaching" trained workers, or of workers bidding up wages as a consequence of acquiring higher levels of qualifications (see also Chapter 4). Yet individuals may be discouraged from shouldering a larger share of job-related training to the extent that resulting qualifications and competencies are not adequately recognised, or that there is large uncertainty about the likelihood of realising a return in the form of higher earnings or improved employability.

There are a number of approaches for addressing these problems of externalities, some of which have been tried by national authorities. One is to employ levies or tax credits as tools to require employers to spend a certain amount on training and thereby reduce the net cost of poaching. A scheme based on this approach exists in France, for example, and was tried out in Australia. Such measures have a mixed record, however, because they create incentives that may encourage inefficient forms of training. In any event, there is no evidence that these measures alone improve the productivity of enterprises or macroeconomic performance (OECD, 1994d).

Other approaches can be adopted to focus on "outputs", so as to make the results of lifelong learning more evident and to establish clearer ownership over them. One such approach is based on improving

the transparency of qualifications and competencies that are acquired through learning outside formal education institutions. Improvements in this regard can enhance the efficiency of labour markets in allocating labour and skills, by making their acquired qualifications and competencies more transparent to employers (OECD, 1994n). At the same time, such measures can increase the efficiency of lifelong learning by making it easier to relate learning outcomes that occur outside formal institutions to those found within such institutions, thereby facilitating the integration of both forms of learning (Colardyn and Durand-Drouhin, 1995).

Achieving greater transparency and protection of the outcomes of employer-supported lifelong learning depends on changes in the financial accounting and reporting practices that influence the reporting and treatment of the costs and benefits of lifelong learning. Such changes might include more detailed disclosure of training and human resource development costs associated with lifelong learning, to distinguish such forms of "investment" from other recurrent costs. Extending the logic further, it might be helpful to find ways of "capitalising" lifelong learning costs in such a way that the value they add to an enterprise is taken into account, perhaps being treated more as an asset (Miller and Wurzburg, 1995).

Finally, there is a need to consider measures to ensure that the lag between the timing of the front end costs of lifelong learning, and the deferred stream of benefits, does not unduly interfere with the financing of lifelong learning. Because there is a lag between when lifelong learning is undertaken and when the costs for it are incurred, it is rational for individuals as well as employers or public authorities to evaluate decisions to invest on the basis of when the benefits are expected, as well as how large the benefits are likely to be. In general, when lifelong learning is undertaken for investment purposes, such as to improve productivity, the investment potential needs to be evaluated in terms of the value of the benefits, compared to the costs. Moreover, if those benefits are expected in the future, their value should be higher than the value of the initial investment to compensate for deferred consumption and the risk associated with expected returns. As discussed in Section C, a "discount rate" is applied to the value of benefits over time, in order to calculate their "present value", which can then be compared to their costs. That said, what is appropriate is not always clear. The choice of the discount rate depends on factors such as the rate of return from other forms of investment and the preference for current consumption. However, even if lifelong learning is treated more as investment, because of externalities and institutional rigidities in capital markets, the lag between the timing of costs and benefits of lifelong learning may inhibit provision. Measures such as changes in financial accounting and reporting practices may overcome some of these problems at the level of the enterprise, where cost can be spread over time through depreciation. But the problems that individuals face in financing their lifelong learning opportunities may require a greater government role, either in setting the "rules of the game" governing financing practices by actors in capital markets, or by acting as lenders. These might be addressed by various approaches to financing lifelong learning, reviewed in the next subsection.

Models for financing lifelong learning

Several basic models for the financing of lifelong learning and its elements have been proposed in the literature (Johnes, 1993; Levin, 1983; Timmermann, 1994 and 1995; Oosterbeek, 1995): *i*) individual drawing rights; *ii*) individual entitlements or vouchers; *iii*) auctions; *iv*) single-employer financing; *v*) self-financing and particularly the "income-contingent loans" variant; and *vi*) parafiscal funds.

The *drawing rights* model is based on a general income-transfer insurance system which aims at regulating, allocating and financing an individual's work, education and leisure, including retirement (Rehn, 1983). The model was part of the blue-print for recurrent education proposed by the OECD in the 1970s (OECD, 1973; Schütze and Istance, 1987). The model has a number of possible advantages, for example in terms of flexibility, scope for individual choice, incentive effects, and the comprehensiveness of the approach envisaged. The main reasons why it failed to catch on in practice are believed to be its inability to address the problem of price distortions at particularly the tertiary level of education, its continued reliance on an extensive role for governments in legislation and finance, and the difficulty of overcoming the co-ordination problems posed by the separation of government into different Ministries and departments.

The basic idea behind educational *entitlements* is that instead of providing the suppliers of education and training with a subsidy, the government allocates vouchers or individual entitlements to students or, in the case of foundation learning, to their parents. Applied to post-compulsory education, the most elaborate and consistent plan is apparently the model proposed by Levin (1983 and 1995). Among the unique features of this model are its comprehensiveness: it addresses the finance of upper secondary and tertiary education as well as the markets for adult education and training, and it influences both the supply and demand side of learning. The most difficult aspect of the proposed voucher scheme is to achieve a good balance between the grants and loans parts of the entitlement. There is a case for increasing the loans part if the demands for learning increase and enrolments rise. The reasoning behind this is that high enrolment levels indicate high expected rates of return; hence the students should bear a larger share of the total costs.

A variant of the entitlements model called the *franchise model* has been proposed by Van Ravens (1994). It is aimed at stimulating non-formal learning at the expense of prolonged initial education. In this arrangement each individual with the proper qualifications receives a lump sum that can be used to cover the costs of educational services and, if necessary, costs of living. The subsidy is made up of different equally-sized layers. The individual can spend the subsidy, but the allowed coverage of the costs decreases with each subsequent layer. In the case of five layers, the first layer may cover all costs. The second layer may cover 90 per cent of the costs, so that the remaining 10 per cent must be covered by other (private) sources. Coverage subsequently decreases to 75, 50 and finally to 25 per cent; in the latter case the individual has to pay for three-quarters of the total cost. In Van Ravens' view this arrangement will stimulate the combination of learning while working. One advantage of this model is that it can be implemented gradually by starting with the final layer and then (if desirable) expanding the system to the remaining layers.

Auction plans for educational services are based on the idea that institutions supplying education and training, for example universities, make bids to the government in order to attract and enrol students. The institutions can bid at a given price, or they can make their own bids, or they can bid a combination of price, quantity and quality. In the United Kingdom, universities are invited to bid for funded students at prices at or below predetermined guide levels.

Single-employer financing of post-secondary education and training has both advantages and disadvantages. Although such an approach might tap additional resources, it hinges on the willingness of employers to put up the resources needed, with the participation of concerned workers. Because this approach risks limiting the post-secondary system to specific vocational training, and to certain categories of personnel, under-investment and market failures are the likely result.

Self-financing approaches require individuals to pay for the their post-compulsory education and training using their own resources, whether these may be household savings, current income or loans which have to be repaid out of future revenue. Self-financing models depend on mechanisms that raise revenues, for example tuition fees. Many OECD countries are experimenting with different approaches to levying tuition fees in tertiary education. Common to these approaches is that the fee falls short of the full cost of the study programme, so that public subsidies remain in place. Williams (1990) identifies five different possibilities for using tuition fees in tertiary education. Tuition fees and other self-financing approaches are attractive because they raise new revenue and because they play on incentives and motivation to learn. But such approaches also have major drawbacks. Firstly, there is the difficulty and cost of administrating the system. Secondly, they assume – quite falsely so – that well-functioning education and capital markets exist, that educational services are competitively priced, and that people are willing to pay for them. Thirdly, self-financing models tend to focus on the supply and demand for formal education in tertiary institutions; they leave open the question of how to pay for adult learning in other settings. Price distortions are particularly pronounced in tertiary education, and they tend to be aggravated by loan provisions. Finally, there is a strong disincentive effect on the demand for further learning by poor youths and other disadvantaged groups. Equality of opportunity is thus adversely affected, and under-investment might result. To counter these problems many OECD countries operate a mixed "loan-grant model", so that the participation of certain target groups can be encouraged through public subsidies. While problems of equity might thus be addressed, at least to some extent, the other drawbacks continue to work against a coherent strategy of encouraging lifelong learning by all and in diverse settings.

The *parafiscal funds* model requires private and public employers to pay a levy based, for example, on the payroll, on labour turnover, capital value or on profits, into training funds administered jointly by government and autonomous foundations. The funds can be used to cover the costs of post-initial vocational education and training as well as continuing education, both of a general and a vocational nature. Major problems are connected to the choice of a basis for calculating the levy. A value-added approach might be the least discriminating among different employers, but raises the question whether small and medium-sized firms should be exempted. Apart from problems of administration and questions concerning the allocation of the funds – should specific programmes be financed, or individual learners, or would the lump-sum financing of institutions be a better solution? – this approach has the important drawback that it might not encourage the demand for learning, especially among disadvantaged groups, the unemployed and those not in the labour force. Another shortcoming is that parafiscal funds would not address the finance of secondary and tertiary education.

The continuing segmentation of education and training sub-systems is reflected in the ways education and training systems are currently financed. Debates refer either to the problems of financing schools, or financing vocational training, or financing tertiary education. A coherent strategy for lifelong learning supposes that a rational financing mode be devised that addresses all of these sub-systems. The foundations, tertiary education and adult learning cannot be considered as entirely separate entities. Given the complexity of the systems and the level of resources that is required in order to pay for lifelong learning, there can be no doubt that the solution is to rely on "mixed" models of finance that combine certain features of all six models described above. It seems also clear that governments should take the lead in devising an appropriate strategy that incorporates the concerns and needs of employers, institutions and individual learners.

Table 8.22 gives a comprehensive summary of the different financing schemes in terms of two criteria, efficiency and equity. The financial arrangement that is best suited to support lifelong learning according to these criteria, is a combination of individual entitlements and substantial income-contingent loans (ICLs). The attractiveness lies both in the possibility of including non-formal learning opportunities and securing equity. Government funding of institutions may resolve equity issues, but it creates inefficiencies in both the labour and education market. At the same time it is mainly focused on initial education. As is clear from Table 8.22, different objectives require different solutions. Education systems differ, as do policy objectives. Education Ministers are most likely to look for an arrangement that i tailored to their constituency and specific interests. However, a commitment to lifelong learning implies a commitment to institutional reform. Financial arrangements are crucial in this respect, both from a distributional point of view and in terms of providing the players (students, parents, employers, governments) with the proper incentives.

F. FINANCING LIFELONG LEARNING: POLICY CONCLUSIONS

There is evidence that various forms of education and training yield economic returns that more than offset their initial costs. This evidence is most comprehensive in its coverage of formal education and training, although some covers non-formal, enterprise-based training as well. The evidence is thinnest with respect to the rates of return on education and training for persons who are most "at risk", and who are targets for high priority attention. However, these are precisely the persons for whom the social benefits of lifelong learning may be substantial and, conversely, for whom the social costs of not participating in lifelong learning may be steepest.

Substantial returns notwithstanding, the affordability of lifelong learning is constrained by its high upfront costs, the presence of externalities that contribute to asymmetry between who pays and who benefits, and the fact that there is considerable time lag between the moment when the costs of various phases of lifelong learning are incurred, and the moment when the benefits are realised. The fact that investment in lifelong learning incurs immediate costs in return for benefits that accrue over time means that individuals, in particular, as well as governments and employers may under-invest. Measures that reduce externalities may help resolve this problem insofar as they reduce the risks inherent in such investments. But additional work is needed to evaluate the feasibility of other financing measures that may make it possible to effectively spread financing burdens over the life-cycle.

Evaluating rates of return to lifelong learning

There is a need for better evidence on the cost-effectiveness of different modes of lifelong learning, and for more particular sub-groups in the population than is presently available. There is also a clear need to better estimate the full range of pecuniary and non-pecuniary costs and benefits. Such work is needed to evaluate where resources are likely to produce the most important benefits, but also to indicate where high social rates of return justify a substantial public role in financing, and where high private rates of return justify a greater private role.

Improving estimates of unit costs in the expansion of lifelong learning

There are important gaps in knowledge on the direct and indirect costs of various teaching and learning approaches. Presently available cost data are highly aggregated, and provide little basis for estimating marginal costs in general, and for particular population sub-groups. New work that evaluates the relative effectiveness of different curricula and learning settings, for example, should also evaluate various aspects of costs.

Adopting a proactive approach to controlling costs of lifelong learning

Aside from evaluating current costs more accurately, there is a need to more aggressively control the cost trajectory of lifelong learning by finding ways of reducing costs. One way is to make sure that any analysis of cost-effectiveness of existing programmes and approaches also examines evidence on how costs might be reduced, or how cost-effectiveness of different interventions might be improved, for example through better targeting of services or changes in governance arrangements. A more general approach is to investigate the functioning of markets for lifelong learning and to determine how they might be made to operate more smoothly.

Improving estimates of the universe of need

Estimating the costs of lifelong learning also depends on assumptions about the numbers of persons involved. Early school-leaving rates or the incidence of literacy deficits in the adult population may provide crude benchmarks by which to estimate numbers of persons whose needs should be addressed, as part of a comprehensive strategy for lifelong learning. But such first-order approximations need to be linked to more detailed methods for evaluating such factors as labour market experience, and personal development plans.

Addressing externalities

Aside from controlling costs, another key to improving the finance of lifelong learning is to ensure that there are suitable incentives for the various actors to undertake the necessary investments. Strategies in this area should address three main factors:

– improving the transparency of learning outcomes so that individuals and employers know what they are gaining from lifelong learning;

– better protecting the lifelong learning investment by ensuring that markets – capital markets included – treat the costs and value of qualifications acquired in lifelong learning in such a manner as to reflect the timing of costs and benefits;

– evaluating the feasibility and effectiveness of training inducements such as levies and tax credit, as mechanisms for encouraging the efficient allocation of resources to lifelong learning.

LIFELONG LEARNING FOR ALL

Table 8.1. **Social rates of return to levels of education in selected OECD countries, by gender and ISCED level, 1992**

(percentage)

	Men				Women			
	Lower secondary education	Upper secondary education	Tertiary education, short duration	Tertiary education, long duration	Lower secondary education	Upper secondary education	Tertiary education, short duration	Tertiary education, long duration
Belgium[1]	..	3.5	15.7	7.5	..	2.6	5.7	12.9
Denmark	..	11.4	3.8	10.9	..	11.2	3.6	8.2
Finland	..	7.6	12.8	15.1	..	5.9	13.6	14.4
France	..	5.9	17.6	15.9	..	9.2	18	11.9
Germany	..	11.3	16.5	13.9	..	7.1	6.7	9.3
Netherlands[1]	8.8	11.2	6.9	9.9	9.5	15.4	1.7	7.6
Spain[2]	11.2	10.4	..	10.8	13.5	9.8	..	12.9
Sweden	..	6.9	8.2	11.8	..	6	7.4	10
Switzerland	..	13.2	12.8	7.5	..	18	8.6	4.9
United States	10.8	19	10.5	12.9	5.1	18.6	12.5	12.2

Note: .. Data not available.
1. 1989 data.
2. 1991 data.
Source: Alsalam and Conley (1995), p. 94.

Table 8.2. **Private return to schooling in United States and United Kingdom, based on Mincer-type wage equations**

United States

Author(s)/date	Sample/year	Rates of return	Percentage	Notes
Angrist and Krueger (1991)	1980 Census (men).	*Cohort born during* 1940-49 (all) 1930-39 (all) 1930-39 (black)	6.0 to 7.1 6.3 to 9.3 4.0 to 6.7	Employ ordinary least squares (OLS) and two-stage least squares (TSLS).
Ashenfelter and Krueger (1994)	Sample of 495 twins, surveyed in 1991.		8.4 to 17.9	Use a variety of techniques, including OLS, generalized least squares (GLS), and instrumental variables (IV).
Card and Krueger (1992a)	1980 Census.	*Cohort born during* 1920-29 1930-39 1940-49	*Average rates of return* 5.07 6.27 7.44	Returns vary by State, due partly to differences in the quality of education. Returns are higher for younger workers.
Card and Krueger (1992b)	Census data for 1960, 1970, and 1980.	*Year* 1960 1970 1980	*Black* *White* 3.04 6.04 3.91 6.58 4.33 5.80	Black/White differences due in large part to differences in the quality of education.
Cohn and Khan (1995)	1985 wave of the Michigan Panel Study Income Dynamics (PSID).	Required schooling: Overschooling: Underschooling:	7.7-9.8 4.9-5.9 -3.8--4.4	Employ definitions of required, over- and underschooling suggested by – and obtain results similar to those of – Sicherman (1991) and Verdugo & Verdugo (1989).
Hersch (1991)	414 male and female employees of warehouse and manufacturing firms in Eugene, Oregon, 1986.	Required school: Overschooling: Underschooling:	*Males* *Females* 6.1 6.4 2.3 2.2 (ns) -0.6 (ns) -3.9 (ns)	ns = not statistically significant.
Heywood (1994)	1989 Current Population Survey (CPS).	*Years of schooling completed* 8 12 16	8.3 13.2 20.3	Rates vary by union status. Rates for "sheepskin" years are higher than what would be expected from rates for the two previous years.

Table 8.2. **Private return to schooling in United States and United Kingdom, based on Mincer-type wage equations** (cont.)

United States

Author(s)/date	Sample/year	Rates of return	Percentage				Notes
Kroch and Sjoblon (1994)	1973 (CPS), and PSID, panel data, 1967-80.	Sample/Race-Sex group	*White men*	*White women*	*Black men*	*Black women*	Major focus of study is on "screening". Includes in some equations the variable "rank" ("the individual's position in the distribution of educational attainment for his/her cohort"). The screening argument is rejected.
		CPS, rank included	7.8	6.8	4.2	8.8	
		PSID, rank included	6.9	7.8	5.9	6.4	
		PSID, rank included	9.4	3.9	2.8	5.1	
Low and Ormiston (1991)	National Longitudinal Survey Youth, 1981.	Standard Mincerian coefficients	*Men* 5.86	*Women* 4.71			Focus on role of risk in returns to schooling. Show that the returns decline as the degree of risk aversion rises.
		Including risk and risk aversion	0.64 to 5.27	0.45 to 4.35			
Neumark and Korenman (1994)	National Longitudinal Survey Youth, 1982-Sisters.	Standard OLS and fixed effects:	*Men* 5.1-7				Focus on biases in returns to education caused by heterogeneity and endogeneity. Argue that bias may not be noticed unless both effects are considered together.
		TSLS: White females:	2.0-8.1				
		Black females:	2.7-7.0				
Wellington (1993)	PSID, 1976 and 1985.	Year/Group	*White males*	*White females*			Also includes data on returns to training.
		1976	5.2	8.1			
		1985	5.7	8.2			

LIFELONG LEARNING FOR ALL

Table 8.2. **Private return to schooling in United States and United Kingdom, based on Mincer-type wage equations** (cont.)

United Kingdom

Author(s)/date	Sample/year	Rates of return	Percentage				Notes
Bennett et al. (1993)	General household survey, 1985-88.	A-Levels Higher Education	Males 6 7	Females 10 6			Rates vary by father's education. Higher returns to vocational schooling.
Griffiths and Saunders (1979)	Survey of earnings of qualified manpower, 1966-67, and various sources for 1973.	Internal rates of return: Private Social	Males 1967 8.2 5.3	Males 1973 10.8 8.3	Females 1967 12.1 11.0	Females 1973 8.9 6.6	Calculate an Alpha of 0.68 for males and 0.76 for females.
Harmon and Walker (1993)	Family expenditure survey, 1978-86.	*Dummy variable coefficients in wage equation for:* School leaving age 16 17 18 19 20 21 and higher	*Males* 0.11 0.12 0.17 0.20 0.23 0.37	*Females* 0.06 0.09 0.17 0.16 0.23 0.29			Returns differ by manual versus non-manual jobs, the latter doing much better. Returns to voluntary schooling at age 16 are much lower for males and slightly higher for females. Also estimate an equation with a cubic function of the variable "years of schooling beyond compulsory age".
Moghadam (1990), cited in Johnes (1993), p. 36	Unknown, 1978-85.	*Year* 1978 1979 1980 1981 1982 1983 1984	*Percent differential* 28 28 39 22 46 92 65	*Implied rate of return* 4.7 4.7 6.5 3.7 7.7 15.3 10.9			"Percent differential" refers to the differential "between those who left full-time education at 21 years and those (otherwise identical) persons who left full-time education at 15 years".

Source: Cohn and Addison (1995).

Table 8.3. **Private rate of return to schooling in the Netherlands, based on Mincer-type wage equations**

Author(s)/date	Sample/year	Rates of return	Percentage Males	Females	Notes
Hartog and Oosterbeek (1988)	Representative sample of labour force, 1982.	Required schooling Overschooling Underschooling	7.6 6.5 -1.9	5.2 3.7 -4.0	Required schooling is reported by the worker; over/underschooling is defined as the difference between required and actual schooling.
Groot and Oosterbeek (1994)	Brabant survey 1983; sample of persons born in the Dutch province of North-Brabant in 1940.	Actual years Effective years Skipping years Repeating years Inefficient years Drop-out years	4.3 6.5 -8.9 ns ns 5.0	8.3 12.3 ns ns ns ns	Controlled for estimated cognitive ability (IQ). Effective years are defined as the theoretical duration of the education attained. Inefficient years are defined as the years in excess of the shortest period necessary to obtain a certain qualification. Drop-out years are defined as the number of years enrolled in a certain type of education without completion.
Oosterbeek and Van Ophem (1995)	Brabant survey 1983; subsample of males.	Actual years 6 7 8 9 10 11-12 13-16 > 16	9.0 8.3 8.2 8.1 7.5 7.0 5.7 3.4		Maximum-likelihood estimates obtained in a model where schooling is endogenous and the returns to schooling interact with estimated cognitive ability (IQ).
Oosterbeek (1992)	Representative sample of males in the labour force, 1985, 1986, 1988.	1985 1986 1988	4.3 4.2 4.5		OLS estimates using only years of schooling, work experience and work experience squared as regressors.
Hartog, Oosterbeek and Teulings (1994)	Representative survey of males in the labour force, 1979, 1985, 1989.	1979 1985 1989	8.9 7.2 7.3		Weighted Least Squares estimates using data grouped by level of education and age.
Gelderblom, 't Hoen and De Koning (1994)	Representative sample of labour force, 1990.	Effective years	3.0		Includes also contractual hours and contractual hours squared.

ns = not statistically significant.
Source: Oosterbeek (1995).

Table 8.4. **Returns to labour market programmes, United States, 1987-89**[1, 2]

(US dollars and annual percentage increase)

Strategy service subgroup	Adult males		Adult females	
	$ impact	Per cent	$ impact	Per cent
Classroom training	378	4.1	1 214	13.9
	(608)		(566)	
On-the-job training/ job search assistance	1 214	13.9	1 064	17.1
	(1 418)		(1 409)	
Other services	−20	−0.2	148	2.4
	(463)		(773)	

1. Figures in parentheses show actual earnings impact over the full 18-month follow-up period.
2. Impact of Title-IIA of the Job Training Partnership Act during the last two quarters of the 18-month follow-up period.
Source: Cohn and Addison (1995).

Table 8.5. **Effectiveness of active labour market programmes**

	Study	Data	Training programme	Results
United States	Card and Sullivan (1988)	A cohort of male participants in the Comprehensive Employment and Training Act programme	The Comprehensive Employment and Training Act programme (CETA)	Participation in CETA increases the probability of employment in the three years after training by 2 to 5 percentage points. Classroom training programmes appear to have had significantly larger effects than on-the-job programmes although the estimated effects of both kinds of programmes are positive. CETA participation appears to have increased both the probability of moving into employment and the probability of continuing employment.
United States	Bassi (1984)	A sample of CETA participants from the Continuous Longitudinal Manpower Survey 1975-76	The Comprehensive Employment and Training Act programme (CETA)	Women appear to benefit substantially from manpower training programmes, while no significant earnings effect were found for male participants. There is evidence of non-random selection or "creaming" in training programmes.
United States	Ashenfelter and Card (1985)	Adult males and females from the 1976 Current Population Survey	The Comprehensive Employment and Training Act programme (CETA)	The training effects for adult males who participated in CETA in 1976 are small: at most in the order of 300 current dollars per year. For adult females the effect is unambiguously positive and in the order of 800-1 500 current dollars per year.
United States	Lalonde (1986)	Disadvantaged workers lacking basic job skills, including women on AFDC (Aid for Families with Dependent Children), ex-drug addicts, ex-criminal offenders, and high school drop-outs from both sexes.	The National Supported Work Demonstration (NSW): a work experience and counselling programme	The earnings of AFDC females were 851 dollars higher than they would have been without the NSW programme, while the earnings of male participants were 886 dollars higher.
United States	Haveman and Hollister (1991)	Survey of impact studies of training programmes	Various training programmes in the United States	A survey of studies shows that in general employment and training programmes have had their greatest impact and largest social returns for those who have had the least previous labour market experience and are the most disadvantaged. Intensive, residential skill-training programmes for youth may be very effective. For seriously disadvantaged males, there is little evidence pointing to any particular employment and training policy as effective.

Table 8.5. **Effectiveness of active labour market programmes** (cont.)

	Study	Data	Training programme	Results
United States	Bell and Orr (1994)	Data from the AFDC Homemaker-Home Health Aid Demonstrations, 1983-86	Four to eight weeks of training for families receiving AFDC	The training and subsidised employment programmes produced significant increases in earnings and reductions in welfare dependence in at least one of the first two post-demonstration years in six out of the seven demonstration States. The estimated earnings gains ranged from over 1 200 dollars per year to nearly 2 600 dollars in 1984.
United states	Bartel (1995)	Personnel records of a large manufacturing firm, 1986-90	Days spent in formal training in the past year	Training increases wage growth and job performance. The rate of return of training for the company is about 20 to 35%.
Netherlands	Ridder (1986)	A survey of participants in training programmes in 1979 who were surveyed in 1982	Several training, recruitment and employment programmes in 1979	Females and minorities benefit from training programmes and still more from employment programmes. Recruitment programmes have a favourable effect on the average employment spell of young workers and women. Minority workers do not benefit from these programmes. Employment programmes lengthen the spell of employment of young workers, female and minorities (in this order). Employment programmes are more effective than recruitment programmes, and these are more effective than training programmes. The labour market position of participants in training programmes is better than that of participants in recruitment programmes, which again is better than that of participants in employment programmes.
Denmark	Jensen, Pedersen, Smith and Westergard-Nielsen (1990)	Information from public registers in the Danish Longitudinal Database	All training programmes offered by the Labour Market Training Board, mainly directed towards the low-skill manual labour market	The effects of training on subsequent wages are rather small. For groups with good initial employment conditions a significantly positive effect is found on wages, while a negative wage effect is found for participants with high initial unemployment. The same strong dependency on initial employment conditions are found for the effects of training on subsequent unemployment.
Sweden	Björklund and Moffitt (1987)	Data from the Swedish Level of Living Surveys 1974 and 1981	Government manpower training programme: classroom and other forms of training in a large variety of fields	The expected wage gain of training for participants is 10%, while the expected wage gains for non-participants is negative. Expansion of the training programme would lower the effects; a reduction of the programme would increase its efficiency.

Source. OECD.

Table 8.6. **The productivity of training in high-tech and low-tech regimes in selected manufacturing industries in Chinese Taipei, 1986**

Industry[2]	Output elasticity		Marginal product of training[1]		Ratio of marginal product in high-tech versus low-tech manufacturing industries
	High-tech	Low-tech	High-tech	Low-tech	
Textiles	0.15	0.08	44.73	26.39	1.70
Apparel	0.12	0.10	16.02	13.29	1.21
Paper and publishing	0.13	0.14	55.10	34.08	1.62
Chemicals	0.14	0.11	94.56	67.99	1.39
Plastics	0.14	0.08	62.35	34.38	1.81
Electric/electronics	0.24	0.09	74.56	32.39	2.30
Transportation equipment	0.13	0.09	58.10	34.47	1.69

1. The apparently high marginal products of training reflect the fact that the training variable measures spending in the current year; thus, the outcome (marginal product) is the result of current spending plus earlier spending. This fuller measure of training effort was not possible because of the cross-sectional nature of the data used.
2. Based on 2-digit International Standard Industry Classification.
Source: Aw and Tan (1995), Table 7, p. 23.

Table 8.7. **Returns to training at work for young workers, 1980s**

Type of training	Return (%)	Author
Formal employer provided training	7	Lynch (1992)
	10.8	Lillard and Tan (1986) Mincer (1988)
	9.5	
Previous employer provided training	0	Lynch (1992)
Previous off-the-job training	5	Lynch (1992)
Apprenticeship	13	Lynch (1992); Blanchflower and Lynch (1994)

Source: Cohn and Addison (1995), Table 7.

Table 8.8. **Returns to on-the-job training**

	Study	Data	Definition of training	Results
United States	Duncan and Hoffman (1978, 1979)	Heads of households and spouses aged 18-64 who worked at least 500 hours in 1975: data from Panel Studies on Income Dynamics	On-the-job training	Time spent in training increases earnings by 6 to 10% with returns similar for men and women, Blacks and Whites.
United States	Mincer (1988)	Data on employees taken from the Panel Survey of Income Dynamics 1968-82	Information on the length of time of training required during the current job	The effect of a year with training on wage growth was 4.4%. The effect of training on wage growth was greater (9.5%) at younger ages than at older ages (3.6%).
United States	Brown (1989)	Data on employees taken from the Panel Survey of Income Dynamics 1976 and 1978	The amount of training on the job needed to become qualified	On average training increases wages by 11 to 20%.
United States	Barron, Black and Loewenstein (1989)	Data on young male new hires at low wages at firm level taken from Employment Opportunity Pilot Project survey	Training in hours by new hires and by their supervisors and co-workers during the first three months of employment at the firm	In a two-year period, training raised wages by 7.5% to 15% per year.
United States	Holzer (1990)	Data on young male new hires at low wages at firm level taken from Employment Opportunity Pilot Project survey	Training in hours by new hires and by their supervisors and co-workers during the first three months of employment at the firm	Training positively related to supervisor's productivity growth ratings and wage growth ratings.
United States	Bishop (1991)	Data on young male new hires at low wages at firm level taken from Employment Opportunity Pilot Project survey	Training in hours by new hires and by their supervisors and co-workers during the first three months of employment at the firm	On average training increases productivity by 22%. Training has a smaller effect on wage growth than on productivity growth.
United States	Bartel (1991)	A survey of human resources policies and practices in American businesses: the Columbia Business School Human Resources Survey	The percentage of occupations in the business for which formal training is conducted	Formal training has a positive and significant effect on labour productivity, only when no account is taken of capital intensity.
United States	Lynch (1992)	Individuals who were between 14 and 21 years old in 1979: the National Longitudinal Survey 1979-1985	Company training, apprenticeship, and training outside the firm	All types of training significantly increase wages of young workers. A week of training increases wages by around 0.3%.
United States	Blanchflower and Lynch (1994)	Sample of young workers from the National Longitudinal Survey Youth Cohort 1979-88	Company training, apprenticeship and training obtained outside the firm	Training provided by previous employers has no effect on wages; company training with current employer increases wages by 8%. Off-the-job training increases wages by 4%. Apprenticeship increases wages for men by 20% but has no effect on female wages.
United States	Bishop (1994)	Data on young male new hires at low wages at firm level taken from Employment Opportunity Pilot Project survey	Training in hours by new hires and by their supervisors and co-workers during the first three months of employment at the firm	Formal training at previous employers increases initial productivity by 9.5%, but has no effect on wages.

Table 8.8. **Returns to on-the-job training** *(cont.)*

	Study	Data	Definition of training	Results
Great Britain	Booth (1991)	Data on employees taken from the British Social Attitudes Survey 1987	Formal job-related training courses and seven types of informal training during the two years prior to the survey	For men the participation in training increases earnings by 11.2%. For women participation in training increases earnings by 18.1%. An extra two weeks of training increases male earnings by 8.8% and female earnings by 15.1%.
Great Britain	Blanchflower and Lynch (1994)	A longitudinal survey of 23-year-old persons born in 1958: the National Child Development Survey 1958-81	Company sponsored training and apprenticeship	Company sponsored training increases wages by 2%; apprenticeship training increases wages by 5%.
Great Britain	Dolton, Makepeace and Treble (1994)	Young people aged 16 who completed their compulsory schooling during the year 1985-86: the Youth Cohort Study	Youth Training Scheme (YTS), off-the-job training and on-the-job training	YTS lowers earnings for women, but increases earnings by around 5% for men. On-the-job training increases earnings for men by 7% and for women by 3%. Off-the-job training increases male earnings by 6% and female earnings by 7.5%.
Great Britain	Blundell, Dearden and Meghir (1994)	A longitudinal survey of 33-year-old persons born in 1958: the National Child Development Survey 1958-91	On- and off-the-job employer provided courses and privately initiated training courses	Employer provided training, particularly on- and off-the-job employer provided training with a person's current employer, significantly increases earnings. Earnings effects of training are between 8 to 15%.
Great Britain	Elias, Hernaes and Baker (1994)	Same as Blundell, Dearden and Meghir (1994)	Formal apprenticeships, qualifications obtained while employed, and other educational courses taken since leaving school	Completion of apprenticeship training significantly increases wages for men but not for women. No other training variable has any significant effect on wages.
Great Britain	Higgins (1992)	Longitudinal data for people who reached the minimum school-leaving age in 1984: the National Youth Cohort Study 1985-86	Youth Training Scheme (YTS)	Youth training reduces individual wages by around 8%.
Great Britain	Theodossiou and Williams (1995)	Full-time employees aged 20-60 in 1986: the Social and Economic Life Initiative data	Training received from employer	There is a significant effect of tenure on the pay of employees who are heavily trained by the employer.
Great Britain	Groot and Oosterbeek (1995)	Employees in 1991 taken from the British Household Panel Survey	Training that was part of present employment and any other training during the past year	On-the-job training increases wages by 15%.

Table 8.8. **Returns to on-the-job training** (cont.)

	Study	Data	Definition of training	Results
France	Laulhé (1990)	Employees aged 15 and over in 1985: data from 1985 Survey of Professional Qualifications Training	Employer-sponsered training	Persons who received some training were much less likely to go from employment to unemployment and more likely to experience occupational mobility.
Netherlands	Groot, Hartog and Oosterbeek (1994)	Employees aged 43 in 1983: the Brabant cohort data	Company-related training	The unconditional wage effect of training is 8%. For participants in training the average wage gain is 21%. For non-participants the wage gains would have been negative.
Netherlands	Groot (1994)	Survey among employers about training for workers, 1992	Enterprise-related training	On average training increases productivity by 16% and wages by 12%.
Norway	Elias, Hernaes and Baker (1994)	A sample drawn from the birth cohorts of 1956-58, interviewed in 1975 and 1981	Educational careers after completion of compulsory school	Training does not significantly increase earnings.
Spain	Alba-Ramirez (1994)	Data on companies with 200 or more workers: the Collective Bargaining in Large Firms data 1979	How many workers have attended training courses in 1988	Training significantly increases labour productivity and wages.

Source: OECD.

Table 8.9. **Enrolment gaps by level of education and age group, 1992**

(thousands)

| | Level of education | | | | |
| | Early childhood | Secondary | Tertiary | | |
	3-6 year-olds	14-17 year-olds	18-21 year-olds	22-25 year-olds	Total
North America					
Canada	508	65	4	70	74
United States	3 753	614	0	824	824
Pacific Area					
Australia	494	114	47	119	166
Japan[1]	. .	0	. .	. .	. .
New Zealand	9	15	9	20	29
European Community					
Belgium	0	0	0	41	41
Denmark	68	7	47	0	47
France	0	23	42	127	169
Greece	135	49	21	71	92
Ireland	68	15	7	22	29
Netherlands	169	0	46	28	75
Spain	217	246	61	66	128
United Kingdom	427	357	297	432	729
Other Europe – OECD					
Austria	80	. .	53	4	57
Finland	135	3	23	0	23
Norway	64	2	29	2	31
Sweden	124	4	66	16	82
Switzerland	127	10	66	21	87
Turkey	4 714	2 525	795	453	1 249

Note: . . Data not available.

1. Enrolment in early childhood education and development programmes occurs in different types of institutions that fall under the authority of different Ministries. Consequently, the exact enrolment gap cannot readily be estimated.

Source: OECD Education Database.

Table 8.10. **Estimated costs of closing the enrolment gaps in early childhood education, 1992**

(3-6 years-olds)

	Total cost (million US$)	As a percentage of gross domestic product	As a percentage of total public expenditure	As a percentage of public education expenditure
North America				
United States	12 065	0.21	0.54	3.84
Pacific Area				
Japan[1]	. .	. .	. .	. .
New Zealand	17	0.04	. .	0.54
European Community				
Belgium	0	0	0	0
Denmark	429	0.46	0.74	5.99
France	0	0	0	0
Ireland	118	0.25	0.58	4.50
Netherlands	393	0.15	0.25	2.65
Spain	456	0.09	0.19	1.92
United Kingdom	797	0.08	0.20	1.67
Other Europe – OECD				
Austria	263	0.18	0.35	3.10
Finland	847	1.12	1.84	13.47
Norway	468	0.60	. .	. .
Sweden	753	0.51	0.77	6.71
Switzerland	240	0.15	0.44	2.65

Note: . . Data not available.

1. See note to Table 8.9.

Source: OECD Education Database.

Table 8.11. **Estimated costs of closing the enrolment gaps in lower and upper secondary education, 1992**

(14-17 year-olds)

	Total cost (million US$)	As a percentage of gross domestic product	As a percentage of total public expenditure	As a percentage of public education expenditure
North America				
United States	3 970	0.07	0.18	1.26
Pacific Area				
Japan	0	0	0	0
New Zealand	38	0.08	. .	1.22
European Community				
Belgium	0	0	0	0
Denmark	35	0.04	0.06	0.49
France	134	0.01	0.02	0.22
Ireland	42	0.09	0.20	1.59
Netherlands	0	0	0	0
Spain	773	0.15	0.33	3.26
United Kingdom	1 565	0.17	0.38	3.27
Other Europe – OECD				
Finland	12	0.02	0.03	0.20
Norway	13	0.02	. .	. .
Sweden	26	0.02	0.03	0.23

Note: . . Data not available
Source: OECD Education Database.

Table 8.12. **Estimated costs of closing the enrolment gaps in both university and non-university tertiary education (full-time), 1992**

	Total cost (million US$)			As a percentage of gross domestic product			As a percentage of total public expenditure			As a percentage of public education expenditure		
	18-21 year-olds	22-25 year-olds	Total	18-21 year-olds	22-25 year-olds	Total	18-21 year-olds	22-25 year-olds	Total	18-21 year-olds	22-25 year-olds	Total
North America												
Canada	49	869	918	0.01	0.16	0.17	0.02	0.32	0.34	0.13	2.29	2.42
United States	0	9 786	9 786	0	0.17	0.17	0	0.44	0.44	0	3.12	3.12
Pacific Area												
Australia	308	787	1 095	0.11	0.27	0.38	0.27	0.69	0.95	1.91	4.89	6.80
New Zealand	52	123	175	0.11	0.26	0.36	..	..	..	1.66	3.92	5.57
European Community												
Belgium	0	281	281	0	0.15	0.15	0	0.26	0.26	0	2.47	2.47
Denmark	315	0	315	0.34	0	0.34	0.55	0	0.55	4.40	0	4.40
France	253	766	1 019	0.02	0.07	0.09	0.04	0.13	0.18	0.42	1.26	1.68
Ireland	52	160	212	0.11	0.34	0.45	0.26	0.78	1.04	1.98	6.07	8.06
Netherlands	501	303	804	0.19	0.11	0.30	0.32	0.19	0.51	3.38	2.04	5.42
Spain	232	250	482	0.04	0.05	0.09	0.10	0.11	0.20	0.98	1.05	2.03
United Kingdom	4 468	6 507	10 975	0.48	0.69	1.17	1.10	1.60	2.69	9.34	13.60	22.94
Other Europe – OECD												
Austria	310	21	331	0.21	0.01	0.22	0.41	0.03	0.44	3.66	0.24	3.90
Finland	201	0	201	0.27	0	0.27	0.44	0	0.44	3.19	0	3.19
Norway	250	20	269	0.32	0.03	0.35	..	..	..	..	..	..
Sweden	471	115	586	0.32	0.08	0.39	0.48	0.12	0.60	4.19	1.03	5.22
Switzerland	849	275	1 125	0.54	0.17	0.71	1.56	0.50	2.06	9.38	3.04	12.43

Note: .. Data not available.
Source: OECD Education Database.

Table 8.13. **Education expenditure by function[1], 1992**

	Percentage of total expenditure			Percentage of current expenditure		
	Current	Capital	Compensation of teachers	Compensation of other staff	Compensation of all staff	Other current expenditure
North America						
Canada	93.1	6.9	54.1	20.2	74.3	25.7
United States	91.6	8.4	58.4	24.6	83.0	17.0
Pacific Area						
Australia	..	..	..	..	..	..
Japan[2]	84.9	15.1	50.9	15.0	65.9	34.1
New Zealand	..	..	..	..	..	..
European Community						
Belgium	98.9	1.1	75.7	2.6	78.4	21.6
Denmark[2]	92.9	7.1	47.8	23.9	71.7	28.3
France	91.6	8.4	..	..	83.5	16.5
Germany (FTFR)[2]	90.9	9.1	..	..	83.4	16.6
Greece	..	..	..	..	..	..
Ireland[2]	95.1	4.9	77.8	8.5	86.3	13.7
Italy[2]	91.8	8.2	64.7	16.7	81.4	18.6
Luxembourg	..	..	..	..		..
Netherlands	94.6	5.4	..	..	76.5	23.5
Portugal[2]	93.4	6.6	..	..	92.1	7.9
Spain	89.7	10.3	..	..	86.0	14.0
United Kingdom	94.9	5.1	57.7	17.7	75.4	24.6
Other Europe – OECD						
Austria	88.0	12.0	53.3	16.2	69.5	30.5
Finland	96.0	4.0	58.9	18.0	76.9	23.1
Iceland	..	..	..	..	..	..
Norway[2]	93.3	6.7	..	..	76.3	23.7
Sweden	..	..	..	..	..	..
Switzerland[2]	84.3	15.7	71.5	14.4	85.9	14.1
Turkey	..	..	..	..	..	..
Country mean	**92.1**	**7.9**	**61.0**	**16.2**	**79.2**	**20.8**
OECD total	**91.0**	**9.0**	**57.7**	**21.1**	**79.8**	**20.2**

Note: .. Data not available.
1. Public and government-dependent private institutions.
2. Public institutions only.
Source: OECD (1995d), Education at a Glance – OECD Indicators, p. 105.

Table 8.14. **Examples of higher education cost functions**

Index of unit costs for distance learning methods,
Open University, United Kingdom
(the cost of print methods for 125 students = 1.00)

Method	Number of students per annum		
	125	625	1 250
Print	1.00	0.24	0.14
Audio cassettes	1.34	0.50	0.39
Audio conferencing	2.73	1.57	1.41
Radio	5.70	1.14	0.57
Educational television broadcast	43.10	8.42	4.21

Source: Bates (1995).

Table 8.15. **Examples of higher education cost functions:**
comparison of teaching costs for different modes of instruction, Australia, 1989-90[1]

Activity	Costs by mode of study, Australian dollars		
	Off-campus	On-campus face-to-face	On-campus mixed mode
Preparation			
Academic input	59	No cost	59
Editing	28		28
Text input	10		10
Distance Education Centre infrastructure	40		40
Subtotal	*137*		*137*
Production			
Audio	10		
Video	0	No cost	Costs recovered
Computer Managed Learning	0		
Printing/Binding	34		
Subtotal	*44*		
Delivery			
Teaching	208	308	246
Examination	12	4	4
Postage/Handling	31	0	1
Student support	17	20	20
Library	10	30	30
Capital	34	50	50
Equipment	53	80	80
University management/infrastructure	147	210	210
Subtotal	*512*	*700*	*641*
Total	693	700	778

1. Estimates based on 90 students.
Source: Taylor and White (1991), p. 33.

Table 8.16. **Adults likely to be in need of basic education and training:**
numbers of 25-64 year-olds in the labour force with lower secondary education or less, 1992[1]

	Men	Women	Total
North America			
Canada	1 572 000	1 002 000	2 574 000
United States	7 784 000	4 750 000	12 535 000
Pacific Area			
New Zealand	253 000	228 000	481 000
European Community			
Belgium	1 040 000	595 000	1 635 000
Denmark	405 000	428 000	833 000
France	4 866 000	4 132 000	8 997 000
Germany	1 853 000	2 276 000	4 129 000
Ireland	401 000	127 000	528 000
Italy	8 535 000	4 157 000	12 692 000
Netherlands	1 161 000	747 000	1 908 000
Spain	5 762 000	2 694 000	8 457 000
United Kingdom	3 010 000	2 996 000	6 006 000
Other Europe – OECD			
Austria	331 000	372 000	703 000
Finland	393 000	345 000	737 000
Norway	166 000	128 000	294 000
Sweden	596 000	478 000	1 074 000
Switzerland	223 000	289 000	512 000
Turkey	8 476 000	3 311 000	11 787 000
Total	**46 826 000**	**29 055 000**	**75 880 000**

1. Refers to ISCED 0 plus ISCED 1 plus ISCED 2.
Source: OECD Education Database.

Table 8.17. **Adults likely to be in need of basic education and training, 1994**

(26- to 65-year-olds with low literacy proficiency[1])

	Age	Percentage	Number
Canada	26-35	38.8	1 938 448
	36-45	35.8	1 713 030
	46-55	54.0	1 884 600
	56-65	67.5	1 652 585
	26-65	100.0	7 188 663
Germany	26-35	35.1	4 971 915
	36-45	40.1	4 688 091
	46-55	42.4	4 364 656
	56-65	58.6	5 832 458
	26-65	100.0	19 857 120
Netherlands	26-35	25.1	661 385
	36-45	33.4	797 258
	46-55	48.3	971 313
	56-65	63.1	911 795
	26-65	100.0	3 341 751
Sweden	26-35	14.3	176 319
	36-45	24.8	293 136
	46-55	26.5	323 300
	56-65	45.5	382 200
	26-65	100.0	1 174 955
United States	26-35	44.5	18 649 505
	36-45	43.2	17 928 432
	46-55	49.6	14 921 664
	56-65	62.2	13 008 508
	26-65	100.0	64 508 109

1. Document literacy levels 1 and 2 combined, as implemented by the International Adult Literacy Survey.
Sources: OECD and Statistics Canada (1995).

Table 8.18. **Unit costs of selected labour market training programmes**

	Costs	Participant	Costs/Participant	
	(million local currency)	(starting)	(local currency)	US$
France (1993)				
Training programmes for the unemployed	27 494	585 694	46 943	7 142
Training of employed because of structural adjustment	349	225 112	1 550	236
Adult education	3 619	391 920	9 234	1 405
Germany (1994)				
Training for unemployed adults and those at risk	13 397	713 893	18 766	8 924
Further education and training	504	25 502	19 763	9 398
Netherlands (1994)				
Vocational training centres	232	24 100	9 627	4 510
Framework regulation for training	199	59 000	3 373	1 580
Vocational guidance and training centres	42	10 600	3 962	1 856
Women's vocational training institutions	10	1 000	10 000[1]	4 685
Industry-based (sectorial) training	50	8 000	6 250	2 928
New Zealand (1991/1992)				
Training for unemployed adults and those at risk (ACCESS)	156	68 070	2 287	1 484
Sweden (1990/1991)				
Training for unemployed adults and those at risk (course costs)	3 335	77 900	42 811	4 644
Training for employed adults	175	20 700	8 454	917

1. 1993 data.
Source: OECD, Active Labour Market Programme Database.

Table 8.19.   **Cost scenarios for extending lifelong learning to the least qualified**[1]

	Scenario A[2]		Scenario B[3]	
	Unit costs (US$)	Total costs As % GDP	Unit costs (US$)	Total costs As % GDP
Germany (FTFR)	8 924	2.7	4 300	1.3
Netherlands	4 142	2.9	4 300	3.0
New Zealand	. .	. .	2 700	2.7
Sweden	4 644	3.3	6 100	4.4

Note: . . Data not available.
1.   See estimates in Table 8.16.
2.   Scenario A: Costs based on labour market programme costs. *Source:* Table 8.18.
3.   Scenario B: Costs based on secondary education unit costs. *Source:* Annex Table A.62.

Table 8.20.   **Cost scenarios for extending lifelong learning to adults with low literacy proficiency**[1]

	Scenario A[2]		Scenario B[3]	
	Unit costs (US$)	Total costs As % GDP	Unit costs (US$)	Total costs As % GDP
Germany	8 924	11.8	4 300	5.7
Netherlands	4 142	5.1	4 300	5.3
New Zealand	. .	. .	2 700	. .
Sweden	4 644	3.7	6 100	4.8

Note: . . Data not available.
1.   See estimates in Table 8.17.
2.   Scenario A: Costs based on labour market programme costs. *Source:* Table 8.18.
3.   Scenario B: Costs based on secondary education unit costs. *Source:* Annex Table A.62.

Table 8.21.   **Duration**[1] **of adult education and training courses, 1994**[2]

(by type of financial support)

	Employer supported ?	Duration		
		Low	Medium	High
Canada (English)	Yes	84	13	3
	No	36	19	45
Canada (French)	Yes	72	28	0
	No	37	18	45
Germany	Yes	70	20	10
	No	50	25	25
Netherlands	Yes	74	18	9
	No	43	19	38
Poland	Yes	66	24	10
	No	40	33	27
Switzerland (French)	Yes	68	17	15
	No	51	25	24
Switzerland (German)	Yes	74	16	10
	No	60	17	23
United States	Yes	86	11	2
	No	54	17	30

1.   Low: 0-59 hours. Medium: 60-300 hours. High: > 300 hours.
2.   Based on the first reported course being taken in the six months preceding the interview.
Sources: OECD and Statistics Canada (1995).

Table 8.22. **Evaluation of financing schemes for lifelong learning**

Model	Promotes efficiency in the education market[1]	Promotes efficiency in the labour market[2]	Lifts liquidity constraints[3]	Takes account of externalities[4]	Promotes spreading learning activities over the life-time[5]	Promotes equal access[6]	Results in net subsidies towards highly educated
Drawing rights	No	No, because of taxes	Yes	Yes, but very crude	Perhaps	Yes	No
Entitlements without loans	No	No, because of taxes	Yes	Yes, but very crude	Yes	Yes	Yes, if some persons do not use their entire entitlement
Entitlements with substantial ICL[7]	Yes	Yes, but disincentive to work for low-income earners	Yes	Yes	Yes	Yes, but some reservations	No
Franchise	Only in later years	No, because of taxes	Only in first years	Yes, in a very elegant way	Yes	Yes, but only in first years	Yes, if some persons do not use their entire franchise
Auctions	Yes	n.a.[8]	n.a.[8]	n.a.[8]	n.a.[8]	n.a.[8]	n.a.[8]
Single employer	Yes, but not in formal education	Yes	Only to the extent that training is specific and workers have a low probability to quit	No	Yes	No	No
Self-financing without loans	Yes	Yes	No	No	No	No	No
Self-financing with ICL	Yes	Yes, but disincentive to work for low income earners	Yes	No	No	Yes, but some reservations	No
Self-financing with graduate tax	Yes	No, disincentive to work for low income earners and disincentive to accept job with high salary	Yes	No	No	Yes	No
Self-financing with mortgage loans and income dependent grants	Yes	Yes, but disincentive for low income earners	Not really	No	No	Yes	Yes

Table 8.22. **Evaluation of financing schemes for lifelong learning** (cont.)

Model	Promotes efficiency in the education market[1]	Promotes efficiency in the labour market[2]	Lifts liquidity constraints[3]	Takes account of externalities[4]	Promotes spreading learning activities over the life-time[5]	Promotes equal access[6]	Results in net subsidies towards highly educated
Parafiscal funds	Yes, but not in formal education	No, because a payroll tax is levied	Not really	To some extent	Yes	No	Yes
Government funding of institutions	No	No, because of taxes	Yes	Yes, but very crude	No	Yes	Yes

1. *Efficiency in education.* This is a broad concept, but for an economist it requires equality of social marginal revenue and social marginal cost. This in turn requires that the tuition fees charged to students equal marginal cost of production minus the value of externalities. (A slightly weaker rule is that tuition fees are proportionate instead of equal to marginal costs minus the value of externalities.)

2. *Efficiency in the labour market.* Some of the arrangements affect the conditions for efficiency in the labour market. One mechanism is that the repayment of loans gives disincentives to work or to accept a job with a high salary. The other mechanism is that public financing of education requires taxes and, except for lump sum taxation, levying taxes increases the difference between gross cost of labour to an employer and the net earnings of a worker.

3. *Lifting liquidity constraints.* One of the most important reasons for governments to intervene in post-compulsory education is that without intervention many people may face serious liquidity constraints. They may have no access to funds, or only against very unfavourable terms. With mortgage loans, the constraint is not really lifted since repayment is due within 10 or 15 years. This merely shifts the liquidity constraint from the education years to the period immediately after education is finished. With parafiscal funds, payroll taxes are levied from the employer. However, to the extent that the employer can shift the tax to the workers, the workers bear the burden of the payroll tax. The extent to which the tax is shifted depends in the elasticities of labour demand and labour supply.

4. *Externalities.* The only reason to provide general subsidies to post-compulsory education is the existence of externalities. Many observers are rather cynic with regard to this point. Most, if not all, of the revenues of post-compulsory education are received by the persons who attained it. Nevertheless, for some studies or courses, externalities are plausible. A financing scheme can take account of that, by differentiating subsidies according to the perceived externalities.

5. Stimulating lifelong learning.

6. Equity in education has two dimensions. The first is that a poor social background is no hindrance to enrol (equal access); the second is that on a lifetime basis, the persons who received more education are not subsidised by the persons that received less education.

7. ICLs = Income Contigent Loans.

8. Not applicable, the auction model is a partial model and no conclusions can be drawn with regard to most of the criteria.

Source: Oosterbeek (1995).

267

Annex

EVIDENCE AND KEY STATISTICS

Table A.1. **Proportion of 0-14, 25-34 and 25-44 year-olds in the population, 1960-2010**

(percentage of population)

		1960[1]	1970[1]	1980[1]	1990[1]	2000[2]	2010[2]
Australia[3]	0 to 14	30.1	28.8	25.3	21.9	20.8	19.4
	25 to 34	13.6	13.3	16.2	16.5	15.1	13.3
	25 to 44	27.4	25.3	28.3	31.6	30.4	27.6
Belgium	0 to 14	23.5	23.6	20.1	18.2	17.7	16.9
	25 to 34	13.9	12.1	15.0	15.9	13.9	12.0
	25 to 44	26.5	25.4	26.7	30.5	29.6	25.8
Canada	0 to 14	33.5	30.2	22.7	20.7	20.6	19.5
	25 to 34	13.9	13.1	17.3	18.5	14.1	12.8
	25 to 44	27.0	25.1	29.2	34.2	31.2	26.2
Czech Republic[4]	0 to 14	25.4	21.3	23.4	21.5	16.6	13.3
	25 to 34	13.6	13.0	16.5	13.5	14.9	15.6
	25 to 44	25.7	25.9	28.5	29.5	28.3	30.7
Denmark	0 to 14	25.2	23.3	20.8	17.0	18.0	16.8
	25 to 34	12.4	13.7	15.4	15.0	14.9	11.5
	25 to 44	25.7	25.2	28.5	30.1	29.6	26.4
France	0 to 14	26.4	24.8	22.3	20.2	18.9	17.6
	25 to 34	14.1	12.1	15.8	15.2	14.4	12.8
	25 to 44	25.7	25.2	27.0	30.0	29.0	26.8
Germany	0 to 14	21.3	23.2	18.5	16.1	15.3	13.2
	25 to 34	13.3	15.1	13.4	16.4	14.9	12.1
	25 to 44	24.4	27.8	28.2	29.7	31.6	27.5
Italy	0 to 14	24.8	24.6	22.3	16.7	14.5	13.5
	25 to 34	15.4	13.7	13.8	15.2	16.0	12.0
	25 to 44	28.0	27.5	26.7	28.6	31.1	28.2
Japan	0 to 14	30.2	24.0	23.6	18.4	15.3	15.3
	25 to 34	16.8	16.8	17.0	12.9	14.8	12.6
	25 to 44	28.5	31.8	32.0	28.9	27.3	27.3
Spain	0 to 14	27.4	27.9	26.6	19.7	15.0	14.1
	25 to 34	15.7	12.5	13.4	15.5	16.7	14.2
	25 to 44	29.0	26.4	25.1	28.2	32.0	30.9
Sweden	0 to 14	22.0	20.8	19.6	17.9	20.0	18.9
	25 to 34	12.1	13.6	15.1	13.8	13.6	11.2
	25 to 44	26.3	25.1	28.0	28.4	27.0	24.5
United Kingdom	0 to 14	23.3	24.3	20.9	19.0	19.5	18.2
	25 to 34	12.8	12.5	14.2	15.3	14.8	12.3
	25 to 44	26.4	24.2	26.1	29.1	29.6	26.7
United States	0 to 14	31.0	28.3	22.5	21.7	21.8	20.3
	25 to 34	12.7	12.4	16.5	17.3	14.1	12.9
	25 to 44	26.1	23.6	27.9	32.4	30.1	26.3

1. Data are United Nations demographic estimates.
2. Data are from the United Nations Populations Division's medium variant population projections.
3. Australian Bureau of Statistics, 1995, *Series A Population Projections* data. Reference month: June.
4. See Note 3, Table 1.2.
Source: United Nations (1994), *World Population Prospects, 1950-2010.* Data for the Czech Republic were provided by the Czech Statistical Office.

Table A.2. **Indicators of growth and dispersion of communication technologies, 1982 and 1992**

	Telephone mainlines per 100 inhabitants		Business mainlines per 100 employees in labour force		Cellular mobile subscribers CAGR (%)	Penetration of facsimile machines CAGR (%)
	1982	1992	1982	1992	1988-92[1]	1988-92[1]
North America						
Canada	42.0	59.2	16.1	39.8	55.1	41.4
United States	46.2	56.5	29.5	42.6	52.0	73.2
Pacific Area						
Australia	36.8	48.7	22.9	37.9	64.3	33.3
Japan	34.7	46.4	24.3	28.5	63.0	28.9
New Zealand	36.9	44.4	16.0	25.4	47.6	35.1
European Community						
Belgium	27.8	42.5	..	25.2	32.5	58.1
Denmark	45.9	58.1	..	22.9	19.3	48.5
France	35.7	52.5	..	14.5	45.0	65.0
Germany	36.8	43.9	..	14.7	77.6	64.7
Greece	25.9	43.6	21.7	37.1	..	40.6
Ireland	16.7	31.4	20.1	32.0	52.4	65.5
Italy	25.9	41.0	16.9	23.9	120.0	83.6
Luxembourg	37.9	60.6	..	38.2	35.7	35.1
Netherlands	36.9	48.7	9.5	22.5	49.8	54.7
Portugal	12.2	30.6	8.5	13.3	137.5	68.8
Spain	21.1	40.5	24.4	29.0	98.4	38.1
United Kingdom	33.9	45.2	14.5	24.1	53.8	28.4
Other Europe – OECD						
Austria	32.2	43.9	..	..	46.9	36.0
Finland	39.9	54.4	..	31.7	36.2	57.9
Iceland	38.9	53.9	..	26.5	25.0	32.4
Norway	34.6	52.9	..	29.3	17.8	29.3
Sweden	59.6	68.2	21.3	31.0	29.6	..
Switzerland	46.5	60.3	23.5	32.5	62.6	47.1
Turkey	3.2	16.1	3.5	14.2	58.0	43.1
OECD average	**35.3**[2]	**47.5**[2]	**15.0**[3]	**27.7**[3]	**52.5**	**48.8**

Note: .. Data not available.
1. Compound annual growth rate (CAGR) calculated in constant 1990 prices deflated the purchasing power parities (PPP) index.
2. Weighted average.
3. Simple average of available data. Weighted average is slightly lower for both years.
Source: OECD (1995a), *Communications Outlook*, Tables 4.2, 4.3, 4.7 and 7.6.

Table A.3. **Shares of high-technology industries in total manufacturing, 1970 and 1992**

(percentage)

	Exports		Value added	
	1970	1992	1970	1992
North America				
Canada	9.0	13.7	10.2	11.2[1]
United States	25.9	37.7	18.2	23.7[2]
Pacific Area				
Australia	2.8	9.6[3]	8.9	10.4[2]
Japan	20.2	36.1	16.4	22.2[2]
New Zealand	0.7	4.4	. .	. .
European Community				
Belgium	7.2	10.0	. .	. .
Denmark	11.9	18.2	9.3	12.3
France	14.0	23.4	12.8	18.8
Germany	15.8	20.6	15.3	20.8
Greece	2.4	4.3	. .	. .
Ireland	11.7	39.4	. .	. .
Italy	12.7	15.1[3]	13.3	13.2[2]
Luxembourg	7.2	10.0	. .	. .
Netherlands	16.0	19.8	15.1	18.6
Portugal	7.6	12.1	. .	. .
Spain	6.1	14.0	. .	. .
United Kingdom	17.1	30.9	16.4	14.5
Other Europe – OECD				
Austria	11.4	17.7	. .	. .
Finland	3.2	13.4	5.9	10.7
Iceland	0.1	0.7	. .	. .
Norway	4.7	10.3	6.6	9.4
Sweden	12.0	21.0	12.8	14.5
Switzerland	30.2	32.9	. .	. .
Turkey	1.8	5.8	. .	. .

Note: . . Data not available.
1.   1989.
2.   1990.
3.   1991.
Source: OECD (1994*d*), *The OECD Jobs Study: Evidence and Explanations*, Part I, Table 4.12, p. 149.

Table A.4. **Employment shares for blue- and white-collar workers, 1981 and 1991**[1]

(per cent of total employment)

	Blue collar		White collar	
	1981	1991	1981	1991
North America				
Canada	29.5	24.5	65.1	71.1
United States[2]	28.2	26.0	68.1	71.1
Pacific Area				
Australia[3]	36.3	35.6	56.6	59.4
Japan	37.8	35.0	52.1	57.9
New Zealand[4]	29.0	24.9	59.9	64.3
European Community				
Belgium[5]	35.3	32.9	61.1	63.4
Denmark[2]	31.6	29.8	65.4	65.1
Germany[6]	35.4	31.9	58.4	61.2
Greece[7]	30.8	29.5	39.5	47.5
Ireland[2]	28.9	27.6	53.6	58.0
Netherlands[8]	24.6	24.2	68.1	70.5
Portugal	37.3	32.6	33.8	47.6
Spain	39.0	37.1	42.8	51.7
United Kingdom[9]	30.7	28.4	65.3	68.6
Other Europe – OECD				
Austria[10]	36.4	34.8	54.1	57.1
Finland[2]	29.5	25.2	58.5	64.7
Norway[7]	31.9	26.1	58.5	65.9
Sweden	31.2	28.3	63.2	68.2
Turkey	. .	25.3	. .	28.2
Unweighted average	32.4	29.5	53.9	60.1

Note: . . Data not available.
1. See OECD (1994c), Annex 2.B for definitions of blue- and white-collar workers.
2. Data refer to 1983 and 1991.
3. Data for 1991 refer to Australian Standards Classification of Occupations, 1986.
4. Data refer to 1987 and 1990.
5. Data refer to 1983 and 1990.
6. Data refer to 1982 and 1991 and to the Former Territory of the Federal Republic.
7. Data refer to 1982 and 1991.
8. Data refer to 1987 and 1991.
9. Data refer to 1984 and 1990.
10. Data refer to 1984 and 1991.
Source: OECD (1994c), *Employment Outlook*, Table 2.3, p. 82.

Table A.5. **Annual hours worked per person per year, 1870-1992**

	1870	1880	1890	1909	1913	1929	1938	1950	1960	1970[1]	1983	1992
Canada	2 964	2 871	2 789	2 707	2 605	2 399	2 240	1 967	1 877	1 890	1 730	1 719
France	2 945	2 852	2 770	2 688	2 588	2 297	1 848	1 989	1 983	1 962	1 711	1 666
Germany	2 941	2 848	2 765	2 684	2 584	2 284	2 316	2 316	2 083	1 949	1 733	1 588
Italy	2 886	2 795	2 714	2 634	2 536	2 228	1 927	1 997	2 059	1 969	1 764	..
Japan	2 945	2 852	2 770	2 688	2 588	2 364	2 391	2 272	2 432	2 201	2 095	1 965
United Kingdom	2 984	2 890	2 807	2 725	2 624	2 286	2 267	1 958	1 913	1 735	1 607	..
United States	2 964	2 871	2 789	2 707	2 605	2 342	2 062	1 867	1 794	1 889	1 787	1 776

Note: .. Data not available.
1. Break in series for all countries except Japan (break occurs in 1983 figure) and United Kingdom (historical series throughout). New series include part-time work.
Sources: The data for 1870 to 1960 are from Carnoy and Castells (1995). From 1970 onwards, the data are from OECD (1994c), *Employment Outlook,* Table B, p. 196.

Table A.6. **Size and composition of part-time employment, 1973-93**[1]

(percentage)

	Part-time employment as a proportion of employment					
	Men			Women		
	1973	1983	1993	1973	1983	1993
North America						
Canada	4.7	7.6	9.7	19.4	26.1	26.4
United States	8.6	10.8	10.9	26.8	28.1	25.3
Pacific Area						
Australia	3.7	6.2	10.3	28.2	36.4	42.3
Japan	6.8	7.3	11.4	25.1	29.8	35.2
New Zealand	4.6	5.0	9.7	24.6	31.4	35.7
European Community						
Belgium	1.0	2.0	2.1[2]	10.2	19.7	28.1[2]
Denmark	..	6.6	10.1[2]	..	44.7	36.7[2]
France	1.7	2.6	3.6[2]	12.9	20.0	24.5[2]
Germany	1.8	1.7	2.2[2]	24.4	30.0	30.7[2]
Greece	..	3.7	2.8[2]	..	12.1	8.4[2]
Ireland	..	2.7	..	..	15.5	..
Italy	3.7	2.4	2.9[2]	14.0	9.4	11.5[2]
Luxembourg	1.0	1.0	1.3	18.4	17.0	16.5
Netherlands	..	7.2[3]	13.4[2]	..	50.1[3]	62.9[2]
Portugal	..	2.5[4]	4.3	..	16.5[4]	11.2
Spain	..	..	2.3	..	..	14.3
United Kingdom	2.3	3.3	6.3[2]	39.1	42.4	45.0[2]
Other Europe – OECD						
Austria	1.4	1.5	1.6[2]	15.6	20.0	20.5[2]
Finland	..	4.5	6.2	..	12.5	11.2
Norway	5.9	7.7[3]	9.7	46.5	63.3[3]	47.6
Sweden	..	6.3[3]	9.1	..	45.9[3]	41.4

Note: .. Data not available.
1. The definition of part-time work is not fully consistent across OECD countries, and data are not comparable in a strict sense.
2. 1992.
3. Break in series after 1983.
4. 1979.
Source: OECD (1994c), *Employment Outlook*, Table D, pp. 198-199.

Table A.7. **The relative size of the population aged 5 to 14, 1970-94**[1]

(percentage)

	1970	1971	1972	1973	1974	1975	1976	1977	1978	1979	1980	1981	1982	1983	1984	1985	1986	1987	1988	1989	1990	1991	1992	1993	1994
North America																									
Canada	21.5	21.0	20.5	19.9	19.2	18.5	17.8	17.1	16.5	15.9	15.4	15.0	14.7	14.5	14.3	14.1	14.0	13.9	13.9	13.8	13.8	13.7	13.6	13.6	13.5
United States	19.9	19.6	19.2	18.7	18.2	17.7	16.7	16.2	16.2	15.7	15.3	15.0	14.7	14.5	14.3	14.2	14.1	14.1	14.1	14.1	14.1	14.2	14.2	14.2	14.3
Weighted mean	*20.0*	*19.7*	*19.3*	*18.8*	*18.3*	*17.8*	*17.3*	*16.7*	*16.2*	*15.7*	*15.3*	*15.0*	*14.7*	*14.5*	*14.3*	*14.2*	*14.1*	*14.1*	*14.1*	*14.1*	*14.1*	*14.1*	*14.1*	*14.2*	*14.2*
Mexico	27.9	27.9	28.0	28.0	28.1	28.2	28.4	28.6	28.8	28.9	28.9	28.7	28.4	28.0	27.6	27.1	26.5	26.0	25.4	24.9	24.5	24.2	23.9	23.7	23.5
Pacific Area																									
Australia	19.4	19.2	19.0	18.8	18.6	18.4	18.2	18.1	18.0	17.8	17.6	17.2	16.9	16.5	16.1	15.8	15.4	15.2	14.9	14.7	14.6	14.5	14.4	14.3	14.3
Japan	15.5	15.4	15.3	15.2	15.3	15.4	15.6	15.8	16.0	16.1	16.2	16.2	16.1	15.9	15.7	15.3	15.0	14.5	14.0	13.5	13.1	12.7	12.3	11.9	11.6
New Zealand	21.2	21.1	20.9	20.7	20.4	20.2	19.9	19.7	19.4	19.1	18.8	18.4	18.0	17.5	17.1	16.7	16.3	16.0	15.7	15.5	15.2	15.1	15.0	14.9	14.9
Weighted mean	*16.1*	*15.9*	*15.8*	*15.8*	*15.8*	*15.9*	*15.9*	*16.1*	*16.3*	*16.4*	*16.4*	*16.4*	*16.2*	*16.0*	*15.7*	*15.4*	*15.1*	*14.6*	*14.2*	*13.7*	*13.3*	*12.9*	*12.6*	*12.3*	*12.0*
European Community																									
Belgium	16.1	16.0	15.9	15.7	15.5	15.3	15.0	15.0	14.7	14.3	14.0	13.7	13.4	13.1	12.9	12.7	12.5	12.4	12.3	12.2	12.1	12.0	12.0	11.9	11.9
Denmark	15.4	15.4	15.5	15.5	15.5	15.4	15.3	15.3	15.1	14.9	14.7	14.5	14.2	13.9	13.6	13.3	12.9	12.4	12.0	11.7	11.4	11.1	11.0	10.9	10.9
France	16.5	16.5	16.4	16.3	16.2	16.1	15.9	15.9	15.7	15.6	15.4	15.2	15.0	14.8	14.5	14.3	14.1	14.0	13.8	13.7	13.6	13.5	13.4	13.3	13.3
Germany (FTFR)	15.6	15.8	16.0	16.1	16.1	15.7	15.2	15.2	14.6	14.0	13.4	12.7	12.1	11.5	11.0	10.7	10.5	10.4	10.4	10.4	10.5	10.7	10.8	11.0	11.1
Greece	16.1	16.1	16.2	16.3	16.2	16.2	16.0	16.0	15.8	15.6	15.4	15.2	14.9	14.7	14.5	14.4	14.2	14.1	14.0	13.9	13.7	13.4	13.0	12.6	12.2
Ireland	20.6	20.5	20.4	20.3	20.3	20.3	20.3	20.3	20.4	20.4	20.4	20.3	20.1	20.0	19.8	19.7	19.6	19.6	19.6	19.5	19.3	19.0	18.6	18.2	17.7
Italy	16.0	16.2	16.3	16.4	16.4	16.4	16.3	16.3	16.2	16.1	15.9	15.6	15.3	15.0	14.7	14.2	13.8	13.3	12.8	12.3	11.8	11.4	11.0	10.7	10.4
Luxembourg	15.0	15.2	14.9	15.3	15.2	14.8	14.5	14.2	14.2	13.7	13.5	12.9	12.6	12.3	11.8	11.4	11.4	11.3	11.2	11.4	11.3	11.2	11.0	10.9	11.0
Netherlands	18.2	18.2	18.1	18.0	18.0	17.8	17.6	17.3	16.9	16.5	16.1	15.6	15.0	14.5	13.9	13.4	13.0	12.6	12.4	12.3	12.0	11.9	11.9	11.9	11.9
Portugal	18.9	19.0	19.0	19.0	18.9	18.7	18.4	18.4	18.0	17.7	17.4	17.1	16.9	16.7	16.5	16.3	16.1	15.9	15.6	15.3	15.0	14.6	14.1	13.7	13.3
Spain	18.4	18.5	18.4	18.4	18.3	18.2	18.1	18.1	17.9	17.8	17.6	17.5	17.3	17.1	16.9	16.6	16.3	15.8	15.4	14.9	14.3	13.8	13.2	12.7	12.2
United Kingdom	16.1	16.3	16.4	16.4	16.3	16.1	15.9	15.9	15.6	15.3	14.9	14.5	14.0	13.6	13.2	12.9	12.6	12.5	12.4	12.3	12.3	12.4	12.5	12.7	12.8
Weighted mean	*16.5*	*16.6*	*16.7*	*16.7*	*16.6*	*16.4*	*16.2*	*16.2*	*15.9*	*15.6*	*15.2*	*14.9*	*14.5*	*14.2*	*13.8*	*13.5*	*13.2*	*13.0*	*12.8*	*12.6*	*12.4*	*12.3*	*12.2*	*12.1*	*12.0*
Other Europe – OECD																									
Austria	16.2	16.5	16.6	16.8	16.8	16.7	16.4	16.1	15.7	15.2	14.7	14.2	13.6	13.1	12.6	12.2	12.0	11.8	11.7	11.6	11.6	11.6	11.7	11.7	11.8
Czech Republic[2]	14.3	14.1	13.8	13.6	13.6	13.7	14.0	14.0	14.2	14.5	14.8	15.3	15.7	16.1	16.5	16.6	16.6	16.5	16.2	15.7	15.2	14.6	14.1	13.6	13.2
Finland	17.0	16.8	16.5	16.3	15.9	15.6	15.2	14.8	14.4	14.0	13.6	13.3	13.1	12.9	12.8	12.8	12.8	12.9	13.0	13.1	13.1	13.0	13.0	12.8	12.7
Iceland	22.5	21.7	21.4	21.1	20.5	20.2	20.0	19.4	19.2	18.6	18.4	18.2	18.0	17.8	17.6	17.4	17.2	17.0	16.9	16.7	16.5	16.3	16.2	16.0	15.8
Norway	16.0	16.0	16.0	16.0	16.1	16.1	16.1	16.1	16.1	16.0	15.8	15.5	15.2	14.7	14.3	13.9	13.5	13.1	12.8	12.5	12.4	12.2	12.2	12.3	12.3
Sweden	13.6	13.7	13.8	13.9	13.9	14.0	14.0	14.0	14.0	13.9	13.7	13.5	13.3	13.0	12.7	12.4	12.2	11.9	11.7	11.6	11.5	11.5	11.5	11.6	11.8
Switzerland	15.6	15.7	15.8	15.9	15.9	15.7	15.6	15.3	14.9	14.6	14.1	13.6	13.1	12.6	12.2	11.8	11.5	11.3	11.1	11.1	11.0	11.1	11.1	11.2	11.4
Turkey	25.7	25.7	25.5	25.4	25.3	25.3	25.4	25.6	25.8	25.8	25.7	25.4	25.0	24.5	23.9	23.5	23.0	22.6	22.2	21.9	21.7	21.6	21.7	21.7	21.8
Weighted mean	*20.1*	*20.2*	*20.1*	*20.1*	*20.1*	*20.1*	*20.3*	*20.3*	*20.3*	*20.3*	*20.3*	*20.1*	*19.9*	*19.6*	*19.3*	*18.9*	*18.7*	*18.4*	*18.1*	*17.9*	*17.8*	*17.7*	*17.7*	*17.7*	*17.8*

1. Percentage of 5- to 14-year-old people in the total population. The total population includes all persons residing in the country, regardless of citizenship, educational or labour market status. Data for the 1970-94 period are United Nations demographic estimates.
2. The data for 1970-1994 are from the demographic yearbook published by the Czech Statistical Office.
Source: United Nations (1994), *World Population Prospects 1950-2010* and national data submissions.

Table A.8. **The relative size of the population aged 5 to 14 and 15 to 24, 1994[1]**

(percentage)

	Age group	
	5 to 14	15 to 24
North America		
Canada	13.5	13.5
United States	14.3	13.8
Weighted mean	*14.2*	*13.7*
Mexico	23.5	21.4
Pacific Area		
Australia[2]	14.3	15.5
Japan	11.6	15.1
New Zealand	14.9	15.8
Weighted mean	*12.0*	*15.1*
European Community		
Belgium	11.9	12.8
Denmark	10.9	13.7
France	13.3	14.2
Germany (FTFR)	11.1	12.0
Greece	12.2	14.2
Ireland	17.7	18.1
Italy	10.4	14.6
Luxembourg	11.0	12.7
Netherlands	11.9	13.5
Portugal	13.3	16.0
Spain	12.2	16.5
United Kingdom	12.8	13.3
Weighted mean	*12.0*	*13.9*
Other Europe – OECD		
Austria	11.8	12.9
Czech Republic[3]	13.2	16.4
Finland	12.7	12.4
Iceland	15.8	15.8
Norway	12.3	13.9
Sweden	11.8	12.6
Switzerland	11.4	12.1
Turkey	21.8	19.1
Weighted mean	*17.8*	*16.8*
Weighted mean of all countries	*14.3*	*15.0*

1. Data are United Nations demographic estimates.
2. Australian Bureau of Statistics, 1995, *Series A Population Projections* data. Reference month: June.
3. The data are from the demographic yearbook published by the Czech Statistical Office.
Source: United Nations (1994), *World Population Prospects 1950-2010.*

Table A.9. **The relative size of the population aged 5 to 14, forecast 1994-2010[1]**

(percentage)

	1994	1995	1996	1997	1998	1999	2000	2001	2002	2003	2004	2005	2006	2007	2008	2009	2010
North America																	
Canada	13.5	13.5	13.5	13.5	13.6	13.6	13.7	13.7	13.8	13.8	13.7	13.7	13.6	13.5	13.3	13.2	13.0
United States	14.3	14.3	14.4	14.4	14.5	14.6	14.6	14.6	14.6	14.5	14.4	14.3	14.2	14.0	13.8	13.6	13.5
Weighted mean	*14.2*	*14.2*	*14.3*	*14.4*	*14.4*	*14.5*	*14.5*	*14.5*	*14.5*	*14.4*	*14.4*	*14.2*	*14.1*	*13.9*	*13.8*	*13.6*	*13.4*
Mexico	23.5	23.3	23.1	22.9	22.7	22.4	22.2	22.0	21.7	21.4	21.1	20.8	20.4	20.0	19.7	19.3	18.9
Pacific Area																	
Australia[2]	14.3	14.3	14.2	14.2	14.1	14.0	13.9	13.8	13.8	13.7	13.7	13.6	13.5	13.4	13.3	13.2	13.1
Japan	11.6	11.3	11.0	10.7	10.4	10.2	10.1	10.0	10.0	10.0	10.0	10.0	10.1	10.1	10.2	10.3	10.3
New Zealand	14.9	15.0	15.1	15.2	15.4	15.5	15.6	15.6	15.6	15.6	15.4	15.3	15.2	15.0	14.8	14.6	14.4
Weighted mean	*12.0*	*11.7*	*11.5*	*11.2*	*11.0*	*10.9*	*10.7*	*10.7*	*10.6*	*10.6*	*10.6*	*10.7*	*10.7*	*10.7*	*10.8*	*10.8*	*10.8*
European Community																	
Belgium	11.9	11.9	11.9	11.9	11.9	11.9	11.8	11.8	11.8	11.8	11.7	11.7	11.6	11.6	11.5	11.4	11.4
Denmark	10.9	10.9	11.1	11.3	11.5	11.8	12.0	12.1	12.2	12.3	12.3	12.3	12.2	12.1	12.0	11.8	11.6
France	13.3	13.2	13.1	13.1	12.9	12.8	12.7	12.6	12.5	12.4	12.4	12.3	12.2	12.1	12.0	11.9	11.8
Germany (FTFR)	11.1	11.1	11.1	11.1	11.0	10.8	10.7	10.5	10.3	10.2	10.0	9.8	9.6	9.5	9.3	9.2	9.0
Greece	12.2	11.8	11.4	11.1	10.7	10.4	10.2	10.0	9.9	9.9	9.8	9.8	9.8	9.7	9.7	9.7	9.7
Ireland	17.7	17.2	16.7	16.2	15.7	15.2	14.8	14.5	14.3	14.2	14.2	14.1	14.2	14.2	14.3	14.4	14.5
Italy	10.4	10.2	10.1	9.9	9.9	9.8	9.8	9.7	9.7	9.7	9.7	9.7	9.7	9.6	9.5	9.5	9.4
Luxembourg	11.0	10.8	10.7	10.9	10.8	10.9	10.8	11.0	11.1	11.1	11.3	11.2	11.4	11.6	11.6	11.6	11.6
Netherlands	11.9	12.0	12.1	12.2	12.2	12.3	12.4	12.4	12.4	12.4	12.3	12.2	12.1	12.0	11.8	11.6	11.4
Portugal	13.3	12.9	12.6	12.3	12.1	12.0	11.8	11.8	11.8	11.8	11.8	11.8	11.7	11.7	11.6	11.5	11.4
Spain	12.2	11.7	11.3	10.9	10.6	10.3	10.1	9.9	9.8	9.7	9.7	9.6	9.6	9.6	9.6	9.6	9.6
United Kingdom	12.8	12.9	13.0	13.1	13.1	13.1	13.1	13.1	13.1	13.0	13.0	12.9	12.8	12.6	12.5	12.4	12.2
Weighted mean	*12.0*	*11.9*	*11.8*	*11.7*	*11.6*	*11.5*	*11.4*	*11.3*	*11.2*	*11.2*	*11.1*	*11.0*	*10.9*	*10.8*	*10.7*	*10.6*	*10.5*
Other Europe – OECD																	
Austria	11.8	11.8	11.9	11.9	11.9	11.8	11.8	11.8	11.8	11.8	11.7	11.7	11.6	11.5	11.3	11.2	11.1
Czech Republic[3]	13.2	13.0	12.8	12.6	12.5	12.3	12.0	11.6	11.3	11.0	10.7	10.4	10.1	9.8	9.5	9.3	9.2
Finland	12.7	12.6	12.5	12.5	12.5	12.4	12.5	12.4	12.5	12.5	12.5	12.4	12.4	12.3	12.2	12.2	12.1
Iceland	15.8	15.6	15.9	15.7	15.5	15.7	15.6	15.8	15.7	15.5	15.7	15.6	15.5	15.3	15.2	15.1	15.0
Norway	12.3	12.5	12.6	12.8	13.0	13.1	13.3	13.4	13.5	13.6	13.7	13.7	13.7	13.6	13.5	13.5	13.3
Sweden	11.8	12.0	12.2	12.5	12.8	13.0	13.2	13.4	13.5	13.5	13.5	13.5	13.4	13.3	13.2	13.0	12.9
Switzerland	11.4	11.5	11.6	11.7	11.8	11.9	12.0	12.0	12.1	12.1	12.1	12.1	12.0	12.0	11.8	11.7	11.6
Turkey	21.8	21.8	21.8	21.8	21.7	21.6	21.5	21.3	21.1	20.8	20.6	20.3	20.0	19.7	19.4	19.1	18.8
Weighted mean	*17.8*	*17.9*	*17.9*	*17.9*	*18.0*	*17.9*	*17.9*	*17.8*	*17.7*	*17.5*	*17.4*	*17.2*	*17.0*	*16.8*	*16.6*	*16.3*	*16.1*

1. Data for 1994 are United Nations demographic projections. Data for the 1995-2010 period are from the United Nations Populations Division's medium-variant population projections.
2. Australian Bureau of Statistics, 1995, *Series A Population Projections* data. Reference month: June.
3. The data for 1995-2010 are from projection made by the Czech Statistical Office (Projection of the population of the Czech Republic until the year 2020. Czech Statistical Office, Praha, 1995). The data for 1994 are from the demographic yearbook published by the Czech Statistical Office.

Source: United Nations (1994). *World Population Prospects 1950-2010*, and national data submissions.

Table A.10. **Population aged 25-64 that has attained a specific highest education level, 1981-92**[1, 2, 3]

(percentage)

		Men and women				Women			
		0/1/2	3	5	6/7	0/1/2	3	5	6/7
Australia	1989	45	25	21	10	52	12	28	8
	1991	44	25	21	10	52	13	28	8
	1993	48	29	10	13	58	20	10	12
Austria	1989	35	60	×	5	45	50	×	5
	1992	32	61	×	7	42	52	×	6
Belgium	1989	63	20	10	7	65	19	11	4
	1992	55	25	11	9	56	24	14	6
Canada	1981	40	37	12	11	39	40	13	9
	1989	29	41	15	15	28	43	16	13
	1992	29	30	26	15	28	33	26	13
Denmark	1981	50	36	4	11	56	30	5	9
	1988	43	40	7	11	48	35	9	8
	1992	41	40	6	13	46	35	7	13
Finland	1982	55	31	7	8	56	31	6	6
	1989	42	40	8	10	43	42	8	7
	1992	38	43	8	10	38	45	9	9
France	1981	61	29	3	7	65	24	4	6
	1989	52	34	7	7	56	30	8	5
	1992	48	36	6	10	52	33	6	9
Germany (FTFR)	1989	22	61	7	10	31	59	3	7
	1992	18	61	10	12	25	60	7	8
Greece	1981	76	16	2	6	79	16	2	3
Ireland	1989	62	23	7	7	59	27	8	6
	1992	58	25	9	8	54	29	9	7
Italy	1989	74	20	..	6	77	19	..	5
	1992	72	22	..	6	74	21	..	5
Netherlands	1990	45	36	13	6	52	32	13	3
	1992	42	37	×	21	48	34	×	18
New Zealand	1981	67	12	16	5	72	8	17	3
	1990	43	25	22	9	49	17	27	7
	1992	44	33	13	11	49	25	17	9
Norway	1981	34	51	8	7	37	50	9	4
	1989	23	55	12	11	24	56	12	8
	1992	21	54	13	12	22	55	13	10
Portugal	1989	92	2	2	4	91	2	4	3
	1991	86	8	2	5	86	7	2	5
Spain	1981	90	5	..	6	93	3	..	4
	1989	80	10	..	9	83	9	..	8
	1992	77	10	3	10	80	9	2	9
Sweden	1981	51	33	6	10	52	31	7	9
	1992	30	45	13	13	29	45	14	12
Switzerland	1989	21	53	16	10	27	58	9	6
	1992	19	60	13	8	25	63	7	5
Turkey	1992	86	9	..	5	91	6	..	3
United Kingdom	1984	46	40	6	8	52	34	9	5
	1989	37	48	7	9	43	42	8	6
	1992	32	50	8	11	38	45	9	8
United States	1981	20	45	14	22	20	49	13	18
	1989	18	46	12	23	18	49	12	20
	1992	16	54	7	24	16	56	7	21

Notes to Table A.10:

Notes: .. Data not available. × Data included in another category.
1. For the classification by level of education, the ISCED standard is used as applied by national authorities. The points in time for which data is presented differ between countries due to data availability.
2. ISCED refers to the International Standard Classification for Education. This classification, developed principally by UNESCO, is used by countries and international agencies as a means of compiling internationally comparable statistics on education. According to ISCED, educational programmes may be classified as follows (OECD, *Education at a Glance*, 1995d, p. 367):
    – ISCED 0 Education preceding the first level (early childhood education).
    – ISCED 1 Education at the first level (primary).
    – ISCED 2 Education at the lower secondary level.
    – ISCED 3 Education at the upper secondary level.
    – ISCED 5 Education at the tertiary level, first stage, of the type that leads to an award not equivalent to a first university degree.
    – ISCED 6 Education at the tertiary level, first stage, of the type that leads to a university degree or equivalent.
    – ISCED 7 Education at the tertiary level, second stage, of the type that leads to a post-graduate university degree or equivalent.
    – ISCED 9 Education not definable by level.
3. The data are from the Census (1.3.1991).

Definitions are as follows:

Australia
The data do not refer to the age group 25 to 64 but to the group 25 to 69.
1989: 0.6 per cent of total omitted due to missing classification by level.
1993: The classification of education has been made according to the new ABS Classifications of Qualifications, which corresponds better to ISCED than the old classification. In order to enable the use of this classification, data are reported for 1993 instead of 1992. The main difference to the data for 1991 is that some educational programmes have been reclassified from ISCED 5 to ISCED 3. ISCED 0/1/2 reported as ISCED 2. Reference month: February.

Austria
1989: ISCED 5 graduates are reported at ISCED 6/7 level.
1992: Classifications for ISCED levels 3 to 6/7 are based on the highest diploma received; ISCED levels 0,1 and 2 refer to the number of years of schooling obtained. Because of the data structure, ISCED 5 graduates are reported at ISCED 6/7 level.

Belgium
1992: The unemployed are defined as people who are "full-time" unemployed and who receive unemployment benefits. On average 8 per cent of the unemployed are not classified by ISCED level.

Canada
1981, 1989: ISCED 3 was not explicitly coded prior to 1991. Estimates for ISCED 3 were calculated using persons with 12 or more years of school and having not post-secondary credentials for all provinces except Quebec where persons with 11 or more years of schooling were used. This may produce a slight over-estimate for ISCED 3.
1992: Classification is based on the average number of years of schooling for ISCED levels 0/1 and 2. ISCED 3 includes those who report having received a secondary school certificate or diploma. Classification for ISCED levels 5 and 6/7 is based on actually obtained diplomas and degrees. The increase of the ratio of the population with ISCED 5 is partly a result of ongoing efforts to improve the classification of post-secondary educational programmes.

Denmark:
1981, 1988 and 1992: Classification for ISCED 0/1/2 is based on the number of years of schooling obtained; completed compulsory education is classified as ISCED 2. ISCED levels 3, 5, 6 and 7 are based on the highest diploma and degree received. Criteria for the national classification correspond to ISCED, i.e. final qualifications, years of schooling and qualifications required for admission. Data are for the total population and based on actual information from institutions on completion except for a part of the 50-64 year-olds where data are self-reported census survey data. In 1991, a number of studies were classified from ISCED 5 to ISCED 6.

Finland
Adult education and apprenticeship programmes are excluded.
1982, 1989, 1992: ISCED 0/1/2 reported as ISCED 2.

France
Classification is based on diplomas for all levels except ISCED 0/1. ISCED level 3 is very complex as it refers to general, vocational and professional education. The professional programmes at ISCED level 3 lead to three separate diplomas.
1989: 3.2 per cent of total omitted due to missing classification by level.
1992: To avoid underestimation of the number of people in the higher ISCED categories, the number of people with higher qualifications than suggested by their diploma has been estimated. The estimates have been adjusted accordingly. 0.1 per cent of total omitted due to missing classification by level.

Germany
1989: The survey data refer to the population living in the former territory of the Federal Republic of Germany (FTFR). Only obtained diplomas or degrees are considered in classifying persons at ISCED levels 3 to 7.
1992: The survey data refer to the populations living in the territory of the former German Democratic Republic (TFGDR) as well as in the former territory of the Federal Republic of Germany (FTFR). Only obtained diplomas or degrees are considered in classifying persons at ISCED levels 3 to 7. The data include 11.1 per cent non-response, which was proportionally redistributed across the ISCED levels.

Ireland
Classification to ISCED level is made by level of certificate, with the exception of levels 0 and 1, where the number of years of schooling is used. A significant number of people who have completed apprenticeship programmes equivalent to upper secondary education are classified at ISCED level 2. Post-secondary vocational courses are classified at ISCED level 3, and non-university tertiary education at ISCED level 5. The proportion of women with upper secondary education is likely to be over-estimated due to the classification of a predominantly male population with apprenticeship classifications at ISCED 2 level.
1989: 0.7 per cent of total omitted due to missing classification by level.
1992: 0.4 per cent of total omitted due to missing classification by level.

Netherlands
Classification is based on self-reported information, collected by means of a labour force survey, concerning the highest diploma or degree obtained in regular as well as in adult education. Senior secondary vocational education is totally classified at the ISCED 3 level. A new scheme currently under development proposes to classify the 3- and 4-year programmes (MBO) as non-university tertiary education.
1990: 0.2 per cent of total omitted due to missing classification by level.
1992: All post-secondary education is classified as ISCED 6/7.

New Zealand

The data do not refer to the age group 45 to 54 but to the group 45-64 years of age.

1990: 0.7 per cent of total omitted due to missing classification by level.

1992: 1.5 per cent of total omitted due to missing classification by level.

Norway

1989: 1.8 per cent of total omitted due to missing classification by level.

1992: Persons for whom the level of educational attainment is unknown have been allocated to ISCED 0/1. The figures given for these categories are therefore equivalent to "unknown".

Portugal

1991: One per cent or less of the total is not classified by level. Missing data were proportionally redistributed.

Spain

1981: ISCED 5/6/7 reported as ISCED 6/7. ISCED 5 is of little significance.

1989: ISCED 5/6/7 reported as ISCED 6/7. ISCED 5 is of little significance.

1992: ISCED 5/6/7 reported as ISCED 6/7. In this year the programmes of *"Formación Profesional de Segundo Grado"* have been reclassified from ISCED 3 to ISCED 5.

Sweden

1992: The data are based on the national register of population and educational attainment, which contains information about issued certificates at ISCED levels 5 and 6/7. Around 20 per cent of the classifications at level 5 and 10 per cent at level 6/7 are based on self-reported information. Until 1968, persons who had passed an examination of a general programme at ISCED level 3 were awarded a diploma. The classification of persons educated at a later date is not based on diplomas but on the completion of ISCED levels 2 and 3. ISCED 0/1/2 reported as ISCED 2. 4.9 per cent of total omitted due to missing classification by level.

Switzerland

1989: 5.5 per cent of total omitted due to missing classification by level.

1992: Apprentices have been defined as being in full-time education. In previous years they were defined as full-time employed. 1.4 per cent of total omitted due to missing classification by level.

Turkey

1992: Classification is based on latest diploma or degree obtained. ISCED level 0 is excluded. The uneven gender distribution of the total population may to some extent be due to this.

United Kingdom

Data on females are based on the age group 55-59 instead of 55-64 and on the age group 25-59 instead of 25-64.

1989: 1.0 per cent of total omitted due to missing classification by level.

1992: ISCED level 3 (defined as beginning at about 14 to 15 years of age and lasting about 3 years) is interpreted for the United Kingdom as covering all persons with O level or A level examination passes, or their equivalent. Most vocational qualifications are included in ISCED level 3. 0.1 per cent of total omitted due to missing classification by level.

United States

1992: In 1992, the educational attainment question in the Current Populations Survey was changed. ISCED 3 now excludes a small number of individuals who have completed grade 12 but did not receive a diploma or its equivalent. In addition, ISCED 3 includes a large number of people with some tertiary education but no credential. ISCED 5 only includes individuals who received an Associate degree, a credential awarded in programmes normally requiring two years of full-time study. Compared to statistics published in earlier editions of *Education at a Glance* (OECD), the change will increase the percentage of the population whose highest educational attainment is ISCED 3 and will decrease the percentage whose highest educational attainment is ISCED 5.

Sources are as follows:

Australia

1989: OECD Education Database.

1991: Database on labour force status and educational attainment, February 1991.

1993: Australian Bureau of Statistics, *Labour Force Status and Educational Attainment in Australia.*

Austria

1989: Micro-census of the Austrian Central Statistics Office, averages for 1989.

1992: Micro-census of the Austrian Central Statistics Office, averages for 1992.

Belgium

1989: OECD Education Database.

1992: Labour Force Survey 1992. The unemployment register in April 1992 has been used for data on the number of unemployed.

Canada

1981: OECD Education Database.

1989: OECD Education Database.

1992: Canadian Labour Force Survey.

Denmark

1981, 1988 and 1992: Statistical register of the labour force and register of statistics on unemployment.

Finland

1982: OECD Education Database.

1989: OECD Education Database.

1992: The Register of Completed Educational Programmes and Degrees. Labour Force Survey 1992.

France

1981: OECD Education Database.

1989: OECD Education Database.

1992: Labour Force Survey, March 1992.

Germany

1989: OECD Education Database.

1992: Labour Force Survey, 1992.

Greece
1981: OECD Education Database.

Ireland
1989: OECD Education Database.
1992: Labour Force Survey, 1992.

Italy
1989: OECD Education Database.
1992: Labour Force Survey, 1992.

Netherlands
1990: OECD Education Database.
1992: Labour Force Survey, 1992.

New Zealand
1981: OECD Education Database.
1990: OECD Education Database.
1992: Household Labour Force Survey, 1992.

Norway
1981: OECD Education Database.
1989: OECD Education Database.
1992: Labour Force Survey, 1992.

Portugal
1989: OECD Education Database. Average figure from four quarterly labour force surveys conducted in 1991.

Spain
1981: Labour Force Survey, 1981.
1989: Labour Force Survey, 1989.
1992: Labour Force Survey, 1992.

Sweden
1981: OECD Education Database.
1992: The Register of Educational Attainment for the Population. Labour Force Survey, 1992.

Switzerland
1989: OECD Education Database.
1992: Labour Force Survey, 1992.

Turkey
1992: Household Labour Force Survey, 1992.

United Kingdom
1984: OECD Education Database.
1989: OECD Education Database.
1992: Labour Force Survey, 1992.

United States
1981: OECD Education Database.
1989: OECD Education Database.
1992: Current Population Survey, March 1992.

Table A.11. **Average annual change in educational attainment for the population aged 25 to 64, 1981-92[1, 2]**

(percentage)

	Men and women				Women			
	0/1/2	3	5	6/7	0/1/2	3	5	6/7
Canada								
Difference 1981-92	−11.1	−7.1	14.5	3.6	−10.9	−6.9	13.1	4.7
Average annual change	*−1.0*	*−0.6*	*1.3*	*0.3*	*−1.0*	*−0.6*	*1.2*	*0.4*
Denmark								
Difference 1981-92	−8.6	4.2	1.7	2.8	−10.3	4.8	2.2	3.4
Average annual change	*−0.8*	*0.4*	*0.2*	*0.3*	*−0.9*	*0.4*	*0.2*	*0.3*
Finland								
Difference 1982-92	−16.3	11.8	1.6	2.8	−18.3	13.1	2.1	3.1
Average annual change	*−1.6*	*1.2*	*0.2*	*0.3*	*−1.8*	*1.3*	*0.2*	*0.3*
France								
Difference 1981-92	−12.8	7.8	2.2	2.8	−13.8	8.8	2.2	2.8
Average annual change	*−1.2*	*0.7*	*0.2*	*0.3*	*−1.3*	*0.8*	*0.2*	*0.3*
New Zealand								
Difference 1981-92	−23.4	20.8	−3.7	6.3	−23.0	17.3	0.0	5.7
Average annual change	*−2.1*	*1.9*	*−0.3*	*0.6*	*−2.1*	*1.6*	*0.0*	*0.5*
Norway								
Difference 1981-92	−12.5	2.8	4.4	5.2	−14.9	5.0	4.0	5.9
Average annual change	*−1.1*	*0.3*	*0.4*	*0.5*	*−1.4*	*0.5*	*0.4*	*0.5*
Spain								
Difference 1981-92	−12.6	5.2	3.0	4.4	−13.0	5.7	2.0	5.2
Average annual change	*−1.1*	*0.5*	*0.3*	*0.4*	*−1.2*	*0.5*	*0.2*	*0.5*
Sweden								
Difference 1981-92	−21.0	11.8	6.7	2.5	−24.0	14.1	7.1	2.8
Average annual change	*−1.9*	*1.1*	*0.6*	*0.2*	*−2.2*	*1.3*	*0.6*	*0.3*
United Kingdom								
Difference 1984-92	−13.7	9.9	1.3	2.5	−14.5	11.2	0.7	2.5
Average annual change	*−1.7*	*1.2*	*0.2*	*0.3*	*−1.8*	*1.4*	*0.1*	*0.3*
United States								
Difference 1981-92	−3.7	9.2	−7.0	1.7	−3.9	6.6	−6.1	3.4
Average annual change	*−0.3*	*0.8*	*−0.6*	*0.2*	*−0.4*	*0.6*	*−0.6*	*0.3*

1. This table shows the estimated average annual changes in population shares for below upper secondary education, for upper secondary education, for non-university tertiary education, and for university tertiary education. Included are all persons in the age group 25-64. Annual changes have been calculated over the period indicated. For countries for which the available data covered less than 5 years, no annual changes were calculated.
2. For the definitions of the education levels, see note 2 in Annex Table A.10.

Source: See Annex Table A.10.

Table A.12. **Proportion of the population in four age groups that had attained at least upper secondary education, 1992**

(percentage)

	25 to 34	35 to 44	45 to 54	55 to 64
North America				
Canada	81	78	65	49
United States	86	88	83	73
Pacific Area				
Australia[1]	57	56	51	42
New Zealand	60	58	55	49
European Community				
Belgium	60	51	38	24
Denmark[2]	67	61	58	44
France	67	57	47	29
Germany	89	87	81	69
Ireland	56	44	35	25
Italy	42	34	21	12
Netherlands	68	61	52	42
Portugal[3]	21	17	10	7
Spain	41	24	14	8
United Kingdom	81	71	62	51
Other Europe – OECD				
Austria	79	71	65	50
Finland	82	69	52	31
Norway	88	83	75	61
Sweden	85	78	63	46
Switzerland	87	84	77	70
Turkey	21	14	9	5
Weighted mean OECD	*72*	*69*	*60*	*48*

1. 1993.
2. Of the 25- to 34-year-olds a relatively large number are still enrolled in education. Data may therefore understate the true values.
3. 1991.
Source: OECD Education Database; see Annex Table A.10.

Table A.13. **Educational attainment of women and men, aged 25-34 and 55-64, 1992[1]**

(percentage differences)

	Age 25-34		Age 55-64		Difference (in %)[1]	
	Men	Women	Men	Women	Age 25-34	Age 55-64
North America						
Canada	3.9	4.0	3.0	2.7	1.4	−9.4
United States	3.8	3.8	3.5	3.2	1.3	−7.9
Pacific Area						
Australia[2]	3.3	3.1	2.9	2.6	−4.4	−11.4
New Zealand	3.0	3.0	2.6	2.3	−2.3	−10.3
European Community						
Belgium	3.2	3.2	2.1	1.8	1.8	−16.1
Denmark	3.2	3.3	3.0	2.7	2.0	−10.0
France	3.3	3.3	2.1	1.7	0.1	−15.3
Germany	3.5	3.4	3.5	2.7	−4.3	−21.7
Ireland	2.9	3.0	2.0	2.0	3.8	0.0
Italy	2.6	2.6	1.7	1.4	−0.1	−14.7
Netherlands	3.4	3.4	2.9	2.3	−2.2	−21.9
Portugal[3]	1.7	1.9	1.3	1.2	9.4	−9.3
Spain	2.8	2.9	1.5	1.3	2.8	−15.4
United Kingdom	3.5	3.3	3.0	2.7	−3.6	−10.1
Other Europe – OECD						
Austria	3.1	3.0	2.8	2.4	−3.2	−13.6
Finland	3.4	3.4	2.7	2.6	6.6	−5.1
Norway	3.6	3.7	3.1	2.8	2.1	−10.1
Sweden	3.5	3.6	3.0	2.9	1.0	−2.8
Switzerland	3.7	3.2	3.5	2.8	−12.5	−19.3
Turkey	1.9	1.5	1.3	1.1	−21.0	−13.6

1. The data indicate the difference in the "expected" level of educational attainment between men and women in the age group 25-34 and 55-64 years of age. The differences are expressed in percentage points. The underlying metric for the calculation of the expected level of educational attainment is the ISCED level obtained. ISCED level 0/1 is assigned a scale value of 1, ISCED level 5/6/7 is assigned a scale value of 6, and ISCED level 6/7 is assigned a scale value of 6.5.
2. 1993.
3. 1991.
Source: See Annex Table A.10.

Table A.14. **Labour force participation rate by level of education for persons between 25 and 64 years of age, 1981-92[1]**

		Men and women				Women			
		Primary or less	Lower secondary	Upper secondary	Tertiary	Primary or less	Lower secondary	Upper secondary	Tertiary
North America									
Canada	1981	60.4	70.0	77.1	85.6	37.7	50.4	62.4	73.1
	1989	56.3	71.2	80.7	88.5	38.1	56.5	70.8	81.9
	1992	52.0	68.8	79.9	87.0	37.3	55.4	72.0	81.2
United States	1981	53.3	62.8	73.6	82.9	34.5	46.4	61.3	71.1
	1989	55.2	64.4	78.5	87.1	38.5	50.3	69.2	79.3
	1992	53.9	64.2	79.7	88.1	38.2	49.7	70.7	81.9
Pacific Area									
Australia	1989	51.9	67.1	82.5	79.9	34.6	52.8	58.9	70.3
	1991	48.1	62.9	79.8	79.8	34.4	50.0	59.5	71.6
	1993	×	65.1	80.2	86.3	×	53.4	62.2	79.0
New Zealand	1981	67.4	74.0	82.1	81.9	47.3	57.3	55.8	65.9
	1990	63.8	76.8	78.9	81.6	51.9	67.2	61.3	73.2
	1992	63.4	77.2	79.1	84.8	50.3	68.8	65.8	77.6
European Community									
Belgium	1989	41.1	68.9	78.7	88.5	26.0	49.9	66.2	82.0
	1992	45.8	67.1	78.8	86.9	31.2	50.3	67.5	81.3
Denmark	1981	. .	73.3	87.8	91.8	. .	64.6	79.9	87.9
	1988	. .	73.9	90.2	94.2	. .	68.4	87.3	92.1
	1992	. .	73.0	88.9	93.6	. .	68.3	86.6	92.4
France	1981	60.4	75.2	84.3	88.2	45.3	60.1	70.6	80.7
	1989	56.1	75.1	83.8	89.2	45.8	62.3	73.3	83.8
	1992	55.1	76.9	83.5	87.8	45.3	65.6	74.9	83.1
Germany	1989	. .	50.2	73.4	87.9	. .	38.4	59.8	74.5
	1992	. .	57.0	76.7	88.3	. .	46.1	67.3	81.8
Ireland	1989	51.8	63.6	67.8	84.6	20.5	32.6	48.7	72.4
	1992	50.5	65.5	70.7	84.9	22.8	36.9	54.3	75.0
Italy	1989	46.9	71.3	80.1	90.6	26.7	48.6	68.5	86.2
	1992	45.6	71.7	79.8	90.7	26.0	50.2	69.3	86.4
Netherlands	1990	45.5	61.3	76.1	85.4	27.9	43.0	60.6	75.8
	1992	45.1	62.1	77.0	85.4	28.8	44.8	63.2	77.4
Portugal	1989	69.9	72.4	72.6	72.7	59.8	65.5	65.7	65.7
	1991	63.3	82.1	88.4	94.2	46.0	73.7	85.2	93.3
Spain	1981	54.5	69.7	78.0	85.1	24.1	42.9	47.1	74.8
	1989	53.2	73.4	81.8	86.5	28.1	50.3	64.8	81.4
	1992	53.4	73.6	80.2	87.0	30.5	52.8	65.9	81.0
United Kingdom	1984	. .	69.6	82.2	86.1	. .	58.0	66.8	76.1
	1989	. .	68.7	83.5	88.7	. .	59.8	72.3	81.7
	1992	. .	64.5	82.1	87.7	. .	54.2	71.4	80.4
Other Europe – OECD									
Austria	1989	. .	53.0	74.6	89.2	. .	41.1	58.2	84.0
	1992	. .	55.7	76.2	89.5	. .	45.0	63.2	83.2
Finland	1982	×	76.9	88.2	91.6	×	71.5	83.5	86.4
	1989	×	71.1	87.2	90.7	×	67.6	84.0	87.0
	1992	×	69.8	84.7	89.1	×	66.4	80.1	86.0
Norway	1981	58.1	68.8	81.9	89.8	45.3	54.9	69.2	83.2
	1989	. .	69.0	84.2	92.7	. .	57.9	76.6	89.3
	1992	. .	66.4	83.2	91.0	. .	56.4	76.7	87.7
Sweden	1981	77.0	85.3	90.0	93.0	67.7	78.4	84.5	91.1
	1989	. .	84.6	93.2	95.7	. .	78.8	91.0	94.9
	1992	×	86.2	93.0	94.8	×	81.0	91.2	94.0
Switzerland	1989	. .	70.6	80.3	90.1	. .	57.8	66.2	75.6
	1991	. .	72.3	81.3	91.7	. .	61.2	68.2	76.8
	1992	. .	71.7	82.2	92.2	. .	61.3	70.2	80.2
Turkey	1992	57.3	70.3	74.7	90.2	31.9	21.0	41.3	82.2

Notes: . . Data not available. × Data included in another category.
1. The labour force participation rate is calculated as the percentage of the population that belongs to the labour force. The labour force is defined in accordance with *OECD Labour Force Statistics*.
Source: See Annex Table A.10.

Table A.15. **Number of full-time students in all levels (except pre-primary), 1975-92**[1, 2, 3]

(per 100 persons in the population aged 5-29)

	Total enrolment									
	1975	1980	1985	1986	1987	1988	1989	1990	1991	1992
North America										
Canada	54.5	49.2	52.7	53.2	53.7	54.3	54.9	55.6	56.9	58.0
United States	55.6	51.7	50.2	50.3	50.7	51.3	51.7	52.6	53.1	54.2
Pacific Area										
Australia	..	..	..	52.1	52.5	53.0	53.1	..	53.9	..
Japan	47.6	53.7	..	..	..	..	57.6	57.1	56.5	55.7
New Zealand	55.1	55.6	50.9	50.9	51.4	51.6	52.7	53.5	54.6	55.6
European Community										
Belgium	..	..	51.5	52.1	51.8	51.3	52.3	52.6	52.9	53.9
Denmark	53.2	54.8	55.6	55.6	55.7	55.6	55.5	55.2	54.8	54.9
France	51.3	52.6	55.1	55.2	55.4	56.1	56.9	57.1	57.7	58.4
Germany (FTFR)	51.3	52.6	53.0	51.9	50.9	50.8	50.4	49.6	49.8	50.3
Greece	..	..	..	..	..	..	..	..	..	50.0
Ireland	51.1	50.0	52.4	52.8	53.3	54.1	55.0	55.9	56.1	56.4
Italy	50.8	50.8	48.4	47.8	47.1	47.0	48.3	48.9	48.4	50.0
Luxembourg	..	..	..	40.7	40.4	41.2	40.7	..	..	..
Netherlands	51.0	52.6	52.3	52.5	52.1	51.8	51.2	51.1	51.2	54.4
Portugal	..	..	..	..	..	45.6	..	..	44.4	..
Spain	..	..	53.9	54.6	55.0	55.4	55.9	56.4	56.6	56.9
United Kingdom	..	..	48.5	47.9	47.2	46.8	51.0	47.1	48.0	51.9
Other Europe – OECD										
Austria	40.5	43.1	49.2	49.7	49.2	49.1	49.1	49.4	49.1	50.5
Finland	49.2	51.6	53.2	53.8	54.6	55.5	56.8	58.3	60.4	60.8
Norway	49.5	51.5	52.6	51.9	51.4	50.7	49.7	53.6	54.2	54.6
Sweden	..	51.2	52.2	51.5	50.9	50.7	50.3	49.8	49.7	50.2
Switzerland	41.2	42.8	49.4	48.7	48.2	47.8	47.8	48.0	48.1	49.1
Turkey	36.1	34.2	37.7	31.3	37.3	38.1	38.2	38.8	39.3	39.7

Note: .. Data not available.

1. Due to the revision of the *OECD Education Statistics* questionnaire in 1985 there may be some differences in coverage prior to that date.
2. Students enrolled in primary, secondary or tertiary education are counted regardless of their ages. Students enrolled in early childhood education are excluded, even if they are 5 years or older.
3. Enrolment in public and private institutions.

Source: OECD Education Database.

Table A.16. **Schooling expectancy for a 5-year-old child[1], 1985-94[2]**

(head counts)

	1985	1986	1987	1988	1989	1990	1991	1992	1994
North America									
Canada	. .	. .	. .	. .	. .	. .	. .	. .	17.1
United States	15.0	15.1	15.2	15.4	15.3	15.5	15.5	15.6	15.6
Pacific Area									
Australia	. .	. .	. .	. .	. .	. .	15.2	. .	15.9
New Zealand	. .	. .	. .	14.4	. .	14.8	15.6	15.1	15.8
European Community									
Belgium	. .	. .	. .	. .	. .	. .	. .	16.5	16.9
Denmark	14.5	14.6	14.7	14.7	14.8	14.8	14.9	15.6	16.2
France	14.8	14.9	15.0	15.1	15.4	15.5	15.6	15.9	16.2
Germany (FTFR)[3]	15.6	15.6	15.6	. .	. .	. .	. .	15.9	16.4
Greece	. .	. .	. .	. .	. .	. .	. .	13.7	13.9
Ireland	. .	. .	. .	. .	. .	. .	. .	14.8	15.1
Luxembourg	. .	13.0	13.1	13.3	13.1	. .	. .	. .	. .
Netherlands	15.2	15.2	15.3	15.4	15.5	15.5	15.7	16.2	16.8
Portugal	. .	. .	. .	. .	. .	. .	13.1	. .	. .
Spain	. .	. .	. .	. .	. .	. .	. .	. .	16.1
United Kingdom	14.8	15.2	14.9	14.9	14.1	15.3	15.3	14.8	14.8
Other Europe – OECD									
Austria	. .	. .	. .	. .	. .	. .	. .	. .	14.9
Czech Republic	. .	. .	13.9	14.0	13.8	13.8	13.7	13.6	13.7
Finland	14.0	. .	. .	. .	. .	14.8	. .	15.4	15.9
Norway	14.0	14.1	14.2	14.3	14.5	15.1	15.4	15.7	16.2
Sweden	13.4	13.5	13.4	13.4	13.4	13.4	13.4	15.1	15.7
Switzerland	14.3	14.4	14.4	14.5	14.6	14.7	14.8	15.2	15.3
Turkey	. .	. .	. .	. .	6.2	6.8	8.3	8.3	8.9

Note: . . Data not available.

1. The expectation of participation is obtained by adding the net enrolment rates for each year of age from 5 to 29 and dividing the result by 100. The indicator therefore presents the hypothetical duration of schooling for a 5-year-old child, assuming a constant length of studies during the ensuing years. Expectancy rates are calculated using head counts. Note that the results would be slightly affected if part-time schooling was not taken into account: the loss would be half a year or more for New Zealand, Norway, the United Kingdom and the United States.
2. No data available for 1993.
3. 1994 covers the whole of Germany.
Source: OECD Education Database.

Table A.17. **Net rates of participation in full-time secondary education, 1985[1]**

(percentage of year group)

					Age					
	14	15	16	17	18	19	20	21	22	23
North America										
Canada	97.4	97.8	93.8	69.0	31.0	9.4	7.3	–	–	–
United States	100.9	91.0	89.6	79.3	18.9	3.4	1.8	0.5	0.6	0.2
Pacific Area										
Australia	104.7	77.5	13.9	1.4	0.5	0.7	–	–	–	–
Japan	98.6	95.4	92.2	94.2	..	..	..	..	..	..
New Zealand	101.7	89.1	67.6	32.9	6.4	2.2	0.1	–	–	–
European Community										
Belgium	98.2	96.6	90.0	80.9	40.4	17.9	9.5	2.3	0.3	0.2
Denmark	99.6	98.1	89.5	73.9	64.9	44.8	24.5	12.8	7.0	4.2
France	94.8	94.9	89.5	77.2	40.2	15.0	2.8	0.4	0.2	0.1
Germany (FTFR)	94.8	95.4	95.8	92.1	76.4	45.5	21.7	10.3	10.9	1.0
Ireland	95.0	90.7	79.0	57.2	21.0	3.7	3.6	1.5	..	..
Italy	80.5	63.2	52.2	44.4	33.8	10.2	3.6	1.5	0.8	0.7
Luxembourg										
Netherlands	98.3	98.4	92.7	77.4	50.8	26.4	12.4	5.1	2.1	0.8
Portugal	42.2	40.3	39.6	35.4	28.5	21.8	19.7	8.7	5.9	5.2
Spain	86.2	73.5	58.0	50.7	26.6	14.0	6.2	5.3	4.3	3.3
United Kingdom	99.2	99.0	48.7	30.9	8.7	2.3	1.1	0.6	0.5	0.3
Other Europe – OECD										
Austria	94.8	88.2	85.5	78.0	42.9	13.6	4.8	2.6	1.8	1.9
Finland	94.8	95.9	88.1	81.6	65.3	21.9	13.8	13.8	10.7	7.0
Norway	99.4	99.9	83.8	75.3	60.2	22.9	11.2	8.2	6.1	4.2
Sweden	98.6	94.8	90.3	82.3	45.9	10.2	4.6	3.5	2.8	2.5
Switzerland	93.3	92.4	84.2	82.2	73.3	49.2	21.3	8.7	4.1	2.6
Turkey	40.2	31.6	29.0	13.1	8.9	4.6	2.1	1.3	0.0	0.0

Notes: .. Data not available. – Magnitude is either negligible or zero.
1. For the methodology for the calculation of net enrolment rates see Table 1.10.
Source: OECD Education Database.

Table A.18. **Net rates of participation[1] in full-time secondary education, 14-23 year-olds, 1994**

(percentage of year group)

	Age									
	14	15	16	17	18	19	20	21	22	23
North America										
Canada	96.5	96.2	93.8	72.0	40.1	16.2	14.6	..	..	..
United States	96.8	96.8	95.0	82.9	26.3	7.1	1.4	0.8	0.4	0.2
Mexico	56.2	46.5	38.9	29.9	17.8	8.5	5.2	3.3	2.2	1.6
Pacific Area										
Australia	98.0	92.7	81.5	61.6	15.7	4.5	4.4	0.9	0.6	0.6
Japan	100.0	98.5	95.1	91.9	1.3	–	–	–	–	–
New Zealand	99.7	100.0	89.9	70.8	26.6	8.8	4.2	2.6	1.9	1.7
European Community										
Belgium	98.9	100.7	100.5	97.1	52.0	27.0	14.1	3.4	1.3	0.5
Denmark	94.7	98.0	93.7	78.6	62.6	43.7	27.2	16.8	10.5	6.8
France	98.3	96.8	96.0	90.0	60.9	34.1	14.7	4.8	1.7	0.4
Germany	98.3	97.7	95.8	91.2	81.9	57.3	31.2	15.9	21.2	2.1
Greece	85.7	80.9	81.6	57.0	17.5	8.4	6.1	3.7	2.6	1.6
Ireland	96.9	93.7	92.2	74.8	34.3	11.0	3.9	..	..	–
Netherlands	98.9	98.6	96.8	87.2	64.7	41.8	25.8	14.4	8.1	4.8
Spain	100.0	93.9	81.8	74.3	42.9	25.2	19.1	12.0	7.7	3.7
United Kingdom	98.0	94.9	73.0	57.3	18.4	5.7	2.7	1.8	1.4	1.1
Other Europe - OECD										
Austria	98.8	95.0	92.2	86.4	55.5	21.5	7.8	4.1	1.2	1.0
Czech Republic	99.7	99.8	88.1	62.5	24.9	3.6	0.9	0.4	–	–
Finland	99.6	99.6	95.9	91.3	80.3	23.9	17.5	16.1	13.6	9.1
Norway	98.9	99.2	93.7	89.7	81.4	34.6	19.9	13.9	10.3	7.1
Sweden	99.4	96.6	96.2	95.5	82.2	21.0	5.9	2.7	2.2	1.7
Switzerland	97.9	95.9	86.3	82.1	74.5	51.5	22.3	8.6	4.4	2.7

Notes: .. Data not available. – Magnitude is either nil or negligeable.
1. For the methodology for the calculation of net enrolment rates see Table 1.10. It should be noted that the enrolment rates in this table refer only to secondary education. There are additional enrolments in tertiary education especially at ages not matching the typical age range for secondary education enrolment. For net enrolment rates in tertiary education, see Table 1.10.
Source: OECD Education Database.

Table A.19. **Number of full-time students in upper secondary education, 1975-92**[1, 2, 3]

(per 100 persons in the population aged 5-29)

	1975	1980	1985	1986	1987	1988	1989	1990	1991	1992
North America										
Canada	12.5	11.2	10.6	10.6	10.6	10.8	10.8	10.9	11.1	11.6
United States	7.3	7.2	10.3	10.4	10.5	10.4	10.0	9.7	9.6	9.5
Pacific Area										
Australia	6.9	. .	6.5	6.8	7.4	7.9	7.9	. .	8.3	ǀ 6.2
Japan	9.7	10.5	12.0	12.2	12.4	12.8	13.2	13.5	13.5	13.2
New Zealand	6.6	7.8	7.5	7.8	8.3	8.8	9.3	9.5	9.9	10.4
European Community										
Belgium	. .	. .	. .	. .	. .	. .	. .	. .	15.3	15.4
Denmark	7.4	10.5	12.1	12.3	12.6	12.7	12.9	12.8	12.8	13.0
France	8.7	9.8	9.6	9.9	10.2	10.8	11.6	12.0	12.3	12.3
Germany (FTFR)	8.8	10.9	15.2	15.3	14.9	14.6	13.9	13.0	12.3	12.0
Greece	6.8	8.1	. .	. .	. .	. .	. .	. .	. .	11.2
Ireland	6.1	6.6	8.5	8.7	8.9	9.2	9.5	10.1	10.2	10.5
Italy	10.0	11.3	11.8	12.1	12.5	12.9	14.6	15.5	15.3	16.0
Luxembourg	8.3	8.7	. .	10.9	10.8	10.7	10.0	. .	. .	. .
Netherlands	5.1	6.7	8.7	9.1	9.3	9.4	9.4	9.3	9.1	ǀ 12.7
Portugal	. .	. .	5.4	5.0	5.5	6.1	. .	. .	7.7	. .
Spain	9.0	12.1	12.4	12.9	13.2	14.1	14.8	15.7	16.4	17.2
United Kingdom	11.2	12.7	12.7	12.6	12.5	12.2	16.2	11.7	11.7	12.7
Other Europe – OECD										
Austria	8.0	9.3	16.4	16.5	16.1	15.7	15.1	15.1	14.6	14.5
Finland	9.4	12.2	13.2	13.0	12.9	12.9	12.8	13.2	14.3	14.4
Norway	9.2	10.4	12.4	12.7	12.3	12.2	12.4	14.7	15.0	15.1
Sweden	7.4	9.2	11.1	10.7	10.4	10.4	10.5	10.4	10.5	10.7
Switzerland	3.2	4.2	13.9	13.8	13.8	13.6	13.5	13.2	12.8	ǀ 11.7
Turkey	3.3	3.7	3.8	3.9	4.1	4.3	4.4	4.6	4.9	5.4

Notes: . . Data not available. Vertical bars indicate a break in the series.
1. Due to the revision of the OECD Education Statistics questionnaire in 1985 there may be some differences in coverage prior to that date.
2. Students enrolled in primary, secondary or tertiary education are counted regardless of their ages. Students enrolled at the pre-primary level of education are excluded, even if they are 5 years or older.
3. Enrolment in public and private institutions.
Source: OECD Education Database.

Table A.20. **Number of full-time students in tertiary education, 1975-92**[1, 2, 3]

(per 100 persons in the population aged 5-29)

	1975	1980	1985	1986	1987	1988	1989	1990	1991	1992
North America										
Canada	6.7	5.9	8.6	8.9	9.0	9.1	9.2	9.3	9.8	10.1
United States	6.6	7.0	7.4	7.4	7.5	7.7	7.9	8.2	8.3	8.7
Pacific Area										
Australia	4.5	5.1	..	3.9	4.3	4.7	4.9	..	5.6	6.9
Japan	4.3	4.7	..	6.0	6.2	6.5	6.8	7.1	7.4	7.8
New Zealand	2.5	2.9	3.0	3.2	3.5	3.9	4.5	4.8	5.3	5.9
European Community										
Belgium	4.2	5.1	6.0	6.2	6.3	6.5	6.7	7.1	7.3	7.5
Denmark[4]	6.1	6.5	6.8	7.0	7.1	7.4	7.7	8.2	8.6	9.4
France	4.9	4.9	6.4	6.6	6.6	6.8	7.2	7.7	8.3	9.0
Germany (FTFR)	3.6	4.2	7.1	7.3	7.5	7.8	8.1	8.2	8.5	8.9
Greece	3.4	3.4	..	..	..	..	..	..	..	4.9
Ireland	2.4	2.7	3.3	3.5	3.6	3.8	4.1	4.4	4.6	5.1
Italy	4.6	5.2	5.5	5.6	5.4	5.8	6.2	6.6	7.1	7.8
Luxembourg	..	..	..	0.7	0.7	0.8	0.8	..	..	..
Netherlands	4.9	6.2	5.5	5.6	5.7	6.1	6.2	6.5	6.9	7.4
Portugal	0.3	0.3	3.0	2.8	2.8	2.9	..	..	4.0	..
Spain	3.7	4.4	5.4	5.9	6.2	6.7	7.1	7.5	8.0	8.6
United Kingdom	2.5	3.2	2.9	2.9	3.0	3.0	3.2	3.4	3.7	4.2
Other Europe – OECD										
Austria[5]	3.2	3.4	6.5	6.9	7.2	7.6	7.9	8.4	8.7	9.3
Finland	5.0	6.2	7.3	7.7	8.1	8.6	9.2	9.8	10.4	10.4
Norway	3.8	3.8	4.9	4.7	5.2	5.4	5.0	6.9	7.6	8.2
Sweden	5.6	6.2	6.5	6.4	6.4	6.5	6.6	6.7	7.0	7.5
Switzerland	3.1	3.6	4.0	4.1	4.3	4.4	4.6	4.7	4.9	5.0
Turkey	1.5	1.0	1.6	1.7	1.8	1.9	2.1	2.4	2.6	2.8

Note: .. Data not available.
1. Due to the revision of the *OECD Education Statistics* questionnaire in 1985 there may be some differences in coverage prior to that date.
2. Students enrolled are counted regardless of their ages.
3. Enrolment in public and private institutions.
4. Enrolment at October 1st, 1991 and 1992.
5. The number of students at ISCED level 6/7 is slightly overestimated due to multiple counts.
Source: OECD Education Database.

Table A.21. **Employees who received training**[1] **and its duration, 1994**

(percentage)

	Received training	Length of training			
		1 week	1-4 weeks	1-6 months	> 6 months
Canada	38	32	12	24	33
Netherlands	38	18	8	35	39
Poland	15	30	23	29	18
Sweden	43	49	33	13	6
Switzerland	42	25	17	28	30
United States	42	41	15	25	20

1. Percentage of the employed population. Since the previous six months.
Sources: OECD and Statistics Canada (1995).

Table A.22. **Sweden: number of employees who received training by age, 1982-94** [1]

(percentage of the employed population)

Age group	1982	1986	1987	1989	1990	1992	1993	1994
16-24	11	16	20	26	27	23	14	23
25-34	17	24	27	32	32	34	22	37
35-44	18	27	29	38	38	41	27	43
45-54	17	23	28	34	37	37	25	44
55-64	11	26	18	24	27	30	20	36
Total	15	22	25	31	33	34	23	38

1. Refers to the first six months of the year.
Source: Statistics Sweden, Personalutbildningsregistret.

Table A.23. **United Kingdom: participation in job-related training** [1] **by age, 1984-90**

(percentage of the employed population) [2]

Age group	1984	1986	1987	1988	1989	1990
16-19	20.2	22.3	21.3	23.0	22.9	25.2
20-24	13.5	16.1	16.8	18.7	19.3	20.5
25-29	11.4	13.5	13.9	15.9	16.7	17.7
30-39	9.3	10.9	12.6	13.9	15.3	15.8
40-49	6.2	7.4	8.9	10.5	12.1	13.5
50-59	1.5	4.3	4.9	6.0	7.5	8.3
60-64 [3]	2.0	2.3	1.9	2.7	3.2	4.1
Total	9.1	10.8	11.7	13.3	14.4	15.4

1. "Training" includes both on-the-job and off-the-job training; four-week reference period.
2. Excluding the self-employed and people on government schemes.
3. Men only.
Source: Labour Force Survey, 1984; 1986-90 (preliminary estimates for 1990).

Table A.24. **Denmark: students in public adult education and continuing vocational training, 1980-93**

(full-time equivalents enrolments, head counts)

	1980	1981	1982	1983	1984	1985	1986	1987	1988	1989	1990	1991	1992	1993
General programmes	22 300	22 600	22 800	23 300	23 100	23 300	22 600	22 000	23 200	23 100	24 500	24 800	24 700	24 500
Folk high school	5 400	5 900	6 400	6 600	6 600	6 400	6 000	5 900	6 000	6 300	6 400	6 600	6 800	6 900
"Day" high school	100	200	400	500	600	700	1 000	1 200	1 800	2 400	3 000	3 600	4 900	6 300
Immigrant education	..	..	..	..	..	..	..	5 200	5 300	5 200	5 200	5 700	5 700	5 200
Open University	15 600	15 700	15 800	16 000	16 600	17 100	18 300	19 000	19 100	19 200	22 900	21 400	21 500	21 200
Adult vocational training/short programmes	7 300	8 600	9 800	9 400	9 000	9 000	8 800	8 600	8 800	8 300	7 800	7 900	8 400	9 200
Adult vocational training/long programmes	..	..	..	..	..	100	500	700	600	400	500	600	400	400
Pre-vocational training	2 600	2 600	2 600	2 600	2 700	2 400	1 800	1 700	1 600	1 700	1 800	1 800	1 600	1 600
Leisure-time education	18 800	19 000	20 700	21 500	21 600	21 800	21 900	20 900	20 900	21 500	21 700	21 900	23 100	24 300
Other	6 300	6 500	6 800	7 000	7 000	7 000	7 000	7 400	7 600	7 700	8 200	8 200	8 500	8 700
Total of above	78 400	81 100	85 300	86 900	87 200	87 800	87 900	92 600	94 900	95 800	102 000	102 500	105 600	108 300
Adults in regular formal education	13 600	14 000	14 400	15 100	15 800	17 100	18 500	19 800	21 200	21 700	22 200	22 700	23 200	24 000
Total adults in public adult education, in continuing training and in regular education	92 000	95 100	99 700	102 000	103 000	104 900	106 400	112 400	116 100	117 500	124 200	125 200	128 800	132 300

Note: .. Data not available.
Source: Statistics Denmark; Ministry of Education, Denmark.

Table A.25. **Denmark: public expenditure on adult education and training, 1980-93**

(million DKr, 1993 prices)[1]

	1980	1981	1982	1983	1984	1985	1986	1987	1988	1989	1990	1991	1992	1993
General programmes	654	679	713	709	694	699	702	711	741	771	800	827	845	840
Folk high school	542	652	555	586	594	624	641	653	647	706	717	744	764	778
"Day" high school	7	15	20	28	35	40	55	70	100	135	170	200	266	315
Immigrant education	..	..	..	..	..	..	..	307	276	270	276	270	267	261
Open University	260	262	265	270	272	260	270	280	282	284	338	318	328	354
Adult vocational training/short programmes	733	855	906	930	898	940	995	980	1 049	996	960	984	1 064	1 159
Adult vocational training/long programmes					8	38	43	43	38	37	38	35	36	
Pre-vocational training	194	194	194	194	199	202	183	180	171	155	155	150	141	141
Leisure-time education	1 005	1 063	1 078	1 050	1 038	1 073	1 065	1 084	1 058	1 073	1 063	1 065	1 066	1 200
Other	346	379	381	384	380	392	403	439	445	452	461	469	487	518
Total	*3 741*	*4 099*	*4 112*	*4 151*	*4 110*	*4 238*	*4 352*	*4 747*	*4 812*	*4 880*	*4 977*	*5 065*	*5 263*	*5 602*
Adults in regular formal education	598	616	634	665	698	752	814	870	933	954	976	998	1 014	1 062
Total public expenditure	*4 339*	*4 715*	*4 746*	*4 816*	*4 808*	*4 990*	*5 166*	*5 617*	*5 745*	*5 834*	*5 953*	*6 063*	*6 277*	*6 664*

Note: .. Data not available.
1. Expenditure include tuition fees, which in 1993 amounted to about 3 per cent of total expenditure for general programmes, 37 per cent for folk high schools, 30 per cent for Open University, and 54 per cent for leisure-time adult education.

Source: Statistics Denmark; Ministry of Education, Denmark.

Table A.26. **Germany (FTFR): institutions,
courses and enrolments in adult education, 1965-93**

	Institutions [1]	Courses	Enrolments [2]
1965	5 870	77 837	1 695.7
1970	5 237	109 881	2 227.3
1975	4 289	195 546	3 761.0
1980	4 817	301 444	4 633.0
1981	4 906	308 380	4 676.8
1982	5 050	303 215	4 551.9
1983	4 919	311 427	4 606.6
1984	4 834	327 167	4 773.5
1985	4 801	334 993	4 826.3
1986	4 683	360 463	5 184.3
1987	4 762	377 877	5 336.9
1988	4 910	398 792	5 568.0
1989	4 805	409 975	5 595.7
1990	4 837	415 973	5 581.3
1991 [3]	4 884	427 657	5 680.7
1992 [3]	4 801	441 443	5 893.1
1993 [3]	4 613	456 243	6 023.4

1. Including external departments.
2. Thousands.
3. Including lecture series.
Source: Federal Ministry of Education, Science, Research and Technology, 1994-95, *Basic and Structural Data; Education Statistics for the Federal Republic of Germany.*

Table A.27. **Germany: expenditure on education
by the federal government, the *Länder* and local authorities according to expenditure areas, 1965-92**

(DM billion)

	Expenditure on education and training [1]	
	Total	Further education and training
1965	15 676	293
1970	27 759	581
1971	34 876	697
1972	39 255	820
1973	44 624	965
1974	52 130	928
1975	56 835	1 054
1976	58 093	1 284
1977	60 407	1 517
1978	64 674	1 831
1979	69 936	2 124
1980	77 127	2 291
1981	80 873	2 374
1982	81 832	2 379
1983	82 605	2 411
1984	83 151	2 636
1985	85 264	2 951
1986	88 722	3 137
1987	91 893	3 216
1988	93 113	2 894
1989	96 254	2 986
1990	102 795	3 217
1991	112 152	3 654
1992 [2]	118 727	3 999

1. Net expenditure. Former territory of the Federal Republic only.
2. By the federal government and the *Länder*.
Source: Federal Ministry of Education, Science, Research and Technology, 1994-95, *Basic and Structural Data; Education Statistics for the Federal Republic of Germany.*

Table A.28. **France: development of private sector[1] continuing training financed by public authorities and enterprises, 1984-93**

(Metropolitan France)

	1984	1985	1986	1987	1988	1989	1990	1991	1992	1993
Students (millions)										
National government	849	871	881	900	1 191	1 228	1 431	1 400	1 523	1 595
Regional government	320	385	353	391	418	432	426	466	439	422
Enterprises	2 343	2 386	2 689	2 828	3 077	3 270	3 390	3 464	3 586	3 695
Total	*3 512*	*3 642*	*3 864*	*4 043*	*4 522*	*4 930*	*5 247*	*5 330*	*5 548*	*5 712*
Training hours[2] (millions)										
National government	221	243	227	262	324	346	348	412	409	475
Regional government	82	79	80	96	108	113	124	136	126	123
Enterprises	132	142	191	206	201	252	272	301	300	301
Total	*435*	*464*	*494*	*550*	*614*	*711*	*744*	*849*	*835*	*899*
Expenditure (millions)										
National government	11 000	12 500	14 000	13 500	17 300	19 600	21 500	22 400	23 800	24 100
Regional government	2 500	2 800	3 000	3 300	3 400	3 100	3 400	3 400	4 000	4 300
Enterprises	18 900	20 700	24 800	27 000	30 700	35 200	39 100	41 900	44 900	44 800
UNEDIC[3]					800	2 400	3 300	5 000	7 600	12 900
Total	*32 400*	*36 000*	*41 800*	*43 800*	*52 200*	*60 300*	*67 300*	*72 700*	*80 300*	*86 100*

1. Not included: training of civil servants, apprentices and entry into employment programmes for 16- to 25-years-olds.
2. Number of students multiplied by training duration.
3. Union nationale pour l'emploi dans l'industrie et le commerce.
Source: Ministry of Education, Higher Education, Research and Vocational Integration (1995), *Repères et références statistiques sur les enseignements et la formation*, Paris.

Table A.29. **Direct expenditure per student in pre-primary education from public sources, 1985-92** [1, 2]

(constant 1992 US dollars)

	1985	1986	1987	1988	1989	1990	1991	1992
North America								
United States	2 928	2 967	3 224	3 309	3 511	3 933	4 127	3 210
Pacific Area								
Japan	..	..	..	..	..	..	..	3 020
New Zealand	..	..	..	..	..	..	..	1 900
European Community								
Belgium	2 245	2 278	2 248	2 235	2 276	2 265	2 308	2 350
Denmark	2 571	2 646	2 814	3 358	3 402	..	..	6 300
France	..	..	..	..	..	..	2 224	2 580
Germany (FTFR)	..	..	..	..	..	..	..	3 350
Ireland	1 327	1 267	1 370	1 278	1 302	1 399	1 566	1 750
Italy	..	..	..	..	..	..	..	3 280
Netherlands	..	..	..	..	..	..	..	2 230
Portugal	..	..	..	..	..	..	1 548	..
Spain	912	905	949	1 028	1 145	1 414	1 827	2 090
United Kingdom	1 726	2 048	2 163	2 209	2 225	2 160	2 296	1 860
Other Europe – OECD								
Austria	2 369	2 365	2 271	2 179	2 250	2 290	2 467	3 280
Czech Republic	..	..	..	..	..	..	..	1 240
Finland	..	..	..	..	..	..	..	6 280
Norway	4 410	5 272	5 960	6 359	6 344	6 027	6 462	7 350
Sweden	..	2 804	2 868	2 751	2 634	2 587	2 571	6 070
Switzerland	..	..	..	..	..	..	2 074	1 890
Country average	*2 311*	*2 506*	*2 652*	*2 745*	*2 788*	*2 759*	*2 679*	*3 335*

Notes: .. Data not available. Vertical lines denote break in series.
1. The number of students used to calculate expenditure per student from public sources is the number enrolled in public schools or in private schools that are predominantly publicly funded.
2. Direct expenditure per student from public sources is calculated by dividing direct government expenditures for educational institutions at the corresponding level of education by the corresponding full-time equivalent enrolment. The result is converted into US dollars using the purchasing power parity (PPP) exchange rate for GDP.
Source: OECD Education Database for enrolment and expenditure data. The PPP exchange rates are published in *OECD National Accounts.*

Table A.30. **Direct expenditure per student in primary education from public sources, 1985-92** [1,2]

(constant 1992 US dollars)

	1985	1986	1987	1988	1989	1990	1991	1992
North America								
United States	4 356	4 585	4 872	4 994	5 259	5 213	5 322	5 600
Pacific Area								
Japan	..	..	..	..	..	..	..	3 530
New Zealand	..	..	..	..	..	..	..	2 030
European Community								
Belgium	2 227	2 212	2 144	2 132	2 117	2 127	2 202	2 390
Denmark	3 563	3 531	3 924	4 123	4 188	4 437	4 520	4 220
France	..	..	..	..	..	..	2 664	2 900
Germany (FTFR)	..	..	..	..	..	..	..	2 980
Ireland	1 320	1 332	1 414	1 352	1 370	1 426	1 585	1 770
Italy	..	..	..	..	..	..	..	4 050
Netherlands	..	..	..	..	..	..	..	2 560
Portugal	1 327	1 368	1 495	1 817	..	1 927	2 169	..
Spain	1 436	1 440	1 496	1 643	1 799	1 797	1 913	2 030
United Kingdom	2 331	2 484	2 655	2 726	2 788	2 891	2 872	3 120
Other Europe – OECD								
Austria	3 444	3 511	3 597	3 539	3 487	3 519	3 673	4 010
Finland	..	..	..	..	..	..	..	3 850
Norway	3 397	3 878	4 264	4 384	4 253	3 871	3 994	4 480
Sweden	..	5 094	5 272	5 529	5 266	5 260	5 623	4 840
Switzerland	..	..	..	..	..	..	5 600	3 560
Turkey	..	..	..	..	..	..	581	
Country average	*2 600*	*2 944*	*3 113*	*3 224*	*3 392*	*3 247*	*3 286*	*3 407*

Note: .. Data not available.
1. The number of students used to calculate expenditure per student from public sources is the number enrolled in public schools or in private schools that are predominantly publicly funded.
2. See Note 2, Annex Table A.29.
Source: OECD Education Database for enrolment and expenditure data, and *OECD National Accounts.*

Table A.31. **Direct expenditure per student in secondary education from public sources, 1985-92**[1, 2]

(constant 1992 US dollars)

	1985	1986	1987	1988	1989	1990	1991	1992
North America								
United States	5 271	5 520	5 705	5 839	6 067	6 533	6 653	6 470
Pacific Area								
Japan	..	..	..	..	..	..	..	3 900
New Zealand	..	..	..	..	..	..	..	2 620
European Community								
Belgium	5 269	5 165	4 938	5 050	4 973	4 795	5 140	5 150
Denmark	5 035	4 984	5 276	5 479	5 534	5 290	5 529	4 940
France	..	..	..	..	..	..	4 770	5 430
Germany (FTFR)	..	..	..	..	..	..	..	4 260
Ireland	2 273	2 255	2 416	2 339	2 359	2 399	2 558	2 770
Italy	..	..	..	..	..	..	..	4 700
Netherlands	..	..	..	..	..	..	..	3 310
Portugal	1 755	1 798	1 862	1 887	..	..	2 430	..
Spain	1 994	2 015	2 128	2 375	2 591	2 701	2 807	2 790
United Kingdom	3 856	4 325	4 660	4 973	2 788	2 891	4 374	4 390
Other Europe – OECD								
Austria	3 935	4 055	4 244	4 310	4 441	4 623	4 811	6 420
Finland	..	..	..	..	..	..	..	4 820
Norway	4 807	5 240	5 500	5 668	5 674	5 142	5 527	6 200
Sweden	..	6 227	6 219	5 949	5 987	6 279		6 050
Switzerland	..	..	..	..	..	..	6 747	..
Turkey	..	..	..	..	..	..	518	..
Country average	*3 799*	*4 158*	*4 295*	*4 387*	*4 703*	*4 720*	*4 322*	*4 639*

Notes: .. Data not available. Vertical lines denote break in series.
1.   The number of students used to calculate expenditure per student from public sources is the number enrolled in public schools or in private schools that are predominantly publicly funded.
2.   See Note 2, Annex Table A.29.
Source: OECD Education Database for enrolment and expenditure data, and *OECD National Accounts.*

Table A.32. **Direct expenditure per student in tertiary education from public sources, 1985-92**[1,2]

(constant 1992 US dollars)

	1985	1986	1987	1988	1989	1990	1991	1992
North America								
Canada	..	..	..	..	..	..	9 915	| 12 350
United States	10 201	10 958	11 185	11 277	9 743	11 989	12 133	11 880
Pacific Area								
Australia	..	..	..	..	..	..	..	6 600
Japan	..	..	..	..	..	..	..	11 850
New Zealand	..	..	..	..	..	..	..	6 080
European Community								
Belgium	7 084	7 216	6 897	..	6 447	6 165	6 410	6 590
Denmark	8 552	8 756	8 326	8 788	8 809	8 315	7 900	6 710
France	..	..	..	..	..	..	4 893	6 020
Germany (FTFR)	..	..	..	..	..	..	..	6 550
Ireland	5 162	5 262	5 892	5 269	4 979	5 516	5 744	7 270
Italy	..	..	..	..	..	..	..	5 850
Netherlands	..	..	..	..	..	..	..	8 720
Portugal	3 725	4 958	6 254	6 989	6 816	..	6 334	..
Spain	1 903	2 007	2 308	2 474	2 769	3 150	3 333	3 770
United Kingdom	..	..	..	..	..	..	9 891	10 370
Other Europe – OECD								
Austria	6 544	7 359	6 947	6 820	6 702	6 356	6 622	5 820
Czech Republic	..	..	..	..	..	..	..	3 590
Finland	..	..	..	..	..	..	..	8 650
Norway	7 841	9 232	9 397	9 556	10 105	8 611	8 641	8 720
Sweden	..	..	..	..	7 460	8 652	8 801	| 7 120
Switzerland	..	..	..	..	..	..	15 094	| 12 900
Turkey	..	..	..	..	..	..	2 873	..
Country average	*6 377*	*6 969*	*7 151*	*7 310*	*7 092*	*7 344*	*7 756*	*7 871*

Notes: .. Data not available. Vertical lines denote break in series.
1.   The number of students used to calculate expenditure per student from public sources is the number enrolled in public institutions or in private ones that are predominantly publicly funded.
2.   See Note 2, Annex Table A.29.
Source: OECD Education Database for enrolment and expenditure data, and *OECD National Accounts.*

Table A.33. **Ratio of students to teaching staff in early childhood education, 1985-92[1, 2, 3]**

	1985	1986	1987	1988	1989	1990	1991	1992
North America								
Canada	17.9	17.7	17.7	17.2	16.6	16.9	. .	. .
Pacific Area								
Japan	. .	. .	. .	. .	19.5	19.3	18.9	18.5
European Community								
Belgium	. .	. .	. .	. .	. .	. .	. .	18.4
Denmark	18.4	17.7	16.5	15.8	15.7	14.1	13.6	10.7
France	. .	. .	. .	. .	. .	. .	27.5	26.0
Germany (FTFR)	. .	. .	. .	. .	. .	. .	23.8	23.9
Ireland	. .	. .	28.9	28.4	29.2	28.9	27.9	27.2
Italy	14.8	15.0	14.5	13.9	13.9	13.9	. .	13.3
Netherlands	20.2	19.5	19.9	19.6	20.3	20.9	21.2	25.9
Portugal	. .	. .	. .	. .	. .	. .	22.2	. .
Spain	29.5	28.5	27.7	26.7	25.9	25.7	24.8	23.4
United Kingdom	. .	. .	27.2	27.8	28.9	28.4	27.8	38.1
Other Europe – OECD								
Austria	21.8	22.3	22.2	22.0	21.7	21.3	20.9	18.3
Finland	. .	. .	. .	. .	. .	. .	. .	12.5
Turkey	19.8	16.5	16.6	16.7	16.2	15.5	16.8	16.6

Notes: . . Data not available. Vertical bars indicate a break in the series.
1. The student:teacher ratio is obtained by dividing the number of full-time equivalent students at a given level of education by the number of full-time equivalent teachers at the same level.
2. Note that the student:teacher ratio is not an indicator of class size. The fact that one country has a lower ratio of students to teachers does therefore not necessarily mean that classes are smaller or that pupils receive larger amounts of instruction. The relationship between the student:teacher ratio and either average class size or the amount of instruction per student is complicated by variations among countries in the length of the school year, the number of hours that a student attends class each day, the length of a teacher's working day, the number of classes or students for which a teacher is responsible, and the division of the teacher's time between teaching and other duties.
3. Note further that all children in early childhood education are counted as full-time even though they may attend school only half-day.
Source: OECD Education Database.

Table A.34. **Ratio of students to teaching staff in primary and secondary education, 1985-92[1]**

	1985	1986	1987	1988	1989	1990	1991	1992
North America								
Canada	16.9	16.6	16.5	16.2	15.9	15.9	. .	. .
United States	. .	. .	. .	. .	. .	. .	15.3	15.3
Pacific Area								
Australia	. .	. .	. .	. .	. .	. .	. .	15.6
Japan	20.7	20.6	20.3	19.9	19.5	19.0	18.5	17.9
New Zealand	. .	. .	19.4	19.4	19.0	. .	. .	18.1
European Community								
Belgium	. .	. .	. .	. .	. .	. .	. .	9.8
Denmark	12.2	11.9	11.6	11.3	11.1	11.0	10.9	10.2
France	. .	. .	. .	. .	. .	. .	. .	16.3
Germany (FTFR)	19.4	18.8	18.4	18.0	17.8	17.5	17.5	17.1
Ireland	. .	. .	. .	. .	. .	. .	. .	20.8
Italy	11.1	10.9	10.6	10.1	10.1	10.1	9.9	9.5
Netherlands	16.3	16.0	15.3	15.3	15.4	. .	. .	. .
Spain	21.7	21.3	21.3	20.8	20.0	19.0	18.6	18.0
United Kingdom	. .	. .	17.1	17.2	16.7	17.3	17.2	17.4
Other Europe – OECD								
Austria	11.4	11.2	10.7	10.5	10.3	10.2	10.1	10.2
Sweden	11.7	11.5	11.4	11.3	11.0	10.8	10.5	11.6
Turkey	27.1	27.3	27.3	27.6	27.7	27.3	27.7	26.8

Note: . . Data not available.
1. See notes to Annex Table A.33.
Source: OECD Education Database.

Table A.35. **Ratio of students to teaching staff in tertiary education, 1985-92**[1]

	1985	1986	1987	1988	1989	1990	1991	1992
North America								
United States	..	..	..	..	..	..	15.6	15.8
Pacific Area								
Australia	..	..	..	..	..	..	9.4	14.3
Japan	11.7	11.4	11.5	11.7	11.8	11.8	12.1	12.2
New Zealand	..	..	..	..	..	..	..	13.8
European Community								
Belgium	..	..	..	..	..	..	13.1	17.5
France	..	..	..	..	..	..	..	17.8
Germany (FTFR)	10.7	10.9	10.9	10.8	10.8	11.0	10.8	10.7
Ireland	10.7	10.8	12.6	13.1	13.6	14.2	14.3	15.0
Italy	29.2	28.3	25.9	26.8	28.8	29.4	31.7	..
Netherlands	10.2	10.3	10.4	10.6	10.6	12.0	13.2	13.9
Portugal	..	..	..	..	..	..	11.4	..
Spain	22.0	23.7	25.0	24.8	24.1	24.0	23.4	22.6
United Kingdom	..	..	..	..	11.4	12.2	12.8	14.0
Other Europe – OECD								
Austria[2]	15.5	15.8	16.3	16.7	16.6	16.4	16.5	13.8
Turkey	19.0	20.5	20.7	19.4	20.6	21.4	21.8	23.1

Notes: .. Data not available. Breaks in series are indicated by a vertical line.
1. See notes to Annex Table A.33.
Source: OECD Education Database.

Table A.36. **Graduation rates[1] in upper secondary education, 1985-92**

(percentage)

	1985	1986	1987	1988	1989	1990	1991	1992
North America								
Canada	70.3	72.2	69.8	66.1	66.8	69.4	71.5	68.4
United States	73.5	73.5	74.1	74.6	73.1	72.2	73.8	75.7
Pacific Area								
Australia	..	..	..	..	..	..	..	87.8
Japan	..	90.5	91.6	90.0	90.8	92.2	91.9	92.2
New Zealand	..	..	..	..	..	..	..	..
European Community								
Belgium	..	..	..	..	..	..	..	77.1
Denmark	87.2	81.7	96.9	99.7	100.7	97.7	100.8	99.1
France	64.1	68.0	68.5	71.0	71.6	71.4	74.8	78.2
Germany (FTFR)	102.6	106.4	107.1	107.1	110.1	107.3	108.1	109.8
Greece	..	..	..	..	..	..	..	84.3
Ireland	..	..	..	..	81.6	80.6	82.1	103.8
Italy	39.3	39.6	40.8	43.3	46.4	45.9	50.6	58.9
Luxembourg	..	..	..	..	..	..	..	..
Netherlands	57.6	68.4	65.8	67.8	72.5	76.8	82.0	95.6
Portugal	22.5	19.5	22.7	..	..	..	50.2	..
Spain	52.4	51.7	51.2	55.9	56.0	62.5	63.8	74.9
United Kingdom	..	..	..	..	..	..	..	81.7
Other Europe – OECD								
Austria	..	..	..	80.8	88.1	88.1	88.4	91.6
Norway	72.5	74.3	75.2	77.2	79.0	81.2	91.0	95.6
Sweden	79.5	79.3	77.7	83.3	83.4	79.5	80.2	83.0
Switzerland	85.3	86.8	87.5	88.6	89.3	88.8	89.3	82.6
Turkey	19.1	20.9	21.1	22.2	22.1	23.8	27.9	29.2

Notes: .. Data not available. Vertical bars indicate a break in series.
1. Graduation rates are calculated as the ratio of upper secondary graduates to the number of persons in the population who are at the typical age at which persons in that country complete the corresponding educational programme. Upper secondary graduates are persons who successfully complete the final year of upper secondary education (success may or may not be established through a final examination). As a consequence, graduation rates may exceed 100 per cent because graduation can occur before or after the theoretical age of graduation.
Source: OECD Education Database.

Table A.37. **Graduation rates[1] in general upper secondary education, 1985-92**

(percentage)

	1985	1986	1987	1988	1989	1990	1991	1992
North America								
Canada	70.3	72.2	69.8	66.1	66.8	69.4	71.5	..
United States	73.5	73.5	74.1	74.6	73.1	72.2	73.8	..
Pacific Area								
Australia	..	..	..	..	..	..	..	..
Japan	..	63.8	65.5	64.3	65.3	66.8	67.0	67.4
New Zealand	16.1	19.0	23.6	25.8	30.3	31.1	34.8	..
European Community								
Belgium	..	..	..	..	..	..	..	34.9
Denmark	30.2	28.7	28.1	29.7	30.2	32.8	32.1		48.7
France	19.9	21.2	22.0	24.5	26.0	27.7	30.4	32.3
Germany (FTFR)	19.7	19.7	20.0	20.5	20.5	21.0	22.3	24.3
Greece	..	..	..	..	..	..	..	60.1
Ireland	66.9	66.7	70.1	69.5	72.5	71.7	73.1	76.6
Italy	15.6	15.2	15.1	15.8	16.8	16.6	18.1	21.8
Luxembourg	..	..	..	..	..	..	..	..
Netherlands	29.3	29.6	28.6	29.4	30.0	30.8	31.6	35.4
Portugal	18.0	16.1	17.7	..	..	..	43.6	..
Spain	25.9	25.4	26.3	27.9	30.5	33.3	33.6		43.6
United Kingdom	..	..	..	..	..	..	..	63.6
Other Europe – OECD								
Austria	14.5	14.3	14.5	14.4	15.2	14.2	13.8	15.0
Finland	42.9	42.5	43.6	42.6	43.8	44.3	44.7	45.4
Norway	35.6	34.5	34.6	34.7	33.7	35.8	40.3	40.3
Sweden	20.8	19.6	17.8	17.8	18.2	18.9	19.7	21.8
Switzerland	16.6	16.1	16.1	15.5	16.0	16.8	17.5	16.1
Turkey	10.8	12.1	11.7	12.6	12.7	13.2	15.8	16.8

Notes: .. Data not available. Vertical bars indicate a break in series.
1. The methodology used for the calculation of graduation rates is explained in Annex Table A.36.
Source: OECD Education Database.

Table A.38. **Graduation rates[1] in vocational and technical upper secondary education, 1985-92**

(percentage)

	1985	1986	1987	1988	1989	1990	1991	1992
North America								
Canada	..	..	..	..	..	..	..	..
United States	..	..	..	..	..	..	..	..
Pacific Area								
Australia	..	..	..	..	..	..	..	..
Japan	..	26.7	26.1	25.7	25.4	25.4	24.9	24.8
New Zealand	..	..	..	..	..	..	..	27.6
European Community								
Belgium	..	..	..	..	..	..	..	41.3
Denmark	57.0	53.0	69.0	70.2	70.5	65.0	68.7	50.4
France	44.2	46.7	46.5	46.6	45.7	43.7	44.4	45.9
Germany (FTFR)	82.9	86.7	87.1	86.6	89.6	86.3	85.8	85.5
Greece	..	..	..	..	..	..	..	24.2
Ireland	..	..	..	..	9.1	8.9	9.0	27.2
Italy	23.7	24.4	25.8	27.5	29.6	29.3	32.5	37.1
Luxembourg	..	..	..	..	..	..	..	..
Netherlands	28.3	38.8	37.2	38.3	42.5	46.0	50.4	60.3
Portugal	4.5	3.3	5.0	..	..	..	6.6	..
Spain	26.6	26.2	24.9	28.0	25.5	29.2	30.2	31.3
United Kingdom	..	..	..	..	..	..	..	16.6
Other Europe – OECD								
Austria	..	..	..	66.3	72.8	73.9	74.7	76.6
Finland	79.9	76.5	76.9	73.3	73.9	75.2	77.8	84.1
Norway	36.9	39.7	40.6	42.5	45.3	45.4	50.7	55.4
Sweden	58.8	59.7	59.9	65.6	65.2	60.6	60.5	61.1
Switzerland	68.7	70.7	71.4	73.1	73.3	72.1	71.8	66.6
Turkey	8.3	8.8	9.4	9.6	9.4	10.6	12.1	12.5

Notes: .. Data not available. Vertical bars indicate a break in series.

1. The methodology used for the calculation of graduation rates is explained in Annex Table A.36. Vocational education includes technical and apprenticeship programmes. To obtain the number of graduates for general and vocational programmes, countries with differentiated upper secondary institutions have reported the number of graduates by type of institutions attended.

Source: OECD Education Database.

Table A.39. **Graduation rates[1] in tertiary university education, 1985-92**

(percentage)

	1985	1986	1987	1988	1989	1990	1991	1992
North America								
Canada	27.0	28.7	31.3	33.3	35.8	37.3	38.7	37.7
United States	32.6	33.6	34.9	36.8	38.9	40.2	41.3	39.1
Pacific Area								
Australia	..	..	25.6	27.7	28.6	..	33.6	36.4
Japan	24.9	24.6	23.8	25.6	24.9	23.7	25.2	25.3
New Zealand	16.8	19.2	20.3	19.3	18.7	20.5	21.8	25.1
European Community								
Belgium	12.7	11.3	10.7	12.6	17.6	17.6	13.4	14.7
Denmark	16.5	16.4	16.0	15.8	18.7	21.3	23.8 |	31.3
France	11.4	11.5	12.2	12.9	13.8	14.8	16.2	..
Germany (FTFR)	15.3	15.0	15.1	15.2	14.9	14.5	14.7	14.6
Greece	..	..	..	..	..	..	..	12.3
Ireland	15.5	17.8	18.4	20.0	19.3	19.6	19.2	21.3
Italy	9.0	9.0	9.1	9.5	10.5	10.3	10.9	12.3
Luxembourg	..	..	..	..	..	..	..	..
Netherlands[2]	7.0	7.5	8.8	12.0	11.1	8.9	9.0 |	27.4
Portugal	6.3	5.4	6.6	..	..	..	..	..
Spain	14.4	15.0	16.4	17.5	18.4	19.3	20.4	20.9
United Kingdom	..	..	..	..	..	..	..	28.7
Other Europe – OECD								
Austria	7.2	6.9	7.4	7.9	7.3	8.5	8.6	8.8
Finland	15.4	15.9	16.2	19.9	18.8	19.4	20.3	22.2
Norway	26.6	23.9	29.2	29.6	31.3	34.1	38.0 |	26.4
Sweden	16.8	15.1	15.2	14.6	14.1	13.3	13.9	15.3
Switzerland	9.3	9.4	9.7	9.9	9.8	9.9	10.0	10.7
Turkey	3.6	4.6	5.7	5.9	6.5	6.7	6.7	6.6

Notes: .. Data not available. Vertical bars indicate a break in series.
1. The methodology used for the calculation of graduation rates is explained in Annex Table A.36.
2. Data in 1992 include non-university tertiary graduates.
Source: OECD Education Database.

Table A.40. **United States: mean verbal and mathematics proficiency scores on Scholastic Aptitude Test, 1976-93**

(college-bound high school seniors)

	1976	1977	1978	1979	1980	1981	1982	1983	1984	1985	1986	1987	1988	1989	1990	1991	1992	1993
Verbal	431	429	429	427	424	424	426	425	426	431	431	430	428	427	424	422	423	424
Mathematics	472	470	468	467	466	466	467	468	471	475	475	476	476	476	476	474	476	478

1.   See Chart 1.36 for explanations.
Source: National Center fo Education Statistics (1994), *The Condition of Education*, p. 64 and p. 228.

Table A.41. **United States: mean science proficiency scores, by sex and age, 1970-92** [1]

	Total			Male			Female		
	Age 9	Age 13	Age 17	Age 9	Age 13	Age 17	Age 9	Age 13	Age 17
1970	225	255	305	228	257	314	223	253	297
1973	220	250	296	223	252	304	218	247	288
1977	220	247	290	222	251	297	218	244	282
1982	221	250	283	221	256	292	221	245	275
1986	224	251	288	227	256	295	221	247	282
1990	229	255	290	230	258	296	227	252	285
1992	231	258	294	235	260	299	227	256	289

1.   The science proficiency scale has a range from 0 to 500. The science tests are administered as part of the National Assessment of Educational Progres since 1970.
Source: National Center of Education Statistics (1994), *The Condition of Education*, p. 56.

Table A.42. **Ratios of mean annual earnings by educational qualifications, early 1970s-90s** [1, 2, 3, 4]

(population 25 to 64 years of age)

Country/education level	Early 1970s	Late 1970s	Early 1980s	Middle/late 1980s	Early 1990s	Five-year change 1970s	Five-year change 1980s/ early 1990s
Australia, men							
Level E/Level A	2.03	1.87	1.74	1.70	1.79	−0.16	0.02
Level E/Level B	1.95	1.72	1.65	1.52	1.62	−0.23	−0.02
Level E/Level C	1.83	1.67	1.61	1.49	1.60	−0.16	−0.01
Level E/Level D	1.27	1.36	1.28	1.19	1.33	0.09	0.03
Australia, women							
Level E/Level A	2.07	1.74	1.70	1.70	1.71	−0.33	0.01
Level E/Level B	1.94	1.55	1.52	1.51	1.61	−0.39	0.05
Level E/Level C	1.88	1.56	1.70	1.49	1.70	−0.32	0.00
Level E/Level D	1.27	1.34	1.37	1.32	1.33	0.07	−0.02
Austria, men							
Level E/Level A	..	..	..	..	1.74	..	..
Level E/Level B	..	..	..	..	1.26	..	..
Level E/Level C	..	..	..	..	1.36	..	..
Austria, women							
Level E/Level A	..	..	..	..	1.58	..	..
Level E/Level B	..	..	..	..	1.14	..	..
Level E/Level C	..	..	..	..	1.20	..	..
Canada, men							
Level E/Level A	2.09	1.69	..	1.90	2.08	−0.33	0.16
Level E/Level B	1.75	1.54	..	1.70	1.71	−0.20	0.07
Level E/Level D	1.49	1.37	..	1.52	1.51	−0.10	0.06
Canada, women							
Level E/Level A	2.44	2.00	..	2.22	2.23	−0.36	0.10
Level E/Level B	1.85	1.65	..	1.82	1.80	−0.17	0.06
Level E/Level D	1.42	1.42	..	1.59	1.53	0.00	0.05
Denmark, men							
Level E/Level A	..	..	1.58	1.59	1.61	..	0.02
Level E/Level B	..	..	1.39	1.42	1.31	..	−0.04
Level E/Level C	..	..	1.37	1.40	1.42	..	0.03
Level E/Level D	..	..	1.32	1.31	1.34	..	0.01
Denmark, women							
Level E/Level A	..	..	1.46	1.39	1.36	..	−0.06
Level E/Level B	..	..	1.33	1.27	1.21	..	−0.07
Level E/Level C	..	..	1.35	1.28	1.26	..	−0.05
Level E/Level D	..	..	1.15	1.17	1.15	..	0.00
France, men							
Level E/Level A	3.85	4.23	..	3.81	..	0.27	−0.26
Level E/Level B	1.88	2.38	..	2.42	..	0.36	0.03
Level E/Level C	3.08	3.47	..	3.20	..	0.28	−0.17
Level E/Level D	1.74	2.46	..	2.35	..	0.51	−0.07
France, women							
Level E/Level A	3.11	3.20	..	3.11	..	0.06	−0.06
Level E/Level B	1.67	2.02	..	2.13	..	0.25	0.07
Level E/Level C	2.36	2.53	..	2.49	..	0.12	−0.03
Level E/Level D	1.45	1.77	..	1.71	..	0.23	−0.04
Germany, men							
Levels D and E/Level A	..	..	2.00	1.94	..	..	−0.06
Levels D and E/Level C	..	..	1.64	1.64	..	..	0.00
Levels B, D and E/Level A	..	..	1.50	1.95	2.02	..	0.37
Levels B, D and E/Level C	..	..	1.25	1.29	1.27	..	0.01
Germany, women							
Levels B, D and E/Level A	..	..	1.77	2.26	2.01	..	0.17
Levels B, D and E/Level C	..	..	1.76	1.70	1.46	..	−0.21

Table A.42. **Ratios of mean annual earnings by educational qualifications, early 1970s-90s** [1,2,3,4] *(cont.)*

(population 25 to 64 years of age)

Country/education level	Early 1970s	Late 1970s	Early 1980s	Middle/late 1980s	Early 1990s	Five-year change 1970s	Five-year change 1980s early 1990s
Japan, men							
Level E/Level A	1.32	1.30	..	1.36	1.36	−0.02	0.02
Level E/Level B	1.31	1.25	..	1.28	1.28	−0.05	0.01
Level E/Level D	0.98	1.11	..	1.34	1.36	0.11	0.10
Japan, women							
Level E/Level A	1.65	1.59	..	1.59	1.62	−0.05	0.01
Level E/Level B	1.40	1.32	..	1.36	1.38	−0.07	0.02
Level E/Level D	1.11	1.21	..	1.22	1.24	0.08	0.01
Netherlands, men							
Level E/Level A	..	..	1.96	1.86	..	..	−0.10
Level E/Level B	..	..	1.56	1.52	..	..	−0.04
Level E/Level C	..	..	1.68	1.64	..	..	−0.04
Level E/Level D	..	..	1.34	1.23	..	..	−0.11
Netherlands, women							
Level E/Level A	..	..	2.20	1.87	..	..	−0.32
Level E/Level B	..	..	2.00	1.62	..	..	−0.38
Level E/Level C	..	..	1.90	1.62	..	..	−0.38
Level E/Level D	..	..	1.50	1.27	..	..	−0.23
Norway, men							
Level E/Level A	..	..	1.43	1.32	1.35	..	−0.05
Level E/Level B	..	..	1.35	1.25	1.26	..	−0.07
Norway, women							
Level E/Level A	..	..	1.26	1.31	1.25	..	−0.01
Level E/Level B	..	..	1.19	1.26	1.26	..	0.04
Sweden, men							
Level E/Level A	1.68	..	1.37	1.57	1.55	−0.22	0.09
Level E/Level B	1.44	..	1.22	1.30	1.36	−0.16	0.07
Level E/Level C	1.54	..	1.31	1.40	1.34	−0.16	0.01
Level E/Level D	1.27	..	1.55	1.12	1.13	0.20	−0.21
Sweden, women							
Level E/Level A	1.76	..	1.49	1.36	1.51	−0.19	0.01
Level E/Level B	1.67	..	1.47	1.34	1.54	−0.14	0.04
Level E/Level C	1.59	..	1.40	1.24	1.37	−0.14	−0.01
Level E/Level D	1.31	..	1.24	1.13	1.16	−0.04	−0.04
United Kingdom, men							
Level E/Level A	1.83	1.69	..	1.87	2.04	−0.14	0.17
Level E/Level B	1.52	1.32	..	1.47	1.53	−0.20	0.09
Level E/Level C	1.51	1.55	..	1.65	1.79	0.04	0.10
Level E/Level D	1.22	1.29	..	1.27	1.31	0.07	0.01
United States, men							
Level E/Level A	1.92	1.94	..	2.33	2.47	0.02	0.20
Level E/Level B	1.55	1.57	..	1.73	1.89	−0.02	0.12
Level E/Level D	1.36	1.41	..	1.48	1.58	0.04	0.07
Unites States, women							
Level E/Level A	1.85	1.78	..	2.15	2.32	−0.07	0.21
Level E/Level B	1.49	1.47	..	1.64	1.83	0.02	0.14
Level E/Level D	1.29	1.29	..	1.36	1.46	0.00	0.07

Note: .. Data not available.

1. Ratios are multiplied by 100.
2. Relative earnings from work are defined as the mean annual earnings from work of individuals with a certain level of educational attainment divided by the mean annual earnings from work of individuals with the respective other level of education. Calculations are based solely on persons with incomes from work during the reference period.
3. Portions of the disparities are due to differences in the number of working hours between the educational groups. On average, persons with higher levels of educational attainment tend to have more working hours per year than those with lower levels of education, which may have to do with differences in propensity to take on and ability to find full-time work.
4. In many cases, the national levels of education used for this indicator do not strictly correspond to the standard ISCED definition for the levels of education. An explanation of the national classifications of educational levels is given below.

Sources and definitions:

Australia
Earnings refer to mean annual earned income, including self-employment income for full-year, full-time workers. Data for all years were taken from the following publications of the Australian Bureau of Statistics: for 1973/74, *Income Distribution,1973-74, Part 1*, Catalogue No. 6502.0, and for 1978/79, *Income Distribution, Australia, 1978-79*, Catalogue No. 6502.0 and *Social Indicators*, No. 4, Catalogue No. 4101.0. For 1985/86, *1986 Income Distribution Survey: Persons with Earned Income*, Catalogue No. 6546.0, and for 1989/90, *1990 Survey of Income and Housing Costs and Amenities: Persons with Earned Income*, Catalogue No. 6546.0. Early 1970s refers to 1973/74, late 1970s to 1978/79, early 1980s to 1981/82, middle/late 1980s to 1985/86, and early 1990s to 1989/90.

Austria
Data refer to median net monthly earnings of wage and salary earners for a standardised working week. Apprentices, part-time white-collar workers and public sector employees in education and research are excluded. Data are from the June 1989 Microzensus as presented in I. Wolf and W. Wolf (1991), *How Much Less: Earnings Disparities Between Women and Men in Austria*, Austrian Federal Ministry of Labour and Social Affairs, Vienna, Table 13.

Canada
Data refer to mean annual gross earnings of full-time workers, including self-employment income. Data are based on the Survey of Consumer Finances and were taken from various issues of *Earnings of Men and Women*, Statistics Canada. Early 1970s refers to 1973, late 1970s to 1979, middle/late 1980s to 1989 and early 1990s to 1991.
The earnings ratios are based on the 1971, 1981 and 1986 Household Censuses. Earnings refer to weekly wages (annual earnings divided by weeks worked) in the year prior to the survey. Thus the data refer to 1970, 1980 and 1985. Only men who worked at least 40 weeks with annual earnings greater than $1 200 and weekly earnings less than $5 000 in 1981 Canadian dollars, and with self-employment income not greater than 25 per cent of wage and salary income, are included. Education level B refers to those with 11-13 years of schooling.

Denmark
Data refer to the mean daily gross wage calculated as yearly wages divided by days worked per year. Data exclude those working less than 30 hours per week, those who received sickness benefits for more than 13 weeks during the year and all persons working less than 13 weeks. The information is derived from a longitudinal sample of individuals taken from administrative records. All data were supplied by the Ministry of Economic Affairs. Early 1980s refers to 1980, middle/late 1980s to 1985 and early 1990s to 1989.

France
Data refer to mean annual income, net of social security contributions, and including bonuses and royalties, 13th month pay and any payments in kind. The data are based on the *Formation et Qualifications Professionnelles* survey for 1970, 1977 and 1985, as presented in C. Baudelot and M. Glaude (1990), "Les diplômes paient-ils de moins en moins?", *Données sociales*, INSEE, Paris, pp. 103-108. Early 1970s refers to 1970, late 1970s to 1977 and middle/late 1980s to 1985.

Germany
All data are based on the German Socio-economic Survey. The figures refer to median gross monthly earnings of male, full-time, full-year workers for the year prior to the survey and includes one-twelfth of 13th and 14th months pay, and one-twelfth of holiday allowances. The data for women refer to average gross wages (excluding all fringe benefits) for the month prior to the interview and includes all workers irrespective of hours worked over the month.

Japan
All data are based on the yearly Basic Survey on Wage Structure referring to regular employees in firms of 10 or more employees. Earnings refer to total monthly cash earnings plus one-twelfth of annual special earnings including bonuses. Data for 1973, 1989 and 1992 were taken directly from the published results of the survey. Early 1970s refers to 1973, late 1970 to 1979, middle/late 1980s to 1989 and early 1990s to 1992.

Netherlands
The data are from the Yearly Survey on Earnings of 1985 and 1989. Earnings refer to standardised gross hourly wages of persons aged 16-64. The wage figure for educational level A was calculated as an unweighted average of reported earnings for the groups *lager onderwijs* (less than lower secondary), *uitgebreid lo algemeen* (second level, first stage of general education track) and *uitgebreid lo beroeps* (second level first stage of vocational track). Data in Annex Table A.43 are also from the Yearly Survey on Earnings of 1985 and 1989, but refer to average monthly earnings (excluding overtime) of full-time workers and exclude the agricultural sector. The data were supplied by the Central Bureau of Statistics. Education level C was not available separately and, therefore, the data shown for level B include both levels B and C.

Norway
Data are based on the Level of Living surveys. Earnings refer to mean hourly wages of employees, estimated as reported before-tax hourly, weekly, fortnightly or monthly wages divided by the corresponding usual hours worked in the main occupation. Early 1980s refers to 1983, middle/late 1980s to 1987 and early 1990s to 1991.

Sweden
Data for 1974 and 1981 are based on the Level of Living surveys, while data for subsequent years are based on the Household Market and Nonmarket Activities surveys. Earnings refer to gross hourly earnings. For those not paid on an hourly basis, they were calculated as reported weekly or monthly gross earnings divided by the corresponding reported hours worked. All data are unweighted. Early 1970s refers to 1974, early 1980s refers to 1981, middle/late 1980s to 1988 and early 1990s refers to 1991.

United Kingdom
Data are from the General Household Survey. The sub-sample used refers to full-time male employees aged 16 to 64. Earnings refer to real weekly earnings. For 1974, weekly earnings are based on all earnings, bonuses, tips, commissions in all jobs during the year divided by total weeks worked. Weekly earnings are estimated as usual gross earnings (including tips and bonuses), per pay period from the employee's main job divided by the usual number of weeks in each pay period. All data are unweighted. Early 1970s refers to 1974, late 1970s to 1979, middle/late 1980s to 1989 and early 1990s to 1991.

United States
Data are from the March Current Population Survey as published in the annual U.S Bureau of the Census Current Population Reports, P-60 Series. Data refer to mean gross annual earnings, including income from self-employment, for full-time, full-year workers aged 18 and over. Neither the structure of the survey nor the manner of handling missing earnings information or the top-coding of earnings has remained constant. But it is unlikely that the broad trends are greatly affected by these factors.
Early 1970s refers to 1975, late 1970s to 1979, middle/late 1980s to 1989 and early 1990s to 1992.

Education classifications for earnings comparisons:

Australia
Level A = Left school at age 14 or 15.
Level B = Left school at the age of 18 or over (in the 1973/74 survey it is left school at age 17 or over).
Level C = Trade certificate (in the 1973/74 survey it is trade level qualification).
Level D = Non-trade certificate or diploma (in the 1973/74 survey is non-degree tertiary qualification).
Level E = Degree.

Austria
Level A = Elementary school without apprenticeship.
Level B = Completed education in school offering higher general education.
Level C = Completed education in schools offering medium level vocational training.
Level E = University.

Canada
Level A = 0 to 8 years of education.
Level B = Some or completed high school (beginning with the 1990 survey, a distinction has been made between some high school and completed high school).
Level D = Some post-secondary or post-secondary certificate or diploma.
Level E = University degree.

Denmark
Level A = Basic elementary (*Grundskole*), pre-vocational education and no schooling.
Level B = *Gymnasium* or equivalent.
Level C = Non-academic vocational education/training.
Level D = Short post-secondary schooling.
Level E = University degree and medium length post-secondary schooling.

France
Level A = No diploma or initial education.
Level B = *Baccalauréat général*.
Level C = CAP or BEP.
Level D = *Baccalauréat* plus 2 years.
Level E = *Grande école*.

Germany
For full-time, full-year males only:
Level A = No qualifications, including graduates of *Hauptschule* or *Realschule* who did not complete either an apprenticeship or graduated from a full-time vocational school.
Level C = Completed apprenticeship, or graduated from a full-time vocational school or technical training.
Level E = Completed either *Hochschule* or *Fachhochschule*.
Other German data:
Level A = No certificate and no occupational training.
Level C = Elementary certificate (*Hauptschule* or *Realschule*) or lower level apprenticeship training.
Level B/D/E = *Abitur* degree, higher occupational training (*Fachhochschule*) or university degree.

Japan
Level A = Elementary and lower secondary education.
Level B = Upper secondary education.
Level D = Junior college or college of technology.
Level E = University.

Netherlands
Level A = *Lager onderwijs* (less than lower secondary), *Uitgebreid lo algemeen* (secondary, first level of general education track) and *Uitgebreid lo beroeps* (secondary, first level of vocational track).
Level B = *Middelbaar onderwijs algemeen* (upper secondary general track).
Level C = *Middelbaar onderwijs beroeps* (upper secondary vocational track).
Level D = *Hoger beroeps onderwijs* (higher-level technical studies).
Level E = *Wetenschappelijk onderwijs*(university).

Norway
Level A = *Ungdomsskolenivå* (primary school) and *Gymnasnivå* (secondary school level 1).
Level B = *Gymnasnivå* (secondary school level 2).
Level E = University level.

Sweden
Level A = Completed old compulsory schooling level (6-8 years), or old compulsory schooling and one year of vocational training, or completed new compulsory schooling (*grundskola* of 9 years) or an older counterpart (*realskola* of 9-10 years).
Level B = High school degree (old *student examen* and new *gymnasium* of 12 years).
Level C = Completed new compulsory schooling and at least one year of vocational training.
Level D = High school degree and at least one year of post-secondary vocational education.
Level E = University degree.

United Kingdom
Level A = No qualifications, miscellaneous non-vocational qualifications (including CSE grades 2-5), miscellaneous apprenticeships, clerical or commercial qualifications without O levels, less than five O levels.
Level B = GCE A level.
Level C = Less than five O levels with clerical or commercial qualifications, City and Guilds Craft or Ordinary Certificate, more than five O levels, and Advanced or final City and Guilds Certificates, Ordinary National Certificate or diploma, BEC/TEC National, General or Ordinary.
Level D = Nursing or teaching (non-graduate) qualifications, and Higher National Certificate or Diploma, BEC/TEC Higher certificate or diploma, City and Guilds full technological certificate, and qualifications from colleges or professional institutions above GCE A level but below degree level.

United States
Level A = Less than 4 years of high school.
Level B = 4 years of high school.
Level D = Less than 4 years of college or university.
Level E = At least 4 years of college or university.

Source: OECD (1994d), *The OECD Jobs Study: Evidence and Explanations*, Table 7.A.1, pp. 160-161.

Table A.43. **Earnings differentials by educational attainment of young and older men, early 1970s-90s**

(ratio of mean annual earnings by qualifications, ages 25 to 34 and 45 to 54)

Differentials by age group		Early 1970s	Late 1970s	Early 1980s	Middle/late 1980s	Early 1990s	Five-year change 1970s	Five-year change 1980s/ early 1990s
Level E/Level A								
Australia	25-34	1.78	1.55	1.39	1.44	1.54	-0.23	0.08
	45-54	2.21	2.00	1.93	1.97	1.98	-0.21	0.03
Japan	25-34	1.16	1.15	..	1.21	1.24	-0.01	0.03
	40-49	1.75	1.75	..	1.62	1.61	0.00	-0.05
Netherlands	23-34	..	..	..	1.58	1.52	..	-0.06
	45-64	..	..	..	2.28	2.15	..	-0.13
United States	25-34	1.60	1.69	..	2.08	2.21	0.09	0.20
	45-54	2.14	2.02	..	2.53	2.50	-0.15	0.18
Level E/Level B								
Australia	25-34	1.63	1.41	1.20	1.37	1.35	-0.22	0.08
	45-54	2.04	1.81	2.20	2.01	1.67	-0.23	-0.30
Japan	25-34	1.11	1.10	..	1.15	1.16	-0.01	0.02
	40-49	1.46	1.44	..	1.36	1.36	-0.01	-0.03
Netherlands [1]	23-34	..	..	..	1.40	1.38	..	-0.01
	45-64	..	..	..	1.69	1.69	..	0.00
United States	25-34	1.28	1.27	..	1.53	1.64	-0.01	0.14
	45-54	1.60	1.62	..	1.79	1.84	0.02	0.08
Level E/Level D								
Australia	25-34	1.27	1.29	1.08	1.21	1.28	0.02	0.12
	45-54	1.48	1.49	1.38	1.31	1.43	0.01	0.03
Japan	25-34	1.11	1.09	..	1.12	1.12	-0.01	0.01
	40-49	1.21	1.24	..	1.28	1.24	0.02	0.00
Netherlands	23-34	..	..	..	1.28	1.17	..	-0.11
	45-64	..	..	..	1.35	1.25	..	-0.10
United States	25-34	1.17	1.18	..	1.32	1.40	0.01	0.08
	45-54	1.41	1.32	..	1.59	1.71	-0.11	0.15
Level E/Level C								
Australia	25-34	1.60	1.44	1.31	1.25	1.38	-0.16	0.04
	45-54	2.14	1.93	1.88	1.81	1.81	-0.21	-0.04

Note: .. Data not available.
1. For the Netherlands, educational Level B includes upper secondary vocational (defined as Level C in Table A.42) and general upper secondary education.
Source: See Annex Table A.42.

Table A.44. **Percentage of children with special learning needs who are enrolled in schools outside the mainsteam education system, late 1980s[1]**

	Early childhood education	Primary education	Secondary education
Pacific Area			
Japan	..	0.33	0.44
European Community			
Belgium	0.55	3.90	3.40
France	0.30	2.00	3.70
Greece	0.10	1.40	0.12
Ireland	..	1.00	0.90
Netherlands	0.71	5.64	2.48
Spain	0.50	0.90	0.20
Other Europe – OECD			
Finland	..	6.21	3.70
Norway	..	0.21	0.38

Notes: .. Data not available.
1. Data refer to selected years from 1987 to 1991.
Source: OECD (1995h), p. 41.

Table A.45. **Federal budget allocations for Head Start and enrolments in the programme, United States, 1975-95**

	Federal expenditure (millions US$)	Enrolments (thousands)
1975	404	..
1980	735	376
1985	1 075	452
1990	1 448	541
1991	1 952	584
1992	2 202	621
1993	2 776	713
1994	3 326	741
1995	..	752

Note: .. Data not available.
Source: United States Department of Education (1994a), *Digest of Education Statistics*, Tables 349 and 360.

Table A.46. **Distribution of 9-year-olds in various types of grouping for reading instruction, 1991**[1,2]

(percentage distribution)

	No grouping	Ability groups	Interest groups	Age groups	Other
North America					
Canada (British Columbia)	57	19	7	2	15
United States	31	45	4	12	7
Pacific Area					
New Zealand	6	83	4	0	7
European Community					
Belgium (French community)	71	16	9	1	3
Denmark[3]	26	38	17	0	19
Germany (TFGDR)	24	55	9	0	12
Germany (FTFR)	63	32	3	0	2
Greece	84	9	4	1	2
Ireland	49	49	1	1	0
Netherlands	9	87	0	2	2
Portugal	69	14	13	0	4
Spain	89	8	1	1	1
Other Europe – OECD					
Finland	66	13	14	1	6
Iceland	41	48	3	1	7
Switzerland	52	16	12	1	20

1. Based on data collected for the International Association for the Evaluation of Educational Achievement reading literacy study.
2. Standard errors of estimates are given in OECD (1995d), p. 359.
3. "No grouping" is probably underestimated due to an inaccurate translation in the Danish survey.
Sources: Elley (1992) and OECD (1995d), *Education at a Glance – OECD Indicators*, p. 172.

Table A.47. **Transitions in initial education and training, 1985 and 1992**[1]

(total, net full-time enrolment rates by age)

	Age 16		Age 17		Age 18	
	1985	1992	1985	1992	1985	1992
North America						
Canada	94	96	69	72	31	37
United States	90	91	79	72	19	21
Pacific Area						
Australia	14	79	. .	59	. .	14
Japan	92	95	94	90	. .	. .
New Zealand	68	88	33	66	6	21
European Community						
Belgium	90	97	81	94	40	50
Denmark	90	92	74	80	65	69
France	90	92	77	87	40	59
Germany (FTFR)	96	95	92	93	76	82
Ireland[2]	79	88	57	70	21	33
Italy	52	. .	44	. .	34	. .
Netherlands	93	97	77	91	51	68
Portugal	40	. .	35	. .	29	. .
Spain[3]	58	76	51	67	27	36
United Kingdom[4]	49	75	31	55	9	19
Other Europe – OECD						
Austria	86	90	78	85	43	54
Finland[2]	88	95	82	86	65	80
Norway	84	93	75	87	60	77
Sweden	90	89	82	87	46	60
Switzerland	84	85	82	82	73	74
Turkey	29	39	13	34	9	20

Note: . . Data not available.
1. Total enrolments in secondary and tertiary education.
2. Figures by single age are estimates.
3. Participation rates do not take into account the students whose age is unknown – about 3 per cent in upper secondary education.
4. If part-time students are considered, the enrolment rates are substantially higher. In 1992, 15 per cent of 16-year-olds, 20 per cent of 17-year-olds, and 17 per cent of 18-year-olds, were enrolled on a part-time basis.
Source: OECD Education Database.

Table A.48. **Youth labour force participation and unemployment, 1983 and 1994[1]**

(percentage of labour force and population)

	Youth unemployment rate		Youth labour force participation rate		Youth employment/population ratio	
	1983	1994	1983	1994	1983	1994
North America						
Canada	19.7	16.5	66.7	62.9	53.6	52.5
United States	17.2	12.5	67.1	66.4	55.6	58.1
Pacific Area						
Australia	17.9	16.2	69.1	68.4	56.7	57.3
Japan	4.5	5.5	44.2	47.6	42.2	45.0
New Zealand	. .	15.0	. .	66.0	. .	56.1
European Community						
Belgium[2]	23.9	18.4	43.9	34.4	33.4	28.1
Denmark[2]	18.9	14.6	65.3	70.5	52.9	60.2
France	19.7	27.5	45.7	30.7	36.7	22.3
Germany[2]	11.0	8.2	58.0	56.9	51.6	52.2
Greece[2]	23.1	28.8	42.7	38.6	32.9	27.5
Ireland[2]	20.1	25.1	58.6	46.9	46.9	35.1
Italy[2]	30.5	30.6	44.6	39.9	31.0	27.7
Luxembourg	6.8	4.4	60.2	47.7	56.1	45.6
Netherlands	24.9	10.2	51.5	61.7	38.7	55.4
Portugal[2]	18.3	12.0	67.5	48.3	55.1	42.4
Spain	37.6	42.8	57.6	49.1	35.9	28.1
United Kingdom[2]	. .	17.3	. .	71.1	. .	58.8
Other Europe – OECD						
Finland	10.5	30.9	57.1	44.6	51.1	30.9
Norway	7.7	7.4	61.8	55.4	57.1	51.3
Sweden	8.0	16.6	65.4	49.6	60.2	41.4
Switzerland	. .	5.7	. .	63.7	. .	60.1

Note: . . Data not available.
1. Youth refers to ages 15-24. Unemployment and labour force participation rates are defined in accordance with *OECD Labour Force Statistics*. Vertical bar indicates a break in the series.
2. 1994 is 1993.
Source: OECD (1995*j*), *Employment Outlook*, Table B, p. 205.

Table A.49. **Monthly flows into and out of unemployment**

		Inflow[1,2]		Outflow[2,3]	
		Total	15-24	Total	15-24
North America					
Canada	1994	2.3	4.1	27.5	36.4
United States	1994	1.7	3.8	37.6	46.4
Pacific Area					
Australia	1994	0.9	1.9	14.4	17.0
Japan	1994	0.4	0.8	14.4	25.5
New Zealand	1994	1.1	2.3	17.7	21.5
European Community					
Belgium	1993	0.4	0.9	8.6	11.7
Denmark	1993	1.8	3.5	21.4	29.4
France	1994	0.4	0.5	3.0	4.4
Germany	1993	0.6	0.8	9.0	13.9
Greece	1993	0.3	1.0	4.7	6.1
Ireland	1992	0.6	0.9	3.8	5.5
Italy	1992	0.4	0.8	9.5	9.6
Netherlands	1993	0.2	0.4	6.4	11.4
Portugal	1993	0.3	0.6	15.3	19.2
Spain	1994	0.6	1.1	2.7	3.9
United Kingdom	1993	0.7	1.7	9.3	11.4
Other Europe – OECD					
Finland	1993	2.8	4.2	13.6	22.6
Norway	1994	0.7	1.2	21.6	38.8
Sweden	1994	1.1	2.3	18.4	28.2

1. Inflows refer to those unemployed for less than one month (two months in the case of Finland).
2. Working-age population (15-64 years) less the unemployed for inflows; total unemployment for outflows.
3. The number of outflows is estimated on the basis of the difference between the average monthly level of inflows and the monthly average change in unemployment (calculated over one year).
Source: OECD (1995*j*), Table 1.9, pp. 27-28.

Table A.50. **Distribution of employment by enterprise tenure, 1991**[1]

	Australia	Canada	Finland	France	Germany[2]	Japan[2]	Netherlands[2]	Norway[3]	Spain[4]	Switzerland	United Kingdom	United States	Unweighted average
Current tenure (%)													
Total	100.0	100.0	100.0	100.0	100.0	100.0	100.0	100.0	100.0	100.0	100.0	100.0	100.0
Under 1 year	21.4	23.5	11.0	15.7	12.8	9.8	24.0	14.9[6]	23.9	17.6	18.6	28.8	18.6
1-2 years	13.2	20.0[5]	12.8	10.7	10.3	16.1[5]	15.5	11.0[6]	7.7	11.7	12.4	11.6	..
2-5 years	25.9	11.9[5]	24.5	15.6	17.9	11.5[5]	22.9	18.0[6]	14.8	20.7	23.9	21.3	..
Under 5 years	60.6	55.4	49.2	42.0	41.0	37.4	62.4	43.9[6]	46.4	49.9	54.8	61.7	50.4
5-10 years	16.2	15.2	16.7	16.2	17.8	19.7	11.4	19.7	14.0	16.8	16.1	11.7	16.0
10-20 years	15.2	19.4	21.4	25.6	24.5	23.6	15.2	24.1	21.3	18.8	19.3	17.8	20.5
20 and more	8.1	10.0	12.8	15.8	16.7	19.3	11.0	12.3	18.4	13.8	9.6	8.8	13.0
Unknown	..	..	..	0.4	..	..	..	..	..	0.8	0.1	..	..
Median tenure (years)													
All persons	3.5	4.1	5.2	7.5	7.5	8.2	3.1	6.5	6.3	5.0	4.4	3.0	5.4
Average tenure (years)													
All persons	6.8	7.8	9.0	10.1	10.4	10.9	7.0	9.4	9.8	8.8	7.9	6.7	8.7

Note: .. Data not available.
1. The data are not perfectly comparable across countries, because of differences in data sources, population and sector coverage, reference years, and definitions. For more details, consult the source.
2. 1990.
3. 1989.
4. 1992.
5. One year and under three years; three years and under five years.
6. Under 21 months, 21 months and under 33 months, 33 months and under 57 months, under 57 months.
Source: OECD (1993b), Table 4.1, p. 121.

Table A.51. **Transition systems and youth unemployment, 1992**[1]

Type of vocational education	Youth unemployment, percentage of population	Youth unemployment, percentage of labour force	Adult unemployment rate, percentage of workforce 25-64 years
Predominantly work-based			
Austria	2.7	. .	3.6
Germany	3.2	7.2	6.2
Switzerland	3.2	. .	2.5
Hybrid			
Denmark	7.5	15.2	10.6
Predominantly institution-based			
France	7.1	20.8	8.8
Japan	2.0	3.8	. .
Netherlands	6.5	7.8	5.6
Sweden	6.3	11.5	3.8
United Kingdom	11.2	15.4	8.4
United States	8.9	14.2	6.6

Note: . . Data not available.

1. Youth unemployment is measured both as a percentage of all persons in the population aged 15-24 years, and as a percentage of the labour force aged 15-24 years. Because of the differences in the enrolment rates among countries, the labour force participation rates differ significantly. It is for this reason that youth unemployment is expressed not only as a percentage of the labour force, which is the conventional approach, but also as a percentage of the whole cohort aged 15 to 24 years.

Sources: OECD (1995d), *Education at a Glance – OECD Indicators,* Table C12(b), p. 42; and OECD (1995j), *Employment Outlook,* Table P, p. 218.

Table A.52.   **Participants in labour market training programmes**

(percentage of the labour force)

	Training for unemployed adults and those at risk		Training for employed adults		Support of apprenticeship and related general youth training	
	1990/91	1993/94	1990/91	1993/94	1990/91	1993/94
North America						
Canada	1.2	2.8	0.7	0.2	–	–
United States[1]	0.9	0.7	–	–	0.1	0.1
Pacific Area						
Australia	1.9	3.6	..	0.4	0.7	0.8
New Zealand	5.0	5.3	–	–	0.3	0.3
European Community						
Belgium	1.9	2.5	5.6	6.0	–	–
Denmark[2]	1.3	4.2	5.4	7.9	–	–
France	2.5	3.2	1.9	1.6	2.0	1.9
Germany[3]	3.7	1.9	0.5	0.1	0.2	0.2
Greece	0.1	0.2	0.9	1.1	0.3	0.3
Ireland[4]	1.6	..	1.8	..	0.7	..
Italy	–	–	–	–	3.3	2.1
Netherlands	1.6	1.4	–	–	0.8	0.7
Portugal	0.1	0.6	1.0	2.1	0.8	0.6
Spain	1.5	0.4	0.4	0.2	–	–
United Kingdom[5]	1.1	0.9	–	–	0.8	0.5
Other Europe – OECD						
Austria	1.3	–	..	–	..	–
Finland	1.4	3.3	–	–	0.3	0.6
Norway	2.7	3.6	–	–	..	..
Sweden	1.7	3.0	0.5	0.5	–	–
Switzerland	0.1	1.1	0.1	0.1	–	–

Notes: .. Data not available; – Nil or less than half of the last digit used.
1. 1993/94 is 1992/93.
2. 1990/91 is 1990; 1993/94 is 1994.
3. 1990/91 is 1991; 1993/94 is 1994. Figures refer to the whole of Germany.
4. 1990/91 is 1991.
5. Excluding Northern Ireland.
Source: OECD (1995j), Employment Outlook, Table T, pp. 222-229.

Table A.53.   **Participation in job-related continuing education and training**[1]

(percentage of the employed population aged 25-64, by level of education)

		Lower secondary education or less	Upper secondary education	Tertiary education	Total
During the 12-month period preceding the survey					
Canada	1991	13	25	40	30
Finland	1990	28	47	74	46
France[2]	1992	13	31	46	27
Germany[3]	1991	11	23	41	27
Norway	1991	17	33	57	37
Sweden[4]	1993	21	34	53	36
Switzerland	1993	16	39	52	38
United States[5]	1991	10	30	54	38
During the 4-week period preceding the survey					
Denmark	1991	6	14	25	15
Ireland[6]	1992	2	4	8	4
Spain	1992	1	6	7	3
United Kingdom	1992	4	10	19	11

1.   A definition of job-related continuing education and training for adults is given in OECD (1995k), p. 148.
2.   The data on continuing education and training are related to training provided or financed by the employers. Due to employers' legal obligation to provide continuing education and training, there are administrative data sources available that give the number of employed who have participated in training during a given year. The labour force surveys give data on the number of participants in continuing education and training on the day of the survey.
3.   Training of students over 25 years old in vocational schools and in the dual system in the framework of initial training is not considered to be continuing vocational education. Forms of continuing vocational education other than courses are also not considered.
4.   The data refer to continuing education and training provided or sponsored by the employer. The data were collected in the Labour Force Survey of June 1993. The reference period in the survey was six months. The number of people involved in training during a 12-month period is assumed to be 150 per cent of the training rate during six months. Labour market training is not included.
5.   Respondents were asked to list up to four adult education activities or courses taken in the past 12 months, and to indicate whether or not they were taken for credit towards a degree and whether or not they were completed. The data are restricted to those who indicated that the main reason for participation was: a) to improve, advance, or keep up to date on the current job; b) to train for a new job or a new career and; c) for other employment or career-related reasons.
6.   Job-related training for the employed includes training related to employment in the workplace and in an educational institution.
Source: OECD (1995d), Education at a Glance – OECD Indicators.

Table A.54.   **Participation by age in job-related continuing education and training**[1]

(percentage of the employed population aged 25 to 64, by age groups)

		Age groups			Total
		25-34 years	35-44 years	45-64 years	
During the 12-month period preceding the survey					
Canada	1991	32	35	23	30
Finland	1990	51	49	40	46
France	1992	43	27	11	27
Germany	1991	33	29	21	27
Norway	1991	40	42	30	37
Sweden	1993	36	33	41	36
Switzerland	1993	42	41	34	38
United States	1991	37	43	33	38
During the 4-week period preceding the survey					
Denmark	1991	17	17	11	15
Ireland	1992	5	4	2	4
Spain	1992	6	2	1	3
United Kingdom	1992	12	12	8	11

1.   See Annex Table A.53.
Source: OECD (1995d), Education at a Glance – OECD Indicators.

Table A.55. **Percentage of respondents who thought it was "very important" for decisions to be taken by schools themselves, 1993-94[1]**

	What subjects are taught	How subjects are taught	Amount of time spent teaching each subject	How the school budget is spent	Teacher selection and promotion	Teachers' salaries and working conditions	Items average within each country
North America							
United States	53	60	57	64	67	57	59.8
European Community							
Belgium (Flemish community)	22	41	27	36	39	26	31.9
Denmark	20	32	16	34	31	12	24.0
France	34	56	51	50	59	43	48.7
Netherlands	15	35	22	31	47	24	28.9
Portugal	44	55	50	56	51	37	48.8
Spain	13	19	17	19	20	13	16.9
United Kingdom	39	50	44	57	50	32	45.3
Other Europe – OECD							
Austria	31	36	28	33	31	18	29.6
Finland	18	35	26	40	34	22	28.9
Sweden	23	38	24	51	44	17	32.8
Switzerland	18	32	21	22	26	14	22.0
Country average for each item	**27.7**	**40.6**	**31.8**	**41.0**	**41.6**	**26.2**	

1. The data come from a questionnaire distributed to a sample of the general public in each of the participating OECD countries. The questionnaire referred specifically to the final years of compulsory secondary education and a common set of questions were asked in all countries. The organisation of the survey was undertaken within each country and the surveys were administered by reputable national survey organisations. The recommended sample size was 1 000 individuals.

Sources: OECD (1995l) and OECD (1995n).

Table A.56. **Perceived confidence in school subjects and cross-curricular qualities, 1993-94**

Respondents who viewed subjects as important and who thought they were well taught, and respondents who thought personal attitudes and attributes were important and that they were well developed

	Average confidence in important subjects (per cent)	Average confidence in important qualities (per cent)
Austria	78	63
Belgium (Flemish community)	72	58
Denmark	75	69
Finland	77	55
France	84	62
Netherlands	64	51
Portugal	58	58
Spain	46	37
Sweden	40	18
Switzerland	76	63
United Kingdom	63	47
United States	63	59
Country average	**66.2**	**53.4**

Source: OECD (1995l), *Public Expectations of the Final Stage of Compulsory Education*, Table C23, p. 132.

Table A.57. **Number of teaching hours per year, by level of public education, 1992**

	Primary education	Lower secondary education	Upper secondary education (general)	Upper secondary education (vocational)
North America				
United States	1 093	1 042	1 019	. .
Pacific Area				
New Zealand	790	897	813	. .
European Community				
Belgium	840	720	660	849
France	944	632	. .	. .
Germany (FTFR)	790	761	673	679
Ireland	951	792	792	792
Italy	748	612	612	612
Netherlands	1 000	954	954	. .
Portugal	882	648	612	612
Spain	900	900	630	630
United Kingdom	. .	669	. .	. .
Other Europe – OECD				
Austria	780	747	664	714
Finland	874	798	760	855
Norway	749	666	627	627
Sweden	624	576	528	612
Turkey	900	1 080	1 080	1 692
Country average	**858**	**781**	**745**	**789**

Note: . . Data not available.
Source: OECD (1995d), *Education at a Glance – OECD Indicators.*

Table A.58. **Staff employed in education as a percentage of the labour force, 1992**

	Public and private education[1,2]			
	Teachers	Pedagogical staff	Support staff	All staff
North America				
United States	2.7	1.5	2.1	6.2
Pacific Area				
Australia	2.9	0.3	1.2	4.2
Japan	2.4	..	0.7	3.1
European Community				
Belgium	4.8	0.6	0.6	6.0
Denmark	3.3	1.6	0.9	5.7
France	3.3	..	..	5.5
Italy	4.2	0.4	0.8	5.5
Other Europe – OECD				
Finland	3.1	..	..	5.1

Note: .. Data not available.
1. Data refer to full-time equivalent staff.
2. Public and private education; primary, secondary and tertiary levels of education.
Source: OECD (1995d), *Education at a Glance – OECD Indicators.*

Table A.59. **Index of computer use for instruction
in four subjects, 1989 and 1992[1]**

	Yield score[2]	
	1989	1992
Austria	27.6	74.1
Germany	35.9	55.4
Japan	14.9	37.3
Netherlands	37.9	63.0
United States	55.1	66.1

1. The subjects are mathematics, science, mother tongue and technology or computer education.
2. The index is based on a yield score that shows the degree of computer use in four subjects in grades 7, 8 and 9 of lower secondary schools using computers.
Source: Brummelhuis (1995), p. 53.

Table A.60. **Expenditure on educational R&D as a percentage of total expenditure on education and of total expenditure on R&D**

(in millions of local currency and at current prices)

		Total public and private educational R&D expenditure (a)	Total public and private educational expenditure (b)	Total public and private R&D expenditure (c)	a/b (%)	a/c (%)
Australia	1990-91	78	21 043	5 091[1]	0.37	1.53
Austria	1989	143	. .	22 967		0.62
Canada	1991-92	118[2]	49 022	10 289	0.24	1.15
Finland	1991	120[3]	41 455	10 171	0.29	1.18
Ireland	1991-92	3[3]	1 638	318	0.18	0.94
Netherlands	1991	98	31 340	10 381	0.31	0.94
New Zealand	1991-92	7	. .	644[4]	. .	1.09
Sweden	1991-92	231[1,2]	100 286	41 352[4]	0.23	0.56
United Kingdom	1991-92	53[3]	. .	12 619	. .	0.42

Note: . . Data not available.

1. Data for 1990.
2. Likely to be underestimated since only data for the tertiary education sector are included.
3. Likely to be underestimated since data are not available for the private non-profit sector. In Finland a potentially more important source of underestimation is the lack of data on expenditure on land, buildings and other capital items for educational R&D. In Ireland and the United Kingdom, the non-inclusion of central overheads attributable to educational R&D in the tertiary education sector is a potentially more important source of underestimation.
4. Data for 1991.

Source: OECD (1995*u*), p. 45.

Table A.61. **Education and earnings, 1992**[1]

	Men			Women		
	Early childhood, primary and lower secondary education	Non-university tertiary education	University education	Early childhood, primary and lower secondary education	Non-university tertiary education	University education
North America						
Canada[2]	81	107	162	72	116	174
United States	66	120	164	65	130	170
Pacific Area						
Australia[2]	88	121	158	90	124	175
New Zealand	74	85	118	73	98	154
European Community						
Belgium	86	115	149	78	137	164
Denmark[2]	86	110	146	86	111	135
France	87	127	174	81	131	142
Germany	88	116	170	84	114	175
Italy[2]	84	x	134	86	x	116
Netherlands	84	x	132	73	x	147
Portugal[3]	65	124	179	67	117	188
Spain[2]	78	x	138	71	x	149
United Kingdom	80	121	171	70	156	206
Other Europe – OECD						
Austria	85	x	146	81	x	134
Finland[2]	93	132	192	94	132	176
Norway	80	131	165	76	131	157
Sweden	88	118	160	92	119	156
Switzerland	76	127	152	67	126	152

Note. x Data included in another category.
1. Ratio of mean annual earnings by level of educational attainment to mean annual earnings at upper secondary level (multiplied by 100) in the population 25 to 64 years of age, by gender.
2. 1991 data.
3. 1993 data.
Source. OECD (1995d), *Education at a Glance – OECD Indicators*, p. 233.

Table A.62. **Unit costs per student by level of education, 1992[1]**

	Level of education[2]		
	Early childhood	Secondary	Tertiary (full-time)
North America			
Canada	. .	. .	12 400
United States	3 200	6 500	6 600
Pacific Area			
Australia	. .	. .	11 900
Japan	3 000	3 900	11 900
New Zealand	1 900	2 700	6 100
European Community			
Belgium	2 300	6 700	6 900
Denmark	6 300	4 900	6 700
France	2 600	5 900	6 000
Germany (FTFR)	3 400	4 300	6 600
Ireland	1 800	2 800	7 300
Netherlands[3]	2 300	4 300	10 800
Spain	2 100	3 100	3 800
United Kingdom	1 900	4 400	15 100
Other Europe – OECD			
Austria	3 300	6 400	5 800
Finland	6 300	4 800	8 700
Norway	7 400	6 200	8 700
Sweden	6 100	6 100	7 100
Switzerland	1 900	. .	12 900

Note: . . Data not available.
1. Expressed in US dollars, adjusted using purchasing power parities (PPP). Rounded to nearest 100 dollars.
2. Public institutions only.
3. Public and government dependent private institutions.
Source: OECD (1995d), *Education at a Glance – OECD Indicators*, Table F.03, pp. 88-92.

Table A.63. **Percentage of adult education and training courses that are employer-supported, 1994[1]**

(by duration of training)[2]

	Duration			Total
	Low	Medium	High	
Canada (English)	57	28	4	37
Canada (French)	45	39	0	30
Germany	45	32	18	37
Netherlands	54	38	13	40
Poland	56	36	23	44
Switzerland (French)	46	30	20	36
Switzerland (German)	46	39	16	38
United States	66	45	6	51

1. Based on the first reported course being taken in the six months preceding the interview.
2. Low: 0-59 hours. Medium: 60-300 hours. High: > 300 hours.
Sources: OECD and Statisctics Canada (1995).

BIBLIOGRAPHY

ALBA-RAMIREZ, A. (1994), "Formal training, temporary contracts, productivity and wages in Spain", *Oxford Bulletin of Economics and Statistics,* Vol. 56, pp. 151-170.

ALSALAM, N. and CONLEY, R. (1995), "The rate of return to education: A proposal for a new indicator", in *Education and Employment,* OECD (1995k), Paris.

ANGRIST, J.T. and KRUEGER, A.B. (1991), "Does compulsory school attendance affect schooling and earnings?", *Quarterly Journal of Economics,* Vol. 106, No. 4, pp. 979-1014.

ARROW, K.J. (1973), "Higher education as a filter", *Journal of Public Economics,* Vol. 2, pp. 193-216.

ASHENFELTER, O. and CARD, D. (1985), "Using the longitudinal structure of earnings to estimate the effect of training program", *Review of Economics and Statistics,* pp. 648-660.

ASHENFELTER, O. and KRUEGER, A.B. (1994), "Estimates of the economic return to schooling from a new sample of twins", *American Economic Review,* Vol. 84, December, pp. 1157-1173.

Australian Department of Employment, Education and Training (1995), *The First Years of Tertiary Education in Australia. A Thematic Review Prepared for the Education Committee of the OECD,* Canberra.

Australian Education Council (1992), *National Report on Schooling in Australia,* Statistical Annex, Curriculum Corporation, Carlton, Victoria.

AUSUBEL, J.H. and GRUBLER, A. (1994), "Working less and living longer: Long-term trends in working time and time budgets", mimeo, OECD, Paris.

AW, B. and TAN, H.W. (1995), "Training, technology and firm-level productivity in Taiwan" (Chinese Taipei), prepared for the conference on Enterprise Training Strategies and Productivity, mimeo, The World Bank, Washington, DC, June.

BARNETT, W. (1992), "Benefits of compensatory pre-school education", *Journal of Human Resources,* Vol. 27, No. 2, pp. 279-312.

BARNOW, B. (1987), "The impact of CETA programmes on earnings: A review of the literature", *Journal of Human Resources,* Vol. 22, pp. 157-193.

BARRON, J.M., BLACK, D.A. and LOEWENSTEIN, M.A. (1989), "Job matching and on-the-job training", *Journal of Labor Economics,* Vol. 7, pp. 1-19.

BARTEL, A. (1991), "Employee training programs in US business", in D. Stern and J.M.M. Ritzen (eds.), *Market Failure in Training? New Economic Analysis and Evidence on Training of Adult Employees,* Springer-Verlag, Berlin, pp. 99-134.

BARTEL, A. (1995), "Training wage growth and job performance: Evidence from a company database", *Journal of Labor Economics,* Vol. 13, pp. 401-425.

BARTEL, A. and SICHERMAN, N. (1995), "Technological change and the skill acquisition of young workers", National Bureau of Economic Research, Working Paper 5107, New York.

BASSI, L. (1984), "Estimating the effect of training programs with non-random selection", *Review of Economics and Statistics,* Vol. 66, pp. 36-43.

BATES, T. (1995), *Technology, Open Learning and Distance Education,* Routledge Studies in Distance Education, London.

BECKER, G.S. (1962), "Investment in human capital: A theoretical analysis", *Journal of Political Economy,* Vol. 70, pp. 9-49.

BECKER, G.S. (1975), *Human Capital: A Theoretical and Empirical Analysis with Special Reference to Education,* National Bureau of Economic and Social Research, New York.

BELL, D. (1973), *The Coming of Post-industrial Society: A Venture in Social Forecasting,* Basic Books, New York.

BELL, S. and ORR, L. (1994), "Is subsidised employment cost effective for welfare recipients? Experimental evidence from seven state demonstrations", *Journal of Human Resources,* Vol. 30, pp. 42-61.

BENGTSSON, J. (1985), "Recurrent education", *International Encyclopedia of Education,* Vol. 7, Pergamon Press, Oxford.

BENNETT, R., GLENNERSTER, H. and NEVISON, D. (1993), *Learning Should Pay,* British Petroleum Educational Service, Poole, Dorset, United Kingdom.

BERG, I. (1970), *Education and Jobs: The Great Training Robbery,* Praeger, New York.

BISHOP, J. (1987), "The recognition and reward of employee performance", *Journal of Labor Economics,* Vol. 5, S36-S56 (supplement).

BISHOP, J. (1989a), "Occupational training in high school: When does it pay off?", *Economics of Education Review*, Vol. 8, pp. 1-15.

BISHOP, J. (1989b), "Job performance, turnover and wage growth", Working Paper 88-03, New York State School of Industrial and Labor Relations, Cornell University, New York.

BISHOP, J. (1991), "On-the-job training of new hires", in D. Stern and J.M.M. Ritzen (eds.), *Market Failure in Training? New Economic Analysis and Evidence on Training of Adult Employees*, Springer Verlag, Berlin, pp. 61-98.

BISHOP, J. (1994), "The impact of previous training on productivity and wages", in L.M. Lynch (ed.), *Training and the Private Sector: International Comparisons*, University of Chicago Press, Chicago, Illinois, pp. 185-186.

BISHOP, J. (1995), *The Impact of Curriculum-based External Examinations on School Priorities and Student Learning*, Working paper 95-30, Center for Advanced Human Resource Studies, Cornell University, New York.

BJÖRKLUND, A. (1991), "Evaluation of labour market policy in Sweden", *Evaluating Labour Market and Social Programmes. The State of a Complex Art*, OECD, Paris, pp. 73-88.

BJÖRKLUND, A. and MOFFITT, R. (1987), "The estimation of wage gains and welfare gains in self-selection models", *The Review of Economics and Statistics*, Vol. 64, pp. 42-49.

BLACKBURNE, L. (1992), "Nursery children get Head Start", *Times Educational Supplement*, 24 July.

BLANCHFLOWER, R. and LYNCH, L.M. (1992), "Training at work: A comparison of US and British youths", Discussion Paper 78, Economic and Social Research Council, London School of Economics, London.

BLANCHFLOWER, R. and LYNCH, L.M. (1994), "Training at work: A comparison of US and British youths," in L.M. Lynch (ed.), *Training and the Private Sector: International Comparisons*, University of Chicago Press, Chicago, Illinois.

BLAUG, M. (1970), *Introduction to the Economics of Education*, Penguin Books, Harmondsworth.

BLUNDELL, R., DEARDEN, L. and MEGHIR, C. (1994), "The determinants and effects of work-related training in Britain", mimeo, University College, London.

BOOTH, A. (1992), "Job-related formal training: Who receives it and what is it worth", *Oxford Bulletin of Economics and Statistics*, Vol. 53, pp. 281-294.

BOUND, J. and JOHNSON, G. (1992), "Changes in the structure of wages in the 1980s: An evaluation of alternative explanations", *American Economic Review*, Vol. 82, pp. 371-392.

BREMER, L. and VAN DER WENDE, M. (1995), *Internationalising the Curriculum in Higher Education*, Nuffic Papers 3, Netherlands Universities Foundation for International Co-operation, The Hague.

BROWN, J. (1989), "Why do wages rise with tenure? On the-job training and life cycle wage growth within firms", *American Economic Review*, Vol. 79, pp. 971-991.

BRUMMELHUIS, A.C.A. (1995), *Models of Educational Change: The Introduction of Computers in Dutch Secondary Education*, Onderzoekscentrum Toegepaste Onderwÿskunde, Twente University, Enschede.

BUECHTEMANN, C. and RYAN, P. (1996), "The school to work transition", *International Handbook of Labour Market Policy and Policy Evaluation*, Social Science Research Center, Berlin.

CAPPELLI, P. (1993), "Are skill requirements rising? Evidence for production and clerical jobs", *Industrial and Labor Relations Review*, Vol. 46, pp. 515-530.

CARD, D. and KRUEGER, A.B. (1992a), "Does school quality matter? Returns to education and the characteristics of public schools in the United States", *Journal of Political Economy*, Vol. 100, No. 1, pp. 1-40.

CARD, D. and KRUEGER, A.B. (1992b), "School quality and black-white relative earnings: A direct assessment", *Quarterly Journal of Economics*, Vol. 107, February pp. 151-200.

CARD, D. and SULLIVAN, D. (1988), "Measuring the effect of subsidised training programs on movements in and out of employment", *Econometrica*, Vol. 56 pp. 497-530.

CARNOY, M. and CASTELLS, M. (1995), "Sustainable flexibility: A prospective study on work, family and society in the information age", mimeo, Stanford university Stanford, CA.

CHAFEL, A. (1992), "Funding Head Start: What are the issues?", *American Journal of Orthopsychiatry*, Vol. 62. No. 1, January, pp. 9-21.

CHO, S.J. (1994), "Five-year plan for new economy and vocational and technical education system", prepared for the OECD seminar on Education and Training for the Workforce, Seoul, 30 May-1 June.

CHUBB, J. and MOE, T. (1993), "The forest and the trees: A response to our critics", in E. Rasell and R. Rothstein (eds.), *School Choice: Examining the Evidence*, Economic Policy Institute, Washington, DC.

COHN, E. and ADDISON, J. (1995), "The economic returns to lifelong learning", mimeo, OECD, Paris.

COHN, E. and KHAN, S.P. (1995), "The wage effects of overschooling revisited", *Labour Economics*, Vol. 2.

COLARDYN, D. (1994), "Certification of adult education", *International Encyclopedia of Education*, 2nd Edition, Pergamon Press, Oxford, Vol. 2, pp. 62-65.

COLARDYN, D. and DURAND-DROUHIN, M. (1995), "Recognising skills and qualifications", *The OECD Observer*, April/May, pp. 12-16.

COLLETTA, N. (1994), "Formal, non-formal and informal education", *International Encyclopedia of Education*,

2nd Edition, Pergamon Press, Oxford, Vol. 4, pp. 2364-2369.

Committee for Economic Development (1985), *Investing in Our Children,* New York.

Committee for Quality Assurance in Higher Education, Australia (1995), *Report on 1994 Quality Reviews,* Vol. 1 and 2, Australian Government Publishing Service, Canberra.

CROSS, K.P. (1981), *Adults as Learners,* Jossey-Bass, San Francisco.

CURRIE, J. and THOMAS, D. (1993), "Does Head Start make a difference?", National Bureau of Economic Research, Working Paper No. 4406, July.

Danish Ministry of Education (1993), "Education and training for all young people", National contribution to the OECD Education Committee activity on "combating failure at school", Copenhagen.

Danish Ministry of Education (1994), *Danish Youth Education: Problems and Achievements,* Report to the OECD, Copenhagen.

Direction de l'évaluation et de la prospective (DEP) (1994), *L'étude de l'école,* ministère de l'Éducation nationale, DEP, Paris.

DOLTON, P. (1992), "The market for qualified manpower in the United Kingdom", *Oxford Review of Economic Policy,* Vol. 8, pp. 103-129.

DOLTON, P., MAKEPEACE, G. and TREBLE, J. (1994), "Public and private sector training of young people in Britain", in L.M. Lynch, (ed.), *Training and the Private Sector: International Comparisons,* University of Chicago Press, Chicago, Illinois, pp. 261-282.

DRUCKER, P.F. (1994), "The age of social transformation", *The Atlantic Monthly,* November, pp. 53-80.

DUNCAN, G. and HOFFMAN, S. (1978), "Training and earnings", in G. Duncan and J. Morgan, (eds.), *Five-thousand American Families: Patterns of Economics Progress,* Institute for Social Research, Ann Arbor, Michigan, pp. 105-150.

DUNCAN, G. and HOFFMAN, S. (1979), "On-the-job training and earnings differences by race and sex", *Review of Economics and Statistics,* Vol. 61, pp. 594-603.

Dutch Ministry of Education and Science (1989), *Richness of the Uncompleted: Challenges Facing Dutch Education,* The Hague.

EBUCHI, K. (1989), *Foreign Students and Internationalisation of Higher Education. Proceedings of OECD/Japan Seminar on Higher Education and the Flow of Foreign Students,* Research Institute for Higher Education, Hiroshima University, Hiroshima.

ECKSTEIN, M.A. and NOAH, H.J. (1993), *Secondary School Examinations: International Perspectives on Policies and Practices,* Yale University Press, New Haven.

EICHER, J.C. and CHEVALLIER, T. (1993), "Rethinking the finance of post-compulsory education", *International Journal of Educational Research,* Vol. 5, pp. 445-519.

ELIAS, P., HERNAES, E. and BAKER, M. (1994), "Vocational education and training in Britain and Norway", in L.M. Lynch (ed.), *Training and the Private Sector: International Comparisons,* University of Chicago Press, Chicago, Illinois, pp. 283-289.

ELLEY, W.B. (1992), *How in the World do Students Read?,* Grindeldruck, Hamburg.

Employment Department, United Kingdom (1994), *Modern Apprenticeships,* Young People and Work Branch, Sheffield.

ENDSLEY, R. (1993), "Parent involvement and quality day care in proprietary centers", *Journal of Research in Childhood Education,* Vol. 7, No. 2, pp. 53-61.

European Round Table of Industrialists (1995), *Education for Europeans. Towards the Learning Society,* Brussels.

EUROSTAT (1995), *Les chiffres clés de l'éducation dans l'Union européenne,* European Communities, Luxembourg.

EURYDICE (1994a), *Pre-school and Primary Education in the European Union,* Commission of the European Communities, Brussels.

EURYDICE (1994b), *Measures to Combat Failure at School: A Challenge for the Construction of Europe,* Commission of the European Communities, Brussels.

FAURE, E., HERRERA, F., KADDOURA, A.R., LOPES, H., PETROVSKY, A.V., RAHNEMA, M. and WARD, F.C. (1972), *Learning to Be: The World of Education Today and Tomorrow,* UNESCO, Paris.

French Ministry of Higher Education and Research (1993), "Quelques aspects de la politique française sur l'internationalisation de l'enseignement supérieur", Statement prepared for the CERI seminar on "Higher Education in a New International Setting", mimeo, OECD, Paris.

French Ministry of National Education (1994), "The French Education System: Background Report to the OECD", Paris.

GARDNER, H. (1987), *The Mind's New Science: A History of the Cognitive Revolution,* Basic Books, New York.

GELDERBLOM, A., 'T HOEN, N.B.J.G. and DE KONING, J. (1994), *Wat wordt men wijzer van onderwijs?,* OSA, Ministry of Labour, The Hague.

GOODLAD, J. (1984), *A Place Called School,* McGraw-Hill, New York.

GORDON, J. and JALLADE, J-P. (1995), "La mobilité étudiante au sein de l'Union Europénne : Une analyse statistique", in C. Kaufmann, J. Milquet and A. Philippart (eds.), *Student Mobility in Europe,* French Community of Belgium, and European Commission, Brussels.

GREENHALGH, C. and STEWART, M. (1987), "The effects and determinants of training", *Oxford Bulletin of Economics and Statistics*, Vol. 49, pp. 171-190.

GRIFFITHS, G. and SAUNDERS, A. (1979), "Returns on investment: A note on male and female higher education in the United Kingdom, 1966-1973", *Public Finance Quarterly*, Vol. 7, January, pp. 110-121.

GROOT, W. (1993), "Over-education and the returns to enterprise-related schooling", *Economics of Education Review*, Vol. 12, pp. 299-309.

GROOT, W. (1994), "Bedrijfsopleidingen goed voor loon en produktiviteit", *Economisch Statistische Berichten*, No. 3988, pp. 1108-1111.

GROOT, W. (1995), "Type specific returns to enterprise-related training", *Economics of Education Review*, Vol. 14 (4), pp. 323-333.

GROOT, W. and OOSTERBEEK, H. (1994), "Earnings effects of different components of schooling: Human capital versus screening", *Review of Economics and Statistics*, Vol. 76, pp. 317-321.

GROOT, W. and OOSTERBEEK, H. (1995), "Determinants and wage effects of participation in on- and off-the-job training", Research Memorandum 95-122, Tinbergen Institute, Rotterdam.

GROOT, W., HARTOG, J. and OOSTERBEEK, H. (1994), "Returns to within-company schooling of employees: The case of the Netherlands", in L.M. Lynch (ed.), *Training and the Private Sector: International Comparisons*, University of Chicago Press, Chicago, pp. 299-307.

GROSSMAN, M. and KAESTNER, R. (1995), "Social benefits of education: Health", presented at the conference on Social Benefits of Education: Can They be Measured?, Office Educational Research and Improvement, US Department of Education, Washington, DC, January.

GRUBB, W.N. (1992), "Post-secondary vocational education and the sub-baccalaureate labor market: New evidence on economic returns", *Economics of Education Review*, Vol. 11, September, pp. 225-248.

GRUBB, W.N. (1995), "Post-secondary education and the sub-baccalaureate labor market: Corrections and extensions", *Economics of Education Review*, Vol. 14, September.

GRUBB, W.N., DAVIS, G., PLIHAL, J. and LUM, J. (1991), "The cunning hand, the cultured mind: Models for integrating vocational and academic education", National Center for Research in Vocational Education, University of California, Berkeley, California.

GRUBER, K.H. (1995), "Comparative comments on educational research and development in Austria, Germany and Switzerland", in *Educational Research and Development in Austria, Germany and Switzerland*, OECD, Paris.

HALSEY, A.H. (1961), *Ability and Educational Opportunity*, OECD, Paris.

HANSEN, S.L. (1994), "Lost talent: Unrealised educational aspirations and expectations among US youth", *Sociology of Education*, Vol. 67, pp. 159-183.

HARMON, C. and WALKER, I. (1993), "Schooling and earnings in the UK – Evidence from the ROSLA experiment", *Economic and Social Review*, Vol. 25, October pp. 77-93.

HARTOG, J. and OOSTERBEEK, H. (1988), "Education allocation and earnings in the Netherlands: Over schooling?", *Economics of Education Review*, Vol. 7 pp. 317-321.

HARTOG, J., OOSTERBEEK, H. and TEULINGS, C. (1994) "Age, wage and education in the Netherlands", in P. Johnson and K.F. Zimmerman (eds.), *Labour Markets in an Ageing Europe*, Cambridge University Press Cambridge.

HAVEMAN, R. and HOLLISTER, R. (1991), "Direct job creation: Economic evaluation and lessons for the United States and Western Europe", in A. Björklund B. Haveman, R. Hollister and B. Holmlund (eds.) *Labour Market Policy and Unemployment Insurance* Clarendon Press, Oxford.

HAVEMAN, R.H. and WOLFE, B.L. (1984), "Schooling and economic well-being", *Journal of Human Resources*, Vol. 19, pp. 377-407.

HEBENSTREIT, J. (1994), "The future of technology in post-secondary education", presented at the OECD conference on Learning Beyond Schooling, OECD, Paris December.

HENIG, J.R. (1994), *Rethinking School Choice: Limits of the Market Metaphor*, Princeton University Press, Princeton, New Jersey.

HERSCH, J. (1991), "Education match and job match", *Review of Economics and Statistics*, Vol. 73, pp. 140-144.

HEYWOOD, J.S. (1994), "How widespread are sheepskin returns to education in the US?", *Economics of Education Review*, Vol. 13, September, pp. 227-234.

HIGGINS, N. (1992), "The effectiveness of YTS in Britain: An analysis of sample selection in the determination of employment and earnings", presented at the OEP conference on Vocational Training in Britain and Europe, September.

HOLZER, H. (1988), "The determinants of employee productivity and earnings", National Bureau of Economic Research, Working Paper 2782, New York.

HOLZER, H. (1990), "The determinants of employee productivity and earnings", *Industrial Relations*, pp. 403-422.

HOPKINS, D. (1994), "Primary effect 'lasts to GCSE'", *Times Educational Supplement*, 9 September.

HOWE 2nd, H. (1994), "The systemic epidemic", *Education Week*, 13 July.

HOWE 2nd, H. (1995), "Uncle Sam is in the classroom!", *Phi Delta Kappan*, pp. 374-377, January.

HULL, D and PARNELL, D. (1991), "Tech. prep. associate degree: Win/win experience", Center for Occupational Research and Development, Waco, Texas.

HUNGERFORD, T. and SOLON, G. (1987), "Sheepskin effects in the returns to education", *Review of Economics and Statistics*, Vol. 69, pp. 175-177.

HUSÉN, T. (1969), *Talent, Opportunity and Career*, Almqvist and Wiksell, Stockholm.

HUSÉN, T. (1979), *The School in Question: A Comparative Study of the School and the Future in Western Societies*, Oxford University Press, London.

HUSÉN, T. (1987), *The Learning Society Revisited*, Pergamon Press, Oxford.

HUSÉN, T., TUIJNMAN, A.C and HALLS, W.D. (1992), *Schooling in Modern European Society: A Report of the Academia Europaea*, Pergamon Press, Oxford.

ILLICH, I. (1968), *De-schooling Society*, Penguin Books, Harmondsworth.

Irish Department of Education (1995), *Charting our Education Future: White Paper on Education*, Dublin.

ISHIDA, H., MULLER, W. and RIDGE, J.M. (1996), "Class origin, class destination, and education: A cross-national study of ten industrial nations", *American Journal of Sociology* (forthcoming).

Japanese Ministry of Education, Sciences and Culture (1994), *Education in Japan: A Graphic Presentation*, Tokyo.

Japanese Ministry of Education, Sciences and Culture (1995), *New Direction in School Education: Fostering Strength for Life*, Tokyo.

JAROUSSE, J.P., MIGNAT, A. and RICHARD, M. (1992), "La scolarisation maternelle à deux ans: effets pédagogiques et sociaux", *Education et Formation*, IREDU-CNRS (Institut de Recherche en Économie de l'Éducation – Centre National de Recherche Scientifique), Université de Bourgogne, April-June.

JENSEN, P., PEDERSEN, P., SMITH, N. and WESTERGARD-NIELSEN, N. (1990), "Measuring the effects of labour market training programs", mimeo, Department of Economics, University of Aarhus.

JOBST, E. (1995), "Finance and governance in a federal system: The German case", in OECD/CCET, *Education in a Federal System: Seminar Papers*, Paris, pp. 63-70.

JOHNES, G. (1993), *The Economics of Education*, Macmillan, London.

JORGENSON, D.W. and FRAUMENI, B.M. (1989), "Investment in education", *Educational Researcher*, Vol. 18 (4), pp. 35-44.

JUHN, C., MURRAY, K.M. and PIERCE, B. (1993), "Wage inequality and the rise in the returns to skill", *Journal of Political Economy*, Vol. 101, pp. 410-442.

KAWANOBE, S., YAMADA, T., TANAKA, M., KAJITA, M., YAMAMOTO, Y., ICHIKAWA, S., KIMURA, H. and INOUE, S. (1993), *A Study on Lifelong Education in Selected Industrialised Countries*, National Institute for Educational Research, Tokyo.

KEARNS, D.T. and DOYLE, D.P. (1988), "Winning the brain race: A bold plan to make our schools competitive", Institute for Contemporary Studies, San Francisco, California.

KEATING, P.J. (1994), *Working Nation: Policies and Programs*, Australian Government Publishing Service, Canberra.

KELLAGHAN, T., SLOANE, K., ALVAREZ, B. and BLOOM, B.S. (1993), *The Home Environment and School Learning: Promoting Parental Involvement in the Education of Children*, Jossey-Bass, San Francisco, California.

KILLEEN, J., WHITE, M. and WATTS, A.G. (1992), *The Economic Value of Careers Guidance*, Policy Studies Institute, London.

KIRSCH, E. (1994), "Les CAP par unités capitalisables dans la sidérurgie : une conversion réussie", *Formation Emploi*, Vol. 32, pp. 7-18.

KLOPROGGE, J.A. (1991), "Reducing educational disadvantages: Developments in the educational priority programme in the Netherlands", mimeo, OECD/CERI, Paris.

KNUTSEN, A.E. (1995), "The GOALS study: Analysis and implications", in *Measuring What Students Learn*, OECD (1995p), Paris.

KOGAN, M. (1988), *Education Accountability: An Analytic Overview*, Hutchinson, London.

KROCH, E.A. and SJOBLON, K. (1994), "Schooling as human capital or a signal: Some evidence", *Journal of Human Resources*, Vol. 29, Winter, pp. 156-180.

LALONDE, R. (1986), "Evaluating the econometric evaluations of training programs with experimental data", *American Economic Review*, Vol. 76, pp. 604-620.

LAULHÉ, P. (1990), "La formation continue: Un avantage pour les promotions à un accès privilégié pour les jeunes et les techniciens", *Economie et Statistique*, pp. 3-8.

LAYARD, R. and PSACHAROPOULOS, G. (1974), "The screening hypothesis and the returns to education", *Journal of Political Economy*, Vol. 82, pp. 985-998.

LENK, H. (1994), "Value changes and the achieving society: A social philosophical perspective", in *OECD Societies in Transition: The Future of Work and Leisure*, OECD (1994e), Paris.

LEVIN, H.M. (1995), "Long-term strategies for coherence in the finance of lifelong learning", mimeo, OECD, Paris.

LEVIN, H.M. and SCHÜTZE, H.G. (eds.) (1983), *Financing Recurrent Education: Strategies for Increasing Employment, Job Opportunities and Productivity*, Sage Publications, London.

LILLARD, L.A. and TAN, H.W. (1986), *Private Sector Training: Who Gets It and What Are Its Effects?*, Rand Monograph No. R-3331-DOL/RC, The Rand Corporation, Santa Monica, California.

LILLARD, L.A. and TAN, H.W. (1992), "Private sector training: Who gets it and why", in R. Ehrenberg (ed.), *Research in Labor Economics*, Vol. 13, pp. 162.

LIMA, R.F. (1995), "Training in Mexico: Evidence from the national employment, wages, technology and training survey", mimeo, presented at the conference on Enterprise Training Strategies and Productivity, The World Bank, Washington, DC, June.

LOW, S.A. and ORMISTON, M.B. (1991), "Stochastic earnings functions, risk, and the rate of return to schooling", *Southern Economic Journal*, Vol. 57, No. 4, pp. 1124-1132.

LYNCH, L.M. (1991), "Private sector training and its impact on the earnings of young workers", *American Economic Review*, Vol. 82, pp. 299-312.

LYNCH, L.M. (1992), "Private sector training and the earnings of young workers", *American Economic Review*, March, pp. 299-312.

LYNCH, L.M. (1994), *Training and the Private Factor: International Comparisons*, University of Chicago Press, Chicago, Illinois.

LYNCH, L.M. (1995), "Employer provided training in the manufacturing sector: First results from the United States", prepared for the conference on Enterprise Training Strategies and Productivity, The World Bank, Washington, DC, June.

MACLURE, A. and DAVIES, P. (eds.) (1991), *Learning to Think, Thinking to Learn*, proceedings of the 1989 OECD conference organised by the Centre for Educational Research and Innovation (CERI), Pergamon Press, Oxford.

MANKIW, G., ROMER, D. and WEIL, D. (1992), "A contribution to the structure of economic growth", *Quarterly Journal of Economics*, Vol. 106, pp. 407-437.

MAYNARD, R.A. (1995), "The social benefits of education: Family structure, fertility and child welfare", mimeo, presented at a conference on "Social Benefits of Education", Office for Educational Research and Improvement, US Department of Education, Washington, DC, 5 January.

McDONNELL, L.M. and ELMORE, R.F. (1987), "Getting the job done: Alternative policy instruments", *Educational Evaluation and Policy Analysis*, Vol. 9 (2), pp. 133-152.

McGUINNESS, A.C. (1995), "Higher education policy in the United States: Towards a more aggressive role", in OECD/CCET and European Commission/PHARE (eds.), *Higher Education Policy for Economies in Transition: National Strategies and Future Dimensions for Regional Co-operation*, Paris, pp. 51-64.

McLAUGHLIN, T.H. (1994), "Politics, markets and schools: The central issues", in D. Bridges and T.H. McLaughlin

(eds.), *Education and the Market Place*, Falmer Press London.

McMAHON, W.W. (1995), "Conceptual framework for the analysis of the social returns to education", mimeo prepared for the Education and Training Division OECD, Paris.

MEURET, D., PROD'HOM, J. and STOCKER, E. (1995) "Comparison of decision-making structures in education systems: A review of the quantitative approach" in *Measuring the Quality of Schools*, OECD (1995r), Paris pp. 35-58.

MIDDLETON, J., ZIDERMAN, A. and van ADAMS, A (1993), *Skills for Productivity: Vocational Education and Training in Developing Countries*, Oxford University Press, London.

MILLER, R. and WURZBURG, G. (1995), "Investing in human capital", *The OECD Observer*, April/May, pp. 16-19.

MINCER, J. (1974), *Schooling, Experience and Earnings*, National Bureau of Economic Research, New York.

MINCER, J. (1988), "Job training, wage growth, and labor turnover," Working Paper No. 2690, National Bureau of Economic Research, New York, March.

MOFFIT, R. (1992), "Incentive effects of the US welfare system: A review", *Journal of Economic Literature*, Vol. 30, pp. 1-61.

MOGHADAM, R. (1990), "Wage determination: an assessment of returns to education, occupation, regional and industry in Great Britain," Center for Economic Performance Discussion Paper 8, London School of Economics, London.

MUSGRAVE, R.A. (1959), *The Theory of Public Finance*, McGraw-Hill Book Company, New York.

National Academy of Sciences (1984), *High Schools and The Changing Workplace: The Employers' View*, Report of the Panel on Secondary School Education and the Changing Workplace, National Academy Press, Washington, DC.

National Center for Education Statistics (NCES) (1994), *The Condition of Education*, US Department of Education, Washington, DC.

National Union of Teachers (1992), *Testing and Assessing Six- and Seven-year-olds*, Hamilton House, London.

NEUMARK, D. and KORENMAN, S. (1994), "Sources of bias in women's wage equations: Results using sibling data", *Journal of Human Resources*, Vol. 29, Spring, pp. 379-405.

New Zealander Ministry of Education (1995), *Thematic Review of Tertiary Education*, Wellington.

OECD (1962), *Policy Conference on Economic Growth and Investment in Education*, Paris.

OECD (1973), *Recurrent Education. A Strategy for Lifelong Learning*, Paris.

OECD (1974), *The Teacher and Educational Change: A New Role*, Paris.

OECD (1975), *Recurrent Education. Trends and Issues*, Paris.

OECD (1977-81), *Learning Opportunities for Adults*, Vol. 1-5, Paris.

OECD (1981), *Children and Society: Issues for Pre-school Reforms*, Paris.

OECD (1982), *In-Service Education and Training of Teachers: A Condition for Educational Change*, Paris.

OECD (1988a), *Ageing Populations: The Social Policy Implications*, Paris.

OECD (1988b), *New Technologies in the 1990s: A Socio-Economic Strategy*, Paris.

OECD (1989), "Decentralisation and school improvement: New perspectives and conditions for change", mimeo, Paris.

OECD (1990a), *The Teacher Today: Tasks, Conditions, Policies*, Paris.

OECD (1990b), "Assessment and recognition of skills and competencies: Developments in France", in *Further Education and Training of the Labour Force*, mimeo, Paris.

OECD (1990c), *Employment Outlook*, July, Paris.

OECD (1991a), *Employment Outlook*, July, Paris.

OECD (1991b), "The lifelong learner in the 1990s", mimeo, Paris.

OECD (1992a), *Technology and the Economy: The Key Relationships*, Paris.

OECD (1992b), *Main Economic Indicators – Historical Statistics 1960-1990*, Paris.

OECD (1992c), *Public Educational Expenditure, Costs and Financing: An Analysis of Trends 1970-1988*, Paris.

OECD (1992d), *High-quality Education and Training for All*, Paris.

OECD (1992e), *Schools and Business: A New Partnership*, Paris.

OECD (1992f), *Education at a Glance – OECD indicators*, Paris.

OECD (1992g), *Employment Outlook*, July, Paris.

OECD (1992h), *Decentralisation and Educational Building Management: The Impact of Recent Reforms*, Paris.

OECD (1992i), *New Technology and Its Impact on Education Buildings*, Paris.

OECD (1992j), *OECD International Education Indicators – A Framework for Analysis*, Paris.

OECD (1993a), *Education at a Glance – OECD indicators*, Paris.

OECD (1993b), *Employment Outlook*, July, Paris.

OECD (1993c), *Review of National Policies for Education: Switzerland*, Paris.

OECD (1993d), *Curriculum Reform – Assessment in Question*, Paris.

OECD (1994a), *Information Technology Outlook*, Paris.

OECD (1994b), *Industrial Policy in OECD Countries, Annual Review*, Paris.

OECD (1994c), *Employment Outlook*, July, Paris.

OECD (1994d), *The OECD Jobs Study: Evidence and Explanations, Parts I and II*, Paris.

OECD (1994e), *OECD Societies in Transition: The Future of Work and Leisure*, Paris.

OECD (1994f), *The Curriculum Redefined. Schooling for the 21st Century*, Paris.

OECD (1994g), *Vocational Training in Germany: Modernisation and Responsiveness*, Paris.

OECD (1994h), *Economic Survey: United States*, Paris.

OECD (1994i), *Apprenticeship: Which Way Forward?*, Paris.

OECD (1994j), *Vocational Education and Training for Youth: Towards Coherent Policy and Practice*, Paris.

OECD (1994k), *Vocational Training in the Netherlands: Reform and Innovation*, Paris.

OECD (1994l), *Quality in Teaching*, Paris.

OECD (1994m), *Making Education Count: Developing and Using International Indicators*, Paris.

OECD (1994n), *The OECD Jobs Study: Facts, Analysis, Strategies*, Paris.

OECD (1994o), *Evaluating Innovation in Environmental Education*, Paris.

OECD (1994p), *School: A Matter of Choice*, Paris.

OECD (1995a), *Communications Outlook*, Paris.

OECD (1995b), *Trends in International Migration, Annual Report*, Paris

OECD (1995c), *Economic Outlook*, Vol. 57, June, Paris.

OECD (1995d), *Education at a Glance – OECD Indicators*, Paris.

OECD (1995e), *The OECD Jobs Study – Implementing the Strategy*, Paris.

OECD (1995f), *Our Children At Risk*, Paris.

OECD (1995g), *Schools under Scrutiny*, Paris.

OECD (1995h), *Integrating Students with Special Needs into Mainstream Schools*, Paris.

OECD (1995i), *Learning Beyond Schooling: New Forms of Supply and New Demands*, Paris.

OECD (1995j), *Employment Outlook*, July, Paris.

OECD (1995k), *Education and Employment*, Paris.

OECD (1995l), *Public Expectations of the Final Stage of Compulsory Education*, Paris.

OECD (1995m), *Reviews of National Policies for Education – Denmark*, Paris.

OECD (1995n), *Evaluation and the Decision-Making Process in Higher Education: French, German and Spanish Experiences*, Paris.

OECD (1995o), *Decision-Making in 14 OECD Education Systems*, Paris.

OECD (1995p), *Measuring What Students Learn*, Paris.

OECD (1995q), *Continuing Professional Education of Highly-Qualified Personnel*, Paris.

OECD (1995r), *Measuring the Quality of Schools*, Paris.

OECD (1995s), *Redefining the Place to Learn*, Paris

OECD (1995t), *Schools for Cities*, Paris.

OECD (1995u), *Educational Research and Development: Trends, Issues and Challenges*, Paris.

OECD (1995v), *Performance Standards in Education: In Search of Quality*, Paris.

OECD (1995w), "Employment dynamics in firms", Employment, Labour and Social Affairs Committee, mimeo, Paris.

OECD (1995x), *Environmental Learning for the 21st Century*, Paris.

OECD (1995y), *OECD Education Statistics, 1985-1992*, Paris.

OECD (1995z), *Reviews of National Policies for Education – Sweden*, Paris.

OECD (1996a), *Measuring What People Know – Human Capital Accounting for the Knowledge Economy*, Paris.

OECD (1996b), *Reviews of National Policies for Education – France*, Paris.

OECD (1996c), *Education Reform and School Autonomy: Approaches, Experience, Effects*, Paris.

OECD (1996d), *Assessing and Certifying Occupational Skills and Competences in Vocational Education and Training*, Paris.

OECD (1996e), *Evaluating and Reforming Education Systems*, Paris.

OECD and STATISTICS CANADA (1995), *Literacy, Economy and Society: Results of the First International Adult Literacy Survey*, Paris and Ottawa.

OFSTED, Department for Education (1994), "Failure at school", National contribution to the OECD Education Committee Activity on "Combating failure at school", mimeo, London.

OOSTERBEEK, H. (1992), *Essays on Human Capital Theory*, University of Amsterdam, Amsterdam.

OOSTERBEEK, H. (1995), "Innovative ways to finance education and its relation to lifelong learning", mimeo, OECD, Paris.

OOSTERBEEK, H. and VAN OPHEM, H. (1995), "Human capital technology and schooling choices", TRACE discussion paper 95-90, University of Amsterdam, Amsterdam.

OPPER, S., TEICHLER, U. and CARLSON, J. (1990), *The Impact of Study Abroad Programmes on Students and Graduates*, Jessica Kingsley Publishers, London.

OSBORNE, R.J. and FREYBERG, P. (1985), *Learning in Science: The Implications of Children's Science*, Heinemann, London.

OSBORNE, D. and GAEBLER, T. (1993), *Reinventing Government: How the Entrepreneurial Spirit is Transforming the Public Sector*, Plume, New York.

PAPADOPOULOS, G. (1994), *Education 1960-1990: The OECD Perspective*, OECD, Paris.

PENCAVEL, J. (1990), "The contribution of higher education to economic growth and productivity: A review", CPER Discussion Paper Series, Stanford University, Stanford, California.

PERRATON, H. (1993), "Distance learning and the internationalisation of higher education", mimeo, prepared for the Centre for Educational Research and Innovation (CERI), OECD, Paris.

PSACHAROPOULOS, G. (1984), "The contribution of education to economic growth", in J.W. Kendrick (ed.), *International Comparisons of Productivity and Causes of the Slowdown*, Ballinger Publishing Co., Cambridge, pp. 340-356.

PSACHAROPOULOS, G. (1993), *Returns to Investment in Education: A Global Update*, The World Bank, Washington, DC.

Qualifications Authority, New Zealand (June 1995), *Submission to the OECD Review Team on Tertiary Education Policies*, Wellington.

RAIZEN, S. (1994), "Learning and work: The research base", in *Vocational Education and Training for Youth: Towards Coherent Policy and Practice*, OECD (1994j), Paris.

REHN, G. (1983), "Individual drawing rights", in H.M. Levin and H.G. Schütze (eds.), *Financing Recurrent Education: Strategies for Increasing Employment, Job Opportunities, and Productivity*, Sage, Beverly Hills, California.

REPLOGLE, E. (1994), "Community: What two programmes show us about the right focus for Head Start", *Children Today*, Vol. 23, No. 2, pp. 23-26.

RIDDELL, C. (1991), "Evaluation of manpower and training programmes: The North American experience", in *Evaluating Labour Market and Social Programmes: The State of a Complex Art*, OECD, Paris, pp. 43-73.

RIDDER, G. (1986), "An event history approach to the evaluation of training, recruitment and employment programmes", *Journal of Applied Econometrics*, Vol. 1, pp. 109-126.

RILEY, J. (1976), "Information, screening and human capital", *American Economic Review*, Vol. 66, pp. 254-260.

RIST, R.C. (1970), "Student social class and teacher expectations: The self-fulfilling prophesy in ghetto education", *Harvard Educational Review*, Vol. 66, pp. 411-451.

RIZO, F.M. (1995), "The roles of federal and regional governments in the management of educational systems:

A Mexican experience", in *Education in a Federal System: Seminar Papers,* OECD/CCET, Paris, pp. 63-70.

ROSENSTOCK. L. (1991), "The walls come down: The overdue reunification of vocational and academic education", *Phi Delta Kappan,* Vol. 72(*b*), pp. 434-436.

RUMBERGER, R.W. (1995), "Dropping out of middle school: A multi-level analysis of students and schools", *American Educational Research Journal,* Vol. 32, pp. 583-625.

SCHULLER, T. (1992), "Age, gender and learning in the lifespan", in A.C. Tuijnman and M. van der Kamp (eds.), *Learning Across the Lifespan: Theories, Research, Policies,* Pergamon Press, Oxford.

SCHULTZ, T.W. (1967), "The rate of return in allocating investment resources to education", *Journal of Human Resources,* Vol. 7, pp. 293-309.

SCHÜTZE, H.G. and ISTANCE, D. (1987), *Recurrent Education Revisited,* Almqvist and Wiksell, Stockholm.

SELDEN, R. (1994), "How indicators have been used in the USA", in K.A. Riley and D. Nuttall (eds.), *Measuring School Quality,* The Falmer Press, London

SHAVIT, Y. and BLOSSFELD, H.P. (1993), *Persistent Inequality,* Westview Press, Boulder, Colorado.

SICHERMAN, N. (1991), "Over-education in the labour market", *Journal of Labor Economics,* Vol. 9 (2), pp. 101-122.

SKILBECK, M. (1990), *Curriculum Reform: An Overview of Trends,* OECD, Paris.

SKILBECK, M. (1994), "National strategies for school reform: Trends and issues", mimeo prepared for the international conference on Changing Educational Structures and Practice, University of Warwick, Coventry, 15 April.

SLAVIN, R.E. (1995), *Cooperative Learning: Theory, Research, Practice,* 2nd Edition, Allyn and Bacon, Boston, Massachusetts.

SMITH, R.M. (1994), "Learning to learn: Adult education", *International Encyclopedia of Education,* 2nd Edition, Pergamon Press, Oxford, Vol. 6, pp. 3345-3349.

SMITH, V.D. (1995), "Social values for education: Environment", mimeo, presented at the conference on Social Benefits of Education, Office for Educational Research and Improvement, US Department of Education, Washington, DC, 5 January.

SMITH, M.S. and LEVIN, J. (1995), "Coherence, assessment and challenging content", in *Performance-based Student Assessment: Challenges and Possibilities,* National Society for the Study of Education, New York.

Spanish Ministry of Education and Sciences, Centre of Research, Evaluation and Documentation (1994), *School Effectiveness and Education Resource Management in Spain,* Madrid.

SPENCE, M. (1974), *Market Signalling: Information Transfer in Hiring and Related Processes,* Harvard University, Boston, Massachusetts.

STAGER, D. (1995), "Economics of technology-based learning and training on the information highway", report of the Working Group on Learning and Training of the Information Highway Advisory Council, Canada, March, mimeo, pp. 43-50.

STERN, D. (1994), "Human resources development in the learning-based economy: Roles of firms, schools and governments", mimeo presented at the conference on Employment and Growth in the Knowledge-based Economy, Copenhagen, 7-8 November.

STERN, D. and RITZEN, J.M.M. (1991), *Market Failure in Training? New Economic Analysis and Evidence on Training of Adult Employees,* Springer-Verlag, Berlin.

STERN, D., RABY, M. and DAYTON, C. (1992), *Career Academies: Partnerships for Reconstructing American High Schools,* Jossey-Bass, San Francisco, California.

STERN, D., STONE, J.R. III, HOPKINS, C., McMILLION, M. and CRAIN, R. (1994), *School-based Enterprise: Productive Learning in American High Schools,* Jossey-Bass, San Francisco, California.

STERN, D., FINKLESTEIN, N., STONE, J.R., LATTING, J. and DORNSIFE, C. (1995), *School-to-work: Research on Programmes in the United States,* The Falmer Press, London, and Taylor, New York.

STEVENS, B. and MICHALSKI, W. (1994), "Long-term prospects for work and social cohesion in OECD countries: An overview of the issues", in *OECD Societies in Transition: The Future of Work and Leisure,* OECD (1994e), Paris.

STIGLITZ, J.E. (1975), "The theory of screening, education, and the distribution of income", *American Economic Review,* Vol. 65, pp. 283-300.

STUEBING, S. (1995), "A place to learn: A study of technology and the design of learning environments", mimeo, OECD, Paris.

SUTTON, P. (1994), "Lifelong and continuing education", *International Encyclopedia of Education,* 2nd Edition, Pergamon Press, Oxford, pp. 3416-3422.

Swedish Ministry of Education and Science (1992), *The Swedish Way Towards a Learning Society: Report to the OECD,* Stockholm.

TAYLOR, J.C. and WHITE, V.J. (1991), *The Evaluation of the Cost-effectiveness of Multimedia Mixed-mode Teaching and Learning,* Australian Government Publishing Service, Canberra.

TEULINGS, C.N. (1995), "The wage distribution model of the assignment of skills to jobs", *Journal of Political Economy,* Vol. 103, pp. 280-315.

THEODOSSIOU, I. and WILLIAMS, H. (1995), "Employer-provided training and tenure effects on earnings", mimeo, University of Aberdeen, Aberdeen.

THUROW, L. (1970), *Investment in Human Capital*, Wadsworth Publishing Co., Belmont.

TIMMERMANN, D. (1994), "Lifelong education: Financing mechanisms", in *International Encyclopedia of Education*, 2nd Edition, Vol. 6, pp. 3422-3425.

TIMMERMANN, D. (1995), "Problems in the financing of recurrent education", mimeo, OECD, Paris.

TITMUS, C.J. (1994), "Concepts, principles and purposes of adult education", *International Encyclopedia of Education*, 2nd Edition, Pergamon Press, Oxford, pp. 111-120.

Tourism Council (1995), "European Union travel and tourism: Towards 1996 and beyond", mimeo, Brussels, April.

TRIER, U.P. and PESCHAR, J. (1995), "Cross-curriculum competencies: Rationale and strategy for developing a new indicator", in *Measuring What Students Learn*, OECD (1995*p*), Paris.

TUIJNMAN, A.C. (1989), *Recurrent Education, Earnings and Well-being: A Longitudinal Study of Swedish Men*, Almqvist and Wiksell, Stockholm.

TUIJNMAN, A.C. (1994), "Adult education: Overview", *International Encyclopedia of Education*, 2nd Edition, Pergamon Press, Oxford, pp. 143-152.

TUIJNMAN, A.C. and BRUMMELHUIS, A.C.A. (1993), "Predicting computer use in six systems: Structural models of implementation indicators", in W.J. Pelgrum and T. Plomp (eds.), *The IEA Study of Computers in Education: Implementation of an Innovation in 21 Education Systems*, Pergamon Press, Oxford.

TUIJNMAN, A.C. and POSTLETHWAITE, T.N. (1994), *Monitoring the Standards of Education*, Pergamon Press, Oxford.

United Nations (1994), *World Population Prospects, 1950-2010*, New York.

United States Department of Education (1994*a*), *Digest of Education Statistics*, National Center for Education Statistics, Washington, DC.

United States Department of Education (1994*b*), *National Assessment of Vocational Education: Final Report to Congress*, Vol. I-IV, Office of Educational Research and Improvement, Washington, DC.

VAN RAVENS, J. (1994), "The franchise model: A prototype of a new funding mechanism", mimeo presented at the Max Goote seminar on Vouchers, Amsterdam, June.

VELZEN, W.G. van, EKHOLM, M.M., HAMEYER, M.U. and ROBIN, D. (1985), *Making School Improvement Work: A Conceptual Guide to Practice*, ACCO, Leuven.

VERDUGO, R.R. and VERDUGO, N.T. (1989), "The impact of surplus schooling on earnings: Some additional findings", *Journal of Human Resources*, Vol. 24 (3), pp. 629-643.

VICKERS, M. (1994), "Skill standards and skill formation: Cross-national perspectives on alternative training strategies", *Jobs for the Future*, Boston, Massachusetts.

VIJLDER, F.J. de (1993), "Post-compulsory education: Participation, government responsibilities and funding mechanisms. Some experiences from the Netherlands", Eenheid Strategisch Beleid, Ministry of Education, Science, and Culture, Zoetermeer.

WAGNER, A. (1996), "Financing higher education: New approaches, new issues", *Higher Education Management*, Vol. 8.1, OECD, Paris.

WAGNER, A. and SCHNITZER, K. (1991), "Programme and policies for foreign students and study abroad: The search for approaches in a new global setting", *Higher Education*, Vol. 22, pp. 275-288.

WALBERG, H.J., HEARTEL, J. and WANG, M. (1993), "The knowledge base for school learning", *Review of Educational Research*, Vol. 63 (3), pp. 249-294.

WELLINGTON, A.J. (1993), "Changes in the male/female wage gap, 1976-85", *Journal of Human Resources*, Vol. 28, Spring, pp. 383-411.

WENDE, C.M., van der (1995), "Internationalising the curriculum in higher education: Draft synthesis report" mimeo prepared for the Centre of Educational Research and Innovation (CERI), OECD, Paris.

WILDAVSKY, A. (1979), *Speaking Truth to Power: The Art and Craft of Policy Analysis*, Little, Brown and Company, Boston, Massachusetts.

WILLIAMS, G. (1990), *Financing Higher Education: Current Patterns*, OECD, Paris.

WILLIAMS, G. (1994), "Reforms and potential reforms in higher education finance", mimeo prepared for the Twelfth General conference of IMHE Member Institutions, OECD, Paris.

WINDHAM, D.M. (1979), "Economic analysis and the public support of higher education: The divergence of education", in D.M. Windham (ed.), *Economic Dimensions of Education*, National Academy of Education, Washington DC.

WITTE, A. (1995), "Social benefits of education: Crime", mimeo presented at the conference "Social Benefits of Education, Office for Educational Research and Improvement, US Department of Education, Washington, DC, January."

World Bank (1995), *Global Economic Prospects and the Developing Countries*, The World Bank, Washington, DC.

WRINGE, C.A. (1994), "Markets, values and education", in D. Bridges and T.H. McLaughlin (eds.), *Education and the Market Place*, Falmer Press, London.

YOSHIMOTO, K. (1994), "Education and training in Japan", mimeo prepared for the OECD seminar on Education and Training for the Workforce, Seoul, 30 May-1 June.

YOUNG, M. (1958), *The Rise of the Meritocracy*, Penguin Books, London.

ZIGLER, E. and MUENCHOW, S. (1994), *Head Start: The Inside Story of America's Most Successful Educational Experiment*, Basic Books, New York.

MAIN SALES OUTLETS OF OECD PUBLICATIONS
PRINCIPAUX POINTS DE VENTE DES PUBLICATIONS DE L'OCDE

ARGENTINA – ARGENTINE
Carlos Hirsch S.R.L.
Galería Güemes, Florida 165, 4° Piso
1333 Buenos Aires   Tel. (1) 331.1787 y 331.2391
Telefax: (1) 331.1787

AUSTRALIA – AUSTRALIE
D.A. Information Services
648 Whitehorse Road, P.O.B 163
Mitcham, Victoria 3132   Tel. (03) 9210.7777
Telefax: (03) 9210.7788

AUSTRIA – AUTRICHE
Gerold & Co.
Graben 31
Wien I   Tel. (0222) 533.50.14
Telefax: (0222) 512.47.31.29

BELGIUM – BELGIQUE
Jean De Lannoy
Avenue du Roi 202 Koningslaan
B-1060 Bruxelles   Tel. (02) 538.51.69/538.08.41
Telefax: (02) 538.08.41

CANADA
Renouf Publishing Company Ltd.
1294 Algoma Road
Ottawa, ON K1B 3W8   Tel. (613) 741.4333
Telefax: (613) 741.5439
Stores:
61 Sparks Street
Ottawa, ON K1P 5R1   Tel. (613) 238.8985
12 Adelaide Street West
Toronto, ON M5H 1L6   Tel. (416) 363.3171
Telefax: (416)363.59.63

Les Éditions La Liberté Inc.
3020 Chemin Sainte-Foy
Sainte-Foy, PQ G1X 3V6   Tel. (418) 658.3763
Telefax: (418) 658.3763

Federal Publications Inc.
165 University Avenue, Suite 701
Toronto, ON M5H 3B8   Tel. (416) 860.1611
Telefax: (416) 860.1608

Les Publications Fédérales
1185 Université
Montréal, QC H3B 3A7   Tel. (514) 954.1633
Telefax: (514) 954.1635

CHINA – CHINE
China National Publications Import
Export Corporation (CNPIEC)
16 Gongti E. Road, Chaoyang District
P.O. Box 88 or 50
Beijing 100704 PR   Tel. (01) 506.6688
Telefax: (01) 506.3101

CHINESE TAIPEI – TAIPEI CHINOIS
Good Faith Worldwide Int'l. Co. Ltd.
9th Floor, No. 118, Sec. 2
Chung Hsiao E. Road
Taipei   Tel. (02) 391.7396/391.7397
Telefax: (02) 394.9176

**CZECH REPUBLIC –
RÉPUBLIQUE TCHÈQUE**
Artia Pegas Press Ltd.
Narodni Trida 25
POB 825
111 21 Praha 1   Tel. (2) 242 246 04
Telefax: (2) 242 278 72

DENMARK – DANEMARK
Munksgaard Book and Subscription Service
35, Nørre Søgade, P.O. Box 2148
DK-1016 København K   Tel. (33) 12.85.70
Telefax: (33) 12.93.87

EGYPT – ÉGYPTE
Middle East Observer
41 Sherif Street
Cairo   Tel. 392.6919
Telefax: 360-6804

FINLAND – FINLANDE
Akateeminen Kirjakauppa
Keskuskatu 1, P.O. Box 128
00100 Helsinki
Subscription Services/Agence d'abonnements :
P.O. Box 23
00371 Helsinki   Tel. (358 0) 121 4416
Telefax: (358 0) 121.4450

FRANCE
OECD/OCDE
Mail Orders/Commandes par correspondance :
2, rue André-Pascal
75775 Paris Cedex 16   Tel. (33-1) 45.24.82.00
Telefax: (33-1) 49.10.42.76
Telex: 640048 OCDE
Internet: Compte.PUBSINQ @ oecd.org
Orders via Minitel, France only/
Commandes par Minitel, France exclusivement :
36 15 OCDE
OECD Bookshop/Librairie de l'OCDE :
33, rue Octave-Feuillet
75016 Paris   · Tel. (33-1) 45.24.81.81
(33-1) 45.24.81.67
Dawson
B.P. 40
91121 Palaiseau Cedex   Tel. 69.10.47.00
Telefax: 64.54.83.26

Documentation Française
29, quai Voltaire
75007 Paris   Tel. 40.15.70.00

Economica
49, rue Héricart
75015 Paris   Tel. 45.78.12.92
Telefax: 40.58.15.70

Gibert Jeune (Droit-Économie)
6, place Saint-Michel
75006 Paris   Tel. 43.25.91.19

Librairie du Commerce International
10, avenue d'Iéna
75016 Paris   Tel. 40.73.34.60

Librairie Dunod
Université Paris-Dauphine
Place du Maréchal-de-Lattre-de-Tassigny
75016 Paris   Tel. 44.05.40.13

Librairie Lavoisier
11, rue Lavoisier
75008 Paris   Tel. 42.65.39.95

Librairie des Sciences Politiques
30, rue Saint-Guillaume
75007 Paris   Tel. 45.48.36.02

P.U.F.
49, boulevard Saint-Michel
75005 Paris   Tel. 43.25.83.40

Librairie de l'Université
12a, rue Nazareth
13100 Aix-en-Provence   Tel. (16) 42.26.18.08

Documentation Française
165, rue Garibaldi
69003 Lyon   Tel. (16) 78.63.32.23

Librairie Decitre
29, place Bellecour
69002 Lyon   Tel. (16) 72.40.54.54

Librairie Sauramps
Le Triangle
34967 Montpellier Cedex 2 Tel. (16) 67.58.85.15
Telefax: (16) 67.58.27.36

A la Sorbonne Actual
23, rue de l'Hôtel-des-Postes
06000 Nice   Tel. (16) 93.13.77.75
Telefax: (16) 93.80.75.69

GERMANY – ALLEMAGNE
OECD Publications and Information Centre
August-Bebel-Allee 6
D-53175 Bonn   Tel. (0228) 959.120
Telefax: (0228) 959.12.17

GREECE – GRÈCE
Librairie Kauffmann
Mavrokordatou 9
106 78 Athens   Tel. (01) 32.55.321
Telefax: (01) 32.30.320

HONG-KONG
Swindon Book Co. Ltd.
Astoria Bldg. 3F
34 Ashley Road, Tsimshatsui
Kowloon, Hong Kong   Tel. 2376.2062
Telefax: 2376.0685

HUNGARY – HONGRIE
Euro Info Service
Margitsziget, Európa Ház
1138 Budapest   Tel. (1) 111.62.16
Telefax: (1) 111.60.61

ICELAND – ISLANDE
Mál Mog Menning
Laugavegi 18, Pósthólf 392
121 Reykjavik   Tel. (1) 552.4240
Telefax: (1) 562.3523

INDIA – INDE
Oxford Book and Stationery Co.
Scindia House
New Delhi 110001   Tel. (11) 331.5896/5308
Telefax: (11) 332.5993
17 Park Street
Calcutta 700016   Tel. 240832

INDONESIA – INDONÉSIE
Pdii-Lipi
P.O. Box 4298
Jakarta 12042   Tel. (21) 573.34.67
Telefax: (21) 573.34.67

IRELAND – IRLANDE
Government Supplies Agency
Publications Section
4/5 Harcourt Road
Dublin 2   Tel. 661.31.11
Telefax: 475.27.60

ISRAEL – ISRAËL
Praedicta
5 Shatner Street
P.O. Box 34030
Jerusalem 91430   Tel. (2) 52.84.90/1/2
Telefax: (2) 52.84.93

R.O.Y. International
P.O. Box 13056
Tel Aviv 61130   Tel. (3) 546 1423
Telefax: (3) 546 1442

Palestinian Authority/Middle East:
INDEX Information Services
P.O.B. 19502
Jerusalem   Tel. (2) 27.12.19
Telefax: (2) 27.16.34

ITALY – ITALIE
Libreria Commissionaria Sansoni
Via Duca di Calabria 1/1
50125 Firenze   Tel. (055) 64.54.15
Telefax: (055) 64.12.57
Via Bartolini 29
20155 Milano   Tel. (02) 36.50.83

Editrice e Libreria Herder
Piazza Montecitorio 120
00186 Roma   Tel. 679.46.28
                               Telefax: 678.47.51

Libreria Hoepli
Via Hoepli 5
20121 Milano   Tel. (02) 86.54.46
                               Telefax: (02) 805.28.86

Libreria Scientifica
Dott. Lucio de Biasio 'Aeiou'
Via Coronelli, 6
20146 Milano   Tel. (02) 48.95.45.52
                               Telefax: (02) 48.95.45.48

JAPAN – JAPON
OECD Publications and Information Centre
Landic Akasaka Building
2-3-4 Akasaka, Minato-ku
Tokyo 107   Tel. (81.3) 3586.2016
                               Telefax: (81.3) 3584.7929

KOREA – CORÉE
Kyobo Book Centre Co. Ltd.
P.O. Box 1658, Kwang Hwa Moon
Seoul   Tel. 730.78.91
                               Telefax: 735.00.30

MALAYSIA – MALAISIE
University of Malaya Bookshop
University of Malaya
P.O. Box 1127, Jalan Pantai Baru
59700 Kuala Lumpur
Malaysia   Tel. 756.5000/756.5425
                               Telefax: 756.3246

MEXICO – MEXIQUE
OECD Publications and Information Centre
Edificio INFOTEC
Av. San Fernando no. 37
Col. Toriello Guerra
Tlalpan C.P. 14050
Mexico D.F.
                Tel. (525) 606 00 11 Extension 100
                               Fax: (525) 606 13 07

Revistas y Periodicos Internacionales S.A. de C.V.
Florencia 57 - 1004
Mexico, D.F. 06600   Tel. 207.81.00
                               Telefax: 208.39.79

NETHERLANDS – PAYS-BAS
SDU Uitgeverij Plantijnstraat
Externe Fondsen
Postbus 20014
2500 EA's-Gravenhage   Tel. (070) 37.89.880
Voor bestellingen: Telefax: (070) 34.75.778

**NEW ZEALAND –
NOUVELLE-ZÉLANDE**
GPLegislation Services
P.O. Box 12418
Thorndon, Wellington   Tel. (04) 496.5655
                               Telefax: (04) 496.5698

NORWAY – NORVÈGE
NIC INFO A/S
Bertrand Narvesens vei 2
P.O. Box 6512 Etterstad
0606 Oslo 6   Tel. (022) 57.33.00
                               Telefax: (022) 68.19.01

PAKISTAN
Mirza Book Agency
65 Shahrah Quaid-E-Azam
Lahore 54000   Tel. (42) 353.601
                               Telefax: (42) 231.730

PHILIPPINE – PHILIPPINES
International Booksource Center Inc.
Rm 179/920 Cityland 10 Condo Tower 2
HV dela Costa Ext cor Valero St.
Makati Metro Manila   Tel. (632) 817 9676
                               Telefax: (632) 817 1741

POLAND – POLOGNE
Ars Polona
00-950 Warszawa
Krakowskie Przedmieácie 7   Tel. (22) 264760
                               Telefax: (22) 268673

PORTUGAL
Livraria Portugal
Rua do Carmo 70-74
Apart. 2681
1200 Lisboa   Tel. (01) 347.49.82/5
                               Telefax: (01) 347.02.64

SINGAPORE – SINGAPOUR
Gower Asia Pacific Pte Ltd.
Golden Wheel Building
41, Kallang Pudding Road, No. 04-03
Singapore 1334   Tel. 741.5166
                               Telefax: 742.9356

SPAIN – ESPAGNE
Mundi-Prensa Libros S.A.
Castelló 37, Apartado 1223
Madrid 28001   Tel. (91) 431.33.99
                               Telefax: (91) 575.39.98

Mundi-Prensa Barcelona
Consell de Cent No. 391
08009 – Barcelona   Tel. (93) 488.34.92
                               Telefax: (93) 487.76.59

Llibreria de la Generalitat
Palau Moja
Rambla dels Estudis, 118
08002 – Barcelona
                (Subscripcions) Tel. (93) 318.80.12
                (Publicacions) Tel. (93) 302.67.23
                               Telefax: (93) 412.18.54

SRI LANKA
Centre for Policy Research
c/o Colombo Agencies Ltd.
No. 300-304, Galle Road
Colombo 3   Tel. (1) 574240, 573551-2
                               Telefax: (1) 575394, 510711

SWEDEN – SUÈDE
CE Fritzes AB
S–106 47 Stockholm   Tel. (08) 690.90.90
                               Telefax: (08) 20.50.21

Subscription Agency/Agence d'abonnements :
Wennergren-Williams Info AB
P.O. Box 1305
171 25 Solna   Tel. (08) 705.97.50
                               Telefax: (08) 27.00.71

SWITZERLAND – SUISSE
Maditec S.A. (Books and Periodicals - Livres
et périodiques)
Chemin des Palettes 4
Case postale 266
1020 Renens VD 1   Tel. (021) 635.08.65
                               Telefax: (021) 635.07.80

Librairie Payot S.A.
4, place Pépinet
CP 3212
1002 Lausanne   Tel. (021) 320.25.11
                               Telefax: (021) 320.25.14

Librairie Unilivres
6, rue de Candolle
1205 Genève   Tel. (022) 320.26.23
                               Telefax: (022) 329.73.18

Subscription Agency/Agence d'abonnements :
Dynapresse Marketing S.A.
38, avenue Vibert
1227 Carouge   Tel. (022) 308.07.89
                               Telefax: (022) 308.07.99

See also – Voir aussi :
OECD Publications and Information Centre
August-Bebel-Allee 6
D-53175 Bonn (Germany)   Tel. (0228) 959.120
                               Telefax: (0228) 959.12.17

THAILAND – THAÏLANDE
Suksit Siam Co. Ltd.
113, 115 Fuang Nakhon Rd.
Opp. Wat Rajbopith
Bangkok 10200   Tel. (662) 225.9531/2
                               Telefax: (662) 222.5188

TUNISIA – TUNISIE
Grande Librairie Spécialisée
Fendri Ali
Avenue Haffouz Imm El-Intilaka
Bloc B 1 Sfax 3000   Tel. (216-4) 296 855
                               Telefax: (216-4) 298.270

TURKEY – TURQUIE
Kültür Yayinlari Is-Türk Ltd. Sti.
Atatürk Bulvari No. 191/Kat 13
Kavaklidere/Ankara
                      Tel. (312) 428.11.40 Ext. 2458
                               Telefax: (312) 417 24 90
Dolmabahce Cad. No. 29
Besiktas/Istanbul   Tel. (212) 260 7188

UNITED KINGDOM – ROYAUME-UNI
HMSO
Gen. enquiries   Tel. (171) 873 8242
Postal orders only:
P.O. Box 276, London SW8 5DT
Personal Callers HMSO Bookshop
49 High Holborn, London WC1V 6HB
                               Telefax: (171) 873 8416
Branches at: Belfast, Birmingham, Bristol,
Edinburgh, Manchester

UNITED STATES – ÉTATS-UNIS
OECD Publications and Information Center
2001 L Street N.W., Suite 650
Washington, D.C. 20036-4922 Tel. (202) 785.6323
                               Telefax: (202) 785.0350

Subscriptions to OECD periodicals may also be
placed through main subscription agencies.

Les abonnements aux publications périodiques de
l'OCDE peuvent être souscrits auprès des
principales agences d'abonnement.

Orders and inquiries from countries where Distribu-
tors have not yet been appointed should be sent to:
OECD Publications Service, 2, rue André-Pascal,
75775 Paris Cedex 16, France.

Les commandes provenant de pays où l'OCDE n'a
pas encore désigné de distributeur peuvent être
adressées à : OCDE, Service des Publications,
2, rue André-Pascal, 75775 Paris Cedex 16, France.

                                       1-1996

OECD PUBLICATIONS, 2, rue André-Pascal, 75775 PARIS CEDEX 16
PRINTED IN FRANCE
(91 96 06 1) ISBN 92-64-14815-9 – No. 48603 1996